LSAT®

STRATEGIES, PRACTICE, AND REVIEW

2011

KAPLAN

PUBLISHING

New York

© 2010 Kaplan, Inc.

Published by Kaplan Publishing, a division of Kaplan, Inc.
1 Liberty Plaza, 24th Floor
New York, NY 10006

Materials used in this book were adapted from the following sources:

Martin V. Melosi, "Hazardous Waste and Environmental Liability: A Historical Perspective," *Houston Law Review,* Volume 25: 741, 1988. Reprinted by permission.

Wendy S. Zeligson, "Pool Coverage, Press Access, and Presidential Debates: What's Wrong with This Picture?" *Cardozo Law Review,* Vol. 9, 1988. Reprinted by permission.

Dan W. Brock and Allen E. Buchanan, "The Profit Motive in Medicine," *Journal of Medicine and Philosophy,* Vol. 12, 1987. Reprinted by permission.

Fred Anderson, "The Republic Reborn by Steven Watts," *American Historical Review,* Vol. 94, No. 2 (April 1989), p. 516. Reprinted by permission.

Judith Olans Brown, Phyllis Tropper Baumann, and Elaine Miller Melnick, "Equal Pay for Jobs of Comparable Worth: An Analysis of the Rhetoric," *Harvard Civil Rights & Civil Liberties Review,* No. 1, Winter 1986. © 1988, the President and Fellows of Harvard College. Reprinted by permission.

Ward & Trent, et al. *The Cambridge History of English and American Literature.* New York: G. P. Putnam's Sons, 1907–21.

National Cancer Institute, "Molecular Test Can Predict Both the Risk of Breast Cancer Recurrence and Who Will Benefit From Chemotherapy." Posted 12/10/2004. www.cancer.gov/newscenter

Reynolds, Anne, "Nazi Looted Art: The Holocaust Records Preservation Project, Part 1," *Prologue,* Fall 2002, Vol. 34, No. 3. Viewed 24 December 2004, U.S. National Archives and Records Administration at www.archives.gov/publications.

Wollstonecraft, Mary, *A Vindication of the Rights of Woman.* Printed at Boston by Peter Edes for Thomas and Andrews, Faust's statue, No. 45, Newbury Street, 1792.

Printed in the United States of America

10 9 8 7 6 5 4 3 2 1
ISBN-13: 978-1-4195-4992-2

Kaplan Publishing books are available at special quantity discounts to use for sales promotions, employee premiums, or educational purposes. For more information or to purchase books, please call the Simon & Schuster special sales department at 866-506-1949.

CONTENTS

PART THREE: PRACTICE TESTS AND EXPLANATIONS

PART FOUR: GETTING INTO LAW SCHOOL

Part One

THE LSAT

CHAPTER 1: AN INTRODUCTION TO THE LSAT

The Law School Admissions Test (LSAT) is probably unlike any other test you've taken in your academic career. Most tests you've encountered in high school and college have been content based—that is, they required you to recall and be conversant with a certain body of facts, formulas, theorems, or other acquired knowledge.

But the LSAT is a skills-based test. It doesn't ask you to repeat memorized facts or to apply learned formulas to specific problems. In fact, all you'll be asked to do on the LSAT is think—thoroughly, quickly, and strategically. There's no required content to study!

Sound too good to be true? Well, before you get the idea that you can skate into the most important test of your life without preparing, remember that learning skills and improving your performance takes practice. You can't cram for the LSAT.

ABOUT THE LSAT

The LSAT is a standardized test written by the Law School Admission Council (LSAC) and administered four times each year. The test is a required component of your application to all American Bar Association-approved law schools as well as some others.

The LSAT is designed to measure the critical reading, data management, and analytical thinking skills that are necessary (according to the governing bodies of law schools) for success in the first year of law school. The good news is that these skills will serve you well throughout law school and on into your profession life. So consider your LSAT preparation an investment in your learning process as well as your career.

You may already possess some level of LSAT-tested skills. But you probably haven't yet mastered how to use those skills to your best advantage in the context of a standardized, skill-based test that requires careful time management.

The LSAT is also a test of endurance—five 35-minute blocks of multiple-choice testing plus a 35-minute writing sample. Add in the administrative details at both ends of the test and a 10- to 15-minute break midway through, and you can count on being in the test room for at least four and a half hours. It's a grueling experience, but it's not as bad if you are familiar with the test and ready to handle every section. You want to approach the test with confidence and rigor so you can maintain your focus, limit your stress, and get your highest score on test day. That's why it's so important to take control of the test, just as you will take control of the rest of the application process.

Our material is as up-to-date as possible at the time of this printing, but LSAC test specifications may change at any time. Thus, please check our website at kaptest.com/LSAT for the latest news and updates.

How Do I Register for the LSAT?

Be sure to register as soon as possible, as your preferred test site can fill up quickly. You can register for the LSAT in any of three ways.

1. Online: You can sign up at lsac.org.
2. Telephone: You can call LSAC at (215) 968-1001.
3. Mail: You can complete the registration form provided in the *Law School Admission Information Book*. The book is free and is available at undergraduate advising offices and law schools. You can also request a copy through LSAC.

If you have additional questions about registration, contact the LSAC by phone or by email at lsacinfo@lsac.org.

The LSAT Question Types

The LSAT consists of five multiple-choice sections: two Logical Reasoning sections, one Logic Games section, one Reading Comprehension section, and one unscored "experimental" section that will look exactly like one of the other multiple-choice sections. At the end of the test, there will be a Writing Sample section in which you'll have to write a short essay. Here's how the sections break down:

Section	Number of Questions	Minutes
Logical Reasoning	24–26	35
Logical Reasoning	24–26	35
Logic Games	22–24	35
Reading Comprehension	26–28	35
"Experimental"	23–28	35
Writing Sample	n/a	35

The five multiple-choice sections can appear in any order, but the Writing Sample always comes last. A 10- or 15-minute break will come between the third and fourth sections of the test.

Each section is covered in its own chapter. You'll be answering roughly 125 multiple-choice questions (101 of which are scored) over the course of three intense hours. That's an average of just a little over a minute per question, not counting the time required to read passages and set up games. Clearly, you're going to have to move fast. But don't let yourself get careless. Taking control of the LSAT means increasing the speed only to the extent you can do so without sacrificing accuracy.

First, just familiarize yourself with the sections and the kinds of questions asked on each section.

Logical Reasoning

What It Is: The Logical Reasoning sections consist of 24–26 questions, each based on a "stimulus" in the form of a paragraph or a dialogue between two speakers. You will evaluate the logic and structure of arguments and identify proper inferences from the statements. As in law school and the practice of law, you will be asked to find underlying assumptions, strengthen and weaken arguments, determine logical flaws, and identify parallel argument structures. You will need the critical reasoning skills that enable you to analyze a stimulus and make judgments accordingly.

Why It's on the Test: Law schools want to see whether you can understand, analyze, evaluate, and manipulate arguments and draw reliable conclusions—as every law student and attorney must. This question type makes up half of your LSAT score, so you know that the law schools value these skills.

Logic Games

What It Is: There are 22–24 questions in the Logic Games (aka Analytical Reasoning) section, based on four games with five to seven questions each. They require an ability to reason clearly and deductively from a given set of rules or restrictions under tight time restrictions. Games require systematic technique and the proper use of scratchwork.

Why It's on the Test: The section tests your command of detail, your formal deductive abilities, your understanding of how rules limit and order behavior (which is the very definition of law itself), and your ability to cope with many pieces of data simultaneously to solve problems.

Reading Comprehension

What It Is: The Reading Comprehension section consists of three single passages, 450–550 words each, and a set of two short passages that together total 450–550 words. Each passage is followed by five to eight questions. The topics are chosen from the areas

 READ MORE

When you finish this program, there's more practice on the tougher questions, games, and passages in Kaplan's *LSAT Advanced*.

of social science, humanities, natural science, and law. Because content is not tested, no outside knowledge is required.

Why It's on the Test: Reading Comprehension tests your ability to understand quickly the gist and structure of long, difficult prose—just as you'll have to do in law school and throughout your career.

The Writing Sample

What It Is: The Writing Sample comes at the end of your LSAT day. You will read a paragraph that presents a problem and two options to address that problem. Each option will have strengths and weaknesses, and you must argue in favor of one option based on the given criteria. There is no right or wrong answer, and the writing sample is unscored. However, law schools will receive a copy of your essay along with your LSAT score.

Why It's on the Test: The Writing Sample shows law schools your ability to argue for a position while attacking an opposing argument under timed conditions. In addition, it may be used to verify that your writing style is similar to that in your personal statement.

HOW THE LSAT IS SCORED

You'll receive one score for the LSAT ranging between 120 and 180 (no separate scores for Logical Reasoning, Logic Games, and Reading Comprehension). There are roughly 101 scored multiple-choice questions on each exam:

- About 52 from the two Logical Reasoning sections
- About 22 from the Logic Games section
- About 27 from the Reading Comprehension section

Your **raw score**, the number of questions that you answer correctly, will be multiplied by a complicated scoring formula (different for each test, to accommodate differences in difficulty level) to yield the **scaled score**—the one that will fall somewhere in that 120–180 range—which is reported to the schools.

Because the test is graded on a largely preset curve, the scaled score will always correspond to a certain percentile, also indicated on your score report. A score of 160, for instance, corresponds roughly to the 80th percentile, meaning that 80 percent of test takers scored at or below your level. The percentile figure is important because it allows law schools to see where you fall in the pool of applicants.

All scored questions are worth the same amount—one raw point—and there's no penalty for guessing. That means that you should always fill in an answer for every question, whether you get to that question or not.

What's a "Good" LSAT Score?

Of course, what you consider a good LSAT score depends on your own expectations and goals, but here are a few interesting statistics.

If you got about half of all of the scored questions right (a raw score of roughly 50), you would earn a scaled score of roughly 147, putting you in about the 30th percentile—not a great performance. But on the LSAT, a little improvement goes a long way. In fact, getting only one additional question right every 10 minutes would give you a raw score of about 64, pushing you into the 60th percentile—a huge improvement.

SAMPLE PERCENTILES

Percentile	Approx. Scaled Score (Range 120–180)	Approx. Raw Score
99th percentile	174	~94 correct out of 101
95th percentile	168	~88 correct out of 101
90th percentile	164	~82 correct out of 101
80th percentile	160	~76 correct out of 101
75th percentile	157	~71 correct out of 101
50th percentile	152	~61 correct out of 101

Note: Exact percentile-to-scaled-score relationships vary from test to test.

So you don't have to be perfect to do well. On most LSATs, you can get as many as 28 questions wrong and still remain in the 80th percentile or as many as 20 wrong and still be in the 90th percentile. Most students who score 180 get a handful of questions wrong.

Although many factors play a role in admissions decisions, the LSAT score is usually one of the most important. And—generally speaking—being average won't cut it. The median LSAT score is somewhere around 152. And if you're aiming for the top, you've got to do even better. The median LSAT scores accepted by the best law schools in the country, such as Yale, Stanford, and Columbia, range from the high 160s to the low 170s. That translates to a percentile figure of 95 and up.

In the next chapter, you'll start to learn how to approach—and master—the test in a general way. As you'll see, knowing specific strategies for each type of question is only part of your task. To do your best, you have to approach the entire test in the proper spirit, with the proactive, take-control kind of thinking it inspires—the LSAT mindset.

LSAT CHECKLIST

Choose a Test Date

☐ The LSAT is given four times each year—February, June, September/October, and December—at designated locations around the world. Factors to consider in selecting a date include (1) when you will have time to prepare for the test, (2) whether you would receive your LSAT score before the application deadlines at the schools to which you will apply, and (3) whether you might take the LSAT more than once. Because the scores are scaled, there is no test time that will yield better scores. The fall test is typically the most popular.

Complete Your LSAT and CAS Registrations

☐ Registering for the LSAT and the Credential Assembly Service (CAS) are two separate processes and need not be done at the same time. They have different deadlines and fees, and you must sign up for both during the law school application process. You can register for each online at lsac.org, by mail, or by phone at (215) 968-1001.

Create an LSAT and Test-Prep Calendar to Schedule Your Practice and Track Important Deadlines

☐ On a calendar, mark your test date and work back from that day to block out the weeks you have to prepare for the test. Fill in your regular responsibilities, including school, work, trips, appointments, and so on. Add the time you will set aside to practice to get ready for test day. Also include important LSAT and CAS registration dates and deadlines.

Ensure That You're Prepared for Test Day

☐ Familiarize yourself with the test.

☐ Learn the Kaplan methods and practice them using the problems and tests included in this book. Be sure to review the explanations for every problem, including why the correct answer is right and why the other four are wrong. Consider the time you have available before test day and focus your practice time where you have the greatest opportunity to add points and raise your score.

☐ Download additional LSAT prep materials (sample questions with explanations and an additional prep test) at no cost at lsac.org.

☐ Check out kaptest.com/LSAT to find free practice events at a Kaplan Center near you.

Check Out Your Test Center

- ☐ Know the directions to your test center and where you can park.

- ☐ Consider visiting the test center in advance to get a feel for the place.

- ☐ Be aware that the room number you are provided with may not be your actual testing room.

- ☐ Use Kaplan's exclusive "Test Site Rater" at kaptest.com/testsites for information from former test takers about desk space, noise levels, proctors, and more.

Pack for Test Day at Least One Day in Advance

- ☐ Admission ticket

- ☐ Valid picture ID

- ☐ LSAT Survival Kit (see chapter 7)

The Day of the Test

- ☐ Make sure you have your LSAT admission ticket and acceptable ID.

- ☐ Make sure you have your LSAT Survival Kit.

- ☐ Dress in layers so you can adjust to the room's temperature.

CHAPTER 2: TAKE CONTROL OF THE TEST

The Strategy and Practice chapters will arm you with the tools you need to do well on the LSAT. But you must wield those tools in the right spirit. This involves taking a certain stance toward the entire test.

THE RIGHT ATTITUDE

Those who approach the LSAT as an obstacle and rail against the necessity of taking it don't fare as well as those who see the LSAT as an opportunity to show off the reading and reasoning skills that law schools are looking for, and to distinguish themselves from the rest of the applicant pack. With that in mind:

- Look at the LSAT as a challenge, but try not to obsess over it; you certainly don't want to psyche yourself out of the game.

- Remember that the LSAT is important, but this one test will not single-handedly determine the outcome of your life.

- Try to have fun with the test. Learning how to match your wits against the test makers can be very satisfying, and the skills you'll acquire will benefit you in law school and in your career.

- According to a Harris poll, more people get into law school with a Kaplan LSAT course than ***all other major test prep companies combined***.* So always remember—you've trained with Kaplan, the leader in LSAT preparation! You have the tools you need and the know-how to use those tools.

*People refers to adults who took the LSAT and a course to prepare for it, were accepted into law school and participated in the survey. The Harris Interactive® online study for Kaplan was conducted between December 6th and 21st, 2007, among 149 U.S. adults who applied to and were admitted into law school, of whom 125 took the LSAT and a course to prepare for it.

CONFIDENCE

Confidence in your ability leads to quick, sure answers and a sense of well-being that translates into more points. Confidence feeds on itself, and unfortunately, so does self-doubt. If you lack confidence, you end up reading sentences and answer choices two, three, or four times, until you confuse yourself and get off track. This leads to timing difficulties that perpetuate the downward spiral, causing anxiety and a tendency to rush.

If you subscribe to the LSAT mindset, however, you'll gear all of your practice toward taking control of the test. When you've achieved that goal—armed with the principles, techniques, strategies, and methods in this book—you'll be ready to face the LSAT with confidence.

STAMINA

The LSAT is a grueling experience, and some test takers simply run out of gas before it's over. To avoid this, take full-length practice tests in the weeks before the test. That way, five sections plus a writing sample will seem like a breeze (well, maybe not a breeze, but at least not a hurricane). On the other hand, don't just rush from one practice test right into another. Learn what you can from your review of each test; then work on your weaknesses and build your strengths before tackling another full-length test.

 **READ MORE**

Get as much test practice as possible. Order PrepTests from LSAC to use as your final practice tests.

In addition to taking the Practice Tests included in this book, you can buy additional practice tests published by LSAC. Look for them in the LSAT Prep Materials section at lsac.org.

TEST EXPERTISE

Every LSAT question, no matter how hard, is worth a single point. And because there are so many questions to do in so little time, it's foolish to spend three minutes getting a point for a hard question and then not have time to get a couple of quick points from two easy questions later in the section.

Given the combination of limited time and all questions being equal in weight, you've got to develop a way of handling the test sections to make sure you get as many points as you can, as quickly and easily as you can. Here are the principles that will help you do that.

 **READ MORE**

Come back and reread this section occasionally to be sure you don't overlook any strategies.

ANSWER QUESTIONS IN THE ORDER THAT'S BEST FOR YOU

One of the most valuable strategies to help you finish sections in time is to recognize and deal first with the questions, games, and passages that are easier for you. Temporarily skip those that promise to be difficult and time consuming. Come back to them at the end, and if you run out of time, you're much better off not getting to questions you may have had difficulty with than missing easier ones. (Because there's no wrong-answer penalty, always fill in an answer to every question on the test, whether you get to it or not.)

Remember, LSAT questions, games, and passages are not presented in *exact* order of difficulty; in fact, the test makers scatter easy and difficult questions throughout the section, in effect rewarding those who get to the end. For example, if you find Sequencing games particularly easy, seek out the Sequencing games in the Logic Games section and do it first.

Know That There Will Be Difficult Questions

It's imperative that you remain calm and composed while working through a section. Don't be rattled by one hard Logic Game, Logical Reasoning question, or reading passage. Part of the job of a top-notch test taker is to avoid investing time where the payoff is questionable. Expect to find at least one difficult passage or game on every section; you won't be the only one to have trouble with it. The test is curved to take the tough material into account. Understand that part of the test maker's goal is to reward those who keep their composure.

Control Time Instead of Letting Time Control You

The last thing you want is to have time called on a section before you've gotten to half the questions. It's essential, therefore, that you pace yourself. You should have a sense of the average time you have to do each question so you know when you're exceeding the limit and should start to move faster.

Keeping track of time is also important for guessing. It pays to leave time at the end to guess on any questions you couldn't answer. You'll have a very good chance of getting lucky on one or two questions.

Grid in Answers Efficiently

You not only have to pick the right answers, you also have to mark those right answers on the answer grid in an efficient and accurate way. It sounds simple, but it's extremely important: Don't make mistakes filling out your answer grid! When time is short, it's easy to get confused going back and forth between your test book and your grid. Here are a few methods of avoiding mistakes:

(1) **Always Circle Answers You Choose:** Circle the correct answers in your test booklet but don't transfer the answers to the grid right away. That wastes too much time. Circling your answers in the test book will also make it easier to check your grid against your book.

(2) **Grid About Five Answers at Once:** Transfer your answers after every five questions, or at the end of each Reading Comp passage or Logic Game, or at the end of a two-page spread in your test booklet (find the method that works best for you). You won't keep breaking your concentration to mark the grid, so you'll save time and improve accuracy.

(3) **Always Circle Questions You Skip:** Put a big circle in your test book around the number of any question you skip (or circle the whole question). When you go back, it will be easy to locate these questions. And if you accidentally skip a box on the grid, you can more easily check your grid against your book to see where you went wrong.

(4) **Save Time at the End for a Final Grid Check:** Take time at the end of every section to check your grid. Make sure you've got an oval filled in for each question in the section. Remember, an unanswered question has no chance of earning a point.

MANAGING STRESS

Some test stress is normal and good; it's a motivation to study, and the adrenaline that gets pumped into your bloodstream helps you stay alert and think more clearly. But high stress levels can make it difficult to concentrate, and you can't work under stress for prolonged periods without exhausting yourself. Practice using techniques to get stress under control and learn which of them will work best for you during the test.

Take Control

Research shows that if you don't have a sense of control over what's happening in your life, you can easily end up feeling helpless and hopeless. Try to identify the sources of the stress you feel. Which of these can you do something about?

Set Realistic Goals

Facing your problem areas gives you some distinct advantages. What do you want to accomplish in the time remaining? Make a list of realistic goals. You can't help feeling more confident when you know you're actively improving your chances of earning a higher test score.

Focus on Your Strengths

Make a list of your strengths that will help you do well on the test. Recognizing your own strengths is like having reserves of solid gold. You'll be able to draw on your reserves as you need them. And every time you recognize a new area of strength, solve a challenging problem, or score well on a practice test, you'll increase your reserves.

Imagine Yourself Succeeding

Close your eyes and imagine yourself in a relaxing situation. Breathe easily and naturally and think of a real-life situation in which you scored well on a test or did well on an assignment. Focus on this success. Now turn your thoughts to the LSAT and keep your thoughts and feelings in line with that successful experience. Don't make comparisons between them; just imagine yourself taking the upcoming test with the same feelings of confidence and relaxed control.

Exercise

Whether it is jogging, biking, yoga, or a pickup basketball game, physical exercise stimulates your mind and body and improves your ability to think and concentrate. A surprising number of students fall out of the habit of regular exercise, ironically because they're spending so much time prepping for exams.

Eat Well

Good nutrition helps you focus and think clearly. Eat plenty of fruits and vegetables; low-fat protein such as fish, skinless poultry, beans, and legumes; and whole grains such as brown rice, whole-wheat bread, and pastas. Don't eat a lot of sugar, high-fat snacks, or salty foods.

Keep Breathing

Conscious attention to breathing is an excellent way to manage stress. Most of the people who get into trouble during tests take shallow breaths: They breathe using only their upper chests and shoulder muscles and may even hold their breath for long periods of time. Breathe deeply in a slow, relaxed manner.

Stretch

If you find yourself getting spaced out or burned out as you're studying for or taking the test, stop for a brief moment and stretch. Stretching will help to refresh you and refocus your thoughts.

Avoid Drugs

Using drugs (prescription or recreational) specifically to prepare for and take a big test is self-defeating. Mild stimulants like coffee or cola can sometimes help as you study because they keep you alert. But too much of them can lead to agitation, restlessness, and insomnia.

STRATEGIES AND PRACTICE

CHAPTER 3: **LOGICAL REASONING**

- Anatomy of a Logical Reasoning Question
- Kaplan's 4-Step Method for Logical Reasoning
- Common Question Types
- Section Management
- Helpful Hints to Improve Your Performance

The fact that Logical Reasoning makes up half of your LSAT score is actually good news, because you already have most of the skills you need for the section. In fact, we all do. But the LSAT tests your ability to use those skills thoroughly, quickly, and strategically.

ANATOMY OF A LOGICAL REASONING QUESTION

Each logical reasoning question begins with either a paragraph or a dialogue between two speakers. This "stimulus" is followed by a question and then five multiple-choice answers.

KAPLAN'S 4-STEP METHOD FOR LOGICAL REASONING

This method applies to all logical reasoning questions regardless of the question type. You will work through each question by taking the following steps.

STEP 1: IDENTIFY

Read the question stem to identify the question type. This step may seem counter-intuitive because the question is not presented first, so it will take some practice. However, reading the question first lets you identify the question type and, ultimately, determine your task as you read the stimulus. Instead of just reading the stimulus to get it read and contemplating the content, you will read it to pull specific information that will help you answer the question. Be sure to keep track of words and phrases that tell you the question type.

STEP 2: UNTANGLE

Take apart the stimulus based on the question type identified in step 1. "Unpack" the stimulus to get the information you will need to answer the particular question.

STEP 3: PREDICT

Think critically about the answer. This step is very important—yet it is the one you will be most tempted to skip. Don't! *Thinking critically* means now that you've found the information you need, put it together and think about the answer. It need not be in complete sentences or formal language. You just need enough to move to the next step and sort through the answers. You also have to be flexible—be ready to spot an answer that is similar but not an exact replica of your prediction.

This step will make you slow in the beginning, but give it a chance. Once you practice it and get better, it will actually make you faster and more accurate. Without this step, you are more likely to get distracted by wrong answers and to waste time analyzing each answer.

STEP 4: EVALUATE

Review the answer choices and determine which one matches your prediction. That's right—literally ask yourself if the answer matches your prediction. Hopefully, one answer will stand out for you. If not, eliminate wrong answers and consider the common wrong answer traps. More on that later.

COMMON QUESTION TYPES

Now that you've seen the Kaplan Method for Logical Reasoning, let's look at the common question types you'll be asked. The first four question types represent half of the points available in the two scored Logical Reasoning sections, so we start with them. We refer to them together as the *assumption family of questions*.

ASSUMPTION FAMILY OF QUESTIONS: ASSUMPTION, STRENGTHEN, WEAKEN, AND FLAW

These four question types all contain an argument. In logical reasoning, the word *argument* doesn't mean a conversation in which people are shouting at one another. Instead, think of an argument as a piece of text in which an author puts forth a set of ideas or a point of view and attempts to support it.

Success in answering these question types depends on your ability to break an argument down into its core components: conclusion and evidence. The **conclusion** is the main point the author is making, and the **evidence** is the information offered by the author to support the conclusion. There is no general rule about where the conclusion and evidence appear in the argument. The conclusion could be the first sentence, followed by the evidence; it could be the last sentence, with the evidence preceding it; or it could be any sentence in between. Placement of the conclusion and evidence is a stylistic issue and not necessarily indicative of the argument structure.

Keywords are commonly used in logical reasoning stimuli to signal the conclusion and evidence. Look for words such as *therefore*, *hence*, *thus*, and *so* to identify the conclusion. Words such as *because*, *since*, and *for* point to the evidence.

If the argument structure is not so obviously identified, give the stimulus the one-sentence test: What statement would the author choose to keep if limited to a single sentence? That statement will probably be the conclusion.

Consider the following stimulus:

> The Brookdale Public Library will require extensive physical rehabilitation to meet the new building codes passed by the town council. For one thing, the electrical system is inadequate, causing the lights to flicker sporadically. Furthermore, there are too few emergency exits, and even those are poorly marked and sometimes locked.

Suppose that the author of this argument were allowed to keep only one sentence to convey her meaning. Do you think that she would waste her lone opportunity on the statement "The electrical system at the Brookdale Public Library is inadequate, causing the lights to flicker sporadically?" Would she walk away satisfied that she had gotten her main point across? Of course not. Given a single opportunity, she would have to state the first sentence: "The Brookdale Public Library will require extensive physical rehabilitation to meet the new building codes passed by the town council." This is her conclusion. If you pressed her for her reasons for making this statement, she would then cite the electrical and structural problems with the building.

Once you identify the argument's conclusion and evidence, determine the author's assumption. An **assumption** is an unstated piece of evidence that is required for the conclusion to be valid, and identifying it is critical to answer the four questions types that make up the assumption family of questions.

While you need the same building blocks (conclusion, evidence, and assumption) for all four question types, you will use them in different ways to answer the questions. Just one more reason to read the question first. Keep reading to learn more.

Assumption Questions

LSAT assumption questions ask you for the assumption the author makes to go from the evidence provided to the conclusion.

You can spot an assumption question from words like *assumes, depends on,* and *presupposes.* Here are some of the ways assumption questions are worded on the LSAT.

- Upon which one of the following *assumptions* does the author rely?
- Which one of the following, if *added to* the passage, will make the conclusion logical?
- The validity of the argument *depends on* which one of the following?

> Allyson plays volleyball for Central High School. *Therefore,* Allyson must be more than six feet tall.
>
> Which one of the following is assumed in the argument above?

1. **Identify:** The word *assumed* tells you this is an assumption question.
2. **Untangle:** Based on the keyword *Therefore,* you should recognize the second sentence as the conclusion. The first sentence supports the conclusion and thus serves as evidence. Allyson must be more than six feet tall because she plays volleyball for Central High School.
3. **Predict:** To find the assumption, you need to bridge the gap from the evidence to the conclusion.

> Allyson playing volleyball + *assumption* → Allyson is over 6 feet tall.

Notice the mismatched terms between the evidence and conclusion. The evidence talks about volleyball, and the conclusion discusses being over 6 feet tall. The assumption must bring the two terms together. So the prediction is that all volleyball players for Central High School are more than six feet tall.

4. **Evaluate:** Take your prediction and compare it to the multiple-choice answers. The selection that matches is your answer.

In more difficult assumption questions, the answers may not be as obvious and easy to find or predict. So to test whether an assumption really is necessary to the argument, apply the Denial Test. Simply negate the statement and see if the argument falls apart. If it does, you've got the correct assumption. If, on the other hand, the argument is unaffected, the choice is wrong.

What if it's not true that all volleyball palyers for Central High School are more than six feet tall? Can you still logically conclude that Allyson must be taller than six feet? No, you can't. Sure, it's possible that she is, but just as possible that she's not. By denying the statement, then, the argument falls to pieces; it's simply no longer valid. And that's our conclusive proof that the statement is a necessary assumption of this argument.

Don't forget that the Denial Test only works when the question stem is looking for a necessary element—not all assumption questions can be attacked this way.

Weaken Questions

Weaken questions ask for information that can be added to the argument to make the conclusion less likely. Weakening an argument does not mean you need to disprove it, only that you need to make it less plausible.

Words that indicate a weaken question include *weaken*, *calls into question*, *casts doubt on*, and *seriously damages*. Sample LSAT weaken question stems are these:

- Which one of the following, if true, *most seriously weakens* the argument above?
- Which one of the following, if true, *casts the most doubt* on the argument above?

Don't let the "if true" part fool you. It just tells you to accept the truth of the choice right off the bat, no matter how unlikely it may sound to you.

Consider the stimulus used before but with a different question.

> Allyson plays volleyball for Central High School. *Therefore,* Allyson must be more than six feet tall.
>
> Which one of the following, if true, would most weaken the argument?

1. **Identify:** The word *weaken* tells you this is a weaken question.
2. **Untangle:** Actively read the stimulus the same way as you would an assumption question to find the conclusion and evidence. Then connect the evidence to the conclusion through the assumption. The difference here is that you work with those pieces to identify something to make the conclusion less likely to happen.
3. **Predict:** To weaken the argument, you can break down the assumption, attack the conclusion, or find an alternative possibility. Some examples that would weaken the argument in this case: Some volleyball players can jump 3 feet off the ground. Height can hinder the ability of volleyball defensive specialists to get down to the ball quickly. Sabrina Taylor, an Olympic volleyball hopeful and former Central High standout, is 5' 8".
4. **Evaluate:** Next take your prediction and compare it to the multiple-choice answers. The selection that matches is your answer.

Strengthen Questions

Strengthen questions are on the opposite side of the coin from weaken questions. They ask for information that can be added to the argument to make the conclusion more likely. Strengthening an argument does not mean you must make it true, just that you make it more plausible.

Strengthen questions will use words such as *strengthen* and *support* and will look like the following on test day:

- Which one of the following, if true, *provides the most support* for the conclusion in the argument above?
- Which one of the following, if true, *most strengthens* the argument?

Let's continue with the same stimulus.

> Example: Allyson plays volleyball for Central High School.
> *Therefore*, Allyson must be more than six feet tall.
>
> Which one of the following, if true, most supports the statement above?

1. **Identify:** The word *support* and the fact that the support is directed from the answer to the text tells you this is a strengthen question.
2. **Untangle:** Just as before, identify the conclusion, evidence, and assumption. In this case, however, work with those blocks to find a statement to make the conclusion more likely to happen.
3. **Predict:** To strengthen the argument, you can bolster the assumption, support the conclusion, or eliminate alternative possibilities. Possible ways to strengthen this argument: Only players over 6 feet tall can block above the net. Everyone on the Central High School volleyball team is over 6 feet tall.
4. **Evaluate:** Armed with your prediction, review the multiple-choice answers and find the one that matches.

Flaw Questions

Flaw questions want you to determine the error the author makes in going from the evidence to the conclusion. Sometimes you will be asked for a general description of the flaw: The argument is most vulnerable to which one of the following criticisms? You may also be asked for a more specific flaw: The argument's reasoning is flawed because the argument overlooks the possibility that . . . ? In both cases, the argument is flawed, and your job is to identify the error in reasoning. In the second example, however, you are given the flaw and asked to apply it in the context of the stimulus.

Common language for flaw questions includes words such as *flaw, error in reasoning, vulnerable to criticism*, and *questionable because*. Sample question stems include the following:

- The reasoning is flawed in the argument because . . .
- The argument is potentially misleading because the author fails to consider . . .

Try a variation on our previous example.

> All players on the Central High School volleyball team are over 6 feet tall. *Therefore*, all high school volleyball players are more than six feet tall.
>
> The argument is flawed because it . . .

1. **Identify:** The word *flawed* tells you this is a flaw question.

2. **Untangle:** Unpack the conclusion and evidence from the stimulus and bridge the gap to find the assumption. The word *therefore* points us to the last sentence as the conclusion. And just why are all high school volleyball players more than six feet tall? According to this author, it's because all players on the Central High team are over 6 feet tall. The evidence talks about Central players, while the conclusion refers to all high school volleyball players. So the author must assume that the Central players are representative of all high school players.

3. **Predict:** Because this is a flaw question, you can take for granted there is a flaw. Your job is to determine how the argument is flawed. Here, you can describe the flaw as an "unwarranted assumption" or an "unrepresentative sample."

4. **Evaluate:** Find the answer that matches your prediction.

The following is a list of some common flaws that appear on the LSAT and an example of each type.

- **Unwarranted assumption:** Her battery works. Therefore, her cell phone is charged. (The unwarranted assumption is that the battery working is the only thing needed to ensure the cell phone is charged.)

- **Necessity versus sufficiency:** If we have dinner at home, then Mike went to the grocery store. I saw Mike picking up groceries today, so we must be having dinner at home. (Dinner at home necessitates Mike shopping. Mike's shopping is necessary for us to have dinner at home, but if he shops, we may still go out for dinner.)

- **Representativeness:** When I was your age, mint chocolate chip was my favorite ice cream flavor. Therefore, I'll be sure to serve mint chocolate ice cream at your birthday party. (My ice cream preference may not be representative of what you and your friends like.)

- **Scope shift:** Only 15 percent of the school children have been to Washington, D.C. Therefore, the school children must not know a lot about our government. (The evidence talks about traveling to our nation's capital. The conclusion talks about knowledge of government. A scope shift occurs in the argument.)
- **Alternative possibilities:** If Olivia is in class, she turns off her cell phone. So if her phone is off, she must be in class. (Olivia may turn off her phone for other reasons as well.)
- **Causation versus correlation:** In the summer, the Osborne family goes swimming often. They also eat a lot of ice cream in the summer. Therefore, swimming makes them want to eat ice cream. (Swimming and eating ice cream may be related as summer activities, but the argument does not tell us anything about causation.)
- **Opinion versus fact:** The restaurant review said this restaurant has great food. Therefore, it must be great. (One person's saying something is so does not necessarily make it true.)
- **Number versus percentage:** The new vice president for marketing wants to eliminate half of the manager positions and a quarter of the assistant positions. Therefore, she is getting rid of more manager spots than assistant jobs. (Percentages without numbers are flawed on the LSAT. She could be eliminating 50 percent of 10 manager spots and 25 percent of 100 assistant jobs.)

This list is not exhaustive, but it does give you a place to start when thinking about what's gone wrong. If a question does not fit neatly into a classic flaw category, take a good look at the argument, accept there is a flaw in using that evidence to support that conclusion, and find what it is.

INFERENCE QUESTIONS

Inference questions ask you which answer can be inferred from the stimulus. Unlike in everyday inferences, the answer *must* be true based on the information provided. Inference questions are different from the question types you've seen so far in that they typically consist of a set of facts, not an argument.

Inference questions are identifiable from words like *must be true*, *logically follows*, *can be inferred*, and *supports*. You already saw *support* as an indicator of a strengthen question as well. Here is how to tell them apart: Determine the direction of the support. If the text supports the answer, it is an inference question. If the answer supports the text, it is a strengthen question.

Here are some sample question stems:

- Which one of the following *can be properly inferred* from the statements above?
- The statements, if true, *most strongly support* which one of the following?

- If the statements above are true, which one of the following *must also be true?*

Take a look at the following example.

> Allyson plays volleyball for Central High School, despite the team's rule against participation by nonstudents.
>
> Which one of the following must be true based on the statement above?

1. **Identify:** The phrase *must* be true identifies this question as an inference.

2. **Untangle:** As you read the stimulus, accept each statement as true, make any connections between them, and translate any formal logic statements. The stimulus tells us that Allyson plays volleyball for Central even though the team has a rule against nonstudents playing on the team.

3. **Predict:** Inference questions are the only exception to Kaplan's logical reasoning method. Inferences are hard to predict because there can be so many possibilities. It is hard to know exactly what the test maker is thinking. So just make sure you know what the stimulus says.

4. **Evaluate:** Review each answer and ask yourself if it must be true based on what you read. In this case, an answer that said, "Allyson is not a student at Central High School," would be a correct choice.

It is important to remember that

- the correct answer to an inference question will not require any information beyond the stimulus. So the further the answer gets from the stimulus, the more you will know it is wrong.

- a valid inference need not be fancy. It may just be a simple summary of the stimulus.

- extreme wording in inference answers should make you wary. The correct answer cannot be more or less extreme than the stimulus. Words like *never, always, some,* and *must* should be noted so you can match the scope of the text to the answer.

- the correct inference need not come from the entire stimulus. It may just be a rephrasing of one sentence or a combination of sentences.

PRINCIPLE QUESTIONS

Principle questions ask you to find a general rule that accounts for the author's position. More specifically, you may be given a specific situation and asked to fit it into a global generality. Or it could be the reverse—you are given a general rule and asked to identify a situation that exemplifies it. Sometimes you will be asked to find a specific situation in the answer that falls under the same general rule exemplified by the situation in the stimulus.

Principle questions include words like *principle*, *policy*, or *proposition*. Here are some sample stems include:

- Which one of the following *principles* provides the greatest support for the claim made in the passage?
- Which of the following *principles*, if valid, most helps to justify the reasoning above?
- Which one of the following most closely conforms to the *principle* illustrated above?

Try this:

> Marvin's grandmother fell and broke her leg while walking through the parking lot. She has a lot of trouble getting around on her own, and the doctor recommended she not be left at home alone. Therefore, Marvin should provide a home for his grandmother while she is recuperating.
>
> The author's position most closely conforms to which one of the following principles?

1. **Identify:** The word principles identifies this question as a principle question.
2. **Untangle:** Your job is to sum up the argument and put it into general terms that could be applied to other arguments. Here, Marvin's grandmother is incapacitated and can't be left alone. So, the argument concludes, Marvin should move her in with him while she recovers.
3. **Predict:** You are looking for a summary of the argument in broad terms; something like, "If a relative is in need, you should do your best to help that person, regardless of personal inconvenience." Notice the general nature of the principle. It does not specifically mention Marvin or his grandmother or the exact situation of the stimulus. Instead, the general situation (helping a relative in need) is addressed.
4. **Evaluate:** Match the correct answer to your prediction.

Oftentimes, principle questions mimic other logical reasoning questions. You may be asked for a principle that justifies (strengthens) or weakens the author's argument, a principle that underlies the argument (assumption), or something that must be true based on the principle (inference). If you recognize the wording of another question type in a principle question, use that knowledge to untangle the stimulus.

PARALLEL REASONING QUESTIONS

Parallel reasoning questions require you to identify the choice that contains the same kind of reasoning as that presented in the stimulus. The correct answer is based on the argument's form, not its content. Many test takers avoid the parallel reasoning questions because of the length of the stimulus and each answer. By following the Kaplan Method, however, you can get points from these questions. Read on.

Common parallel reasoning identifiers are *parallel to* or *similar to*. Check out these sample question stems.

- The reasoning above is most closely *paralleled* in which one of the following?
- The pattern of reasoning is *similar to* that exhibited in which one of the following?
- Which one of the following exhibits faulty reasoning *most similar to* the flawed argument above?

Try this:

> Coach Walker has her best recruiting class ever this year along with several experienced players. They work well as a team, they are dedicated, and they are motivated to win. *Therefore,* the Buckeye University soccer team will definitely win the conference championship this year.
>
> Which one of the following arguments has a pattern of reasoning most like the one in the argument above?

1. **Identify:** The *pattern of reasoning most* like language tells you this is a parallel reasoning question.
2. **Untangle:** Read the stimulus looking for the conclusion and evidence. Then characterize the conclusion. In this case, the conclusion is "The Buckeye University soccer team will definitely win the conference championship this year." It is a prediction of something that will absolutely happen supported by unquantifiable evidence.

   Other common conclusion types besides prediction are recommendation, comparison, assertion of fact, if/then, and value judgment. The conclusions must also match in terms of other considerations. Look at whether the conclusion is positive or negative and whether it is qualified in any way through words such as likely or impossible.
3. **Predict:** You are looking for an answer with a conclusion that is in the form of a positive prediction supported by qualitative evidence.

4. **Evaluate:** Match the correct answer to your summary of the argument structure. First find the conclusion of each answer to determine if it is a positive prediction. If not, eliminate it—there is no need to check the rest of that answer. If you have more than one answer left after checking the conclusions, go back to those and compare the evidence structure.

Again, focus on the form of the argument, not its content. Don't let yourself be drawn to a choice based on its subject matter. A stimulus about music may have an answer choice that also involves music, but that doesn't mean that the reasoning in the two arguments is similar.

METHOD OF ARGUMENT QUESTIONS

Method of argument questions ask you to demonstrate an understanding of how an author's argument is put together, not what it says. You will describe in general terms how the author makes her point. The key skill—once again—involves being able to analyze the structure of an argument.

Method of argument language includes phrases such as *argumentative technique*, *argumentative strategy*, and *responds to . . . by*. Some sample question stems follow.

- Which one of the following describes the author's *argumentative strategy*?
- James *responds to* Michael by . . .

Try this example:

> Company president: The consultant reviewed our operation and determined the company needs to double production at the Ohio plant. *Therefore*, we must increase production right away to reach that goal.
>
> The author uses what technique to make his argument?

1. **Identify:** The word technique tells you that this is a method of argument question.
2. **Untangle:** The stimulus will either be presented as a paragraph or as a conversation between two people. Read the stimulus looking for the conclusion and evidence and look for how they are put together. Also, pay attention to the keywords used to provide structure and flow to the argument.
3. **Predict:** Here, the company president presents an expert's review to conclude that production must increase.
4. **Evaluate:** Find the answer that matches the prediction.

PARADOX QUESTIONS

Paradox questions ask you to make something that does not appear to make sense into something that does. A paradox exists when an argument contains two or more inconsistent statements. The correct answer will reconcile the seemingly inconsistent statements while allowing them all to be true.

Paradox language includes phrases like *solve the apparent paradox*, *resolve the discrepancy*, and *explain*. Here are some sample question stems.

- Which one of the following *solves the mystery* presented above?
- Which one of the following, if true, *explains the surprising result*?

Try this example:

> Fifty-seven percent of the registered voters in this district claimed to support the Democratic candidate, yet the Republican candidate won the election with 55 percent of the vote.
>
> Which of the following would resolve the apparent discrepancy above?

1. **Identify:** *Resolve the apparent discrepancy* tells us that this is a paradox question.
2. **Untangle:** Read the stimulus looking for the paradox. What does not make sense? Here, the Republican won the election, even though more registered voters preferred the Democrat.
3. **Predict:** To reconcile this paradox, you need to provide an explanation that accounts for a majority of registered voters supporting the Democrat but the Republican winning—something like the Democratic supporters did not show up at the polls in the numbers expected. Reconcile the seemingly contradictory elements of the argument by showing that the group of registered voters is not identical to the group of people who actually voted in the election.
4. **Evaluate:** Compare your prediction to the answer choices and choose the match.

POINT AT ISSUE QUESTIONS

These questions involve a conversation between two speakers and ask you to identify the issue on which they take differing opinions. To see where two arguments differ, separately compare their conclusions and their evidence. The trick is to stay within the scope of both speakers' arguments; the point at issue can't be something that one speaker raises but the other doesn't address at all. The correct answer will describe a point addressed by both speakers and about which the speakers hold conflicting views.

Point at issue questions include words like *A and B disagree over whether* and *the point at issue between them is*. Take a look at the following sample stems.

- Scott and Jack *disagree over whether* . . .
- The *point at issue between* the two candidates is . . .

Here is an example:

> Andrew: We should present documentary evidence to support our client's claims. The materials were created in the course of business and have lots of information.
>
> Deb: I want to put an expert on the stand. The information is complicated, and the jury will find it easier to understand if we introduce the data through testimony.
>
> Andrew and Deb disagree over which one of the following?

1. **Identify:** The phrase *disagree over* tells us that this is a point at issue question.
2. **Untangle:** Andrew wants to present documentary evidence, and Deb wants to introduce testimonial evidence to make their client's case.
3. **Predict:** Both speakers are strategizing the client's case and how to present it. They differ, however, on the best way to do that.
4. **Evaluate:** Look for an answer that acknowledges the speakers' disagreement about how best to present their client's case.

MAIN POINT QUESTIONS

Main point questions are exactly what they sound like. They ask you to find the author's central claim in his argument. Key conclusion words such as *therefore* and *thus* will point you to the main point. However, they are often missing in main point questions. Be on the lookout for the author's disagreement, use the one-sentence test introduced earlier in this section, or combine sentences to identify the conclusion.

Main point clues are terms like *main idea* and *conclusion*. You will see question stems such as these:

- Which one of the following most accurately expresses the *main point* of the argument?
- Which one of the following is the *main conclusion* of the argument?

Here is an example:

> Most people prefer to take the scenic route when traveling to Franklintown and enjoy the countryside. However, that takes too much time. I always take the direct route on I-71.
>
> What is the main conclusion of the argument?

1. **Identify:** *Main conclusion* says this is a main point question.
2. **Untangle:** The author disagrees with the route choice most people take to Franklintown and identifies a problem with it—it takes too long. What is the author's solution? Take the direct route.
3. **Predict:** Look for the main point in the author's disagreement and combine statements. Here the author disagrees about the best route and says he takes I-71. In other words, the best route to Franklintown is I-71.
4. **Evaluate:** Find an answer choice that matches your summary.

ROLE OF A STATEMENT QUESTIONS

Role of a statement questions include a statement from the stimulus (usually verbatim) and ask you to determine the role it plays in the argument. We have learned already that the main components of an argument are the conclusion and evidence, so read the stimulus looking for the identified statement, the conclusion, and the evidence. If the statement from the question stem does not fit neatly into a conclusion or evidence designation, think about what the author is trying to do with the statement.

Role of a statement terminology includes plays which one of the following roles, *figures in the argument*, and *plays which part*. Here are some sample question stems:

- The assertion that the company must increase production *plays which of the following roles* in the president's argument?
- The statement that Allyson plays volleyball for Central High School *figures in the argument* in which of the following ways?

Let's see how this works with an example:

> Although voters embrace the idea of clean air, they are weary of the high cost of environmental cleanup. Therefore, I will recommend to the senator that she vote against the environmental bill as it now stands.
>
> The statement that voters are weary of the high cost of environmental cleanup plays which one of the following roles in the argument above?

1. **Identify:** The role of the statement question is identified by the phrase *plays which one of the following roles.*

2. **Untangle:** Your task is to find the phrase from the question in the stimulus and determine the role it plays in the argument. Once you find the phrase, break down the argument into conclusion and evidence. In this example, the conclusion is found in the last sentence with the keyword *therefore.* The first sentence indicates why the recommendation will be made to the senator and, consequently, serves as evidence.

3. **Predict:** The phrase that voters are weary of the high cost of environmental cleanup is part of the evidence. So the prediction is just that, or a statement that defines evidence.

4. **Evaluate:** Determine an answer that matches your prediction.

SECTION MANAGEMENT

Not all logical reasoning questions are created equally. Some are easier, and some are more difficult. Because each question is worth the same toward your score, you want to manage the Logical Reasoning section to get as many points as you can. Remember, law schools don't see which answers you get right and wrong. They just get a final score. So don't belabor one question. Move on. It's better to decide in 10 seconds that the question is hard and will take you a while so you should skip it than to invest 3 minutes in it and still end up guessing. Use your time where you can get points.

We will talk later about the Logic Games and Reading Comprehension sections, in which you can reorder the four games and the four passages to take control of the section and set yourself up to get the most points you can. That will not work in the Logical Reasoning sections. You can't preview all the questions and reorder them. It would take too long.

The level of difficulty typically goes up as you move through a Logical Reasoning section. Of course, you'll find a difficult question or two early in the section. Such placement rewards test takers who answer skillfully or skip a tough question and punishes test takers who insist on sticking with a question regardless of time wasted. You'll also find easier questions toward the end of the section, rewarding those who get there and penalizing those who get bogged down and never get to the end.

Difficult questions generally include some combination of a longer or more confusing stimulus, formal logic, tougher answer choices, and parallel reasoning (considered a high-difficulty question type). The important lesson is that you recognize questions that are more challenging for you and use that knowledge to decide whether to skip a question or not. Just remember to circle a question you skip so you can refer to it later. Also, make sure you are bubbling your answers properly on the grid sheet.

One more point about managing the Logical Reasoning section—the difficulty level tends to spike around questions 14 to 22. Practice working through questions 13, 14, or 15 (or wherever there is a natural page break) and then turn to the end of that section and work back toward the middle from there. For example, you can work through the first four pages, then turn to the last page and the last question of the section and begin working backwards. That means you will get to the "danger zone" at the end. If you are running out of time, you want to run out of time where the questions are harder and you might need to guess anyway.

HELPFUL HINTS TO IMPROVE YOUR PERFORMANCE

Use Formal Logic in Logical Reasoning

Identifying, translating, and understanding formal logic statements is imperative for your success on the LSAT. Your ability to manipulate formal logic statements allows you to transform a complex statement into a more manageable format. Whether you're tackling a tough logical reasoning stimulus or analyzing logic game rules, a strong command of formal logic is critical to building your accuracy and efficiency on the LSAT.

For LSAT purposes, formal logic is all about conditional statements. These statements tell you that a certain condition is sufficient to know that the necessary result will happen. So you must be able to break statements down into sufficient elements (trigger/cause) and necessary conditions (result/effect). The most basic form of formal logic is an if/then statement.

For example, if Emerson travels to Europe, then she must have a valid passport. In other words, a valid passport is necessary for Emerson's trip to Europe. Just knowing that Emerson takes a trip to Europe is sufficient for you to know that she has a valid passport.

However, if Emerson has a valid passport, does she have to take a trip to Europe? Not necessarily. She may or may not. Just knowing she has a valid passport does not tell us whether she takes a trip to Europe or anywhere for that matter. The valid passport is necessary, but not sufficient, for Emerson to take a trip to Europe. The result is necessary for the condition to occur, but the result is never sufficient by itself to know whether the condition must occur.

Keywords help you recognize formal logic and indicate which part of the statement is sufficient (trigger/cause) and which part is necessary (result/effect).

Sufficient Words (Trigger/Cause) X	→	Y Necessary Words (Result/Effect)
If		Then
Any		Only
All		Only if
Every		Not/Never/No…unless
When(ever)		Not/Never/No…without
Sufficient/Enough/Guarantee		Necessary/Needed/Required
Cause		Effect
Each		Must

In other words, you must identify the X and the Y. So no matter what text form you find the formal logic in, your goal is to translate the statement back to the basic X → Y.

Remember, there are six basic statements in which the X is always the sufficient condition and Y is always the result. All of these statements mean the same thing and can be taken to the simplest version (If X, then Y). For example, let's look at the first statement, "If you apply to law school, then you h ave to take the LSAT." The X, the sufficient element, is applying to law school. The Y, the necessary result, is taking the LSAT. How would the different translations be stated?

Formal Logic in Text Form	Formal Logic in Equation Form
If you apply to law school, then you take the LSAT.	If X, then Y
All students who apply to law school have to take the LSAT.	All X are Y
Only students who have taken the LSAT are applying to law school.	Only Y are X.
You are applying to law school only if you have taken the LSAT.	X only if Y.
No student applies to law school unless he or she has taken the LSAT.	No X unless Y.
If you do not take the LSAT, then you cannot apply to law school.	If not Y, then not X. (contrapositive of all five statements)

Thus, if you find a statement in any of the previous text forms or their variations, you translate it into the matching equation. From the equation, you identify the X and the Y and create the "If X, then Y," statement. Now what? You form the contrapositive.

The contrapositive is the only other statement you can know to be true based on the "If X, then Y," statement. Put simply, the contrapositive is equally valid as the original statement and is nothing more than another way to express the truth of the original statement.

To form the contrapositive, you take three steps.

1. Reverse the terms around the arrow.
2. Negate both terms.
3. Any *and* changes to *or*; any *or* changes to *and*. (This step only applies to complex formal logic statements.)

Let's continue with the previous example. What's the contrapositive for the first statement, "If you apply to law school, then you have to take the LSAT"? We've already identified this if/then statement as formal logic, determined the X and the Y, and created the matching equation.

$$X \rightarrow Y$$

Apply to law school $\rightarrow$ Take the LSAT

1. Reverse the terms around the arrow to get $Y \rightarrow X$.
2. Negate both terms to get Not $Y \rightarrow$ Not X.
3. The statement included no *and* and no *or*, so the contrapositive is Not take the LSAT $\rightarrow$ Not apply to law school.

You must be clear on the deductions you can and can't make based on formal logic statements. Here is another example: If I yell loudly at my cat Adrian, he will run away. My yelling loudly at my cat Adrian is sufficient for me to know he will run away. But it's not necessary. My cat might run if I throw water at him, even if I don't yell loudly. The *if* side of the statement gives me the X, and the *then* side gives me the Y. So here is what I get.

Sufficient	$\rightarrow$	Necessary
X	$\rightarrow$	Y
Yell at cat	$\rightarrow$	Cat runs away
Not Y	$\rightarrow$	Not X (contrapositive)
Cat does not run away	$\rightarrow$	Did not yell at cat

Given that the statements above are true, which one of the following statements must also be true?

1. If I don't yell loudly at my cat Adrian, he will not run away.
2. If my cat Adrian has run away, then I yelled at him.
3. If my cat Adrian has not run away, then I did not yell loudly at him.

The third statement, the contrapositive, is the only one of the three that's inferable from the original. There is no way to tell what happens if I don't yell loudly at my cat Adrian. It is not a trigger. I also don't know what happens if my cat Adrian has run away. That is not a trigger either.

Let's try one more example: If Spencer votes, he is registered and he is 18 or older.

Sufficient	$\rightarrow$	Necessary
X	$\rightarrow$	Y and Z
Votes	$\rightarrow$	Registered and 18+
Not Y or Not Z	$\rightarrow$	Not X (contrapositive)
Not registered or not 18+	$\rightarrow$	Did not vote

So from the original statement and the contrapositive, we know what happens if Spencer votes, and we know what the result is if Spencer is not registered or if he's not 18 or older. That's it. There is *no* trigger for (so you can't know the result of) Spencer's not voting. You also can't know the result if Spencer is registered and he's 18 or older. Again, that is not a trigger.

One more important point about formal logic: It is not the order of the conditions that makes them sufficient and necessary. Rather, the language of the conditions determines whether a condition is sufficient or necessary.

ANSWER THE QUESTION BEING ASKED

It's disheartening when you fully understand the author's argument and then lose the point by supplying an answer to a question that wasn't asked. For example, when you're asked for an inference supported by the argument, it does you no good to jump on any choice that might be true. Likewise, if you're asked for an assumption, don't be fooled into selecting a choice that merely restates a piece of the author's stated evidence.

When asked why they chose a particular wrong choice, students sometimes respond by saying such things as "Well, it could be true, right?" and "Look, it says so right there," pointing to the stimulus. Well, that's simply not good enough. The question stem doesn't ask, "Which one of the following looks vaguely familiar to you?" It asks for something very specific. You must follow the test makers' line of reasoning to the correct response.

Also, be on the lookout for "reversers"—words such as *least* and *except,* which are easy to miss but entirely change what you're looking for among the choices.

ELIMINATE WRONG CHOICES FIRST IF YOU HAVE TO GUESS

One or more of the wrong answer choices on any question will fall into patterns that, with practice, you'll quickly recognize. Any wrong choice you can eliminate improves your chance of choosing the correct answer. On logical reasoning questions, common wrong answer types are these:

- **Outside scope:** As you just saw, these are very common. These answers will focus on immaterial or irrelevant information that is outside the scope of the argument. They are usually within the same topic, though, so be careful!
- **Extreme:** Unless the language of the argument is extreme, choices using words like *always, never, none, all,* and *every* are most likely wrong.

- **Distortion:** Some choices use language or ideas from the stimulus but misapply them conspicuously.
- **Half right, half wrong:** Some choices join a correct statement with an incorrect one; don't be hasty and choose your answer without reading the entire choice.
- **180:** Choices that are exactly the opposite of the correct one are common, especially on questions that ask for exceptions or on strengthen/weaken questions.
- **Irrelevant comparison:** These answer choices often involve statistical evidence that compares two things that are unrelated or have no effect on the validity of the argument.

PRACTICE PROBLEM

Let's try this question together before you head into the practice sets.

> A study of 20 overweight men revealed that each man experienced significant weight loss after adding SlimDown, an artificial food supplement, to his daily diet. For three months, each man consumed one SlimDown portion every morning after exercising and then followed his normal diet for the rest of the day. Clearly, anyone who consumes one portion of SlimDown every day for at least three months will lose weight and will look and feel his or her best.
>
> Which one of the following is an assumption on which the argument depends?
>
> (A) The men in the study will gain back the weight they lost if they discontinue the SlimDown program.
>
> (B) No other dietary supplement will have the same effect on overweight men.
>
> (C) The daily exercise regimen was not responsible for the effects noted in the study.
>
> (D) Women will not experience similar weight reductions if they adhere to the SlimDown program for three months.
>
> (E) Overweight men will achieve only partial weight loss if they do not remain on the SlimDown program for a full three months.

1. READ THE QUESTION STEM FIRST: IDENTIFY

Quite clearly, this is an Assumption question. Before reading the first word of the stimulus, you know that the conclusion will lack an important piece of supporting evidence. Now turn to the stimulus, already on the lookout for this missing link.

2. Untangle the Stimulus: Analyze

The first sentence introduces a study of 20 men using a food supplement, resulting in weight loss for all 20. The second sentence describes how they used it: once a day for three months, after morning exercise. So far so good; it feels as if it's building up to something. The keyword *clearly* usually indicates that some sort of conclusion follows, and in fact it does, in the third sentence: Anyone who has one portion of the product daily for three months will lose weight too.

Read critically! If you read quickly, the conclusion might seem to say that anyone who follows the same routine as the 20 men will have the same results, but it actually says that anyone who consumes the product in the same way will have the same results. You should have begun to sense the lack of crucial information at this point. The evidence in the second sentence describes a routine that includes daily exercise, whereas the conclusion focuses only on the supplement. The conclusion, therefore, doesn't stem logically from the evidence. This blends seamlessly into Step 3.

3. Think Critically About the Answer: Predict

As expected, the argument is beginning to look as if it has a serious shortcoming. In simplified terms, the argument is "A bunch of guys did A and B for three months and had X result. If anyone does A for three months, that person will experience X result too." The author must be assuming that A (the product), not B (exercise), was the determining element. So you might prephrase: "Something about exercise needs to be cleared up." That's it. All you need is an inkling of what the question is looking for, and in this case, it seems that if you don't shore up the exercise issue, the argument is invalid. Turn to Step 4, which is . . .

4. Review the Answer Choices: Evaluate

Since you were able to prephrase something, it's best to skim the choices looking for it. And there's your idea, stated in a very LSAT-like manner, in (C).

In questions based on the recognition of evidence and conclusions in arguments, once you grasp the structure of the argument and have located the author's central assumption, you should be able to answer any question the test throws at you. This one takes the form of an Assumption question, but it could just as easily have been a Weaken question:

> Which one of the following, if true, casts the most doubt on the argument above?

Answer: Daily exercise contributed significantly to the weight loss experienced by the men in the study.

And here's a Flaw question that could have been based on the same stimulus:

> **The author's reasoning is flawed because it . . .**

Answer: . . . overlooks the possibility that the results noted in the study were caused by daily exercise rather than by the consumption of SlimDown.

So there you have it—a quick demonstration of how to use the strategies and techniques outlined in this chapter to work through the complete Logical Reasoning process. Apply these techniques on the following practice sets and in the Logical Reasoning sections of your Practice Tests in this book. Pay careful attention to all of the answer explanations, even for the questions you got right.

LOGICAL REASONING PRACTICE

SET ONE

<u>Directions:</u> This test consists of questions that ask you to analyze the logic of statements or short paragraphs. For each question, you are to choose the answer you consider correct on the basis of your common-sense evaluation of the statement and its assumptions. Although a question may seem to have more than one acceptable answer, there is only one answer, and it is the one that does not entail making any illogical, extraneous, or conflicting assumptions about the question. These questions do not presuppose any knowledge of formal logic on your part.

1. In his long and epochal career, Beethoven was both synthesizer and innovator, the supreme classicist who startled the musical world of his time by his bold surges forward toward the chromaticism to come. But because his later music made so much use of unprecedented dissonance, a few cynical critics have suggested that the composer's progressively worsening deafness must have weakened his ability to imagine and produce consistently harmonious music. In other words, he was writing what he misheard, according to these critics. I maintain that, on the contrary, if the deaf Beethoven had been trying to create in a medium he had known intimately but could no longer manipulate successfully, he would have been all the more likely to _____.

    Which one of the following best completes the passage above?

    (A) depend heavily upon the rules of conventional harmony to produce predictable sounds

    (B) compose dissonances from his inability to hear what he had written

    (C) rely upon his own judgment in deciding what type of music to compose

    (D) avoid cynical criticism by composing only consistently harmonious music

    (E) suspect that his ear had become so untrustworthy that he should end his career before full maturation

2. Many factors affect the home-building industry, but the number of single-family homes under construction generally rises as interest rates decline. Contractors are able to plan their hiring schedules and order essential building materials in response to reliable predictors of the movement of prevailing interest rates.

    It can be inferred from the passage above that

    (A) the price of building materials rises when interest rates decline.

    (B) no factor affecting home building is as reliable a predictor as interest rates.

    (C) assessments of growth in the housing industry are sometimes based upon expected fluctuations of interest rates.

    (D) a contractor does not order building materials until a hiring schedule is set up.

    (E) most housing being built today is single-family housing.

3. Experts on the American political process have long agreed that voters like a certain amount of combativeness, even aggressiveness, in a presidential candidate. A poll just after the 1988 election, however, showed that many people had been annoyed or disgusted with the campaign and had not even bothered to vote. In addition, many voters felt that most candidates were "nonpresidential." Campaigns that feature combativeness have therefore become counterproductive by causing voters to lose respect for the combative candidate.

Which one of the following, if true, most seriously weakens the argument?

(A) Many presidential campaigns have been memorable because they were full of surprises.

(B) The poll cited does not specifically show that combative campaigning was responsible for voter disaffection.

(C) Even before 1988, many voters were skeptical about politicians, particularly candidates for president.

(D) What seems to be aggressiveness is really assertiveness, a necessary quality for keeping one's name in the public eye.

(E) Political campaigning is a means of giving voters essential information on which they must base their decisions.

4. The federal government currently interferes blatantly in the relationship between parent and child. The Internal Revenue Service provides a child care or dependent's deduction on the annual income tax return. In effect, the government, by rewarding some providers of support, determines which taxpayers are to be considered worthy enough to care for dependents.

Which one of the following, if true, weakens the argument above?

(A) A taxpayer need only attach the appropriate schedule to the tax form to apply for the deduction.

(B) The deduction is likely to offer a proportionately greater benefit to the lower-income taxpayer.

(C) A child must be living at home with the provider of support in order to qualify as a dependent.

(D) The deduction actually affects a fairly small percentage of taxpayers.

(E) The deduction is available to anyone who supplies the principal support of a dependent.

5. Detective-adventure series and other action programming on prime-time television have been criticized for inciting some viewers, male adolescents in particular, to commit acts of violence. The most carefully engineered studies have not, however, supported this assumption. Rather, it seems likely that someone who is frustrated and resentful and, therefore, prone to violence is drawn to the kind of programming that shows characters who release their frustrations in acts of violence.

Which one of the following would provide the most logical concluding sentence for the paragraph above?

(A) In fact, action programming probably helps a frustrated viewer release hostility without resorting to violence.

(B) Moreover, there are studies that indicate that male adolescents are more likely than other viewers to believe that the world shown in action programming is realistic.

(C) In other words, an unusual interest in action programming may be an indication of a violence-prone personality rather than an incitement to violence.

(D) Be that as it may, action programming continues to grow in popularity with the American TV audience.

(E) Therefore, the reasonable observer of the American scene will conclude that action programming should be banned from prime-time viewing hours.

Questions 6–7

Although the legislative process in our democratic government is based on the proposition that Congress must represent the interests of the majority of its constituents, this principle that the majority rules is frequently contradicted by the efforts of lobbyists. Minority interests with the wherewithal to finance hard-sell lobbying campaigns can distort an elected official's sense of public opinion, thereby exercising a destructive influence over political decisions.

6. The argument above depends upon the truth of which one of the following assumptions?

(A) The democratic process is a reflection of our capitalist economic system.

(B) The democratic process requires that minority interests be protected by constitutional amendment.

(C) Minority interests cannot be protected without spending large sums of money on lobbying activities.

(D) The democratic process cannot function properly unless the activities of big business are restrained.

(E) The democratic process depends on the ability of all members of society to have equal influence on the legislative process.

7. Which one of the following, if true, would most weaken the argument above?

(A) The majority opinion on many political issues is ill informed and unconsidered.

(B) Elected officials are rarely influenced by pressures of lobbying campaigns.

(C) Interest groups can accumulate large sums of money through fund-raising activities.

(D) All groups and interests are entitled to hire professional lobbyists to represent their cause.

(E) There is no clear-cut majority position on many political issues facing Congress.

8. If we reduce the rate of income taxation, people will spend a larger portion of their gross incomes on consumer goods. This will stimulate economic growth and result in higher salaries and, thus, in higher government revenues, despite a lower rate of taxation.

   Which one of the following arguments most closely resembles the reasoning in the statements above?

   (A) If we reduce the amount of overtime our employees work, production costs will decline, and our total income will thus increase.

   (B) If we make it harder to participate in the school lunch program, people will have to pay for more of their food, and farm income will therefore increase.

   (C) If a movie is classified as obscene, more people will want to see it, and the morals of the general community will be corrupted more than they would be otherwise.

   (D) If we give our employees more paid holidays, their efficiency while actually on the job will improve, and our total productivity will thus increase.

   (E) If we give our children more spending money, they will learn to manage their finances better and will thereby realize the virtue of thrift.

9. If a judge is appointed for life, she will make courtroom decisions that reflect the accumulated wisdom inherent in this country's judicial history, relying upon the law and reason rather than upon trends in political thinking. If, on the other hand, the judge is appointed or elected for short terms in office, her decisions will be heavily influenced by the prevailing political climate. In sum, the outcome of many court cases will be determined by the method by which the presiding judge has been installed in her post.

   Each of the following, if true, provides support for the argument above EXCEPT

   (A) Surveys indicate that judges enjoy their work and want to remain in office as long as possible.

   (B) Judges appointed for life are just as informed about political matters as are judges who must run for re-election.

   (C) The rulings of judges who must run for re-election are generally approved of by the voters who live in their elective districts.

   (D) Most judges appointed for life hand down identical rulings on similar cases throughout their long careers.

   (E) Only judges who are selected for short terms of office employ pollsters to read the mood of the electorate.

10. Advertisement: Savvy shoppers know that the Fall Sale at Thompson's gives you great savings on clothes for the whole family. When you make at least one purchase in each of the men's, women's, and Children's departments during the sale, you'll receive a voucher for 50 percent off any purchase in the Housewares department. If you're working to clothe the family on a budget, don't miss the Fall Sale at Thompson's!

    Which one of the following provides the most serious criticism of the above advertisement?

    (A) Many shoppers may not make a purchase in each department during September.

    (B) The savings advertised are for housewares, not for clothing.

    (C) The length of the sale is not specified in the advertisement.

    (D) A purchase in the Housewares department is much more expensive than a purchase in the Women's department.

    (E) The sale does not take into account other discounts that customers may redeem.

11. It is possible for a panhandler to collect a considerable amount of money from passersby if she can convince them that she is destitute and that begging is the only way for her to help herself. If, on the other hand, passersby get the impression that they are being conned or that the panhandler is just being lazy, they will not give her anything at all.

    Which one of the following statements can be most reliably concluded from the passage above?

    (A) Most panhandlers are unwilling to work.

    (B) If someone begs when she does not need to, people will not give her any money.

    (C) Most passersby would give a panhandler money if they thought that she was not conning them.

    (D) Passersby often base their decision of whether or not to give money to a panhandler on their impressions of her and her honesty.

    (E) People who give money to panhandlers are not influenced by how much change they have in their pockets when they decide the amount of money they will give.

12. Dr. Kells is a better physician than Dr. Li. This is obvious because in a recent survey, their mutual patients rated Dr. Kells as the better physician.

    The argument above assumes that

    (A) patient rating is a valid indicator of the quality of a physician.

    (B) patients will rate a doctor as "better" if they feel more comfortable with that doctor.

    (C) the better doctor will be the one with greater experience.

    (D) the better doctor is the one from whose care patients benefit more.

    (E) there are no doctors better than Dr. Kells.

13. Although temporary and contract employees can play an important role in completing projects and adjusting to seasonal work flow, they are not an adequate substitute for a full-time, permanent staff. To thrive, the company needs workers who are not just skilled and efficient but who also have a personal connection to their work and a dedication to the company. A staff made up of contract or temporary employees is incomplete at best.

The author of this passage assumes that

(A) temporary employees are detrimental to a company's success.

(B) companies should encourage temporary employees to feel dedicated to their employers.

(C) seasonal work flow is not an important factor in assessing an employee's suitability for work.

(D) temporary employees lack connection and commitment to the companies that hire them.

(E) permanent employees are more skilled and efficient than are temporary employees.

SET TWO

1. We gave working parents the opportunity to use a trial membership to our new Flash Fitness Centers. More than 85 percent found this convenient new workout to be very effective. If you're a parent who is crunched for time, Flash Fitness is the quick solution!

Which one of the following statements is the most serious criticism of the advertisement above?

(A) Working parents are not necessarily representative of the general population.

(B) Other fitness centers are just as convenient and effective as Flash Fitness.

(C) The fact that working parents found Flash Fitness effective does not mean that it was quick.

(D) *Effective* is a subjective term and makes no representation as to a measurable degree of success.

(E) Most people do not consider convenience as an important factor when choosing a fitness center.

2. Ranjit was extremely upset when he received a failing grade in his engineering class because he had attended every class, participated in class discussions, and turned in every project except for the 3-D modeling project. He concluded that the grade was unfair, because other students who had not turned in the 3-D modeling project had passed the class.

Based on the information contained in the passage, it is reasonable to infer that

(A) Ranjit has never failed a class before.

(B) Ranjit received a failing grade primarily because he didn't turn in the 3-D modeling assignment.

(C) Ranjit received above-average scores on all of his assignments except the 3-D modeling project.

(D) Ranjit believes that he received a failing grade primarily because he did not turn in the 3-D modeling project.

(E) Ranjit's performance was above average in comparison to students in other engineering courses.

3. Several of the older pieces in the City Opera Company's costume shop, made from rare vintage fabrics, have become threadbare and worn from improper storage and exposure to light. Luckily, the original seamstress saved the extra fabric from the creation of these costumes. Utilizing the seamstress's original patterns and these pieces of fabric, the costume designer will be able to restore the costumes to their original fabric quality.

Which of the following statements, if true, would most strengthen the author's argument?

(A) The costume designer will be able to duplicate the original seamstress's careful technique.

(B) The heavy traffic and difficulty in maintaining a steady climate make the costume shop a less than ideal location for storage of the costumes.

(C) The seamstress anticipated that the costumes would eventually need repairs.

(D) The fabric that was put aside when the costumes were made has not itself been damaged by improper storage.

(E) Garment storage techniques were not advanced enough at the time the costumes were made to prevent them from becoming damaged.

4. Due to a dramatic drop in population, Academy B, known as one of the city's best schools, closed. Many of its teachers got jobs in suburban school districts well known for their excellent schools. They returned to Academy B when it reopened two years later and have all remained there; the school is again considered one of the finest in the city.

   Which one of the following can be most reasonably inferred from the statements above?

   (A) The quality of education at Academy B vastly improved only because its teachers worked in other excellent schools.

   (B) Academy B reopened because its board recognized the high quality of the teachers' work.

   (C) When Academy B reopened, some suburban school teachers left their jobs.

   (D) The teachers in the district's other schools did not have an opportunity to teach at Academy B when it reopened.

   (E) Although the teachers in the district's other schools were inferior to those at Academy B, the closing of the school had no real effect on the district's quality of education.

5. Proponents of writing programs have reacted with uncritical enthusiasm to recent studies showing an increase in writing programs in high schools. The majority of these classes, however, utilize creative writing techniques rather than the traditional practice in reading texts and writing and revising expository text. Unfortunately, by concentrating on a less practical type of expression, these programs will actually have the undesirable effect of decreasing the numbers of high school graduates who are skilled at expository writing.

   The author's conclusion relies on which of the following beliefs?

   (A) Introducing an expository writing requirement for graduation would lead to the abandonment of most creative writing classes.

   (B) When students have a choice, more of them will enroll in a creative writing course than in an expository writing course.

   (C) Creative writing courses fail to provide the skills necessary to be an effective expository writer.

   (D) Continued emphasis on creative writing courses will eventually reduce the pool of qualified instructors of expository writing.

   (E) Most high school graduates today have at least average skills in expository writing.

6. Figures from other cities conclusively disprove the commonly held belief that magnet school programs in Minneapolis caused the extremely long waiting lists for certain schools. Some cities with magnet school programs have no waiting lists for schools at all, while in other cities with no magnet programs, parents send their children to schools in other areas because the classes in their neighborhood elementary schools are so crowded.

The author of the argument is assuming which of the following?

(A) Because magnet school programs offer different programs than other schools, parents' decisions to add their children to the waiting lists must be motivated by an interest in that particular school.

(B) Because magnet school programs have not caused long school waiting lists in every case, they have not caused the increase in Minneapolis.

(C) Because magnet school programs in other cities did not cause school waiting lists to grow, their impact has been beneficial.

(D) Minneapolis's magnet school program fostered long waiting lists because it did not sufficiently anticipate the number of interested families.

(E) Despite magnet school programs, waiting lists for schools in Minneapolis are minimal.

7. Researchers in the harbor town of Osceola have determined that the channeling of recycled wastewater into the harbor is endangering the health of the town's residents. A sharp increase in cases of the intestinal illness giardia has been directly attributed to bacteria that began to appear in drinking water supplies immediately following the implementation of the wastewater recycling program. The researchers have proposed adding the synthetic enzyme tripticase to the water during recycling. The addition of this enzyme would solve the health problem by eliminating the bacteria that causes giardia.

Which one of the following statements, if true, most weakens the researchers' argument?

(A) The tripticase enzyme also acts to break down bacteria causing intestinal conditions other than giardia.

(B) Globally, giardia is one of the least common and the least severe of all known illnesses related to the consumption of contaminated drinking water.

(C) No other illnesses aside from giardia have increased significantly in Osceola since the wastewater recycling program began.

(D) Giardia may be caused by the ingestion of contaminated food as well as contaminated drinking water.

(E) The tripticase enzyme also breaks down the chlorine that is essential to maintaining a safe drinking water supply.

8. Fairfield College's dean of English noticed that average scores on the year-end freshman English assessment have been significantly lower since 1998 than they were prior to that year. She also realized that in 1998, the freshman English classes had been moved from a 2 P.M. time slot to an 8 A.M. time slot. The dean, pointing out that students perform better when they are wide awake, concluded that test scores would increase if the English class were moved back to the afternoon time slot.

The dean's argument assumes that which of the following is true?

(A) Classroom space could be made available for the English class meeting at 2 P.M.

(B) Numerous factors could account for the drop in test scores.

(C) Other colleges with higher English test scores have classes that meet later in the day.

(D) Students are more likely to be wide awake during the afternoon than they are early in the morning.

(E) The quality of the English professors' instruction has little or no effect on the students' test scores.

9. It is more expensive to live far from an interstate than near one, not because of the cost of commuting but because of the decrease in property values associated with proximity to an interstate. Interstates are located in urban areas, and although homes in urban areas generally command higher prices than those in less populated areas, the presence of an interstate nearby can cause a large decrease in property values. The property values of homes far from an interstate are not subject to this decrease. As a result, rural and suburban homes that are far from an interstate are generally more expensive than urban homes that are near one.

The above argument is based on which one of the following assumptions?

(A) Interstates are built only in neighborhoods that are made up primarily of single-family homes.

(B) The property value loss associated with having an interstate nearby is greater than the gain associated with being located in an urban area.

(C) Urban homes typically have less square footage than homes in suburban and rural areas.

(D) Homeowners who live near an interstate are more likely to raise their property values by remodeling.

(E) Most homes have approximately the same property value when factors of location are not taken into consideration.

10. When Han came home from work, she discovered that although the doors and windows were all closed, her security alarm had gone off, something that can happen only if the alarm is set off by strong winds or the vibrations of a large vehicle. Earlier that morning, the alarm had been set off by a large truck passing by, but Han had turned off the alarm again before she departed. The forecast called for a 40 percent chance of windy weather. Because the truck had already left the neighborhood when Han left for work, the second alarm must have been activated by a strong wind.

    The speaker's conclusion about how the second alarm was activated assumes which one of the following?

    (A) It is easy to tell the difference between an alarm activated by windy weather and one activated by the vibrations of a large vehicle.

    (B) The vibrations of a vehicle are more likely to set off an alarm than is windy weather.

    (C) No large vehicles have passed by Han's house since the truck left earlier in the morning.

    (D) The alarm was set off because it is too sensitive to movement.

    (E) Every time a large vehicle passes by, the alarm will be set off.

11. From the eighth through the 19th century, the Japanese imperial power underwent a period of steady decline. This is often wrongly attributed to a fundamental bias in Japanese society ensuring that clan loyalty was always more important than loyalty to any emperor. A close look at the evidence, however, reveals that even as late as the Kamakura period in the 13th and 14th centuries, military dictators with the title "shogun" ruled in the name of the emperor and exercised a strong, centralized power.

    Which one of the following, if true, would most seriously weaken the argument?

    (A) Many Japanese followed the shogun because they feared his power and not because they were loyal.

    (B) The Kamakura shogunate collapsed in 1333, and Japan experienced 200 years of civil war.

    (C) The shoguns came from independent clans and ruled without concern for the emperor.

    (D) During the earlier Heian period, from the years 794 to 1185, the power of the shoguns was far less than that of the emperor.

    (E) Many historians believe that geography and the system of taxation were more crucial than clan loyalty in undermining imperial power.

Questions 12–13

The moral condemnation, voiced by some segments of the public, of the students arrested recently while demonstrating at City Hall is an error. We should keep in mind that, more than 200 years ago, our forefathers dumped tea in Boston Harbor in defiance of the British.

12. Which one of the following would be the most effective response for the author's opponents in disputing his argument?

(A) It is unpatriotic to demonstrate in front of a City Hall.

(B) Students are too inexperienced to understand the consequences of demonstrations.

(C) In today's world, one's beliefs and conscience are rarely the motivation behind one's actions.

(D) The American patriots who threw tea into Boston Harbor had some public support for their cause.

(E) Simply because some past demonstrations by citizens are considered justified does not mean all such acts are justified.

13. Which one of the following best describes the author's method of argument?

(A) He attacks the public for its manifest hypocrisy.

(B) He argues from a general principle of rebellion to a specific instance of that rebellion.

(C) He argues from a specific instance of rebellion to a general principle concerning the justification of all rebellion.

(D) He draws an analogy between the students' actions and the actions of patriots now deemed justified.

(E) He argues from the lack of sufficient evidence concerning the students' actions to a conclusion supporting the students' actions.

SET THREE

1. The problem with arms reduction is that it is an illusory concept benefiting none. Even though designated stockpiles are being reduced, the weapons race continues, as the destructive power of new technologies and remaining arsenals is enhanced in order to maintain the pre-existing firepower. Thus, although it fosters an illusion of progress, arms reduction does nothing to curtail the proliferation of weaponry, and all must continue to live under the constant threat of annihilation.

Which one of the following, if true, would most strengthen the author's argument?

(A) Arms reduction allows steady maintenance of the existing balance of power.

(B) No arms limitation proposals have aimed at completely eliminating a nation's armament stockpile.

(C) The five largest military powers have increased funding for new weapons in each of the last 10 years.

(D) The distinction between offensive and defensive weapon systems is often merely a matter of interpretation.

(E) Arms limitation treaties have only accounted for the elimination of 15 percent of the total firepower possessed by the five largest military powers.

2. These so-called pacifists are either the victims or the propagators of a false logic. They claim that weapons reductions would result in a so-called climate of peace, thereby diminishing the likelihood of conflicts leading to war. But what are the facts? In the past 10 years, during which time we have seen increased spending for such defense requirements as state-of-the-art weapons systems and augmented combat personnel, there have been fewer military actions involving our forces than in any previous decade in the twentieth century. Our own installations have not been attacked, and our allies have rarely found it necessary to ask for our armed support. In other words, defense readiness is, in the real world, the most efficient peacemaking tool.

Which of the following is an assumption underlying the conclusion of the passage above?

(A) Military actions involving our forces can be instigated by any of a number of different factors.

(B) Our buildup of weapons systems and combat personnel has prevented our adversaries from increasing their own spending on defense.

(C) The increased defense spending of the past 10 years has lessened the need for significant military expenditure in future decades.

(D) At the present time, state-of-the-art weapons systems and the augmentation of combat personnel are equally important to a nation's resources.

(E) The number of military actions involving our forces would have been greater in the past decade if we had not increased our defense spending.

3. A free press always informs the public of all aspects of a country's current military operations, except for cases in which the safety of troops or the success of a mission would be jeopardized by the public's knowing.

Which one of the following adheres most closely to the principle set forth above?

(A) A free press would publish editorials supporting a current military campaign but could repress dissenting opinions regarding the campaign.

(B) An unfree press would release information on the country's prisoners of war taken during a current military campaign, unless such information would hamper efforts to secure the prisoners' release.

(C) A free press would accurately report the number of casualties suffered on both sides of a battle but could withhold information regarding the possible targets for a future military strike.

(D) An unfree press would print inflammatory accounts of an international event to garner public support for an unpopular war.

(E) A free press would reveal any new information regarding the country's past involvement in secret military operations as soon as that information became available.

4. The Meisman Art Center recently discovered an early work by the renowned painter Marin Dillard, who became famous for work produced during a 10-year period late in her lifetime. This new painting dates to approximately 35 years earlier than her previously known earliest work. What is surprising about the discovery is that, even though a significant amount of time passed between the creation of this and Dillard's later paintings, the style of the new piece is indistinguishable from that of Dillard's other work. This new discovery helps to elucidate an exciting new facet of Dillard's life and work.

It can be inferred that the author of the above passage believes that

(A) Dillard became famous on the merits of all her work, not just the later pieces.

(B) despite the assertions of the art historians who discovered it, the painting in question was not created by Marin Dillard.

(C) it is likely that the recently discovered painting was actually created much later than experts have claimed.

(D) art historians have not been sufficiently thorough in their attempts to make note of stylistic differences between the new piece and Dillard's later work.

(E) 35 years is an unusually long time for an artist to work without showing any change in artistic style.

5. Salesperson: These computers are marked down dramatically, because two-thirds of the hard drives stop working within a year of their purchase.

Customer: That isn't a problem. I'll buy three, so I will be certain to have one that continues working after a year.

The customer's reasoning is faulty in that he mistakenly assumes that

(A) just because a computer doesn't work in one instance doesn't mean it won't work in another instance.

(B) although the computers don't always continue to work, they are likely to do so for this customer.

(C) one out of any three computers will continue working after a year.

(D) the effectiveness of the computers is not dependent upon who uses them.

(E) the price of three marked-down computers is less than the price of one full-price computer.

6. The human resources department at Luna Systems recently changed its open-door policy, which had allowed employees to view or add information to their human resources portfolios upon request. The portfolios are now accessible only to staff in the human resources department. Many employees are upset with the change—which was initiated by the chair of human resources, Andrea McCarthy—and believe that she does not have the company's best interests in mind. However, McCarthy has been a loyal employee of Luna for 12 years, as is clearly evidenced by the records contained in her human resources portfolio.

The author's conclusion about McCarthy assumes which one of the following?

(A) Only long-term employees of the human resources department are permitted to add information to employee portfolios.

(B) Employees' requests to view portfolios are usually motivated by a desire to get a fuller picture of their job performances.

(C) Salary increases are usually based in part on favorable feedback received from customers and supervisors.

(D) The open-door policy was instituted to give supervisors a more accurate picture of an employee's performance.

(E) The information in McCarthy's human resources portfolio is an accurate record of her employment at Luna Systems.

7. Toy manufacturer: This rubber ball is costly to make. We should switch to a less costly brand of rubber for this product.

Marketing analyst: But the ball sells so well because of its superior bouncing properties. No other material performs as well. We should stick with what we know we can sell.

The speakers above disagree over which one of the following issues?

(A) Whether the rubber used for this ball is more expensive than other available materials

(B) Whether this product regularly meets its sales quotas

(C) Whether the company should make the rubber ball from a different brand of rubber

(D) Whether customer priorities should factor into product development decisions

(E) Whether other rubber materials perform as well as the material currently used

8. Although Bidwell raises several good points in his criticism of the exclusive nature of the academic arena, his piece as a whole is poorly written, resulting in a confusing and distracting experience for his readers. For example, chapter 6 accuses academics of dwelling in an "ivory tower" when it discusses their tendency to work in isolation without looking for concrete connections to the world. Perhaps this description was more accurate when Bidwell was a student, but I am certain that college campuses today have neither towers nor white buildings.

The author of this passage has failed to recognize an instance of which of the following in Bidwell's writing?

(A) Generalization

(B) Deduction

(C) Reasoning through counterexample

(D) Figurative language

(E) Irony

9. Several of the concepts for the company's new advertising campaign can immediately be recognized as effective based on prior knowledge of the market alone. Past experience has shown us, however, that some concepts can be shown to be effective only when the campaign is launched and studies of its effects are undertaken.

Which of the following can be logically inferred from the passage above?

(A) It may be impossible to determine the effectiveness of some aspects of the new campaign until after the campaign has launched.

(B) Many concepts for the company's new advertising campaign are too closely related to those of prior campaigns to be effective.

(C) It is likely that there are effective concepts that have not yet been proposed for the company's new campaign.

(D) The company is less likely to find success with an untested concept than with one that has been launched and studied.

(E) Many of the concepts that are identified as effective based on prior knowledge of the market have been abandoned before being launched and studied.

10. Holt: The most effective and accurate way of determining the level of need for a food shelf in our neighborhood is by distributing an anonymous questionnaire at the next meeting of the Concerned Neighbors Committee. Nearly all of the meeting attendees are neighborhood residents, and because the responses are anonymous, people will be assured of confidentiality. We can then create an accurate picture of the need for emergency food services in our area.

Which one of the following provides the most serious criticism of the argument above?

(A) The plan overlooks the fact that a significant number of people who would use a food shelf may not be members of the Concerned Neighbors Committee.

(B) The anonymous nature of the questionnaire prevents neighborhood organizations from identifying families who might benefit from a food shelf.

(C) The plan does not provide a reliable means of determining the level of need for food shelves in adjacent neighborhoods.

(D) The plan does not distinguish between households that would use a food shelf and those that simply have a tight food budget.

(E) The plan overlooks the fact that some people surveyed may lie because they are embarrassed by their need for emergency food services.

11. Some commentators have theorized that candidate Steven Perez and incumbent Senator Marlin Ray have a great deal of common ground in their platforms. However, the two candidates could not be more different, as evidenced by the following quotes from the men themselves. Steven Perez eloquently expressed his concern about crime when he said, "Our priority must be increasing police presence to provide safe streets for our children as they walk to school, come home, and fall asleep at night." Compare this to the words of Senator Ray, who said to reporters, "You can hire as many police officers as you like, but one factor in keeping the streets safe is teaching children how to express themselves without violence."

    Which of the following statements offers the most effective criticism of the argument above?

    (A) It assumes that all candidates share the same beliefs about important issues.

    (B) It draws a conclusion about the differences between the two platforms based on information about the candidates' positions on a single issue.

    (C) It confuses the danger of criminals on the street with the danger of violence among children and teenagers.

    (D) It fails to present the argument of the opposing viewpoint.

    (E) It concludes that a public statement is an accurate indication of a politician's beliefs but provides evidence to the contrary.

12. Alisa is the stockroom coordinator at World Imports, where she is responsible for unpacking new merchandise as it arrives in the store. She estimates that 3 percent of new items in the furniture department are broken or irreparably damaged in transit, while 9 percent of each equally sized shipment to the kitchen department arrives too damaged to sell. Since these items must be disposed of, increasing total costs, this statistic shows that it costs World Imports three times as much to stock kitchen items as furniture items.

    Which of the following statements points out a major flaw in the reasoning above?

    (A) The cost of stocking an item is influenced by many factors besides the percentage of each shipment that is damaged in transit.

    (B) The individual shipments on which these breakage rates are based are too small to support statistical generalizations about all shipments.

    (C) Imports Etc., another housewares store, uses a different shipping company and experiences only a 1.5 percent breakage rate for furniture and a 6 percent breakage rate for kitchen items.

    (D) A certain amount of breakage during shipping is unavoidable, and all import businesses experience similar losses.

    (E) The company's kitchen items have become famous because they are produced in a remote Central American village, making breakage during shipping unavoidable.

13. Principal Tsang demands that the English department justify its departure from the prescribed curriculum. By moving away from the texts selected by the school board, she claims, we have left the senior class ill-prepared for the mandatory literature exit exam. What she fails to realize, however, is that the new material we introduced this school year was brought in with the aim of giving students an opportunity to hone their writing skills and experience a broader range of cultures through literature. We expressed these goals in a letter sent to students' parents earlier this fall. As a department, we are baffled by Principal Tsang's opposition to students in this school learning new and important skills.

    Which one of the following points out the principle flaw in the reasoning of the argument?

    (A) There is no guarantee that the new materials will improve students' writing skills.

    (B) The skills gained because of the new curriculum will not necessarily outweigh the skills lost by not studying the previous curriculum.

    (C) Principal Tsang is concerned with the effects of the new curriculum, not with the intent of the new curriculum.

    (D) The authors' claim concerning the intent of the curriculum change is impossible to verify.

    (E) Students who passed last year's exam had read books from a wide range of cultures.

ANSWERS AND EXPLANATIONS

ANSWER KEY

Set One	9. B	4. C	13. D	8. D
1. A	10. B	5. C	**Set Three**	9. A
2. C	11. D	6. B	1. C	10. A
3. B	12. A	7. E	2. E	11. B
4. E	13. D	8. D	3. C	12. A
5. C	**Set Two**	9. B	4. E	13. C
6. E	1. C	10. C	5. C	
7. B	2. D	11. C	6. E	
8. D	3. D	12. E	7. C	

DIAGNOSTIC TOOL

Tally up your score and write down your results below.

Total Correct: _____ out of 39

Percentage Correct: # you got right × 100 ÷ 39: _____

DIAGNOSE YOUR RESULTS

Look back at the questions you got wrong and think back on your experience answering them.

Step 1: Find the Roadblocks

Did you struggle to answer some questions? To improve your score, you need to pinpoint exactly what element of these "roadblocks" tripped you up. To do that, ask yourself these two questions.

Am I weak in the skills being tested?

Logical Reasoning questions test your skills in evaluating arguments and formulating or assessing a plan of action. Were you unable to identify the various components of any given argument or to digest the dense language? If so, you need more practice with complex reasoning skills.

The Kaplan Logical Reasoning principles and methods in this book can help you focus on and develop the specific skills you need to work through these questions thoroughly, quickly, and strategically.

Was it the question type that threw me off?

Then you need to become more comfortable with it! Go back to the beginning of this chapter and review the Kaplan principles and methods. Make sure you understand them and know how to apply them. These strategies help to improve your speed and efficiency on Test Day. You also need to be very familiar with the nine Logical Reasoning question types. Finally, get as much practice as you can so you grow more at ease with this question type.

Step 2: Find the Blind Spots

Did you answer some questions quickly and confidently but get them wrong anyway? When you come across wrong answers like these, you need to figure out what you thought you were doing right, what it turns out you were doing wrong, and why that happened! The best way to do that is to **read the answer explanations!**

They give you a detailed breakdown of why the correct answer is correct and why all the other answer choices are wrong. This helps to reinforce the Kaplan principles and methods for each question type and helps you figure out what blindsided you so it doesn't happen again. Also, just as with your roadblocks, try to get in as much practice as you can.

Step 3: Reinforce Your Strengths

Read through all the answer explanations for the questions you got right. Again, this helps to reinforce the Kaplan principles and methods for each question type, which in turn helps you work more efficiently so you can get the score you want. Now keep your skills sharp with more practice.

As soon as you are comfortable with all the LSAT question types and Kaplan methods, complete a full-length practice test under timed conditions. In this way, practice tests serve as milestones; they help you to chart your progress! So don't save them all for the final weeks.

If you are aiming for that top score, TRY OUT Kaplan's *LSAT Advanced*, which includes only the toughest LSAT questions and most focused strategies.

You can also visit **kaptest.com/LSAT** for more details on Kaplan's online and classroom-based options. Kaplan uses only real LSAT questions, so you get the most comprehensive, testlike experience.

SET ONE

1. A

You have to fill in the blank. You'll want to get an idea of the direction in which the passage is going so that you can extrapolate to the most likely ending.

The passage begins by labeling Beethoven as both an innovator—meaning he brought music forward, moving towards what the passage says was "the chromaticism to come" (whatever that is)—and a synthesizer, presumably not the Moog variety but someone who "put it all together"; that is, who also worked with classical forms. *But*—a keyword of contrast here—some critics said that Beethoven's innovations (his work with dissonance) were *not* some kind of wonderful experimentation but merely

a manifestation of his increasing deafness—hence, they represent an unharmonious flaw in his later music.

The author doesn't hold with this interpretation. She does, after all, label them "cynical critics." And she says, "I maintain that, on the contrary . . . ," another signal that the author is about to take issue. If Beethoven's deafness was (as is alleged) impairing his ability to handle his musical medium, then he would have been all the more likely to do . . . what? Well, she wants to finish with a statement of a contrary effect. Her argument is this: If the cause the cynics describe were, in fact, the case (if deafness made Beethoven less competent), then there would be an opposite effect, an effect something like (A). A less competent Beethoven would have played it safe by producing conventional music. (B) directly echoes the opinion of the cynical critics—it doesn't stand in contrast to it—so it's not an opinion that would be cited to bolster the author's own feelings about Beethoven. Jumping to (E)—which seems to agree that Beethoven was losing his abilities towards the end of his career—you can see that (E), too, is more in line with the view of the cynical critics. (C)'s sentiment is somewhat in line with that of the author; it makes a bit of sense in that it suggests that Beethoven composed what he wanted to compose. But it doesn't act as a clear contrast to the notion that Beethoven composed dissonant music because his hearing was impaired and didn't know what sounds he was making, so it doesn't act in a satisfactory way to fill in the blank. Finally, (D) brings up the issue of "harmonious music," which you want. But by assigning a motive to Beethoven—that he was trying to defuse critical response—(D) goes far afield. No such reference to motive has a place in the argument as written.

2. C

The stimulus isn't much of an argument, is it? It's a series of flat statements on the topic of interest rates, which are cited as having an inverse relationship with the building of single-family dwellings: As rates go down, construction goes up. In line with that (says the second sentence), contractors order building materials based on predictions of which way interest rates will go. This should make sense. All of this is in line with (C).

And remember, when you're asked what can be inferred from the passage, you really want something that must be true—something in line with the scope and point of view. (C) is just a broader rephrasing of the relationship cited in the stimulus and is thus the best answer. Note that the choice is rendered even more reasonable by its use of the qualifier *sometimes*. Because it's not an extreme statement with no exceptions possible, it's easy to sign on to (C) as a reflection of the author's equally moderate views.

(A) brings up the cost of building materials, but because the passage says nothing at all about the costs of home building—there isn't a single reference to costs—it goes beyond the scope. You can't infer that those who sell building materials raise their prices in response to the greater demand they expect from the lower interest rates. (B) distorts the paragraph. Interest rates are cited as a good predictor, *not* the best. As for (D), just because the author mentions hiring schedules before mentioning orders for new materials does not mean that one of those things must come first on the builder's agenda. (E) is an unwarranted inference since the author's only concern is one type of dwelling, the single-family home. You cannot fairly extrapolate from this paragraph to any statement about the home building industry in general.

3. B

The argument of the passage is not closely reasoned, as you may have noticed in the use of "however" in the second sentence. The adverb implies that what follows is a refutation of the first sentence. In fact, there is no such clear, logical relationship: There need not be a conflict between the notion that American voters prefer a combative presidential candidate and the poll showing voter disaffection in 1988. Because the writer assumes the connection, he concludes that this disaffection, added to the feeling of many voters that the candidates were not "presidential," proves that aggressive candidates are not gaining voter respect. As we have seen, the logical error occurs in the writer's assumption that "people had been annoyed" by the "combativeness, even aggressiveness" of candidates and not by something else. His argument is seriously weakened, therefore, if, as stated in (B), the poll did not reveal that voters were annoyed by combativeness in the campaign. Furthermore, there is no indication that any of the candidates actually were combative or aggressive.

(A) is completely off the point. The issue is not whether the 1988 campaign was "memorable" but whether it revealed a change in voter attitudes toward combativeness. (C) refers to a general attitude on the part of many voters, but the passage is confined to an argument about specific attitudes that the author feels were created by specific events of the 1988 election. A prior climate of public skepticism would not damage the argument unless we knew that combativeness did not play a role in those earlier elections. In (D), an attempt is made to soften the charge of aggressiveness by redefining it as a somewhat more admirable and arguably essential quality for a politician. Even if this were true, however, the passage is concerned with public perceptions rather than with a discussion of the merits of what looks like combativeness. (E) is an interpretation of events that, however legitimate in itself, has no effect on the basic argument of the passage. This choice addresses a general concept, not the specific 1988 campaign and the specific topic of the effectiveness of combative campaigning styles.

4. E

Always watch for tone words; the charge in this stimulus that the government interferes "blatantly," wrongly using its bureaucratic power, alerts you immediately to the author's opinion.

It seems that the IRS gives a child care deduction to certain people who provide support to a dependent. The complaint is that the government exercises unfair control in its choice of which people receive this deduction. The author believes that the government can have no justifiable basis on which to make this decision and is in effect deciding which people are worthy of caring for dependents and which are not.

The choice that most weakens this argument is (E). If the tax deduction is, as (E) says, available to anyone who is the principal supporter of a dependent, then that answers the implicit charge that the government has arbitrarily set itself up to decide people's personal worth. If the

IRS, in other words, is using an appropriate criterion that is applied equitably to all, then the charge that the deduction is being selectively used to decide people's worth is groundless. (A) might have fooled you because it seems to be saying that anyone who wants the deduction can have it. But it really says that anyone who attaches the appropriate schedule may apply for the deduction; they won't necessarily get it. The fact that the IRS will consider anyone doesn't mean that it isn't (as the author alleges) making the final decision on inappropriate criteria, choosing people arbitrarily on the basis of what it deems to be their personal worth. (B) mentions the deduction but is otherwise beyond the argument's scope, going off on the interesting but irrelevant topic of the relative size of the deduction for lower-income taxpayers. As for (C), even if it were true, the government might still be reaching its decision as to who gets the deduction based on improper criteria. All (C) gives us is one of those criteria—the requirement that a dependent be a coresident. But perhaps the other criteria are just as objectionable as the author seems to feel they are. Finally, (D)'s implication that only a few people will get the deduction is another error in scope, because (D) has nothing to do with the main issue, which is the government's methods or motives. The "weakener" you need has to demonstrate that the government—contrary to what the author believes—is awarding the deduction based on proper criteria.

5. C

The author counters the view that violent TV shows incite people to commit violent acts. A correlation has been noticed—and a correlation, of course, is an acknowledgment that two phenomena accompany each other, whether or not they're causally related—between watching TV violence and committing violent acts. Apparently, it's true that people who watch violent shows are more likely to commit violent crimes than those who don't watch those shows. And this finding might well suggest that the TV shows are causing the viewers to commit the crimes. But the author believes that the correlation is better explained in another way—that violence-prone people tend to watch violent shows because they feel an affinity to the violence-prone

characters of the shows. So to the author, the critics cited in the first sentence are guilty of confusing cause and effect. The TV shows don't make the viewer violence-prone; rather, it's frustration and resentment that make people violence-prone and make these people watch violent TV programs.

The passage ends abruptly without a proper conclusion—for obvious reasons, because you're asked to come up with that yourself. The best answer is (C), which takes the author's argument to its logical conclusion: A person's addiction to action TV shows may reveal something about that person's tendency towards violence, but it doesn't constitute an inducement to commit violence. (A) goes too far. It states that the effect of action shows is salutary. But that doesn't at all follow from the argument, which merely contends that the crime-and-TV-show correlation can be explained in an alternative way. (B) raises the issue of who finds the action programs realistic. This issue comes from left field. You're looking for a summation of the given argument. (B) introduces a new point. (D) is irrelevant—you would never expect a paragraph about whether action TV leads to violence to end with a quick reference to action shows' general popularity. And it's more likely that the author would disagree with (E) than end her discussion with it. In a way, her views are a defense of action programming against the charge of aiding and abetting violent crime. Therefore, (E)'s call for a ban on action shows is uncalled for.

6. E

In the stimulus for questions 6 and 7, the conclusion is expressed in the main clause of the first sentence: Lobbyists have a negative effect on the principle of "the majority rules" as practiced in Congress. The reason for that conclusion—the evidence—comes in the second sentence: Wealthy minority interests can afford to finance lobbyists, who pressure elected officials. These lobbyists make the officials believe that the opinions of the lobby are held by the people at large. So, the argument goes, some people (namely, the rich interest groups) have a greater influence on decision making than do others. And this, it's alleged, thwarts majority rule.

Thinking about a key assumption connecting this evidence to that conclusion—and that's what question 6 asks for—note that the author jumps from the idea that lobbyists distort Congress's sense of public opinion to the conclusion that lobbyists undermine the majority-rule concept. To make this leap, the author must be assuming that all members of society have to have equal influence on legislation for majority rule to work. All the evidence says is that lobbyists distort Congress's sense of public opinion—it doesn't claim that the opinion of the majority is completely silenced. The majority-rule principle (according to this passage) implies that Congress should represent the interests of the majority of its constituents. So by asserting that the lobbyists muck things up, the author must be taking for granted that all members of society have to be heard from, have to have equal influence. That's what (E) says. (A)'s reference to capitalism takes it way, way beyond the scope of the argument. The only connection between money and the argument's content is tangential—the idea that money helps the lobbyists distort Congress's sense of public opinion. (A) blows that out of proportion. (B), meanwhile, is too specific. To say that minority interests have to be protected by constitutional amendment is to propose a specific solution that the author need not be assuming or signing on to. (C) is off the point because the argument is about protecting majority interests—the concept of majority rule is what's allegedly in danger here. (This could be brought up as an objection to (B), as well.) Finally, (D) plays off your possible assumption that the minority interests in the passage are big-business fat cats, but as far as the passage goes, it may be the case that other minority interests, ones not connected with big business at all, engage in lobbying too.

7. B

Now there's another major assumption at work here—it's not among the answer choices for question 6, but it's the key to question 7. The author is assuming that Congress, bullied and influenced by the lobbyists, goes about the act of legislating under that influence. He's assuming (in short) that lobbyists' efforts are, by and large, successful. But if, as (B) says, it's a rare day when an elected official is at all moved by a lobbying campaign, then the lobbyists are not successful. That in turn defuses the author's concerns about the danger to majority

rule. Thus, (B) is an excellent weakener and the correct answer.

(A) is no good because the argument isn't about the quality of the majority opinion; the author is only concerned with whether the majority's opinion is being sufficiently represented. (C) supports the argument: If interest groups can (as it says) raise a lot of cash, they can then use the cash for lobbying purposes—the exact sort of situation that has the author all bent out of shape. As for (D), even if groups are entitled to employ lobbyists, it doesn't weaken the author's claim that the effect of lobbyists is dangerous. There are many things all of us are entitled or permitted to do that may not be good for us or for society. Finally, even if, as (E) says, the majority position were not one definite position but a mush of many, the author wants Congress to have a clear view that that is the case. Despite (E), the lobbyists may still muddy Congress's view, as the author alleges.

8. D

To look for an argument that "resembles" the stimulus is to find parallel reasoning—a structure that is as close as possible to the original. The stimulus says that if you lower taxes, people will buy more things, stimulating economic growth, which in turn will raise salaries, which in turn will bring in more money for the government. You're not concerned here with whether this is a sound program but with how it's put together. The bottom line is, what you have here is something of a paradox: Begin by lowering taxes, which (you'd assume) would lower government revenues, and in the end, government revenues will increase. Engaging in a particular action will (in the end) give you a result that's the opposite of what you expected.

And that's what you get in correct (D). Though it would be reasonable to expect that more employee days off would reduce productivity (because they'd be spending less time on the job), in fact productivity will be greater, the exact opposite effect. The chain of events described in the stimulus may be a little longer—it has more steps—than (D), but its overall shape is very similar. (A) presents no paradox. You would expect that reducing overtime would bring down costs and increase total income. (B) departs from the stimulus's pattern. It has the government changing the rules about the school lunch program and farmers—a third party—reaping a benefit. (C)'s plan carries a bit of irony in its assertion that rating a movie "X" ends up corrupting the morals of the community. But as in (B)—and unlike correct (D)—the agent who performs the first action here (the censor) is not the one who reaps the ultimate benefit. (E) may be even less of a paradox than (A). It is not at all surprising that a kid given more practice managing money ends up learning the value of thrift.

9. B

Four of the five answer choices in question 9 support the logic, so you'll be looking for a statement that either weakens it or has no effect on it. The conclusion is that the way a judge came into his or her job, thus how much job security he or she has, often determines how a case will come out—that judges decide differently depending on whether they were elected or appointed for life or only for a short term. In the end, the author evidently believes that the wiser judge is the life-term judge.

Because the author provides nothing concrete to back up this claim, the answer choices have many opportunities to support the reasoning. (A) supports the idea that the short-term judges are likely to be moved by the prevailing political climate. If, as (A) says, they really want to keep their jobs, they will be more likely to decide the way the voters want them to decide in order to improve their election chances. Likewise, (C) supports that connection between the approval of the voters (which is necessary for re-election, of course) and the voters' view of the judge's decisions by showing that short-term judges "happen" to rule in a way the voters approve of. And if you jump ahead to (E), you get perhaps the strongest support for the allegation that short-term judges worry about the mood of the voters—according to (E), they're the only judges who use pollsters, whose sole purpose is to track public opinion. (D) lends support to the other part of the argument—the view of lifelong judges. (D) implies that those judges, as alleged by the author, do turn a blind eye to the vicissitudes of politics.

(B) claims that long-term judges keep their ear to the political ground as much as short-term judges do; that

damages the distinction between judges raised in the argument.

10. B

This question asks us to criticize the logic in an advertisement. We are told that the Fall Sale offers savings on clothing. The supporting evidence is that if you purchase clothing in three different departments, you receive a discount off of a purchase in the Housewares department. (B) points out that, although the sale is advertised as offering "great savings on clothes for the whole family," the only discount available is on housewares.

(A) isn't a criticism of the argument because it focuses on people who are outside the scope of the offer, those who won't make the purchases required to get the coupon. As for (C), the length of the sale doesn't affect whether shoppers are saving money on clothes. The comparison in (D) is irrelevant—it may speak to whether or not the shopper saves money overall, but it does not address the actual claim made, that the consumer will save money *on clothing*. It's certainly possible that the coupon will help some shoppers save some money but not, contrary to the ad's claims, on clothes. Similarly, other discounts, (E), don't have any impact on the validity of the claim that this sale will save shoppers money on clothing.

11. D

You're asked for a conclusion. The stimulus argument describes two factors that influence whether or not, and how much, passersby will give to panhandlers. First, if passersby find a panhandler to be destitute and forced to beg, they may give quite a bit of money. Second, and on the other hand, if passersby think they are being conned or that the panhandler is lazy, they won't give anything. Thus, the most reliable conclusion is (D). People decide whether to give to a panhandler based on how they perceive her—as sincere or as lazy and dishonest.

As soon as you realize that the passage is only about how people's perceptions influence their reactions, you can eliminate a couple of wrong answers. The passage never tells you whether most panhandlers are lazy or not, (A). The same problem exists in (B). You don't know that some beggars can't fool passersby. (C) is a misreading of the first condition. Appearing truly needy is necessary for getting money from passersby; it need not be sufficient. Furthermore, (C) speaks of most passersby, which needn't be true at all. Perhaps most people never give money to panhandlers. And (E) concludes that a completely new factor, the amount of change one has, doesn't influence the decision making of passersby. There are no grounds for concluding this. The stimulus presents some factors in the decision making, but it never says that these are the only factors.

12. A

This short argument concludes that Dr. Kells is a better physician than Dr. Li. The evidence, which is very brief, is that their patients rate Kells as a better doctor. As always in an Assumption question, we're looking for the missing piece that ties the evidence (that patients rate Kells the better doctor) to the conclusion (that Kells *is* the better doctor). If the ratings of patients provide a solid basis for determining who is the better doctor, then the argument is solid. That's a perfect match for (A). (B) does nothing to tie ratings to actual quality. Instead, it introduces a new factor, the patients' comfort level with a doctor, which is outside scope. Likewise, (C) and (D) introduce new factors ("greater experience" and "from whose care patients benefit more") without filling the gap between ratings and actual quality. (E) needn't be true for the argument to be valid; the conclusion claims only that Kells is better than Li, not better than *everyone*.

13. D

The author concludes that a staff made up of contract or temporary employees is "incomplete at best." Why? The evidence says it's because a company needs workers who have a personal connection to their work and a dedication to the company. We're looking for the author's assumption—the missing piece that ties the idea that we need dedicated, connected workers to the idea that temporary workers aren't enough. The author must believe that temporary workers *aren't* dedicated and connected. Otherwise, temporary employees would indeed be an acceptable substitute for permanent staff. (D) sums up this assumption nicely. (A) distorts the point; the author states only that temporary staff by

themselves are inadequate, not that they cause the company any harm. (B) might be tempting because it suggests a possible remedy for the problem the author raises, but that's not what we've been asked for. We're looking for the missing piece that leads to the conclusion that temporary workers are *not enough*. The idea that they could be encouraged to develop that dedication actually weakens the conclusion. (C) directly contradicts the author's statement that temporary and contract workers can play an important role with regard to seasonal work flow. (E) is another distortion: The passage mentions that skilled and efficient employees are important to a company but doesn't attribute those qualities to either group.

SET TWO

1. C

The conclusion is that for parents who are crunched for time, Flash Fitness is the "quick solution." The evidence, however, doesn't have anything to do with being quick—it tells us that working parents "found this convenient new workout to be very *effective*." Predict: The fact that the workout was effective doesn't demonstrate that it was quick. There's no evidence for "quick" at all, as set forth in correct choice (C).

Note that none of the wrong choices address quickness, which is the new element introduced in the conclusion. (A) may be true, but it is not a serious criticism of the ad, since time-crunched parents are the target audience (so we really don't care whether the rest of the world would like the program). The information in (B) is irrelevant. The ad makes no claim that Flash Fitness is more effective or convenient than other fitness centers, only that it is an effective and convenient center. (D) may be true, but it's not important, because the conclusion of the argument is that the program is a "quick" solution—we're not trying to prove effectiveness. (E) is also irrelevant. While it may be true that some people are not concerned with convenience when choosing a fitness center, this ad attempts to appeal to those who do have that concern.

2. D

Ranjit thinks it was unfair that he failed the class because other students who neglected to turn in the same project that he failed to turn in passed the class. Therefore, he must believe that the failure to turn in that project was the *reason* he failed the class, or at least a substantial factor. Note the subtle difference between correct choice (D), which says just that, and wrong choice (B), which suggests that we know the *actual* reason for the failure rather than simply understanding Ranjit's position. All of the information given relates to Ranjit's assessment, *not* to the actual reasons for the grade, so (B) is beyond the scope of the information provided. We have no information about Ranjit's other classes and, therefore, cannot draw any conclusions about his grades in them (as (A) asks us to do). The information in the passage tells us that Ranjit turned in all of his other assignments but nothing about his scores. (E) takes us even further outside scope by comparing Ranjit's performance to students in other classes—students who were never mentioned in the stimulus.

Whether or not Ranjit has ever failed a class before is irrelevant, because his grade is based on his record in this specific class, so (A) is incorrect. As for (C), Ranjit may have received above-average scores on his other assignments, but then again, he may not. We know only that he turned in the assignments; we have nothing on which to base any inferences about how he did on them.

3. D

The author concludes that the costume designer will be able to restore the original fabric quality of the garments that have been damaged through improper storage. The evidence? We have access to the original patterns and the original fabric. It's fabric quality that's at issue, so the success or failure of the author's plan hinges on the fabric. If, as the author assumes, it's in its original condition, then it will work and the costumes can be restored to their original fabric quality. Otherwise, the pattern, however detailed, would yield another garment made of damaged fabric. Therefore, (D) would strengthen the argument by providing support for an assumption that is central to the designer's plan.

(A) is outside the scope—our focus is on the quality of the fabric, not the technique. (B) addresses the causes of the damage, which are irrelevant to the question of whether or not the fabric quality can be restored. (C) introduces an element—what the original seamstress may or may not have anticipated—that has no bearing on the likelihood that the original fabric quality can be restored. (E) may look tempting at a glance, but it talks about the damage to the *costumes*, not to the remaining fabric—and it's the quality of the remaining fabric that will control the success or failure of the restoration.

4. C

Because this is an Inference question, we're not looking for evidence and conclusion. There's no argument here, just straight information. Summarize what you know as you read: Academy B was known as one of the best schools, but it closed. Many teachers went to good suburban schools, and then when Academy B reopened, they came back, and it's again enjoying an excellent reputation. What else do we *know for sure* based on what we've just read? (C) says that some suburban teachers left their jobs when Academy B reopened. We know that because we know that some Academy B teachers were working as suburban teachers while the Academy was closed and that they've now returned to Academy B and stayed there.

(A) is incorrect because we don't have enough information to draw any conclusions about the impact of the teachers' experience in the suburban schools. We also have no information about the reasons the school reopened, as (B) asserts, nor about either the quality of other teachers in the district or overall district quality as set forth in (E). (D) might appear tempting because we're told that the teachers from the suburban schools all returned to Academy B and stayed there, but that doesn't mean that there aren't other openings available—only "many" of the teachers went to the suburban schools, and we don't know whether the school reopened with exactly the same number of teachers it had originally, anyway.

5. C

The author's conclusion is that the recent increase in popularity of high school-level writing classes will decrease the number of graduates who are capable of producing effective expository writing. The evidence is that most of these newly popular classes use creative writing techniques. The assumption that links this evidence with the conclusion is that creative writing techniques will not help students become effective expository writers. Correct choice (C) says exactly that: Creative writing courses won't give students the skills to be good expository writers. If they *will*, of course, then the argument fails. Incorrect choice (A) brings up the idea of a writing requirement, which is outside scope. The key to this argument is the question as to whether the new classes—which primarily use creative writing techniques—will increase or decrease effective expository writing among high school graduates. (B) makes an irrelevant comparison, which may be tempting at a glance because it contains all the right keywords. As in any Assumption question, keep your eye on the gap you're trying to fill between the evidence and conclusion, and you won't be misled by choices like this. (D) introduces an entirely new element—that of qualified instructors. (E) is irrelevant to the author's conclusion, which relates to the projected increase/decrease in expository skills, *not* their current level.

6. B

There is no connection between magnet school programs in Minneapolis and long waiting lists for school there, this passage concludes, because no such connection can consistently be found in other cities. Correct choice (B) connects the evidence (magnet schools didn't cause waiting lists in other cities) with the conclusion (therefore, they didn't cause waiting lists in Minneapolis, either). (A) is outside the scope; the argument is concerned with the link (or lack thereof) between the magnet program and the waiting lists, not the motivations of the parents *within* that program. (C) introduces another out-of-scope element: the benefits of the magnet programs. Our only concern is with the causal relationship between the magnet programs and the waiting lists. (D) directly contradicts the author, who said the magnet programs were *not* the cause of the waiting lists. (E) is also contradictory; the author states

clearly that there are "extremely long" waiting lists for some schools.

7. E

The problem: Channeling recycled wastewater into the harbor seems to have brought dangerous bacteria into this town's drinking water. The solution: Researchers recommend adding the enzyme tripticase to the water to eliminate those pestilent bacteria, which in turn will "solve the health problem." Because you're looking to weaken this argument, ask yourself if there could be a problem with this solution. It removes the bacteria, which will only solve the health problem if tripticase itself doesn't introduce any other problems. If, however, tripticase merely replaces one problem with another, as (E) has it, then the author's conclusion about its effectiveness as a solution is weakened.

Okay, so tripticase is supereffective because it solves the giardia problem as well as others. This certainly doesn't weaken the author's argument that tripticase is an effective solution (even though other illnesses are technically outside the scope), so eliminate (A). The frequency and severity of giardia worldwide isn't the issue here—the author addresses the effectiveness of a solution for the health problems of a certain town that originated in response to the channeling of recycled wastewater, so (B) is wrong. Other illnesses are irrelevant to this consideration, as was mentioned above in (A). Therefore, eliminate (C). The author discusses water-induced cases of giardia, so cases that arise from other causes aren't within the argument's scope, so (D) is also wrong.

When you're asked to weaken or strengthen an argument, remember to evaluate the impact that each answer choice has on that argument without questioning the information you're given. Assume that the stimulus is true and reconsider it in light of each answer choice. Does the new information make the conclusion more or less plausible? Don't question the information; just focus on its impact on the argument.

8. D

The dean concludes that moving the English class back to the afternoon would increase student scores and offers two pieces of evidence for that: the correlation between the change in time slot and the drop in scores and the fact that students perform better when wide awake. She's making two key assumptions here, either of which could be the correct answer: The first is that there's a causal relationship between the time change and the drop in scores; the second is that the causal relationship is triggered by students not being wide awake at 8:00 A.M. (D) is a perfect match for the second. Remember that some Assumption questions will contain more than one possible Assumption, so you should be adaptable in those infrequent instances where your assumption doesn't match.

(A) is not relevant because the dean isn't concerned with whether it is practical to change the class meeting time, only whether test scores would go up if the time were changed. (B) would actually weaken the author's argument, since it suggests that class time may not be the only factor that causes the low test scores. (C) might provide some support for the author's conclusion, but it's not a necessary component of the argument, and the question stem asked for an assumption the argument was based on—that means a necessary but unstated piece of evidence. (E) is outside the scope, because the argument relates strictly to the causal relationship between the time change and the drop in scores.

9. B

The argument concludes that it is more expensive to live far from an interstate than near one. The only evidence for this claim is the fact that property values drop in areas that are closer to interstates. However, we're told that most interstates are in urban areas, where property values are higher to start with. For the author's conclusion to be true, we must assume that the decline due to proximity to an interstate is greater than the increase due to urban location. (B) states this assumption clearly. Remember that you're looking for something that ties the evidence (being near an interstate lowers property values) to the conclusion (that homes in urban areas near interstates are less expensive than those in suburban/rural areas far from interstates). The core issue is *property values*, and (A) and (C) have nothing to do with property values. Don't fall into the trap of analyzing what impact things like square footage and single-family areas *might*

have on property values. (D), far from being a missing component of the argument, would undermine the idea that those homes near the interstate were less expensive. (E) looks tempting because it equalizes costs before taking the location into account, but it does nothing to resolve the two competing impacts on the cost (urban location versus proximity to interstate).

10. C

The author concludes that windy weather must have set off the alarm. Her evidence is that only windy weather or a large truck could have done it, and the large truck that had set the alarm off earlier was already gone. The gap between the evidence and conclusion is fairly clear here—we're presented with evidence that one specific truck couldn't have set off the alarm, but perhaps there are other trucks. Our author seems to assume that there were not other trucks that could have set off the alarm: a perfect match for (C).

(A) introduces an irrelevant distinction—we're interested only in whether the facts that (1) only wind or a truck could have caused this and (2) the truck Han saw this morning is gone, taken together, mean that wind must have set off the alarm. (B) also raises an irrelevant distinction—and one that would argue *against* the author's conclusion rather than adding supporting evidence. (D) may or may not be true, but it has no impact on the argument, which seeks only to determine that it was wind (versus a truck) that set off the alarm. (E) certainly needn't be true for the author to reach her conclusion—she's attributing the alarm to *wind*, not to a truck. Don't be fooled by familiar language in an answer choice—keep your eye on the gap you identified before you started looking at the choices!

11. C

The author's argument is that the decline in Japanese imperial power was not due to a fundamental bias favoring clan loyalty over loyalty to the emperor. The evidence supporting this claim is that for hundreds of years during this period of decline, centralized power was held by shoguns, who ruled in the name of the emperor. The assumption here is that the rule of the shoguns was in fact imperial rule rather than clan-based rule. In the passage, you're given little information about this. Choice (C) claims that, in fact, the shoguns were representative of the different clans and ruled with little regard for the emperor. This denies the assumption and makes the example of the shoguns a piece of evidence for the author's opponents.

(A) does not weaken the argument, because you're essentially concerned with *who* held power rather than *why* they held power. It does deny that there was loyalty involved, but that doesn't greatly weaken the claim made. (B) gives a piece of history that implies nothing about the type of rule the shoguns exercised nor about the object of people's loyalty and obedience. (D) reduces the power of the shoguns during the early part of the period being discussed and gives it to the emperor. Because the author mentions the shoguns as an example of the reach of imperial power, their later ascendance does not weaken the argument. (E), too, provides another reason for the decline of the imperial power and so would strengthen the author's case, not weaken it.

12. E

The author's conclusion is that the public is in error in its condemnation of the students who were arrested. The evidence is an analogy drawn between the students' actions (which in all likelihood broke the law) and the actions of the patriots in Boston, who dumped tea into the harbor. The implied conclusion here is that since history has justified the violent actions of the patriots, it will probably do the same for the students' actions. The best response to this line of reasoning is to point out that merely because one such incident of rebellion (the Boston Tea Party) has proved justified is no reason to assume that any such incident is, or will later appear, justified. That's correct choice (E).

(A) fails because it just begs the question. The author is arguing that it may in fact be patriotic, or at least justified, to demonstrate in front of City Hall. So (A) just ignores his argument. (B) points out that students are too inexperienced to understand the consequences of their demonstration. But is this a reason to condemn their demonstration? Their demonstration could be the morally correct act yet not be fully understood in all its consequences. So (B) is dealing with a different issue.

(C) is a general, cynical statement but has no obvious bearing on the argument. Perhaps the students' act was one of those few that are based on beliefs and conscience. (D) says only that the patriots had some support. Yet we don't know for sure that the students haven't had some support. Secondly, (D) speaks of support for the patriots' cause, whereas it's their actions that the author is using in his analogy.

13. D

The author uses a case of justified rebellion as an analogy to argue that the students' actions may very well have been justified. That's choice (D).

(A) goes too far. He accuses the public of not keeping the patriots in mind, not of purposely ignoring the Boston Tea Party. There really is no general principle of rebellion here, as the author compares only two particular instances of rebellion, so (B) and (C) are incorrect. (E) is incorrect because the author never says that we don't have sufficient evidence to condemn the students. His point is that we're overlooking an important and relevant precedent.

SET THREE

1. C

The author concludes that the benefits of arms reduction are merely illusory. The evidence presented is that even though some weapons are reduced, other weapons not covered by the treaty are increased to account for those that are reduced. In other words, if the superpowers agree to cut their tank forces in half, they will also double their navies or some other arsenal not covered by the reduction treaty. This argument is most strengthened by choice (C). Choice (C) tells us that the five largest military powers have increased funding for new weapons in each of the last 10 years. This supports the author's assertion that whatever firepower is reduced by the arms limitation treaties is reacquired through new weapons.

(A) says that the balance of power remains in spite of arms control. However, the balance of power is a proportion, and even though it is unchanged, the amount of firepower might well be reduced. (B) doesn't strengthen the argument because although no proposals have called for the elimination of weapons, they might still account for a reduction in the number of weapons. (D) comes from left field, introducing irrelevant outside knowledge. The author lumps all arms together, so this distinction is irrelevant to the argument as given. (E) actually contradicts the author's claim by stating that 15 percent of the firepower possessed by the largest military powers really has been cut. Even if this is not a great reduction, it contradicts the author's argument, which is that no reduction has been achieved through arms limitation.

2. E

The author refutes some "so-called pacifists" (that's his phrase) who, you learn by inference, have been calling for weapons reductions to create a climate of peace. The author believes that a "climate of peace" has been created by increased military spending and supports this claim by pointing to the number of attacks on this country and its allies. Fewer attacks, it is said, have occurred, and the author sees a causal connection.

Now the assumption underlying this causal connection is your goal in question 2, and you find it in (E). It has to be true that had defense spending not gone up, the number of attacks on this country and its allies would have increased. Otherwise there would be no causal connection between the two phenomena, as the author claims. (A) is irrelevant. The author doesn't refer to what causes the attacks but simply asserts that military readiness can prevent them. With regard to (B), the author doesn't tell you how and why more defense spending has prevented military actions, just that it has done so. And the author makes no claim about the future of peace or of military spending, (C).

The thrust of the argument is toward the past and what past spending has done. Whether all this readiness can permit future cuts is a matter upon which the author doesn't speculate. Finally, (D)'s equation of weapons and personnel is silly, specious, and irrelevant. Both are mentioned as key elements of the current peace climate, and both have benefited from having more money available. But if the author has an opinion as to which (weapons or personnel) are more valuable, he's keeping it to himself.

3. C

You're asked for a situation that conforms to a principle, so your best bet is to understand the principle thoroughly, then test the choices against this understanding. The author offers an absolute truth with two restrictions. First the rule: A free press always reports all information about a country's military operations. There are two cases, and only two cases, in which this might not be true: (1) if such information would jeopardize the safety of the troops and (2) if such information would jeopardize the success of a mission. With such clear rules, we'll be looking for the answer choice that follows them faithfully.

To make answer choice (A) work, you'd have to assume that such dissenting opinions would jeopardize the troops and/or the success of the mission. This choice supports no such assumption, so based on the information that it alone provides, it is not consistent with the stimulus's principle. (B) and (D) discuss unfree presses and, therefore, fall outside the scope of the argument. The rules pertain only to a free press, and we can't infer how an unfree press would behave in regard to these issues. Answer choice (C) succeeds where (A) fails because, while it doesn't directly state that the publication of future military targets would jeopardize the success of a mission, the link between the two is far clearer and more logical. According to the principle, a free press *could* withhold information that endangers the troops or mission, and it's reasonable to say that the info discussed in (C) could fall into that category. (E) The principle deals with *current* military operations and, therefore, doesn't shed any light on what's appropriate behavior in regard to previous engagements. Clandestine past military operations are outside the scope.

No correct answer choice will require you to make a significant, unfounded assumption in order to make it work. The right answer choice will be correct on its own merit, without requiring you to introduce extra information.

4. E

Correct choice (E) is supported by the author's statement that it is "surprising" that Dillard's early and late work are so similar in style, despite the 35-year gap between the two stages. If the author is surprised by this fact, then we can infer that she believes that such a time period would normally cause a change in the artist's style.

(A) contradicts the passage, which clearly states that Dillard became famous for works produced late in her lifetime. (B), (C), and (D) all indicate some form of skepticism about the discovery or the available information on Dillard's work. However, the author's statement that the newly discovered painting uncovers a new facet of Dillard's life and work clearly indicates that she accepts the historians' identification, examination, and dating of the piece at face value.

5. C

The key to solving a question about a "misunderstanding" is to examine the second person's statement and see what understanding of the original statement is implied therein. Here, the customer says that he will have at least one functioning computer as long as he purchases three. This is true only if one out of any three given computers would continue working, (C). In reality, of course, the salesperson meant that any given computer has a one-third chance of continuing to function; all three computers might fail.

(A) is incorrect, because the customer's plan would then not be "certain to have" a computer that still worked after a year. (A) would imply that the customer would keep trying computers until he found one that worked, not buy three computers in order to have one that worked. (B) and (D) are incorrect because the identity of the person using the computer (whether it is this customer or another) is outside scope of the stimulus. (E) may be an assumption the customer is making, since he otherwise might be more likely to buy a full-price computer, but we have no evidence that this is what he thought the salesperson said—the only thing we know for sure is that he thinks if he buys three computers, he'll have one that works.

6. E

There's a lot of information here about the policy change and reaction to it, but the question stem directs us to the end of the stimulus: The author's conclusion "about McCarthy" is simply that she's been a loyal employee for 12 years. How do we know? The author

offers her personnel file as evidence. Whether or not we can draw any conclusion about McCarthy based on the personnel file depends on the accuracy of the file. If it's accurate, it's a basis to draw conclusions about McCarthy's work history with Luna, but if it's not, then it's useless as evidence. The author, then, must assume that the information in the file is accurate. That's (E). It could be true that only long-term human resources staff can add items to portfolios, (A), but don't lose sight of what you're looking for—we need the missing piece that allows us to draw conclusions about McCarthy's work history at Luna from her personnel file. (B) certainly seems to make sense, but it doesn't plug that gap between McCarthy's personnel file and drawing conclusions about her work history at Luna. (C) provides a good explanation of why employees would want to add information to their portfolios, but fails to address the validity of McCarthy's personnel file as evidence of her loyalty. As for (D), the reason for the policy is irrelevant to this question, since our focus is on the use of McCarthy's personnel file as evidence. Note that all of the wrong answer choices here address the policy change, rather than focusing on the piece of the stimulus referred to in the question stem. Because the bulk of the text relates to that change, it will be tempting for students who haven't used the question stem to direct their reading to focus there as well.

7. C

This is a Point at Issue question that basically asks, "What are they fighting about?" Look to see where they disagree. The marketing analyst only disputes the manufacturer's conclusion; each person presents completely different evidence. They can only disagree about something that they both discuss, and the only thing that meets that criterion in this dialogue is the conclusion. Therefore, they disagree about whether the company should switch to a less expensive brand of rubber, or (C).

(A) The manufacturer certainly assumes that other brands cost less, but the analyst in no way disputes this or even directly mentions it. Both seem to agree that other brands would cost less. (B) is not addressed by either person. The analyst mentions sales but not sales *quotas*, and the manufacturer doesn't even get close to discussing sales. (D), like (B), brings up an issue that neither person directly addresses. Even if you thought the analyst's comments might have some relevance to customer preferences, the analyst never addresses them directly, and the manufacturer never gets near this subject. (E) is addressed by the analyst but not by the manufacturer, whose argument deals only with cost.

Notice that all of the wrong answer choices mention issues that would be more relevant to the analyst's comments than the manufacturer's. Don't neglect the first argument; the right answer will have to be something discussed with different opinions by both people.

8. D

The author believes that Bidwell has incorrectly used the expression *ivory tower*, because in her experience, buildings that have towers or are ivory colored are not to be found on college campuses. However, the passage tells us that Bidwell uses the term when he "discusses [academics'] tendency to work in isolation without looking for concrete connections to the world." Even if you aren't familiar with the terminology, you should recognize that Bidwell isn't claiming that academics reside in tall white buildings. The expression *ivory tower* is an example of figurative language. Bidwell is implying that academics are distant from, and untouched by, the real world. (D) is the correct answer.

If you were unfamiliar with the term *ivory tower*, you could have used the context of the passage and the process of elimination to find the answer. To make a generalization, (A), is to draw a general conclusion from a specific set of events or circumstances. The author of this passage generalizes when she states that no college campuses have white buildings or towers, but this is not a generalization that she has failed to see in Bidwell's writing. (B), a deduction, is a conclusion formed on the basis of given information; there's nothing like that in the passage. There is no support for (C); a counterexample is a fact that disproves a generalization, but no generalization is found here. Lastly, irony, (E), is a situation in which the actual result or sequence of events is the opposite of what would be expected. An example of irony would be if the author of this passage discovered

that her office were being relocated to the tower of a white building on campus.

9. A

The stimulus tells us that there are at least two sources of effective concepts for a company's advertising campaign: those that are recognizable as such based on previous knowledge of the market and those that are shown to be effective only when used to launch a campaign. We don't know which kind the current campaign consists of or whether it might be a mix. Therefore, we can infer that we may not be able to judge the effectiveness of all aspects of the campaign prelaunch—because we won't if it contains any elements that fall into the latter category.

(B) distorts the role of "prior knowledge" and "past performance" in the stimulus. (C) is probably true—but we have no information in the passage from which to draw that conclusion. Avoid answer choices that seem reasonable but can't be tied directly to the stimulus. Similarly, (D) brings in an element that is not found in the passage. The passage draws a distinction between the two types of concepts, but it does not state which of them has more merit. As far as we know, both types are effective and fulfill the company's needs. (E) is outside scope: Our concern is the point at which effectiveness can be assessed.

10. A

Mr. Holt concludes that an anonymous survey at the next Concerned Neighbors Committee meeting is the best way to gather accurate information about the need for a food shelf. His evidence is that the people at the meeting are largely from the neighborhood and the anonymity will encourage them to answer honestly. (A) provides the best criticism of Mr. Holt's logic by pointing out that the sample of neighborhood residents attending the meeting may not be large enough or may not be representative. If the survey might fail to reach a significant number of potential food shelf clients, then Holt's plan will not be effective.

(B) is outside scope. The purpose of the survey is to determine whether there is a need, not to target specific beneficiaries. (C) is also outside scope—we're only looking to determine the need in *this* neighborhood. (D) introduces an irrelevant element. We're only concerned with those who might use a food shelf. If some people lie on the survey, (E), then its results might be slightly skewed, but the author has taken measures to minimize that by making the survey anonymous, so he hasn't overlooked the issue.

11. B

The author believes that these two opposing quotations reflect the dramatically different platforms of two candidates for a Senate seat. However, a candidate's platform may be made up of many issues, so one narrow conflict is not sufficient to demonstrate, as the author claims, that there is not "a lot of common ground." Perhaps these two candidates have identical positions on fiscal issues, education, etc. (A) directly contradicts the author's illustration, which shows two candidates who do not share the same beliefs on a particular issue. (C) attempts to mislead by referencing a familiar detail, but it doesn't reach the core of the argument—that these two candidates don't have a lot of middle ground because they disagree about this one point. (D) is true, but it's not a flaw. A valid argument need not include evidence for the opposing viewpoint. (E) might look tempting, since the author does assume that the candidates' quotations here express the totality of their views on an issue, but he does not provide any evidence to show that this is not the case. Beware of answer choices that start strong and take a wrong turn.

12. A

The author concludes that World Imports spends three times as much on kitchen items as it does on furniture. The evidence is that 3 percent of the furniture arrives at the store too damaged to sell, while 9 percent of the kitchen items arrive in the same condition. While the math might look good, this is a classic case of statistics being used to support a conclusion they don't actually support at all. The author attempts to convince us that since three times as much kitchen merchandise is damaged, it must be three times as expensive to stock kitchen merchandise as furniture. The problem, of course, is that the cost of stocking items is reliant on more than simply the breakage rate. Some items are more expensive than others, some are heavier (and therefore more expensive to ship) . . . the list could go on. All you

really need to know is that other factors impact the cost, leading to correct choice (A).

(B) is tempting, in that inadequate and unrepresentative samples are often at the core of a flaw question, but in this case, we have no information about the shipments on which we can make that determination. (C) is simply a distraction; the varying breakage rates at World Imports's competitors have nothing to do with the argument at hand, which deals exclusively with World Imports's products. The mention of competitors takes us outside the scope of the argument. (D) suggests that a minimum amount of breakage is inevitable, but that doesn't impact the assessment of relative costs, which is really what we're interested in. (E) says merely that long-distance shipping is unavoidable . . . this also has no impact on the relationship between breakage and cost.

13. C

The primary flaw in the authors' reasoning is that they respond by defending their *intentions*, while the principal's concern is clearly for the actual impact. (C) is therefore correct; the issue here is not the motivation behind the change but the effects that came out of it. (A) and (B) deal with the effectiveness of the new curriculum. But the authors never implied that the curriculum was guaranteed to improve writing skills, (A), or that it would be more beneficial than the old curriculum, (B). They merely stated that the change was well intentioned. (D) is irrelevant since the principal is unconcerned with motivations. (E) is outside scope— students who passed last year's exam weren't using the curriculum in question.

CHAPTER 4: **LOGIC GAMES**

- Anatomy of a Logic Game
- Kaplan's 5-Step Method for Logic Games
- Types of Logic Games
- Section Management
- Helpful Hints to Improve Your Performance
- Practice Tips

Initially, nothing inspires more fear in the hearts of LSAT test takers than Analytical Reasoning—the Logic Games section. The skills tested on this section may seem unfamiliar. However, this particular section will likely be the easiest for you to improve upon in the course of your LSAT studies; that is, you will quickly see dramatic improvement in this section by just implementing a few key strategies.

To start, it may help you to re-examine the reason this section is included on the test— the major analytical skills that the Logic Games section is designed to measure:

- **Organization:** The ability to assimilate efficiently, both in your head and on the page, the amount of data in each game
- **Mental agility:** The ability to maintain enough flexibility to apply the data in various ways to each question
- **Memory:** The ability to retain the work done in the initial setup stage while focusing on any new information in the question stem
- **Concentration:** The ability to stay focused on the task at hand and not let your mind wander

Logic games are most troublesome to those test takers who don't have a clearly defined method of attack. And that's where Kaplan's 5-Step Method for Logic Games, game- and section-specific strategies, and helpful hints will help, streamlining your work so you can rack up points quickly and confidently.

ANATOMY OF A LOGIC GAME

Each logic game has three distinct parts: an introductory paragraph, a list of rules, and a set of questions with multiple-choice answers. The initial paragraph presents an everyday situation along with a cast of characters and an action to be done to the characters. The introduction may also provide additional information to structure the game further.

The scenario is followed by a list of indented rules that limit the action of the game. Some rules will be definite, and other rules will be more ambiguous.

A set of five to seven questions follows the rules. Some of the questions can be answered from the original scenario and rules. Other questions will include additional information to be used for answering that question only.

KAPLAN'S 5-STEP METHOD FOR LOGIC GAMES

1. OVERVIEW

Read the first paragraph, stop, and answer the SEAL questions.

Situation:	What is the situation, or where does the game take place?
Entities:	What is the cast of characters or game pieces you will play with?
Action:	What action will you do to the entities?
Limitations:	Are there any other pieces of information you have not used yet from the first paragraph?

The LSAT uses four common actions or a combination of them in games. They are sequencing, matching, distribution, and selection. In other words, you will need to sequence, match, distribute, and/or select entities. If you need to do a combination of actions, we call that a hybrid game.

2. SKETCH

Draw a simple picture of the game, including the entities and a framework, on a blank portion of the test booklet page, typically at the top or bottom of the page. Scratch paper is not provided for the LSAT, and you want your sketch to be neat and accessible. The exact sketch will be determined by the action of the game.

3. RULES

Analyze and convert each rule into a visual representation. In other words, take each rule out of the text and draw it directly into your sketch, if possible. If not, draw the rule to the side of your sketch.

4. DEDUCTIONS

Determine if you can combine rules to make any deductions. More simply, now that you've seen all the game information, is there anything else that you know? Kaplan uses the BLEND acronym to guide the process.

B	loc of entities:	Two or more entities moving or working together in a sketch
L	imited options:	When a game can only work out a limited number of ways (usually two)
E	stablished entities:	Entities that are placed definitively in particular locations
N	umbers:	Ratios and numerical restrictions that impact a game's possible outcomes
D	uplicates:	Entities that appear in more than one rule

5. QUESTIONS

Read all of the questions first, then begin to attack them systematically. Approximately half of the questions can be answered from your initial work in steps 1 through 4. The other questions will add a condition for purposes of that question only. The rule of thumb with "if" questions is to resketch them.

You must have a solid command of the limited number of logic games question stems. When you take a few seconds to recognize the question type, characterize the answer choices, and apply the appropriate process, your work becomes more efficient—and more accurate.

Acceptability Questions

If the question asks which choice would be "acceptable," one answer choice will satisfy all the rules; each wrong choice will violate at least one rule.

New "If" Questions

When the question adds a new "if" condition, treat the "if" as a new rule and draw a new sketch if necessary.

Complete and Accurate List Questions

Answer the other questions first; their sketches will help you answer these. Use the choices to decide what possibilities you have to test.

Could [Not] versus Must [Not] Questions

Focus on the nature of the right and wrong answer choices:

If the question reads . . .	The right answer will be . . .
Which one of the following statements could be true?	. . . a statement that could be true, and the four wrong choices will be statements that must be false.
Which one of the following statements cannot be true?	. . . a statement that cannot be true, and the four wrong choices will be statements that either must be true or merely could be true.
Which one of the following statements must be true?	. . . a statement that must be true, and the four wrong choices will be statements that could be false.
All of the following statements could be true EXCEPT . . .	. . . a statement that must be false, and the four wrong choices will be statements that could or must be true.
All of the following statements must be true EXCEPT . . .	. . . a statement that could be false, and the four wrong choices will be statements that must be true.
Which of the following statements could be false?	. . . a statement that could be false, and the four wrong choices will be statements that must be true.
Which one of the following statements must be false?	. . . a statement that must be false, and the four wrong choices will be statements that either must be true or could be true.

You'll have a chance to see these major logic games principles in action when you review the explanations to the games in the practice set and Practice Tests in this book.

TYPES OF LOGIC GAMES

Logic games come in four basic varieties: sequencing, matching, distribution, and selection. If more than one action takes place in a game, it is a hybrid.

SEQUENCING

Logic games requiring sequencing skills—those that involve putting entities in order—have long been a test maker's favorite. In a typical sequencing game, you may be asked to arrange the cast of characters numerically from left to right, from top to bottom, in days of the week, in a circle, and so on. The sequence may be a matter of degree—say, ranking the eight smartest test takers from 1 to 8. Or it may be based on time, such as one that involves the order of shows broadcast on a radio station. Occasionally, there are two or even three orderings to keep track of in a single game.

Strict and Loose Sequences

There are two types of sequencing games. In a **strict** sequencing game, the placement of entities is very strictly defined. You may be told, for example, that "A is third," or that "X and Y are adjacent," and so on. These are definite, concrete pieces of information, and the game centers around placing as many people into definite spots as possible. In contrast, in a **loose** sequencing game, your job is to rank the entities only in relation to one another. You're usually never asked to determine fully the ordering of the cast of characters. Instead, the relationships between the entities constitute the crux of the game.

Typical Sequencing Game Issues

The following is a list of the key issues in sequencing games, each followed by a corresponding rule—in some cases, with several alternative ways of expressing the same rule. At the end, these rules will be used to build a miniature logic game so that you can see how rules work together to define and limit a game's action. These rules all refer to a scenario in which eight events are to be sequenced from first to eighth.

Issue	Sample Rules
Which entities are concretely placed in the ordering?	X is third.
Which entities are forbidden from a specific position in the ordering?	Y is not fourth.
Which entities are next to, adjacent to, or immediately preceding or following one another?	X and Y are consecutive. X is next to Y. No event comes between X and Y.
Which entities cannot be next to, adjacent to, or immediately following one another?	X does not immediately precede or follow Q. X is not immediately before or after Q. At least one event comes between X and Q. X and Q are not consecutive in the sequence.
How far apart in the ordering are two particular entities?	Exactly two events come between X and Q.
What is the relative position of two entities in the ordering?	Q comes before T in the sequence. T comes after Q in the sequence.

How a Sequencing Game Works

Now see how rules like those above might combine to create a simple logic game.

> Eight events—Q, R, S, T, W, X, Y, and Z—are being ordered from
> first to eighth.
>
> X is third.
>
> Y is not fourth.
>
> X and Y are consecutive.
>
> Exactly two events come between X and Q.
>
> Q occurs before T in the sequence.

How would you approach this simplified game? With eight events to sequence, draw
eight dashes in an open spot on your game page and number them one through eight.
Then list the entities.

Q R S T W X Y Z

___	___	___	___	___	___	___	___
1	2	3	4	5	6	7	8

Next work your way through the rules. Rule 1: X is third.

___	___	X	___	___	___	___	___
1	2	3	4	5	6	7	8

Rule 2: Y is not fourth.

___	___	X	___	___	___	___	___
1	2	3	4	5	6	7	8
			Y̶				

Rule 3: X and Y are consecutive. X is third, and Y cannot be fourth. Therefore, Y must
be second.

___	Y	X	___	___	___	___	___
1	2	3	4	5	6	7	8

Rule 4: Exactly two events come between X and Q. Because Q can't obey this rule coming
before X—there isn't enough room—it must come after X. Put X in the sixth space.

___	Y	X	___	___	Q	___	___
1	2	3	4	5	6	7	8

Rule 5: Q occurs before T in the sequence. So T must be either seventh or eighth.

This is an example of how the rules work together to build a sequencing game. You'll see how this works in the sequencing games on the Practice Tests; pay careful attention to the written explanations.

MATCHING

As their name implies, matching games ask you to match up one set of entities to another set of entities—often working with many characteristics at once. For example, a game may involve three animals, each assigned a name, a color, and a particular size. It's no wonder test takers get bogged down in these questions—there's a lot to keep track of.

Some people dislike matching games because they feel bombarded with information and don't know where to start. Organization is especially crucial to get the points for these questions. A table or grid sketch will be helpful.

Center the sketch around the most concrete entity and build into the table or grid the more fluid entity. Visualize the action and create a mental picture or a sketch that puts the elements into a logical order. If you think through the scenarios and don't get scared off by their seeming complexity, you can find matching games accessible and even fun.

Typical Matching Game Issues

The following is a list of the key issues in matching games, each followed by a corresponding rule or set of rules.

All of these rules refer to a situation in which you have three animals—a dog, a cat, and a goat. Each animal has a name (Bimpy, Hank, and Jiming), a color (brown, black, or white), and a size (large or small).

Issue	Rule
Which entities are matched up?	The dog is brown.
	The black animal is small.
Which entities are not matched up?	Bimpy is not white.
	The goat is not large.
Which entity's matchups depend on the matchups of other entities?	If the cat is large, then Hank is brown.
	If the white animal is small, then Jiming is not the dog.

Notice that these last rules take the form of if/then statements, which means that the contrapositive can be employed.

Remember, the **contrapositive** is formed by reversing and negating the terms of an if/then statement. For the first, you get this:

> If Hank is NOT brown, then the cat is NOT large.

Taking the contrapositive of the second rule results in this statement:

> If Jiming IS the dog, then the white animal is NOT small.

Both of these new pieces of information are just as powerful as any of the indented rules given in the game's introduction.

How Matching Games Work

You know the drill by now. Now take some of the rules above and form them into a mini logic game:

> A rancher owns three animals—a dog, a cat, and a goat.
> The animals are named Bimpy, Hank, and Jiming. One of the animals is brown, one is black, and one is white. Two of the animals are large and one is small.
>
> The dog is brown.
>
> The black animal is small.
>
> Bimpy is not white.
>
> The goat is not large.
>
> If the cat is large, then Hank is brown.

In this game, you are matching two sets of entities: attributes to animals. The animals are the most concrete entity, so list them across the top of your table. The attributes will change, so list them down the side.

	Dog	Cat	Goat
Name: B H J			
Size: L L S			
Color: br bl wh			

Now draw in the rules. Rule 1: The dog is brown—that's straightforward enough. Rule 2: The black animal is small. You don't know where either attribute is yet, but you know they go together. So draw them off to the side. The same goes for Rule 3: Bimpy is white.

	Dog	Cat	Goat		
Name: B H J					B
Size: L L S				S	wh
Color: ~~br~~ bl wh	br			bl	

Rule 4: The goat is not large. Think about this before you fill in anything. There are only two sizes, large and small. So if the goat is not large, it has to be small. Based on Rule 2 then, the goat is also black. So the cat must be white and named Bimpy. Because only one of the animals is small, according to the introduction, the cat and the dog must be large.

	Dog	Cat	Goat		
Name: ~~B~~ H J		B			B
Size: ~~L L~~ S	L	L	S	S	wh
Color: ~~br bl wh~~	br	wh	bl	bl	

Rule 5: If the cat is large, then Hank is brown. We already know that the cat is large, so Hank must be brown. We also know that the dog is brown; therefore, it is named Hank. The only name left over, Jiming, must belong to the goat.

	Dog	Cat	Goat		
Name: ~~B H J~~	H	B	J		B
Size: ~~L L~~ S	L	L	S	S	wh
Color: ~~br bl wh~~	br	wh	bl	bl	

Just by drawing in the rules and making some deductions along the way, you can complete the sketch and have everything you need to answer the questions.

DISTRIBUTION

In distribution games, you are given a set of entities and asked to divide the entities into subgroups. You're not concerned with the order of the entities but rather the size of the subgroups, which entities go where, and which entities can and cannot be with each other.

Typical Distribution Game Issues

Here are the issues involved in distribution games along with the rules that govern them. These rules refer to a scenario in which all the members of a group of eight entities—Q, R, S, T, W, X, Y, Z—have to be distributed into three different classes.

Issue	Rule
Which entities are concretely placed in a particular subgroup?	X is placed in Class 3.
Which entities are barred from a particular subgroup?	Y is not placed in Class 2.
Which entities must be placed in the same subgroup?	X is placed in the same class as Z. Z is placed in the same class as X. X and Z are placed in the same class.
Which entities cannot be placed in the same subgroup?	X is not placed in the same class as Y. Y is not placed in the same class as X. X and Y are not placed in the same class.
Which entity's placement depends on the placement of another entity?	If Y is placed in Class 1, then Q is placed in Class 2.

How Distribution Games Work

These rules can combine to form a miniature distribution games.

> Eight students—Q, R, S, T, W, X, Y, and Z—must be subdivided into three different classes—Classes 1, 2, and 3.
>
> X is placed in Class 3.
>
> Y is not placed in Class 2.
>
> X is placed in the same class as Z.
>
> X is not placed in the same class as Y.
>
> If Y is placed in Class 1, then Q is placed in Class 2.

A good sketch for distribution games begins with the subgroups at the top of a table and a list of the entities above that.

Q R S T W X Y Z

1	2	3

Then use the rules and make deductions to determine the placement of the entities and how many go in each subgroup. Rule 1: X is placed in Class 3—that's easy to put in our table.

Rule 2: Y is not placed in Class 2. While this rule tells you where Y is not, you can turn it into a positive statement because there are only two places Y can go. If Y is not in 2, it must be in Class 1 or Class 3.

Rule 3: X is placed in the same class as Z. We know X is in Class 3 because of rule 1, so Z is also in Class 3.

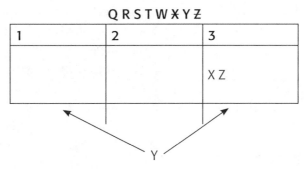

Rule 4, X is not placed in the same class as Y, prohibits Y from being in the same class as X. So you now know Y cannot be in Class 3, and you already know that Y cannot go in 2 (see rule 2). Therefore, Y must go in Class 1.

Rule 5 tells us that if Y is placed in Class 1 (as it is here), then Q is placed in Class 2.

QRSTWXYZ

1	2	3
Y	Q	X Z

And that, in simplified form, is the dynamic of a distribution game. For more complex distribution games, check out the practice set and Practice Tests.

SELECTION

In selection games, you are given a set of entities and asked to choose some for inclusion in the group and to reject the others. In other words, you are picking a smaller group from a larger group. Sometimes the test makers specify an exact number for the smaller group; sometimes they don't. In a common variation, the initial group of entities is itself broken into subgroups at the start of the game. An example would be a farmer choosing five animals from a group of three cows, four horses, and two goats.

Typical Selection Game Issues

The following is a list of the key issues in selection games, each followed by a corresponding rule and, in some cases, with several alternative ways of expressing the same rule. At the end, again, these rules will be used to build a miniature logic game.

These rules all refer to a scenario in which you are to select a subgroup of four from a group of eight entities—Q, R, S, T, W, X, Y, and Z.

Issue	Rule
Which entities are definitely chosen?	Q is selected.
Which entities rely on a different entity's selection in order to be chosen?	If X is selected, then Y is selected. X will be selected only if Y is selected. X will not be selected unless Y is selected.
Which entities must be chosen together or not at all?	If X is selected, then Y is selected. If Y is not selected, then X is not selected.
Which entities cannot both be chosen?	If R is selected, then Z is not selected. If Z is selected, then R is not selected. R and Z won't both be selected.

How Selection Games Work

You can combine these rules to create a rudimentary grouping game of selection:

> A professor must choose a group of four books for her next seminar. She must choose from a pool of eight books—Q, R, S, T, W, X, Y, and Z.
>
> Q is selected.
>
> X is not selected unless Y is selected.
>
> R is selected only if Z is not selected.
>
> If Y is selected, then S is chosen and T is not.

A selection game sketch starts with the list of entities. If you know the number of entities chosen, draw that number of dashes below the list. There is no need to number them because the order in which they are selected or placed is not at issue in a selection game. (If it is, a second action, sequencing, is added to this game, and it becomes a hybrid game.) If you don't know the number of entities selected, draw the list of entities without dashes. Circle and cross out entities as they are chosen or rejected.

Q R S T W X Y Z

——— ——— ——— ———

Rule 1: Q is selected. So put Q in the sketch.

Q̶ R S T W X Y Z

Q___ ——— ——— ———

The other rules can't be built directly into the sketch, since they are based on formal logic and describe eventualities (what the result is *if* something else happens). Translate the formal logic rules and draw them to the side of your sketch. Be sure to write out the contrapositive of each rule as well. Rule 2: No X is selected unless Y is selected. Rule 3: R is selected only if Z is not selected. And finally, Rule 4: If Y is selected, then S is chosen and T is not. Line up the arrows underneath each other so you can quickly scan the triggers to the left of the arrows. You only know what happens if those triggers are "pulled."

Q̶ R S T W X Y Z

Q̲ ___ _____ _____ _____

X	$\rightarrow$	Y
No Y	$\rightarrow$	No X
R	$\rightarrow$	No Z
Z	$\rightarrow$	No R
Y	$\rightarrow$	S and No T
No S or T	$\rightarrow$	No Y

Formal logic rules will take effect whenever a question adds new hypothetical information. For instance, say a question reads: "If Y is selected, which one of the following could be true?" Y is chosen for purposes of this question only, and you resketch, near the question if possible. In this case, there is no need to rewrite the formal logic rules. They are still available to you in your original sketch. Now add Y to the sketch and scan the formal logic rules to see if choosing Y triggers a result. It does, so add S to the sketch and eliminate T.

Q̶ R S T̶ W X Y̶ Z

Q̲ ___ Y̲ ___ S̲ ___ _____

No other rules come into play, so check the answers. A correct answer to this question could be that R is selected. And that, in a nutshell, is how a simplified selection game works.

HYBRID

Some LSAT logic games have more than one action. The most common hybrid games combine sequencing with matching and sequencing with distribution. However, any combination is fair game. Typically, you will see one and at the most two hybrid games in a section. They provide a way for the test maker objectively to raise the difficulty level of the game. Just remember, though, not every tough game is a hybrid and not all hybrid games are difficult. You will have to determine the setup for the game and keep track of the actions. However, the Kaplan 5-Step Method applies just as well to hybrid games as it does to the single-action games.

The key issues for any hybrid game are the same as those for each of the component skills—sequencing, matching, distribution, and selection—discussed above. And while organization is important to all logic games, it is especially critical in hybrid games because you are working with more information. One more note about hybrid games: Consider whether the questions involve one action or another. It is helpful to understand how each action works in the game on its own as well as how it works in conjunction with other actions.

Now that you have some logic games background, it's time to see how you can marshal that knowledge to approach games systematically and get the points. Let's work through a hybrid game together.

QUESTIONS 1–2

> Five workers—Mona, Patrick, Renatta, Saffie, and Will—are scheduled to clean apartments on five days of a single week, Monday–Friday. There are three cleaning shifts available each day—a morning shift, an afternoon shift, and an evening shift. No more than one worker cleans in any given shift. Each worker cleans exactly two shifts during the week, but no one works more than one cleaning shift in a single day.
>
> Exactly two workers clean on each day of the week.
>
> Mona and Will clean on the same days of the week.
>
> Patrick doesn't clean on any afternoon or evening shifts during the week.
>
> Will doesn't clean on any morning or afternoon shifts during the week.
>
> Mona cleans on two consecutive days of the week.
>
> Saffie's second cleaning shift of the week occurs on an earlier day of the week than Mona's first cleaning shift.

1. Which one of the following must be true?

   (A) Saffie cleans on Tuesday afternoon.

   (B) Patrick cleans on Monday morning.

   (C) Will cleans on Thursday evening.

   (D) Renatta cleans on Friday afternoon.

   (E) Mona cleans on Tuesday morning.

2. If Will does not clean on Friday, which one of the following could be false?

   (A) Renatta cleans on Friday.

   (B) Saffie cleans on Tuesday.

   (C) Mona cleans on Wednesday.

   (D) Saffie cleans on Monday.

   (E) Patrick cleans on Tuesday.

Part Two: Strategies and Practice
Logic Games | **89**

Though only two questions accompany this game, a typical logic game will have five to seven questions.

1. OVERVIEW

The situation here is an apartment building that you want to clean. The entities are the five workers—Mona, Patrick, Renatta, Saffie, and Will (known to their friends as M, P, R, S, and W). The game asks you to distribute the workers among five days of the week and then order them in the morning, afternoon, and evening shifts. The actions are distribution and sequencing, so this is a hybrid game.

Now let's consider the limitations: everything in the initial paragraph you have not used yet. (As an aside, the setup never contains extra information to fool you in any way. If information is included, it's there for a reason and will be useful to you.) So what else is there? First, no more than one worker cleans in any given shift. That means that either one or no workers clean in a shift. Second, each worker cleans exactly two shifts during the week. So each worker will be in our sketch two times. Last, each worker can only appear on the schedule once in a day. So now you know that each worker will be scheduled on two different days. Put it all together, and you learn that 10 out of the 15 available shifts will be taken and five will be empty.

2. SKETCH

Remember, a sketch includes the entities and a framework to put them in. So what makes the most sense? You want to distribute the workers over five days and then sequence them in the shifts. Ultimately, you want to make a schedule. Common sense tells you to put the days across the top and the shifts down the side. Each worker will be on the schedule twice, so list each one twice. Also, five shifts will be empty—you can identify them with X's.

M M P P R R S S W W X X X X X

	M	T	W	Th	F
Morn					
Aft					
Eve					

3. RULES

Rule 1: Exactly two workers clean each day. So at the end of each day, expect to find two workers and one empty shift. Put an X on each day or write something like "2 a day" to remind you of this rule.

M M P P R R S S W W X X X X X

	M	T	W	Th	F
Morn					
Aft					
Eve					
	X	X	X	X	X

Rule 2: M and W clean on the same days, and that holds for both of the days they clean. Since you don't know which days or in which order, block them together off to the side.

M M P P R R S S W W X X X X X

	M	T	W	Th	F	
Morn						
Aft						MW
Eve						
	X	X	X	X	X	

Rule 3: P does not clean on the afternoon or evening shifts. Turn that in to a positive statement, and you know that P can only clean in the mornings.

Rule 4: W does not clean on any morning or afternoon shifts. Therefore, he must clean in the evenings.

M M P P R R S S W W X X X X X

	M	T	W	Th	F		
							MW
Morn						P…P	
Aft							
Eve						W…W	
	X	X	X	X	X		

Rule 5: M cleans on two consecutive days of the week. Since M and W clean on the same days, that means W cleans on two consecutive days as well. Also, W cleans during the evening shift, so M cleans earlier during the morning or afternoon shift.

M M P P R R S S W W X X X X X

	M	T	W	Th	F		M M
Morn						P…P	. .
Aft							. .
Eve						W…W	. .
	X	X	X	X	X		W W

Rule 6: S's second shift occurs on an earlier day of the week than M's first shift. Therefore, S cleans twice before M is on the schedule.

M M P P R R S S W W X X X X X

	M	T	W	Th	F	
Morn						P...P
Aft						
Eve						W...W
	X	X	X	X	X	

S...S...M M
..
..
..
W W

4. DEDUCTIONS

Work through BLEND. Are there any Blocs of entities? Yes, MM in particular. Try putting the bloc across the schedule on the different days. Because S . . . S must be to the left of the bloc, the earliest M can be on the schedule is Wednesday. Therefore, MM can be placed on Wednesday and Thursday or Thursday and Friday.

That takes us to Limited options. You now know that there are two possible places for M on the calendar. If sketching both options gives you additional information and further "limits" the game, draw them out.

M M P P R R S S W W X X X X X

	M	T	W	Th	F	
Morn						P...P
Aft						
Eve			W	W		W...W
	X S	X S	X M	X M	X	

S...S...M M
..
..
..
W W

M M P P R R S S W W X X X X X

	M	T	W	Th	F	
Morn						P...P
Aft						
Eve				W	W	W...W
	X	X	X	X M	X M	

S . . . S

S...S...M M
..
..
..
W W

Now check Established entities. You can establish almost all the workers on particular days based on where M and W are because no other workers can be scheduled with them. You can't set the workers in specific shifts, however.

M M P P R R S S W W X X X X X

①	M	T	W	Th	F	
Morn					P	P…P
Aft						
Eve			W	W		W…W
	P/R X S	P/R X S	X M	X M	X R	

S . . . S . . . M M
. .
. .
. .
W W

M M P P R R S S W W X X X X X

②	M	T	W	Th	F	
Morn						P…P
Aft						
Eve				W	W	W…W
	X	X	X	X M	X M	

←————————————→

S . . . S
P . . . P
R . . .R

S . . . S . . . M M
. .
. .
. .
W W

Numbers and Duplicates don't provide any additional information. So move from the deduction step on to the questions.

5. QUESTIONS

This is where you'll see how all the work you did up front pays off. Question 1 offers no new "if" information; it simply asks what must be true. And because you've already deduced a few things that *must be* true, you can scan the choices for one that matches any of your newly discovered pieces of information. It doesn't take long to spot choice (C)—your big deduction staring you right in the face. Circle (C) and move on. (Just for the record, (A), (B), and (D) could be true but need not be, while (E), as you discovered earlier, is impossible.)

Question 2 contains a hypothetical: no Will on Friday. One glance at your sketch says you've got option 1. You've already done the hard work. Check the answers.

This question asks for a statement that could be false—which means that the four wrong choices will all be things that must be true. And in fact, choices (A) through (D) match the situation in this question perfectly, while (E) merely could be true: Patrick's first cleaning shift of the week could be on Tuesday, but it just as easily could be on Monday as well. (His second shift must be on Friday.) (E) is the only choice that could be false.

Be sure to apply the 5-Step Method and the strategies and techniques discussed when you work through the following practice sets and all your Practice Tests.

SECTION MANAGEMENT

Section management means taking control of a section so you can get the most points out of it. The goal is to attack the section in a way to take control of your time, get your easier points up front, build in time for your tougher games, and gain confidence in the process. In the Logic Games section, you can take several steps to manage the section.

First of all, preview all four games and reorder them from the easiest game for you to the most difficult. There are six factors to consider when you preview the games and put them in your own order. They relate to the game setup and the game questions.

Game Setup Factors

1. **Concreteness:** Look for words in the setup like *must*, *exactly*, and *only* to identify information that is specific and absolute.
2. **Simplicity:** Identify games with a single action as opposed to multiple actions.
3. **Familiarity:** Find the games that you recognize and have worked with before.
4. **Brevity:** Use your judgment: There's a tradeoff between lots of text to read and additional information you can use to structure the game.

Game Question Factors

5. ***If's* and difficult questions:** Pay attention to types of questions, levels of difficulty, and questions that begin with *if*.
6. **Number of questions:** Determine the number of questions—all other issues being equal, the more questions there are, the bigger payoff you can get from one game setup.

No one factor will make a game easy or hard, and unfortunately, there is no exact formula to determine game order. You must keep these factors in mind and practice ordering the games. Ultimately, you want to preview all four games inside of a minute.

Even if you are working on one game, first scan it and decide whether you would put it in the first or second half of your order. When you are done with the game, evaluate your choice. Would you choose the same order again? Why or why not? What can you look for in the next game to help you put the games in the best order for you?

Second, keep moving through the section. Each question is worth the same amount, and law schools do not know where you earn your points—they just see a total score.

A third section management tool deals with bubbling the answer grid. In the Logic Games section, we recommend completing a game and marking the answers together before moving to the next game. The idea is to identify the correct circles and to keep from misbubbling.

Fourth, reorder the questions so you answer the questions up front that require the least work. Generally speaking, answer logic games questions in the following order:

1. Acceptability questions
2. Must questions
3. If Must questions
4. Could questions
5. If Could questions
6. Complete and Accurate List questions

Most importantly, slow down in the beginning to master your logic games skills and practice the timing. You cannot get faster until you have the proper foundation from which to work.

HELPFUL HINTS TO IMPROVE YOUR PERFORMANCE

KNOW THE KAPLAN METHOD

The 5-Step Method guides you through the information so you can take it in and use it accurately and efficiently to answer questions and earn points.

KNOW THE RULES

The LSAT measures critical thinking, and virtually every sentence in Logic Games has to be filtered through some sort of analytical process to be of any use. So it's not enough just to copy a rule off the page (or shorthand it); it's imperative that you think through its full meaning, including any implications it might have. And don't limit this to the indented rules; statements in introductions are very often rules that warrant the same meticulous consideration.

Say a game's introduction sets up a scenario in which you have three boxes, each containing at least two of the following three types of candy—chocolates, gumdrops, and mints—and then you get the following rule:

> Box 2 does not contain any gumdrops.

What does that rule say? *There aren't any gumdrops in Box 2.* But what does that rule *mean* in the context of the game? That Box 2 *does* contain chocolates and mints. Each box contains at least two of three things. If you eliminate one of the three things from any particular box, the other two things *must* be in that box.

Moreover, part of understanding what a rule means is being clear about what the rule *doesn't* mean. Take a look at this rule:

Rule: If Bob is chosen for the team, then Eric is also chosen.

Means: Whenever Bob is chosen, Eric is too.

Doesn't mean: Whenever Eric is chosen, Bob is too.

Remember the discussion of formal logic in chapter 3 on Logical Reasoning with its if/then statements and sufficient condition and necessary results? If I yell loudly at my cat, he will run away. That means that whenever I yell at him loudly, he runs away. But, just as important, it *doesn't* mean that whenever he runs away, I've yelled at him.

KEEP A CLEAN, READABLE MASTER SKETCH

Find an open space on the game page and set up your master sketch. You will not receive any scratch paper, so keep your sketch neat and accessible.

Developing good scratchwork will help your performance on logic games. For each game, you'll find it helpful to create a master sketch that encapsulates the game's information in an easy-to-follow form. This gives your eye a place to gravitate towards when you need information and helps to solidify in your mind the action of the game, the rules, and whatever deductions you made.

Keep scratchwork simple—you get no points for beautiful diagrams, and the less elaborate the sketch, the more time you'll have for thinking and answering questions. Pay careful attention to the scratchwork suggestions in the explanations to the games in the practice set and Practice Tests.

The goal of the scratchwork is to condense a lot of information into manageable, user-friendly visual cues. Jot down each rule in quick shorthand. (Remember, however, shorthand is useful only if it reminds you at a glance of the rule's meaning. You need to understand your own notes!) You should never have to look back at the game itself once you get to the questions. It's much easier to remember and apply rules written like so:

B → E

No G in 2

than those written like so:

If Bob is chosen for the team, then Eric is also chosen.

Box 2 does not contain any gumdrops.

But such notation is only helpful if you know what the arrow means and use it consistently. If you develop personal shorthand that's instantly understandable to you, you'll have a decided advantage on test day.

REVIEW THE RULES BETWEEN QUESTIONS

Notice we said "review," not "study." Glancing at your master sketch to remind yourself of the rules is especially helpful after the first few questions to make sure the rules are fresh in your mind. Reviewing rules is also useful after "if" questions to erase any conditions from your mind that were specific to that question.

THINK IN COMPLETE SENTENCES

You will write A → B, but you need to be thinking what the abbreviation means: "If I buy apples, then I also buy bananas." The abbreviation is easier to remember and work with but is confusing if you don't have the larger meaning in mind.

THINK "MUSTS"

Focus on what is certain and what must be true.

TURN NEGATIVES INTO POSITIVES

Suppose a game setup tells you that seven friends will each participate in one of three activities: Ping-Pong, bowling, or dancing. A rule says that Jack does not bowl or dance. From that rule, you know what Jack does not do, and you can also determine by eliminating two of the three activities that Jack must play Ping-Pong. Positive rules are easier to work with than negative rules.

DRAW OUT A QUESTION'S NEW "IFS"

When a question starts with *if* or something similar, a new rule is added to the game for purposes of that question only. You will incorporate that new rule by drawing a new sketch for that question. Do not draw on your master sketch or attempt to do the work in your head. Instead, find a blank space on the game page, preferably close to the question. Redraw the master sketch, include the new rule, make any deductions, and then answer the question. In other words, work back through the Kaplan Method for logic games. The time spent is worth it: In the time it takes to complain about redrawing, you could have completed the task!

CHARACTERIZE THE ANSWER CHOICES

Be sure you know what the question is so you know what kind of answer to find. If a question asks, "Which one of the following must be false?" then the correct answer is always false and the four wrong answers could be true. Without characterizing the question and answer choices, it is easy to mix up the answers and, ultimately, answer the wrong question.

LABEL EACH QUESTION'S SCRATCHWORK

If you don't have room to do your scratchwork next to the question, be sure to identify it so you can use it properly for another question if applicable.

PRACTICE TIPS

METHOD FIRST, SPEED LATER

Begin your practice by mastering Kaplan's Logic Games Method and work on timing later. Start by building your skills before you worry about getting faster. Getting faster does not mean you are answering questions correctly. Let's say it another way: It does not matter how fast you get the answers wrong. Many students start their LSAT preparation thinking that timing is their biggest problem. Does this sound familiar? "If I had all the time in the world, I could get every answer right." The trouble is, you have exactly 35 minutes to play four games and answer 22 to 24 questions in the Logic Games section.

A basketball player first learns the fundamentals of the game doing repeated dribbling, passing, and shooting drills. Then the ball player practices plays that put the skills together and adds scrimmages to practice game situations. In the process, the player works out to improve strength, agility, and endurance. The more comfortable with the skills and the more fit the player is, the more quickly the player can "read" the situation on the floor, make decisions, and respond in a game. No basketball player starts by playing games against rival teams. Practice your LSAT-taking skills the same way.

SLOW DOWN TO GO FASTER

To gain time in Logic Games, spend time practicing Kaplan's steps 1–4 so you become more efficient and more accurate at thinking through and analyzing the game setup and rules, drawing sketches, and making deductions. Yes, we know the points come from answering questions correctly in step 5. However, if you rush through steps 1–4 to get right to the questions in step 5, we also know you end up redoing the same work for each question. Spend a little extra time up front.

LOGIC GAMES PRACTICE

SET ONE

Directions: Each group of questions is based on a passage or a set of conditions. You may wish to draw a diagram to answer some of the questions. Choose the best answer for each question.

Questions 1–5

Six people—Matt, Ned, Qi, Stanley, Tonga, and Vladimir—are sitting around a rectangular table with six seats, one at the head of the table, one at the foot, and two on each long side of the table. The chairs are numbered 1 through 6 in a clockwise fashion, beginning with the chair at the head of the table, such that Chairs 1 and 4, 2 and 6, and 3 and 5 are directly across the table from each other.

Consecutively numbered chairs are considered adjacent. Chairs 1 and 6 are also considered adjacent.

Ned is sitting in Chair 1 or Chair 4.

Stanley and Tonga are sitting in adjacent chairs on one long side of the table.

Qi and Stanley are not sitting in adjacent chairs.

1. Which one of the following could be the seating arrangement of the six people in Chairs 1 through 6, respectively?

   (A) Ned, Vladimir, Tonga, Stanley, Matt, Qi

   (B) Vladimir, Stanley, Tonga, Ned, Matt, Qi

   (C) Qi, Matt, Ned, Stanley, Tonga, Vladimir

   (D) Ned, Tonga, Qi, Vladimir, Stanley, Matt

   (E) Qi, Vladimir, Matt, Ned, Tonga, Stanley

2. If Vladimir is sitting in Chair 4, then which one of the following pairs must be sitting in adjacent seats?

   (A) Matt and Ned

   (B) Matt and Qi

   (C) Ned and Qi

   (D) Ned and Stanley

   (E) Stanley and Vladimir

3. If Qi is sitting in Chair 1, then which one of the following must be sitting adjacent to her?

   (A) Ned

   (B) Matt

   (C) Stanley

   (D) Tonga

   (E) Vladimir

4. If Stanley and Vladimir are sitting in adjacent chairs, then Matt could be sitting in any of the following EXCEPT

   (A) Chair 1.

   (B) Chair 2.

   (C) Chair 3.

   (D) Chair 5.

   (E) Chair 6.

5. If Stanley is sitting in Chair 3 and Matt is sitting in Chair 6, then which one of the following pairs CANNOT sit directly across the table from each other?

   (A) Ned and Qi

   (B) Ned and Vladimir

   (C) Qi and Stanley

   (D) Qi and Vladimir

   (E) Stanley and Vladimir

<u>Questions 6–11</u>

A salesperson will display nine cheeses in three groups of three cheeses each. The groups are labeled A, B, and C. Four of the cheeses—F, G, H, and J—are domestic cheeses, and five—P, Q, R, S, and T—are imported cheeses. Each cheese will be displayed in exactly one of the three groups. The display must meet the following conditions:

At least one cheese in each group must be a domestic cheese.

F must be displayed with two imported cheeses.

Q must be displayed in Group C.

S must be displayed in Group A.

Neither F nor J nor R can be displayed in the same group as Q.

6. If both P and T are displayed in Group B, then which one of the following must be true?

(A) F is displayed in Group A.

(B) G is displayed in Group A.

(C) H is displayed in Group A.

(D) J is displayed in Group A.

(E) R is displayed in Group A.

7. Which one of the following statements must be true?

(A) If F and R are displayed together, they are displayed in the same group as S.

(B) If G and H are displayed together, they are displayed in the same group as Q.

(C) If G and T are displayed together, they are displayed in the same group as F.

(D) If H and J are displayed together, they are displayed in the same group as P.

(E) If R and S are displayed together, they are displayed in the same group as J.

8. All of the following are groups of three cheeses that can be displayed together in Group B EXCEPT

(A) F, P, and R.

(B) G, H, and T.

(C) G, J, and R.

(D) J, P, and T.

(E) J, R, and T.

9. If G is displayed in Group A, then which one of the following could be true?

(A) H is displayed in Group A.

(B) J is displayed in Group B.

(C) P is displayed in Group A.

(D) R is displayed in Group A.

(E) T is displayed in Group C.

10. If both H and P are displayed in Group B, then which one of the following must be the cheeses displayed in Group A?

(A) F, J, S

(B) F, R, S

(C) F, S, T

(D) J, S, R

(E) J, S, T

11. If J is displayed in Group B, then which one of the following CANNOT be true?

(A) F and R are displayed in the same group.

(B) G and R are displayed in the same group.

(C) H and S are displayed in the same group.

(D) R and S are displayed in the same group.

(E) S and T are displayed in the same group.

SET TWO

Questions 1–5

A doctor is scheduled to see seven patients—Quincy, Roland, Selena, Thurman, Vivian, Wilma, and Xavier—between the hours of 9 A.M. and 5 P.M. All appointments last exactly one hour and start at the top of the hour. There are no appointments scheduled during lunch. The schedule for the appointments must conform to the following conditions:

Xavier is scheduled as either the first or last appointment.

Selena's appointment is scheduled earlier than Thurman's appointment.

Thurman's appointment is exactly one hour before Vivian's appointment.

If Roland's appointment is scheduled for 12 P.M., then Thurman's appointment is scheduled for 3 P.M.

Lunch is scheduled for 1 P.M. and is one hour long and there are no other breaks scheduled for the day.

1. Which one of the following could be a list of the patients in the order of their scheduled appointments, from 9 A.M. to 4 P.M.?

    (A) Xavier, Quincy, Roland, Thurman, Vivian, Selena, Wilma

    (B) Quincy, Selena, Wilma, Roland, Xavier, Thurman, Vivian

    (C) Roland, Quincy, Selena, Wilma, Thurman, Vivian, Xavier

    (D) Xavier, Thurman, Vivian, Wilma, Selena, Roland, Quincy

    (E) Selena, Thurman, Vivian, Roland, Wilma, Quincy, Xavier

2. Which one of the following must be FALSE?

    (A) Roland's appointment is scheduled for 4 P.M.

    (B) Quincy's appointment is scheduled for 2 P.M.

    (C) Wilma's appointment is scheduled for 10 A.M.

    (D) Vivian's appointment is scheduled for 10 A.M.

    (E) Selena's appointment is scheduled for 9 A.M.

3. If Roland is scheduled for 12 P.M., then which of the following must be true?

    (A) Xavier is scheduled for 9 A.M.

    (B) Selena is scheduled for 2 P.M.

    (C) Wilma is scheduled for 11 A.M.

    (D) Quincy is scheduled for 11 A.M.

    (E) Vivian is scheduled for 3 P.M.

4. Which of the following patients CANNOT be scheduled for 2 P.M.?

    (A) Quincy

    (B) Roland

    (C) Selena

    (D) Thurman

    (E) Vivian

5. If Roland's appointment is exactly one hour before Thurman's appointment, which choice contains two alternative appointments, either of which could be true?

    (A) Quincy's appointment is at 2 P.M.; Wilma's appointment is at 2 P.M.

    (B) Thurman's appointment is at 10 A.M.; Vivian's appointment is at 10 A.M.

    (C) Selena's appointment is at 3 P.M.; Vivian's appointment is at 3 P.M.

    (D) Thurman's appointment is at 2 P.M.; Selena's appointment is at 2 P.M.

    (E) Roland's appointment is at 12 P.M.; Thurman's appointment is at 12 P.M.

Questions 6–10

Each of six vacationers—Cedric, Dolores, Fredrick, Gloria, Hedwig, and Jorge—will visit one of three cities—Lisbon, Madrid, or Novosibirsk—for exactly one month, according to the following conditions:

Each of the vacationers visits one of the cities with either one or three of the other vacationers, and no two groups contain exactly the same number of tourists.

Hedwig visits a different city than Jorge.

Dolores visits the same city as Gloria.

Cedric visits either Lisbon or Madrid.

If Jorge visits Novosibirsk, Dolores visits Novosibirsk with him.

6. Which of the following could be true for the one-month vacation?

   (A) Fredrick and Hedwig visit Madrid. Cedric, Dolores, Gloria, and Jorge visit Novosibirsk.

   (B) Dolores, Fredrick, Gloria, and Jorge visit Lisbon. Cedric and Hedwig visit Madrid.

   (C) Dolores, Gloria, and Jorge visit Lisbon. Cedric, Fredrick, and Hedwig visit Madrid.

   (D) Cedric and Fredrick visit Lisbon. Dolores, Gloria, Hedwig, and Jorge visit Madrid.

   (E) Cedric, Fredrick, Gloria, and Hedwig visit Lisbon. Dolores and Jorge visit Novosibirsk.

7. Which of the following must be FALSE?

   (A) Fredrick visits the same city as Hedwig.

   (B) Cedric visits the same city as Hedwig.

   (C) Cedric visits the same city as Fredrick.

   (D) Jorge visits Lisbon.

   (E) Jorge visits Madrid.

8. If Hedwig visits Novosibirsk, which one of the following must be true for the one month vacation?

   (A) Cedric visits Lisbon.

   (B) Jorge visits Madrid.

   (C) Dolores visits Novosibirsk.

   (D) Gloria visits Lisbon.

   (E) Fredrick visits Novosibirsk.

9. If Gloria visits Madrid, which one of the following must be FALSE?

   (A) Fredrick visits Madrid.

   (B) Hedwig visits Madrid.

   (C) Hedwig visits Novosibirsk.

   (D) Jorge visits Novosibirsk.

   (E) Jorge visits Lisbon.

10. Which one of the following could be FALSE?

    (A) Dolores visits a city with exactly three of the other five students.

    (B) Gloria must visit Madrid if Hedwig visits Novosibirsk.

    (C) Fredrick must visit Novosibirsk if Jorge visits Novosibirsk.

    (D) Gloria visits a city with exactly three of the other five students.

    (E) Cedric must visit Lisbon if Fredrick visits Madrid.

SET THREE

Questions 1–5

Seven instructors—J, K, L, M, N, P, and Q—teach adult education courses at a community college. Each instructor teaches during exactly one semester: the fall semester, the spring semester, or the winter semester. The following conditions apply:

K teaches during the winter semester.

L and M teach during the same semester.

Q teaches during either the fall semester or the spring semester.

Exactly twice as many instructors teach during the winter semester as teach during the fall semester.

N and Q teach during different semesters.

J and P teach during different semesters.

1. Which one of the following could be an accurate matching of instructors to semesters?

    (A) M: the fall semester; P: the spring semester; Q: the fall semester

    (B) J: the winter semester; L: the winter semester; P: the winter semester

    (C) L: the fall semester; N: the spring semester; P: the winter semester

    (D) J: the fall semester; M: the winter semester; N: the spring semester

    (E) K: the spring semester; L: the winter semester; P: the winter semester

2. Which one of the following CANNOT be true?

    (A) L teaches during the fall semester.

    (B) M teaches during the spring semester.

    (C) M teaches during the winter semester.

    (D) N teaches during the spring semester.

    (E) P teaches during the fall semester.

3. If exactly one instructor teaches during the spring semester, which one of the following must be true?

    (A) J teaches during the winter semester.

    (B) L teaches during the fall semester.

    (C) M teaches during the winter semester.

    (D) P teaches during the spring semester.

    (E) Q teaches during the fall semester.

4. Each of the following contains a list of instructors who can all teach during the same semester EXCEPT

    (A) J, K, M.

    (B) J, L, M.

    (C) K, L, P.

    (D) K, P, Q.

    (E) L, M, P.

5. Which one of the following could be a complete and accurate list of instructors who do not teach during the winter semester?

    (A) J, L, Q

    (B) J, Q

    (C) L, M, Q

    (D) N, P, Q

    (E) N, Q

Questions 6–10

Eight albums are to be played at a party. Two of the albums are country—G and H, three of the albums are dance—J, K, and L, and three of the albums are folk—M, N, and P. The two country albums are to be played consecutively, the three dance albums are to be played consecutively, and the three folk albums are to be played consecutively. The following conditions apply:

Each album is played exactly once.

The dance albums are played after the country albums or after the folk albums, but not after both.

Album N is played before album P and album G is played before album H.

No two albums are played at the same time.

6. Which of the following statements must be FALSE?

    (A) Album G is played first.

    (B) Album G is played seventh.

    (C) Album H is played second.

    (D) Album H is played seventh.

    (E) Album M is played third.

7. Which of the following could be true?

    (A) Album G is played second.

    (B) Album G is played eighth.

    (C) Album K is played first.

    (D) Album N is played second.

    (E) Album N is played third.

8. Which of the following CANNOT be an accurate list of the albums that are played second, third, and fourth?

    (A) N, M, J

    (B) P, M, J

    (C) N, P, K

    (D) H, J, K

    (E) H, K, L

9. If album P is played immediately before album M, then which one of the following statements could be true?

    (A) Album P is played first.

    (B) Album P is played sixth.

    (C) Album M is played third.

    (D) Album M is played seventh.

    (E) Album M is played second.

10. If albums K and N are played consecutively, but not necessarily in that order, which of the following statements must be FALSE?

    (A) Album N is played before album M.

    (B) Album J is played before album L.

    (C) Album L is played before album J.

    (D) Album M is played before album H.

    (E) Album G is played before album K.

ANSWERS AND EXPLANATIONS

ANSWER KEY

Set One	Set Two	Set Three
1. B	1. C	1. D
2. B	2. D	2. A
3. D	3. A	3. C
4. A	4. E	4. D
5. D	5. A	5. D
6. E	6. B	6. D
7. B	7. C	7. D
8. B	8. E	8. A
9. E	9. D	9. C
10. B	10. B	10. D
11. C		

DIAGNOSTIC TOOL

Tally up your score and write down your results below.

Total Correct: _____ out of 31

Percentage Correct: # you got right × 100 ÷ 31: _____

DIAGNOSE YOUR RESULTS

Look back at the questions you got wrong and think back on your experience answering them.

Step 1: Find the Roadblocks

Could you simply not wrap your head around some Logic Games? To improve your score, you need to pinpoint exactly what elements of these roadblocks tripped you up. To do that, ask yourself these two questions.

Am I weak in the skills being tested?

Logic Games are a complex LSAT question type that tests your analytical reasoning skills. They not only assess whether you are able to assimilate the data being presented in each game, they also test your ability to organize the data according to different rules and to remember the work you did in the setup stage while focusing on the new information in each question stem.

The Kaplan Logic Games principles in this book can help you focus on the specific skills required for tackling the complicated, multifaceted data presented to you in Logic Games. If you need more help in this department, TRY OUT the *Kaplan Logic Games Workbook*. It contains proven methods for improving data organization and concentration, as well as techniques for increasing speed and accuracy on the hardest questions.

Was it the question type that threw me off?

Then you need to become more comfortable with it! Go back to the beginning of this chapter and review the Kaplan principles and methods for Logic Games. Make sure you understand them and know how to apply them. Also, make sure are you very familiar with the types of Logic Games you are likely to encounter on Test Day.

Also, get as much practice as you can so you grow more at ease with Logic Games. For even more practice, TRY OUT the *Kaplan Logic Games Workbook*, which includes only real LSAT questions with practice sets for each type of Logic Game and two full-length Logic Games practice sections!

Step 2: Find the Blind Spots

Did you answer some Logic Game questions quickly and confidently but get them wrong anyway? When you come across wrong answers like these, you need to figure out what you thought you were doing right, what it turns out you were doing wrong, and why that happened. The best way to do that is to **read the answer explanations!**

They give you a detailed breakdown of why the correct answer is correct and why all the other answer choices are wrong. This helps to reinforce the Kaplan principles and methods for each question type and helps you figure out what blindsided you so it doesn't happen again. Also, just as with your roadblocks, try to get in as much practice as you can.

Step 3: Reinforce Your Strengths

Read through all the answer explanations for the ones you got right. Again, this helps to reinforce the Kaplan principles and methods for each question type, which in turn helps you to work more efficiently so you can get the score you want. Now keep your skills sharp with more practice.

As soon as you are comfortable with all the LSAT question types and Kaplan methods, complete a full-length practice test under timed conditions. In this way, practice tests serve as milestones; they help you to chart your progress! So don't save them all for the final weeks.

If you are aiming for that top score, try the *LSAT Advanced*, which includes only the toughest real LSAT questions and most focused strategies.

You can also visit **kaptest.com/LSAT** for more details on Kaplan's online and classroom-based options. Kaplan uses only real LSAT questions, so you get the most comprehensive, testlike experience.

SET ONE

Questions 1–5

This game involves placing people around a table, and it's pretty straightforward. The table is clearly described, maybe even too clearly. It's awfully wordy for what it has to say.

There is a rectangle in which Chairs 1 and 4 are at opposite ends, the head and foot, with Chairs 2 and 3 adjacent to each other on one side and Chairs 5 and

6 adjacent on the other. You go clockwise around the table, the rules tell you, and, although you might have figured it out for yourself, you're even told exactly which chairs are opposite which. So this all turns out to be pretty simple to sketch.

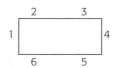

Rule 2 says Ned is in Chair 1 or 4. Of course, that means he is either at the head or foot of the table. You could have written a note to yourself at the top of the page: "N head or foot." And as a result, each time you drew the table to answer a question, you would have seen that note and remembered right away to put Ned at one end of the rectangular table.

Same thing for the other rules. You could have written in big letters "ST" at the top of the page to remind yourself that those two characters, Stanley and Tonga, have to be next to each other along one of the table's two long edges. Alternatively, you might have written "ST = 2 and 3 or 5 and 6." That's just another way of noting the relevant information. And there's no need to do much more with Rule 4 than write something like "Q not = S," a reminder always to separate Qi and Stanley.

1. B

Armed with all that information, you should be able to make short work of question 1, which asks for the one and only one acceptable sequence. Ned has to be in Chair 1 or 4. That means that choice (C) is unacceptable since (C) puts him in Chair 3. Cross out (C); there's no point in ever looking at it again. Next, remember that Stanley and Tonga have to be adjacent, and that eliminates choice (D), which puts two people between S and T in either direction. Moreover, they have to be adjacent along a long side of the table; that is, in Chairs 2 and 3 or 5 and 6. This eliminates choice (A), in which they are next to each other but Stanley is sitting in Chair 4; that is, at the foot of the table.

Nothing seems to have violated Rule 4 yet, but dollars to doughnuts, one choice will. And it turns out to be choice (E). You can't have Q in 1 and S in 6 because that, according to the first rule, counts as adjacency. You're left with choice (B), which must be okay since the other four choices violate rules. (B) is correct, although you needn't bother to check it at this point as long as you're sure the others are wrong. Just choose (B) and move on.

2. B

A quick sketch for question 2 puts V in Chair 4 and should immediately put Ned in Chair 1. (Ned has to be in one or the other, and since someone else is in 4, he has to be in Chair 1). On one side of the table, as always, you put Stanley and Tonga. You don't know which side right now. That leaves two people, Qi and Matt, and they, too, will be along one long side of the table. That's all that's left. So when question 2 asks who has to be next to each other, you should look for Qi and Matt, and you'll find them in correct choice (B). All of the other pairs *could* be adjacent but needn't be. So it's choice (B), and you're done with that one almost as quickly as you started.

3. D

Question 3 can be done very quickly too. Putting Qi in Chair 1, as you're told to do, means that Ned goes to Chair 4 this time. That leaves Stanley and Tonga, once again, along one of the long sides. But remember Rule 4: You have to separate Qi and Stanley. Therefore, Qi, who will have to sit next to either S or T since she's at the head, will be next to Tonga for sure, choice (D). Ned, choice (A), is opposite Qi. Stanley, choice (C), can't be next to her. And certainly, either Matt, choice (B), or Vladimir, choice (E), will have to be next to Qi, too, although you cannot choose between them. So it's Tonga, choice (D).

4. A

Question 4 asks, "Where could Matt *not* be?" The rules tell you very little about Matt, so build on the concrete information you're given about the other characters and see where that leaves Matt at the end.

Stanley and Vladimir are next to each other, you're told to assume. Stanley and Tonga are likewise next to each other, right? So both V and T will flank S at the table. However, you specifically know that Stanley and Tonga take up one long side of the table. This means that Vladimir will have to end up at one end of the table or

the other, either the head or the foot. Well, the other end, the head or the foot, is reserved for Ned. So if you look at the answer choices with the head and the foot going to Vladimir and Ned, there's no way that Matt or anyone else, besides those two, could occupy Chair 1 or Chair 4. The former has been chosen as the correct answer, choice (A). As for the others, Matt could take any of those. He and Qi will occupy 2 and 3 or 5 and 6, but more than that you don't know. So it's choice (A).

5. D

Question 5, in its exploration of who can or cannot sit across from whom, explicitly places two people in chairs and allows you to do likewise with a third. Specifically, if Stanley is in Chair 3, Tonga (who again has to be next to Stanley along a long side of the table) has to take the other chair along that side, Chair 2. Stanley is in 3, Tonga in 2, and Matt in 6. Now at this point, a lot depends on the placement of Ned. Both Chair 1, the head, and Chair 4, the foot, are available to him. If Ned is in Chair 1, the head (that is, between Tonga on his left and Matt on his right), that leaves two chairs, 4 and 5, available to Qi and Vladimir. But Qi can't take Chair 4 while Stanley is in Chair 3. Rule 4 forbids it. So you would have to have Vladimir in 4 and Qi in 5. Under those circumstances, you would have choice (C), Qi and Stanley opposite each other in Chairs 5 and 3, respectively, and also choice (B), Ned and Vladimir opposite each other at the ends of the table.

But suppose Ned's in Chair 4 at the foot. With Matt in 6, Ned in 4, Stanley in 3, and Tonga in 2, the possibilities are slightly more numerous. Chairs 1 and 5 remain for Qi and Vladimir, with no restrictions as to who is in which. Under those circumstances, you could certainly have Ned in 4 opposite Qi in 1, leaving Vladimir in 5 opposite Stanley in 3. Thus, (A) and (E) must be rejected. Either is a possibility. But under no circumstances will you ever see Qi and Vladimir opposite each other (as it turns out, in none of these scenarios did you see that), and that makes choice (D) correct.

Questions 6–11

After previewing the setup and rules, you see that this game asks you to distribute nine cheeses into three groups of three cheeses each—a Grouping game of distribution. There are four domestic cheeses—F, G, H, and J—and five imported cheeses—p, q, r, s, and t (it can help to keep the entities separate if you use CAPS for one group and lower case letters for the other). The three groups are A, B, and C. The two key issues will be these:

1) What cheese is in what group?
2) What cheeses can, must, or cannot be selected with what other cheeses?

You've got three groups of three each. Set this up as you might in real life. Just list the three groups with three dashes under each. Be sure you also list the two types of cheeses:

DOMESTIC   *imported*
  F G H J   p q r s t

  <u>A</u>   <u>B</u>   <u>C</u>

— — —   — — —   — — —

1) It's best to build a rule directly into the master sketch whenever you can. One of the cheeses in each group must be domestic. Make a note of this in the sketch; placing a "D" under one of the dashes in each group should suffice.

2) You don't know which group F is in, but F must always be accompanied by two imports—no domestics allowed in a group with F.

3) q, an imported cheese, goes in Group C. Build this right into the sketch.

4) s goes in Group A. That's another imported cheese definitely set.

5) Whew. Three rules in one. Be careful when you unpack this rule. Take it one step at a time. First of all, F can't be in the same group as q. Secondly, J can't go in the same group as q, and finally, r can't go with q either. Your mind is probably jumping ahead and combining this rule with Rule 3, and that's a good thing. It means that you're getting used to looking for deductions.

Time to take a closer look at Rule 5 (and Rule 3). Don't just write "No F q." Ask yourself "What does that mean?"—q is in Group C, so F must be in either A or B.

J, too, can't go with q. Again, this means that J must go in either Group A or Group B. Finally, r can't go with q, so r must also go in A or B.

Keep going. There's more to be deduced here. F and J and r each must go in either Group A or Group B. Can these entities go in the same group? Rule 2 told you that F must go in a group with two imports. r is an import, so F and r could go in the same group, but J is a domestic. No way could F and J go in the same group. So F must go in Group A or B, and J must go in the other.

As with all games, take a moment to work through the numbers aspect of the game. Here that means looking at Rule 1. Each group must have at least one domestic cheese. Rule 5 said that F and J (two domestics) can't go with q in Group C, but Group C must have at least one domestic. What domestic cheeses are left? G and H are the only other domestics. One of this pair must ALWAYS go in Group C. You can bet that one or two answer choices will try to put them both elsewhere. Now you're thinking like the test makers.

Finally, it's a good idea to identify the "floaters" in each game. These are those entities that don't appear in any rules or deductions. They will serve to fill in the remaining slots after you've placed all the other entities. Here, the "floaters" are p and t, two imported cheeses.

Here's what you have going into the questions:

DOMESTIC			*imported*		
F G H J			p q r s t		
<u>A</u>		<u>B</u>			<u>C</u>
— <u>s</u> —		— — —			G/H q
D		D			D
F + 2 imp.		F + 2 imp.			No F
J		J			No J
r		r			No r
F ≠ J		F ≠ J			

6. E

You know that each group must have at least one domestic cheese. Because p and t (both imports) are in Group B, the remaining cheese must be domestic. We deduced in Rule 5 that r, an import, must be in Group A or B. The last cheese in B must be domestic, so r must go in Group A, choice (E).

(A) No, F could go in group B with p and t.

(B) No, G could be in Group C.

(C) No, H could be in Group C.

(D) No, J could go in Group B with p and t.

When you're given new information, get it down in the test booklet. Then ask yourself, "What entities does this new information affect?" Go back to your master sketch and the rules.

7. B

A "must be true" question with no new information often signals that the test makers are asking for a key deduction. However, you can tell that that's probably not the case here because of the complex answer choices. Each choice is like a question in itself. You can count on spending a good deal of time here. This question is a candidate for skipping the first time around if you need to preserve time because there's not much to do except try out each choice.

(A) Could F and r be together and not be in the group with s (that's Group A)? Sure they could. Here are the complete groupings that show choice (A) needn't be true: A—J s t, B—F p r, C—G H q.

(B) Could G and H be together and not be in the group with q? No way. We saw up front that J and F can't be with q (Rule 5), and because each group needs at least one domestic, either G or H must be with q. (B) must be true and is the answer. On Test Day, you'd stop right here and go on to the next question. For the record, here are groupings that show the remaining choices needn't be true (you may have come up with other acceptable groupings to dispose of these choices):

(C) and (D) A—J H s , B—F p r, C—G q t

(E) A—F s r, B—J G r, C—H p q

To prove that a choice in a "must be true" question is wrong, find an exception to the choice, an acceptable situation that shows that the choice could be false.

8. B

This takes a slightly different form than most Acceptability questions, but it's still an Acceptability question. You're asked to find the one unacceptable Group B among the choices. What do we know about Group B? We deduced that either F or J must always go in Group B (see above for a reminder of how we deduced that). Every acceptable Group B must therefore contain either F or J. Scan the choices. Choice (B) doesn't include F or J, and it tries to place both G and H in Group B—wrong on both counts. Remember, one of G or H must always go in Group C.

Always keep in mind exactly what the question is asking. If you had mistakenly thought that this question was asking for the one acceptable choice instead of the one unacceptable one, you would have been very confused.

9. E

G is in Group A. What rules or deductions will you use to deal with G? Questions 2 and 3 both were answered by realizing that either G or H must go in Group C. Here G is in A, so H must go in Group C. What else do you know about G? G is a domestic cheese, so F, which must be grouped with two imports, can't be in A. The only other choice for F is Group B. F and J can't be in the same group, so J must go in Group A. So far, we have G, J, and s in Group A; F and r in Group B; and H and q in Group C. Who's left? p and t will fill in the slots: one in Group B and the other in Group C. Don't hesitate to redraw your master sketch whenever needed. Here's what this question's sketch would look like:

A	B	C
G̲ s̲ J̲	F̲ r̲ p̲/t̲	H̲ q̲ p̲/t̲

Scan the choices; t could indeed be in Group C. (E) could be true and is the answer.

(A) No, H is in Group C.

(B) No, J is in Group A.

(C) No, p is in Group B or C.

(D) No, r is in Group B.

Work with any new information that you're given. Keep asking yourself, "In what rules and deductions have I seen this entity before?" and "What do I know about this entity?"

10. B

H is a domestic cheese, so F can't join H and p in Group B (Rule 2). Because F can't, J must be the one to fill out Group B. F's only other choice is Group A. r must go in Group A because B is now full. We're looking for Group A, and now we have it: F, r, and s—choice (B).

Only do the work required to answer the question. You could have taken the deductions further and filled out Group C, but there's no need to. The question is asking about Group A, so that's the only group you're interested in.

11. C

What does it mean for J to be in Group B? It means that F must be in Group A—by now, splitting these two entities up between Groups A and B should be instinctual. Other than that, there's not much else to deduce: r, as usual, can go in either A or B, and our perpetual floaters p and t can pretty much go anywhere. What leads to the answer here is the situation of G and H. These two domestic cheeses can both join q in C, or they can split up between B and C. The one thing neither of them can do is end up in Group A because that's where F is in this question, and F's companion cheeses are always both imports. (C) is therefore impossible—for H to be displayed with s (in Group A) it would have to be in the same group as F, which is a no-no.

For (A) and (D), there's no problem here—r can go in Group A with F and s while the remaining entities fill out Groups B and C in any one of a number of different ways. For (B), G and r can join J in Group B as long as H joins q in Group C. Then p and t can fill in the remaining slots in Groups A and C.

For (E), the situation just described in (B) above works; just put t in Group A along with F and s and p in Group C along with H and q.

SET TWO

Questions 1–5

In this Sequencing game, you're asked to put seven patients in order according to their scheduled appointments. The natural way to picture this is to create eight empty spaces with the time of the appointment above each one, starting with 9 A.M. Try to find a way to build each rule into the sketch as you read over each one. Create your own visual diagrams and then compare them to the ones here. You might like our visual aids better, or you might prefer your own symbols. Either way, the goal is to create a visual language that you can use to help yourself answer all LSAT Logic Games questions.

Xavier can only have the appointment at 9 A.M. or 4 P.M. Note this limitation on your graph. Selena must come before Thurman, but the rule does not say exactly when. Make a note showing the link between S and T. Thurman and Vivian must be scheduled for back-to-back appointments, with Thurman's being the first. You can combine this with the previous clue to give you a link among S, T, and V. With three letters integrated into this clue, you can expect it will be important.

If Roland is at 12 P.M., then Thurman must be scheduled for 3 P.M. From a previous clue, you know that Vivian must be scheduled at 4 P.M. This gives you a connection among R, T, and V but only if R = 12.

There is one last point to make: Q and W have no limitations placed on them whatsoever. This information may help when determining what "must be true." Since the two elements are identical, what must be true of one will also be true of the other.

$$Q, R, S, T, V, W, X$$

$$\boxed{S \ldots T}$$
$$+$$
$$\boxed{TV}$$
$$=$$
$$\boxed{S \ldots TV}$$

if R = 12, T = 3

Ⓠⓦ

/x						x/
9	10	11	12	1	2	3	4

(with an ☒ placed under the 1)

No one can be scheduled for 1 P.M., the hour designated for lunch. Place a blocked out X there to designate this.

Before you start with the questions, be sure you have considered all the implications of each rule. Xavier can only be at the two ends of the schedule. Because Selena is before Thurman and Vivian is directly after Thurman, then Selena must go before both Thurman and Vivian. This means that Selena *cannot* have either the 3 P.M. or 4 P.M. appointment.

Now that you've taken the time to consider all the important implications of each rule, you should be all set to jump into the questions and rack up some points.

1. C

This is an Acceptability question, so grab each rule and see which choices violate that rule. The correct answer is the one that violates no rules. The first rule, Xavier at either 9 A.M. or 4 P.M., eliminates (B). The second rule, Selena is scheduled before Thurman, eliminates (A) and (D). Rule 3, Thurman is immediately before Vivian, doesn't help eliminate any answer choices. However, the fourth rule, placing Roland at 12 P.M. and Thurman at 3 P.M., eliminates answer (E). Only (C) is left.

2. D

This question asks you to identify the one patient who cannot have the designated appointment time given in the answer choices. A good place to begin would be to see which rules, if any, govern the patients in the answer choices. Rule 4 is only relevant if Roland is scheduled for 12 P.M., and answer (A) schedules him at 4 P.M. There are no limitations governing the placement of Quincy and Wilma; therefore, they could be scheduled for 2 P.M. and 10 A.M., respectively. Rule 2 states that Selena must be scheduled some time before Thurman, and answer (E) clearly does this by giving Selena the first appointment at 9 A.M. Rule 3 states that Vivian must be scheduled immediately after Thurman. Therefore if Vivian is scheduled for 10 A.M., Thurman must have the first appointment at 9 A.M. However, Rule 2 clearly places Selena before Thurman, and if Thurman is scheduled for 9 A.M., there would be no place to schedule Selena and Rule 2 would be violated. Therefore, (D) must be false.

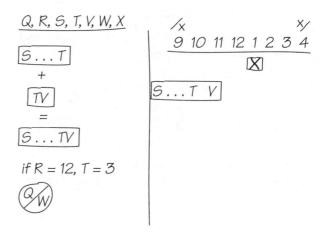

3. A

If Roland is scheduled for 12 P.M., then Thurman is at 3 P.M. and Vivian is at 4 P.M. With Vivian in the 4 P.M. slot, Xavier must be scheduled for 9 A.M. Answer (A) is just waiting for you to pick up an easy point.

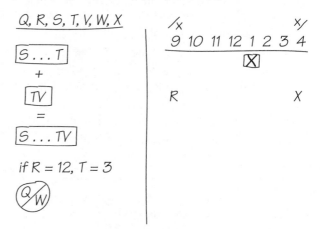

4. E

On your scratchwork, you should have factored in Rule 5, which gives you the doctor's lunchtime. The question asks who can't be scheduled immediately after the doctor's lunch. According to Rule 3, Thurman is scheduled exactly one hour before Vivian, so if Vivian is scheduled for 2 P.M., then Thurman must be scheduled for 1 P.M., which coincides with the doctor's lunch. Therefore Vivian *cannot* have a 2 P.M. appointment.

Q, R, S, T, V, W, X

$$\boxed{S \ldots T}$$
$+$
$$\boxed{TV}$$
$=$
$$\boxed{S \ldots TV}$$

if R = 12, T = 3

Ⓠ/W

```
/x                    x/
9 10 11 12 1 2 3 4
           ☒

           S...T V
              ☒
```

(A) is correct. Vivian would be restricted only to the
12 P.M. and 4 P.M. appointments. Therefore, (B) and (C)
are incorrect. Thurman would be restricted to the
11 A.M. and 3 P.M. appointments, and therefore (D) and
(E) are incorrect.

Questions 6–10

This game asks you to distribute six vacationers among
three cities: call it a Grouping game of Distribution. The
six vacationers are Cedric, Dolores, Fredrick, Gloria,
Hedwig, and Jorge (who can be referred to as C, D, F,
G, H, J) and the vacation cities are Lisbon, Madrid,
and Novosibirsk (l, m, n). The easiest way to set up the
game is to create three columns, one for Lisbon, one for
Madrid, and one for Novosibirsk (l, m, and n), and leave
room below each to designate which vacationers go to
which city.

5. A

Some questions, such as this one, will add an extra rule
or condition that they want you to incorporate into the
existing rules given in the setup to solve for the answer.
Follow the same steps you took when you were reading
the setup; visualize how the new rule affects the game
and think of any deductions or implications the new rule
will have. For this question, Roland must now be placed
immediately before Thurman, and Thurman is still placed
immediately before Vivian. Therefore, Roland, Thurman,
and Vivian now form a three-hour chunk of appointments
that cannot be separated. Because Selena still has to
come before Thurman, the only two places this group
of appointments can fit are 10 A.M.–12 P.M. (Roland,
Thurman, and Vivian, respectively) or 2 P.M.–4 P.M. If
the group is placed in the 10 A.M.–12 P.M. appointments,
then Selena must have the 9 A.M., and Xavier has the
4 P.M. This leaves Quincy and Wilma to have the 2 P.M.
and 3 P.M. appointments, and either of them can have the
2 P.M.

C, D, F, G, H, J

2·4·0 (one city empty)

No H·J

$$\boxed{DG}$$

if $J_n = \boxed{DJ}$

. . . .

F*

if $J_n = \boxed{DGJ}_n$ and Ⓗ$_n$

```
/c      c/
l   m      n
```

Your diagram might look similar to the one pictured
above. The first rule states that each vacationer is
accompanied by either one or three of the other
vacationers. This means that there can only be two
groups of vacationers to divide among three cities,
so one city will be left empty. The second rule is that
Hedwig and Jorge will each be in one of the separate
groups. Denote this in some way on your graph. The
third rule states that Dolores and Gloria must visit the
same city together. The fourth rule states that Cedric
must be in Lisbon or Madrid. Place this on your graph

Q, R, S, T, V, W, X

$$\boxed{S \ldots T}$$
$+$
$$\boxed{TV}$$
$=$
$$\boxed{S \ldots TV}$$

if R = 12, T = 3

Ⓠ/W

```
/x                       x/
9 10 11 12 1 2 3 4
              ☒

S  R  T  V ☒ W/Q  Q/W  X

X     S/W/Q   ☒  R  T  V
```

in some form. The fifth rule tells you that if Jorge is in Novosibirsk, then Dolores is in Novosibirsk with him.

Remember to take a closer look at all the rules to see if any deductions can be made or implications drawn from each one. You can deduce from the first rule that you should have one group of two vacationers in any given city and one group of four vacationers in another city. You also know from this rule that one column in your chart, which represents one of the cities, must be left blank. Also, consider the first three rules together. Dolores and Gloria must be in the same city together. If they consist of the group of two vacationers, then the remaining four vacationers must all be together, including Hedwig and Jorge, which violates Rule 2. Therefore, Dolores and Gloria must be part of the group of four. Fredrick has no limitations on him.

Finally, if Jorge visits Novosibirsk, then Dolores visits Novosibirsk; therefore, Dolores *and* Gloria both visit because they are always together. Because D and G are in the group of four, the fourth person must be Fredrick because Cedric is in either Lisbon or Madrid and Hedwig cannot be in the same city as Jorge. Now, let's see how all this applies to the questions.

6. B

This is the familiar Acceptability question. Apply each rule to the answer choices, eliminating all answers that violate a rule. The first rule states that the vacationers are divided into a group of two and a group of four, eliminating (C). The second rule states that Hedwig and Jorge must be in separate cities, so get rid of (D). The third rule states that Dolores and Gloria must be in the same city, eliminating (E). The fourth rule states that Cedric cannot be in Novosibirsk, so choice (A) is out. The remaining answer choice, (B), is the correct response.

7. C

Questions that ask for an answer choice that "must be false" mean that you can eliminate any answer choice that *could* be true. Based on the answer from question 6, eliminate (B) and (D), since they show that Cedric and Hedwig could be together and that Jorge could be in Lisbon. Answer (A) could also be eliminated, because

it would be possible for Fredrick to visit the same city as Hedwig with the remaining four vacationers in the second group. The trickiness of this question is in the fact that there are no explicit limitations regarding Cedric and Fredrick. But if you were to place them in the same city, they would either be their own group of two or half of a group of four. If they were their own group of two, then the remaining four vacationers must make up the second group and must contain both Hedwig and Jorge, a clear violation of the second rule. If they were half of a group of four, then the other two vacationers would be either Dolores and Gloria (since they must be together) or Hedwig and Jorge. Both choices leave Hedwig and Jorge together in the same group, a clear violation of the second rule. Therefore, (C) must be false—Cedric cannot be in the same city as Fredrick.

8. E

If Hedwig visits Novosibirsk, then Jorge cannot visit Novosibirsk and must be with Cedric in either Lisbon or Madrid. Because there can only be groups of two or four, the remaining three vacationers (Dolores, Fredrick, and Gloria) could all join Hedwig in Novosibirsk, or Dolores and Gloria (they must be together) could join Cedric and Jorge in Lisbon or Madrid and Fredrick could join Hedwig in Novosibirsk. Either way, Fredrick is in Novosibirsk, and (E) is correct.

9. D

If Gloria visits Madrid, then Dolores must also be in Madrid. But if Jorge is in Novosibirsk, then Dolores and Gloria have to be there with him. So Jorge cannot visit Novosibirsk; (D) is correct.

10. B

Since the question is asking for what "could be false," you can eliminate any answer choice that *must* be true. Remember the deduction you made about Dolores and Gloria? They had to be in the group of four; therefore, (A) and (D) must be true and can be eliminated. Remember question 7? You determined that Cedric cannot be in the same city as Fredrick, and since Cedric must be in either Lisbon or Madrid, if Fredrick is in one, then Cedric must be in the other. Eliminate (E) because it must be true. If Jorge visits Novosibirsk, then Dolores and Gloria must also visit Novosibirsk, which means one of the remaining three vacationers (Cedric, Fredrick, or Hedwig) must also visit Novosibirsk to complete the group of four. Cedric must be in Lisbon or Madrid, and Hedwig cannot be in the same city as Jorge; therefore, Fredrick must be in Novosibirsk, and (C) must be true. If Hedwig is in Novosibirsk, Gloria and Dolores could be in any of the three cities. (B) is the only answer choice that could be false.

SET THREE

Questions 1–5

Seven instructors—J, K, L, M, N, P, and Q—each teach during exactly one of three semesters. In other words, you have to distribute the seven instructors among the three semesters. So this is another grouping game of distribution, and the key issues will be these:

- Which instructors can, must, or cannot teach during which semesters?

- Which instructors can, must, or cannot teach during the same semester as which other instructors?

- How many instructors teach during each semester?

A list of the entities and three columns (one for each of the semesters) will allow you to keep track of the action here.

J   K   L   M   N   P   Q

Fall	Spring	Winter

1) Here's a concrete rule: You can place K in the winter column permanently.

2) Rule 2 is a familiar enough Grouping rule. L and M are always together. "Always LM," captures this.

3) Rule 3 can be built in directly, with arrows pointing to the fall and spring semesters.

4) The winter semester gets twice as many as the fall semester. Okay, what does that mean in the context

of this game? With seven instructors, there really aren't that many ways to split them up so that exactly twice as many wind up in the winter semester. So how many combinations are there? If one instructor taught in the fall, then you'd need two in the winter, and the remaining four would teach during the spring semester. Or you could have two in the fall, four in the winter, and one in the spring. That's it. It's either 1/4/2 or 2/1/4. You can't have three or more in the fall, since that would force you to have six or more in the winter, and that's no good because there are only seven instructors.

5) and 6) are familiar enough grouping rules. You cannot have an NQ, and we cannot have a JP.

The Big Deduction here was the 1/4/2 or 2/1/4 breakdown of the instructors. This essentially comes straight out of Rule 4, but if you noticed it at this point, it's okay, too. From here, you could have explored different scenarios, seeing if they set off any chains of inferences, but nothing else qualifies as a major deduction. On to the questions!

THE FINAL VISUALIZATION

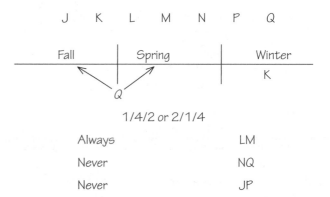

THE QUESTIONS

1. D

This is a harder Acceptability question than most since we're only given part of the lineup. You may have been forced to work out scenarios for each choice. Only (B) and (E) contain a straightforward violation of a rule. (According to Rule 6, we can't have J and P together, and according to Rule 1, K teaches during the winter). The rest of the choices require some work.

(A) With Q and M in the fall, you need L there as well (Rule 2). That's three in the fall, which is no good, because it would force you to place six in the winter.

(C) If L is in the fall, then so is M. Because the fall can hold no more, Q must go in the spring (Rule 3). That leaves K, J, P, and N for the winter. But we can't have J and P together, so (C) doesn't work. So (D) is correct by the process of elimination.

(D) For the record: Placing J, M, and N as the stem dictates means you must also place L in the winter. Because the winter now has three instructors, it will need a fourth to satisfy the 2/1/4 distribution. We also need to split up J and P. So you can place Q in the fall and P in the winter, and you have an acceptable arrangement.

Fall	Spring	Winter
J	N	K
Q		M
		L
		P

Acceptability questions are usually quick points, but they can be harder when you only see part of the arrangement. Often, the wrong choices in these questions don't contain obvious violations of the rules. Rather, they violate the rules by virtue of their implications for the other entities.

2. A

This one was quick if you worked out the scenario in (C) from the previous question. In that choice, you saw what happens when you put L in the fall: You need to put M there as well, and you're forced to place J and P together in the winter. So you can never put L (or M, for that matter) in the fall, and choice (A) is correct.

If you didn't see this, you still could have attacked this question strategically by postponing working on it until after you've built some acceptable scenarios from the other questions. (B) must be true. (E) could be true, and both (C) and (D) are true based on the correct answer to the Acceptability questions.

Postpone working on questions when your work on the other questions will eliminate some choices.

Don't forget about the correct answer to the Acceptability question. It often eliminates a few wrong choices elsewhere.

3. C

If only one instructor teaches in the spring, then we have a 2/1/4 setup. You've seen we can't place L and M in the fall because that would force J and P together in the winter. So L and M teach in the winter, and (C) is correct.

(A), (D), and (E) are all possible only. (B) is impossible. L teaches in the winter.

Sometimes a game's questions are similar to each other. So once you build some experience, you should be able to make inferences more quickly as the game goes on.

4. D

Here's another question that allows you to benefit from previous work. In the last question, we had K, L, and M together in the winter. They could be joined by either J or P without any violations. Once you know that we can have KLMJ or KLMP together, you can eliminate all four wrong choices because they all contain a subset of one of those groups. You also might have spotted correct choice (D) directly: K must be in the winter, and Q can never be in the winter. So (D) is correct. Use your previous work whenever possible. It saves time.

5. D

Who doesn't teach in the winter semester? Since the winter semester has either two or four instructors, either three or five instructors don't teach during the winter semester. So (B) and (E) are wrong. Eliminating the other wrong choices was a little harder.

(A) splits up L and M, in violation of Rule 2. (C) places J and P in the winter and thus violates Rule 6. So (D) is correct. For the record, we could place Q and P in the fall; N in the spring; and K, L, M, and J in the winter.

Numbers deductions are key in Grouping games. Always look for minimums and maximums, then use that information to cut down on your work later on.

Note that the challenge with this game was timing. Lots of people could find the right answers given unlimited time, but the real challenge is to find the right answers as quickly as possible. Take a second look at your work on these questions and ask yourself how you could have used good test-taking strategies to save time. Then practice these strategies until you apply them automatically.

Questions 6–10

This game involves placing eight albums of three different genres in playing order. Since you are both distributing the albums among the genres and ordering them from first to last, this would be a Hybrid game of Sequencing and Grouping. First, organize the setup. The two country albums are G and H; the three dance albums are J, K, and L; and the three folk albums are M, N, and P. The next part of the setup informs you that all genre albums are to be played consecutively. This means that albums G and H will be played consecutively; albums J, K, and L will be played consecutively; and albums M, N, and P will be played consecutively. Your sketch work should be concerned with organizing the order in which the genres will be played and the order of the albums within each genre. Now take a look at the rules to see what restrictions you will have on the "action" of the game.

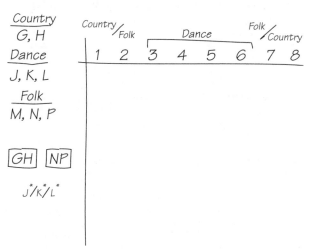

Take a look at the first and last rule. If each album is to be played only once and no two albums can be played at the same time, then you will have exactly eight spaces to place the eight different albums. The next rule—that dance albums are to be played after the country or folk albums but not after both—tells you that the dance albums must be played in the middle. Organize your sketch accordingly.

For the third rule, mark on your sketch under the folk genre that album N is played before album P. This connects N and P in a loose manner. Under the country genre, mark that album G is played before album H. That's another similar connection, this time of GH. Since there are only two albums in the country genre, note that the sequence must always be G, then H. Although it's not listed, you can see that at this moment, items J, K, and L have no limitations concerning them. This fact may come in handy. Now take a look at the questions.

6. D

Because the question asks for the one answer that must be false, eliminate any choice that could be true. If the country genre was played first, then album G could be played first, eliminating (A). If the genre sequence were folk-dance-country, and because there are three albums for both folk and dance, then the seventh album would be the first country album and would be album G. Eliminate (B). Following the same setup as (A), if album G is first, then album H must be second. Eliminate (C). However, if album H is played seventh, the country genre must be played last, which means album G would be played eighth and Rule 3 would be violated. Therefore, (D) must be false. To state it another way, if H is seventh, then to preserve the GH rule, G must be sixth, leaving a big hole in the eighth spot. That won't do. (E) could be true by following the setup of (B), placing the folk genre first.

Country
G, H

Dance
J, K, L

Folk
M, N, P

[GH] [NP]
J'/K'/L'

	Country/Folk		Dance			Folk/Country	
1	2	3	4	5	6	7	8
					G	H	_

empty! ↘

Country
G, H

Dance
J, K, L

Folk
M, N, P

[GH] [NP]
J'/K'/L'

	Country/Folk		Dance			Folk/Country	
1	2	3	4	5	6	7	8
[N	P]	M	J/K /L			G	H

7. D

Because you're looking for the answer choice that could be true, all four wrong choices must be false. It is usually easier to eliminate what must be false than to play out all of the possibilities. Choice (A) places G, a country album, second. Country albums can be first and second, but there's another rule involving G—it has to come before H (another country album). That means that if the country albums are played first and second, G would have to be first—(A) cannot be true and can be eliminated. The same analysis rules out (B)—if the country albums are seventh and eighth, then G must be seventh to leave room for H to follow. (C) is impossible because K is a dance album and the dance albums come in the middle, after either country or folk. (D) works: MNP could be in slots 1, 2, and 3, respectively. If this isn't immediately apparent, though, just hold on to this choice and move on to (E), which can be authoritatively ruled out because N must precede P. If the folk albums are in slots 1, 2, and 3, then N can be no later than second without violating the third rule. That leaves only (D).

8. A

The question asks which answer choice *cannot* be a list of albums that are played second, third, and fourth. This means you can eliminate all answer choices that could be the albums played second, third, and fourth. If the country genre is played first, then you know that album H must be the second album. Because there are no limitations on the order of the dance albums, both (D) and (E) are possible lists. The remaining three answer choices play the folk genre first, which means that album N must be played before album P. (A) violates this rule. If album N is played second and album M played third, then album P must be played first, which violates Rule 3.

Country
G, H

Dance
J, K, L

Folk
M, N, P

[GH] [NP]
J'/K'/L'

	Country/Folk		Dance			Folk/Country	
1	2	3	4	5	6	7	8
[P	N]	M	J				

wrong

9. C

This question gives you an extra conditional statement to work into the already established rules. If album P is played immediately before album M and album N must be played before album P (Rule 2), then the folk genre must be played in the order of N, P, and M. If the folk genre is played first, then album N would be played first, album P would be played second, and album M would be played third. If the folk genre was played last, then album N would be played sixth, album P would be played seventh, and album M would be played eighth. These are the only possible positions for the albums to be played in. (C) is the only choice that could be true.

Country
G, H

Dance

J, K, L

Folk

M, N, P

GH   NP

J˙/K˙/L˙

Country/Folk		Dance			Folk/Country		
1	2	3	4	5	6	7	8
G	H	J/L	L/J	K	N	P	M

Country
G, H

Dance

J, K, L

Folk

M, N, P

GH   NP

J˙/K˙/L˙

NPM

Country/Folk		Dance			Folk/Country		
1	2	3	4	5	6	7	8
N	P	M	J/ /K	L/	G	H	
G	H	J/K/L/			N	P	M

or

10. D

Another condition has been added in this question (albums K and N are to be played consecutively.) It is misleading that the question tells you they do not have to be played in that particular order, because they do. Since album N must be played before album P, as stipulated in Rule 3, the folk genre could not be played first, ending with album N and starting the dance genre with album K. Therefore, the country genre must be played first. The dance genre, as stipulated in Rule 2, must be played second and end with album K, and the folk genre is then played last, starting with album N. (D) must be false since the country genre, which album H belongs to, is played before the folk genre, which album M belongs to.

CHAPTER 5: READING COMPREHENSION

- Anatomy of a Reading Passage
- Kaplan's 5-Step Method for Reading Comprehension
- A Word about Comparative Reading
- Section Management
- Helpful Hints to Improve Your Performance

Does this sound familiar? You see a passage and you read it. Then you move to the first question and go back to reread the passage, looking for information to answer the question. Next you review each answer, double-checking each one against the text. While this process could work if the test was untimed, it is inefficient for the LSAT. The biggest struggle in the Reading Comp section is to give up old ways of reading and adapt another methodology designed to help you be more efficient and accurate on test day. However, your highest score depends on it.

ANATOMY OF A READING PASSAGE

The Reading Comprehension section is made up of three passages of 450 to 550 words each plus a set of paired passages with a total of 450 to 550 words together. Five to eight questions follow each of the three passages and the passage set.

The subjects for LSAT Reading Comp passages are taken from four general areas: social sciences, natural sciences, the humanities, and law. Typically, each subject is represented in the section, and all the information you need to answer questions is in the passage itself. In other words, prior content knowledge is not necessary. The passages can be long, dense, and difficult—not unlike some of the material you'll face in law school and your career. So right now is a good time to start shoring up your reading skills.

KAPLAN'S 5-STEP METHOD FOR READING COMPREHENSION

STEP 1: READ THE PASSAGE STRATEGICALLY

Reading critically is a key LSAT skill and one that will serve you well in law school and beyond. To answer LSAT questions accurately and within the 35-minute time limit, you need a way to read the passage once and take in the information you need as you go. This skill is a different way of reading than most of us used in college. The good news is that Kaplan knows the questions that will be asked and the type of information you need to pull out as you read to answer those questions.

Let's say it another way: You are not reading the passage to become an expert on the topic, and you will not be asked to write a research report or opinion piece. Instead, you will be asked specified question types to score points.

To be prepared, you must read the passage looking for specific information.

Identify Topic, Scope, Purpose, and Main Idea

The **topic** is the broad subject matter of the passage (e.g., world hunger). It is objective in nature and will almost always appear within the first few sentences of the first paragraph.

Like the topic, the **scope** is objective and identifies the piece of the topic the author will address in the passage (e.g., new technology to solve world hunger). Again, keep your eye out for it in the first paragraph.

The **purpose** refers to why the author is writing the passage (e.g., to describe a new technology and its promising uses). The purpose might be to argue, explain, illustrate, rebut, advocate, describe, etc.

The **main idea** is where the purpose takes the author; that is, the point the author is arguing, explaining, etc. about the topic (e.g., biochemical engineering helps address world hunger in a variety of ways). The purpose and main idea can be presented anywhere in the passage, even at the very end. Pay specific attention to them because everything else in the passage will support them.

Create a Passage Road Map

The "road map" is a summary you write next to each paragraph that tells you what kind of information is in the paragraph. Building on the example from above, the first paragraph may be a description of the problem of world hunger. Paragraph two may include examples of past, unsuccessful efforts to address world hunger. Paragraph three may introduce biochemical engineering and the ways it can be used to address world hunger.

In school, you often read to memorize information for an exam. Content memorization will not get you points on the LSAT. In fact, the passage remains right in front of you. So you don't need to memorize anything. Instead, you need to know where to find information to answer questions and, ultimately, score points.

A concise road map helps you in the following ways: (1) to anticipate where an author is going with an argument or line of reasoning, (2) to locate and mark the critical portions of the text, (3) to anticipate from where in the passage the test makers will draw their questions, and (4) to research correct answers quickly and confidently.

Circle Keywords

Reading comp passages are full of structural signals: keywords or phrases that help the author string ideas together logically. They allow you to infer a great deal about content, even if that content is obscure or difficult. The six types of keywords are as follows:

1. **Logic:** Words or phrases that indicate evidence (*because, since, for*) and conclusion (*therefore, consequently, it follows that, thus*)

2. **Contrast:** Words or phrases that signal a difference of opinion or shift in ideas (*but, however, although, by contrast, despite*)

3. **Continuation:** Words or phrases that show agreement or additional support for a thought (*further, moreover, likewise, additionally, also*)

4. **Illustration:** Words or phrases that mark examples and illuminate a thought (*for example, in the case of*)

5. **Emphasis/Opinion:** Words or phrases that indicate a point of view and the information's level of importance (*most of all, especially, very, argued that, unfortunately, critically*)

6. **Sequence/Chronology:** Words or phrases that outline steps or indicate timing (*in the 19th century... but today, first... second... finally, before*)

All authors use keywords. But authors of reading comp passages use them with special frequency, largely as a way of rewarding strategic readers. So don't just find and circle the keywords. Think about what they signal, what that means in the structure of the passage, and what you can anticipate ahead.

In summary, reading strategically means reading actively. You are not just reading to get the passage read. You are reading to pull out information you will need to answer questions. Specifically, you are looking for the topic, scope, purpose, main idea, road map, and keywords. That means asking yourself questions as you read the passage. Don't get to the end and then ask yourself where to find those pieces. And here's a rule of thumb for all you note takers: The more you underline in the passage and the more you write off to the side of the passage, the more you are focused on the details and missing the structure and gist.

STEP 2: READ THE QUESTION

The question provides two pieces of information. First, it includes words and phrases to help you identify the question type. The Reading Comp section features four kinds of questions. Second, the question typically includes a clue directing you to a specific part of the passage to find the answer.

Let's start with the four reading comp question types and how to identify them.

Global Questions

Global questions ask about the passage as a whole—the main idea, purpose, and organization. Typically, each passage will have a global question at the beginning of the question set. If there is a second global question, it is usually found toward the end of the question set.

Common question stems include these:

- Which one of the following best states the main idea of the passage?
- The main purpose of the passage is to...
- Which one of the following best describes the contents of the passage?

Detail Questions

Detail questions ask for specific information stated in the passage and can be answered directly from the text. Most students find these to be the easiest reading comp questions because they're the most concrete.

Sample question stems include the following:

- According to the passage, the council was divided on the issue of...
- According to the author, the flu virus cannot occur in the absence of which one of the following?
- The passage states...
- The statement declares that...

Inference Questions

Inference questions are the most common question type in Reading Comp, with about 10 or more appearing in the section. They ask you to read between the lines of the passage, not outside them. Just as in Logical Reasoning, an **inference** is a statement that must be true based on the passage. In other words, it will follow from the passage but will not be stated directly. Instead, the answer will be hinted at or implied. The harder you have to work to justify an answer based on the text, the less likely it is the correct choice.

Unlike those in Logical Reasoning, Reading Comp inferences can often be predicted if the question clues are descriptive enough. Occasionally, the stem won't contain specific information, in which case you simply have to work your way through the choices until you find the one that is supported by the text. When evaluating the answer choices, keep the relevant ideas firmly in mind.

Extracting valid inferences from Reading Comp passages often requires recognizing that information can be expressed in different ways. You will need to paraphrase the relevant text or make a deduction.

Sample question stems include the following:

- It can be inferred from the passage that...
- The passage suggests that...
- The author implies that...
- The critics would most probably agree with which one of the following statements?

Logic Questions

You will see approximately six logic questions in the Reading Comp section. They come in two distinct forms: function questions and reasoning questions.

- **Reasoning:** These questions are similar to Logical Reasoning questions; treat them exactly as you would the same type of question in the Logical Reasoning section. The reasoning question types most often seen in Reading Comp are assumption, strengthen, weaken, principle, and parallel reasoning.
- **Function:** Logic function questions include a piece of the text in the form of a phrase, example, quote, and so on. and ask you what role or function that piece of information serves in the passage.

Common question stems include these:

- The Obama example is included primarily to...
- The experiment described in paragraph 2 serves to...
- The author discusses conflict for the purpose of...

In addition to clueing you in to the question type, the wording of the question will send you back to a particular part of the passage, narrowing your research. Keep your eye out for these five types of clues.

1. **Proper names and nouns:** By *names* and *nouns*, we mean individuals; groups (e.g., critics, scientists, artists); and other concepts such as ideas, beliefs, and theories. They are all included in a passage to demonstrate an attitude or a point of view and are often the subject of one or more questions. For example,

- The environmentalists are mentioned in the passage in order to...
- The author would most likely agree with which one of the following statements?

   Pay particular attention to proper nouns and names as you read a passage. When they appear in a question, your circle or margin note will guide you back to the right place in the passage.

2. **Line references:** We love line references because they make it so easy to go back to the text. Don't make the mistake, though, of going back to the exact line and just re-reading it. Read the line in context by looking at the surrounding sentences, circled keywords, and your road map note. By the way, line references don't always indicate a detail question, as many mistakenly believe. They are most often found in inference and logic function questions.

3. **Direct quotes:** Think about who said the phrase when you see a direct quote in a question. Was it the author, or was it someone else? Ask yourself why that person said it; that is, for what purpose the person said it.

4. **Paragraph references:** When a question mentions a particular paragraph, consider the gist of the whole paragraph in the context of the passage.

5. **Content clues:** Content clues refer to descriptive words and phrases that highlight a point of emphasis or opinion from the passage. Again, look at the clue in context.

STEP 3: RESEARCH THE RELEVANT TEXT

Now that you know the question type and the clue, you can return to the passage with a specific purpose in mind and find the answer to the question. Sometimes just establishing that information appears in a particular paragraph will be enough to answer a question, but many answer choices are traps for those who try to rely on memory.

To answer global questions, review the critical elements you identified in step 1: topic, scope, purpose, main idea, and your road map.

For detail questions, use the clues in the question to direct you back to the relevant part of the text. The answer can be quite close to or just a summary of the information you find.

At step 3 for inference questions, remember that the answer must follow from the passage. Read between the lines and combine statements as necessary.

Use the appropriate logical reasoning strategy for logical reasoning questions. Finally, check the context of the identified part of the text and ask yourself why the author put it there.

STEP 4: THINK CRITICALLY ABOUT THE ANSWER

Prephrase what you think the correct choice will be. This step will prevent you from falling for distracters. Just as with Logical Reasoning, this step is critical to accuracy and efficiency in choosing the correct answer. It is also the step you are most likely to avoid—but you shouldn't. Predicting the answer takes patience and focus, both important skills you must practice and give yourself time to hone. The time spent will pay off in points on test day! We know the right answer is one of the five choices there in front of you. But going over and over the answers and comparing them back and forth with the text wastes a lot of time and promotes falling into wrong answer traps.

STEP 5: EVALUATE THE ANSWER CHOICES

The preparation you've done will help you zero in on the right choice. Finding the choice that matches your prediction is the surest, most efficient approach, but you can eliminate wrong choices if necessary.

Classic wrong answer traps include answers that

- are outside the scope (choices that go beyond the scope of the passage or particular argument of focus).
- give the opposite response (a 180).
- misuse a detail.
- present a distortion.
- use extreme language.
- give half right and half wrong information.

The test maker has to write four of the five answers to be incorrect and makes them incorrect for a particular reason. If you become familiar with the common wrong answer types, you will get better at eliminating them and choosing correct answers with confidence.

Keep in mind that all LSAT questions have one right answer and four wrong answers. Notice we did not say that some answers are OK but not as good as the correct answer. Answers are not correct in degrees. They are right, or they are wrong.

A WORD ABOUT COMPARATIVE READING

The comparative reading piece includes two shorter passages titled Passage A and Passage B. They will be written by different authors and not necessarily be written in response to each other. Expect them to have the same topic. The scopes may be close, but the purpose of each will be different. Not all passage pairs will have the same relationship. For example, passages could agree or disagree on a major point, or one passage might establish a hypothesis while the other supports the hypothesis.

The comparative reading passage set is similar to the other reading comp passages in some ways and different in others. Similarities include the following: the length of the passages; the subject matter being from the humanities, social sciences, natural sciences, or law; the number of questions; the types of questions, and the amount of time allocated. Differences include the fact that there are two short passages instead of one, the fact that most questions have a comparative element, and the importance of recognizing agreement and disagreement between the two passages.

SECTION MANAGEMENT

You want to manage the Reading Comp section just as you do the Logic Games section to get the most points you can out of it. Start with your easiest passage up front and build to your most difficult passage. Again, you want to earn points right away and as quickly as possible in the 35 minutes you're given.

Start by scanning all the passages and determining the order in which you will tackle them. Practice this initially without time pressure, but on test day, you ant to spend only 30 to 60 seconds on this. There is no objective formula to determining passage order but rather factors to consider. Then you must choose the order based on what you know works best for you. Here are some criteria to keep in mind when ordering the passages:

- **Author's point of view:** Does the author have an opinion, and how clear is it?
- **Clarity of language:** Is the language dense or straightforward, technical or simplistic?
- **Clarity of organization:** How many paragraphs make up the passage? Are there few paragraphs, so you have to impose the structure? Or are there more paragraphs, allowing you to rely on the author's organization?
- **Number, length, and difficulty of questions:** What question types are available? How long are the answers? How many questions are there? In other words, how many points are available from one passage? Remember: More questions are not always better if the passage is difficult for you. Remember, you might be able to get through two passages with five questions each more quickly and get more points than if you spent a lot of time on a hard passage with eight questions.
- **Personal preference and familiarity:** How comfortable and/or knowledgeable are you with the subject? This factor can be tricky because personal preference does not always add up to more points. You may not like natural science and have no college training in natural science, but if the passage is well organized, you still can read it critically and get points from it. An abstract social science passage may feel more familiar but be more difficult to road map.

Here is a word about outside knowledge. It is not necessary on the LSAT, and sometimes it can actually be harmful. The Reading Comp section is "closed research." That is, everything you'll need to answer every question is included in the passage. Correct answers must reflect only what the passage says or implies. So don't let your own knowledge or opinions interfere with answering questions correctly.

You can also manage the section by doing all your work for a passage and then transferring the answers to the grid sheet. This way, you focus on the critical reading and research and cut down on misbubbling.

Finally, you can choose the order of the questions. Consider doing global questions first. You know where they usually show up in a question set, and you will have just completed the critical reading identifying the global elements. Plus, doing global questions first helps you solidify your grasp of the passage. Detail questions, especially those with line references, are good candidates to tackle next. Many test takers benefit from leaving the more difficult logic or inference questions for last. In particular, leave questions without line references and "except" questions for last.

This, of course, is only a suggested order. With practice, you may want to revise it, taking into account your own strengths for each question. Just be sure to ask yourself: "Can I answer this question quickly?"

HELPFUL HINTS TO IMPROVE YOUR PERFORMANCE

Start by practicing the Kaplan Method. At first it will feel cumbersome and awkward, and it will slow you down. However, your mastery will improve, and your answers will get more accurate. Then you can practice your timing and endurance.

Now let's try the 5-Step Method on an actual LSAT-strength Reading Comp single passage

For the time being, we've just included the question stems of the questions attached to this passage, because you don't want to get into answer choices until later. Remember that on test day, you don't have to do the passages in order, either—pick your best shots first.

It has been suggested that post–World War II concepts of environmental liability, as they pertain to hazardous waste, grew out of issues regarding municipal refuse collection and disposal and industrial waste disposal in the period 1880–1940. To a great degree,

(5) the remedies available to Americans for dealing with the burgeoning hazardous waste problem were characteristic of the judicial, legislative, and regulatory tools used to confront a whole range of problems in the industrial age. At the same time, these remedies were operating in an era in which the problem of hazardous waste had yet to be recognized. It is

(10) understandable that an assessment of liability was narrowly drawn and most often restricted to a clearly identified violator in a specific act of infringement of the property rights of someone else. Legislation, for the most part, focused narrowly on clear threats to the public health and dealt with problems of industrial pollution meekly if at all.

(15) Nevertheless, it would be grossly inaccurate to assume that the actions of American politicians, technologists, health officials, judges, and legislators in the period 1880–1940 have had little impact on the attempts to define environmental liability and to confront the consequences of hazardous waste. Taken as a whole, the precedents of

(20) the late 19th through the mid-20th century have established a framework in which the problem of hazardous waste is understood

Remedies 4 HW problem typical of industrial age

Yet, problem still new

By liability fell on indivi & specific acts

and confronted today. Efforts at refuse reform gradually identified the
immutable connection between waste and disease, turning eyesores
into nuisances and nuisances into health hazards. Confronting the

(25)   refuse problem and other forms of municipal pollution forced cities
to define public responsibility and accountability with respect to the
environment. A commitment to municipal services in the development
of sewers and collection and disposal systems shifted the burden
of responsibility for eliminating wastes from the individual to the

(30)   community. In some way, the courts' efforts to clarify and broaden the
definition of public nuisance were dependent on the cities' efforts to
define community responsibility themselves.

The courts retained their role as arbiter of what constituted private
and public nuisances. Indeed, fear that the courts would transform

(35)   individual decisions into national precedents often contributed to the
search for other remedies. Nonetheless, the courts remained an active
agent in cases on the local, state, and national level, making it quite
clear that they were not going to be left out of the process of defining
environmental liability in the United States. In the case of hazardous

(40)   waste, precedents for behavior and remedial action were well developed
by 1940. Even though the concept of hazardous waste is essentially
a post–World War II notion, the problem was not foreign to earlier
generations. The observation that the administrative, technical, and
legal problems of water pollution in the 1920s were intertwined is

(45)   equally applicable to today's hazardous waste problem.

Health hazards
Cities confront probs

courts were active on
all levels

Topic: Hazardous waste
Scope: P-WWII concept of Env. liability
Purpose: Hist/Legis of P-WWII HW problems
Main Idea: 19th/20th established today's framework

1. According to the author, the efforts by cities to define public
   responsibility for the environment resulted in which of the
   following?

2. Which of the following, if substituted for the word *immutable*
   (line 23), would LEAST alter the author's meaning?

3. With which one of the following statements would the author
   be most likely to agree?

4. The author's primary purpose is to discuss...

5. The tone of the author's discussion of early attempts to deal
   with waste and pollution problems could best be described
   as...

6. According to the passage, judicial assessments of liability in waste disposal disputes prior to World War II were usually based on...

7. The passage suggests that responses to environmental problems between 1880 and 1940 were relatively limited in part because of...

1. READ THE PASSAGE STRATEGICALLY

The first few sentences introduce the topic: hazardous waste. The scope—the specific angle the author takes on the topic—seems to be the post–World War II concept of environmental liability. It's been suggested that this has some connection to issues from 1880–1940; latter-day remedies are "characteristic of the judicial, legislative, and regulatory tools used to confront a whole range of problems in the industrial age." Because hazardous waste liability concepts had their roots in an era that predated the recognition of hazardous waste, the author believes that liability assessment and the ensuing legislation regarding hazardous waste were both "narrowly drawn."

However, the keyword *nevertheless* at the beginning of the next paragraph indicates that a contrast is coming. This sentence harks back to and solidifies the connection between the actions and policies from 1880–1940 and the concept of environmental liability, which is the author's main idea.

Lines 19–22 ("Taken as a whole... confronted today") restate the main idea. There's a description of the gradual recognition of hazardous waste and some repercussions of the efforts to define the problem and assign responsibility. Note that there's some talk about individual versus community responsibility and the role of cities, but don't fuss over the specifics. If there's a question on these issues, you'll know where to look.

The first part of the last paragraph deals with the courts' role. The last three sentences reinforce the main idea.

2. READ THE QUESTION STEM

Be clear about what each question asks and be prepared to skip questions early on. Look at the question stems for this passage scanning for Global questions—especially *main idea* or *primary purpose*. If you come across the following question, you should attempt it with the passage fresh in your mind:

4. The author's primary purpose is to discuss...

3. RESEARCH THE RELEVANT TEXT IN THE PASSAGE

In this case, your road map or a quick review of the gist of each paragraph will suffice.

4. MAKE A PREDICTION

If you read critically, you will have already formed an idea of the author's purpose.

5. GO TO THE ANSWER CHOICES

    (A) contrasts in the legislative approaches to environmental liability before and after World War II.

    (B) legislative trends that have been instrumental in the reduction of environmental hazardous wastes.

    (C) the historical and legislative context in which to view post–World War II hazardous waste problems.

    (D) early patterns of industrial abuse and pollution of the American environment.

    (E) the growth of an activist tradition in American jurisprudence.

Choice (C) has the right elements: the connection to the author's main idea ("the historical and legislative context... to view... waste problems") and the correct topic and scope: hazardous waste, post–World War II.

Choice (A) misinterprets the passage structure—no such contrast is presented.

(B) is tempting; legislative trends were discussed, but not in enough depth to be the author's primary purpose. And the discussion hinges on defining liability for hazardous wastes and doesn't specifically discuss any factor "instrumental in the reduction of environmental wastes." (D) and (E) both violate the topic and scope of the passage (notice that neither even mentions the topic of hazardous wastes).

 **READ MORE**

There's plenty of practice with REAL, challenging Reading Comp sets in Kaplan's *LSAT 180.*

Question 5, focusing on tone, is another Global question that you may wish to answer early on. Continuing to scan the questions, the one with the line reference, question 2, may have caught your eye. This type simply tests your understanding of a certain word in a particular context, and because it tells you exactly where in the passage the word is, you might try this one next. Questions 1 and 6 are clearly Detail questions, so you might do those next, beginning with the one that seems the most familiar. The Inference questions, 3 and 7, are probably good to save for last.

Try one Detail question and one Inference question, repeating steps 2–5 of Kaplan's method.

2. READ THE QUESTION STEM

Here's the complete form (with answer choices) of question 6:

    6. According to the passage, judicial assessments of liability in waste disposal disputes prior to World War II were usually based on

        (A) excessively broad definitions of legal responsibility.

        (B) the presence of a clear threat to the public health.

(C) precedents derived from well-known cases of large-scale industrial polluters.

(D) restricted interpretations of property rights infringements.

(E) trivial issues such as littering, eyesores, and other public nuisances.

Mark key phrases (like "according to the passage" and "prior to World War II"), if it helps you to keep focused on what's required. Look for clues—like proper nouns and names, line or paragraph references, or direct quotes—that will lead you to the answer.

3. Research the Relevant Text in the Passage

Pre–World War II judicial assessments of liability should ring a bell—they were discussed in the first paragraph.

4. Make a Prediction

The answer is " . . . an assessment of liability was narrowly drawn and most often restricted to a clearly identified violator in a specific act of *infringement of the property rights* [emphasis added] of someone else."

5. Go to the Answer Choices

The correct choice, (D), is a direct paraphrase.

(E) is a common type of wrong answer; it consists of wording taken straight from the passage but, unfortunately, the wrong part of the passage. Don't choose an answer simply because you recognize some of the words or phrases in it; this common trap snags many careless test takers. (B) is another classic wrong answer—the 180 choice. This choice actually represents the opposite of what's stated or implied in the passage. According to the author, pre–World War II was "an era in which the problem of hazardous waste had yet to be recognized."

2. Read the Question Stem

Here the inference question:

3. With which one of the following statements would the author be most likely to agree?

(A) The growth of community responsibility for waste control exemplifies the tendency of government power to expand at the expense of individual rights.

(B) Although important legal precedents for waste control were established between 1880 and 1940, today's problems will require radically new approaches.

(C) While early court decisions established important precedents involving environmental abuses by industry, equally pressing matters, such as disposal of municipal garbage, were neglected.

(D) Because environmental legislation between 1880 and 1940 was in advance of its time, it failed to affect society's awareness of environmental problems.

(E) The historical role of U.S. courts in defining problems of hazardous waste and environmental liability provides valuable traditions for courts today.

Note words like "author…most likely to agree" to understand that the question asks for an inference.

3. Research the Relevant Text in the Passage

You want something the author would agree with; what do you know about the author's opinions? The first sentence of the second paragraph says that it would be "inaccurate to assume" (an opinion) that the actions of judges and legislators had little impact on defining liability and confronting the issue. This implies that the courts had a positive impact, which is bolstered by lines 19–22 and 39–43.

4. Make a Prediction

You want a choice that discusses the positive effects of the courts and one that is in line with the author's tone (in this case factual and evenhanded), as well as the content.

5. Go to the Answer Choices

Notice how correct choice (E) sounds like an offshoot of the author's main idea. The first sentence of the second paragraph says that it would be wrong to assume that the actions of judges and legislators had little impact on defining liability and confronting the issue. This implies that the courts had a positive impact, which is bolstered by lines 39–43. Combine that with the statement in lines 19–22: "Taken as a whole, the precedents of the late 19th through the mid-20th century have established a framework in which the problem of hazardous waste is understood and confronted today."

Choice (A) offers a judgment taken from the community/individual responsibility issue, something the author never does; he or she simply says that the burden shifted from one to the other. And there's no reason to believe that the author would agree with (B), either. While he or she would certainly agree with the first part, nothing indicates that the author would advocate radical new approaches for today's problems. Both of these choices fail to match the author's tone and are outside the scope of the passage.

READING COMPREHENSION PRACTICE

SET ONE

Directions: Each passage in this test is followed by several questions. After reading the passage, choose the best answer to each question. Your replies are to be based on what is stated or implied in the selection.

Passage for Questions 1–7

Various factors influence voter preference in U.S. presidential elections, but perhaps none is so persuasive as a candidate's performance on nationally televised debates just prior to the

(5) election. Newspapers and television news programs generally attempt to provide thorough coverage of the debates, further augmenting the effect of good or bad candidate performances. In this way, the news media fulfill the traditional

(10) role of educating the public and enabling voters to make better informed decisions about elected officials. However, the same media that bring live debates into millions of living rooms across the nation also limit the availability of debate cover-

(15) age by use of "pool" coverage, the sharing of news coverage with other news organizations. When typical pool situations arise, one of the major networks covers the event, and a "feed" is created so other broadcasters may have access to the same

(20) coverage. Individual broadcasters are unable to convey a unique account to their viewers. The pool system limits the news-gathering ability of television news organizations and denies viewers an opportunity to gain maximum insight from

(25) the debate. The First Amendment freedoms afforded the press exist largely to ensure that the public benefits from the free flow of information. Some commentators suggest that the purpose of a free press is to inform citizens about matters

(30) of public concern. Others, however, believe that the value of free press lies in its ability to foster a marketplace of ideas in which the best options prevail. Presidential debates embody all these

considerations. Not only do candidates provide

(35) information about matters of utmost interest, they also offer diverse views on how to approach the major issues. Given television's ability to further the informational and marketplace-of-ideas goals of the First Amendment, debate coverage should

(40) be diverse as possible.

What difference does it make whether viewers saw a "tight shot" of one candidate or a "two-shot" of both candidates at a given time? The answer depends on what happens, when it happens, and

(45) whether the pool director anticipated it or was fortunate enough to have captured it anyway. It may be argued that none of this matters. The important thing, the argument goes, is that viewers will know generally what happened. According

(50) to this line of reasoning, the number of news organizations covering an event—and even which ones—would be irrelevant. But courts have held differently: "It is impossible to treat two news services as interchangeable, and it is only by cross

(55) lights from varying directions that full illumination can be secured." Undoubtedly, there are some circumstances in which pool coverage is the only way to cover an event. But these few situations must not foster a casual acceptance of pool

(60) implementation in other situations.

1. It can be inferred that the author's primary objection to the pool system of covering presidential debates is that it

   (A) restricts the public's access to a diversity of ideas and information.

   (B) limits the number of people who have access to debates on television.

   (C) undermines candidates' ability to persuade voters.

   (D) dissuades voters from exercising their right to choose between candidates.

   (E) contributes to an overreliance by the public on televised accounts of political issues.

2. The author would probably assert that the opinion of the court presented in the second paragraph is

(A) useful but biased.

(B) reflective of an unfortunate trend.

(C) overly permissive.

(D) substantially correct.

(E) commendable but ineffective.

3. In the first paragraph, the author cites two opinions concerning the benefits provided to society by a free press primarily in order to

(A) suggest the range of benefits that potentially would be provided by competitive coverage of presidential debates.

(B) indicate that some of the defenses of pool coverage contradict one another.

(C) criticize the assumptions held by some commentators on journalism.

(D) contend that First Amendment freedoms do not apply to presidential debates.

(E) reconcile different points of view in an effort to reach a more acceptable definition of press freedom.

4. It can be inferred from the passage that a proponent of the pool system of debate coverage would be most likely to defend that viewpoint with which of the following remarks?

(A) Broadcasters rarely betray their political preferences in debate coverage.

(B) Although imperfect, pool coverage is the only practical means of reporting most political events.

(C) Presidential debates are too complex to be covered thoroughly by any one broadcaster.

(D) Broadcasters are prevented by public opinion from presenting biased coverage.

(E) Small differences in style of coverage do not significantly affect the amount of information conveyed to viewers.

5. The author warns that the use of pool coverage in situations in which it may be needed may lead to other situations in which

(A) public events covered by the media are subjected to undue analytical scrutiny.

(B) broadcasters accept further limitation of their First Amendment freedoms.

(C) the informational content of news events is diminished.

(D) pool coverage is relied upon when it is in fact undesirable.

(E) broadcasters suffer increasing erosion of their capacity for news gathering.

6. The author's argument that the pool system "denies viewers an opportunity to gain maximum insight from the debate" (lines 23–25) would be most WEAKENED if it could be shown that

(A) candidates' debate performances rarely make a difference of more than a few percent in voting results.

(B) most debate viewers form their opinions primarily on the basis of postdebate commentary presented separately by each network.

(C) candidates' posture and mannerisms during debates are as important in forming voter opinion as their actual words.

(D) few viewers of televised debates bother to read follow-up commentary in newspapers and magazines.

(E) competitive coverage would provide viewers with a wider variety of interpretations on which to base their opinions.

7. Which of the following titles best describes the content of the passage?

   (A) Debate Coverage: How It Changes Voters' Opinions

   (B) The "Pool" System: A Limitation on Public Access to Information

   (C) The "Pool" System: Its Benefits Versus Its Impracticalities

   (D) First Amendment Press Rights: How They Conflict with Presidential Politics

   (E) Televised Debates: Their Role in Presidential Politics

Passages for Questions 8–12

Passage A

In the late 1990s and early 2000s, a variety of nontraditional mortgage products became popular for home buyers who might not have qualified for conventional financing. Some of these loans
(5) allowed purchasers to spread payments over 50 years instead of the traditional 15- to 30-year period, radically increasing the interest paid over the life of those loans and slowing the rate at which equity accrued. Other loans began with interest-
(10) only payments for a year or two, meaning that no equity at all accrued during that time. The most popular of these subprime loans were adjustable-rate loans— loans with shifting interest rates.

The industry stood to make a greater profit on
(15) subprime loans, and brokers were soon actively selling them to borrowers who could have qualified for more favorable, less expensive traditional loans, particularly when the homes purchased were in lower-income and minority-populated
(20) areas. Usually, no projections were offered as to the amount of monthly mortgage payments after the loans adjusted, and many borrowers were unprepared for the "payment shock" when rates adjusted: Some payments increased by several hundred
(25) dollars per month.

Many borrowers were assured that they would be able to refinance their loans before the increase kicked in. For hundreds of thousands of home owners, however, the reality was quite different.
(30) The fact that they'd accrued little or no equity during the period of lower payments combined with a slump in the housing market meant that many homeowners facing increased payments owed more than their homes were worth. The end
(35) result was hundreds of thousands of foreclosures in 2006 and 2007, with more than 2.2 million projected by the end of 2008.

Passage (B)

Irresponsible consumer borrowing patterns in the few years surrounding the turn of the century have had an impact that will likely affect the economy of the United States for many years to come.
(5) Perhaps the blame doesn't fall entirely on the borrowers: The culture of instant gratification and the impression painted by the popular marketing machine that is so pervasive in our society certainly created the impression that it was every person's
(10) right to attain home ownership and the American dream regardless of financial position.

Unfortunately, we are all paying for that unrealistic optimism today. The mortgage companies and special divisions that sprang up to meet this
(15) demand are going out of business at an astonishing rate as their clientele find themselves unable to meet the mortgage payments they agreed to just a few short years ago. Banks and investors that shared the risks of these ventures are experiencing
(20) hundreds of billions of dollars in losses, and there appears to be no relief in sight as home values plummet in response to the growing number of crisis sales and foreclosure properties on the market. Thus, local economies are hit simultaneously
(25) with deteriorating housing markets and mass layoffs as the affected companies tighten their belts or close their doors.

8. The authors of the two passages would most likely agree about which of the following?

   (A) Overly ambitious home buyers have created circumstances that will negatively affect the economy as a whole.

   (B) Mortgage brokers should not have offered these high-cost subprime loans to borrowers without providing more extensive information about the risks associated with them.

   (C) The declining value of real property has played a role in the economic problems related to the increase in foreclosures.

   (D) Homeowners with little or no equity are at a greater risk of losing their homes when payments adjust or other economic factors shift .

   (E) It is not realistic for every American to aspire to own his or her own home.

9. Which of the following best describes the relationship between the passages?

   (A) Both examine the problems homeowners are facing, but they reach different conclusions about the root causes of that problem.

   (B) Passage A describes a problem, and Passage B explains the origins of the problem and its anticipated impact.

   (C) The passages consider the same set of circumstances from differing perspectives.

   (D) Passage B refutes the conclusions set forth in Passage A.

   (E) The passages propose differing solutions to the same socioeconomic dilemma.

10. The authors of the two passages would most likely strongly disagree about

   (A) the extent of the impact of the increase in foreclosures on the economy as a whole.

   (B) whether or not subprime loans should have been offered to some of the homeowners who are currently facing foreclosure on such loans.

   (C) the number of homeowners who will ultimately lose their property as a result of the combination of economic factors impacting the housing market today.

   (D) the extent of the risk the current issues in the mortgage lending industry pose to investors.

   (E) which parties are primarily responsible for the difficulties currently faced by homeowners with subprime mortgage loans.

11. The author of Passage B expresses concern that

   (A) more than 2 million homeowners are likely to lose their homes in the immediate future.

   (B) buyers will continue to borrow irresponsibly, aggravating the already difficult economic conditions surrounding home ownership.

   (C) many buyers were treated unfairly or misled into taking on mortgage loans that were ultimately not in their best interests.

   (D) the decline in the housing market and increase in foreclosure rates are having a negative impact on the larger economy.

   (E) mortgage brokers who offered subprime loans to borrowers who could have qualified for traditional mortgage loans may face sanctions.

12. The authors of the two passages differ in their assessment of the impact of the increase in subprime mortgage foreclosures primarily in that

    (A) the author of Passage A expects the consequences to be much more serious than does the author of Passage B.

    (B) the author of Passage A takes a much broader view of the potential ramifications than does the author of Passage B.

    (C) the two authors are concerned with different aspects of the fallout from the increase in foreclosures.

    (D) the author of Passage B does not believe that the average homeowner will face significant losses because of the increase in foreclosure rates.

    (E) the author of Passage A is concerned with longer-range consequences than is the author of Passage B.

SET TWO

Passage for Questions 1–7

It is in his attack on the abstract and individualistic doctrine of the "rights of man" that Edmund Burke develops most fully his philosophy of society and breaks most decisively
(5) with the mechanical and atomic political theory which, inherited from John Locke, had dominated the thought of the 18th century. Over and against the view of the state as the product of a "contract" among individuals, whose "rights" exist
(10) prior to that contract and constitute the standard by which at every stage the just claim of society on the individual is to be tested, he develops the conception of the individual as himself the product of society, born to an inheritance of rights
(15) (which are "all the advantages" for which civil society is made) and of reciprocal duties, and, in the last resort, owing these concrete rights (actual rights which fall short in perfection of those ideal rights "whose abstract perfection is their practical

(20) defect") to convention and prescription. Society originates not in a free contract but in necessity, and the shaping factor in its institutions has not been the consideration of any code of abstract pre-existent rights ("the inherent rights of the people")
(25) but "convenience."

And, of these conveniences or rights, two are supreme, government and prescription, the existence of "a power out of themselves by which the will of individuals may be controlled" and the
(30) recognition of the sacred character of prescription. In whatever way a particular society may have originated—conquest, usurpation, revolution ("there is a sacred veil to be drawn over the beginnings of all government")—in process of
(35) time, its institutions and rights come to rest upon prescription. In any ancient community such as that of France or Britain, every constituent factor, including what we choose to call the people, is the product of convention. The privileges of every
(40) order, the rights of every individual, rest upon prescription embodied in law or established by usage. This is the "compact or agreement which gives its corporate form and capacity to a state," and, if it is once broken, the people are a number
(45) of vague, loose individuals and nothing more. Alas! They little know how many a weary step is to be taken before they can form themselves into a mass, which has a true politic personality.

There is, therefore, no right of revolution, or
(50) rebellion at will. The "civil, social man" never may rebel except when he must rebel. Revolution is always the annulment of some rights. It will be judged in the last resort by the degree in which it preserves as well as destroys and by
(55) what it substitutes for what it takes away. At its best, revolution is "the extreme medicine of the constitution," and Burke's quarrel with the Assembly (which ruled during the French Revolution) is that they made it "its daily bread";
(60) that, when the whole constitution of France was in their hands to preserve and to reform, they elected only to destroy.

1. The primary purpose of the passage is to

   (A) expound upon Burke's belief that there exists a sovereign right for citizenry to revolt when one can be assured that they will create a vastly superior, wholly new system of government.

   (B) explain Burke's unique concept that the state is formed through a pact individuals choose to make, forfeiting some of their inherent rights for longer-term success of the group.

   (C) determine the extent to which Burke believed in the ability of the individual to govern himself solely as a solitary individual.

   (D) explain Burke's philosophy of the necessity of societies, the importance of evolved prescriptions, and the impact of these needs on the right of revolution.

   (E) define Burke's belief that a sovereign ruler must be chosen to lead a society.

2. The passage suggests which of the following about the relationship between the individual and revolution?

   (A) The individual has the right to rebel at will, because there is historical precedent for revolution.

   (B) Revolution is inherently destructive to at least some of the rights in any given society.

   (C) It is the individual's choice to pursue revoltion, but they should do it only when they intend to totally overhaul the existing system.

   (D) There is no need for revolution, because individuals are free within themselves to alter their realities.

   (E) Revolution is an extension of the individual's agreement with the social contract.

3. The author indicates that, for Burke, the customs that exist regarding how individuals are treated result primarily from

   (A) existing laws and traditions that have evolved in a society, regardless of the origins of those practices or the society itself.

   (B) the creation and enforcement of the rules of society by a sovereign ruler.

   (C) the individual's decision as to whether to participate in society or to focus on individual freedoms independent of society.

   (D) ever-shifting trends and societal perspectives.

   (E) the manner in which the society was originally formed.

4. Each of the following is a component of Locke's philosophy with which the author tells us that Burke disagrees EXCEPT

   (A) the individual is endowed with the ideal right to choose whether or not to be part of society.

   (B) society is subject to reassessment as membeship evolves.

   (C) society originates from necessity rather than by the will of individuals.

   (D) the individual's experience of society is formed by the choices he or she makes.

   (E) governments are created by the individual.

5. With which of the following statements about Edmund Burke would the author of this passage most likely agree?

   (A) Burke believed that it was critical to avoid change in the predictable rules of society.

   (B) Burke was a free thinker who felt that adaptability and frequent restructuring were key to maintaining effective government.

   (C) Burke was an optimist who sought to demonstrate that society was an individualist's utopia.

   (D) Burke accepted that moderate changes in society were sometimes necessary.

   (E) Burke was an individualist who believed that the needs of members of society were paramount to those of society as a whole.

6. The author indicates that, in Burke's view, revolutionary zeal serves primarily as

   (A) the ultimate solution for the political dissatisfaction of the general populace.

   (B) a means of disguising more subtle and manipulative political processes.

   (C) an ultimately difficult solution to dissatisfaction with society that may spawn more problems than it solves.

   (D) the understandable emotional outpouring of individuals who have discovered that their social contract is being violated.

   (E) the conscious decision of citizens to alter their inherent rights.

7. Based on the passage, which of the following would be most likely to be the subject of a work by Locke?

   (A) An analysis of the basis of society's right to make claims on individuals.

   (B) The right of rulers to dictate social doctrines even in the absence of the consent of the people.

   (C) Society's inability to create new social mores.

   (D) The importance of tradition and evolved prescription in society's construction.

   (E) The importance of a person's social position in determining his or her worth.

Passage for Questions 8–14

A new test can predict the risk of breast cancer recurrence and may identify women who will benefit most from chemotherapy, according to research supported by the National Cancer
(5) Institute (NCI). These results suggest that almost half of over 50,000 U.S. women diagnosed with estrogen-dependent, lymph-node-negative breast cancer every year are at low risk for recurrence and may not need to go through the discomfort
(10) and side effects of chemotherapy.

The test is based on levels of expression (increased or decreased) of a panel of cancer-related genes. This panel is used to predict whether estrogen-dependent breast cancer will come back.
(15) Scientists on this study also will present new results indicating that the same test can predict which women benefit most from chemotherapy. Women with low risk of breast cancer recurrence—about half of the women in the recent
(20) study—do not appear to derive much benefit from chemotherapy.

The researchers used tissue samples and medical records from women enrolled in clinical trials of the cancer drug tamoxifen, which blocks the effect
(25) of estrogen on breast cancer cells. These women had a kind of breast cancer defined as estrogen-receptor-positive, lymph-node-negative. This kind of breast cancer needs estrogen to grow but has

not spread to the lymph nodes. Currently, many
(30) American women with this type of breast cancer
do receive chemotherapy in addition to hormonal
therapy.

Using samples from 447 patients and a
collection of 250 genes, 16 cancer-related genes
(35) were found that worked best. The scientists created
a formula that generates a "recurrence score"
based on the expression patterns of these genes
in a tumor sample. Ranging from 1 to 100, the
recurrence score is a measure of the risk that a
(40) given cancer will recur.

The results validate the ability of the recurrence
score to predict risk of recurrence. Using biopsy
tissue and medical records from another tamoxifen trial, researchers divided 668 women into low,
(45) intermediate, and high risk of recurrence groups.
Fifty-one percent were in the low-risk group (with
a score of less than 18); 22 percent were at intermediate risk (recurrence score 18 or higher but
less than 31); 27 percent were at high risk (a score
(50) of 31 or higher).

These risk group divisions correlated well with
the actual rates of recurrence of breast cancer
after 10 years. There was a significant difference
in recurrence rates between women in the low-
(55) and high-risk groups. In the low-risk group, there
was a 6.8 percent rate of recurrence at 10 years;
in the intermediate- and high-risk categories, these
rates were 14.3 and 30.5 percent, respectively. Up
to a recurrence score of 50, rates of recurrence
(60) increased continuously as the recurrence score
increased. These trends held across age groups and
tumor size. The same test has also been used to
predict how beneficial chemotherapy will be for
women with estrogen-receptor-positive, lymph-
(65) node-negative breast cancer that are on tamoxifen.

In the treatment study, women with high recurrence scores, who are representative of about 25
percent of patients with this kind of breast cancer,
had a large benefit from chemotherapy in terms
(70) of 10-year recurrence-free rates. Women with low
recurrence scores, who represent about 50 percent
of these patients, derived minimal benefits from

chemotherapy. The group under study was not
large enough to determine whether chemotherapy
(75) is detrimental to the low-risk group. "The test
has the potential to change medical practice by
sparing thousands of women each year from the
harmful short- and long-term side effects associated with chemotherapy," said JoAnne Zujewski,
(80) MD, senior investigator in NCI's Cancer Therapy
Evaluation Program.

8. With which of the following statements
concerning estrogen-dependent, lymph-node-
negative breast cancer would the author be most
likely to agree?

(A) It is essential that these women all participate
in chemotherapy treatment.

(B) The vast majority of women with estrogen-
dependent, lymph-node-negative breast
cancer are at a high risk for recurrence.

(C) Chemotherapy is detrimental to women who
are in the low-risk group for recurrence of
estrogen-dependent, lymph-node-negative
breast cancer.

(D) A significant percentage of the women
diagnosed with this type of cancer do not
need to be treated with chemotherapy.

(E) The drug tamoxifen is the best cure for
women with estrogen-dependent, lymph-
node-negative breast cancer.

9. The author is primarily concerned with discussing

   (A) public interest in breast cancer drugs and how raised awareness has positively affected patients.

   (B) the drawbacks to using drug-testing participants as subjects for the recurrence scale.

   (C) the benefits of testing levels of expression of certain cancer-related genes to predict the likelihood of recurrence of estrogen-dependent breast cancer.

   (D) the effectiveness of the formula that generates a "recurrence score" based on the expression patterns of genes taken from chemotherapy recipients.

   (E) the benefits and the disadvantages of treating patients with estrogen-dependent breast cancer with chemotherapy.

10. According to the study outlined in the passage, which one of the following is an example of a woman who would benefit from chemotherapy?

    (A) One with estrogen-receptor-positive, lymph-node-negative breast cancer who is at a low risk of recurrence

    (B) One who is not taking tamoxifen to treat her estrogen-receptor-positive, lymph-node-negative breast cancer

    (C) One who is taking tamoxifen for her estrogen-receptor-negative, lymphnode-positive breast cancer

    (D) One that had test results showing high levels of increased expression of cancer-related genes

    (E) One with estrogen-receptor-positive, lymph-node-negative breast cancer who is at a high risk of recurrence

11. Which one of the following provides the best description of the organization of the passage?

    (A) A medicine is introduced, and its benefits and side effects are described in greater detail.

    (B) A problem is defined, its potential causes are discussed, and a possible solution is presented.

    (C) A process is outlined, its negative consequences are explained, and predictions are made.

    (D) A process is introduced and explained, its efficacy is discussed, and its potential value is explained.

    (E) A process is critiqued, and its previous history is generalized.

12. Each of the following is mentioned in the passage as a result of the success in assigning recurrence scores to patients being treated for estrogen-receptor-positive, lymph-node-negative breast cancer EXCEPT

    (A) fewer low-risk women will have to undergo chemotherapy as part of their treatment for this form of breast cancer.

    (B) more lower-risk women will utilize hormonal therapy to prevent cancer from coming back.

    (C) doctors will be able to predict more accurately the likelihood of recurrence of this type of cancer.

    (D) doctors now know that age groups and tumor size are less important in detecting recurrence than the expression (increased or decreased) of certain cancer-related genes.

    (E) the importance of chemotherapy in treating patients at a high risk of recurrence is confirmed.

13. According to the passage, the likelihood that a woman with estrogen-dependent, lymph-node-negative breast cancer will have it recur can best be determined by

    (A) the age of the woman at the initial onset of cancer.

    (B) the level of expression of certain genes.

    (C) the size of her initial tumor.

    (D) at what point in her treatment tamoxifen therapy is commenced.

    (E) whether or not she is undergoing or has undergone chemotherapy.

14. It can be inferred from the passage that

    (A) a patient with a recurrence score of 20 would not be likely to benefit from chemotherapy.

    (B) recurrence levels can be accurately predicted only if the patient is taking tamoxifen.

    (C) chemotherapy can increase the risk of recurrence in patients with low recurrence scores.

    (D) some doctors believe that chemotherapy can negatively impact a patient.

    (E) more than half of the women who currently receive chemotherapy as part of their treatment for estrogen-dependent, lymph-node-negative breast cancer are unlikely to benefit from it.

SET THREE

Passage for Questions 1–6

The Nazi Party leadership's interest in art arose early on, and art confiscations began by 1938. The Nazis wanted to rid Germany of art created during the Weimar Republic, the period of 1924–1930,
(5) when Germany was a leading European cultural center, especially in the fields of art, cinema, and literature. Weimar decadence aroused Nazi anger, and Hitler began closing art schools in 1933.

Soon after their rise to power in 1933, the Nazis
(10) purged so-called "degenerate art" from German public institutions. Artworks deemed degenerate by the Nazis included modern French and German artists in the areas of cubism, expressionism, and impressionism. Approximately 16,000 pieces were
(15) removed, and by 1938 the Nazi Party declared that all German art museums were purified. State-sponsored exhibitions of this art followed the Nazi purges, clarifying to Germans which types of modern art were now unacceptable
(20) the new German Reich. Soon after, an auction of 126 degenerate artworks took place in 1939 at the Fischer Gallerie in Lucerne, Switzerland, to raise revenues for the Party. The auctioned paintings by modern masters, many previously
(25) purged from German public institutions, included works by van Gogh and Matisse.

Hitler called for a new art, an art that portrayed the *Volk* and the *Volksgemeinschaft* (*Volk* community) as "a realization not of individual talents
(30) or of the inspiration of a lone genius, but of the collective expression of the *Volk*, channeled through the souls of individual creators." Hitler wanted new cultural and artistic creativity to arise in Germany, with the "folk-related" and "race
(35) conscious" arts of Nazi culture replacing what he called the "Jewish decadence" of the Weimar Republic. According to the Nazis, acceptable and desirable art included Old Flemish and Dutch masters; medieval and Renaissance German art-
(40) works; Italian Renaissance and baroque pieces; 18th-century French artworks; and 19th-century German realist painters depicting the German *Volk* culture.

Art looting that had begun on an ideological
(45) basis became an organized government policy. For Nazi officers seeking social status and promotion within the Party, collecting and giving art con-firmed one's dedication to promoting Nazi racial ideologies in the Reich. It was a way to emulate
(50) Hitler and Göring. Yet some top Nazis deviated from this model. For example, Joseph Goebbels, Reich minister for propaganda, collected artworks

by German expressionists, and Foreign Minister Joachim von Ribbentrop acquired impressionist
(55) paintings by Manet.

The first official rounds of Nazi confiscations began in Austria after the 1938 Anschluss, the annexation of Austria into the German Reich. Art confiscations in Poland began in 1939. Shortly
(60) thereafter, Nazi bureaucratic agencies were established in the newly occupied territories and charged with confiscating art. For example, the collections of Vienna's prominent Jewish families were the first to be taken by the Nazis, and Jews
(65) who did not plan to leave "Greater Germany" were required to register their personal property with the local police. Artworks soon paid for exit visas and taxes.

Many who were persecuted by the Nazis or
(70) who were political opponents did attempt to flee Germany in the mid 1930s. When the Nazis banned the exportation of paper money, wealthy émigrés began to turn their investments into art. Because the Nazis lacked a useable foreign cur-
(75) rency, artworks were often used as an alternative to money. As late as 1939, art could be taken out of Germany only as personal property. Art, thus, became cash for black marketers, Nazis and non-Nazis, and for victims of Nazism who used it as a
(80) safe, liquid asset. Almost all European art dealers who bought and sold to Germans and Nazis took advantage of their ignorant or ill-informed clients in the occupied areas, and both occupier and occupied exploited one another.

1. A Jewish art owner who emigrated in 1935 from Hitler's Germany would most likely

(A) have had little difficulty taking German currency with him.

(B) have had to use art as a means of taking his investments with him.

(C) have been able to leave the country with all of his personal belongings.

(D) have invested substantial sums of money in paintings by Matisse and van Gogh.

(E) have received a fair return for his investment when he sold his art to European art dealers.

2. The passage is primarily concerned with detailing

(A) the ironclad distinctions the Nazi government used to decide which art was "degenerate" and which was acceptable.

(B) how, during the rule of the Nazi regime, art was used for varying financial purposes.

(C) the history of the Nazi movement to purge certain types of art and replace them and the role art came to play in the financial transactions of Germans and the Nazi Party.

(D) the persecution of German, Polish, and Austrian individuals who collected what the Nazis deemed "degenerate art."

(E) the catastrophic effects of Nazi art "purification" on the German art establishment.

3. According to the passage, which one of the following is an example of art that the Nazi government did approve of?

(A) Cubist paintings by modern French and German artists

(B) Paintings that focused on the self-expression of the individual

(C) Works by van Gogh and Matisse

(D) German folk art that depicted the *Volk* community in a positive way

(E) Polish art

4. It can be inferred from the passage that the Nazi treatment of art in the 1930s was motivated, at least in part, by all of the following EXCEPT

    (A) a desire to purge the country of decadent Weimar-era art.

    (B) the confiscation of valuable, saleable works that would earn funds for the government.

    (C) an effort to bring greater focus to acceptable art, like German Renaissance and medieval works.

    (D) a desire to extend the party's actions with regard to art beyond the borders of Germany.

    (E) a desire to promote German impressionist and expressionist painters.

5. Which of the following relationships does the author imply?

    (A) A partial causal link between the belief in individualistic art and *Volk* art

    (B) A correlation between being Jewish and having one's art deemed "degenerate"

    (C) A connection between the destruction of "degenerate" art and the belief that certain modern art was symbolic of "Weimar decadence"

    (D) A causal relationship between the black market art trade and the creation of German currency that could be used abroad

    (E) A direct causal link between collecting art and being termed "degenerate"

6. The author indicates that the Nazi Party intended for art to serve primarily as

    (A) a means of personal expression for German artists.

    (B) a method for Jewish people to transform German currency into exportable funds.

    (C) a way to establish credibility by showing continuity with the Weimar government.

    (D) a way to promote racial tolerance through folk art and a sense of community.

    (E) a method to propagate the Nazi belief in the racial superiority of the *Volk* people.

Passage for Questions 7–12

Women, subjected by ignorance to their sensations, are only taught to look for happiness in love, and adopt metaphysical notions respecting that passion, and frequently in the midst of these
(5) sublime refinements they plump into actual vice. These are the women who are amused by the reveries of the stupid novelists, who, knowing little of human nature, work up stale tales, all retailed in a sentimental jargon, which equally tend to corrupt
(10) the taste, and draw the heart aside from its daily duties.

Females, in fact, denied all political privileges, and not allowed a civil existence, have their attention naturally drawn from the interest of the
(15) whole community to that of the minute parts. The mighty business of female life is to please, and restrained from entering into more important concerns by political and civil oppression, sentiments become events, and reflection deepens what
(20) it should, and would have effaced, if the understanding had been allowed to take a wider range.

Unable to grasp any thing great, is it surprising that they find the reading of history a very dry task, and disquisitions addressed to the under-
(25) standing intolerably tedious, and almost unintelligible? Yet, when I exclaim against novels, I mean when contrasted with those works which exercise the understanding and regulate the imagination.

For any kind of reading I think better than leav-
(30) ing a blank still a blank, because the mind must
receive a degree of enlargement and obtain a little
strength by a slight exertion of its thinking powers.

I have known several notable women, and one
in particular, who was a very good woman—as
(35) good as such a narrow mind would allow her to
be, who took care that her daughters (three in
number) should never see a novel. As she was a
woman of fortune and fashion, they had various masters to attend them, but as the few books
(40) thrown in their way were far above their capacities, or devotion, they neither acquired ideas nor
sentiments, and passed their time in dressing,
quarrelling with each other, or conversing with
their maids by stealth, till they were brought into
(45) company as marriageable.

With respect to love, nature, or their nurses, had
taken care to teach them the physical meaning of
the word; and, as they had few topics of conversation, and fewer refinements of sentiment, they
(50) expressed their gross wishes not in very delicate
phrases, when they spoke freely, talking of matri-
mony.

I recollect many other women who, not led
by degrees to proper studies, and not permit-
(55) ted to choose for themselves, have indeed been
overgrown children; or have obtained, by mixing
in the world, a little of what is termed common
sense; that is a distinct manner of seeing common
occurrences, as they stand detached: but what
(60) deserves the name of intellect, the power of gaining general or abstract ideas, or even intermediate
ones, was out of the question. Their minds were
quiescent, and when they were not roused by sensible objects and employments of that kind, they
(65) were low-spirited, would cry, or go to sleep.

The best method, I believe, that can be adopted
to correct a fondness for novels is to ridicule
them: not indiscriminately, for then it would have
little effect; but, if a judicious person, with some
(70) turn for humor, would read several to a young
girl, and point out both by tones, and apt comparisons with pathetic incidents and heroic characters

in history, how foolishly and ridiculously they
caricatured human nature, just opinions might be
(75) substituted instead of romantic sentiments.

7. The primary purpose of the passage is to

   (A) extol the virtues of novels as a means of
   expanding women's intellectual capacities.

   (B) refute the belief that women are less educated
   and intellectually developed than men.

   (C) explain the relationship between the
   intellectual limitations placed on women of
   the time and the role of novels in their lives.

   (D) catalog the misguided topics most common
   to novels.

   (E) explain the feminist bent of most novels and
   its impact on women's intellectual growth.

8. With which of the following statements about the
place of women in society would the author of
this passage most likely agree?

   (A) A woman's primary function in society is to
   generate income.

   (B) Women, although generally of different
   character and inclination than men, have the
   same opportunities that men do.

   (C) Adult women have rights and responsibilities
   in society that are equal to those of men.

   (D) Men are inferior to women, since women
   are more inclined by nature and their role in
   society to provide pleasure to others.

   (E) The lack of opportunity to involve herself
   in politics and the life of society is one of
   the factors that helps to limit a woman's
   intellectual development.

9. The author cites all of the following as problems EXCEPT

   (A) the limitations on women's intellectual development make them depressed.

   (B) lack of proper sources of education may lead women to believe it is acceptable to swear and speak crudely about sex.

   (C) the lack of proper education of women creates a situation where ignorant women are teaching other women to be ignorant.

   (D) the lack of access to proper reading material keeps women shamefully unaware of the realities of human sexuality.

   (E) women are unable to gain true intellect.

10. According to the passage, in the author's time, a woman's worth was derived from

    (A) her financial and social standing within the community.

    (B) her tendency toward civil-mindedness and political involvement.

    (C) her intellectual capabilities and accomplishments.

    (D) her ability to please.

    (E) her refined manner of speaking.

11. Which one of the following statements, if true, would most weaken the author's negative portrayal of the impact of novels on women?

    (A) They make women want to focus on love.

    (B) They expose women to life outside of their sheltered existences, encouraging them toward vice.

    (C) They make reading fun, increasing the chance that women will move on to reading more intellectually challenging works.

    (D) They teach women how to please the opposite sex so that they can be empowered.

    (E) They provide enjoyable entertainment for women.

12. The text suggests which of the following as a way to get young women to stop reading novels?

    (A) Have a person read passages from some novels to young women and make fun of them.

    (B) Make it clear to young women that all novels deserve their scorn.

    (C) Mothers should have a serious talk with their children about the inaccuracies and oversimplifications in novels.

    (D) An adult should explain to young women that romance is wicked and so they should not read novels, which glorify love.

    (E) Force them to read material at a much higher level so that they can begin to develop their intellects.

ANSWERS AND EXPLANATIONS

ANSWER KEY

Set One				
1. A	9. C	5. D	13. B	6. E
2. D	10. E	6. C	14. D	7. C
3. A	11. D	7. A		8. E
4. E	12. C	8. D	**Set Three**	9. D
5. D		9. C	1. B	10. D
6. B	**Set Two**	10. E	2. C	11. C
7. B	1. D	11. D	3. D	12. A
8. C	2. B	12. B	4. E	
	3. A		5. B	
	4. C			

DIAGNOSTIC TOOL

Tally up your score and write down your results below.

Total Correct: _____ out of 38

Percentage Correct: # you got right × 100 ÷ 38: _____

DIAGNOSE YOUR RESULTS

Look back at the questions you got wrong and think back on your experience answering them.

Step 1: Find the Roadblocks

Did you struggle to answer some questions? To improve your score, you need to pinpoint exactly what element of these "roadblocks" tripped you up. To do that, ask yourself these two questions.

Am I weak in the skills being tested?

Reading Comprehension questions test critical reading skills, such as whether you can summarize the main idea of a passage, differentiate between ideas explicitly stated in a text and those implied by the author, make inferences based on information in a text, analyze the logical structure of a passage, or deduce the author's attitude about a topic from the text. The Kaplan Reading Comp principles and methods in this book can help you focus on and develop the specific reading skills you need for better efficiency and comprehension on test day.

Was it the question type that threw me off?

Then you need to become more comfortable with it! Go back to the beginning of this chapter and review the Kaplan principles and methods. Make sure you understand them and know how to apply them. You also need to be very familiar with the four Reading Comp question types. This will improve your speed and efficiency on test day. Finally, get as much practice as you can so you grow more at ease with this question type.

Step 2: Find the Blind Spots

Did you answer some questions quickly and confidently but get them wrong anyway? When you come across wrong answers like these, you need to figure out what you thought you were doing right, what it turns out you were doing wrong, and why that happened! The best way to do that is to **read the answer explanations!**

They give you a detailed breakdown of why the correct answer is correct and why all the other answer choices are wrong. This helps to reinforce the Kaplan principles and methods for each question type and helps you figure out what blindsided you so it doesn't happen again. Also, just like with your Roadblocks, try to get in as much practice as you can.

Step 3: Reinforce Your Strengths

Read through all the answer explanations for the questions you got right. Again, this helps to reinforce the Kaplan principles and methods for each question type, which in turn helps you work more efficiently so you can get the score you want. Now keep your skills sharp with more practice.

As soon as you are comfortable with all the LSAT question types and Kaplan methods, complete a full-length Practice Test under timed conditions. In this way, Practice Tests serve as milestones; they help you to chart your progress! So don't save them all for the final weeks.

If you are aiming for that top score, try the *LSAT Advanced*, which includes only the toughest real LSAT questions and most focused strategies.

You can also visit **Kaptest.com/LSAT** for more details on Kaplan's online and classroom-based options. Kaplan uses only real LSAT questions, so you get the most comprehensive, testlike experience.

SET ONE

1. A

The first passage is pretty straight forward. It revolves around the author's argument that "pool" coverage of presidential debates stifles the news media's ability to gather and present news. Why does the author find such a limitation on the media alarming? She feels that it denies viewers an opportunity to gain maximum insight from presidential debates—that is, it sets limits on the amount and variety of information that the public receives. That's the passage's main point. Be aware that the author is talking about the actual "shooting" of a news event—the visual image broadcast to the viewer. She feels that a diversity of images is needed to illuminate an event fully. Although she concedes at the end of the passage that pool coverage may be the

only way to cover some events, she cautions against the indiscriminate use of such coverage.

Question 1 asks for the author's primary objection to pool coverage of presidential debates. As noted, the author is primarily concerned with the way pool coverage limits the public's exposure to a variety of viewpoints and information. (A) says exactly that and is the correct answer. The author never charges the pool coverage system with limiting the *number* of people who have access to televised debates. Her point is that it limits the number of *versions* of a debate being offered to people, so (B) is wrong. The author discusses the impact of a candidate's debate performance in the first paragraph. However, when examining the effects of pool coverage, the author clearly is thinking of the effect on the public's ability to judge, not on the candidates' ability to persuade, so (C) is out. (D) involves a similar distortion of the passage's contents. The author claims that pool coverage, by limiting the information viewers receive, hinders the public's ability to choose between candidates, not its right to choose. As for (E), the author salutes TV's ability to bring live debates into millions of living rooms across the country. Her argument doesn't include a discussion of the dangers of an "overreliance" by the public on television.

2. D

Take a look at the second paragraph and see what motivates the author's reference to court opinion. The author begins by anticipating a possible counterargument—that it doesn't matter what specific images people see as long as they know generally what happened. This argument would lead a proponent of pool coverage to say that the number of news organizations covering an event is irrelevant. At the end of the paragraph, the author attacks this counterargument by quoting a court decision. That is, she uses the words of the court to defend her views. If you realize this, you don't even have to look at the quote to infer the author's opinion of the court's findings. She must agree with them, right? The only choice that reflects this level of agreement is (D)—"substantially correct." (B) and (C) are way too negative, and (A) and (E) are not positive enough.

3. A

To answer question 3, take a close look at the second half of the first paragraph. The two benefits of a free press cited there are (1) its ability "to inform citizens about matters of public concern" and (2) its ability "to foster a marketplace of ideas in which the best options prevail." Both benefits are involved when television airs a presidential debate, and the author argues that diversity of coverage would maximize these benefits. (A) paraphrases this argument. The author doesn't mention these benefits as proposed "defenses" of pool coverage, and they certainly don't contradict each other, so (B) is off the mark. (C) is wrong. You more or less know this as soon as you see the verb *criticize*—it just doesn't fit what the author is doing. The same goes for (E); the author does not "reconcile" anything here. In fact, there's no need to—the different views on free press benefits are presented here as being complementary. Finally, (D) is dead wrong—the point of this paragraph is that First Amendment freedoms have a whole lot to do with presidential debates.

4. E

Question 4 asks how a proponent of the pool system would defend her viewpoint. Since the author argues that pool coverage limits the information provided to viewers, you need a choice that would challenge the author's point of view. (A) doesn't address this position. So what if broadcasters only rarely betray their political preferences in debate coverage? Pool coverage still limits viewers to coverage by only one of these broadcasters. (B) could be tempting too, but it also doesn't attack the author's main argument. The author concedes that pool coverage may be the only way to cover some events. But the drawbacks of such coverage still exist for non political events—and you might have to forgo "practicality" at some point in deference to larger issues. (C) strengthens the author's argument. If presidential debates are so complex that one broadcaster cannot cover them properly, we should allow coverage by a number of broadcasters. (D) is similar to (A) and is wrong for the same reason. (By the way, when you see that two or more answer on the LSAT are very similar, it's a strong signal that these are wrong. After all, there can be only

one right answer.) (E) is your last chance—and it's the correct answer. If small differences in style of coverage don't affect the amount of information conveyed to viewers, then the premise to the author's argument is blown out of the water. (E) would be the best remark for a proponent of pool coverage to make in its defense.

5. D

Question 5 is a Detail question. The authorial warning occurs in the last paragraph. There the author expresses the hope that the few situations in which pool coverage is necessary will not "foster … pool implementation in other situations." Unnecessary pool coverage translates to undesirable pool coverage for the author—so (D) is your answer. (A) comes out of left field—the author never mentions the dangers of analysis-crazed media. (Who knows, she might even welcome such a situation. It would provide the public with a lot of information, wouldn't it?) (B) calls attention to the author's fleeting reference—back in the first paragraph—to the First Amendment freedoms afforded the press. But in her discussion of these freedoms, the author never makes the specific argument that pool coverage violates them. So expanded use of pool coverage couldn't be referred to as a "further limitation."

(C) could have been tempting if you made things difficult for yourself. If you thought, "Well, gee, the author thinks pool coverage limits the informational content of presidential debates, so she probably would claim that expanded use of pool coverage would reduce the informational content of other news events, too." But such logical gymnastics shouldn't be necessary on the LSAT. The same thing goes for (E). The author does think pool coverage limits news gathering, but this point never arises in her final warning.

6. B

Question 6 calls your attention to lines 23–25, but you're actually dealing once again with the author's overall argument. The author feels that the pool system "denies viewers an opportunity to gain maximum insight from the debate" because the sharing of news coverage means that viewers are receiving only one set of images— only one version of the debate—not a wide variety representing various viewpoints. According to the author, this prevents individual broadcasters from conveying a unique account of the debate to their viewers. The question asks you to find an answer that would weaken the author's contention that this limitation adversely affects viewers' ability to make voting decisions.

(A) might be tempting. If debate performances don't sway many voters one way or another, what difference does it make what version of the debate they saw? But (A) doesn't address the author's specific argument concerning the effects of the pool system on voter insight. It doesn't matter if a debate doesn't have a major impact on the outcome of an election. What matters—to the author—is that the public has access to as much information as possible when deciding how to vote. So (A) wouldn't weaken the author's argument. (B) reveals a way to alleviate—if not make irrelevant—the limits that the pool system places on the public's access to a variety of ideas. If networks were to wrap up a debate with their own follow-up commentary, providing the public with a diversity of ideas that they then use as a basis for making voting decisions, then the author's objections to the pool system would be weakened. So (B) looks pretty good, but go on to the other choices. (C), (D), and (E) would all strengthen, not weaken, the author's argument. If (C) is correct, then the author's objections to pool coverage are right on the mark—no amount of postdebate coverage could make up for viewers' having access to only one visual version of a debate. If (D) is correct, the importance of televised coverage—and a variety of it—is emphasized all the more. Finally, (E) just restates the author's argument. "Competitive coverage" means the same thing as not using pool coverage.

7. B

Question 7 asks for the title that best describes the content of the passage. Wrong answers in such questions usually involve titles that are either too general or too specific—or those that are totally outside the scope. Take (A), for example. The author doesn't discuss how debate coverage changes voters' opinions, does she? Throw it out! The author also doesn't discuss the benefits or impracticalities of the pool system. Throw (C) out! Does the author discuss how First Amendment press rights

conflict with presidential politics? Nope—forget (D). How about (E)? In the first paragraph, the author does touch on the influence exercised by televised presidential debates. But the brunt of the passage involves the pool system and the limitations it imposes on public access to information. That's (B), your answer—the only choice that accurately reflects the author's main concerns.

For Comparative Reading Passages

Like all comparative reading passages, these two have the same topic: increase in mortgage foreclosures in the late 1990s to early 2000s. They also share a scope: the causes and impact of that increase. Next, we have to identify the purpose/main idea for each passage independently.

Passage A: The author's main idea is that many home buyers were led into poor mortgage decisions and are now paying the price by losing their homes.

Passage B: The main idea in Passage B is that irresponsible borrowing created a problem that will impact the economy as a whole.

Having assessed topic, scope, purpose, and main idea just as we do in regular passages (except that we have two purposes/main ideas), we move on to the one step that differs in reading comparative passages: Before moving on to the questions, we need to get a handle on the relationship between the passages.

The best starting point is to examine each passage's purpose/main idea. Passage A describes the industry factors that led to the large number of subprime loans in the late 1990s and early 2000s and the impact on those home buyers, while Passage B assigns the home buyers a large share of the blame and explores the potential impact on society. But each author writes as though unaware of the other—one passage isn't responsive to the other or a direct rebuttal.

Since comparative passages are so short, we won't need Road Maps. Once we have T/S/P/MI and the relationship between the passages in hand, we can jump into the questions.

8. C

This Inference question asks for common ground between the two authors. Because these two authors don't agree about much, you might be able to predict an answer; if not, simply work through the answer choices looking for some common ground. It is often efficient to attack the "most likely agree" or "most likely disagree" questions in a comparative reading passage in the same way as you would a point-at-issue question. In answer choice (C), both authors explicitly mention declining home values as part of the larger problem. This is the correct answer!

Only the author of Passage B blames the homeowners—and only the author of Passage B discusses the cost to the economy as a whole. Eliminate (A). The author of Passage A suggests that buyers received inadequate information, but there's no indication that the author of Passage B agrees. Eliminate (B). This is explicitly stated by the author of Passage A, but the author of Passage B doesn't address this. This answer choice is a good reminder that "likely" in an Inference question stem requires something more than just the fact that something seems reasonable and doesn't contradict the author—he must have given us a basis for concluding that he'd agree. Eliminate (D). The author of Passage B suggests this when he says that part of the blame falls on the marketing machine that created the impression that it was "every person's right to attain home ownership and the American dream regardless of financial position." However, the author of Passage A doesn't mention this at all. Eliminate (E).

9. C

Relationships-between-the-passage questions are common in comparative reading passages, and fortunately, you've already analyzed that up front. The answer to this question is easy to predict (and you shouldn't even consider looking at the answer choices without formulating the answer in your mind): We determined that both of our authors were examining the increase in mortgage foreclosures but from very different perspectives as far as causes and impacts. That's correct answer choice (C). Don't be put off by the fact that the right answer seems a bit less specific than some of the wrong answer choices—remember that this isn't a Detail question.

(A) is too focused on homeowners—both examine the increase in foreclosures, but the author of Passage B isn't concerned with the problems of the homeowners. (B)—Passage A does more than describe a problem—it also delves into causes and what's likely to come next. (D)—Although the author of Passage B clearly disagrees with Passage A's characterization of the causes of the crisis, he doesn't directly refute any point raised in Passage A. In fact, we already determined that the two passages were entirely independent. (E) Neither author offers a solution.

10. E

Again, rely on the work you've already done. We identified two key differences when assessing the relationship between the passages: The authors disagreed about who was to blame and considered the ramifications from different perspectives. But the second discrepancy wasn't really a point of disagreement—they simply looked at different aspects. That leaves "who is to blame?" That's correct answer choice (E).

(A) is addressed only by the author of Passage B, but we have no reason to believe that the author of Passage A would disagree. (B) might be tempting at a glance, because it appears to speak to the issue of whether the lenders/brokers or the borrowers are to blame. However, while only author A suggests that these loans shouldn't have been offered, the author of Passage B does not contradict that idea. In fact, he would probably agree, although for somewhat different reasons. (C)—Passage A makes a prediction about the number of foreclosures still to come, but the author of Passage B doesn't make any predictions. (D)—Passage A does not talk about investors at all.

11. D

Most questions in comparative reading passages refer to both passages and require you to understand the relationship between them, but the occasional question, like this one, focuses on a single passage. Make sure to focus on that passage and forget everything you read in the other for purposes of such a question. (D) is correct—the second paragraph in Passage B says that investors and economies are suffering.

(A) is a concern expressed by the author of Passage A, not B. (B) is a distortion—the author of Passage B does blame irresponsible borrower behavior, but he doesn't say anything about that trend continuing. (C) is another position set forth by the author of Passage A. (E) isn't suggested by either author.

12. C

Again, revisit the work you did up front. This was one of the two differences we already noted. And what was the difference? Not so much direct disagreement as that the author of Passage A was concerned with the impact on the borrowers, whereas the author of Passage B was focused on investors and the broader economic implications. That's answer choice (C).

(A) is incorrect because each author describes a set of serious consequences; they're simply different ones. You won't be asked to make a judgment like the one that would be required to decide which of their projections is "more serious." (B) is reversed—the author of Passage A focuses only on homeowners, while author B looks at the bigger picture. In (D), the author of Passage B doesn't take any position whatsoever on what will happen to homeowners. With (E), the difference between the two authors' assessments of the consequences isn't about the long or short range; one looks at homeowners and the other looks at investors and society, but there is no clear discrepancy in the time frame.

SET TWO

1. D

The author begins the passage by discussing why Edmund Burke's belief in how governments are formed contrasts with his philosophical forefather John Locke's idealistic belief that people choose to join their governments. Unlike Locke, Burke believed that people are the "product of society, born to an inheritance of rights... and of reciprocal duties" and that government and prescription are paramount and limit the "right" of revolution. (D) is the only answer that encompasses the full scope of the passage. (A) distorts the last paragraph, where the author reports that Burke sees the right of revolution as a limited one of last resort. (B) can't be

the right answer, because Burke felt that people are born into a political system without first consciously making a decision to join it—it is his predecessor, Locke, who believed that societies are formed voluntarily. (C) contradicts Burke's belief that societies exist of necessity and that individuals exist as "a product of society." Finally, (E) is incorrect because Burke never speaks of a particular *form* of government, only of the importance of government and prescription.

2. B

The author clearly states at the beginning of the second paragraph that "there is, therefore, no right of revolution, or rebellion at will," which eliminates (A). The second paragraph states that "revolution is always the annulment of some rights," leading to correct answer (B). Burke took issue with the way that the French Assembly made destroying the existing structure of their government their "daily bread." He believed that the present government should reflect the prescriptions and traditions leading up to it. For this reason, (C) is incorrect. (D) is wrong because the text, while explaining that Burke was not for revolutions, did not say that he was concerned with the individual's freedom. (E) is incorrect because, while Locke's concept of the social contract is discussed (and contrasted with Burke's opinions on how societies are built), revolution is never outlined as an inherent right of the social contract concept.

3. A

Near the beginning of the second paragraph, Burke is quoted as saying, "there is a sacred veil to be drawn over the beginnings of all government." The author goes on to say, "In any ancient community such as that of France or Britain, every constituent factor, including what we choose to call the people, is the product of convention. The privileges of every order, the rights of every individual, rest upon prescription embodied in law or established by usage," leading to correct answer (A). (B) contradicts the idea that the rules are developed over time and passed down through society. (C) lifts language from the passage, but there is no link in the passage between the behavior of individuals and their treatment. (D) is incorrect because the author says the prescriptions that dictate the course of society are evolved and become ingrained, not "evershifting." (E) is not the correct answer, because the author has stated that the origins of a society are cut off from the prescriptions.

4. C

Burke disagreed with Locke's philosophies, which had dominated Western political thought of the 18th century, for many reasons. Because this is an EXCEPT question, it may be most efficient to eliminate the choices that *are* aspects of Locke's philosophy we're told Burke doesn't accept. Correct choice (C) *is* a point of contention between Locke and Burke, but this is Burke's view— Locke believed that individuals "contracted" to form society. If you recognize that immediately, great—if not, eliminate the rest. Burke disagreed with Locke's belief that the individual consciously chose whether or not to be part of the society around them, so eliminate (A). Burke believed that society built upon the prescription and traditions of the past, while Locke said that the claims of society were "continually tested" as it evolved, so (B) is not the answer. (D) can be eliminated, because Burke felt that the way people are treated depends on the customs their society has built up about an individual's treatment. Like (B), (E) is incorrect, because Burke believed that the individual had much less to do with the formation of his or her society, compared to the laws and customs that came before, whereas Locke believed that the "contract" was subject to continual analysis and modification.

5. D

(D) is the statement that the author would most likely agree with—Burke did recognize that some change was required and, indeed, that even revolution was occasionally necessary. In the last paragraph, we're told that he believed that the proper role of the Assembly was to "preserve *and reform*." The same information contradicts (A). Burke stressed the importance of continuity and tradition in government, so (B) can be eliminated. Both (C) and (E) can be eliminated, as Burke's philosophy focused on society as a whole and eschewed individualism.

6. C

The end of the second paragraph discusses Burke's belief that individuals breaking a society are unprepared for the long, difficult road toward re-establishing society. The last paragraph tells us that revolution necessarily destroys some rights and should be undertaken only as a last resort because of the difficulty of rebuilding society. (C) sums up these cautionary words. (A) directly contradicts this idea, claiming that revolution is a *good* solution. The whole last paragraph tells us unequivocally that Burke doesn't believe so. (B) is wrong because other political processes are not discussed in relation to revolution. (D), despite inviting familiar language from the passage, can't be right because it was Locke, not Burke, who believed in a social contract that individuals chose to agree to. (E) again lifts language from the passage, but it's language that relates to the formation of society, not to the role of revolution.

7. A

To answer this question correctly, you must clearly recognize that Burke was attacking the ideology of Locke. Only a very small piece of the passage talks about Locke's beliefs, near the beginning of the first paragraph. Being aware of "who said what" in a passage that sets forth more than one point of view is critical. We learn in the first paragraph that Locke was interested in what he termed the "social contract," where individuals, who are born with certain rights, decide if they want to join society. Locke also believed that participation in society and its claim on the rights of the individual were subject to continual reassessment. (A) describes a work that would elaborate on those points. (B) is incorrect because Locke believed the power of society derived from the consent of its members. (C) may look tempting because the passage talks quite a bit about the importance of evolved prescription and pre-existing societal rights—but those are Burke's views, not Locke's. (D) can be eliminated for the same reason. (E) is also not likely, because Locke believed all people were born with inherent rights.

8. D

In the first paragraph of the passage, the author states that the results of the new test "suggest that almost half of over 50,000 U.S. women diagnosed with estrogen-dependent, lymph-node-negative breast cancer every year are at low risk for recurrence and may not need to go through the discomfort and side effects of chemotherapy." Paragraph 2 includes a paraphrase of this information, and in the last paragraph, the author reiterates, "Women with low recurrence scores, who represent about 50 percent of these patients, derived minimal benefits from chemotherapy." So (D) is the correct answer. Both of these pieces of text contradict wrong answer (A). (B) is incorrect because if almost half of the women diagnosed are at low risk, "the vast majority" can't be at high risk. In fact, information from the study tells us that 27 percent of the subjects were at high risk. (C) is a distortion—we know chemotherapy isn't especially beneficial to these women, but the author specifically stated that the group hadn't been large enough to determine whether or not chemo was detrimental. (E) makes a comparison that's never addressed in the passage—the only thing the author tells us categorically is that chemotherapy seems not to be necessary/beneficial for low-risk women. He says nothing about what *is* the best course of treatment, though tamoxifen might be tempting because it's familiar from the passage.

9. C

Because this is a Global question, look at your topic/ scope/ purpose and your road map before the answer choices. We've already determined that the author's purpose here was to inform us about this test and its benefits, which is a perfect match for answer (C). (A) is outside the scope of the passage—there's no mention of public interest or of a positive impact that's *already* taken place, only the one that is now possible. (B) isn't mentioned at all, although the study group did come from the test group for another drug. (D) may be tempting, in that the author does tell us that the test seems to be effective, but only one small piece of the passage is devoted to the method; the correct answer to a Global question must encompass the passage as a whole. (E) is incorrect because the specific benefits and disadvantages aren't addressed, only the fact that there are benefits for one group but not the other.

10. E

For this Detail question, begin with your road map and look up the answer. Where did the author talk about who would and would not benefit from chemotherapy? The last paragraph. So look back and see what the passage says. The only information we're given is that women at a high risk of recurrence benefit and those at a low risk do not. So who *would* benefit, as the question asks? Someone at a high risk of recurrence, which is (E). Women with low recurrence scores didn't benefit much from chemotherapy, so (A) is wrong. (B) introduces an element that's totally outside the scope of the passage— all of the women studied were taking tamoxifen. (C) also makes the tamoxifen a factor, though we have no means of determining the impact of tamoxifen use on the need for chemotherapy since we have studied only women taking tamoxifen. (D) is wrong because all we're told is that the levels of expression (increased *or* decreased) form the basis for prediction—we don't know the meaning of increased expression in particular.

11. D

This question asks about the general organization of the passage, which you should already have laid out in your road map. Although the details might be a bit complex, the basic structure of the passage isn't too complicated— which is often the case in science-based passages. Correct choice (D) provides a good summary: A process (the new test) is introduced and explained, then its efficacy is discussed (through the data showing the accuracy of its predictions), and finally, the potential benefits (saving women from unnecessary chemotherapy) are set forth. (A) can be eliminated with a glance at the first clause— the passage begins by describing the *test*, not a medicine. Likewise, (B) goes wrong immediately: The passage doesn't begin with a problem but with an announcement of the new test. (C) starts out right, because a process *is* outlined (the process of testing for levels of expression of a panel of cancer-related genes), but no negative consequences are described. (E) takes a wrong turn at "critiqued" and another at "generalized." Either of those verbs alone is enough to eliminate this answer choice.

12. B

In a Detail/EXCEPT question, the most efficient approach is generally to locate those items that *are* found in the passage and eliminate them. (A) is stated directly in the first paragraph. Correct choice (B) is a distortion—hormone therapy is mentioned, but the only treatment option that is discussed in terms of its efficacy or necessity is chemotherapy. We're told in paragraphs 5 and 6 that the recurrence scores are reliable, so we can eliminate (C). (D) can be eliminated because paragraph 6 tells us that the correlation between recurrence scores and actual rates of recurrence are consistent regardless of age group and tumor size. The final paragraph indicates that women with high-recurrence risk benefit greatly from chemotherapy, eliminating (E).

13. B

The result of the recurrence score tests is that by looking at "levels of expression (increased or decreased) of a panel of cancer-related genes" scientists can accurately predict the likelihood of recurrence, so (B) is correct. (A) and (C) are directly contradicted when paragraph 6 states that the findings of the study "held across age groups and tumor size," but an efficient approach to this question won't require elimination—it will require only looking up the correct answer and matching it with (B). Tamoxifen, again, is a red herring. It's mentioned in the passage, but not for its own value as a treatment, so (D) can be eliminated. As for (E), there's a correlation between the recurrence score and chemotherapy, but this answer has it backward, suggesting that chemotherapy determines the likelihood of recurrence when the passage tells us that the likelihood of recurrence determines the need for chemotherapy.

14. D

Because this is a wide-open Inference question with a stem that provides no direction to the appropriate section of the passage, we'll have to go straight to the answer choices. (A) refers to a patient who falls in the intermediate risk group—a group we know very little about, and nothing in terms of the benefits of chemotherapy. (B) ties the success of the test to tamoxifen. It's true that we've only seen the efficacy of the test in the context of patients taking tamoxifen,

but we can't predict that it would be any less accurate in other patients—we simply don't have enough information from the passage to know one way or the other. (C) directly contradicts the last paragraph, which says that we don't have enough information yet to determine whether chemotherapy is detrimental to low risk patients. (D), although similar, refers to the belief of "some doctors," not a provable fact. We know that at least one doctor—the one quoted in the last paragraph—thinks chemotherapy has negative effects because she refers to "harmful short- and long-term side effects." Note also the distinction between the language of (D)'s "negatively impact" a patient versus the more specific (and unsupportable) "increase the risk of recurrence" in (C). (E) is close but distorts the numbers—we're told that *almost half* of the women being treated with chemotherapy could do without it, not "more than half."

SET THREE

1. B

(B) is the correct answer because paragraph 6 explains that in Hitler's Germany, the currency was non-exportable and had to be invested in physical art that would later be sold. This directly contradicts (A). As for (C), the only information we're given about personal property in the passage is that Jews who were not leaving "Greater Germany" were required to register it with the police. Likewise, (D) is unlikely since paragraph 2 states that works by these artists were among those confiscated by the Nazis. The last paragraph states that most European art dealers took advantage of the political situation in Germany to acquire art for less than it was truly worth, so (E) is also unlikely.

2. C

The passage begins by explaining how the Nazi Party undertook to purge certain art (particularly that of the Weimar era) that it deemed decadent, describes that process in more detail, and then sets forth the role that art came to play in financial transactions—a perfect match for (C). (A) can be eliminated readily for two reasons: It's too strong in its terminology ("ironclad distinctions"), and it addresses only a small portion of the passage and, therefore, can't be the correct answer to a Global question. (B) is tempting because the passage does discuss how art was used by the individual and the German government during this time for various financial purposes, but it also fails to take in the passage as a whole. Paragraphs 5 and 6 refer to the treatment and experiences of Jewish people and how art played a role in that, but there is no indication that art collecting was a cause of the persecution or that those who collected art were singled out, so (D) is incorrect. It, too, focuses in on one specific aspect of the passage rather than the global aspects. The effects of Hitler's attitudes about art on the German art world are not the main focus of the piece—it is merely one of the facts the passage touches upon, so (E) is incorrect.

3. D

In paragraph 3, the author explains that Hitler wanted German artists to aspire to creating "a new art, an art that portrayed the *Volk* and the *Volksgemeinschaft* (*Volk* community) as "a realization not of individual talents or of the inspiration of a lone genius, but of the collective expression of the *Volk*, channeled through the souls of individual creators.'" The paragraph goes on to explain that Hitler wanted new German art to be "folk-related" and "race-conscious," taking the place of what he believed to be decadent artists of the previous Weimar regime. So (D) is correct. In the passage's second paragraph, cubist art is one of the types of art listed as being considered degenerate by the Nazis, so (A) is out. (B) can't be right because paragraph 3 explained that Hitler wanted artists to focus on creating what he felt was a "collective expression of the *Volk*," not the artistic expression of the individual. In paragraph 2, the passage lists masterworks by van Gogh and Matisse as some of the "degenerate" artwork that the Nazi government auctioned off to raise money for the regime, so (C) is wrong. The only reference to art in Poland comes in paragraph 5, where the author tells us that art was confiscated in Poland after 1939. The passage doesn't even state explicitly whether this was Polish art or simply art that was in Poland at that time, and it certainly makes no claim of Nazi approval, so (E) is wrong.

4. E

(E) is the exception, because paragraph 2 states this type of art was exactly the type to incur the label "degenerate." There is mention of Party officials collecting such art in paragraph 4, but it's set forth as a deviation, not a party goal. (A) is incorrect because paragraph 1 states that Hitler detested the art of the Weimar period of government that came before it, the passage states in paragraph 3 that he termed it "Jewish decadence." (B) is incorrect, because the Nazi government profited from the art it chose to censor, as outlined in paragraph 2. Paragraph 3 discusses what art of the past and present Hitler wanted to support, and German Renaissance and medieval works were included, so (C) is not the exception. (D) is not the exception either, because paragraph 5 discusses the systematized censorship of art in Austria and Poland.

5. B

(B) is correct because Hitler clearly hated Jewish people and wanted to eradicate their "degeneracy" from Germany in what he saw as its many forms. One of the motivations for the artistic changes set in motion by the Nazi Party was to rid Germany of the "Jewish decadence" of the Weimar era. In paragraph 3, Hitler's belief that art's new direction needed to be in a more collective, less individual approach is discussed, so (A) is not correct. (C) is incorrect because the passage never discusses destruction of art, just that art deemed "degenerate" was sold to make the Nazi Party more money. (D) is wrong because the last paragraph states, "When the Nazis banned the exportation of paper money, wealthy émigrés began to turn their investments into art. Because the Nazis lacked a useable foreign currency, artworks were often used as an alternative to money." So the black market trade did not cause the creation of a useable currency abroad. Paragraph 4 explains, "For Nazi officers seeking social status and promotion within the Party, collecting and giving art confirmed one's dedication to promoting Nazi racial ideologies in the Reich." So (E) is wrong.

6. E

Paragraph 3 describes Hitler's interest in fostering a new type of art, which is "race-conscious" and "folk-related," so (E) is the correct answer. (A) is incorrect because that same paragraph discourages individualism in art. (B) is a tantalizing choice, because the last paragraph does discuss how Jewish people were forced to invest in art to take their money with them when they left Germany, but the passage does not say that the Nazis intended this to be a means of assistance for the Jews. This was just a side result of the policies the Nazi Party had concerning currency. Hitler wished to eradicate what he saw as the "decadent" attitude from the German art world during the Weimar era, so (C) is incorrect. (D) is incorrect because Hitler believed that art should champion the *Volk* people and that other races were inferior.

7. C

We already determined during our passage overview that the author was primarily concerned with explaining the restrictions on women's intellectual development and the way that novels played into those limitations: that's a close match for (C). (A) is clearly incorrect because it directly contradicts the author's negative attitude toward the value of novels. The answer also can't be (B), because she *does* believe men receive better educations than women do. The author discusses the topics common to novels only briefly—it's neither a "catalog" nor the main focus of the passage. Remember that to be correct, a Global answer choice must take in the passage as a whole. (E) is incorrect because the novel's sentimentality and simplistic ideas about how women should be focused on romance—the antithesis of feminism—are part of the reason Wollstonecraft dislikes them, as she explains in paragraph 1.

8. E

In the second paragraph, the author tells us that women's lack of access to political participation narrows their view and "sentiments become events," which is a match for (E). (A) directly contradicts paragraph 2's assertion that the primary business of female life is to please, and (B) is contradicted in various places, in particular paragraph 2's mention of the denial of political privileges and paragraph 6's note that many women were not led to proper studies nor "permitted to choose for themselves." These same references contradict answer (C). The author makes no reference to the superiority or inferiority of

men versus women—only their respective rights and positions in society. Therefore, (D) is a distortion.

9. D

Wollstonecraft is concerned (in paragraph 5) that women learn about sex even without a good education but in a crude and unrefined way, so (D) is correct. The same paragraph describes how that improper learning leads to crude expression, so (B) can't be the exception. In paragraph 6, Wollstonecraft is concerned that women either stay intellectually childish or only learn some street-smart common sense but never "what deserves the name of intellect, the power of gaining general or abstract ideas, or even intermediate ones"; consequently, (E) can't be the exception. She also states in paragraph 6 that these women's minds were inactive from not being used, which caused them to be "low-spirited," and they "would cry, or go to sleep," so (A) is not the exception. In paragraphs 4 and 5, she discusses a mother who tries to raise her daughters to be what she knows to be well educated, but because she herself was only educated as a woman, she did not know what her daughters' education was missing; (C) is not the exception either.

10. D

In the second paragraph of the passage, Wollstonecraft says, "The mighty business of female life is to please," so (D) is correct. In this paragraph, Wollstonecraft also notes that women are denied political privileges and opportunities that might act to get them involved in the working toward the greater good, so (B) is incorrect. Women were unable to work or have money of their own, so (A) is wrong. (C) can't be right, because the main point of Wollstonecraft's passage is that women are not provided with the means to develop any true intellect at all. (E) is a distortion—the coarseness of speech of certain women was mentioned in the passage but not with regard to defining a woman's worth.

11. C

Even though Wollstonecraft is not in favor of women reading novels, she does concede in paragraph 3 that she thinks that any type of reading is "better than leaving a blank still a blank, because the mind must receive a degree of enlargement and obtain a little strength by a slight exertion of its thinking powers." If reading novels were a gateway to reading more intellectually stimulating books, Wollstonecraft's opposition to novels would be negated, so (C) is correct. (E) is wrong, because Wollstonecraft would agree that many women find novels enjoyable, but that that is precisely the problem with them, because novelists "work up stale tales, all retailed in a sentimental jargon, which equally tend to corrupt the taste, and draw the heart aside from its daily duties" (paragraph 1). Likewise, (A) and (D) are wrong because one of Wollstonecraft's main objections to novels is that she feels that novelists tend to focus on love and base sexuality. She states in paragraph 2 that "the mighty business of female life is to please," which keeps them from "entering into more important concerns by political and civil oppression," and she is upset that for these women, love takes on a supreme importance and "sentiments become events, and reflection deepens what it should, and would have effaced, if the understanding had been allowed to take a wider range." (B) is also wrong, because Wollstonecraft would agree that novels encourage women toward vice, and that point supports her negative conclusions about novels.

12. A

In the last paragraph, Wollstonecraft states that she feels that the best way to curb young women's fondness for novels is have a "judicious person, with some turn for humor," read several novels to a young woman and "point out both by tones, and apt comparisons with pathetic incidents and heroic characters in history, how foolishly and ridiculously they caricatured human nature, just opinions might be substituted instead of romantic sentiments." Consequently, (A) is correct. She cautions that an adult not make fun of all novels, because that would "have little effect," so (B) is wrong. (C) is incorrect because Wollstonecraft believed a sense of humor is needed to prove how silly and inaccurate novels are. Throughout the passage, Wollstonecraft bemoans the preoccupation women have with romantic love, but while she appears to feel that this besmirches the grandeur of love, she never states that love itself is evil, so (D) is wrong. As we saw in the example she provides in paragraphs 4 and 5, making young women read books that are much too difficult for them is only going to discourage them from reading quality texts, pushing them toward less illuminating interests, so (E) is also incorrect.

CHAPTER 6: WRITING SAMPLE

- Anatomy of the Writing Sample
- Kaplan's 4-Step Method for the Writing Sample

This section tests your ability to write a clean, concise, and persuasive argument under time constraints. No outside knowledge is necessary.

ANATOMY OF THE WRITING SAMPLE

You are given a prompt consisting of a problem, two criteria or goals that must be met in addressing the problem, and two possible courses of action. You'll have 35 minutes at the end of your LSAT day to make a written case for your position.

Your essay must be confined to the space provided, which is roughly the equivalent of two sheets of standard lined paper. Usually, two or three paragraphs will be enough. Note that there's really no time or space to change your mind or radically alter your essay once you've begun writing, so *plan your argument out carefully before beginning to write*. Make sure to write as legibly as you can.

 READ MORE

The Writing Sample is a factor in admissions decisions. Take it seriously and read on.

The Writing Sample is ungraded, but it is sent to law schools along with your LSAT score. In fact it's the second page admissions committee members see when they open and review your packet from LSAC! Many law schools use the Writing Sample to help make decisions on borderline cases or to decide between applicants with otherwise comparable credentials. Granted, it may not carry the same weight as the scored sections of the test, but since it can impact on your admission chances, your best bet is to take it seriously.

The following is an example of a Writing Sample prompt:

> The *Daily Tribune*, a metropolitan newspaper, is considering two candidates for promotion to business editor. Write an argument for one candidate over the other with the following considerations in mind:
>
> - The editor must train new writers and assign stories.
> - The editor must be able to edit and rewrite stories under daily deadline pressure.

Laura received a BA in English from a large university. She was managing editor of her college newspaper and served as a summer intern at her hometown daily paper. Laura started working at the *Tribune* right out of college and spent three years at the city desk covering the city economy. Eight years ago, the paper formed its business section, and Laura became part of the new department. After several years covering state business, Laura began writing on the national economy. Three years ago, Laura was named senior business and finance editor on the national business staff; she is also responsible for supervising seven writers.

Palmer attended an elite private college where he earned both a BS in business administration and an MA in journalism. After receiving his journalism degree, Palmer worked for three years on a monthly business magazine. He won a prestigious national award for a series of articles on the impact of monetary policy on multinational corporations. Palmer came to the *Tribune* three years ago to fill the newly created position of international business writer. He was the only member of the international staff for two years and wrote on almost a daily basis. He now supervises a staff of four writers. Last year, Palmer developed a bimonthly business supplement for the *Tribune* that has proved highly popular and has helped increase the paper's circulation.

 **READ MORE**

LSAC offers a wide sampling of essay topics with its practice tests. The more of them you examine, the more likely that you'll have relevant ideas prepared for test day.

KAPLAN'S 4-STEP METHOD FOR THE WRITING SAMPLE

1. BRAINSTORM

Before you start to write, read the prompt objectively so you understand the problem, then read the criteria and alternative solutions. Consider the strengths and weaknesses of each option, evaluate them in light of the criteria presented, and then pick your winning solution.

Don't obsess over your position. Nobody really cares which choice you make (for example, whether you choose to support Laura or Palmer). What's important is how well you support your position. Generally, the alternatives are written to be pretty evenly matched, so there's no right or wrong answer. Your essay will either have a well-supported or ill-supported position.

Use the scrap paper provided to brainstorm your essay. Set aside five minutes for this important step. Writing off-topic suggests that you are unable to focus your ideas—or that you don't care.

2. PLAN

Now that you have reviewed the pros and cons of the two options, you must decide which arguments to make and in what order to support your choice and to dismiss the option you reject. Take five minutes for this step to prioritize your thinking and organize your paragraphs.

Use a clear, simple structure to set up your argument. You can decide in advance how to present your response. One possibility is the "winner/loser" format, in which the first paragraph begins with a statement of choice and then discusses the reason why your choice (the winner) is superior. The next paragraph focuses on why the other alternative (the loser) is not as good and should end with a concluding sentence reaffirming your decision. Another possibility is the "criteria" format, in which the first paragraph discusses both the winner and the loser in light of the first criterion, and the second paragraph discusses them both in light of the second criterion.

Mention, but downplay, the strengths of the opposing view. Use sentence structures that allow you to do this, such as, "Even though Palmer won a prestigious national award ...," and then attempt to demonstrate why this is really no big deal. Try to do the same thing for at least one of the winner's obvious weaknesses. Doing so demonstrates that you see the full picture. Recognizing and dealing with possible objections make your argument that much stronger.

Continue using the scrap paper for this step.

3. WRITE

Write well. It sounds obvious, of course, but you should try to make your prose as clean and flawless as you can. Some people get so entangled in content that they neglect the mechanics of essay writing. But spelling, grammar, and writing mechanics are important. Use structural signals to keep your writing fluid and clear, and use transitions between paragraphs to keep the entire essay unified.

Don't simply repeat the facts from the prompt; instead, present them persuasively. Try to offer an interpretation of the facts in light of the stated criteria. If you're arguing for Laura, you can't state simply that "Laura was named senior business and finance editor on the national business staff," and expect the reader to infer that's a good thing. For all we know, being in that position may be a detriment in terms of the criteria—training new writers and working under daily deadline pressure. It's up to you to indicate why certain facts about the winner are positive factors in light of the criteria and vice versa for facts about the loser. Merely parroting what's written in the topic won't win you any points with the law schools.

Your space is limited, so make each sentence count. Be sure to stick with your plan, communicate concisely, and write in the active voice. Use 25 minutes to write your argument. Above all, write legibly.

4. PROOFREAD

Don't skip this step. Save two minutes to proofread your argument and correct spelling and grammatical errors. Planning to proofread also helps ensure that you will complete the essay.

 READ MORE

Check out the *Kaplan LSAT Writing Workbook*! You'll get review and exercises for essential writing basics, organization and time-management strategies, more LSAT practice prompts, and advice on how to write dynamic, successful personal statements for your law school applications!

SAMPLE ESSAY

Using the sample prompt from pages 159–160 to write an essay, using the two lined pages that follow and observing the 35-minute time limit. Then check your essay, making sure it observes the basic principles.

_____

_____

_____

_____

_____

_____

_____

_____

_____

_____

_____

_____

_____

_____

_____

_____

_____

SAMPLE RESPONSE

Compare your answer to the following sample response:

> Both candidates are obviously qualified, but Laura is the better choice. For one thing, Laura has been working at the *Tribune* for eleven years and has, therefore, had plenty of opportunity to learn the workings of the paper. For another, her experience has, been in national rather than international business, and national business will certainly be the focus of the *Tribune's* financial coverage. In her current capacity, she is responsible for writing and editing articles while simultaneously overseeing the work of a staff of seven. Clearly, then, Laura can work under deadline pressure and manage a staff, a capability she demonstrated at an early age as the managing director of her college newspaper. Although Laura's academic credentials may not measure up to Palmer's, her background in English, her history of steady promotions, and her work as senior national business writer—combined with a solid business knowledge and obvious drive for accomplishment—will certainly spur the department to journalistic excellence.

> Palmer's résumé is admirable but is nonetheless inferior to Laura's. True, Palmer has evidently done a fine job managing the international section, but his staff numbers only four, and the scope of the venture is smaller than Laura's. True, Palmer's articles on the impact of monetary policy did win an award in the past, but since he has been working for the *Tribune*, no such honors have been forthcoming. Not only does Palmer lack the English literature background that Laura has, but he also lacks her long experience at the *Tribune*. Furthermore, Palmer's editing experience seems slight, considering the length of his current tenure and the size of his staff, and while he demonstrates competence in the area of international business, he has little experience in the national business area.

> In light of these circumstances, the newspaper would meet its stated objectives best by promoting Laura to the position of business editor.

This generally well-reasoned and well-written essay would be an asset to any applicant's law school admissions file. The writer states his or her choice in the first sentence and then substantiates this choice in a paragraph on the winner and a paragraph on the loser. Notice the way this writer acknowledges, yet rebuts, the winner's flaws and the loser's strengths. Whether or not one agrees with the choice of Laura over Palmer, the essay definitely makes an organized, well-reasoned case for the choice—and that, after all, is what the law schools will be looking for.

Now do the practice essay provided in the following pages.

WRITING SAMPLE PRACTICE

ESSAY ONE

<u>Directions:</u> The scenario presented below describes two choices. In your essay, argue *for* one choice and *against* the other, based on the two specified criteria and the facts provided. There is no right or wrong answer.

Newlyweds Lauren and Michael Tompkins are moving to Centerville, a large city with an active downtown and a network of suburbs. Michael will be starting a new job at a prestigious investment banking firm, and Lauren will be attending graduate school. Keeping the following considerations in mind, write an argument supporting one of the two housing options described.

- The Tompkinses have $20,000 in savings.

- The Tompkinses are planning on starting a family in a few years.

The couple is considering buying a two-bedroom condo in a renovated building downtown. It is within walking distance of Michael's office and near other amenities like restaurants, clubs, museums, and movie theatres, but a trip to the supermarket will entail a long bus ride. Lauren will also have to ride the bus or take the train to the university, which is located in the suburb of Hillsdale. Should the couple buy a car, they will have to pay monthly for parking in the building. Their monthly mortgage and maintenance fees would be $1,000, and the parking fee is an extra $200 per month.

The Tompkinses are also considering renting a three-bedroom house with a driveway in historic Millston, a suburb adjacent to Hillsdale and about 30 minutes outside of the city. The house, though old, is in good condition, and the landlord lives next door. There is a commuter rail station a few blocks from the house. The train runs both downtown and to the university in Hillsdale, though given the house's suburban location, a car would be very useful. With the money they would have used for a down payment on the condo, the Tompkinses could afford a new car. Millston also has excellent public schools. If the Tompkinses sign a two-year lease, the rent including utilities will be $850 per month.

_____

_____

_____

_____

_____

_____

_____

_____

_____

_____

_____

_____

_____

_____

_____

_____

_____

_____

_____

_____

_____

_____

_____

_____

SAMPLE RESPONSE

The Tompkinses should buy the condo in downtown Centerville rather than rent the house in Millston. Given their $20,000 in savings, real estate will prove to be a better investment than a new car for this young couple. Even though the condo seems to cost more in the short run, in the long run, it will more than pay for itself. Michael will likely be required to work long hours, whereas Lauren's schedule will be more flexible, making proximity to his job a priority. The Tompkinses should take advantage of this time before they have children to live in the city and enjoy an urban lifestyle. Michael's job gives him excellent earning potential, so if Lauren finds the commute to her classes via public transportation to be too inconvenient, the couple will soon be able to afford a used car and the additional charge to park it in their building.

The suburban house would be a better choice if the Tompkinses already had children. Its advantages (larger size, good schools) would be most appealing to a larger family. Since the Tompkinses plan to wait a few years before having a child, these advantages are negated by the long commute for Michael and the lack of investment in the rental property. Even though a new car would be nice, it too makes more sense once the couple has kids. Although they would be paying less each month for the house, paying for a rental when they can afford to buy does not make good financial sense.

It would not be prudent for the Tompkinses to make living arrangements best suited to a family with children when their plans to have a baby are still several years off. In these few years, they may decide to move somewhere else entirely, in which case they may be able to make a profit on selling their condo rather than take a loss on the rental of the house.

This essay makes a good case for the writer's choice of the condo over the house. The writer states his or her opinion in the first sentence and then clearly emphasizes the strengths of the condo option in the first paragraph. The second paragraph acknowledges the attractions of the house but convincingly argues that the condo is still a better choice for the Tompkins family. This is the kind of essay law schools will be looking for.

CHAPTER 7: THE FINAL WEEK

Is it starting to feel as though your whole life is a buildup to the LSAT? You've known about it for years, worried about it for months, and now spent weeks in solid preparation for it. As the test gets closer, you may find your anxiety is on the rise.

You shouldn't worry. After the preparation you've received from Kaplan, you're in good shape for the test. To calm any pretest jitters you may have, though, let's go over a few strategies for the days before the test.

THE WEEK BEFORE THE TEST

The week or so leading up to the test should be all about keeping up your skills but avoiding burnout and anxiety. You should do the following:

- Recheck your admission ticket for accuracy; if corrections are necessary, they must be made in writing.
- Practice getting up as early as you'll have to on test day and review test material, preferably your most recent Practice Tests.
- Visit the testing center if you haven't already. This is a good way to ensure that you don't get lost on the day of the test and know where to park.

PRACTICE TIMING

Your test room may or may not have a working clock. Although the proctor will keep the official time, bring your own analog wristwatch to pace yourself in each 35-minute time block. No timers except analog wristwatches are permitted.

It's also best to practice using the timing routine that you'll follow during the real test. Some students find it helpful to set their watches at 25 past the hour for the scored sections (e.g., at 11:25). This way, they know that the section will end exactly when their watch says 12:00. Others reset their watches exactly on the hour at the beginning of each section and know that every section will end 35 minutes later. Still others synchronize their watches with the room clock and follow the proctor's timing guidelines. It doesn't matter which procedure you adopt, or even if you come up with one of your own, just as long as you use it consistently so that keeping track of time on test day is second nature.

THE DAY BEFORE THE TEST: AN LSAT SURVIVAL KIT

You've prepared well to this point. Don't stop now! Relax the day before the test. Remember, the LSAT is not about memorization; it's about skill testing. You want a clear, rested mind. You don't want to be exhausted or burned out.

Put together an "LSAT Survival Kit" containing the following items. Be sure to read the most current LSAC rules about what you can bring and adapt this list as appropriate:

- Your admission ticket
- Appropriate photo ID
- Several No. 2 pencils (slightly dull points fill the ovals best)
- Analog wristwatch
- Pencil sharpener
- Eraser
- Aspirin, antacid, and tissues
- Some water and high-energy, natural sugar snacks (apples, bananas, nuts, trail mix) for the break

Take the night off entirely. Go to see a movie or watch some TV. Try not to think about the test. Get to bed early.

THE DAY OF THE TEST

Get up early, leaving yourself plenty of time.

Read something to warm up your brain like a reading passage or a logic game you've already done—you don't want the LSAT to be the first written material your brain tries to assimilate that day.

Dress in layers for maximum comfort; you'll be able to adjust to the testing room's temperature.

In traveling to the test center, leave yourself enough time for traffic and mass transit delays.

TEST CENTER PROCEDURES

Don't get flustered when they fingerprint you and check your ID as you enter the testing room—this is standard operating procedure. The test administrators do this because occasionally they have reason to believe that some test takers are not exactly who they say they are. If you're on the up and up, you'll have nothing to worry about.

After the test booklets are handed out and you've filled out all of the required inform-ation, the proctor will read the instructions, and the test will begin. Your proctor may or may not write the starting and ending time of each section on a blackboard in front of the room. The proctor will announce a five-minute warning for each section.

TAKING THE TEST

Here are some last-minute reminders to help guide your work on the test:

- Confidence is key. Accentuate the positives, and don't dwell on the negatives!

- Remember you can get a lot of questions wrong and still score high—so don't panic when faced with difficult material.

- Don't get bogged down in the middle of any section. At the end of every section are questions that may be really easy—get to them!

- Transfer your answers methodically and don't leave any answers blank. To ensure accuracy, say the question number and choice to yourself (silently, of course) as you grid.

- Don't be alarmed by extra-tough questions at the beginning. It happens. Skip past tough ones and come back to them later, making sure to circle them in the test booklet.

- Remember your section management skills and use them.

- Preview the Logic Games section before you launch into the questions. Reorder any Reading Comp passages. And save the Logical Reasoning danger zone for the end of the section.

- Don't try to figure out which section is unscored. It can't help you, and you may be wrong.

TEST RHYTHM

Between sections 1 and 2, 2 and 3, and 4 and 5, the proctor will say only: "Time's up on this section. Go on to the next section."

Notice that there's no break here—you must go immediately from one section to the next. Also, if you finish a section early, you're not allowed to move on to another section. They're strict about this one, so watch your step. If you have extra time, spend it looking back over your work on that section alone.

After section 3, you'll be instructed to close your test booklets and take a 10- to 15-minute break. Pay no attention to other people's nervous chatter during the break. Some will say it's the hardest test since the dawn of time; others will say it's so easy they can't believe it. Either kind of comment can rattle you. Instead, plan what you will do at the break to keep yourself focused and get you ready for the second half of the test.

After the break, you'll return to the testing room for the remaining sections. Then, after section 5, your test materials will be collected, and the Writing Sample materials will be handed out.

After the Writing Sample is collected, the test ends, and you're free to get on with your life. For most of you, this means getting back to the rest of the application and admission process we will talk about in Part Four: Getting into Law School.

AFTER THE TEST

Unlike many things in life, the LSAT allows you a second chance. If you end the test really feeling that you've not done as well as you could have, you have the option of canceling your score. Canceling a test means that it won't be scored. It will just appear on your score report as a cancelled test. No one will know how well or poorly you really did—not even you.

ABOUT CANCELLING YOUR SCORE

You will be asked on test day if you want to cancel your score. Kaplan strongly advises against cancelling your score immediately. There's no reason to rush this important decision. You have a few days to decide. Check with LSAC for the specific time line and procedures.

WHEN YOU SHOULD CANCEL

When deciding whether to cancel your score, a good rule of thumb is to make an honest assessment of whether you'll do better on the next test. Wishful thinking doesn't count; you need to have a valid reason to believe that the next time would be different.

Remember, no test experience is going to be perfect. If you were distracted by the proctor's hacking cough this time around, next time you may be even more distracted by construction noise, or a cold, or the hideous lime-green sweater of the person sitting in front of you.

Three legitimate reasons to cancel your test are illness, misbubbling, and personal circumstances that cause you to perform poorly on that particular day. Also, if you feel that you didn't prepare sufficiently, then it may be advisable to cancel your score and approach your test preparation a little more seriously the next time.

But keep in mind that test takers historically underestimate their performance, especially immediately following the test. They tend to forget about all of the things that went right and focus on everything that went wrong. So unless your performance is terribly marred by unforeseen circumstances, don't cancel your test immediately. At least sleep on the decision for one or two nights, and if you still feel you want to do it again, then send in the form. Just remember, cancellations are permanent. Once the form is sent, you can't change your mind.

WHAT THE SCHOOLS WILL SEE

If you do cancel your test and then take it again for a score, your score report will indicate that you've canceled a previous score. Because the earlier test won't be scored, you don't have to worry about this score showing up on any subsequent score report. If you take more than one test without canceling, then all these scores will show up on each score report, so the law schools will see them all. The trend is to use the highest score for admission, although some schools do average multiple scores. Check with individual schools for their policy on multiple scores.

Part Three

PRACTICE TESTS AND EXPLANATIONS

HOW TO CALCULATE YOUR SCORE

STEP 1

For each Practice Test, add together your total number correct for all four sections. This is your raw score.

Section I (# correct) _____

Section II (# correct) _____

Section III (# correct) _____

Section IV (# correct) _____

Total Correct (raw score) _____

STEP 2

Find your raw score on the table below and read across to find your scaled score and your percentile.

Raw Score	Scaled Score	Percentile Rank	Raw Score	Scaled Score	Percentile Rank	Raw Score	Scaled Score	Percentile Rank
0	120	0	23	131	2	46	144	23
1	120	0	24	132	3	47	145	26
2	120	0	25	133	3	48	146	29
3	120	0	26	133	3	49	146	29
4	120	0	27	133	3	50	147	33
5	120	0	28	134	4	51	147	33
6	120	0	29	135	5	52	148	37
7	120	0	30	136	6	53	148	37
8	121	0	31	136	6	54	149	41
9	122	0	32	137	8	55	150	45
10	122	0	33	137	8	56	150	45
11	123	0	34	138	9	57	150	45
12	124	0	35	138	9	58	151	50
13	124	0	36	139	10	59	151	50
14	125	0	37	140	13	60	152	54
15	126	1	38	140	13	61	153	58
16	126	1	39	140	13	62	154	58
17	127	1	40	141	15	63	154	58
18	128	1	41	142	17	64	155	62
19	129	1	42	142	17	65	155	66
20	130	2	43	143	20	66	156	66
21	130	2	44	144	23	67	157	70
22	130	2	45	144	23	68	157	70

Raw Score	Scaled Score	Percentile Rank	Raw Score	Scaled Score	Percentile Rank	Raw Score	Scaled Score	Percentile Rank
69	158	70	80	165	88	91	174	98
70	158	74	81	166	90	92	174	98
71	159	77	82	166	92	93	175	98
72	160	77	83	167	92	94	176	99
73	160	80	84	168	93	95	177	99
74	161	80	85	168	95	96	178	99
75	162	83	86	169	95	97	179	99
76	162	83	87	170	96	98	180	99
77	163	86	88	171	96	99	180	99
78	164	88	89	172	97	100	180	99
79	164	88	90	173	97	101	180	99

PRACTICE TEST 1

LSAT PRACTICE TEST 1 ANSWER SHEET

Remove (or photocopy) the answer sheet and use it to complete the Practice Test.

HOW TO TAKE THE PRACTICE TESTS

Before taking each test, find a quiet place where you can work uninterrupted for about two and a half hours. Make sure you have a comfortable desk and several No. 2 pencils.

Each Practice Test includes four scored multiple-choice sections. Keep in mind that on the actual LSAT, there will be an additional multiple-choice section—the experimental section—that will not contribute to your score, plus an unscored Writing Sample.

Once you start a Practice Test, don't stop (except for a 5- to 10-minute break after the second section) until you've gone through all four sections. Remember, you can review any questions within a section, but you may not go back or forward a section.

Good luck!

Start with number 1 for each section. If a section has fewer questions than answer spaces, leave the extra spaces blank.

Section I

1. Ⓐ Ⓑ Ⓒ Ⓓ Ⓔ	9. Ⓐ Ⓑ Ⓒ Ⓓ Ⓔ	17. Ⓐ Ⓑ Ⓒ Ⓓ Ⓔ	25. Ⓐ Ⓑ Ⓒ Ⓓ Ⓔ
2. Ⓐ Ⓑ Ⓒ Ⓓ Ⓔ	10. Ⓐ Ⓑ Ⓒ Ⓓ Ⓔ	18. Ⓐ Ⓑ Ⓒ Ⓓ Ⓔ	26. Ⓐ Ⓑ Ⓒ Ⓓ Ⓔ
3. Ⓐ Ⓑ Ⓒ Ⓓ Ⓔ	11. Ⓐ Ⓑ Ⓒ Ⓓ Ⓔ	19. Ⓐ Ⓑ Ⓒ Ⓓ Ⓔ	27. Ⓐ Ⓑ Ⓒ Ⓓ Ⓔ
4. Ⓐ Ⓑ Ⓒ Ⓓ Ⓔ	12. Ⓐ Ⓑ Ⓒ Ⓓ Ⓔ	20. Ⓐ Ⓑ Ⓒ Ⓓ Ⓔ	28. Ⓐ Ⓑ Ⓒ Ⓓ Ⓔ
5. Ⓐ Ⓑ Ⓒ Ⓓ Ⓔ	13. Ⓐ Ⓑ Ⓒ Ⓓ Ⓔ	21. Ⓐ Ⓑ Ⓒ Ⓓ Ⓔ	29. Ⓐ Ⓑ Ⓒ Ⓓ Ⓔ
6. Ⓐ Ⓑ Ⓒ Ⓓ Ⓔ	14. Ⓐ Ⓑ Ⓒ Ⓓ Ⓔ	22. Ⓐ Ⓑ Ⓒ Ⓓ Ⓔ	30. Ⓐ Ⓑ Ⓒ Ⓓ Ⓔ
7. Ⓐ Ⓑ Ⓒ Ⓓ Ⓔ	15. Ⓐ Ⓑ Ⓒ Ⓓ Ⓔ	23. Ⓐ Ⓑ Ⓒ Ⓓ Ⓔ	
8. Ⓐ Ⓑ Ⓒ Ⓓ Ⓔ	16. Ⓐ Ⓑ Ⓒ Ⓓ Ⓔ	24. Ⓐ Ⓑ Ⓒ Ⓓ Ⓔ	

right in Section I

wrong in Section I

Section II

1. Ⓐ Ⓑ Ⓒ Ⓓ Ⓔ	9. Ⓐ Ⓑ Ⓒ Ⓓ Ⓔ	17. Ⓐ Ⓑ Ⓒ Ⓓ Ⓔ	25. Ⓐ Ⓑ Ⓒ Ⓓ Ⓔ
2. Ⓐ Ⓑ Ⓒ Ⓓ Ⓔ	10. Ⓐ Ⓑ Ⓒ Ⓓ Ⓔ	18. Ⓐ Ⓑ Ⓒ Ⓓ Ⓔ	26. Ⓐ Ⓑ Ⓒ Ⓓ Ⓔ
3. Ⓐ Ⓑ Ⓒ Ⓓ Ⓔ	11. Ⓐ Ⓑ Ⓒ Ⓓ Ⓔ	19. Ⓐ Ⓑ Ⓒ Ⓓ Ⓔ	27. Ⓐ Ⓑ Ⓒ Ⓓ Ⓔ
4. Ⓐ Ⓑ Ⓒ Ⓓ Ⓔ	12. Ⓐ Ⓑ Ⓒ Ⓓ Ⓔ	20. Ⓐ Ⓑ Ⓒ Ⓓ Ⓔ	28. Ⓐ Ⓑ Ⓒ Ⓓ Ⓔ
5. Ⓐ Ⓑ Ⓒ Ⓓ Ⓔ	13. Ⓐ Ⓑ Ⓒ Ⓓ Ⓔ	21. Ⓐ Ⓑ Ⓒ Ⓓ Ⓔ	29. Ⓐ Ⓑ Ⓒ Ⓓ Ⓔ
6. Ⓐ Ⓑ Ⓒ Ⓓ Ⓔ	14. Ⓐ Ⓑ Ⓒ Ⓓ Ⓔ	22. Ⓐ Ⓑ Ⓒ Ⓓ Ⓔ	30. Ⓐ Ⓑ Ⓒ Ⓓ Ⓔ
7. Ⓐ Ⓑ Ⓒ Ⓓ Ⓔ	15. Ⓐ Ⓑ Ⓒ Ⓓ Ⓔ	23. Ⓐ Ⓑ Ⓒ Ⓓ Ⓔ	
8. Ⓐ Ⓑ Ⓒ Ⓓ Ⓔ	16. Ⓐ Ⓑ Ⓒ Ⓓ Ⓔ	24. Ⓐ Ⓑ Ⓒ Ⓓ Ⓔ	

right in Section II

wrong in Section II

Section III

1. (A) (B) (C) (D) (E)
2. (A) (B) (C) (D) (E)
3. (A) (B) (C) (D) (E)
4. (A) (B) (C) (D) (E)
5. (A) (B) (C) (D) (E)
6. (A) (B) (C) (D) (E)
7. (A) (B) (C) (D) (E)
8. (A) (B) (C) (D) (E)

9. (A) (B) (C) (D) (E)
10. (A) (B) (C) (D) (E)
11. (A) (B) (C) (D) (E)
12. (A) (B) (C) (D) (E)
13. (A) (B) (C) (D) (E)
14. (A) (B) (C) (D) (E)
15. (A) (B) (C) (D) (E)
16. (A) (B) (C) (D) (E)

17. (A) (B) (C) (D) (E)
18. (A) (B) (C) (D) (E)
19. (A) (B) (C) (D) (E)
20. (A) (B) (C) (D) (E)
21. (A) (B) (C) (D) (E)
22. (A) (B) (C) (D) (E)
23. (A) (B) (C) (D) (E)
24. (A) (B) (C) (D) (E)

25. (A) (B) (C) (D) (E)
26. (A) (B) (C) (D) (E)
27. (A) (B) (C) (D) (E)
28. (A) (B) (C) (D) (E)
29. (A) (B) (C) (D) (E)
30. (A) (B) (C) (D) (E)

right in
Section III

wrong in
Section III

Section IV

1. (A) (B) (C) (D) (E)
2. (A) (B) (C) (D) (E)
3. (A) (B) (C) (D) (E)
4. (A) (B) (C) (D) (E)
5. (A) (B) (C) (D) (E)
6. (A) (B) (C) (D) (E)
7. (A) (B) (C) (D) (E)
8. (A) (B) (C) (D) (E)

9. (A) (B) (C) (D) (E)
10. (A) (B) (C) (D) (E)
11. (A) (B) (C) (D) (E)
12. (A) (B) (C) (D) (E)
13. (A) (B) (C) (D) (E)
14. (A) (B) (C) (D) (E)
15. (A) (B) (C) (D) (E)
16. (A) (B) (C) (D) (E)

17. (A) (B) (C) (D) (E)
18. (A) (B) (C) (D) (E)
19. (A) (B) (C) (D) (E)
20. (A) (B) (C) (D) (E)
21. (A) (B) (C) (D) (E)
22. (A) (B) (C) (D) (E)
23. (A) (B) (C) (D) (E)
24. (A) (B) (C) (D) (E)

25. (A) (B) (C) (D) (E)
26. (A) (B) (C) (D) (E)
27. (A) (B) (C) (D) (E)
28. (A) (B) (C) (D) (E)
29. (A) (B) (C) (D) (E)
30. (A) (B) (C) (D) (E)

right in
Section IV

wrong in
Section IV

1   1   1

Section I

Time—35 minutes 26 questions

Directions: This test consists of questions that ask you to analyze the logic of statements or short paragraphs. For each question, choose the answer you consider best on the basis of your commonsense evaluation of the statement and its underlying assumptions. Although a question may seem to have more than one acceptable answer, there is only one best answer, and that is the one that does not entail making any illogical, extraneous, or conflicting assumptions about the question.

1. "Litigiousness" is the habit of unnecessarily taking to court matters that could probably be settled fairly by other means. According to judicial experts, the United States is rapidly becoming the most litigious country in the world. Disputes that could easily have been settled out of court in any number of ways, including binding arbitration, now clog the average court calendar in all parts of the nation.

   Which one of the following statements, if true, best supports the argument?

   (A) An increasing number of court cases involve employee-employer disputes, which can be handled by government administrative boards.

   (B) The greater the number of unnecessary court cases in a society, the larger the number of trial lawyers who are gainfully employed.

   (C) Litigiousness is not necessarily a socially negative trait, since it may encourage shy individuals to defend their own rights.

   (D) Studies of litigiousness may not have taken into account the average American's lack of sophistication about courtroom procedure.

   (E) The litigiousness of urban dwellers can be explained by their feelings of isolation in a forbidding, hostile environment.

2. From the eighth through the 19th century, the Japanese imperial power underwent a period of steady decline. This is often wrongly attributed to a fundamental bias in Japanese society ensuring that clan loyalty was always more important than loyalty to any emperor. A close look at the evidence, however, reveals that even as late as the Kamakura period in the 13th and 14th centuries, military dictators with the title "shogun" ruled in the name of the emperor and exercised a strong, centralized power.

   Which one of the following, if true, would most seriously weaken the argument?

   (A) Many Japanese followed the shogun because they feared his power and not because they were loyal.

   (B) The Kamakura shogunate collapsed in 1333, and Japan experienced 200 years of civil war.

   (C) The shoguns came from independent clans and ruled without concern for the emperor.

   (D) During the earlier Heian period, from the years 794 to 1185, the power of the shoguns was far less than that of the emperor.

   (E) Many historians believe that geography and the system of taxation were more crucial than clan loyalty in undermining imperial power.

GO ON TO THE NEXT PAGE ⇨

3. Factories that want to increase productivity should pay their workers piecemeal, according to how much they produce, rather than on an hourly wage system. Workers who receive a flat rate of, say, two dollars per item will have more incentive to produce as many items as possible than will workers who know that they will receive the same salary regardless of how hard they work.

The argument assumes which one of the following?

(A) Most factories pay their workers in hourly wages.

(B) Most factories want to increase their output whenever possible.

(C) Economic reward is the only incentive that can increase productivity.

(D) A worker who works hard will produce more items than one who does not.

(E) Workers would prefer their pay to be based on the number of items they produce.

4. Advocates of foreign language study have reacted with uncritical enthusiasm to recent surveys showing increased enrollment in college-level foreign language classes. Most of the classes in question, however, employ conversational methods rather than traditional exercises in grammar and rigorous analysis of literary texts. Unfortunately, by providing an easier way of meeting language requirements for the bachelor's degree, these classes will actually have the pernicious effect of decreasing the numbers of graduates who are capable of appreciating the subtleties of another culture's means of expression.

Which one of the following beliefs is necessary for the author's conclusion to be reasonable?

(A) Abolishing the foreign language requirement for the bachelor's degree would allow the abandonment of most conversational language classes.

(B) A conversation course typically attracts more students than a literature course when a choice exists.

(C) Foreign language courses taught conversationally lack the cultural insights provided by traditional courses oriented to grammar and literature.

(D) Continued emphasis on conversation courses will eventually reduce the pool of qualified foreign language instructors.

(E) Most college graduates today have a reading knowledge of at least one foreign language.

GO ON TO THE NEXT PAGE ▷

1 | 1 | 1

Questions 5–6

The socioeconomic status of its family has often been cynically proposed as the determining factor of a child's later intellectual prowess. To test the validity of this belief, infants from underprivileged families were removed from their homes and placed in special schools, where they were taught relatively advanced subjects from the time they were only three months old. These children had an average IQ of 110 by the time they reached school age. It would seem then, that it is the degree of prekindergarten education the child has received, rather than the socioeconomic level of its parents, that determines future intelligence.

5. The author's method of argument is to

   (A) present an alternative conclusion that explains the same evidence.

   (B) argue that children from poorer backgrounds are actually more intelligent than those from richer backgrounds.

   (C) cite specific evidence that supports her own conclusion.

   (D) disprove the statistics presented by opponents.

   (E) suggest that the cause-and-effect relationship presented by her opponents is actually reversed.

6. Which one of the following, if true, would provide the best foundation for a rebuttal of the argument above?

   (A) The degree of prekindergarten education that a child receives is related to its family's socioeconomic status.

   (B) Children from wealthy families who were placed in the same special schools had an average IQ of 110 when they reached school age.

   (C) Families in lower income brackets often have more children and thus cannot give as much attention to each one.

   (D) Children learn more readily between the ages of 5 and 10 than they do between the ages of 1 and 5.

   (E) Few parents at any socioeconomic level attempt to teach their children before the children reach the age of 5.

GO ON TO THE NEXT PAGE ▷

1   **1**   **1**

7. In our society, personality is considered an expression of individuality. We like to see ourselves as self-created, distinct from the influences of the past, bent upon our own development as self. Effects upon us are viewed as intrusions. But in the tribal society of the Bambara peoples, personality is the sum of many parts— less an individual phenomenon than a reflection of the family, less a single unit than an integer of a larger, sustaining tribal identity. Personality is richer because it is not self-centered, maturer because it benefits from diversity, and stronger because it draws its strength from the clan.

The argument has been designed to emphasize the supposed interrelationship between

(A) richness of personality and integration in a society.

(B) individuality of expression and development of the self.

(C) diversity of personality and self-centeredness.

(D) a sustaining tribal identity and the strength of the clan.

(E) development of the self and the intrusion of outside effects.

8. Experts on the American political process have long agreed that voters like a certain amount of combativeness, even aggressiveness, in a presidential candidate. A poll just after the 1988 election, however, showed that many people had been annoyed or disgusted with the campaign and had not even bothered to vote. In addition, many voters felt that most candidates were "nonpresidential." Campaigns that feature combativeness have, therefore, become counterproductive by causing voters to lose respect for the combative candidate.

Which one of the following, if true, most seriously weakens the argument?

(A) Many presidential campaigns have been memorable because they were full of surprises.

(B) The poll cited does not specifically show that combative campaigning was responsible for voter disaffection.

(C) Even before 1988, many voters were skeptical about politicians, particularly candidates for president.

(D) What seems to be aggressiveness is really assertiveness, a necessary quality for keeping one's name in the public eye.

(E) Political campaigning is a means of giving voters essential information on which they must base their decisions.

GO ON TO THE NEXT PAGE ▷

Questions 9–10

It is healthier to eat frozen vegetables than fresh ones, not because of any beneficial property of freezing (which actually robs food of some nutrients) but because of the common practice of harvesting crops before they are ripe. Vegetables are at their most nutritious when they are allowed to ripen in the field. Vegetables picked when ripe would be overripe or even rotten by the time they reached the consumer, so they must be picked early and allowed to ripen in transit. These crops never achieve their full nutritive value. However, the ripening process of vegetables destined for freezing can be stopped soon after harvest. As a result, frozen vegetables are generally more nutritious than the fresh vegetables we buy at the local grocery store.

9. The above argument is based on which one of the following assumptions?

   (A) Frozen food companies freeze only the most nutritious varieties of vegetables.

   (B) Nutritional loss from freezing is less than that from premature harvesting.

   (C) Fresh vegetables are never sold immediately but rather sit on shelves for long periods.

   (D) People never freeze the vegetables they buy at the grocery store.

   (E) All kinds of vegetables ripen at approximately the same rate in the same amount of time.

10. Which one of the following, if true, would most seriously undermine the argument in the passage?

   (A) Overripe vegetables are more nutritious than underripe ones.

   (B) Vegetables destined for freezing and those destined for the grocery store are harvested at the same time.

   (C) Fresh vegetables are refrigerated during transport to prevent excessive spoilage.

   (D) Many consumers who live near farms can purchase vegetables directly from growers.

   (E) Tests have shown that fresh vegetables taste substantially better than frozen vegetables.

11. Running is very beneficial to cardiovascular health, so it is not uncommon for doctors to recommend running to their patients as a means of keeping fit. However, it is well known that running can cause damage to the knees of some runners that may limit future activity and even require surgery. Therefore, physicians should not recommend running to their patients.

Which of the following most closely parallels the logical structure of the argument above?

   (A) Nutritionists have long believed that red wine provided certain health benefits when consumed in moderation, so many recommended small quantities of red wine to their clients. However, it has recently come to light that red wine does not offer the benefits nutritionists originally believed that it did, so nutritionists should no longer recommend red wine.

   (B) Certain types of green vegetables can provide substantial health benefits, so dieticians frequently include them on lists of "good" foods provided to those looking to improve health through better diet. However, those same vegetables can cause blood thickness disorders in some people, so dieticians should stop advocating their consumption.

   (C) Running is only one option when it comes to increasing cardiovascular health; anyone who is in a position to advise cardiac patients should provide a variety of options and be sure not to create the impression that running is the only effective means of building up one's heart.

GO ON TO THE NEXT PAGE ▷

(D) Bicycling is a very healthy sport and one that is accessible to the serious athlete or the average person looking to get some exercise while spending some time outdoors. However, serious injuries are possible, especially when cyclists ride in areas of heavy vehicular traffic. Thus, all cyclists, whether serious athletes or hobbyists, should wear protective gear like helmets and knee pads when riding.

(E) Skydiving is an inherently dangerous activity, and anyone who chooses to jump out of an airplane must realize that some risk of serious injury or even death is involved. However, every activity involves some level of risk, so that alone should not discourage anyone from trying skydiving.

12. The state legislature has before it a bill outlawing capital punishment, and certain lawmakers are doing everything in their power to see that it does not get passed. To these lawmakers I say, go to death row, and it will become obvious that even convicted murderers are people worthy of our mercy.

Which one of the following best describes the author's method of argument?

(A) She suggests a course of action designed to impact her opponents emotionally.

(B) She argues from a general principle to a particular conclusion.

(C) She uses irony to mock her opponents' position.

(D) She attacks the way in which her opponents have presented their view.

(E) She ignores a distinction that is essential to her opponents' case.

13. Lest charity become confused with self-interest, it is well to remember that we can hope to rehabilitate a convicted felon without demanding that he or she be remade in our own image. To insist that the former pusher become a social worker, or the former burglar a bank clerk, is to deny the very individuality of expression that true rehabilitative programs should develop.

Which one of the following sentences best completes the statement of the position put forth in the passage above?

(A) For proper rehabilitation, however, the convicted felon must follow the advice of professionals in choosing a career.

(B) Moreover, forcing an unsuitable career upon the subject for rehabilitation might pressure him or her to return to the criminal life out of frustration.

(C) In particular, it is unlikely that any individual will find self-expression in work that involves reporting daily to an institution.

(D) Furthermore, many a social worker has less knowledge of the motivations behind criminal acts than a felon who has actually committed a crime.

(E) In addition, society has the right to demand that rehabilitated felons take jobs that benefit the society as a whole.

GO ON TO THE NEXT PAGE

14. State revenues from the corporate income tax are seriously threatened by the new trend towards decentralization of corporate headquarters. Many of the companies leaving the city, with its extensive public transportation system, are finding it necessary to import costly executive helicopters to transport personnel to and from isolated locations in the suburbs. Because money spent on these helicopters is deductible from gross corporate income as an expense of doing business, such companies will thus pay lower taxes to the state. We must apply appropriate economic sanctions to avoid the loss of these much-needed tax revenues.

Which one of the following identifies a flaw in the reasoning behind the argument?

(A) The writer fails to suggest alternative modes of transportation less costly than helicopters.

(B) The writer fails to demonstrate that higher personnel transport costs are not offset by other economies at the new corporate headquarters.

(C) The writer fails to consider the increased taxes paid by the helicopter manufacturers as a result of booming business.

(D) The writer fails to consider the higher productivity achieved through rapid helicopter travel.

(E) The writer fails to specify other economic difficulties caused by the corporations' flight from the city.

15. A student at any college within the Metropolitan Consortium for Higher Education is permitted and encouraged to take classes at other member colleges when these complement the offerings of his home institution. Please note, however, that the final determination of credits earned and degree requirements satisfied will remain the prerogative of the student's own academic dean, regardless of any conflicting policies at other institutions. The rules governing a student's course of study depend solely on the institution in which he is officially enrolled; that is, not on his physical presence in a given classroom.

Based on the above policy statement, which of the following must be true?

(A) Any student admitted to a college within the Consortium will be allowed to transfer his enrollment to another member college.

(B) A college may exclude a student enrolled in the Consortium from its nonacademic programs.

(C) Each college's Admissions Office is the sole judge of eligibility to attend its classes.

(D) Students are not required to follow rules of conduct established by colleges at which they are not enrolled.

(E) A student's academic dean can refuse to accept course credits awarded by another college within the Consortium.

GO ON TO THE NEXT PAGE

16. Early in the 20th century, the doctor was a comforter, expected to predict the progress of a disease or to help the patient cope with a struggle or an imminent defeat but not to work miracles. This situation changed with the coming of such drugs as penicillin, insulin, and antibiotics. Add the rapid technological developments of contemporary medicine, and we find the medical professional under pressure to defeat every disease, correct every physical defect, and maximize the patient's quality of life. Society no longer is satisfied with the dedicated efforts of human beings; it now demands perfect performance of technicians as foolproof as the most sophisticated machines.

Which one of the following can be most reasonably inferred from the passage?

(A) Today's physician does not view comforting the patient as part of the job.

(B) The patient today expects results rather than sympathy from the physician.

(C) Medical incompetence is more widespread today than it was in the early 20th century.

(D) As medical technology has advanced, health care workers have become less sensitive to the feelings of their patients.

(E) Because doctors cannot meet the often unrealistic expectations of their patients, they are subjected to an ever-increasing number of malpractice suits.

17. Those who oppose psychological testing of schoolchildren, alleging that teachers will unconsciously "write off" pupils labeled as slow, overlook the fact that a self-fulfilling prophecy is necessarily also a true one. Information about a student's probable development can only help the teacher to arrange an appropriate remedial program.

Which one of the following arguments is most similar in logical structure to that above?

(A) Opponents of long-term testing of newly developed drugs maintain that intensive short-term testing is sufficient to identify possibly dangerous side effects. This ignores the possibility that some side effects may become evident only after decades of use.

(B) Some believe that arms limitations talks should be avoided, since they bring to the fore sensitive issues that may actually escalate tensions. However, arms limitations talks provide the basis for effective action to decrease the danger of widespread destruction.

(C) Claims that hospital diets are often unbalanced and even harmful, because of their high sodium and starch content, are beside the point, since hospitals hire trained nutritionists to design their menus.

(D) The majority of contact lens wearers agree that the benefits of improved vision and physical appearance outweigh the admitted inconveniences of the lenses in comparison to traditional eyeglasses.

(E) Whether the possibility of contagion through door handles and water faucets touched by many people is real or imagined, installation of swinging doors and pedal-controlled wash basins in public restrooms is an easy way to allay such fears.

GO ON TO THE NEXT PAGE ▷

1   **1**   **1**

18. Housing statistics for other cities conclusively disprove the frequently advanced claims that New York City's rent control laws caused the widespread abandonment of apartment houses that the city has suffered in recent decades. Some cities with strict controls on rentals have experienced little abandonment, while in others without controls of any kind, landlords walked away from entire neighborhoods.

The author of the argument is assuming which one of the following?

(A) Because rent control laws restrict landlords' profits, a landlord's decision to abandon his property must be motivated solely by financial considerations.

(B) Because rent control was not the cause of housing abandonment in every case, it was not the cause in the case of New York City.

(C) Because rent control did not lead to housing abandonment in New York City, its net impact on the city has been beneficial.

(D) New York City's rent control laws fostered widespread abandonment of property because they were insufficiently strict.

(E) Despite rent control laws, New York City has experienced only negligible abandonment of rental properties in recent decades.

19. The unexpected plummet of the stock market in September badly shook the economy. For this past holiday season, retail sales comprised a lower percentage of total annual sales than in any of the previous 20 years. Retailers and legislators are worried. New rules that govern trading on the stock exchange may be put into effect.

Which of the following can be inferred from the statements above?

(A) The stock exchange wishes to enlist the aid of the government.

(B) Legislators typically do not become concerned until a real market effect is felt.

(C) New rules governing the trading of stocks will increase the volume of retail sales.

(D) Some legislators believe that the decline in the percentage of retail sales was due to the September stock market fall.

(E) In September, the stock market fell to its lowest point in 20 years.

GO ON TO THE NEXT PAGE

20. It is barbarous in the extreme to equate murder with simple acquiescence in the choice of a pain-wracked, dying friend to find self-deliverance from an onerous life. To assist a friend in suicide is to give solace, to respect the individual's free choice; to murder, of course, is to perform the ultimate act of disrespect for individual civil rights. Both our legislators and our justices must be urged to use reason rather than to respond as they have with traditional prejudice.

It can be inferred from the passage that

(A) the concept of murder in any given society is related to that society's interpretation of the idea of individual rights.

(B) terminally ill patients frequently contemplate suicide.

(C) some of our legislators and our justices do not agree with the author of the passage that assisting a suicide is not an act of murder.

(D) suicide should always be considered an act of self-deliverance, just as murder should be considered an act of disrespect for individual civil rights.

(E) whether or not suicide can be considered a legal act depends upon whether or not the suicide victim is suffering great pain.

21. All candidates for the master's degree who enrolled after 1977 take a seminar on Heidegger, and all candidates for the master's degree who enrolled after 1981 take a seminar on Wittgenstein.

If a student took a seminar on Heidegger but did not take a seminar on Wittgenstein, which one of the following must be true?

(A) The student enrolled prior to 1982.

(B) The student enrolled after 1977 and prior to 1982.

(C) If the student was a candidate for the master's degree, then the student enrolled prior to 1982.

(D) If the student was a candidate for the master's degree, then the student enrolled prior to 1978.

(E) If the student was a candidate for the master's degree, then the student enrolled after 1977 and prior to 1982.

GO ON TO THE NEXT PAGE ▷

1   1   1

22. The proposal to reduce grain prices by mandating a government-controlled price level would _____. Artificially stabilized pricing drains the economy while it encourages inefficient production and discourages individual initiative. To let the forces of the free market operate would be to give efficient producers the advantage they earn.

Which one of the following most logically fills the blank in the passage above?

(A) reward producers who are not responding adequately to market forces

(B) actually have the contrary effect of increasing grain prices

(C) strike a necessary balance between government intervention and a free market economy

(D) make grain available to those who cannot now afford to eat well

(E) allow individual efforts to influence the operation of the free market

23. Samuel Taylor Coleridge must have found the inspiration for "The Rime of the Ancient Mariner" in Hakluyt's 1600 edition of the real-life sea narrative *The Southern Voyage of John Davis*. Although the poet did not mention the 200-year-old work in his notes, both "Mariner" and *Southern Voyage* prominently feature a tale of misfortune resulting from the murder of a bird, a rotting ship drifting out of control in the tropics, and a scene of a dying man cursing his fate. Furthermore, Wordsworth, Coleridge's good friend and occasional collaborator, had an interest in books about actual historical sea voyages and may have owned a copy of Davis's story.

The author of the passage makes his point primarily by

(A) drawing an analogy between literature and seafaring.

(B) reinterpreting a classic literary work.

(C) paralleling an author's work with the events of the author's life.

(D) supporting a claim with circumstantial evidence.

(E) documenting a controversial claim of literary influence.

GO ON TO THE NEXT PAGE

24. Society still wastes incalculable human potential when men and women are denied career advancement because of false but unthinkingly perpetuated age stereotypes. To combat this situation, now and in the future, the mature job applicant should do everything possible to seem young, competent, and energetic—and, once hired, should conceal his or her true age to ensure unbiased treatment from coworkers.

Which one of the following, if true, is most damaging to the argument above?

(A) Harmful age stereotypes can only be destroyed if capable older people reveal their true age.

(B) Neurological studies have found certain changes in brain function to be widespread in those over 65.

(C) Increasing numbers of older people are already finding employment in clerical and food service jobs.

(D) Legislation forbidding age-based discrimination for workers between 40 and 70 has wide popular support.

(E) Improved nutrition can prevent, and to a lesser degree reverse, many of the physical changes traditionally associated with aging.

25. On the desert island off the coast of Long Beach, goats had multiplied in the wild, denuding the hills of ground foliage essential to prevent erosion and drastically reducing their own food supply. It was thought that the introduction of a predator like the coyote, which had overpopulated the Mojave Desert and dangerously thinned its own sources of prey, would naturally stabilize the island ecology.

Which one of the following, if true, is most damaging to the argument?

(A) Neither the coyote nor any of its close relatives has ever been found living naturally on any of the offshore islands along the coast in question.

(B) The goats on the island are all descended from a small herd of domesticated goats and have never experienced the threat of a predator.

(C) As the ground foliage disappears, a prickly cactus native to the island will spread, effectively stopping soil erosion.

(D) The coyote, an effective hunter and rapid breeder, would soon overpower the goats, exhaust its food supply, and experience starvation in great numbers.

(E) In suburban areas at the edge of the Mojave Desert, residents are frightened because coyotes kill household pets.

GO ON TO THE NEXT PAGE ▷

1   **1**   **1**

26. Recent purchases by the Social Documentation Division of the university library have made this collection one of the best in the nation, with a complete and up-to-date range of statistical reference tools, census studies, and the like. All new acquisition funds should therefore be shifted away from the now extensive Social Documentation collection and towards other departments, such as Latin literature and Renaissance art, where the library's deficiencies are most notable.

Which one of the following, if true, most undermines the argument?

(A) Today's emphasis on technology makes such essentially unquantifiable subjects as literature and art less important within the university curriculum.

(B) Despite the completeness of the Social Documentation collection, new computerized study devices are still being developed, and funds should be allotted for their purchase.

(C) Social documentation by its very nature is an ongoing process, and the library must continue to purchase new materials to keep its collection current.

(D) Increased student enrollment in sociology courses may necessitate additional copies of works already in the library's holdings.

(E) To encourage greater library use by students, funds could be shifted not towards additional book acquisition but towards remodeling and enhancing existing lounge areas.

IF YOU FINISH BEFORE TIME IS CALLED, YOU MAY CHECK YOUR WORK ON THIS SECTION ONLY. DO NOT WORK ON ANY OTHER SECTION IN THE TEST.

STOP

Section II

Time—35 minutes 27 questions

Directions: Each selection in this test is followed by several questions. After reading the selection, choose the best response to each question and mark it on your answer sheet. Your replies are to be based on what is stated or implied in the selection.

Traditional justifications of the free speech principle originate in the belief that speech is entitled to greater tolerance than other kinds of activity. A review of the traditional justifications
(5) reveals two distinct models of explanation: the "classical model" and the "fortress model." Although both these models link the need to protect speech to its inherent value, they agree on little else.
(10)   According to the classical model, freedom of speech serves an indispensable function in democratic self-government. Meiklejohn uses the traditional New England town meeting as the paradigmatic setting for a self-governing society. From
(15) this perspective, the free speech principle need only protect political speech—the facts, theories, and opinions relating to any issue on which the citizens must vote. Meiklejohn insists that even extremist views cannot be concealed from voting
(20) citizens if these views bear on any public issue before them. Protection of free speech, including extremist political speech, serves the collective interests of a self-governing society made up of all rational, equal, and fully participating citizens.
(25) This theory is predicated on the belief that speech itself is valuable and thus ascribes positive value to a very broad range of speech, including that which may be offensive to many people.

In contrast to the serene and optimistic outlook
(30) of the classical model, the fortress model is built on a foundation of pessimism, individualism, relativism, and self-doubt. Whereas this model considers freedom of speech necessary to the discovery of truth, it assumes that any belief held by an
(35) individual is likely to prove ultimately false. In this frame, speech represents not so much a free marketplace of ideas as a kind of counsel of despair. From Holmes's perspective, the government and a majority of the people pose a great danger of

(40) intolerance. Despite the high probability that any individual's beliefs will eventually prove to be false, people nonetheless tend to feel certain about them and, consequently, feel justified in requiring others to conform. The fortress model's prescrip-
(45) tion for combating the tendency to censor nonconforming views is to overprotect speech. This strategy provides a broad "buffer zone" that encompasses extremist speech because its protection substantially diminishes the probability that
(50) inherently valuable speech will be suppressed. Even if these views are so extreme that they cannot seriously be considered to contribute to the discovery of truth—like the most extreme views propounded by the Nazis—they still ought not to
(55) be censored, because once unleashed, censorship cannot be reasonably expected to remain confined to worthless views.

Bollinger, rejecting both the classical and the fortress models as inadequate, furnishes a new
(60) model designed to account for the changes in the function of speech attributable to the emergence of a society marked by stability and widespread consensus on essential values. This new model referred to as the "self-restraint" model casts new
(65) light on the free speech principle. Although continuing staunchly to support free speech, the self restraint model inverts the relationship between speech and tolerance. Under the traditional models, the value of tolerance is subordinated to the
(70) value of speech. However, the self-restraint model often subordinates the value of speech to that of tolerance because in a stable, consensual society, the pursuit of self-control, self-discipline, and self-restraint becomes of paramount importance.

GO ON TO THE NEXT PAGE ⟶

2   **2**   **2**   **2**

1. The author is primarily concerned with discussing.

    (A) arguments for and against free speech.

    (B) different theoretical justifications for supporting free speech.

    (C) Bollinger's criticisms of the right of extremist speech.

    (D) Meiklejohn's and Holmes's understanding of free speech principles.

    (E) a new approach to the problem of constitutionally limiting extremist speech.

2. Which of the following is most probably an assumption made by Meiklejohn?

    (A) To make rational decisions, members of a democratic society need to consider all views, even extremist ones.

    (B) Most members of a democratic society would embrace extremist views if exposed to them.

    (C) Many views that are unpopular when first expressed are eventually accepted by the majority.

    (D) Useful social reforms are often originally proposed by extremist groups.

    (E) Protection of free speech is useful only in a small, self-governing community where all can join in decision making.

3. It can be inferred that Meiklejohn's model of free speech would NOT necessarily extend protection to

    (A) speech expressing extremist political viewpoints.

    (B) extremist speech that is not political

    (C) views that reject the basis of democratic government.

    (D) opinions that the majority of citizens find offensive.

    (E) speech that represents the beliefs of individuals rather than of the community.

4. It can be inferred that Holmes would agree with all of the following statements EXCEPT

    (A) to protect useful speech, it is necessary to protect extremist speech.

    (B) views that have little value to society may nevertheless deserve protection.

    (C) censors cannot be trusted to distinguish reliably between worthwhile and worthless views.

    (D) it is potentially less harmful to censor valuable speech than to tolerate extremist speech.

    (E) censorship of extremist views makes it more likely that nonextremist views will also be censored.

5. It can be inferred that all of the following are true of Bollinger's model EXCEPT that it

    (A) assumes that tolerance is inherently valuable in a stable society.

    (B) conceives the relationship between speech and tolerance differently than do the classical and fortress models.

    (C) does not protect speech as fully as the classical and fortress models.

    (D) applies to a society that shares agreement on fundamental values.

    (E) assumes that the justification for protecting free speech may change as society evolves.

GO ON TO THE NEXT PAGE ▷

2   2   2   2

6. Which of the following best describes the organization of the first three paragraphs of the passage?

(A) The author describes two theories and links each to the historical situation in which it was proposed.

(B) The author refers to a traditional way of viewing a question and examines two contrasting approaches that spring from that view.

(C) The author establishes contrasts between two approaches to a question and then explores their points of agreement.

(D) The author discusses two theories and the opposed conclusions that follow from them.

(E) The author summarizes two views of a controversial issue, mentions two questions they cannot answer, and calls for a synthesis.

7. Meiklejohn's and Holmes's understanding of free speech are similar in that both

(A) believe that free speech ultimately leads to the discovery of truth.

(B) favor extending the right of speech to those who express extremist doctrines.

(C) consider that censorship involves the suppression of valuable speech.

(D) justify free speech by referring to the citizen's right to be informed of all views relevant to public issues.

(E) argue that protecting free speech is important mainly because it promotes tolerance as a social value.

Although research in molecular biology has yet to have a major impact on the prevention and treatment of disease, a backlash already seems to be developing. Lay critics as well as members of
(5) the profession have argued that molecular biologists should focus on certain areas, like fertility mechanisms, whereas other areas, like genetics or aging, are possibly dangerous and not worthy of public financial support. These critics believe that
(10) they can channel contemporary biology to fit their own conception of appropriate research. However, the traditional pact between society and scientist, in which the scientist is given responsibility for determining the direction of research, is necessary
(15) if basic science is to be effective. This does not mean that society is at the mercy of science but rather that society, who must determine the pace of scientific innovation, should not attempt to prescribe its directions.

(20)   It is partly the successes of molecular biology that have brought on this questioning. One advance has been the development of the process called recombinant DNA research. Because the method allows genes from any species to be put
(25) into a common type of bacterium, there is a theoretical possibility of hazard. But if safety were the most important consideration about recombinant DNA, then we might expect the debate to focus on the hazards of recombinant DNA experiments.
(30) Instead, many discussions soon turn to a consideration of genetic engineering.

One type of genetic engineering involves altering some body cells so that they can perform needed functions. A second type, involving replacement of
(35) genes in germ cells that transmit their genes to our offspring, presents more of a dilemma because it could change the human gene pool. Both forms, but especially the latter, present perplexing problems: Who is to decide, and how shall they decide,
(40) what genes are malfunctional? These are moral decisions and therefore highly subjective. Although genetic engineering is not the same as recombinant DNA research, the two are rightly linked because recombinant DNA work is hastening
(45) the day when genetic engineering will be a feasible process for use on certain diseases. Because recombinant DNA work is bringing closer the discovery of new medical treatments and is likely to bring other new capabilities, why is there so much

GO ON TO THE NEXT PAGE

2   **2**   **2**   **2**

(50) focus on genetic engineering? I believe that genetic engineering has become a symbol to many people of the frightening potential of modern technology.

Rather than seeing in molecular biology the *(55)* same complex mixtures of appropriate and inappropriate applications that characterize all powerful sciences, many people have allowed a negative catch phrase, "genetic engineering," to dominate discussions. People worry that if the possibility of *(60)* curing a genetic defect by gene therapy should ever become a reality, the inevitable result would be "people made to order." It is being too hastily argued that unless we block recombinant DNA research now, we will never have another chance *(65)* to control our fate.

8. The passage as a whole can be characterized as an attempt to answer which of the following questions?

   (A) What are the likely dangers to society of research in recombinant DNA?

   (B) Should limits be placed on biological research because of the risks that new knowledge can carry for society?

   (C) Does society have valid concerns about the safety of genetic engineering?

   (D) How has public criticism of recombinant DNA research affected the pace of scientific innovation?

   (E) Do hazardous research techniques primarily pose moral or practical problems for biologists?

9. The author suggests which of the following about research into "fertility mechanisms" (lines 6–7)?

   (A) It is the most promising area of study in molecular biology.

   (B) It has attracted both lay and scientific criticism.

   (C) It is an area within which too few scientists are interested in working.

   (D) It is a focus of dissension among various groups in society.

   (E) It is viewed as a relatively uncontroversial area of study.

10. In the argument, the author acknowledges that society should exercise control over which of the following?

   (A) Direction of scientific work

   (B) Application of new medical treatments

   (C) Specific priorities of scientists

   (D) Expenditure of allocated funds

   (E) Rate of scientific advance

11. The passage does NOT provide an answer to which of the following questions?

   (A) Why has molecular biology so far failed to produce many tangible benefits?

   (B) What is the traditional role played by scientists engaged in scientific study?

   (C) Do critics consider some areas of study in molecular biology more acceptable than others?

   (D) Has work in molecular biology raised legitimate questions of moral concern?

   (E) Why have questions concerning recombinant DNA often tended to turn to a discussion of genetic engineering?

GO ON TO THE NEXT PAGE ⟩

2   2   2   2

12. It can be inferred that the author is most likely to agree with which of the following statements about science and society?

   (A) Public constraint of scientific inquiry is one of the social costs of democracy.

   (B) Excessive interference by society can threaten the intellectual freedom and activity upon which all scientific innovation depends.

   (C) As scientists increase their ability to prevent disease, society will gradually lose interest in monitoring scientific research.

   (D) Scientists have a right to block public discussion as a way of keeping society from participating in decisions that do not concern it.

   (E) The current conflict between scientific researchers and their social critics will never be satisfactorily resolved.

13. The author suggests that the debate over genetic engineering has

   (A) failed to examine many of the risks involved in the research.

   (B) fully documented the potential dangers of the research.

   (C) shed light on a related discussion of recombinant DNA research.

   (D) been used to exaggerate the dangers of recombinant DNA research.

   (E) helped to stimulate the development of new medical treatments.

14. The author implies that the probability of "inappropriate applications" (lines 55–56) of new technologies by molecular biologists is

   (F) somewhat more likely than in other fields of research.

   (G) unlikely because most molecular biologists are trained in ethics.

   (H) no more likely than in other fields of scientific research.

   (I) much less likely than in other fields of research.

   (J) unlikely because most researchers work as part of a team.

15. The content and style of the passage suggest the passage was most probably taken from

   (A) a speech given to medical students on the importance of ethics in contemporary medicine.

   (B) a government report outlining the likely impact of contemporary research on society.

   (C) an introduction to current theoretical and practical research in molecular biology.

   (D) a review assessing the progress of molecular biology in the areas of disease prevention and treatment.

   (E) a paper delivered at a seminar devoted to examining the costs and benefits of limiting scientific inquiry.

GO ON TO THE NEXT PAGE

Passage A

The growth of collaborative divorce as an option for couples ending their marriages, especially those with children, has radically changed the landscape of divorce. Finally, some spouses
(5) who are ready to go their separate ways are being encouraged to work together and come up with a plan that both parties can accept, rather than being pushed by attorneys to fight every minor point and rack up legal bills that further strain
(10) finances already damaged by the need to maintain two households with the same amount of income that previously supported just one. There is little reason for most couples to follow the old, adversarial route.

(15)   In the collaborative divorce process, attorneys act as advisors rather than advocates. In fact, both attorneys are required to agree in writing that should the collaborative process break down and a contested divorce ensue, they will withdraw from
(20) the case.

There may be many professionals involved in the collaborative divorce process just as there often are in a contested divorce case, but they're not hired guns there to prove the point most advan-
(25) tageous to the party who is writing the checks; instead, they serve to smooth out the process and guide the parties toward solutions advantageous to all. One emerging model employs a collaborative divorce team that includes two lawyers, two
(30) "divorce coaches," a child specialist, and a financial advisor.

In addition to the emotional and psychological benefits to the parties and their children, collaborative divorce can be substantially less expensive
(35) than a traditional contested divorce case. It is no surprise that the American Bar Association recently issued an ethics opinion speaking favorably of collaborative divorce.

Passage B

Collaborative divorce—like so many facets of the American legal system—is realistically available only to those with significant assets or cash flow. Proponents of the system point to many
(5) benefits in terms of peace, psychological well-being, positive impact on future relations, and lower stress levels for children of divorce. In many cases, those claims may hold true. However, a look at the actual numbers in play quickly reveals how
(10) unrealistic those projected savings may be for many divorce litigants.

One recent study showed collaborative divorce as the second-least-expensive alternative—a distant second to mediation. But the median cost of
(15) collaborative divorce as revealed in that study was in excess of $19,000. That might represent substantial savings over the median contested divorce cost, particularly if that study's median price tag of more than $77,000 for a litigated divorce is
(20) accurate. But given that median incomes across the country range from the low 30,000s to just shy of 100,000, it seems unlikely that the true "average person" is paying $77,000 for a contested divorce—or has enough assets to
(25) justify doing so.

For the real "average family," the price tag for a team of six professionals is out of reach, however favorably it might compare with the hypothetical alternative costs.

GO ON TO THE NEXT PAGE ▷

16. The authors of the two passages would be most likely to disagree about which of the following?

    (A) The advantages of using the collaborative divorce process rather than a full-blown contested divorce proceeding

    (B) The benefit of having additional professionals like financial advisors involved in the divorce process

    (C) The impact the advent of collaborative divorce has had on the average couple seeking a divorce.

    (D) Whether couples should employ the services of other professionals in an effort to work out their difficulties before seeking a divorce

    (E) The desirability of working together versus having an advocate fighting for a client's greatest advantage in a divorce proceeding

17. Which of the following best describes the relationship between the two passages?

    (A) Passage A advocates a system that Passage B recommends against.

    (B) Passage A sets forth evidence of the value of a system, and Passage B refutes that evidence point by point.

    (C) Passage B points out a limitation on the impact of the system advocated by the author of Passage A.

    (D) The authors of Passages A and B reach similar conclusions but employ different reasoning methods

    (E) Passage B provides evidence disproving a specific benefit set forth in Passage A.

18. The author of Passage B would be most likely to challenge the author of Passage A on which point?

    (A) The value of the additional services provided by the "team of professionals" in a collaborative divorce process

    (B) The actual cost of the collaborative divorce process

    (C) The accessibility of the collaborative divorce process to the typical couple seeking a divorce

    (D) The idea that parties seeking a divorce should not strive to maximize their own gain

    (E) The claim that the American Bar Association has indicated support for the collaborative divorce process

19. The authors of the two passages would be most likely to agree on which of the following?

    (A) Collaborative divorce should be more accessible to couples with fewer assets and lower income.

    (B) The collaborative divorce process may be smoother and more peaceful than a traditional contested divorce.

    (C) Children of collaborative divorce have fewer emotional problems after the divorce is final than do children whose parents have divorced through conventional processes.

    (D) The financial advisor plays a particularly important role in the collaborative divorce process.

    (E) Traditional divorce processes should be phased out in favor of collaborative divorce for all couples seeking to end their marriages.

GO ON TO THE NEXT PAGE ⟶

2   **2**   **2**   **2**

20. Which of the following is most analogous to the relationship between the two passages?

   (A) A musician argues that his band should invest in new equipment and outlines the benefits of the change, but another member doesn't think the band can afford to make the investment.

   (B) A professor recommends a very informative new book to all of his colleagues, but a critic points out that because the book is currently available only in Greek, in its present form it will be accessible to only a fraction of those colleagues.

   (C) An attorney argues for an equal division of assets in the split of a business partnership, but one of the partners suggests that they should receive impartial advice from a financial advisor before making any decisions.

   (D) One member of a corporate board proposes undertaking a new project and provides an estimated budget for the project, but another member points out several flaws in the budget and suggests that the project will actually be much more expensive than anticipated.

   (E) Two children get into a fight on the playground at school, and rather than punishing the children, the principal asks the school counselor to intervene and help the children to work out their problems.

21. Which of the following is not mentioned by either author as a potential benefit of the collaborative divorce process?

   (A) Better ability to communicate or work together in the future

   (B) A higher likelihood of arriving at a joint custody arrangement acceptable to both parties

   (C) Lower cost as compared to a litigated divorce

   (D) The possibility of arriving at an outcome that is comfortable for both parties

   (E) An easier process for children of the parties

GO ON TO THE NEXT PAGE ▷

It is interesting to note that the circle and square, not arrows and bullets, saved the Plains Indians from total annihilation. Their survival was encoded and transmitted through the Medicine

(5)　Wheel, which integrated the tribe to the cosmos, to each other, and to the Self within—requirements for any community that seeks to flourish and persist.

The Medicine Wheel integrated the tribe to the

(10)　cosmos and to the recurring cycles of the sun, moon, and stars. Stones were arranged in circles, around which key points were marked. Carefully arranged piles of rock, for example, would mark the sunrise and sunset of the summer solstice, the

(15)　rise of important constellations, and the rise of significant, bright stars. Divided into 28 segments, these circles symbolically represented the 28 houses or "mansions" of the moon, which revolved around the centerpoint, the house of the sun.

(20)　The Medicine Wheel, then, was a solar and stellar observatory. It was the basis of the Plains Indians' calendar, by which time the seasons and the rhythm of tribal life were calculated—agriculture, migration, festivals, and war.

(25)　Although the Medicine Wheel functioned in a cosmic manner, orienting the tribe to time through the movements of the heavenly bodies, it had an equally important mental or psychological function as well. It integrated the members of the

(30)　tribe to each other and to humanity at large. Tribal lore stated that all members of the community began their life at a particular point on the Medicine Wheel, the Great Circle of Life. Because all perspectives pointed toward the Center, there

(35)　was no advantage or disadvantage to any particular point. Yet, although each point on the Circle was considered unique, major personality types were recognized. The Medicine Wheel was divided into four cardinal directions, a quaternity that

(40)　represented four psychological powers. Thus, the Medicine Wheel taught diversity within unity. For example, a tribal member might have her or his

Beginning Place in the South, in the Power of Innocence or Trust. Such a person would then be

(45)　taught to recognize the other Powers of the Medicine Wheel—North, West, and East—by observing and then imitating the qualities of those who possessed Wisdom, Introspection, or Illumination, respectively, as their dominant trait.

(50)　Thus, tolerance for the four different Powers was taught—an important element for any community that wishes to survive. However, tribal members were taught more than tolerance. Each member of the tribe was actually encouraged to

(55)　cultivate the recessive or undeveloped traits of her personality in order to grow as a whole person. Plains Indian training thus raised the passive virtue of tolerance to the active and higher virtue of integration.

22. According to the information in the passage, each of the following is an accurate statement about the Medicine Wheel EXCEPT that

(A) it was integral to the survival of the Plains Indians.

(B) it measured both astronomical cycles and the change of seasons.

(C) its psychological function was more valuable than its cosmic function.

(D) it symbolized the individual as well as the community.

(E) it celebrated the diversity of personality types.

GO ON TO THE NEXT PAGE ⇒

2   2   2   2

23. The passage provides information most useful in answering which of the following questions?

(A) Which forces jeopardized the survival of the Plains Indians?

(B) Which personality traits did the Plains Indians consider to be dominant?

(C) Why were certain constellations considered important in Plains Indian cosmology?

(D) How did the Plains Indians calculate agricultural rhythms and seasonal changes?

(E) Why did the Plains Indians value tolerance and integration?

24. The primary purpose of this passage is to

(A) detail the spiritual beliefs of the Plains Indians.

(B) illustrate how Native Americans overcame adversity through tolerance and integration.

(C) describe both the cosmological and the psychological functions of the Medicine Wheel for the Plains Indians.

(D) suggest that the social value of the Medicine Wheel surpassed its natural value.

(E) analyze the personality traits recognized and valued by the Plains Indians.

25. The passage implies that the primary psychological function of the Medicine Wheel was to

(A) establish a hierarchy of personality traits.

(B) teach individuals to recognize their own personality types as well as those of other tribal members.

(C) encourage tribal members to develop those traits essential to the tribe's survival.

(D) orient tribal members to recurring cosmological and natural cycles.

(E) emphasize the value of passivity and tolerance to the community.

26. Which of the following provides the best title for the passage?

(A) Plains Indian Culture: A Proud Heritage

(B) Visionary Power and Cultural Survival

(C) The Medicine Wheel and Ancient Astronomy

(D) The Medicine Wheel: Instrument of Survival

(E) The Medicine Wheel: Mirror of Native American Psychology

27. Of the following, the author of the passage is most probably

(A) an anthropologist.

(B) an astronomer.

(C) a social psychologist.

(D) a theologian.

(E) an archaeologist.

IF YOU FINISH BEFORE TIME IS CALLED, YOU MAY CHECK YOUR WORK ON THIS SECTION ONLY. DO NOT WORK ON ANY OTHER SECTION IN THE TEST. STOP

3   3   3   3   3

Section III

Time—35 minutes 24 questions

Directions: Each group of questions is based on a set of conditions. You may wish to draw a rough sketch to help you answer some of the questions. Choose the best answer for each question and fill in the corresponding space on your answer sheet.

Questions 1–6

A salesperson will display nine cheeses in three groups of three cheeses each. The groups are labeled A, B, and

C. Four of the cheeses—F, G, H, and J—are domestic cheeses, and five—P, Q, R, S, and T—are imported cheeses. Each cheese will be displayed in exactly one of the three groups. The display must meet the following conditions:

> At least one cheese in each group must be a domestic cheese.
>
> F must be displayed with exactly two imported cheeses.
>
> Q must be displayed in Group C.
>
> S must be displayed in Group A.
>
> Neither F nor J nor R can be displayed in the same group as Q.

1. If both P and T are displayed in Group B, then which one of the following must be true?

    (A) F is displayed in Group A.

    (B) G is displayed in Group A.

    (C) H is displayed in Group A.

    (D) J is displayed in Group A.

    (E) R is displayed in Group A.

2. Which one of the following statements must be true?

    (A) If F and R are displayed together, they are displayed in the same group as S.

    (B) If G and H are displayed together, they are displayed in the same group as Q.

    (C) If G and T are displayed together, they are displayed in the same group as F.

    (D) If H and J are displayed together, they are displayed in the same group as P.

    (E) If R and S are displayed together, they are displayed in the same group as J.

3. All of the following are groups of three cheeses that can be displayed together in Group B EXCEPT

    (A) F, P, and R.

    (B) G, H, and T.

    (C) G, J, and R.

    (D) J, P, and T.

    (E) J, R, and T.

4. If G is displayed in Group A, then which one of the following could be true?

    (A) H is displayed in Group A.

    (B) J is displayed in Group B.

    (C) P is displayed in Group A.

    (D) R is displayed in Group A.

    (E) T is displayed in Group C.

5. If both H and P are displayed in Group B, then which one of the following must be the cheeses displayed in Group A?

    (A) F, J, S

    (B) F, R, S

    (C) F, S, T

    (D) J, S, R

    (E) J, S, T

6. If J is displayed in Group B, then which one of the following CANNOT be true?

    (A) F and R are displayed in the same group.

    (B) G and R are displayed in the same group.

    (C) H and S are displayed in the same group.

    (D) R and S are displayed in the same group.

    (E) S and T are displayed in the same group.

GO ON TO THE NEXT PAGE

3 **3** **3**

Questions 7–12

Fred's Fish Salon serves a special Friday night seafood banquet consisting of seven courses—flounder, grouper, haddock, jumbo shrimp, kingfish, lobster, and mackerel. Diners are free to select the order of the seven courses, according to the following conditions:

> The kingfish is served sometime after the jumbo shrimp.
>
> The grouper is served exactly two courses before the haddock.
>
> The lobster is served sometime before the grouper.
>
> The kingfish is served either fifth or sixth.
>
> The flounder is served second.

7. Which one of the following sequences would make for an acceptable banquet?

   (A) jumbo shrimp, flounder, lobster, mackerel, grouper, kingfish, haddock

   (B) jumbo shrimp, flounder, mackerel, grouper, kingfish, haddock, lobster

   (C) lobster, flounder, grouper, jumbo shrimp, kingfish, haddock, mackerel

   (D) lobster, flounder, jumbo shrimp, kingfish, grouper, mackerel, haddock

   (E) lobster, grouper, jumbo shrimp, haddock, kingfish, flounder, mackerel

8. Which one of the following is a complete and accurate list of the courses in which haddock can be served?

   (A) fifth, sixth

   (B) fourth, fifth, sixth

   (C) fifth, sixth, seventh

   (D) third, fifth, sixth, seventh

   (E) third, fourth, fifth, sixth, seventh

9. If kingfish is the fifth course served, then which one of the following must be true?

   (A) Grouper is the third course served.

   (B) Haddock is the fourth course served.

   (C) Jumbo shrimp is the third course served.

   (D) Lobster is the first course served.

   (E) Mackerel is the seventh course served.

10. Which one of the following would make it possible to determine the exact ordering of the courses?

    (A) Grouper is the fourth course served.

    (B) Haddock is the fifth course served.

    (C) Kingfish is the sixth course served.

    (D) Lobster is the first course served.

    (E) Mackerel is the seventh course served.

11. If kingfish is the sixth course served, then which one of the following CANNOT be true?

    (A) Grouper is the fifth course served.

    (B) Haddock is the seventh course served.

    (C) Jumbo shrimp is the fifth course served.

    (D) Lobster is the third course served.

    (E) Mackerel is the first course served.

12. If mackerel is the third course served, which one of the following must be true?

    (A) Grouper is the fourth course served.

    (B) Haddock is the seventh course served.

    (C) Jumbo shrimp is the first course served.

    (D) Kingfish is the fifth course served.

    (E) Lobster is the fourth course served.

GO ON TO THE NEXT PAGE

3 **3** **3**

Questions 13–18

There are five tin cans in a row, labeled one through five, from left to right. The five cans together contain a total of 10 marbles—4 red, 2 green, 2 blue, 1 orange, and 1 yellow. Each can contains at least one marble.

> The can containing the yellow marble is adjacent to the can containing the orange marble.
>
> The fourth can contains exactly three marbles, of which exactly two are red.
>
> The third can contains exactly two marbles.
>
> Exactly one of the blue marbles is in the second can.
>
> The first can contains no blue marbles.

13. If both green marbles are in the second can, how many marbles does the fifth can contain?

    (F) One

    (G) Two

    (H) Three

    (I) Four

    (J) Five

14. If the fifth can contains the orange marble and nothing else, which one of the following can possibly be a complete and accurate list of the marbles in the third can?

    (A) Two red marbles

    (B) One green marble and one red marble

    (C) One blue marble and one green marble

    (D) One blue marble, one green marble, and one red marble

    (E) One blue marble and two red marbles

15. If the first can contains three marbles, which one of the following CANNOT be true?

    (A) The first can contains a green marble.

    (B) The first can contains a yellow marble.

    (C) The first can contains a red marble.

    (D) The last can contains a yellow marble.

    (E) The last can contains an orange marble.

16. If the fifth can contains exactly two red marbles and one green marble, which one of the following is a complete and accurate list of the marbles in the first can?

    (A) One orange marble

    (B) One green marble

    (C) One yellow marble and one blue marble

    (D) One green marble and one yellow marble

    (E) One green marble and one orange marble

17. If the orange marble is in the third can and a green marble is in the fourth can, which one of the following must be true?

    (A) The first can contains a green marble.

    (B) The fifth can contains a green marble.

    (C) If the third can contains a green marble, then the fifth can contains a blue marble.

    (D) If the fifth can contains a blue marble, then the third can contains a green marble.

    (E) If the fifth can contains a green marble, then the third can contains a blue marble.

18. If the orange marble must be in the same can as two green marbles, which one of the following pairs of cans contains no red marbles?

    (A) The first and second

    (B) The first and third

    (C) The first and fifth

    (D) The second and third

    (E) The second and fifth

GO ON TO THE NEXT PAGE ▷

3 **3** **3** **3**

Questions 19–24

Four children—Peter, Rita, Sam, and Thelma—are in art class. Each child will work alone or in a pair. Each child or pair of children will create a project based on the following guidelines:

> If Peter works with either Sam or Thelma, the pair will create a clay figure. If Peter works by himself, he will create a clay figure.

> If Rita works with Peter, the pair will create a watercolor painting. If Rita works by herself, she will create a mobile.

> If Sam works with either Rita or Thelma, the pair will create a mobile. If Sam works by himself, he will create a watercolor painting.

> If Thelma works with Rita, the pair will create a papier-mache ball. If Thelma works by herself, she will create a papier-mache ball.

19. All of the following could be complete lists of all of the projects created by the children EXCEPT

   (A) clay figure, papier-mache ball.

   (B) mobile, watercolor painting.

   (C) mobile, mobile, clay figure.

   (D) clay figure, clay figure, watercolor painting.

   (E) clay figure, mobile, papier-mache ball, watercolor painting.

20. If no clay figures are created by the children, which one of the following pairs of children must work together?

   (A) Peter and Rita

   (B) Peter and Sam

   (C) Rita and Sam

   (D) Rita and Thelma

   (E) Sam and Thelma

21. If exactly two children work together and that pair creates a mobile, which one of the following could be the projects created by the children who work on their own?

   (A) Clay figure, mobile

   (B) Clay figure, watercolor painting

   (C) Mobile, papier-mache ball

   (D) Mobile, watercolor painting

   (E) Papier-mache ball, watercolor painting

22. If all of the children pair up and exactly one mobile is created, which one of the following pairs of children cannot work together?

   (A) Peter and Rita

   (B) Peter and Thelma

   (C) Rita and Sam

   (D) Rita and Thelma

   (E) Sam and Thelma

23. If all of the children pair up and none of the pairs creates a project that the individual children making up that pair would have created if each worked alone, then which one of the following must be the projects created by the children?

   (A) Clay figure, mobile

   (B) Clay figure, watercolor painting

   (C) Mobile, papier-mache ball

   (D) Mobile, watercolor painting

   (E) Papier-mache ball, watercolor painting

3   **3**

24. Which one of the following CANNOT be true?

   (A) Peter works alone, and exactly one papier-mache ball is created by the children.

   (B) Rita works alone, and exactly one clay figure is created by the children.

   (C) Sam works alone, and exactly two watercolor paintings are created by the children.

   (D) Exactly two mobiles are created by the children.

   (E) Exactly two papier-mache balls are created by the children.

IF YOU FINISH BEFORE TIME IS CALLED, YOU MAY CHECK YOUR WORK ON
THIS SECTION ONLY. DO NOT WORK ON ANY OTHER SECTION IN THE TEST.

STOP

4   **4**   **4**   **4**   **4**   **4**

Section IV

Time—35 minutes 25 questions

Directions: This test is comprised of questions that ask you to analyze the logic of statements or short paragraphs. You are to choose as the answer to each question the one choice you consider best on the basis of your commonsense evaluation of the statement and its assumptions. Although a question may seem to have more than one acceptable answer, there is only one best answer, and it is the one that does not entail making any illogical, extraneous, or conflicting assumptions about the question. These questions do not presuppose any knowledge of formal logic on your part.

1. The mural in the executive dining room was painted more than 40 years ago, and its subsequent exposure to extremes of heat and humidity has caused some of the once-vivid colors to fade. Fortunately, the muralist's preliminary studies included precise instructions for mixing pigments. Using these instructions and his leftover paints, skilled preservationists will be able to restore the mural to its original hues.

   Which one of the following is an assumption on which the conclusion logically depends?

   (A) The preservationists will be able to duplicate the muralist's technique.

   (B) The wide fluctuations in temperature and humidity typical of food service areas make the executive dining room a poor location for a mural.

   (C) The artist foresaw that the colors would fade with time.

   (D) The paints left over from the mural's creation have not themselves changed color.

   (E) Temperature- and humidity-control technology was insufficient at the time of the mural's painting to prevent its subsequent fading.

2. As today's agribusiness concerns standardize cultivation, older plant varieties are often dropped, and many are no longer available in seed form. For the plant breeder, the potential extinction of even ill-tasting and ugly varieties is cause for alarm. Such plants, scorned by backyard gardeners, may well contain desirable traits such as disease resistance and quick maturation.

   Which one of the following can be inferred from the passage?

   (A) Plant breeders seek to develop new varieties of cultivated plants without concern for their taste or appearance.

   (B) In the future, backyard gardeners will be able to choose from a greater variety of plants.

   (C) Individual traits from many plant varieties can be combined into a future hybrid.

   (D) Agribusiness concerns are seeking the extinction of many plant varieties.

   (E) The typical backyard gardener is not concerned with the maturation period of the plants he cultivates.

GO ON TO THE NEXT PAGE

4 4 4 4 4 4

3. Many undeveloped areas of the world suffer from air pollution, even though no factories or combustion engines are in use. Evidently, the connection between industrialization and air pollution has yet to be proved to the dispassionate observer.

Which one of the following most closely parallels the reasoning in the argument above?

(A) A few of his analyses of our capitalization program were overly optimistic. I think we can agree that he does not have the steadiness necessary to manage our banking division.

(B) When the new diet drink was tested at the shopping mall, some people detested the taste. It is safe to assume that most people will like it very much.

(C) Many people who rarely eat red meat have developed cardiac problems. We may conclude, therefore, that a diet including much red meat is not demonstrably harmful to the heart.

(D) Even if more students sign up for gymnastics, the school will still be buying the same amount of equipment for the sport. We must urge our gymnasts to scout out alternative sites for practice.

(E) At first, we hired a famous violinist to teach the music class, but few students improved dramatically. We should have just hired someone who knew only fundamentals.

4. The form of the Petrarchan sonnet fosters a more exquisite literary experience than does the form of the detective novel. We can be assured of this truth by the fact that the best critics, those with delicate sensibilities, inevitably prefer the Petrarchan sonnet to the detective novel. And we know these critics to be superior by their preference for the Petrarchan sonnet.

A proper critique of the logic expressed in the argument above would most likely point out that the author

(A) fails to cite specific critical authorities.

(B) assumes the point he wishes to establish.

(C) generalizes from a specific example to a general rule.

(D) does not provide evidence in support of his conclusion.

(E) fails to provide exceptions to the classification he outlines.

GO ON TO THE NEXT PAGE ⟩

4   4   4   4   4   4

5. When we returned home after our six-month vacation abroad, we found several drinking glasses shattered in place on the kitchen shelf—something that can only happen during a sonic boom or when there is an earth tremor. This must have been the loud noise that we heard not long after we drove off to the airport our last night in this country. Since there was no report on the car radio that night about tremors in the area, which always receive great attention, the glasses must have been shattered by a sonic boom, an occurrence so common that it is never reported.

The speaker's conclusion about the "loud noise" assumes which one of the following?

(A) It is easy to tell the difference between glass shattered by an earth tremor and that shattered by a sonic boom.

(B) A sonic boom always causes more damage in the house than does an earth tremor.

(C) No earth tremor has occurred since the night the family left on their vacation.

(D) The drinking glasses on the shelf were shattered because they were not securely protected.

(E) Every time there is an earth tremor in the area, some of the kitchen glassware will be shattered.

Questions 6 –7

6. Although very few philosophers can be neatly pigeonholed, some general classifications can be made. Most English philosophers, for example, are empiricists. Bradley is an English philosopher. Therefore, Bradley is probably an empiricist.

Which one of the following most closely parallels the reasoning used in the example above?

(A) I do not know who the anonymous author is. I do, however, know who my father is. Thus, the anonymous author is not my father.

(B) Nearly all very tall buildings have elevators. The Cole Monument is a very tall building. Therefore, it probably has an elevator.

(C) Late-night phone calls are irritating. Sue always phones late at night. Thus, Sue's calls are always irritating.

(D) Few French philosophers are materialists. Engels is a materialist. Therefore, Engels is probably not a French philosopher.

(E) Most people who vote do so out of a sense of duty. Therefore, those who do not vote must refrain because of reasons of conscience.

7. It would appear that, for most people in this society at least, monogamy is an essential feature of a healthy marriage. From this, it follows that a healthy marriage must be based on a mutual love between the partners. As Benjamin Franklin once said: "Where there is marriage without love, there will be love without marriage."

Which one of the following best exemplifies Franklin's reasoning?

(A) Because there is no taste in Jim's new diet, there will be tasting outside of it.

(B) Where there is a will there is a way, but where there is no will, there cannot be a way.

(C) While there may be courage without honor, there can be no honor without courage.

(D) Because Susie loves a man she is not married to, she will marry a man she does not love.

(E) Because none of these toys is very expensive, buying all of these toys is affordable.

GO ON TO THE NEXT PAGE

8. Educators have too eagerly embraced the rise, after a decade of decline, in median SAT scores. Unfortunately, this encouraging statistic is actually yet another indictment of our educational system. The scores have risen because fewer students take the tests. In particular, students with disadvantaged backgrounds have become discouraged and have given up their hopes of attending colleges that require the tests. In other words, the low scorers have dropped out of competition, and today's higher median scores reflect an increasingly homogeneous test-taking population of privileged students.

The author argues primarily by

(A) denying the accuracy of his opponents' figures.

(B) finding an alternative explanation for his opponents' evidence.

(C) refining an existing argument.

(D) defending an argument against the claims of his opponents.

(E) suggesting that his opponents may be unduly influenced by self-interest.

9. Recent studies have indicated that a certain type of freshwater cod has more tumors than other species of fish in the Hudson. Long before this phenomenon was recognized, significant strides had been made in clearing the river of chemical and other kinds of industrial pollution thought to promote tumorous growth.

Which one of the following conclusions can most reliably be drawn from the statements above?

(A) There is no causal link between chemical pollution and the tumors on the freshwater cod.

(B) A sudden change in the river environment has had a drastic effect on the freshwater cod.

(C) Efforts to clear the Hudson of chemical and other kinds of industrial pollution have not been vigorous enough.

(D) No other fish but the freshwater cod is susceptible to the effects of chemical and other kinds of industrial pollution.

(E) The mentioned studies provide no evidence that the number of tumors in the freshwater cod is related to the level of industrial pollution in the river.

GO ON TO THE NEXT PAGE ▷

4 **4** **4** **4** **4** **4**

10. Politics is the art of the possible; ideology, the articulation of the desirable. The ideologue will demand free lunch for all, and never alter his cry, but the like-minded politician will accept the offer of half-price lunch tickets or even a partial subsidy of dessert, waiting for another day to press the issue yet again.

In distinguishing between the politician and the ideologue, the author of the passage argues that

(A) the politician, unlike the ideologue, is willing to change his views to suit the occasion.

(B) the ideologue demands everything at once, but the politician sees the practical virtue of gaining a little bit at a time.

(C) a politician will accept whatever is possible, no matter what his announced ideology may be.

(D) the ideologue is more capable of addressing the desires of man, while the politician sees to such practical concerns as food and housing.

(E) neither the politician nor the ideologue is likely to be what he or she pretends to be.

Questions 11–12

The people behind this movement to impeach me charge that I drastically exacerbated our state's unemployment problems. By raising corporate taxes, they claim, I singlehandedly forced many labor-intensive industries to move out of the state. What they fail to realize, however, is that my purpose in increasing the corporate income tax was to raise revenues to fund a statewide jobs program. The remarks I made two years ago before the legislature would bear me out, if my detractors would read the Legislative Record. But no, they prefer to persecute me for wanting to create jobs and ease our state's economic woes.

11. Which one of the following is most similar logically to the response the author makes above?

(A) Emperor Hirohito's claim that, though he was opposed to Japan's invasion of Manchuria, he was powerless to restrain the military from launching it

(B) Benedict Arnold's declaration that, while he did not originally intend to betray the revolutionary army, the injustices he suffered forced him to do so

(C) Galileo's assertion that he had renounced his true beliefs before the Inquisition because failure to do so would have resulted in his conviction as a heretic

(D) Alfred Nobel's contention that he had invented dynamite to be used as a tool of peacetime technology rather than as the destructive weapon it later became

(E) Charles I's pronouncement on the scaffold that his duty had been to care for his subjects as a loving father and that he had done so to the best of his ability

GO ON TO THE NEXT PAGE

4   4   4   4   4   4

12. Which one of the following points out the principal flaw in the reasoning of the argument?

(A) There is no guarantee that a statewide jobs program would be effective in eliminating unemployment.

(B) The number of jobs created by a statewide jobs program would not necessarily offset the number of jobs lost as a result of the tax increase.

(C) The author's constituents want to impeach him because of the effects of his tax increase, not because of the intent of his tax increase.

(D) The author's claim concerning the intent of his tax increase is impossible to verify.

(E) Raising taxes is not an effective method of creating jobs in industry.

13. When I was in high school, the teachers were always warning us against ever using drugs. Yet many of the students freely admitted in later years that they had used drugs regularly in high school. I can only draw the unfortunate conclusion from this that my teachers' warnings were in vain.

Which one of the following claims, if true, would be most useful in refuting the argument of the passage above?

(A) Many of the students who used drugs were aware of the dangers involved because of the teachers' warnings.

(B) Some students use drugs for legitimate reasons.

(C) The school had to compel teachers to warn their students against drug use.

(D) Some of the author's fellow students were persuaded not to use drugs by their teachers' warnings.

(E) Drug use invariably results in bad study habits and poor class attendance.

14. No matter what their early education, some students seem to have more aptitude for mathematics than do others. Students with a facility for numbers usually learn musical theory more quickly than do equally intelligent students whose gifts are not primarily mathematical in nature. College students concentrating in the sciences, or in any other fields that tend to attract math-adept students, typically have less difficulty grasping the logic of compositions of so-called "new music" than do students majoring in the humanities.

Given the accuracy of the statements in the passage above, which one of the following draws the most well-founded conclusion from the passage?

(A) Students who major in the humanities have rarely taken courses in mathematics during the early years of their education.

(B) Students with a facility for numbers are generally more intellectually gifted than are students who major in the humanities.

(C) There is a direct correlation between musical talent and one's aptitude for mathematics.

(D) Students majoring in the humanities are likely to learn musical theory less quickly than are students concentrating in the sciences.

(E) Students who have an aptitude for mathematics do not choose to concentrate in the humanities at the college level.

GO ON TO THE NEXT PAGE

4   4   4   4   4   4

Questions 15–16

Government support for the arts cannot help but interfere with the free flow of the creative process. Monies, inevitably channeled at the dictates of the politically powerful, will accumulate around the established institutions when a certain philosophy prevails, or just as swiftly revert to the more experimental groups when the political pendulum swings. Individual creators will swerve willy-nilly, pursuing the funds at the expense of their own sure and inner-directed development.

15. The author's logic in the argument would be most weakened if which of the following were true?

(A) Approximately the same number of individual creative artists are associated with so-called established institutions as with the more experimental groups.

(B) In assigning monies to the arts, politicians in power heed the advice of committees composed of artists who are well known in their fields.

(C) While it can be argued that political ideas swing in and out of fashion, it is equally arguable that trends in the arts are often short-lived.

(D) Individual artists who produce lasting works of art do not typically tailor their efforts to attract monies, either private or public.

(E) Many people who would not otherwise experience the arts have had the opportunity to do so because of increased government funding over the past few years.

16. Which one of the following conclusions to a final sentence beginning, "As a result, the creative process in this country . . ." would be most appropriate, given the logic of the rest of the paragraph?

(A) would be continually diverted, distracted, and otherwise degraded by the intrusion of governmental decisions into the world of art.

(B) would become the plaything of the politically powerful, inevitably and irretrievably captured by the established institutions.

(C) would dry up entirely in those regions where political representation is weakest and thrive wholesomely in areas dominated by aggressive, successful political leaders.

(D) would be seen at its most exuberant when the political pendulum swings toward support of the experimental groups and at its most moribund when the reverse is true.

(E) might become, at last, the expression of the individual's own inner-directed development rather than a pale reflection of the prevailing political philosophy.

GO ON TO THE NEXT PAGE

17. The advantages of a college education are too precious to be squandered upon students who are not seriously dedicated to learning. Administrators should strenuously enforce the philosophy that enrollment in college is a privilege that must be earned, and earned again. When a student fails a course, he should be dismissed at once so that more deserving applicants can take his place.

Which one of the following, if true, is the best rebuttal of the argument advanced above?

(A) A student should not be expected to fulfill university requirements at the expense of choosing the electives needed for his individual course of study.

(B) The university may not have made the student fully aware of the demands of its curriculum and the intensity of study required.

(C) To dismiss a student who fails a course is to place achievement over the individual's right to education.

(D) Scholarship is only one of the possible contributions that a student might make to the university community.

(E) Personal and other circumstances unrelated to a student's dedication may have interfered with his studies and caused his grades to suffer.

18. The problem with arms reduction is that it is an illusory concept benefiting none. Even though designated stockpiles are being reduced, the weapons race continues, as the destructive power of new technologies and remaining arsenals is enhanced in order to maintain the pre-existing firepower. Thus, although it fosters an illusion of progress, arms reduction does nothing to curtail the proliferation of weaponry, and all must continue to live under the constant threat of annihilation.

Which one of the following, if true, would most strengthen the author's argument?

(A) Arms reduction allows steady maintenance of the existing balance of power.

(B) No arms limitation proposals have aimed at completely eliminating a nation's armament stockpile.

(C) The five largest military powers have increased funding for new weapons in each of the last 10 years.

(D) The distinction between offensive and defensive weapon systems is often merely a matter of interpretation.

(E) Arms limitation treaties have only accounted for the elimination of 15 percent of the total firepower possessed by the five largest military powers.

GO ON TO THE NEXT PAGE ▷

4   **4**   **4**   **4**   **4**   **4**

19. The summer heat wave and drought in the Midwest threaten to cut the 1988 corn harvest by more than one-third. Such a shortfall will undoubtedly lead to higher meat and other food prices in 1989, rises that could be as high as 18.6 percent in 1989 and 20.8 percent in 1990. Either we can ignore this problem, or else we can spend a comparatively small amount now to irrigate some of the major corn fields. Those who believe that we should not spend this money forget that if we do not, we face an imminent food shortage and economic disaster.

    The argument assumes that

    (A) the government can afford the cost of irrigation now.

    (B) irrigation is the only way that the crop yield can be significantly increased.

    (C) the heat wave and drought will persist through 1990.

    (D) irrigation will ensure that corn harvests reach expected yields.

    (E) other agricultural areas are also not expected to meet their anticipated corn yields in 1988.

20. Those who condemn the governor for being unsympathetic to the plight of the automobile industry are just using that allegation as a smokescreen for their own partisan politics. The naive citizen who believes their charges fails to realize that a politician may sometimes appear to be lacking compassion for a special interest group when, in reality, he is just trying to implement a public policy that is beneficial to great numbers of people representing diverse interests.

    Which one of the following, if true, provides the strongest support for the assertion made in the first sentence of the passage?

    (A) Sometimes it is difficult to distinguish between insensitivity to special interest groups and public-spirited devotion to broader concerns.

    (B) The governor's harshest critics are members of automobile workers' unions and politicians with strong ties to the automotive industry.

    (C) Many people who accuse the governor of being unsympathetic to the plight of the automobile industry voted for him in the last election.

    (D) The governor is not a politician who makes a clear distinction between partisan politics and civic responsibility.

    (E) Sometimes a politician believes he is acting in the community's best interest when, in reality, he is just being insensitive to the concerns of a minority group.

GO ON TO THE NEXT PAGE ⟶

21. Without the profound structural changes in the Irish agricultural economy that began with the first grudging acceptance of the potato into the human diet, the great Potato Famine of the 1840s would never have been the disaster it was. Although other staples continued to be cultivated, primarily for export to England, the total dependence of much of the Irish population on potatoes turned the blight-induced failure of several potato crops in the latter part of the decade into a sweeping sentence of death or emigration.

Which one of the following conclusions can most reliably be drawn from the statements in the passage?

(A) The adoption of the potato as the staple of the Irish diet represented a nationalistic rejection of English social patterns.

(B) Other staples are less susceptible to crop failure than is the potato.

(C) Reliance on a single crop made Ireland a fertile ground for revolutionary activity when that crop failed.

(D) Absence of alternative sources of food left much of the Irish population with nothing to eat when the potato crop failed.

(E) Those who resisted the potato when it was introduced into Ireland did so to forestall the potential dangers of a restructured agricultural system.

22. Imagine that upon entering your living room I find that you are reading a book I consider morally repugnant; imagine that in my indignation I steal the volume and burn it or simply rip out the offending pages; and imagine that when you file a complaint you find that my behavior is condoned by the police and the courts. This may seem absurd, but if you replace me in this scenario with certain moralistic individuals, and if you replace your living room with your children's schools and our municipal libraries, the result is a description of a situation that is eating away at the very roots of our constitutional system—the banning of so-called "offensive" books from our library collections.

Which one of the following describes the principal weakness in the author's analogy?

(A) Burning a book is more violent than banning a book.

(B) The police and the courts do not condone the theft of personal property.

(C) Schools and municipal libraries, unlike the reader's living room, are public institutions.

(D) Books that may be suitable for adults may not be suitable for children.

(E) The Constitution does not clearly define what makes a book "offensive" in the eyes of the law.

GO ON TO THE NEXT PAGE ⟶

4   4   4   4   4   4

23. During exam periods, cookie sales in the college cafeteria are high. Cookies are selling well in the cafeteria today, so it must be exam time.

Which one of the following is logically most similar to the argument above?

(A) Proficiency at logical thinking is enough to ensure success in the computer programming field. But there are no computer programmers among my friends, so they must all be illogical.

(B) Someone who thinks logically can become a computer programmer. David thinks very logically, so he can become an excellent programmer.

(C) Skill in thinking logically is one guarantee of success at computer programming; a degree from a prestigious computer science department is another.

(D) A computer programmer must be able to think logically. Rob is a very logical person, so he must be a programmer.

(E) Computer programmers are always able to solve logic problems. None of the students can solve logic problems, so none of them are computer programmers.

24. Deviations from social norms, particularly in such emotionally charged areas as eating, are usually accompanied by defensiveness, self-justification, and attempts at proselytizing others. That eating meat is still fundamental to mainstream American culture can be seen from the fact that most vegetarians, regardless of the specific motivation underlying their diet, express strong feelings about the rightness of their eating pattern and its potential benefits for others.

A logical critique of the argument above would most likely emphasize which one of the following?

(A) The difference between proselytizing and educating others

(B) The failure to consider that not all proselytizers are deviants

(C) The failure to define "mainstream American culture"

(D) The author's evident prejudice against vegetarians

(E) The actual number of vegetarians in America today

GO ON TO THE NEXT PAGE

4   4   4   4   4   4

25. Each and every one of the typists who works at the Ace Employment Agency works overtime. Jonathan Simson works overtime at the Ace Employment Agency. Therefore, Jonathan Simson must be a typist.

Which one of the following is most similar in structure to the above argument?

(A) All rabbits eat carrots. My pet, Scamper, eats carrots, so he must be a rabbit.

(B) All members of the Eastside Racquetball Club purchase raffle tickets. Suzanne Child is a member of the Eastside Racquetball Club. Therefore, she must purchase raffle tickets.

(C) Every woman who chooses to take this drug must be aware of the risks involved. Joanne doesn't like to take risks. Therefore, she will not choose to take this drug.

(D) Every performer who sings at the nightclub is served a free meal. Therefore, if you are hungry, you should arrange to sing at the nightclub.

(E) None of the construction workers at this site belong to a union. Jack Krone is not a construction worker at this site. Therefore, he belongs to a union.

IF YOU FINISH BEFORE TIME IS CALLED, YOU MAY CHECK YOUR WORK ON THIS SECTION ONLY. DO NOT WORK ON ANY OTHER SECTION IN THE TEST. **STOP**

4   **4**

LSAT WRITING SAMPLE TOPIC

Margaret has received $6,500 in an insurance settlement. The money is an unexpected boon to Margaret, who has taught elementary school for the past six years. She is trying to decide which of two possible ways to spend the money. Write an essay explaining why one plan is superior to the other. Two factors should help formulate your decision:

1. Margaret wants to use the money for something that will prove to be of long-range advantage.
2. Margaret is unable to contribute any of her own funds, so the insurance money must cover the entire cost of the plan she selects.

Margaret is considering buying her own car. She has been commuting to work by public transportation but has long desired the personal freedom that having her own car could provide. Since she wants a car that is fully protected under both manufacturer's and dealer's warranties, Margaret has decided against buying a used car, which would have been considerably less expensive. She has also decided against the smaller and less expensive cars because she fears that they would be unsafe in a collision. She has found a midsize car within her price range. The insurance money will leave her with monthly payments only slightly higher than her current transportation costs. Title and insurance will add to the cost, but Margaret feels that by getting two other teachers to join her in a carpool, she can manage the expense. If all goes according to schedule, the car should be paid for within two years.

The insurance money could also be used to pay for a master's degree in psychology. Margaret's ultimate goal is to become a school psychologist, and toward this end, she has been working as a volunteer counselor for a hotline serving runaways and troubled teenagers. Margaret would have to give up this volunteer work to take classes three nights a week at the state university, but she feels that she can keep her current job while studying. The money would fund tuition, books, and incidental expenses but would not be sufficient to cover her expenses for the required six-month internship.

IF YOU FINISH BEFORE TIME IS CALLED, YOU MAY CHECK YOUR WORK ON THIS SECTION ONLY. DO NOT WORK ON ANY OTHER SECTION IN THE TEST. | STOP

PRACTICE TEST ONE: ANSWER KEY

Section I Logical Reasoning	Section II Reading Comprehension	Section III Logic Games	Section IV Logical Reasoning
1. A	1. B	1. E	1. D
2. C	2. A	2. B	2. C
3. D	3. B	3. B	3. C
4. C	4. D	4. E	4. B
5. C	5. C	5. B	5. C
6. A	6. B	6. C	6. B
7. A	7. B	7. A	7. A
8. B	8. B	8. C	8. B
9. B	9. E	9. E	9. E
10. B	10. E	10. B	10. B
11. B	11. A	11. C	11. D
12. A	12. B	12. B	12. C
13. B	13. D	13. A	13. D
14. B	14. C	14. C	14. D
15. E	15. E	15. B	15. D
16. B	16. C	16. B	16. A
17. B	17. C	17. C	17. E
18. B	18. C	18. E	18. C
19. D	19. B	19. D	19. B
20. C	20. B	20. A	20. B
21. C	21. B	21. A	21. D
22. A	22. C	22. D	22. C
23. D	23. D	23. D	23. D
24. A	24. C	24. E	24. B
25. D	25. B		25. A
26. C	26. D		
	27. A		

ANSWERS AND EXPLANATIONS

SECTION I: LOGICAL REASONING

1. A

The author's conclusion is that our nation's courts are currently clogged with disputes that could be solved by other means. The passage contains no real evidence for this, oddly enough; the author merely defines litigiousness and claims that the American judicial system suffers from an excess of it—citing only the opinion of judicial experts, but no real facts. So the answer choice that best supports the passage will be the one that does provide examples or other significant evidence to support the author's claim. Only choice (A) offers the needed examples: an increasing number of court cases involving labor/management disputes that could be settled by government boards.

(B) fails to support the conclusion; it merely indicates an effect of litigiousness—low unemployment among lawyers.

(C) tries to justify litigiousness on the grounds that it has redeeming social value, "since it may encourage shy individuals to defend their own rights." But whether litigiousness per se is a bad thing is not the issue here; the issue is whether or not our legal system suffers from an excess of litigiousness.

(D) would have you doubt the validity of studies of litigiousness, but the passage never mentions any such studies.

(E) attempts to explain the litigiousness of urban dwellers. But the author has not claimed that the courts are backed up by unnecessary lawsuits brought by greedy city dwellers; the claim is that courts everywhere are besieged by unnecessary lawsuits.

2. C

The author's argument is that the decline the Japanese imperial power underwent was not due to a fundamental bias favoring clan loyalty over loyalty to the emperor. The evidence supporting this claim is that for hundreds of years during this period of decline,

centralized power was held by shoguns, who ruled in the name of the emperor. The assumption here is that the rule of the shoguns was in fact imperial rule rather than clan-based rule. In the passage, you're given little information about this. Choice (C) claims that, in fact, the shoguns were representative of the different clans and ruled with little regard for the emperor. This contradicts the assumption and makes the example of the shoguns a piece of evidence for the author's opponents.

(A) does not weaken the argument, because you're essentially concerned with *who* held power rather than *why* they held power. It does deny that there was loyalty involved, but that doesn't greatly weaken the claim made.

(B) gives a piece of history that implies nothing about the type of rule the shoguns exercised or about the object of people's loyalty and obedience.

(D) reduces the power of the shoguns during the early part of the period being discussed and gives it to the emperor. Because the author mentions the shoguns as an example of the reach of imperial power, their later ascendance does not weaken the argument.

(E), too, provides another reason for the decline of the imperial power and so would strengthen the author's case, not weaken it.

3. D

The argument concludes that factories that want to increase productivity should pay workers on a piecemeal scale rather than an hourly wage. In other words, they should pay based on the number of finished products rather than on the time spent working. The evidence provided is that paying on a piecemeal scale will maximize worker incentive; workers will work harder. But does a harder-working factory worker necessarily produce more items? You don't know. Suppose the factory is heavily mechanized or short on raw materials. Suppose, that is, that the number of items a worker can produce is not determined by how hard the worker works but by some other factor. In that case, such a proposal will motivate workers yet not increase productivity. So the author must be assuming choice (D), that workers who work harder will produce more items than those who do not. This assumption is necessary to link the evidence concerning motivation to the conclusion concerning productivity.

(A) is not assumed because it's not necessary that most factories pay an hourly wage, merely that some do so.

(B) is also wrong because it speaks of "most factories." Determine the scope of Logical Reasoning arguments carefully.

(C) is too strong to be a necessary assumption. The author argues that piecemeal pay is an incentive to increase productivity but not that piecemeal pay is the *only* incentive that can increase productivity.

(E), concerning workers' preferences, is clearly outside the argument's scope. What the workers prefer is of no concern to this argument.

4. C

The conclusion of this argument is that the recent surge in popularity of college-level foreign language classes will decrease the number of graduates who are capable of appreciating the subtleties of another culture's means of expression. The evidence is that most of these newly popular classes employ conversational methods. The assumption that links evidence and conclusion is that conversational methods (as distinct from the traditional format of grammar exercises and rigorous analysis of literary texts) will not teach students cultural subtleties. In other words, the author assumes that if you've been trained in the conversational method, you'll be unable to appreciate the subtleties of that foreign culture's means of expression. Choice (C) articulates this assumption and is, therefore, correct.

(A) brings in the extraneous idea of abolishing the foreign language requirement to get rid of the conversation classes. But the author's argument isn't about saving or abandoning the requirement; it's about the effects of different kinds of language classes, so (A) is not assumed.

(B) plays on the assertions made in the first two sentences of the passage: first, that attendance in college-level foreign language classes is up and, second, that most of these classes are conversational in format. However, the author is not assuming that, given a choice, students prefer conversation classes to the more traditional format. This may be the case, but the question of student choice is simply not an issue here.

(D) is plausible: It sounds like a possible long-term effect of what the author considers a surfeit of second-rate classes producing second-rate students. However, (D) is not an assumption of the argument. (D) would probably function better as a further conclusion to the author's argument, but it doesn't link the author's evidence with his actual conclusion.

(E) simply contradicts the entire thrust of the passage, which is that newfangled teaching methods are producing students with inadequate foreign language skills. If the author assumes that most students have a reading knowledge of a foreign language, why would he complain about the new format? Furthermore, if a student has gained this reading knowledge from the now popular conversation classes, the author's argument would be weakened. (E), therefore, cannot be an assumption of the argument.

5. C

The author of the argument disagrees with the "cynical" claim that a child's socioeconomic background is the factor that determines his or her later intellectual capacity. She then presents the results of a study, which show (she claims) that the level of prekindergarten education, not socioeconomic background, actually determines subsequent intellectual prowess. Thus, the best description of the argument is (C).

(A) is wrong because the evidence the author provides is not the same as that on which the "cynical" conclusion was originally based; the study is new evidence that she's come up with.

(B) is contrary to the author's point that socioeconomic background does not determine intelligence.

(D) can't be right, because as far as you know, the author's opponents have not presented any statistics at all.

(E) seems to say that the author has shown that high intelligence causes a high socioeconomic background, which, aside from making no sense, contradicts the author's stated opinion that the two things (socioeconomic background and intelligence) do not correlate.

6. A

The author believes that by demonstrating that the level of prekindergarten education correlates with future intelligence, she has shown that future intelligence is not a result of socioeconomic background. If it is true, as (A) states, that the level of prekindergarten education correlates with socioeconomic background, then all three things correlate, and it becomes likely that future intelligence *and* prekindergarten education are effects of socioeconomic background.

(B) would actually help the author's argument by showing that socioeconomic background has no effect on the children's later intelligence.

(C) doesn't tell you enough to be a good answer; what is the relationship between amount of attention and amount of prekindergarten education?

(D) fails because it sheds no light on the issue of what, if anything, accounts for high intelligence—socioeconomic background or prekindergarten education.

(E) can have no effect on the author's argument, which does not concern how many children receive prekindergarten education but rather what that pre-kindergarten education means for later intelligence.

7. A

This passage sets up a distinction between two apparently different concepts of "personality," as the author views them: our current idea of self-created individuality and the traditional Bambara notion of the individual as part of a larger whole. After contrasting the concepts, he argues that the latter is preferable; the personality that is "the sum of many parts" will be the richer type. In other words, as stated in choice (A), the author believes that richness of personality has a relationship with the degree to which one is integrated with a society; the former follows from the latter.

(B) describes two related aspects of our society's idea of personality. These are similar ideas, however, and are not presented in a relationship that is central to making the main argument of the passage.

(C) is 180. An inaccurate relationship is described. Far from arguing that diversity of personality and selfcenteredness are in any way related, the author explicitly states the reverse.

The relationship in (D) is not discussed by the author; it cannot be reasonably inferred from the passage that he would agree that such a relationship exists.

(E) suggests that the development of the self, according to the concepts described in the first part of the passage, might be affected by the kind of intrusions mentioned, but such a relationship is not presented directly, much less used for purposes of argument.

8. B

The argument of the passage is not closely reasoned, as you may have noticed in the use of "however" in the second sentence. The adverb implies that what follows is a refutation of the first sentence. In fact, there is no such clear, logical relationship: There need not be a conflict between the notion that American voters prefer a combative presidential candidate and the poll showing voter disaffection in 1988. Because the writer assumes the connection, he concludes that the disaffection, added to the feeling of many voters that the candidates were not "presidential," proves that aggressive candidates are not gaining voter respect. As we have seen, the logical error occurs in the writer's assumption that "people had been annoyed" by the "combativeness, even aggressiveness" of candidates and not by something else. His argument is seriously weakened, therefore, if, as stated in (B), the poll did not reveal that voters were annoyed by combativeness in the campaign. Furthermore, there is no indication that any of the candidates actually were combative or aggressive.

(A) is completely off the point. The issue is not whether the 1988 campaign was "memorable" but whether it revealed a change in voter attitudes toward combativeness.

(C) refers to a general attitude on the part of many voters, but the passage is confined to an argument about specific attitudes that the author feels were created by specific events of the 1988 election. A prior climate of public skepticism would not damage the argument, unless we knew that combativeness did not play a role in those earlier elections.

(D) is incorrect. An attempt is made to soften the charge of aggressiveness by redefining it as a somewhat more admirable and arguably essential quality for a politician. Even if this were true, however, the passage is concerned with public perceptions rather than with a discussion of the merits of what looks like combativeness.

(E) is an interpretation of events that, however legitimate in itself, has no effect on the basic argument of the passage. This choice addresses a general concept, not the specific 1988 campaign and the specific topic of the effectiveness of combative campaigning styles.

9. B

The argument concludes that frozen vegetables are healthier than fresh vegetables. The evidence for this claim is the fact that vegetables are most nutritious when allowed to ripen on the vine. This fact must be applied to the farmer's situation. Because of the time necessary to ship fresh produce, fresh produce must be harvested before it's ripe. Thus, fresh produce lacks some of its possible nutritive value. Frozen vegetables, on the other hand, can be allowed to ripen on the vine prior to freezing. Thus, although freezing produce robs them of some nutrients, the fact that they can be vine-ripened adds nutrients. The author's conclusion, that frozen produce is healthier, is only true, however, if the nutritional loss entailed by freezing is less than the loss entailed by premature harvesting. Thus, the argument assumes choice (B).

The author speaks of vegetables in general, not specific vegetables, so (A) is not assumed. Likewise for (E); the

contrast is not between different *vegetables* but rather between different *ways* of harvesting and distributing vegetables.

(C) is not assumed. Even if the fresh produce doesn't sit on the shelf, the author can still argue that it is less nutritious.

(D) is irrelevant. The author is concerned with the nutritional value of the produce prior to any freezing by the consumer.

10. B

Because the author has described a *possible* farming scenario in which frozen vegetables are healthier than fresh vegetables, and because the author has concluded that this scenario has *real* consequences for our diets, the author must be assuming that farms *do* operate as described. The argument, therefore, will be severely weakened by choice (B), which claims that farmers do not operate according to the author's model. If all vegetables are harvested at the same time (which would have to be prematurely), then the frozen vegetables aren't vine ripened, and the author's evidence falls apart.

The relative nutritional content of overripe and underripe vegetables, (A), is irrelevant because the author is speaking only of ripe vegetables. The author's point rests on how these ripe vegetables came to be ripe.

(C) speaks of refrigeration, which is not the same as freezing and, therefore, has no impact on the argument.

(D) speaks of the few consumers who can buy directly from the farm. Yet the author is speaking about the vast majority of consumers who must buy their produce from middlemen.

(E) concerns the taste of the two types of vegetables. The author, though, is concerned solely with nutritional content; nothing about taste will weaken the argument.

11. B

As always, begin with the clearest piece: The conclusion says that someone should not recommend something. Answer choices (A) and (B) both have similar conclusions, but none of the remaining answer choices do. That means that when it comes to assessing the evidence, we can ignore wrong answer choices (C), (D), and (E) altogether and focus in on the two remaining choices. The evidence in the stimulus says that there's a benefit to something, so it's been recommended, but there's also a risk. Correct answer choice (B) is a perfect match—these green vegetables have been recommended by dieticians, but they can cause blood problems. Wrong answer choice (A), on the other hand, says something was *thought* to have a benefit but that turned out not to be true.

Remember: By breaking down the stimulus in a Parallel Reasoning question and checking the clearest piece against each answer choice first, you can save yourself a lot of reading, a lot of comparison, and a lot of opportunities to get bogged down in a wrong answer choice.

12. A

The author argues that the bill outlawing capital punishment should be passed. Her reasoning is that if the opponents of the bill actually visit those who stand to be executed, they will see that these criminals deserve our mercy. The author, then, is not presenting any logical evidence to support her view on the bill; she is appealing to her opponents' emotions—mercy, in particular. Thus, (A) is correct.

(B) is incorrect because aside from incorrectly using emotion as a logical principle, she states no other principle.

(C) is incorrect because there's no reason to believe that her speech is ironic or mocking.

(D) fails because she attacks only the fact that her opponents have not visited death row and felt the appropriate amount of mercy. You're never given a clue as to how they presented their opposing view.

(E) is incorrect because she hasn't ignored some distinction relevant to her opponents' case. When in doubt, try to fit the specific piece—can you name the distinction she ignores? If not, there's probably a good reason for that!

13. B

The author warns us not to confuse charity with self-interest by preventing a convict from exercising free will in the choice of a new career. To do this would be "to deny the very individuality of expression that true rehabilitative programs should develop." You can thus expect a concluding statement that completes this theme—that convicts must be permitted free choice in determining their new careers. Only choice (B) takes this approach. If we try to rehabilitate convicts in careers of *our* choosing, we may frustrate them to the point that they return to a life of crime.

(A) and (E) both contradict the author's message by arguing that someone else should have the power to determine a convict's new career: either professional advisors, (A), or society as a whole, (E).

Even choice (C) is sneakily repressive: Would the author take such a stand with a convict who *wanted* a new career in an institutional setting? Moreover, (C) is a broad generalization that comes from left field.

Finally, the motivation behind the criminal act, choice (D), is irrelevant to the issue of whether a convict should be allowed to choose his or her new career.

14. B

The author recommends a course of action, the application of economic sanctions, because in his view, the relocation of companies from city to isolated suburbs has decreased the contribution made to state revenues by the corporate income tax. How? The new locations require expensive helicopter transportation for personnel; this expense is deductible from corporate tax payments. The assumption here, evidently, is that the corporate moves have not also had the contrary effect upon a company's total deductible business expenses. In other words, as suggested in choice (B), the paragraph takes for granted that "other economies" have not accompanied the move to the suburban locations, thus offsetting the effect of the increased transportation costs and sustaining or possibly raising the total amounts paid in corporate income taxes.

(A) is not a useful criticism of the author's reasoning since it is a given of the situation that helicopter transportation has been found "necessary." The use of the term indicates that reasonable alternatives do not exist.

(C) is based on at least two unwarranted assumptions: that the helicopters are manufactured in the state whose finances are being discussed and that the taxes generated would be at least as great as the amount lost from the taxes of the companies using the helicopters. There is no justification for assuming either of these to be the case. In fact, the helicopters are described as "imported," indicating that they were manufactured elsewhere.

In (D), there is a similar reliance upon unjustified assumptions. While it is possible that helicopter travel in the suburbs might have the effect of increasing productivity above levels in the city (with its mass transit), it is not very likely. Nor do we know that this supposed rise in taxes would be great enough to offset the loss that the author of the passage now deplores.

(E) is incorrect. The author is not required to demonstrate any difficulties other than those mentioned in the passage. As long as helicopter use reduces tax income, the argument stands.

15. E
The Consortium's policy statement tells you that, although a student at any of its colleges may enroll in certain classes at any other member college, the student's own academic dean has final say on whether these courses may be taken for credit or used to satisfy degree requirements. If the academic dean has final say in this matter, then the implication is that he or she can refuse to accept credits awarded by other member colleges for these courses. Thus, choice (E) is the correct answer.

(A) would have you believe that the policy statement was about transferring enrollment from one member college to another and not about the transferring of credits, which is actually the case.

(B) and (D) bring in irrelevant issues never touched upon by the author and not implied by the policy statement; this passage has nothing to do with either

nonacademic programs, choice (B), or codes of conduct, choice (D).

(C) directly contradicts the first sentence of the passage, in which the author tells us that students are "permitted and encouraged" to attend classes at any other member college.

16. B
This passage is a brief history of society's changing view of physicians from the beginning of the 20th century to the present. In sum, you are told that the great strides in combating disease have led patients nowadays to expect that medical professionals, once less able to heal than to give comfort, should always deliver technically proficient service rather than, as (B) would have it, "sympathy." In effect, (B) is a condensed version of the idea expressed in the last sentence of the paragraph.

(A) is incorrect. You are not told how the physician views the job; the emphasis is on the expectations patients may have of medical professionals.

(C) cannot be inferred, for it is the author's main contention that the rapid increase in medical successes has led patients to expect "perfect performance." Even if one were to interpret the phrase "medical incompetence" somewhat differently, as referring to individual failures within the profession, (C) is simply not addressed in the passage; no comparison is made between the competence of physicians in the past and that of today's medical professionals.

(D) goes too far. There is no suggestion here that health care workers have become less sensitive; again, the emphasis is on the patients' expectations.

(E) is beyond the scope, as malpractice suits are never mentioned at all in the passage.

17. B
As in two earlier questions, the point here is to grasp the essential structure of the argument in the passage, then compare it with the logical structure of each of the answer choices. Here, you are asked to select the answer choice with a structure most similar to that of the passage given, in which the author argues that the possible danger of psychological testing of

schoolchildren is outweighed by the likelihood that the results of such testing will benefit students. In other words, an activity should be pursued if the good effects will probably be greater than the possible bad effects. Similarly, (B) states that arms limitation talks should be pursued because increased chances of survival outweigh the possible risks involved. The subjects of the two arguments are different, but the logical structures are similar.

(A) does not argue in favor of pursuing a certain activity (intensive short-term testing of drugs) but attacks it, bringing up an objection that, to the author, affirms the need for the alternative program of long-term testing.

(C) is incorrect. The claim being discussed—that hospitals serve high-sodium, high-starch diets—is merely dismissed with the counterclaim that hospital menus are designed by trained nutritionists (the assumption being that trained nutritionists would not design harmful meals).

The structure of (D) at first seems roughly similar to that of the passage. The good results (improved vision, improved appearance) are contrasted with the bad effects, the inconveniences as compared with eyeglasses. But "inconveniences" do not weaken the possible good of wearing lenses; they are a side effect, not something detrimental to the essential aim of improved vision. In addition, the argument, unlike that of the paragraph, includes a comparison between two alternatives, rather than merely discussing the merits and possible drawbacks of only one.

(E) is an argument for adding devices (swinging doors, pedal-controlled wash basins) to make another device (the public restroom) appear less dangerous, or contagious, than people think it is. Rather than weigh a greater good against a possible lesser evil, this argument contends that the public should be distracted from concern over a perceived, but possibly nonexistent, evil.

18. B

There is no connection between rent control laws in New York and abandonment of apartment houses there, this passage argues, because no such connection can consistently be found in all other cities. We read that some cities without the laws have experienced widespread abandonment, while some cities with the laws have not. In other words, the logic here is aptly summed up in answer choice (B): The rent control laws of New York could not be responsible for abandonment because cities exist where similar laws did not have a similar effect.

The assumption in (A), even if true, would not help explain the apparently conflicting data; after all, it is the author's point of view that the rent control laws do not cause abandonment, but the assumption of (A) would in fact strengthen the likelihood of such a causal connection.

(C) is completely unwarranted. You have no indication that the author believes the laws to be beneficial simply because she argues that they are not responsible for one problem—the abandonment of apartment houses.

(D) is incorrect because it contradicts the author's contention that New York's rent control laws did not foster widespread abandonment of property.

(E) also contradicts the author, who would not use "despite" to refer to laws that she feels have no effect upon abandonment. In addition, she has made abundantly clear that she accepts as a given that abandonment in New York has indeed been "widespread" rather than "only negligible."

19. D

You're told that the September stock market fall shook the economy. Then you're told that retail sales during the holiday season were lower, when compared to the total annual sales, than in any of the previous 20 years. This is followed with the statement that retailers and lawmakers are worried, and that the latter may institute new rules concerning stock trading. Well, what inference leaps out at you? The inference that the stock market plummet is responsible for the fall in retail sales or, at least, those considering the new legislation must believe it is. As a result, (D) is inferable.

(A), and the stock market's wishes, are outside the scope of the passage. Although the legislature is considering rules, we have no indication that the market desires such rules or any other "aid."

(B)—Similarly, the typical habits of legislators are also outside the argument's scope. This argument concerns only the recent market plummet.

(C) All that can be inferred from this piece is that the new rules might protect the market and retail sales, not that they will increase the volume of retail sales.

(E) is not the main point because no indication of the seriousness of previous market falls is given. It was the holiday season retail sales that hit a 20-year low.

20. C

This author argues that an individual ought to be allowed to help a "pain-wracked, dying friend" to commit suicide. To do so would not be an act of murder, according to the author, but a giving of solace and a mark of respect for an individual's free choice. The correct inference can be drawn from the final sentence of the passage, where the author concludes that lawmakers and judges must treat such cases reasonably, instead of responding "as they have with traditional prejudice." You can infer, then, that lawmakers and judges disagree with the author (otherwise, the author would not be trying to win them over to his side). Choice (C) is thus the correct answer: Lawmakers and judges, according to the author, feel that assistance of suicide is murder, and the author wishes to change their minds.

(A) is sensible but cannot be inferred from the passage. A logical inference must be provable, or at least likely, solely on the basis of the given information. The author never discusses his idea in the context of other societies, so you cannot infer a universal application for it.

(B) is far off the mark. The passage says nothing about the thoughts and feelings of the terminally ill; perhaps very few contemplate suicide.

(D) goes too far. The author very carefully describes exactly the type of assistance of suicide he thinks is justified and never implies that the act of suicide is always an act of self-deliverance.

(E) also tries to cover too much ground. The author's case for the legality of suicide assistance rests on the free choice of the victim, not on the amount of pain the victim is suffering.

21. C

The stimulus tells you about courses taken by master's degree candidates. If a master's degree candidate enrolled during or after 1977, then he or she takes a Heidegger seminar. This, of course, does not mean that candidates enrolled during or prior to 1977 do not take a Heidegger seminar. You don't know anything about those people. Furthermore, if a master's degree candidate enrolled after 1981, then he or she takes a Wittgenstein seminar. You're given information about a specific student—that he or she took a Heidegger seminar but not a Wittgenstein seminar—and are asked for an inference about the student. You can infer nothing unless the student is a master's degree candidate, because all your information is limited to this type of student. Thus, choices (A) and (B) need not be true. If the student is a master's degree candidate, then we know that not taking a Wittgenstein seminar means that he or she could not have enrolled after 1981. Thus, as correct choice (C) has it, if the student is a master's degree candidate, he or she must have enrolled prior to 1982. To have enrolled after 1981 and not taken a Wittgenstein seminar would deny the second stimulus statement. As for when prior to 1982 the student enrolled, we haven't a clue. It could have been after 1977, as choice (E) says, which would explain the Heidegger seminar. Yet it could also have been before 1978, as (D) has it. Remember, the stimulus does not say that only those enrolled after 1977 take a Heidegger seminar.

22. A

To fill in the blank correctly, you must understand the basic argument of the paragraph, which links government-stabilized pricing with increased inefficiency and decreased individual initiative. Mirroring this concept is the author's conclusion that the reverse policy would have the reverse effect; efficiency would increase in a free market as efficient producers gain deserved economic rewards. The topic sentence, therefore, must convey the notion that government control of prices would not result in such deserved rewards. On the contrary, as stated in correct answer choice (A), undeserving producers who have been inefficient in a free market would be rewarded.

(B) is nonsensical. The mandated pricing might have any number of economic repercussions, but the price level itself would be lower because the policy would so ordain. Whether the lower prices would reflect economic reality is another matter.

(C) The author has made clear in the passage that she is in sharp disagreement with the proposal to control grain prices. This answer choice incorrectly suggests that the idea represents some sort of happy medium rather than, as the author believes, a wrongheaded policy.

Whereas (D) is a possible effect of the proposal, it is not a topic explored by the author in the rest of the passage and would not logically be raised.

(E) is based on a misreading of the author's economic assumptions. She believes that government should not intervene in what to her is the natural functioning of the free market. She does not suggest that individuals should or could have an effect upon the forces of the market; rather, she praises individuals who know how to exploit those forces efficiently.

23.   D

To prove that a particular sea narrative was partial inspiration for a Coleridge poem, the author of the passage first lists several concrete characteristics that the two works have in common. In addition, he notes that the poet's good friend Wordsworth might have owned a copy of the narrative; the implication is that he shared it with Coleridge. Similar qualities have appeared in works written two centuries apart, and the earlier work could have been available to the author of the more recent work; however, no connection between events has actually been documented in the passage. In other words, the argument relies entirely upon the citation of evidence that is circumstantial, as stated in correct answer choice (D).

(A) is incorrect because the author doesn't create an analogy between seafaring and literature; the author is comparing two literary works about seafaring.

(B) introduces an element that is not found at all in the paragraph. The author has not attempted to reinterpret the poem but merely to explain its genesis; no attention is paid to the meaning of the work.

(C) is incorrect because the parallels adduced in the passage are between two works rather than between one work, "The Rime of the Ancient Mariner," and the life of its creator, Coleridge. The reference to his real-life friendship with Wordsworth is not presented as a parallel to any aspect of the poem, although the author implies that the relationship could have had an effect upon the work.

As you have seen, precisely what the argument in the passage lacks is concrete documentation for this new claim about literary influence. Answer choice (E) is, therefore, incorrect.

24.   A

The argument here is that older workers, to combat societal bias against them, should pretend to be younger, both when applying for work and after being hired. Is this a reasonable strategy? It would not be if, as suggested by answer choice (A), there is the possibility that older workers can effectively combat bias by confronting society with the truth—that maturity in itself does not diminish or destroy the capabilities of all workers. In this case, older people would not only achieve the short-term goal of gaining employment but also attain the long-term goal of making employment more available to their peers.

(B) would tend to reinforce the argument of the passage, since the statement tends to suggest that older men and women are subject to changes that might diminish their capabilities as workers.

At first glance, choice (C) might seem to indicate that the original contention about the waste of human potential has been overstated, but it is possible that these "increasing numbers of older people" have found jobs because they have followed the advice of the author of the passage. Also, it is possible that these jobs, clerical and food service, do not fully utilize the potential of older workers and represent, in fact, the problem stated by the author.

(D) suggests a solution, reinforcing the idea that a problem currently exists. Since the solution has not yet been implemented, the answer choice does not refute the author's argument that deception is necessary at the moment.

(E) might be considered a case of too little, too late. If the basic problem is the need for mature workers to find employment now in the face of age bias, it is not very helpful to learn that they could have avoided, and might indeed be able to reverse, certain problems associated with age. According to the author, older workers are already often capable. False stereotypes, not actual deficiencies, have become a bar to their employment.

25.   D

The suggestion here is that the introduction of a highly successful predator into a closed environment will stabilize the ecology. How? By reducing overpopulation of a basically defenseless animal that has caused, and will continue to cause, environmental damage. We are asked to determine which of the answer choices offers information that would show this plan to be misguided. If (D) were true, one ecological problem would be supplanted by another; the goats, now in danger of starving, would be replaced by ravenous coyotes, who would eventually bring themselves to starvation. This would hardly constitute "stabilization" of the ecology. Choice (D) is correct because it gives a very good reason for not acting upon the argument in the passage.

On the other hand, choice (A) is not to the point, since it is possible that the island environment would be congenial to coyotes; this answer choice does not rule out the coyotes' adaptation to the island environment.

Nor does choice (B) rebut the argument of the passage, for the point is to reduce the number of goats, not to give them a fair shake in terms of dealing with predators.

Only one of the two problems cited in the passage is addressed by choice (C). Even if soil erosion were stopped, the loss of ground foliage would still lead to the distressing result of a whole population of goats starving to death. We have no reason to believe that they can gain sustenance from the native cactus.

(E) is completely irrelevant, because (so far as we know) there are no household pets to be endangered by transplanted coyotes on the wild desert island.

26.   C

The proposal in the passage seems straightforward enough. Now that one division of the university library is superior, why not use incoming monies to upgrade those divisions that are still inferior? What this argument ignores, however, is the possibility that different kinds of effort may be necessary to ensure that different divisions remain "complete and up-to-date." Specifically, the Social Documentation Division, relying as it must upon such materials as census studies and statistics, probably needs to keep making substantial purchases of new materials to "keep its collection current." As described in correct answer choice (C), the division must have access to continued funding because it is concerned with the documentation of "an ongoing process."

(A) is not an effective criticism of the argument in the passage. Even assuming that social documentation as a study is more important to the university community than other disciplines, that is no reason to leave these other areas without adequate funding if there is no further need for monies in the Social Documentation Division. Literature and art may be less important, but they have not been abandoned.

(B) places undue importance on an inessential factor. The new computerized devices do not yet exist; it is not clear what kind of improvement they could bring when perfected. (C) is a better answer than (B) because (C) points to an inherent quality of social documentation that necessitates further funding.

(D) is a weak argument, because it is not definitely known that additional copies will indeed be needed. Rather than hold back money for a possible need, the university would logically address needs that already exist. Furthermore, there is no reason to place a priority on the convenience of sociology students when other areas of the library may be lacking basic resource materials.

(E) shows a misplacement of emphasis. Since the library has deficiencies, the author would respond, the principal effort should be to improve the collection rather than encourage greater use of a flawed collection.

SECTION II: READING COMPREHENSION

Passage 1—Free Speech Passage

Topic and Scope
Free speech; specifically, three theories about speech.

Purpose and Main Idea
The author wants to show the different sides surrounding the argument of free speech.

Paragraph Structure
Paragraph 1 mentions two traditional justifications of the free speech principle, the classical and fortress models. This paragraph is mainly introduction, but read carefully and make note of what you're told: Traditional justifications protect speech more than other actions; the two models agree that speech has an inherent value but otherwise disagree. Paragraphs 2 and 3 explore the two models in detail, associating them with Meiklejohn and Holmes, respectively. The major *difference* between the two models is that Meiklejohn sees the right of free speech in a positive light, as something that helps democratic government, whereas Holmes sees it more negatively, as a safeguard against intolerance. As is often in Reading Comp, this distinction becomes clearer when you get to the questions. Don't worry about pinning it down exactly as you read. Finally, paragraph 4 briefly presents Bollinger's model.

1.   B
The first question is a straightforward Main Idea question; look for a choice that covers the whole passage and gets the author's focus or point of view

right. (B) works best because the three views presented in the passage are all theoretical justifications for free speech (as the very first sentence indicates).

(A) misses the author's point of view; no arguments against free speech are considered. The focus, rather, is on how one justifies the decision to support broad rights of free speech—this is why (B) works better.

(C) and (D) are both too narrow, making the views of one or two theoreticians the author's primary concern, whereas the author is equally concerned with all three. In addition, (C) distorts the discussion of Bollinger, which mentions no criticisms of the right of extremist speech.

(E) is wrong, first, because the author does not claim that his approach is "new" (although Bollinger's may be) and, second, because neither Bollinger nor the author discusses "constitutionally limiting extremist speech"—in fact, the Constitution is never mentioned.

2.   A
Questions 2 and 3 deal with Meiklejohn—paragraph 2. This one asks for an assumption Meiklejohn would make. (A) deals with Meiklejohn's basic argument on "extremist speech" contained in the last three sentences of the paragraph: Extremist views cannot be concealed from citizens who must vote on public issues.

(A) is a necessary assumption because, if it were not true, citizens could make rational decisions without the opportunity to consider extremist views, and Meiklejohn's justification for free speech would fall apart.

(B) is, if anything, an argument against free speech (assuming that Meiklejohn himself is not an extremist)—at any rate, all Meiklejohn says is that one needs to consider extremist views, not embrace them.

(C) and (D) are very similar. Both offer secondary arguments in favor of free speech, but neither is logically necessary to Meiklejohn's justification. Apply the same test as with (A): Assume that (C) isn't true, that no unpopular views have ever been accepted eventually. Meiklejohn would just say, "Even so, people still need to *consider them in order* to make a choice."

So (C) is not an assumption he makes, and the same with (D).

(E) takes Meiklejohn's use of the New England town meeting as a "paradigm" (or model) for free speech and twists it into an idea that's never suggested, that free speech matters only in a community that's like a New England town meeting.

3.   B

More Meiklejohn; you're asked what kind of speech Meiklejohn would NOT necessarily favor extending protection to. Once again, paragraph 2 has the correct answer; we're told in midparagraph that from Meiklejohn's perspective, the free speech principle need protect only *political* speech. So nonpolitical speech is not necessarily protected—choice (B).

(A) and (C) are out because we're told that Meiklejohn *would* favor protecting extremist speech as long as it had relevance to political issues.

Similarly, we're told at the end of the paragraph that Meiklejohn sees a value in preserving a broad range of speech, including that which many people find offensive, (D).

(E) is a detail from paragraph 3; it's Holmes, not Meiklejohn, who regards speech as the expression of individual beliefs.

4.   D

On to Holmes (paragraph 3). The easiest way to understand (D) is to realize that if it were true, a lot of extremist speech and some "valuable" (nonextremist) speech would be censored—exactly what Holmes is not for. More specifically, sentences 6 and 7 of paragraph 3 say that the fortress model "overprotect[s] speech," protecting extremist speech, which "diminishes the probability that inherently valuable speech will be suppressed." So to Holmes, censoring valuable speech is more harmful, not less, than allowing extremist speech (D).

(A) states exactly the opposite of this, exactly what Holmes does believe.

(B) Holmes's idea of protecting "extremist" speech to ensure protection of "valuable" speech implies that

extremist speech is not very valuable and, therefore, supports (B).

(C) follows from the idea of a "buffer zone" and the statement at the end of the paragraph that "once unleashed, censorship cannot be reasonably expected to remain confined to worthless views."

(E) is another way of stating this same idea; it also repeats (in the negative) the earlier idea that protecting extremist speech accomplishes the protection of "valuable" speech, too.

5.   C

On to Bollinger (paragraph 4). Bollinger's is the "self-restraint model," and sentence 3 of this paragraph tells us that "although continuing staunchly to support free speech, the self-restraint model inverts the relationship between speech and tolerance." So it does "staunchly support" free speech, and (C) is not true, or at least, we have no reason to think it is true. This same sentence supports (B), which paraphrases "inverts the relationship" as "conceives the relationship . . . differently."

(A) paraphrases the last sentence—tolerance is part and parcel of the "self-control, self-discipline, and self-restraint" this sentence refers to as valuable in a stable society.

(D) is based on the first sentence of paragraph 4: Bollinger is referring to a society marked by "consensus on essential values."

The same sentence says that Bollinger's model accounts for "changes in the function of speech attributable to the emergence" of such a society—in other words, free speech has a different function in such a society than in earlier societies, (E).

6.   B

This is a variant on the standard "organization of the passage" question—you're asked about the first three paragraphs only: in other words, the introduction, Meiklejohn, and Holmes. The "traditional way of viewing a question" in (B) is referred to in sentence 1; it specifies greater tolerance for speech than action and finds inherent value in speech (sentence 3). The "two contrasting approaches" in (B) are, of course, the classical model (Meiklejohn) and the fortress model (Holmes). So this choice precisely describes paragraphs 1, 2, and 3.

(A) starts well (although it doesn't refer to paragraph 1) but then goes off the track—the author never discusses the historical background of either theory.

(C) is exactly backwards: The author first refers to points of agreement (and they are precious few) and then spends two paragraphs on the disagreements.

However, the conclusions are largely the same, not opposed—both theories support extremist speech, although with different reasoning. Therefore, (D) is incorrect.

(E) starts well, like (A), but the author never mentions unanswerable questions or calls for a synthesis. (Bollinger's view is not a synthesis but a third distinct model, and anyway, the author does not endorse it.)

7.   B

What should stick in your mind is that Meiklejohn and Holmes both defend the right of free speech for extremist views, choice (B).

(A) is not a similarity; we're told in paragraph 3 that the belief that free speech leads to the discovery of truth is specific to Holmes's theory.

The idea that censorship entails suppression of valuable speech is also listed as one of Holmes's views. So (C) is incorrect.

The need to keep the public abreast of all relevant issues is something Meiklejohn stands for (paragraph 2), not Holmes. So (D) is a wrong answer choice.

Finally, the promotion of tolerance as a social value is something that neither thinker stands for—it's described in paragraph 4 as a principle of Bollinger's. Eliminate (E) as well.

Passage 2—Limiting Science

Topic and Scope

Science and society; who should control the direction of scientific research.

Purpose and Main Idea

The author argues that scientists should dictate the path of scientific research.

Paragraph Structure

The gist of this opinionated science passage, the issue and the author's own view, is clear in paragraph 1. Paragraph 2 brings up recombinant DNA research, a possibly hazardous area of research; the paragraph ends by saying that debate inevitably turns to a more volatile issue, genetic engineering. Paragraph 3 explains why genetic engineering is so controversial and allows that recombinant DNA research is related to it. Paragraph 4 is a summary. The author reminds us of the benefits to be derived from recombinant DNA research and suggests that people are overreacting—they're letting a knee-jerk response to genetic engineering determine their thinking on it and recombinant DNA research.

8.   B

This type of Main Idea question, with the choices worded as questions, occurs fairly regularly. Your strategy is the same: You want the choice that conveys the big idea and covers the whole passage.

(B) is best here; it sums up the big issue in one sentence. The wrong choices are typical of those in all Main Idea questions.

(A) and (C) are too narrow; they pick up on details. The danger of recombinant DNA research is mentioned in paragraph 2, but it's never explained (A). As for (C), the author admits in paragraph 3 that there are valid concerns about genetic engineering, but that, too, is subsidiary.

(D) and (E) never happen: There's no discussion of either the effect of criticism on the pace of research, (D), or the moral versus practical problems of hazardous research, (E).

9.   E

This is a simple Detail question. According to the passage, a lot of people, scientists and lay critics alike, agree that "fertility mechanisms" are appropriate areas of biological research in contrast to more dangerous areas like genetics and aging. The clear suggestion is that "fertility mechanisms" are pretty uncontroversial.

(A) and (C)—There's no actual indication of either (A), which was probably meant to tempt you, or (C). Be sure to reread with care.

(B) and (D) both contradict the suggested idea.

10.   E

This refers to another point in paragraph 1. It comes up in the last sentence. The author, arguing that the *direction* of research should not be regulated, grants that society "must determine the pace of innovation." (E) gives a simple paraphrase.

(A) turns the idea around.

(B), application of new treatments, is never mentioned.

(C) and (D) seem confusing, which should have aroused suspicion. Setting specific priorities (C) and controlling fund expenditures (D) could affect either the rate or the direction of research. In any case, neither is mentioned.

(E) is mentioned—it's the clear choice.

11.   A

The idea in (A) comes up at the start of the passage: We're told that molecular biology hasn't yet had a major impact in medical treatment. But we're never told why.

(B) is answered in the middle of paragraph 1: Scientists have traditionally had responsibility for determining the direction of research.

(C) is answered near the beginning: Studies of fertility mechanisms are more acceptable than studies of genetics and aging.

We saw the answer to (D) with question 8: The author admits in paragraph 3 that there are real moral questions.

(E) is answered indirectly in paragraph 4: People's anxieties lead them to substitute a high-pitched polemic against genetic engineering for a reasonable consideration of recombinant DNA research.

12.   B

The stem hints strongly that this is a disguised Main Idea question—you're being asked for a statement about *science* and *society* that the author would agree with. So

you're looking for the statement that's consistent with the author's big idea. The right choice is (B). This is clearly an idea underlying the author's viewpoint.

(A) would weaken that viewpoint.

(C) is 180. The author never suggests that society is about to start losing interest in regulating science. Quite the contrary.

(D) sounds too extreme. There's no advocacy by the author of desperate acts by scientists.

(E) is simply not suggested. In fact, the author clearly thinks it can be settled.

13.   D

This gets back to the idea of genetic engineering being a symbol to people of the "frightening potential of modern science" (end of paragraph 3). The author's point is that some people want to abandon recombinant DNA research because of supposed dangers of genetic engineering. (D) gets to the same basic point. There's simply no suggestion of either (A) or (B).

(C) contradicts the real idea.

(E) gets things twisted; it's recombinant DNA research, not a public debate about genetic engineering, that may yield medical treatments.

14.   C

The clear-cut suggestion in the relevant sentence is that all powerful sciences can be abused. The potential for abuse in molecular biology is no more or less than in any other science.

(A) and (D) simply miss the point.

(B) and (E) sound like nonsense; they're never suggested.

15.   E

This is an Application question. Note that the stem asks you to extrapolate from both the content and style of the passage. Well, the passage essentially represents an opinion, doesn't it? You can easily imagine somebody else writing a passage that comes down on the other side of the same big issue: Society has a right to oversee dangerous research. The choice that's most consistent with the passage's content and style is (E). The passage could easily be one of several papers given at this type of seminar. The other choices are too neutral sounding. Some of them have other problems, too.

(A) is out because the level of information in the passage is wrong for medical students, and the thrust isn't ethics.

(B) is out because a government report would sound unopinionated.

(C) and (D) misrepresent the passage. It's neither a broad outline of current work, (C), nor a look at progress in disease prevention/treatment, (D).

Questions 16–21

Of course, both passages have the same topic: collaborative divorce. The scope of the passages is slightly different, though. In Passage A, the author is primarily concerned with singing the praises of the collaborative divorce process, while Passage B focuses on one specific aspect—the potentially prohibitive cost for many divorcing couples.

Passage A: The author's main idea is that collaborative divorce is a very positive new development beneficial to most divorcing couples. His purpose is simply to illustrate that value for us.

Passage B: The main idea in Passage B is that collaborative divorce is too expensive for the "average" American couple. The author's purpose is simply to argue that point.

Having assessed topic, scope, purpose, and main idea just as we do for regular passages (except that we have two purposes/main ideas), we move on to the one step that differs in reading comparative passages: Before moving on to the questions, we need to get a handle on the relationship between the passages.

The best starting point is to examine each passage's purpose/main idea. Passage A speaks only of the positive aspects and impact of the collaborative divorce process, while Passage B suggests that its implications are much more limited since it is too expensive for many.

Since comparative passages are so short, we won't need road maps. Once we have T/S/P/MI and the relationship between the passages in hand, we can jump into the questions. Remember to look first to see whether any questions refer to only one passage and then follow your usual order of operations with regard to question types.

16. C

Question 16 asks about a point of disagreement between the two authors, and we've already determined the key point of disagreement: The author of Passage B thinks collaborative divorce just isn't realistically affordable for a lot of people. Although the correct answer choice, (C), doesn't explicitly mention cost, keeping that prephrase in mind should allow you to identify it. The correct answer focuses on the breadth of the impact of this new process; author A talks that up, but author B clearly thinks it will be limited because so many people just can't afford to use it. The author of Passage B doesn't offer any argument about the benefits of collaborative divorce, which eliminates answer choices (A), (B), and (E). Wrong answer choice (D) is outside the scope of both passages, because it raises the issue of averting divorce. Our authors are concerned only with the method of divorce.

17. C

"Relationship between the passages" questions are common—almost universal—in comparative reading passages. As with Global questions in other Reading Comprehension passages, you should already have done the work required to answer this question when you initially attacked the passages. We've already determined not only the point of disagreement between the two passages but the fact that the author of Passage A is broadly concerned with the benefits of collaborative divorce, while the author of Passage B primarily concerns himself with one obstacle. Correct answer choice (C) sums that up. (A) is incorrect because the author of Passage B never recommends against collaborative divorce; he simply believes that many people won't be able to afford it. (B) can be eliminated because there's no point-by-point refutation—Passage B is very narrowly focused on one problem. (D) is wrong because the authors don't reach the same conclusion; author A thinks this system is great for everyone, and author B thinks it's only for the select few who can afford it. (E) might be tempting, but the author of Passage B didn't dispute any of the benefits of collaborative divorce—not even that it might be less expensive; he simply said it wasn't realistically available for everyone.

18. C

The correct answer is (C), again focusing directly on the key difference between the two passages. Answer choices (A), (D), and (E) all set forth benefits mentioned by the author of Passage A, but the author of Passage B does not take issue with them. Answer choice (B) may be tempting since it focuses on the cost of the process, which is clearly the major concern of the author of Passage B. In fact, though, the author of Passage A hasn't told us anything about how much the process costs—only that it's less expensive than a traditional contested divorce.

19. B

Remember that the author of Passage B takes no issue with the benefits of collaborative divorce; in fact, he concedes in the first paragraph that many of the pros mentioned by author A may indeed be accurate. Correct answer choice (B) identifies one of those benefits on which the authors seem to agree. (A) is tricky, but author A didn't take any position on making the process more available; his statement that there's little reason for couples to consider the traditional route indicates that he thinks it's already widely available. (C), (D), and (E) all go too far: We know that the process of collaborative divorce may be easier on children but not enough specifics to support (C). There is no basis for weighing the value of one professional against another, as (D) would require. (E) is too extreme: Neither author has mentioned eliminating traditional divorce as an option.

20. B

You've already analyzed the relationship between the passages and answered another question that required identification of that relationship in the abstract, so

don't do that work over again. The author of Passage A talks generally about how good something is; the author of Passage B points out a limitation that makes it inaccessible to many. That's exactly the pattern you see reflected in correct answer choice (B): The professor says the book is great, but someone else points out that a limitation (the fact that it's written in Greek) means many can't benefit from it. Note that many of the wrong answer choices relate to costs or advice from professionals and so look similar to the passages. They might be tempting, but we're concerned here with form, not substance. (A) relates to one specific decision by one specific entity. (C) somewhat mirrors the collaborative divorce scenario, but we're not looking to reflect collaborative divorce—we're looking for a scenario that's parallel to the relationship between the passages. Don't ever lose sight of what you're looking for. (D) may also be tempting, but the author of Passage B isn't poking holes in a proposal or illustrating the cost for a particular project—he's pointing out an obstacle to the widespread applicability of the system as a whole. (E), like (C), reflects the process but not the relationship between the passages.

21. B

This is a Detail question just like any other and should be treated just like a Detail question in a traditional Reading Comprehension passage. The primary difference is that you have to check both passages here. Make sure you have a handle on what you're being asked: You're looking for the one benefit not raised by *either* author. That means as soon as one mentions something as a benefit, it's off the list—for the purposes of this question, it doesn't matter if the other author disagrees. Most of the benefits come from Passage A, so that's a logical place to start matching them up and checking them off. A quick check of Passage A knocks out answer choices (C) and (D), both mentioned in the first paragraph. Passage B takes out (A) and (E) with "positive impact on future relations and lower stress levels for children of divorce." That leaves correct answer choice (B)—although both authors state or imply that there are benefits for children and parents, neither mentions joint custody.

Passage 4—Medicine Wheel
Topic and Scope
Medicine Wheel of the Plains Indians; specifically, its two primary functions.

Purpose and Main Idea
The author asserts that the Medicine Wheel had cosmic and psychological roles in Plains Indians' survival.

Paragraph Structure
Paragraph 1 describes the Medicine Wheel as important to the survival of the Plains people. Paragraph 2 sketches the Medicine Wheel's role in marking the movements of the heavens and describes its function as a calendar. Paragraph 3 concerns the Medicine Wheel's psychological and social functions and says that through it, the Plains Indians recognized diverse personality types, each of which was regarded with respect. Finally, in paragraph 4, the author suggests that the Medicine Wheel conveyed the values of tolerance and integration—values, the author asserts, that are essential to a community's survival.

22. C

This is a straight Detail question in the "all EXCEPT" format. These can be time consuming, so scan the choices to see if any pop out as being wrong. Choice (C) contradicts the idea that the cosmic and psychological functions of the Medicine Wheel were equally valuable (see the first sentence of paragraph 3).

(A) is true; the importance of the Medicine Wheel in the Plains Indians' survival is emphasized in paragraph 1.

(B) is supported by the last two sentences of paragraph 2.

(D) and (E) are both true because paragraph 3 describes the "unity within diversity" that the Medicine Wheel taught.

23. D

Here we have another Detail question. Information in the passage won't help you answer the question posed in choice (A); whereas paragraph 1 suggests that the survival of the Plains Indians was threatened, we're not told *which* forces jeopardized their survival.

Although paragraph 3 talks about different personality traits that the Plains Indians recognized, no particular type was seen as dominant, so (B) is incorrect.

(C) is wrong too: Although paragraph 2 mentions important constellations, we haven't a clue about which those important constellations were.

However, the passage can help us with the question in (D): The last sentence of the second paragraph says that the Plains Indians calculated agricultural rhythms and seasonal changes through the Medicine Wheel.

There isn't an answer for choice (E) in this passage. Yes, the Plains Indians valued tolerance and integration, as paragraph 4 states. Why? We're never told.

24. C

This question asks for the passage's primary purpose or main idea. The passage discusses the two equally important functions of the Medicine Wheel and suggests that it played an integral role in the survival of the Plains Indians. Consequently, choice (C) correctly reflects the passage's gist.

Because the passage never explicitly discusses the spiritual beliefs of the Plains Indians and certainly doesn't concern the much broader topic of Native American spirituality, choice (A) is incorrect.

(B) is also too broad—this passage concerns one Native American nation; it doesn't concern Native Americans in general or their fight against adversity.

(D) is incorrect because the social or psychological value of the Medicine Wheel equalled its cosmic or natural function: Neither was of greater value.

You can eliminate (E) because although personality traits are discussed in paragraph 3 in relation to the psychological function of the Medicine Wheel, you could hardly say that the passage's primary purpose is to analyze these traits.

25. B

The psychological function of the Medicine Wheel is discussed in paragraph 3, and the gist of this paragraph is that through the Medicine Wheel, the Plains Indians recognized major personality types and taught tribal members to recognize, respect, and imitate the qualities of other tribal members with other, equally valuable strengths. Choice (B) captures this.

(A) is wrong because the Medicine Wheel taught equality; it certainly didn't set up any hierarchy of personalities.

(C) is a distortion: Tribal members were encouraged to imitate the traits of people possessing strengths other than their own so that each member would become a richer, more balanced person. The author never suggests that they were encouraged to develop traits that were particularly important to the tribe's survival.

(D) is incorrect because the primary psychological function of the Medicine Wheel had to do with the development of each individual's personality and respect for all tribal members, as described in paragraphs 3 and 4. Orienting members to natural cycles was the Medicine Wheel's primary *cosmological* function, as described in paragraph 2.

(E) is wrong because the passage doesn't suggest that the Medicine Wheel taught passivity; it taught tolerance and integration, as paragraph 4 says.

26. D

"Best title" questions test your knowledge of the passage's main idea. As we described before, this passage concerns the cosmological and psychological functions of the Medicine Wheel and its essential role in the survival of the Plains Indians. Considering that, choice (D) represents a reasonable title for the passage.

(A) misses the passage's focus on the Medicine Wheel.

(B) is way too broad.

(C) comes close to capturing the Medicine Wheel's cosmic function but never mentions its psychological function or role in the Plains Indians,' survival.

(E) is out for a similar reason: It neglects to mention the Medicine Wheel's cosmological function and besides, it's too broad in its general focus on Native American psychology.

27. A

Application questions like this one require you to consider the passage's focus as well as its tone. Considering that this passage concerns an artifact of cosmic, psychological, and spiritual value to a culture, its author is most likely an anthropologist, choice (A). It is unlikely that an astronomer, choice (B), would have devoted three of the four paragraphs discussing topics totally unrelated to astronomy. A social psychologist, (C), probably would have focused more on the thoughts and feelings of the individual members as they relate to the group and less on rituals and beliefs important to a culture's survival. It's likely that a theologian, (D), would have written more explicitly about the religious or spiritual aspects of the Medicine Wheel. You can eliminate choice (E) because an archaeologist probably would have concentrated more on the Medicine Wheel as an artifact, object, or relic: This passage describes the function of the Medicine Wheel and its role in the survival of the Plains Indians, but it hardly goes beyond describing the Medicine Wheel as an arrangement of stones.

SECTION III: LOGIC GAMES

Game 1—Cheese Display

The Action

After previewing the setup and rules, you see that this game asks you to distribute nine cheeses into three groups of three cheeses each—a grouping game of distribution. There are four domestic cheeses—F, G, H, and J—and five imported cheeses—p, q, r, s, and t (it can help to keep the entities separate if you use CAPS for one group and lower case letters for the other). The three groups are A, B, and C. The key issues will be these:

1) What cheese is in what group?
2) What cheeses can, must, or cannot be selected with what other cheeses?

The Initial Setup

You've got three groups of three each. Set this up as you might in real life. Just list the three groups with three dashes under each. Be sure you also list the two types of cheeses.

DOMESTIC   imported

F G H J   p q r s t

A   B   C

___ ___ ___   ___ ___ ___   ___ ___ ___

The Rules

1) It's best to build a rule directly into the master sketch whenever you can. One of the cheeses in each group must be domestic. Make a note of this in the sketch; placing a *D* under one of the dashes in each group should suffice.

2) You don't know which group F is in, but F must always be accompanied by two imports—no domestics allowed in a group with F.

3) q, an imported cheese, goes in Group C. Build this right into the sketch.

4) s goes in Group A. That's another imported cheese definitely set.

5) Whew. Three rules in one. Be careful when you unpack this rule. Take it one step at a time. First of all, F can't be in the same group as q. Secondly, J can't go in the same group as q. Finally, r can't go with q either. Your mind is probably jumping ahead and combining this rule with Rule 3, and that's a good thing. It means that you're getting used to looking for deductions.

Key Deductions

Time to take a closer look at Rule 5 (and Rule 3). Don't just write "No F q." Ask yourself "What does that mean?" Because q is in Group C, F must be in either A or B. J, too, can't go with q. Again, this means that J must go in either Group A or Group B. Finally, r can't go with q, so r must also go in A or B.

Keep going. There's more to be deduced here. F and J and r each must go in either Group A or Group B. Can these entities go in the same group? Rule 2 told you that F must go in a group with two imports. r is an import, so F and r could go in the same group, but J is a domestic.

No way could F and J go in the same group. So F must go in Group A or B, and J must go in the other.

As with all games, take a moment to work through the numbers aspect of the game. Here that means looking at Rule 1. Each group must have at least one domestic cheese. Rule 5 said that F and J (two domestics) can't go with q in Group C, but Group C must have at least one domestic. What domestic cheeses are left? G and H are the only other domestics. One of this pair must *always* go in Group C. You can bet that one or two answer choices will try to put them both elsewhere. Now you're thinking like the test makers.

Finally, it's a good idea to identify the "floaters" in each game. These are those entities that don't appear in any rules or deductions. They will serve to fill in the remaining slots after you've placed all the other entities. Here, the "floaters" are p and t, two imported cheeses.

The Final Visualization

Here's what you have going into the questions:

DOMESTIC   imported

F G H J   p q r s t

A   B   C

___ s ___   ___ ___ ___   G/H q ___

D	D	D
F + 2 imp.	F + 2 imp.	No F
J	J	No J
r	r	No r
F ≠ J	F ≠ J	

The Big Picture

- When you have two or more types of entities, it's vital that you can easily tell them apart. One way is to put one group all in CAPS and the other in lower case letters. You can use your own way (circles and squares, underlining, etc.) as long as it's quick, neat, and effective.

- The setup is the time to think, above all. The drawing is secondary. Consider the implications of each rule and, if you can, build a rule directly into your master sketch instead of rewriting it (as in Rule 1).

- It's very useful to identify the "floaters" in each game. These entities not explicitly tied to any rule or deduction will fill out the spaces in a game. In a "could be true" question, the flexibility of floaters make them likely answer choices. Conversely, a "must be true" question is more heavily based on restrictions, in which case floaters are not as likely to be part of the correct answer.

The Questions

1. E

You know that each group must have at least one domestic cheese. Because p and t (both imports) are in Group B, the remaining cheese must be domestic. We deduced in Rule 5 that r, an import, must be in Group A or B. The last cheese in B must be domestic, so r must go in Group A, choice (E).

(A) No, F could go in group B with p and t.

(B) No, G could be in Group C.

(C) No, H could be in Group C.

(D) No, J could go in Group B with p and t.

Remember: When you're given new information, get it down in the test booklet. Then ask yourself, "What entities does this new information affect?" Go back to your master sketch and the rules.

2. B

A "must be true" question with no new information often signals that the test makers are asking for a key deduction. However, you can tell that's probably not the case here because of the complex answer choices. Each choice is like a question in itself. You can count on spending a good deal of time here. This question is a candidate for skipping the first time around if you need to preserve time, because there's not much to do except try out each choice.

(A) Could F and r be together and not be in the group with s (that's Group A)? Sure they could. Here are the complete groupings that show choice (A) needn't be true: A—J s t, B—F p r, C—G H q.

(B) Could G and H be together and not be in the group with q? No way. We saw up front that J and F can't be with q (Rule 5), and because each group needs at least one domestic, either G or H must be with q. (B) must be true and is the answer. On Test Day, you'd stop right here and go on to the next question. For the record, here are groupings that show the remaining choices needn't be true (you may have come up with other acceptable groupings to dispose of these choices):

(C) and (D) A—J H s, B—F p r, C—G q t

(E) A—F s r, B—J G r, C—H p q

Remember: To prove that a choice in a "must be true" question is wrong, find an exception to the choice; that is, an acceptable situation that shows that the choice could be false.

3. B

This takes a slightly different form than most Acceptability questions, but it's still an Acceptability question. You're asked to find the one unacceptable Group B among the choices. What do we know about Group B? We deduced that either F or J must always go in Group B (see Key Deductions for a reminder of how we deduced that). Every acceptable Group B must, therefore, contain either F or J. Scan the choices. Choice (B) doesn't include F or J, and it tries to place both G and H in Group B—wrong on both counts. Remember, one of G or H must always go in Group C.

Remember: Always keep in mind exactly what the question is asking. If you mistakenly thought that this question was asking for the one *acceptable* choice instead of the one *unacceptable* choice, you would have been very confused.

4. E

G is in Group A. In what rules or deductions are you used to dealing with G? Questions 2 and 3 both were answered by realizing that either G or H must go in Group C. Here G is in A, so H must go in Group C. What else do you know about G? G is a domestic cheese, so F, which must be grouped with two imports, can't be in A. The only other choice for F is Group B. F and J can't be in the same group, so J must go in Group A. So far we have G, J and s in Group A; F and r in Group B; and H and q in Group C. Who's left? p and t will fill in the slots: one in Group B and the other in Group C. Don't hesitate to redraw your master sketch whenever needed. Here's what this question's sketch would look like:

A   B   C

G s J   F r p/t   H q p/t

Scan the choices. t could indeed be in Group C. (E) could be true and is the answer.

(A) No, H is in Group C.

(B) No, J is in Group A.

(C) No, p is in Group B or C.

(D) No, r is in Group B.

Remember: Work with any new information that you're given. Keep asking yourself, "In what rules and deductions have I seen this entity before?" and "What do I know about this entity?"

5. B

H is a domestic cheese, so F can't join H and p in Group B (Rule 2). Because F can't, J must be the one to fill out Group B. F's only other choice is Group A. r must go in Group A because B is now full. We're looking for Group A, and now we have it: F, r, and s, choice (B).

Remember: Only do the work required to answer the question. You could have taken the deductions further and filled out Group C, but there's no need to. The question is asking about Group A, so that's the only group you're interested in.

6. C

What does it mean for J to be in Group B? It means that F must be in Group A—by now, splitting these two entities between Groups A and B should be instinctual. Other than that, there's not much else to deduce. r, as usual, can go in either A or B, and our perpetual

floaters, p and t, can pretty much go anywhere. What leads to the answer here is the situation of G and H. These two domestic cheeses can both join q in C or they can split up between B and C. The one thing neither of them can do is end up in Group A because that's where F is in this question, and F's companion cheeses are always both imports. (C) is therefore impossible—for H to be displayed with s (in Group A) would mean placing H in the same group as F, which is a no-no.

There's no problem with (A) and (D). It can go in Group A with F and s, while the remaining entities fill out Groups B and C in any one of a number of different ways.

(B) works. G and r can join J in Group B as long as H joins q in Group C. Then p and t can fill in the remaining slots in Groups A and C.

The situation just described in (B) above works for (E); just put t in Group A along with F and s, and p in Group C along with H and q.

Remember: Manage your time well. Just because a question is the last one on a game doesn't mean that it's the most difficult. Many, many games on the LSAT have manageable and even easy questions towards the end. If you allow yourself to get caught up in early, difficult questions, you may never get to these later, easier questions.

Game 2—Fish Salon

In this sequencing game, you're asked to put seven courses in order. The natural way to picture this is to simply write 1 through 7 across the page. As you work with each rule, try to find a way to build each rule into the sketch. As it turns out, you can put many of these rules directly into the sketch. K must be served after J. G is served two courses before H. L must be served before G. K is served either fifth or sixth, and F is served second:

1 2 3 4 5 6 7

F (J) . . . K or K

L . . . G _ H

You have quite a few restrictions on the entities, so it's worth the time to consider the implications of these restrictions. F is set at second, K is fifth or sixth, J is served sometime before K, G can't be sixth or seventh, and L must be before G. Therefore, there are only two entities left that can be served seventh: H or M. Also, recognize that because L must come before G, the earliest that G can be served is third.

Even though it looks like there aren't any Big Deductions here, you are given a lot of information. As long as you've taken the time to think through the important implications thoroughly, you should be all set to rack up some points.

The Questions

7. A

Here's an Acceptability question, so grab each rule and see which choices violate that rule. The answer will be the one choice that violates no rules. Rule 1, placing J before K, doesn't eliminate any choices. However, Rule 2, which places G two courses before H, eliminates (C). According to Rule 3, L is served before G, which kills (B). Rule 4 places K fifth or sixth, eliminating (D), and Rule 5 places F second, so (E) must be wrong. You're left with (A), the correct answer.

8. C

It's never too early to start benefiting from your previous work. You're asked for the courses in which haddock could be served. Well, in question 1, you saw haddock served seventh. It could be true then, so it can be true now. Eliminate any choice that doesn't include seventh. Good-bye choice (A). We saw up front that the earliest G can be served is third. Because G is two places to the left of H, the earliest H can be is fifth. Cross off any choice that has H in an earlier course than fifth. Good-bye (B), (D), and (E), which leaves us with (C), the answer.

9. E

If K is fifth, G can't be third because that would require H to be fifth. G can't be sixth or seventh (nowhere for H to go), so G must be fourth. Rule 2 then forces us to

place H sixth. We deduced up front that H or M must always be seventh, so here M must be seventh. Choice (E) must be true and is the answer.

If you *didn't* make the up-front deduction that either M or H must be seventh, then you had a longer road ahead of you. You still knew that F is second, G is fourth, and H is sixth. In this scenario, K must be fifth because it isn't sixth, and we're left with this arrangement:

$$1 \quad 2 \quad 3 \quad 4 \quad 5 \quad 6 \quad 7$$
$$\_ \quad F \quad \_ \quad G \quad K \quad H \quad \_$$

J must be served before K, and L must be served before G. So between them, J and L must occupy the first and the third positions, although we don't know their order. Regardless, there's only one space left for M, and that's seventh, which again is choice (E).

10. B

Again, use your previous work. In question 9, G was fourth and M was seventh, but the ordering was not determined (we didn't know exactly when J or L were served). Therefore, you can eliminate choices (A) and (E). From there, you have to try out each choice. If H is fifth, G must be third (Rule 2) and K must be sixth (Rule 4). We deduced up front that either H or M must be seventh, so here M must be seventh. L must be before G, and the only open spot before G is 1. J is left to fill in the remaining fourth spot. Everything is determined, so (B) is the answer. Choices (C) and (D) both lead to more than one possible ordering.

11. C

Where have you seen K in the sixth slot before? In the right answers to questions 7 and 10, K was sixth, so look at the setups and eliminate choices that mirror either of those choices. If it could be true then, it can be true now. In question 7, G was fifth with K sixth, so cross off (A). In that choice, H was seventh, so eliminate (B). That choice also had L third, so good-bye (D). Could M be first? Sure. Here is the ordering that allows us to kill (E): 1—M, 2—F, 3—L, 4—J, 5—G, 6—K, 7—H. We are left with the answer, choice (C).

If J were fifth, there would be no place for the "G _ H" block.

12. B

The last question of a game isn't always the most difficult or even difficult at all. We deduced up front that the only two entities that could be seventh are M and H. Here M is third, so H must be seventh, choice (B).

If you missed that deduction, you had a longer route to the same answer. If M is third, then where could the G _ H block go? G cannot be third, because M is third, so how about fourth? If G is fourth, then H is sixth, and therefore K is fifth (Rule 4). But J must precede K, and L must precede G. However, there is only one available space before K and G, so this scenario is impossible, which means that G cannot be fourth. The only space left for G is fifth. So G must be fifth, which makes H seventh, and we're left with the same answer, choice (B).

Game 3—Marbles in Cans

One of the most common reasons students run out of time in Logic Games is that they've wasted time rereading the rules over and over again. We see this syndrome most often when, as in this game, there are many variables and many rules. To avoid this problem, you should do two things.

First, take a few extra seconds with each rule. Don't just read it—ponder it. Identify some of its logical implications the first time through. If you've understood a rule thoroughly the first time around, there will be less need to go back to it later.

Second, when putting together a master grid, take pains to incorporate into it as much of the data as you can. Having put the data in one place in an easy-to-readand-recall format, you won't have to go back to the original rules out of desperation: The data will have become part and parcel of your understanding of the entire game and will always be convenient for reference.

Here's how a master grid for this game might have evolved, starting with a basic setup and roster:

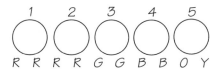

Remember, you can attack the rules in any order you want, as long as you remember to get them all. In an effort to start filling in spaces, let's translate the second and third indented rules for starters:

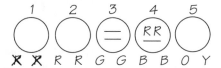

A dash indicates a marble we know is present but whose color is as yet uncertain. Note the way the sketch has been drawn: This student will never, ever be tempted to add any more than two marbles for Can three and 3 marbles for Can 4! Let's incorporate the last two rules:

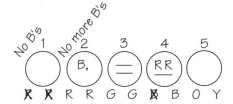

(Notice the comma in Can 2—the student's reminder to himself that more than one marble may go there.)

We've left the first indented rule till last, simply because it's not directly relevant at this moment to the job of filling in the cans. To incorporate it into the work, how about making the roster look like this, eliminating the deadwood while we're at it:

Remember, though, that for a complicated rule, symbolization is not enough! If you take a few seconds to fix the information in your mind—"Wherever the O goes, the Y is in an adjacent can"—chances are you won't forget about it later on.

There is actually one more thing we could add to our master grid, and you may see it if you wonder what we know about Cans 1 and 5. Because no can is empty, we can actually set it up like this:

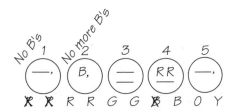

we've accounted for 8 of the 10 marbles!

The Questions

13. A

If (as the stem says) Can 2 gets two green marbles, it will have a total of three. Adding from left to right, 1 + 3 + 2 + 3 + 1 = the full complement of 10. Thus, Can 5 will have only its minimum of one marble, and (A) is correct.

14. C

Your first step should have been to notice that the hypothetical is about Can 5 and that the question asks about Can 3. Doing so helps you organize your work thereafter; it also helps you throw out choices (D) and (E) immediately, because each mentions three marbles even though the third rule clearly states there can only be two marbles in Can 3. Next, you could have realized that if the orange marble is in Can 5, the yellow marble must be adjacent in Can 4. Thus far, things are pretty routine. We next turn our attention to the marbles yet to be placed: R R G G B. That B must go into Can 3, because neither Can 1 nor Can 2 will accept it. This means that choices (A) and (B), neither of which names a blue marble, must also be eliminated. That leaves (C) as the correct answer, and in fact, Can 3 will contain either B and G, as (C) states, or B and R, as it might have stated.

15. B

If Can 1 gets 3 marbles, then once again all 10 marbles have been accounted for (adding from left to right, 3 + 1 + 2 + 3 + 1 = 10). Because Can 2 can only have one marble and already has a blue one, the O/Y group cannot go in Cans 1 and 2. Can 1 can contain neither the O nor the Y; the answer to what cannot be true, therefore, is choice (B), a yellow marble in Can 1,

because this would require the orange to be in Can 2, an impossibility in this question. A red or green marble in Can 1 violates no rules, so (A) and (C) can be true, and because the O/Y group could show up in Cans 4 and 5, it is possible for the last can to contain either a yellow or orange marble, eliminating (D) and (E).

16. B

This is perhaps the first question in the game more or less requiring a full, new grid of its own. After entering the stem info, we're left with this:

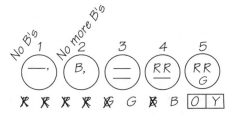

Once again, all 10 marbles are accounted for! The question asks for the possibilities for Can 1, which cannot contain B. Nor can O or Y be included (Can 2 is full here, so we'd have to violate the O/Y rule). That leaves only G—and "one green marble," choice (B), must be correct.

17. C

If the orange marble is in Can 3, then the Y will have to be in adjacent Can 2 or Can 4. But Can 4, according to the stem, is full: It will take a G along with its original two R's for its total of three. Therefore, the Y goes into Can 2:

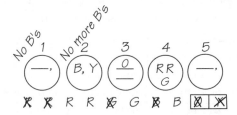

There's still a lot up in the air—four marbles, and we only know where three of them go. That may be a hint that it's one of the if/then choices that will be correct, the "if" clause acting as more information to narrow down the options a bit. In any event, (C) turns out to be the answer. If, as (C) says, the remaining G goes into

Can 3, there would still be a B left, forbidden to Can 1 and Can 2 and thus destined for Can 5. (A) and (B) can be quickly eliminated because the remaining G could just as easily go into Can 3 as into Can 1 or 5. As for (D) and (E), neither one's "if" clause leads inevitably to its "then" clause: Whether Can 5 takes a blue marble, choice (D), or a green marble, choice (E), Can 3 could contain a red marble rather than blue or green.

18.   E

Your intuition was working well if, after seeing the requirement that "G, G, O" go together, your immediate reaction was to ask, "In which can?" Can 3 is surely out because it's only permitted two marbles; beyond that, "G, G, O" have to be the only marbles in a can (otherwise we can't give each can its minimum of one). That rules out Cans 2 and 4. Now, If "G, G, O" were in Can 1, putting the Y into adjacent Can 2 wouldn't leave enough marbles for the other cans. By process of elimination, then, "G, G, O" must go into Can 5.

The Y then goes into Can 4. One B is left to be placed and must go into Can 3 (because Cans 4 and 5 are filled and Cans 1 and 2 can take no more Bs). One of the remaining two marbles (both Rs) must go into Can 1 and the other into Can 3. In the end, it's Cans 2 and 5 that contain no red marbles—choice (E).

Game 4—Art Class

The Action

This game is an example of one of the newest types of game on the LSAT, games that aren't particularly amenable to diagramming. However, this game is just as susceptible to Kaplan's 5-Step Method as any other type. Work systematically, and you'll find that there are quite a few makeable points here. There are four children—Peter, Rita, Sam, and Thelma—in art class. The "action" of the game involves the kids pairing off or working alone and each child or pair of children creating some project. The key issues will be these:

1) When two children pair up, what project will they make?

2) When a child works alone, what project will he or she make?

3) When given a project or set of projects created, what individuals or pairings could or must have accounted for such a result?

The Initial Setup

There's not much to draw here. Make a list of the kids and possible items and be ready to deal with the rules.

The Rules

Take your time when you unpack the information in all of these rules. One mistake in a game like this, and you're in for a long, unproductive ordeal.

1) If Peter and Sam pair up, they'll create a clay figure. If Peter pairs up with Thelma, they'll also create a clay figure. If Peter works on his own, he'll create a clay figure. Carefully make a note of this, something like "Peter and Sam = clay," and "Peter and Thelma = clay," and "Peter alone = clay."

2) Again, we have information about what the children make. This time it's Rita. If Rita and Peter team up, they'll create a watercolor painting. If Rita works alone, she'll create a mobile. Make a note of this in the master sketch.

3) Now it's Sam's turn. If Sam and Rita team up, they'll create a mobile. If Sam and Thelma team up, they'll also create a mobile. If Sam works on his own, he'll create a watercolor painting. Make a note of this.

4) Finally, here's Thelma. If Thelma teams up with Rita, they'll create a papier-mache ball. If Thelma works by herself, she'll also create a papier-mache ball. Again, mark this information down where you can easily access it.

Key Deductions

There are no real deductions, but you must be able to understand how the entities work within the situation. On games such as this one that aren't amenable to diagramming, the key to success is accurately working with the rules. If you need the extra help, you can go through various scenarios of what happens when the different children pair up. For instance, if Peter and

Sam team up, they make a clay figure. If the other two children work alone, they make a mobile (Rita) and a papier-mache ball (Thelma). Going through these "what ifs" can help you get a grasp of the game's workings if you're confused. However, don't spend all day going through countless possibilities.

The Final Visualization

Here's the master sketch. We've divided it up by child to keep it clear, even though this meant including some pieces of information twice:

Peter and Rita = watercolor	*Sam and Peter = clay*
Peter and Sam = clay	*Sam and Rita = mobile*
Peter and Thelma = clay	*Sam and Thelma = mobile*
Peter alone = clay	*Sam alone = watercolor*
Rita and Peter = watercolor	*Thelma and Peter = clay*
Rita and Sam = mobile	*Thelma and Rita = ball*
Rita and Thelma = ball	*Thelma and Sam = mobile*
Rita alone = mobile	*Thelma alone = ball*

The Big Picture

- This game shows why it's so important to depend on thinking rather than drawing for your Logic Games success. If you approach this type of game trying to "draw to win," you'll be very disappointed with the results. In fact, while you didn't have to draw at all to be successful on this game, you *did* have to fully understand the action.

- Accuracy is vital in all Logic Games but especially so in games that aren't amenable to diagramming. If you misread a rule, you're sunk.

- If you see a game like this on your section and it throws you for a loop, skip it. Go for the easier, more accessible points, confident that you're using your time in the best possible way. A game like this would most likely come last in the section (based on previous LSATs), but remember, on your LSAT, this type of game could come earlier, and you don't have to do the games in the order they're presented.

- Just because a game is unfamiliar doesn't necessarily mean that it's hard. There are some very doable questions here—look for them.

The Questions

19. D

Here we have a "reverse" Acceptability question—four of the choices work, and only one has a problem. Check each choice to see if there's a way for the children to create the projects in each.

Peter and Sam pair up to create a clay figure. Rita and Thelma create a papier-mache ball. (A) works, so it isn't the answer.

Sam and Thelma can create a mobile, whereas Peter and Rita make a watercolor painting. (B) is possible and, therefore, isn't the answer either.

Sam and Thelma can pair up to create a mobile. Rita, working alone, can also create a mobile. This leaves Peter to work alone and create a clay figure. (C) can work and isn't the answer.

There are only three ways for the children to make a clay figure: Peter and Sam, Peter and Thelma, and Peter alone. If Peter teams up with Sam or Thelma, he obviously can't also work alone. Therefore, it's not possible for the children to make two clay figures, which means that (D) is the answer.

Nothing in the rules says any of the children must team up. If they all work alone, they would make the items listed in this choice. (E) is possible, which means that it isn't the answer.

Remember: Acceptability questions are valuable for many reasons. They provide an opportunity to see exactly how the entities interact within the given situation. A normal Acceptability question (Which one of the following works?) gives you one valid situation, the "acceptable" answer, which you can use for later reference. A "reverse" Acceptability question like this one is even more valuable because it gives you four—count 'em four—examples of situations that work.

20. A

We don't want any clay figures made. In the last question, we saw that clay figures are created in three situations: Peter and Sam, Peter and Thelma, and Peter alone. If no clay figures are to be created, Peter can't work alone or in any combination that results in the creation of a clay project. Peter must therefore team up with the only child left—Rita. Peter and Rita team up and make a watercolor. Choice (A) is correct.

(B), (C), and (D) are all impossible, based on the fact that we just saw that Peter must pair up with Rita to avoid the creation of a clay project.

(E) is possible: If Peter and Rita work together, the remaining children, Sam and Thelma, could also work together to create a mobile, which is fine in this situation. However, Sam and Thelma could just as easily work on their own. The pair in choice (A) is the only one that's absolutely necessary to satisfy the requirement of the question stem.

Remember: Have a goal in mind—think systematically: "The children can't make any clay figures, so what does that rule out? Okay, what's left?"

21. A

This stem gives us two pieces of information. Exactly two of the children pair up (which means the other two work alone), and the pair creates a mobile. What pairings can create a mobile? Rita and Sam can create a mobile, and Sam and Thelma can create a mobile. We're looking for the projects that the two solo children create. Well, simply try out the two possibilities.

If Rita and Sam pair up, that means that Peter and Thelma work on their own. Peter working alone would create a clay figure, and Thelma working alone would create a papier-mache ball. Unfortunately, clay figure and papier-mache ball isn't an answer choice, so on to the second possibility.

If Sam and Thelma team up, that means that Peter and Rita work on their own. Peter working alone would create a clay figure, and Rita working alone would create a mobile. Clay figure and mobile is choice (A), the correct answer.

Remember: When you have actively pursued the answer and found it, don't waste time checking the other choices. Trust your work. You want to have time to at least look at every question on the section.

22. D

In this one, no one flies solo, so the children must form two teams, exactly one of which we're told will create a mobile. As we just saw in the previous question, the only pairs that can create a mobile are Rita and Sam or Sam and Thelma. In the first case, the two pairs will be Rita/Sam and Peter/Thelma. In the second case, we'd have Sam/Thelma and Rita/Peter. Choices (A) and (E) conform to the second set of pairings, whereas (B) and (C) conform to the first. The only pairing that's impossible is the one found in (D): Rita and Thelma together would leave Sam and Peter for the other pair, in which case we wouldn't get the requisite mobile—we'd get a papier-mache ball and a clay figure, and who needs that? (At least for the sake of this question.) Choice (D) is the pair that can't team up.

Remember: Use your work from previous questions—half the thinking that went into this one was done already in question 21—both questions involve the similar aspect of having one pair create a mobile.

23. D

Read this stem very carefully. The first part is easy enough: The children form two teams. Now for the tougher part. No team creates anything that the individual members of that team would create on their own. Let's start at the top with Peter. Peter working alone would create a clay figure. Who can Peter team up with that wouldn't result in a pair creating a clay figure? Rita is the only one. So Peter and Rita must team up to make a watercolor. Rita working alone wouldn't make a watercolor, so we're fine so far. That leaves only Sam and Thelma, who paired up will create a mobile. Neither Sam working alone nor Thelma working alone create a mobile, so this works out. The children's projects must be a watercolor and a mobile, choice (D).

Remember: Break up complex question stems and take the information one part at a time. If you find a stem confusing, try putting it in your own words.

24. E

Here's a "cannot be true" question with no new information. Not much to do except try each choice. If you can find a situation in which a choice works, it can be true and isn't the answer.

If all four children work alone, Thelma would create the only papier-mache ball. (A) can be true and isn't the answer.

If all four children work alone, Peter would create the only clay figure. (B) can be true and isn't the answer.

Sam working alone creates a watercolor painting. Peter and Rita can pair up and create another watercolor painting. That leaves Thelma working alone to create a papier-mache ball. (C) can be true and isn't the answer.

Rita working alone creates a mobile. Sam and Thelma can pair up and create a mobile. That leaves Peter working alone to create a clay figure. (D) can be true and isn't the answer.

There are only two ways to get a papier-mache ball—Thelma and Rita or Thelma working alone. Because Thelma can't work with Rita and work alone (obviously), the children can't make two papier-mache balls. (E) cannot be true and is the answer.

Remember: Pick easy situations when you attempt to disprove choices in a "cannot be true" question. There's no need to get overly elaborate. In this case, a simple situation is all four children working alone, creating four different projects. This simple and familiar scenario quickly eliminates the first two choices.

SECTION IV: LOGICAL REASONING

1. D

In this passage, we read that a 40-year-old mural has faded because of exposure. It is thought that the vividness of the original colors can be restored by using the muralist's leftover paints and mixing them according to his surviving instructions. Can this ploy work? Only if the leftover paints have not themselves deteriorated or otherwise altered over the years; otherwise, the mixing instructions, however precise, would result in colors unlike the original. Therefore, choice (D) is an assumption that is critical to the preservationists' plans.

(A), on the other hand, is a sweeping assumption. The point is to restore color, not to try to emulate the muralist's personal technique of painting. The latter goal is not the focus of the argument of the passage.

(B) takes the unwarranted line that the executive dining room must have suffered "extremes of heat and humidity" because of side effects from the serving of food. However, the cause of the exposure is not an essential part of the argument, so (B) is not assumed.

(C) invites you to assume that the muralist left his original paints and instructions for the use of later generations, but the "precise instructions" may actually have been for his own use. You have no indication that the paints were set aside for future restoration.

(E) may be true, but it is not necessarily so on the basis of the passage. Perhaps technology was sufficient to prevent fading, but the company did not invest in any form of temperature and humidity control.

2. C

To select the best inference drawn from the passage, you have to read between the lines. In the paragraph, we are explicitly told that the potential extinction of certain ill-tasting or ugly plant varieties is alarming because these plants might also be disease-resistant or have the ability to mature quickly. Why would these desirable traits of unwanted plants appeal to the breeder? It must be that the traits can be passed on to more attractive varieties; specifically, as expressed in choice (C), an attractive plant hybrid can be produced that will include desirable characteristics from two or more different species—good taste from one, disease resistance from another. That explains how a generally undesirable plant can nonetheless be desirable—for one of its traits.

(A) contradicts the passage. As the second sentence implies, many plants may face extinction because of undesirable taste or appearance. Breeders want to save these plants, not because taste and appearance are unimportant but because the plants have other traits that are desirable.

(B) cannot be inferred from the facts given us. We know that many plant varieties have already disappeared; more may disappear in the future.

(D) confuses unintended consequence with basic intent. As the first sentence of the passage explains, the extinction of plant varieties occurs along with the tendency toward standardized cultivation. The goal of the agribusiness concerns is to standardize; it would be unwarranted to say that extinction per se is part of that goal.

In (E), another unwarranted inference has been drawn. As we have read, the typical backyard gardener may indeed scorn certain varieties that nonetheless have a desirable maturation period. The latter is only a secondary characteristic when the aim is, as suggested, to produce plants that taste good or look attractive. It is quite possible, however, that the gardener could be concerned with the maturation period if it were the only difference between two otherwise equally attractive plants.

3. C

In this question, you are being asked to select an argument that resembles in logic the argument about air pollution. Note the logical shape of this argument. According to the writer, we cannot (if dispassionate) make a connection between industrialization and air pollution if the latter occurs without the presence of the former. In other words, we cannot say that a specific cause (X) has a specific effect (Y) unless that specific cause (X) is always associated with that specific effect (Y). Without evaluating the logic of this kind of argument, you will note that it resembles the argument of correct choice (C). In this case, the contention is that we cannot say that eating red meat (the specific cause X) leads to cardiac problems (the specific effect Y) because some people who have cardiac problems (Y) do not eat red meat (X).

The logical structure is quite different from (A). Someone is described as giving occasional evidence of a certain characteristic (unwarranted optimism); this evidence is interpreted or redefined as another quality (lack of requisite steadiness).

The argument of (B) can be broken down this way: If a small portion of a sampling responds one way (e.g., detests the diet drink), the larger portion will have a completely opposite reaction (like it very much). Remember, it is not the quality of logic that concerns us here, but the shape of the argument being advanced in each case. In that regard, (B) does not resemble the original argument.

(D) argues that if more gym students have the same amount of practice equipment available, some will have to go elsewhere to practice. In other words, if there is more demand for a constant supply of a resource, the demand will require other sources of the resource.

Equally dissimilar in structure to the stimulus is (E), in which the cause (a famous violinist) has little effect, so it is argued that a lesser cause (the teacher schooled only in fundamentals) would have a greater effect.

4. B

The author concludes that a more exquisite literary experience is to be had from a Petrarchan sonnet than from a detective novel. The evidence used to support this claim is that the best critics agree with it; the critics with the most delicate sensibilities (whom the author takes to be the best critics) prefer the Petrarchan sonnet to the detective novel. And how do we know that these critics are the best critics? Why, because they prefer the sonnets. Thus, the conclusion (the superiority of the sonnets) is presupposed in the evidence (in the identification of who are the best critics). This is circular reasoning. For this argument to work, some other criterion would be needed to determine the qualifications of the critics. As it now stands, it is logically flawed, and this flaw is described by choice (B). The author assumes the point he wishes to argue.

(A) does a little damage, as the author has never named one of the critical authorities. But that's not the main flaw here; the main flaw is the criterion he used in deciding who the best authorities are.

(C) is incorrect for the simple reason that no specific example is given.

(D) is incorrect because the author does provide evidence—the best critics' opinions. The problem resides in the fact that the evidence is inappropriate.

(E) is incorrect because the author need not provide exceptions; he may not believe that there are any exceptions.

5. C

This passage makes clear that the phenomenon of the shattered glasses could only have been caused by either a sonic boom or an earth tremor. The speaker heard a loud noise just as he was leaving for a vacation abroad, but he did not turn back to investigate. The car radio carried no mention of earth tremors, which are always reported in the area; the speaker assumes that the noise was therefore a sonic boom, which would not have gained broadcast attention. Then it is assumed that the noise heard was connected with the shattering of the glassware. This assumption ignores the possibility that the glasses were broken sometime later, either by another sonic boom or by an earth tremor, while the speaker was in another country and unlikely to hear a report about such a local phenomenon. Choice (C) states this assumption.

(A) proposes a distinction that is not necessary for the argument to work. In fact, if it were possible to tell the difference as suggested in this answer choice, there would be no need for the speculation of the speaker's concluding sentence.

(B) also suggests a distinction that is not an assumption of the speaker's. On the contrary, the extent of the damage is not seen as a clue to its cause, which (on that basis alone) could be either an earth tremor or a sonic boom.

It is of course possible that more secure protection might have prevented the shattering of the glasses, but we have no indication that the speaker assumes so. There (D) is incorrect.

The assumption in (E) is not essential to the speaker's conclusion, which designates a sonic boom rather than an earth tremor as the cause of the shattering. In any event, the speaker states that the breaking of glassware is "something that can only happen during a sonic boom or when there is an earth tremor"—not something that inevitably must happen.

6. B

The argument presented as an example can be short-handed as follows: Most P (for English philosophers) are E (for empiricists). B (for Bradley) is a P. Therefore, B is probably an E. This is mirrored in choice (B), where tall buildings fill the place of English philosophers, elevators replace empiricists, and the Cole Monument stands in for Bradley.

(C) is wrong primarily because the evidence and conclusion express certainty rather than probability. Choice (D), while having similar content, possesses a different form. To be parallel, the second premise would have to read, "Engels is a French philosopher." Furthermore, the use of "few" doesn't parallel the use of "most" in the stimulus. Choice (E) is way off, concluding, with a wild shot in the dark, the reasons people do not vote. The stimulus argument is not concluding reasons but, rather, the probability of a certain description. Choice (A), while interesting in itself, is not parallel. Among other things, it deals only with individuals, rather than groups, and thus lacks the notion of "most" and probability. Furthermore, its conclusion denies a proposed description, whereas that of the stimulus argument affirms a probable description. And perhaps most seriously, the first premise drastically oversimplifies the idea of "knowing," ignoring the possibility that the speaker doesn't know that he knows the anonymous author.

7. A

As presented in the passage, Franklin's argument is not exactly the same as the author's. The author concludes that monogamy is essential to a healthy marriage. Franklin's reasoning is intended to supply evidence for this conclusion. We need only focus on Franklin's reasoning, which amounts to the claim that love is unavoidable. And, while perhaps it ought only to occur within marriage, if it doesn't, then it will occur outside marriage. In other words, if one doesn't love one's spouse, then one will end up loving some other man or woman. So according to Franklin, although love might be best enjoyed within marriage, it will be enjoyed in any case. (A) uses this same reasoning. Taste, inferably good taste, is lacking from Jim's new diet; as a result, Jim will be "tasting" (that is, cheating) outside of his diet. This example uses the same reasoning and even carries with it the idea of "cheating." Love outside of the marriage bond is often frowned on, as is cheating on one's diet.

(B) is not parallel because here there is nothing like love or taste that simply must be satisfied. It's admitted as possible that there is neither a will nor a way. (C) is incorrect because courage is set up as necessary to honor, whereas in the stimulus, neither love nor marriage is necessary to the other. (D) is a different claim than the one made by Franklin. He says that a loveless marriage leads to fooling around; (D) says fooling around leads to a loveless marriage. And (E) isn't even close. It's an inference from evidence about parts to a conclusion about the whole; here, the whole set of toys. Franklin's reasoning is based on nothing like that. (In all likelihood, his reasoning is based on personal experience.)

8.   B

For this passage, you are asked to describe the type of argument used by the author. First, it is important to understand the intent of the passage, which concerns the nationwide rise in median SAT scores. The trend has gratified educators, we read, but the author contends that an accurate interpretation reveals a disturbing truth: Scores have not risen because all students have improved as test takers but because an increasing number of potentially low scorers no longer take the tests, leaving the field to the more privileged students. In other words, the author accepts the basic evidence of optimistic educators—the rise in test scores—but offers a contrasting explanation. The correct answer is, therefore, choice (B).

Self-evidently, (A) is incorrect, because it is essential to the author's argument that he accept "the accuracy of his opponents' figures." (C) would suggest that the author has clarified an explanation of the statistic; in fact, he offers an original explanation that flies in the face of the educators' optimistic reading of the test results. Because his argument is original, (D) cannot apply in this case, for he is articulating a new idea rather than defending one previously stated. In (E), one should not be misled by the author's somewhat facetious reference to the educators' all too eager embrace. Although he has adopted a dry tone toward his opponents and hints that they may have been hasty in their judgment, he in no way suggests that self-interest has clouded their ability to interpret the rise in median SAT scores. (Remember that the question asks for the author's "primary" method of argument.)

9.   E

There are only two sentences in this brief paragraph. Assuming that one logically follows from the other, what conclusion can reasonably be drawn? First, we are told that one Hudson River fish, a cod, suffers more from tumors than do other fish in the river. Second, we learn that pollution thought to cause such growths was being cleaned out of the river long before the cod tumors were discovered. What relationship does the second fact have to the first? The correct choice is (E); that is to say, there is no evident relationship at all between the two facts, at least as far as we can tell from the study. There is certainly no proof of a connection between cod tumors and Hudson River pollution; the former were discovered after the latter began to abate. This is not to say that there isn't a relationship, merely that we have no evidence of a relationship. The other answer choices offer unwarranted conclusions.

(A) The lack of evidence is taken to an illogical extreme (i.e., since there is no evidence that pollution causes the tumors, there must be no connection). But a lack of evidence for one possibility does not prove that its opposite is true. (B) is not only an unjustified conclusion but also plays fast and loose with the facts. There was no "sudden change" in the river, as far as we know; rather, the passage suggests, if anything, an impressive but gradual change in the amount of pollution. More to the point, sudden or not, the change cannot be linked to the appearance of the tumors simply on the basis of the information in the passage. The tumors may have existed long before they were discovered, or they may have been undetectable in their early stages. There is no indication that choice (C) is a reasonable conclusion; on the contrary, the author cites the "significant strides" made. It is always possible that the efforts could be more vigorously pursued, but we have no reason to suspect that to be the case. (D) rides roughshod over logic in two ways—by making the assumption that the Hudson River pollution causes the cod tumors and by assuming that the alleged causal relationship would only affect the freshwater cod. The latter error, presumably, would result from a misreading of the statement that one type of cod has more tumors than other fish swimming the same waters.

10. B

On the one hand, according to the author, the ideologue will "never alter his cry," which is defined as an expression of what is most desired; on the other, the politician is said to accept a partial victory, if only because it is the one possible at the moment, while planning to gain more ground in the future. As stated in correct choice (B), the author's distinction could be interpreted to mean that the former cannot accept a partial victory but demands immediate and complete satisfaction, while the latter believes it sensible to accept the piecemeal nature of progress in the actual world.

This is not to say, however, as choice (A) incorrectly states, that the politician's pragmatism involves shifting views to suit the occasion. He or she may accept a certain reality, as the author would have it, and tailor actions accordingly but not alter any beliefs that are held. The sweeping statement in choice (C) is not justified by the passage. The author does not claim that the typical politician will accept any or all things that are possible; the politician is described as accepting what is possible within his views. The distinction made in choice (D) is also not suggested by the passage, which leaves open the possibility that either politician or ideologue

can equally well address either practical concerns or abstract concepts. (E) is not implied by the passage. As far as the author is concerned, neither politician nor ideologue, despite their use of characteristically different strategies, is necessarily deceitful.

11. D

The author (who is obviously a politician) is defending himself against a call for his impeachment. The call for his impeachment is a response to the author's having raised corporate taxes, thereby forcing many industries out of the state. The resulting loss of jobs has exacerbated the state's unemployment problems. The author's defense consists not of disputing the alleged effects of his corporate tax increase but of pointing out his intentions in raising the tax. He responds to the impeachment call with the reason behind his tax increase. So the form of the reasoning is something like this: "Regardless of the effects of my actions, I had good intentions behind them." Choice (D) mirrors this reasoning: Alfred Nobel created dynamite, which has led to much death and suffering, but he originally intended it to be used in peaceful pursuits.

(A) describes an example in which someone (Hirohito) claims not to be responsible for some wrongheaded undertaking. This is different from the stimulus plea, because the politician never denies responsibility for the tax increase. (B) has Benedict Arnold changing his intentions. This is not the same as having good intentions that go unfulfilled in practice. (C) just provides a sensible reason for Galileo's renunciation. There's no idea here of a distinction between effects and original intentions, so (C) cannot be correct. (E) is incorrect because Charles I is not making a plea to escape responsibility. His intention had presumably been to carry out his duty, and he claimed to have done so as well as he could. There is no hint here of a plea to ignore the effects of his policies in favor of his original intent.

12. C

The principal flaw in the author's reasoning is his unreasonable assumption that his constituents want to impeach him because of his original intentions. This is very unlikely. What has angered his constituents is the effect of the author's policy. Thus (C) is correct; the issue here is the effects of the tax increase, not the purpose behind it.

(A) and (B) are attacks upon the strategy of increasing the corporate tax rate. Yet the author did not imply that this was guaranteed to eliminate unemployment (A). He merely thought it likely to reduce unemployment. (B) points out that the plan could fail and the state could wind up with higher unemployment. Well, this doesn't weaken the author's argument, because he is not arguing that the plan was foolproof, merely that it was well intentioned. (D) is both false and irrelevant. The author tells us that the Legislative Record can verify his claim and, even if it couldn't, the real problem is the nature of his claim—that his intentions are what is important—and not its verifiability. (E) is incorrect because the author does not believe that raising taxes itself will create jobs. The author's idea was that raising taxes will provide revenues and that these revenues could fund a statewide jobs program. Furthermore, (E) ignores the author's principle mistake—the mistake of thinking that his intentions are more important to the issue than his competence.

13.   D

The writer has concluded that the teachers' warnings about drug abuse must have been useless, since many of their students regularly used drugs while attending the school. The keyword here is *many*; not all students became drug users. What about those who did not? It is possible, as choice (D) correctly suggests, that some of the nonusers chose to avoid drugs as a result of the faculty's warnings; this answer choice refutes the argument that the warnings were "in vain."

On the other hand, choice (A) does not. If the intent of a warning is to prevent an act, the teachers' efforts were certainly "in vain," no matter how much educational information was passed along. If, as suggested in (B), some students had defensible reasons for using drugs, we can assume that the teachers' warnings were not directed toward them. Yet the other students did not

have such reasons, and their actions would prove that, for them at least, the warnings had been in vain.

Thus, choice (B) does not refute the main argument of the passage. The statement in choice (C) is not relevant to the discussion: Administration pressure on the teachers could have affected the sincerity of their delivery of warnings, perhaps, but the passage is about the supposed inefficacy of the warnings, not about the possible causes of this lack of effect. Similarly, answer choice (E) introduces information that is off the main point. The passage does not discuss the bad effects of drugs, although we can assume that the teachers did so in their warnings against drug use.

14.   D

The author of this passage claims that there is a correlation between aptitude for mathematics and the ability to learn music theory; in a similar vein, she sees a relationship between a student's attraction to math-related courses and his or her ability to comprehend the composition of contemporary music. From these linked ideas, we can conclude that students in courses not related to math—that is to say, students unlikely to have math aptitude as their principal intellectual gift—would not have as great an ability to learn musical theory as students majoring in subjects that require math aptitude. In slightly different form, this conclusion is expressed in correct answer choice (D).

We have no reason to conclude, as stated in choice (A), that humanities majors have not studied math as younger students. Even if likely to be less gifted in math than others, they could have been required or could have chosen to enroll in math or math-related courses. There is no reason to suspect otherwise. (B) states a relationship that is not at all suggested by the paragraph. In fact, the second sentence makes clear that the author is comparing two types of intelligence that are of equal intellectual luster; the difference is in kind, not intensity. At first glance, answer choice (C) might seem to be a logical conclusion, but the phrase "musical talent" is a misstatement of the author's terms of comparison. She sees a correlation between math aptitude and the ability to understand musical theory and new forms of musical composition. This latter ability is not synonymous with musical talent, which would include the ability to perform or compose or otherwise creatively engage in the musical art. (E) is an unwarranted conclusion. The author believes that students gifted in math are more likely to major in math-related courses than in the humanities; she cites this tendency. She does not go so far, however, as to imply that no student with mathematical aptitude would ever choose to major in the humanities.

15. D

With some force, the author of the passage criticizes government funding of the arts on two counts. First, it will be distributed according to the views of those temporarily in power; second, as a necessary consequence, artists will produce according to changing political realities. In other words, government agencies will not support the best artists but those whose ideas are most acceptable at any given moment; artists will not produce truly individual works but only those that are currently acceptable. The logic of this argument would be seriously weakened if most important artists tended to ignore the lure of government funds or, as in choice (D), the influence of either private or public monies. This answer choice leaves open the possibility that lesser artists will be influenced as the author predicts but weakens the contention that, overall, "the free flow of the creative process" will be interfered with.

The information in (A) would put equal numbers of working artists at each extreme of the political spectrum but does not address their motives. Without more information, then, choice (A) cannot qualify as a refutation of the argument in the passage. (B)—The artists who are "well known in their fields" might well share the political philosophies of the "politicians in power." The participation of the advisory committees would, in that case, exacerbate the problem outlined by the author; politicians and artists of a certain stripe might tend to channel monies to artists or groups of the same stripe. (C) does not weaken the argument of the passage; it is simply not relevant. Interesting

as it may be that both politics and the arts may be characterized by rapid shifts in fashion, that fact would not change the relationship described in the passage between government money and interference with individual creativity.

(E) changes the focus by referring to another aspect of government arts funding: the effect upon audience rather than the effect upon artists. The author has not addressed this issue. While audiences may have increased, they could have been experiencing only those performances or exhibits that had found political favor or had been created, as the author fears, to appeal to the tastes of those disbursing government funds.

16. A

For this question, you are being asked to choose a comprehensive summation of the passage about government funding's possibly harmful effect on the arts. The topic sentence that opens the paragraph lays down the basic charge that such support interferes with creativity. The author, as we have seen, expands upon the point by describing how it can or will do so. As stated in choice (A), a logical conclusion of the argument is that this type of interference with the creative process will be diverting, distracting, and otherwise degrading. These rather overheated terms are in keeping with the polemical tone of the writing; they follow logically from the author's picture of "willynilly" pursuit of government funds.

The first half of (B) seems to follow logically, both in tone and in substance; the author suggests that politicians would adopt such a condescendingly proprietary attitude toward the arts. The second half of (B), however, misses an important point; rather than be "inevitably and irretrievably captured" by one type of institution, the arts would, in the author's view, become the plaything of whichever group held power at a particular moment in a continually shifting process. (C), at first glance, seems logical enough. The author does believe that "the politically powerful" can control arts funding; it would seem likely that the most powerful leaders would divert funds to their own legislative districts. But we must remember that the author does not believe that increased arts funding always correlates with "wholesomely thriving" art. The passage makes clear that, to the author, arts funding is likely to produce debased or insincere art. (D)—There is a misreading of the second sentence of the passage. Experimental groups and established institutions are apparently equal, from the author's point of view; neither is more likely than the other to encourage the individual artist to pursue his or her own path. (E) directly contradicts the intent of the passage. This answer choice describes the state of affairs that the author would like to see occur, but it is the reverse of the supposed effect of government funding of the arts as denounced in the passage.

17.   E

According to the argument of this passage, college students who fail a course should be expelled because their failure indicates a lack of serious dedication to learning. But is that necessarily true in every case? It is possible that even the most dedicated student might encounter an obstacle outside his or her control, as expressed in correct answer choice (E). In that event, it could be the obstacle (e.g., serious illness), not the student's attitude, that leads to failure; thus hindered, the student would be no less "deserving" than others, solely from the evidence of his or her performance in the course, and the argument of the passage would be refuted.

(A) raises an irrelevant issue. The author of the passage condemns a student for failing any course. To imply, as choice (A) does, that some courses are more difficult to pass than others does not tackle the main issue. Equally, the statement in (B) strays from the point. The author would surely argue that, fully informed or not, the student who fails is squandering university resources. The lack of awareness is not extenuating just as, traditionally, ignorance of the law is no excuse. The author would probably agree with (C) but find the statement an affirmation rather than a rebuttal. Clearly, the passage argues resoundingly that academic achievement is the only criterion for continued enrollment in college and admits no such "right" to education. Similarly, although somewhat differently

framed, (D) suggests that factors other than scholarship should be considered. Contributions to the community, however, are secondary to the topic being discussed—the college education itself and the means by which one earns the privilege of participating in it. As outlined by the author, the argument of the passage is not rebutted by the secondary considerations introduced in (D).

18.   C

The author concludes that the benefits of arms reduction are merely illusory. The evidence presented is that even though some weapons are reduced, other weapons not covered by the treaty are increased to account for those that are reduced. In other words, if the superpowers agree to cut their tank forces in half, they will also double their navies or some other arsenal not covered by the reduction treaty. This argument is most strengthened by choice (C). Choice (C) tells us that the five largest military powers have increased funding for new weapons in each of the last 10 years. This supports the author's assertion that whatever firepower is reduced by the arms limitation treaties is reacquired through new weapons.

(A) says that the balance of power remains in spite of arms control. However, the balance of power is a proportion, and even though it is unchanged, the amount of firepower might well be reduced. (B) doesn't strengthen the argument because although no proposals have called for the elimination of weapons, they might still account for a reduction in the number of weapons. (D) comes from left field, introducing irrelevant outside knowledge. The author lumps all arms together, so this distinction is irrelevant to the argument as given. (E) actually contradicts the author's claim by stating that 15 percent of the firepower possessed by the largest military powers really has been cut. Even if this is not a great reduction, it contradicts the author's argument, which is that no reduction has been achieved through arms limitation.

19.   B

The conclusion of this argument is that we must irrigate our corn fields now to prevent a food shortage and economic disaster later. The argument cites some evidence to prove that a disaster is on its way, but then it jumps to the conclusion that irrigation is what's needed to prevent this disaster. That conclusion depends on the claim that irrigation is the only thing that can do the job, choice (B). If there is some other measure that will prevent the disaster, then the conclusion is no longer valid, and irrigation may not be necessary.

(A) addresses the issue of the feasibility of irrigation, whereas the argument discusses only the necessity of irrigation. (C) is irrelevant, since the argument seems to imply that a cut in the 1988 harvest alone could produce price increases in 1989 and 1990. We don't need to know anything about the weather in 1989 and 1990, since it's the 1988 drought that threatens to cause the 1989 and 1990 economic disasters. (D) is too strong. Irrigation does not have to produce harvests of expected yields for the conclusion to be valid; it need only improve the situation significantly, enough to prevent disaster. (E) introduces the issue of other areas' agricultural yields, an issue that is not addressed by this conclusion.

20. B

This question focuses on the first sentence of the passage, which accuses the governor's critics of partisanship. The two groups cited in answer choice (B) would be partisan, by definition, in regard to any "plight of the automobile industry." Therefore, if the statement were true, it would strongly support the idea that the state's chief executive is being attacked by people whose motives are not disinterested.

The general observation in choice (A) may or may not have much merit as an abstract statement. In any case, however, it does not strengthen or weaken the force of the assertion made in the first sentence. There, the motives of the governor's critics are being assessed. (A) addresses a concept brought up later in the passage— the assessment of the motives of a political figure like the governor who is under attack. (C) is irrelevant. Either the sincere critic or the disingenuously partisan critic might have voted for the governor in the past, when the current problems of the automobile industry might not have been an issue.

(D) focuses on the character of the governor, but as we have seen, the assertion being discussed in this question has to do with a specific segment of the public. Furthermore, if (D) is true, the governor is likely to merit honest criticism. This would weaken the author's assertion. (E) takes the wrong focus. Whether or not it accurately reflects the author's point of view (and, logically speaking, we have no evidence either way), it does not directly speak to the assertion made in the first sentence—about the true nature of those who now condemn the governor.

21. D

The author argues that, since much of the Irish population had become totally dependent on the potato for the bulk of its diet, successive failures of the yearly potato crop resulted in a national famine. The question asks for the most logical conclusion of this argument. (D) is the best conclusion, because if much of the population was totally dependent on the potato for its diet, then it follows that much of the population was left without alternative food sources when the potato crops continued to fail.

There's no reason to conclude that the adoption of the potato as a staple of the Irish diet represented a rejection of English social patterns, choice (A), because the author never discusses either nationalism or social patterns. Similarly, the passage tells us nothing about the relative susceptibility of various staples to crop failure, choice (B). All the author tells us about other crops is that they continued to be cultivated but "primarily for export to England."

(C) is also unwarranted; the author never implies that the great Potato Famine caused any revolutionary activity. Instead, the disastrous consequence of the Potato Famine, according to the author, was "a sweeping sentence of death or emigration." (E) cannot be concluded, because although the author asserts that the potato was grudgingly accepted as a staple of the Irish diet, the passage tells us nothing of those who resisted the potato or their motivation in doing so.

22.   C

The author is creating an analogy between the public's banning of books from schools and municipal libraries and the rather absurd hypothetical situation of the author's barging into my living room and taking away the book I am reading. The author hopes we will find the former situation just as absurd as the latter. The comparison on which the analogy is based, however, is weak, and (C) points to the principal weakness. While it is absurd to suggest that the author should have a say in what I read in my own living room, it may not be so absurd to say that certain representatives of the public should have a say in what can be read in public institutions like schools and municipal libraries. My living room belongs to me, not to the author; schools and libraries, on the other hand, belong to every member of the public.

(A) hinges on an irrelevant issue. Whether the book is burned or just banned is not important; what is important here is the parallel between living room and library and the question of whether people can be forbidden to own and read certain types of books. (B) is not a weakness in the analogy, since it only points to a lack of reality in the author's hypothetical situation, a lack of reality that the author intends in order to heighten the situation's absurdity. The author, after all, enjoins us to imagine that the courts condone this behavior. (D) might weaken the analogy between the reader's living room and children's schools, but the analogy between the reader's living room and municipal libraries would remain untouched; thus, (D) is not as strong an answer as (C) is. (E) may raise an interesting problem to be considered in any discussion of censorship, but because it has nothing to do with this particular analogy (remember your question stem!), it can hardly be our correct answer.

23.   D

First, a statement is made about a relationship—during exam periods (whenever X), a rise in cookie sales occurs (then Y). Second, the argument assumes that neither factor in the relationship can occur separately from the other; that is, a rise in cookie sales must

always signal an exam period, just as an exam period, as stated, is always accompanied by increased cookie sales (since Y, therefore X). The logical structure of the argument in (D) is very similar. Because a computer programmer must necessarily have the ability to think logically, it follows, according to this argument, that any logical person (Rob, in this example) must necessarily be a computer programmer. In other words, (D) says: "Whenever X (computer programmer), then Y (logical thinker); because Y (logical thinker), therefore X (computer programmer)."

Note that (A) has a very different structure. One factor, "proficiency at logical thinking," leads to another factor, "success in the computer-programming field." But the nonexistence of this second factor among a group of friends is then said to imply the nonexistence of the first. Put another way, the argument contends that "whenever X, then Y; since not-Y, therefore not-X."

In (B), one factor, a person's ability to think logically, is described as possibly leading to a job as a programmer; further, a specific person's ability to think very logically may possibly make him a very good programmer. Structurally, then, the argument says: "Whenever X, possibly Y; because X, therefore Y."

(C) also differs in structure from the original argument. Here, one factor is presented as having a specific consequence; then a second factor is described as having the same consequence. In this case, we can say: "Whenever X, then Y; but Z will also cause Y."

The structure of (E) slightly resembles that of choice (A). One type of element, computer programmers as a class, is associated with a quality; if students do not possess this quality—the ability to solve logical problems—they cannot be computer programmers. In other words: "Whenever X, then Y; because not-Y, then not-X."

24.   B

In effect, this question asks you to determine what is illogical about the passage. The author begins by claiming that the attempt to proselytize or convert others is, among other characteristics, a likely trait of people whose behavior may not be strictly normal. As an example, he cites the case of vegetarians, who are, in his view, mostly proselytizers. This very tendency, he says, proves that vegetarianism is a deviation from the American social norm of meat eating. What logical objection can be raised to this argument? As expressed in answer choice (B), the author has neglected the possibility that, while social deviation may indeed create proselytizers, it is not therefore true that all proselytizers have been created by a deviation from the social norm. Social deviation may be one cause, but not the only cause, of the urge to proselytize.

The objection cited in choice (A) is less damaging, since it merely offers a less pejorative expression than "proselytizing" without addressing the question of whether or not the activity of "expressing strong feelings," however termed, is always associated with social deviation. Softening the term "proselytizing" does not change the form of the author's reasoning.

(C) suggests that an important term in the author's argument is too vague. In context, however, what he means by "mainstream American culture" is perfectly clear, since it is, by definition, that part of society that follows the social norms.

(D) brings an unwarranted charge. Although the author might seem to feel that social deviants in general have some unattractive qualities, as set forth in the first sentence, he does not reveal a prejudice against vegetarians per se. There is no evidence that his characterization of the behavior of vegetarians is unfair.

(E) seems an attractive choice, because if statistics showed that more than half of all Americans no longer eat meat, the author's conclusion would indeed be mistaken; vegetarianism would be a mainstream activity. This objection cannot be raised, however, if the figures are otherwise. Because we do not know which is the case, we cannot be certain that "the actual number" would weaken the author's main argument. (E) is therefore not as useful a critique as (B), which attacks the logic of the argument.

25. A

This is a Parallel Reasoning question that can be diagrammed with relative ease. The original diagram translates into this: All X (typists at Ace) do Y (work overtime); because Y, therefore X. (A) is parallel: All X (rabbits) do Y (eat carrots); because Y, therefore X.

(B) becomes this: All X (Eastside members) do Y (purchase tickets); since X, therefore Y.

(C) becomes this: All X (drug takers) do Y (become conscious of the risks); because Z (doesn't like risks), therefore not X.

(D) becomes this: All X (nightclub singers) do Y (get served free meal); if Z (hungry), then become X.

If we translate (E)'s first sentence into "All construction workers at this site do not belong to a union," it becomes this: All X (workers at site) do Y (eschew union membership); because not X, therefore not Y. So (E)'s "none" construction isn't parallel to begin with and can't even be made parallel.

PRACTICE TEST 2

LSAT PRACTICE TEST 2 ANSWER SHEET

Remove (or photocopy) the answer sheet and use it to complete the Practice Test.

HOW TO TAKE THE PRACTICE TESTS

Before taking each test, find a quiet place where you can work uninterrupted for about two and a half hours. Make sure you have a comfortable desk and several No. 2 pencils.

Each Practice Test includes four scored multiple-choice sections. Keep in mind that on the actual LSAT, there will be an additional multiple-choice section—the experimental section—that will not contribute to your score, plus an unscored Writing Sample.

Once you start a Practice Test, don't stop (except for a 5- to 10-minute break after the second section) until you've gone through all four sections. Remember, you can review any questions within a section, but you may not go back or forward a section

Good luck!

Start with number 1 for each section. If a section has fewer questions than answer spaces, leave the extra spaces blank.

Section I

1. Ⓐ Ⓑ Ⓒ Ⓓ Ⓔ   9. Ⓐ Ⓑ Ⓒ Ⓓ Ⓔ   17. Ⓐ Ⓑ Ⓒ Ⓓ Ⓔ   25. Ⓐ Ⓑ Ⓒ Ⓓ Ⓔ
2. Ⓐ Ⓑ Ⓒ Ⓓ Ⓔ   10. Ⓐ Ⓑ Ⓒ Ⓓ Ⓔ   18. Ⓐ Ⓑ Ⓒ Ⓓ Ⓔ   26. Ⓐ Ⓑ Ⓒ Ⓓ Ⓔ
3. Ⓐ Ⓑ Ⓒ Ⓓ Ⓔ   11. Ⓐ Ⓑ Ⓒ Ⓓ Ⓔ   19. Ⓐ Ⓑ Ⓒ Ⓓ Ⓔ   27. Ⓐ Ⓑ Ⓒ Ⓓ Ⓔ   # right in
4. Ⓐ Ⓑ Ⓒ Ⓓ Ⓔ   12. Ⓐ Ⓑ Ⓒ Ⓓ Ⓔ   20. Ⓐ Ⓑ Ⓒ Ⓓ Ⓔ   28. Ⓐ Ⓑ Ⓒ Ⓓ Ⓔ   Section I
5. Ⓐ Ⓑ Ⓒ Ⓓ Ⓔ   13. Ⓐ Ⓑ Ⓒ Ⓓ Ⓔ   21. Ⓐ Ⓑ Ⓒ Ⓓ Ⓔ   29. Ⓐ Ⓑ Ⓒ Ⓓ Ⓔ
6. Ⓐ Ⓑ Ⓒ Ⓓ Ⓔ   14. Ⓐ Ⓑ Ⓒ Ⓓ Ⓔ   22. Ⓐ Ⓑ Ⓒ Ⓓ Ⓔ   30. Ⓐ Ⓑ Ⓒ Ⓓ Ⓔ
7. Ⓐ Ⓑ Ⓒ Ⓓ Ⓔ   15. Ⓐ Ⓑ Ⓒ Ⓓ Ⓔ   23. Ⓐ Ⓑ Ⓒ Ⓓ Ⓔ   # wrong in
8. Ⓐ Ⓑ Ⓒ Ⓓ Ⓔ   16. Ⓐ Ⓑ Ⓒ Ⓓ Ⓔ   24. Ⓐ Ⓑ Ⓒ Ⓓ Ⓔ   Section I

Section II

1. Ⓐ Ⓑ Ⓒ Ⓓ Ⓔ   9. Ⓐ Ⓑ Ⓒ Ⓓ Ⓔ   17. Ⓐ Ⓑ Ⓒ Ⓓ Ⓔ   25. Ⓐ Ⓑ Ⓒ Ⓓ Ⓔ
2. Ⓐ Ⓑ Ⓒ Ⓓ Ⓔ   10. Ⓐ Ⓑ Ⓒ Ⓓ Ⓔ   18. Ⓐ Ⓑ Ⓒ Ⓓ Ⓔ   26. Ⓐ Ⓑ Ⓒ Ⓓ Ⓔ
3. Ⓐ Ⓑ Ⓒ Ⓓ Ⓔ   11. Ⓐ Ⓑ Ⓒ Ⓓ Ⓔ   19. Ⓐ Ⓑ Ⓒ Ⓓ Ⓔ   27. Ⓐ Ⓑ Ⓒ Ⓓ Ⓔ   # right in
4. Ⓐ Ⓑ Ⓒ Ⓓ Ⓔ   12. Ⓐ Ⓑ Ⓒ Ⓓ Ⓔ   20. Ⓐ Ⓑ Ⓒ Ⓓ Ⓔ   28. Ⓐ Ⓑ Ⓒ Ⓓ Ⓔ   Section II
5. Ⓐ Ⓑ Ⓒ Ⓓ Ⓔ   13. Ⓐ Ⓑ Ⓒ Ⓓ Ⓔ   21. Ⓐ Ⓑ Ⓒ Ⓓ Ⓔ   29. Ⓐ Ⓑ Ⓒ Ⓓ Ⓔ
6. Ⓐ Ⓑ Ⓒ Ⓓ Ⓔ   14. Ⓐ Ⓑ Ⓒ Ⓓ Ⓔ   22. Ⓐ Ⓑ Ⓒ Ⓓ Ⓔ   30. Ⓐ Ⓑ Ⓒ Ⓓ Ⓔ
7. Ⓐ Ⓑ Ⓒ Ⓓ Ⓔ   15. Ⓐ Ⓑ Ⓒ Ⓓ Ⓔ   23. Ⓐ Ⓑ Ⓒ Ⓓ Ⓔ   # wrong in
8. Ⓐ Ⓑ Ⓒ Ⓓ Ⓔ   16. Ⓐ Ⓑ Ⓒ Ⓓ Ⓔ   24. Ⓐ Ⓑ Ⓒ Ⓓ Ⓔ   Section II

Section III

1.	Ⓐ Ⓑ Ⓒ Ⓓ Ⓔ	9.	Ⓐ Ⓑ Ⓒ Ⓓ Ⓔ	17.	Ⓐ Ⓑ Ⓒ Ⓓ Ⓔ	25.	Ⓐ Ⓑ Ⓒ Ⓓ Ⓔ
2.	Ⓐ Ⓑ Ⓒ Ⓓ Ⓔ	10.	Ⓐ Ⓑ Ⓒ Ⓓ Ⓔ	18.	Ⓐ Ⓑ Ⓒ Ⓓ Ⓔ	26.	Ⓐ Ⓑ Ⓒ Ⓓ Ⓔ
3.	Ⓐ Ⓑ Ⓒ Ⓓ Ⓔ	11.	Ⓐ Ⓑ Ⓒ Ⓓ Ⓔ	19.	Ⓐ Ⓑ Ⓒ Ⓓ Ⓔ	27.	Ⓐ Ⓑ Ⓒ Ⓓ Ⓔ
4.	Ⓐ Ⓑ Ⓒ Ⓓ Ⓔ	12.	Ⓐ Ⓑ Ⓒ Ⓓ Ⓔ	20.	Ⓐ Ⓑ Ⓒ Ⓓ Ⓔ	28.	Ⓐ Ⓑ Ⓒ Ⓓ Ⓔ
5.	Ⓐ Ⓑ Ⓒ Ⓓ Ⓔ	13.	Ⓐ Ⓑ Ⓒ Ⓓ Ⓔ	21.	Ⓐ Ⓑ Ⓒ Ⓓ Ⓔ	29.	Ⓐ Ⓑ Ⓒ Ⓓ Ⓔ
6.	Ⓐ Ⓑ Ⓒ Ⓓ Ⓔ	14.	Ⓐ Ⓑ Ⓒ Ⓓ Ⓔ	22.	Ⓐ Ⓑ Ⓒ Ⓓ Ⓔ	30.	Ⓐ Ⓑ Ⓒ Ⓓ Ⓔ
7.	Ⓐ Ⓑ Ⓒ Ⓓ Ⓔ	15.	Ⓐ Ⓑ Ⓒ Ⓓ Ⓔ	23.	Ⓐ Ⓑ Ⓒ Ⓓ Ⓔ		
8.	Ⓐ Ⓑ Ⓒ Ⓓ Ⓔ	16.	Ⓐ Ⓑ Ⓒ Ⓓ Ⓔ	24.	Ⓐ Ⓑ Ⓒ Ⓓ Ⓔ		

right in
Section III

wrong in
Section III

Section IV

1.	Ⓐ Ⓑ Ⓒ Ⓓ Ⓔ	9.	Ⓐ Ⓑ Ⓒ Ⓓ Ⓔ	17.	Ⓐ Ⓑ Ⓒ Ⓓ Ⓔ	25.	Ⓐ Ⓑ Ⓒ Ⓓ Ⓔ
2.	Ⓐ Ⓑ Ⓒ Ⓓ Ⓔ	10.	Ⓐ Ⓑ Ⓒ Ⓓ Ⓔ	18.	Ⓐ Ⓑ Ⓒ Ⓓ Ⓔ	26.	Ⓐ Ⓑ Ⓒ Ⓓ Ⓔ
3.	Ⓐ Ⓑ Ⓒ Ⓓ Ⓔ	11.	Ⓐ Ⓑ Ⓒ Ⓓ Ⓔ	19.	Ⓐ Ⓑ Ⓒ Ⓓ Ⓔ	27.	Ⓐ Ⓑ Ⓒ Ⓓ Ⓔ
4.	Ⓐ Ⓑ Ⓒ Ⓓ Ⓔ	12.	Ⓐ Ⓑ Ⓒ Ⓓ Ⓔ	20.	Ⓐ Ⓑ Ⓒ Ⓓ Ⓔ	28.	Ⓐ Ⓑ Ⓒ Ⓓ Ⓔ
5.	Ⓐ Ⓑ Ⓒ Ⓓ Ⓔ	13.	Ⓐ Ⓑ Ⓒ Ⓓ Ⓔ	21.	Ⓐ Ⓑ Ⓒ Ⓓ Ⓔ	29.	Ⓐ Ⓑ Ⓒ Ⓓ Ⓔ
6.	Ⓐ Ⓑ Ⓒ Ⓓ Ⓔ	14.	Ⓐ Ⓑ Ⓒ Ⓓ Ⓔ	22.	Ⓐ Ⓑ Ⓒ Ⓓ Ⓔ	30.	Ⓐ Ⓑ Ⓒ Ⓓ Ⓔ
7.	Ⓐ Ⓑ Ⓒ Ⓓ Ⓔ	15.	Ⓐ Ⓑ Ⓒ Ⓓ Ⓔ	23.	Ⓐ Ⓑ Ⓒ Ⓓ Ⓔ		
8.	Ⓐ Ⓑ Ⓒ Ⓓ Ⓔ	16.	Ⓐ Ⓑ Ⓒ Ⓓ Ⓔ	24.	Ⓐ Ⓑ Ⓒ Ⓓ Ⓔ		

right in
Section IV

wrong in
Section IV

1　　　　　　　　　　$\boxed{1}$　　　　　　　　　　**1**

Section I
Time—35 minutes 24 questions

Directions: Each group of questions is based on a set of conditions. You may wish to draw a rough sketch to help you answer some of the questions. Choose the best answer for each question and fill in the corresponding space on your answer sheet.

Questions 1–5

A designer will select exactly two appliance designs and exactly two cabinet designs for the renovation of a house. The available appliance designs are H, J, K, L, and M, and the available cabinet designs are T, V, and W. The selections of appliances and cabinets must be made in accordance with the following conditions:

　　H is selected only if J and W are selected.

　　M cannot be selected unless J is selected.

　　If V is selected, then H is selected.

1. If V is selected, which one of the following must be selected?

　　(A) K

　　(B) L

　　(C) M

　　(D) T

　　(E) W

2. Which one of the following pairs of designs CANNOT be selected together?

　　(A) H and J

　　(B) H and M

　　(C) J and K

　　(D) J and L

　　(E) J and M

3. If J is not selected, which one of the following must be true?

　　(A) H and T are selected.

　　(B) K and L are selected.

　　(C) K and M are selected.

　　(D) L and V are not selected.

　　(E) M and W are not selected.

4. If L is selected, how many distinct combinations of designs can be selected?

　　(A) 1

　　(B) 2

　　(C) 3

　　(D) 4

　　(E) 6

5. If the conditions are altered such that H can be selected without selecting J, but all of the other conditions remain in effect, then which one of the following is a pair of designs that may be selected together?

　　(A) H and M

　　(B) K and M

　　(C) K and V

　　(D) M and V

　　(E) T and V

GO ON TO THE NEXT PAGE

Questions 6–12

For a family portrait, seven members of the Ellis family—Feisal, Gillian, Helen, Ian, Jeremy, Khalia, and Laura—stand in positions numbered one through seven from left to right, according to the following conditions:

> Feisal and Gillian do not stand next to each other.
>
> Exactly two people stand between Helen and Feisal.
>
> Ian and Feisal stand next to each other.
>
> Khalia and Gillian do not stand next to each other.
>
> Helen's position is exactly two places to the left of Gillian's position.

6. Which one of the following is an acceptable arrangement of family members from left to right?

   (A) Feisal, Ian, Helen, Jeremy, Gillian, Laura, Khalia

   (B) Feisal, Ian, Khalia, Helen, Jeremy, Gillian, Laura

   (C) Feisal, Khalia, Ian, Gillian, Jeremy, Helen, Laura

   (D) Jeremy, Feisal, Ian, Laura, Helen, Khalia, Gillian

   (E) Khalia, Jeremy, Ian, Feisal, Gillian, Laura, Helen

7. If Laura stands in position one, then Jeremy must stand

   (A) between Gillian and Helen.

   (B) between Ian and Laura.

   (C) next to Feisal.

   (D) next to Khalia.

   (E) in position seven.

8. If Laura stands next to Feisal, which one of the following CANNOT be true?

   (A) Gillian stands in position seven.

   (B) Ian stands in position one.

   (C) Ian stands between Feisal and Khalia.

   (D) Jeremy stands between Helen and Ian.

   (E) Laura stands between Feisal and Khalia.

9. If Jeremy stands in position seven, how many people stand between Jeremy and Laura?

   (A) None

   (B) One

   (C) Two

   (D) Four

   (E) Five

10. If Ian and Jeremy stand next to each other, how many people stand between Laura and Khalia?

    (A) None

    (B) One

    (C) Two

    (D) Four

    (E) Six

11. If Laura stands next to Khalia, how many people stand between Gillian and Jeremy?

    (A) None

    (B) One

    (C) Two

    (D) Three

    (E) Four

GO ON TO THE NEXT PAGE ⟩

1   1   **1**

12. Which one of the following CANNOT be true?

   (A) Feisal stands next to both Ian and Laura.

   (B) Gillian stands next to both Jeremy and Laura.

   (C) Jeremy stands next to both Gillian and Helen.

   (D) Khalia stands next to both Feisal and Laura.

   (E) Laura stands next to both Feisal and Jeremy.

Questions 13–17

Five sled dogs—Gakido, Hira, Jinook, Kini, and Leinheit—occupy five positions on a racing team. The positions are numbered one through five, and exactly one sled dog occupies each position. The sled dogs are hitched to harnesses as shown below:

The assignment of sled dogs to positions is subject to the following conditions:

   Each harness connects exactly two sled dogs, and sled dogs connected by harnesses are considered adjacent to one another.

   Exactly two sled dogs are experienced and exactly three sled dogs are inexperienced.

   An experienced sled dog must occupy the first position.

   Jinook is an experienced sled dog.

   Gakido is an inexperienced sled dog.

   The experienced sled dogs cannot be adjacent to one another.

   Kini is not adjacent to Leinheit.

13. Which one of the following is an acceptable list of the positions in a single team that could be occupied by inexperienced sled dogs?

   (A) First, second, fifth

   (B) First, third, fourth

   (C) Second, third, fourth

   (D) Second, fourth, fifth

   (E) Third, fourth, fifth

14. If Jinook occupies the fifth position, which one of the following must be true?

   (A) Gakido occupies the second position.

   (B) Hira occupies the third position.

   (C) Leinheit occupies the fourth position.

   (D) The sled dog occupying the third position is experienced.

   (E) The sled dog occupying the fourth position is inexperienced.

15. If Leinheit and Hira occupy the fourth and fifth positions, respectively, then which one of the following must be false?

   (A) Gakido is adjacent to Jinook.

   (B) Gakido is adjacent to Kini.

   (C) Gakido is adjacent to Leinheit.

   (D) Gakido is adjacent to Hira.

   (E) Jinook is adjacent to Kini.

16. If Kini occupies the fifth position, which one of the following would guarantee that an experienced sled dog occupies the fourth position?

   (A) Gakido occupies the second position.

   (B) Gakido occupies the third position.

   (C) Hira occupies the third position.

   (D) Jinook occupies the first position.

   (E) Leinheit occupies the second position.

GO ON TO THE NEXT PAGE

17. If Jinook is adjacent to both Kini and Leinheit, then Hira must be

    (A) adjacent to Gakido.

    (B) adjacent to Jinook.

    (C) adjacent to Kini.

    (D) adjacent to Leinheit.

    (E) adjacent to either Jinook or Leinheit.

Questions 18–24

A veterinarian has scheduled seven animals—Porter, Quint, Rocky, Slacker, Tammy, Venus, and Willoughby—to be examined on a single day, from first to seventh. Each animal will be examined exactly once during the day, and no two animals will be examined at the same time. The order of examinations must conform to the following restrictions:

> Porter is examined immediately before Tammy is examined.
>
> If Quint is examined fifth, Venus is examined sixth.
>
> If Slacker is examined second, Porter is examined third.
>
> Willoughby is examined either fourth or sixth.
>
> Venus is not examined first or fifth.

18. Which one of the following is an acceptable ordering of animal examinations?

    (A) Quint, Slacker, Porter, Tammy, Venus, Willoughby, Rocky

    (B) Quint, Venus, Slacker, Willoughby, Porter, Tammy, Rocky

    (C) Rocky, Slacker, Venus, Willoughby, Porter, Tammy, Quint

    (D) Slacker, Porter, Tammy, Quint, Willoughby, Rocky, Venus

    (E) Slacker, Rocky, Porter, Tammy, Quint, Willoughby, Venus

19. If Slacker is examined second, which one of the following animals must be examined fifth?

    (A) Porter

    (B) Quint

    (C) Rocky

    (D) Tammy

    (E) Willoughby

20. If Quint is examined fifth and Rocky is examined before Willoughby is examined, then which one of the following must be true?

    (A) Porter is examined first.

    (B) Rocky is examined third.

    (C) Slacker is examined seventh.

    (D) Tammy is examined second.

    (E) Willoughby is examined sixth.

21. If Porter is examined third, which one of the following is a complete and accurate list of animals who can be examined fifth?

    (A) Quint

    (B) Slacker

    (C) Quint, Slacker

    (D) Rocky, Slacker

    (E) Quint, Rocky, Slacker

22. If Willoughby is examined immediately after Quint is examined, and Slacker is examined immediately after Venus is examined, then Rocky must be examined

    (A) third.

    (B) fourth.

    (C) fifth.

    (D) sixth.

    (E) seventh.

GO ON TO THE NEXT PAGE ⟩

1   **1**   **1**

23. If Tammy and Venus are both examined sometime after Willoughby is examined, then the number of possible orderings of animal examinations is

    (A) 1
    (B) 2
    (C) 3
    (D) 4
    (E) 5

24. If Rocky is examined fourth, which one of the following could be true?

    (A) Porter is examined third.
    (B) Quint is examined first.
    (C) Slacker is examined second.
    (D) Slacker is examined seventh.
    (E) Tammy is examined seventh.

IF YOU FINISH BEFORE TIME IS CALLED, YOU MAY CHECK YOUR WORK ON THIS SECTION ONLY. DO NOT WORK ON ANY OTHER SECTION IN THE TEST.

STOP

Section II

Time—35 minutes 25 questions

Directions: This test is comprised of questions that ask you to analyze the logic of statements or short paragraphs. You are to choose as the answer to each question the one choice you consider best on the basis of your common-sense evaluation of the statement and its assumptions. Although a question may seem to have more than one acceptable answer, there is only one best answer, and it is the one that does not entail making any illogical, extraneous, or conflicting assumptions about the question. These questions do not presuppose any knowledge of formal logic on your part.

1. Most of the office complexes designed by Valentine Brown have a central open area around which the buildings are grouped. But it is also true that most of the office complexes designed by Mr. Brown have underground walkways between the buildings. So most of the office complexes designed by Valentine Brown combine a central space around which the buildings are grouped with a system of underground walkways between the buildings.

   Which one of the following arguments contains flawed reasoning most similar to the flawed reasoning in the argument above?

   (A) Most of the children in class say that dessert is their favorite meal and that pecan pie is their favorite dessert. So the favorite food of most children in class is pecan pie.

   (B) Excessive reading can weaken a person's eyesight. Excessive reading can also make a person round-shouldered. Excessive reading, therefore, can make a person round-shouldered and near-sighted.

   (C) The majority of customers at Torrance Autos wish to buy a four-door sedan. But the majority of customers at Torrance Autos also wish to purchase a red car. So the majority of customers at Torrance Autos wish to purchase a red, four-door sedan.

   (D) People who spend the most time watching television say they most prefer to watch sports programs and situation comedies. Thus, sports and situation comedies are probably the most frequently watched varieties of programming on television.

   (E) Constance will live only in an apartment that has a playground attached. Philip will live only in an apartment that allows pets. Therefore, if Constance and Philip live together, they will live only in an apartment that has a playground attached and allows pets.

2. Toy manufacturer: This rubber ball is costly to make. We should switch to a less costly brand of rubber for this product.

   Marketing analyst: But the ball sells so well because of its superior bouncing properties. No other material performs as well. We should stick with what we know we can sell.

   The speakers above disagree over which one of the following issues?

   (A) Whether the rubber used for this ball is more expensive than other available materials

   (B) Whether this product regularly meets its sales quotas

   (C) Whether the company should make the rubber ball from a different brand of rubber

   (D) Whether customer priorities should factor into product development decisions

   (E) Whether other rubber materials perform as well as the material currently used

GO ON TO THE NEXT PAGE

2 2 2 **2**

Questions 3–4

Salesperson: The revolutionary new Shepherd's Gate Protection System represents the latest in sheep-tending technology. The built-in sensors recognize the scent of predators from miles around. When your flock is in danger of attack, the electronic gates surrounding the flock will quickly slam shut, keeping any unwanted animals away and your flock safer than ever. Sure, the system is prone to false alarms, but you know what they say: "Better safe than sorry."

3. Which one of the following, if true, most strengthens the salesperson's argument?

   (A) Sheep cannot be injured by the electronic gates when they quickly slam shut.

   (B) Similar electronic protection systems are currently used to protect cattle from attack from predators.

   (C) Roughly half of the incidents in which the gates are activated are triggered by false alarms.

   (D) Some sheep predators have been hunted almost to extinction.

   (E) Flocks of sheep are rarely attacked by predators.

4. The phrase "better safe than sorry" plays which one of the following roles in the argument above?

   (A) It illustrates how a supposedly problematic aspect of the Gate Protection System is actually beneficial.

   (B) It provides additional evidence of the mechanical efficacy of the Gate Protection System.

   (C) It reinforces the notion that false alarms from the Gate Protection System are relatively rare.

   (D) It attempts to diminish the magnitude of a deficiency of the Gate Protection System.

   (E) It introduces a further reason for the need for sheep-tending technology.

5. Administrator: Sandra would not make an effective teacher. She is too lenient to fail students and too critical to reward any students with high marks.

   An assumption central to the argument above is that

   (A) effective teachers fail a certain percentage of their students and reward the rest with high marks.

   (B) a teacher must be capable of either rewarding students with high marks or failing students in order to be effective.

   (C) to fail or reward her students, Sandra must be an effective teacher.

   (D) it is impossible to fail a student and then later reward the same student with high marks.

   (E) if Sandra were less critical, she would reward students with high marks.

GO ON TO THE NEXT PAGE

6. The financial burden imposed by job-related costs is greatest for individuals who make a salary of $30,000 to $40,000 per year and less for those who make much lower or much higher salaries. The reason for this is that individuals in low-paying, entry-level positions making far less than $30,000 per year generally have fewer costs associated with maintaining their jobs, such as wardrobe costs, dry-cleaning, and medical bills due to work-related stress. The burden of these costs increases as one is promoted to higher-ranking positions but then lessens as the salary levels commensurate with further promotions become more than adequate to off set such costs. Jenny, who now makes $40,000 per year as an administrative director, will therefore be less financially burdened over the coming years by costs related to this job.

The argument above depends on which one of the following assumptions?

(A) Jenny will be promoted in the years to come.

(B) Over the next several years, Jenny's employer will provide benefits that help reduce stress-related medical costs.

(C) The $40,000 pay rate is not considered an entry-level salary for Jenny's position.

(D) None of Jenny's coworkers who earn the same salary as Jenny is as burdened as she is by job-related costs.

(E) The costs related to Jenny's previous job were not as high as the costs related to her current position.

7. An individual may become more personally appealing as he or she becomes more physically beautiful. At the same time, however, the positive attention brought on by greater beauty may make the person vain or arrogant, which may decrease his or her personal appeal.

Which one of the following statements is best illustrated by the situation described above?

(A) The link between beauty and personal appeal is entirely superficial.

(B) Traits that appear positive are usually negative.

(C) A characteristic may be both enhanced and reduced by a single factor.

(D) Negative traits can only be balanced by positive traits of equal importance.

(E) Beauty is in the eye of the beholder.

GO ON TO THE NEXT PAGE ⟩

8. Educational consultant: Most school districts today do not provide adequate educations for their students. Teachers do not receive quality training. Moreover, after-school academic programs are limited by tight budgets, and parental involvement in the classroom is at an all-time low. The Prentice School District, however, is looking up; parents and community volunteers are spending more time assisting in classrooms than in previous years.

If the educational consultant's statements are true, which of the following must also be true?

(A) The education provided by the Prentice School District displays at least one component of adequate education more so than it has in the past.

(B) The education provided by the Prentice School District can be considered adequate.

(C) The Prentice School District surpasses others in terms of the quality of education that its students receive.

(D) Many schools currently offer fewer after-school academic programs than do the schools in the Prentice School District.

(E) There is less parental involvement in other school districts than there is in the Prentice School District.

Questions 9–10

A consumer survey of independent feature films revealed that the percentage of action films that received the survey's highest rating was greater than the percentage of romance films that received the highest rating. Yet the survey organizers were probably erroneous in their conclusion that subject matter determines a feature film's popular appeal, since the action films were all directed by filmmakers with at least one hit film to their credit, while the romance films were directed by newer filmmakers, many of whom had not produced a previous film.

9. The statements above, if true, support which one of the following inferences?

(A) Fewer romance films than action films received the survey's highest rating.

(B) There is no relationship between the popular appeal of the feature films evaluated in the survey and any previous successes of the directors of those films.

(C) If consumers were surveyed regarding their impressions of big-budget mainstream films, the percentage of romance films that would receive the survey's highest rating would be lower than the percentage of action films that would receive the highest rating.

(D) Experienced filmmakers are more likely to produce hit films than are new filmmakers.

(E) Among directors with the same number of hit films to their credit, differences in the subject matter of their feature films may not affect the way the films are popularly rated.

GO ON TO THE NEXT PAGE

2   2   2   2

10. Each of the following, if true, supports the author's contention that the organizers misinterpreted the survey data EXCEPT

   (A) the fact that one has directed a previous hit film is a positive indicator of that director's filmmaking talent.

   (B) consumer ratings of a new film are influenced by the previous history of success of the film's director.

   (C) action films generally require larger budgets than romance films and are thus prohibitive for many first-time film directors.

   (D) it is rare for the films of first-time directors to attain the popular appeal of films directed by filmmakers with at least one hit film to their credit.

   (E) directors who have produced a previous hit film generally obtain the largest budgets and attract the most talented and well-known actors for their subsequent films.

11. Candidate: I am worried about the effects that the recent media coverage of my personal life will have on my chances of gaining office. Even though the reports are untrue, some voters interviewed on television, in response to these reports, have already expressed doubts regarding my ability to lead.

   Campaign manager: Your concern is unfounded. Of 1,000 people in this city randomly surveyed by email, only 25 have responded that their perception of your ability to lead has been negatively impacted by the recent media coverage.

   The campaign manager's argument is most vulnerable to criticism on the ground that it fails to acknowledge the possibility that

   (A) future media reports that follow up on the story of the candidate's personal life will further damage the public's perception of the candidate's ability to lead.

   (B) the candidate's main opponent will use the opportunity created by the recent media coverage to conduct her own survey to assess the damage done to her opponent's credibility.

   (C) the voting public would understand that its reaction to the recent media coverage of the candidate's personal life was the intended primary focus of the survey.

   (D) opinions expressed in television interviews are not always the most reliable indicator of how interviewees are likely to act in given situations.

   (E) many of those surveyed who are skeptical of the candidate's ability to lead due to the recent reports did not actually respond to the survey.

GO ON TO THE NEXT PAGE

2 **2**

12. Sarah's principal: Sarah's teacher should spend more individual time with Sarah instead of generating more vocabulary charts for her to memorize. Sarah makes a large number of usage mistakes when she writes and does not seem to have a grasp of basic phonetics. She has yet to memorize one of the vocabulary charts entirely, and she continues to misuse in her writing words she has already learned. Research shows that individual attention is more effective in helping students learn than is rote memorization, so Sarah's teacher is not displaying good judgment in continuing to rely on vocabulary charts to improve Sarah's writing.

Which one of the following statements best describes the function served by the principal's proposal that Sarah's teacher should personally provide Sarah with additional help?

(A) It represents a central assumption of the argument.

(B) It is a conclusion within a larger argument, which supports the main conclusion.

(C) It is a hypothesis that is not supported by evidence in the passage.

(D) It is the conclusion that the rest of the argument upholds.

(E) It is a piece of evidence designed to support the ultimate conclusion of the argument.

13. If too much pressure is exerted on the bottom shelf of a bookcase, the entire bookcase will collapse. Sherry's bookcase has collapsed. Therefore, too much pressure must have been exerted on its bottom shelf.

Which one of the following criticisms best describes a weakness in the argument above?

(A) It supports its conclusion with irrelevant evidence.

(B) It contains a shift in the meaning of the word "collapse" from "partial collapse" to "full collapse."

(C) It concludes that an outcome has been caused by a particular factor that may be only one possible cause of the outcome in question.

(D) It overlooks the possibility that some bookshelves have only one shelf.

(E) It draws an overly broad conclusion from contradictory evidence.

GO ON TO THE NEXT PAGE ⇨

2   2   2   2

14. College dean: Parker College provides a great deal of financial aid to its students. This year, every registered student is receiving either a student loan or a scholarship.

    Financial aid officer: Then all of our registered students have loans this year, because every student who received a scholarship this year also received a student loan.

    In which one of the dialogues below does the pattern of reasoning most closely parallel the reasoning presented above?

    (A) Florist: We are pleased with the mixed bouquets that your company delivered, each of which contained either beautiful orchids or vibrant red roses.

        Flower wholesaler: Then most of the bouquets delivered also had a silver rose, because most of the bouquets containing orchids this week also had a silver rose.

    (B) Grandmother: I am so proud of this family! Each of us has attended either Branston College, the school you attend, or Browning College.

        Grandson: Then I may be the first to attend both, because I am thinking of transferring to Browning.

    (C) Psychiatrist: Ward A patients are generally improving; each now receives either an antidepressant or an antischizophrenic drug.

        Nurse: Ward B patients must also be improving, because they also receive either an antidepressant or antischizophrenic drug.

    (D) Margaret: The hospital is encouraging all patients to eat more vegetables. Tonight every patient ordered either peas or corn.

        Cafeteria worker: Every patient who ordered corn tonight also ordered peas. So every patient ordered peas tonight.

    (E) Contractor: The architect's design calls for ornate crown moldings to be added to the west wing or east wing but not both.

        Foreperson: The moldings will be more obtrusive on the smaller west wing, so we will have to add them to the east wing.

15. A passenger vehicle is defined as any fully enclosed four-wheeled vehicle with room to transport at least one other passenger in addition to the driver. A semi truck, though it may have enclosed room to transport one non driving passenger, always has more than four wheels. A jeep, though it may have four wheels and room to carry a driver and additional passengers, is rarely fully enclosed. A postal van, though it may be enclosed and have four wheels, usually does not have room to transport passengers other than the driver.

    If the statements in the passage above are true, which one of the following must also be true?

    (A) If an automobile is neither a semi truck, nor a jeep, nor a postal van, then it is not a fully enclosed four-wheeled vehicle.

    (B) If an automobile is not a semi truck, or a jeep, or a postal van, then it is a passenger vehicle.

    (C) If a jeep is fully enclosed with four wheels and room to carry nondriving passengers, then it is both a jeep and a passenger vehicle.

    (D) Postal vans are more like passenger vehicles than are semi trucks.

    (E) Some postal vans may be considered to be jeeps.

GO ON TO THE NEXT PAGE

2   **2**   **2**   **2**

16. As long as we must offer remedial programs in our doctoral courses, we cannot say that the open admissions programs in our colleges have succeeded. In fact, were our high schools more successful, we would have no need for open admissions in our colleges. We must admit that the practice of passing more people farther along into higher education has merely delayed their realization of their disadvantages rather than equalized their advantages.

Which one of the following educational reforms would the author be most likely to support?

(A) Elimination of the open admissions program

(B) Elimination of remedial programs at the doctoral level

(C) Improvement of practices in secondary education

(D) A higher teacher-student ratio in low-income areas

(E) More stringent promotion standards

17. A certain laboratory is studying the incidence of fatal liver damage in rats. Sixty-five percent of all rats whose environments exposed them to low levels of the toxin sulfur dioxide died of liver disorder. Ninety percent of all rats who died of liver disorder, however, were not exposed to any environmental toxins.

Which one of the following would provide a feasible explanation for the statistics above?

(A) Environmental and nonenvironmental causes of liver disease in rats are mutually exclusive.

(B) There is only one cause of fatal liver disease in rats.

(C) Environmental toxins are not particularly dangerous to the livers of rats.

(D) Only a small portion of the entire group of rats studied was exposed to environmental sulfur dioxide.

(E) Most rats will not suffer from exposure to low levels of sulfur dioxide.

18. Children never develop strong self-esteem if they are guided by critical adults. Therefore, if children are not guided by critical adults, they will develop strong self-esteem.

The flawed pattern of reasoning in which one of the following arguments is most similar to that in the argument above?

(A) Even though Hannah studies hard, she does not make good grades. Therefore, Hannah should not try to make good grades by studying hard.

(B) Telephone solicitors who have bad phone manners do not sell any products. Therefore, telephone solicitors with low sales records must have bad phone manners.

(C) Using the store's new knitting machine, the knitting store owner made twice as many sweaters yesterday as she did the day before. Therefore, if she uses the knitting machine again tomorrow, she will make twice as many sweaters as she did today.

(D) Puppies who are not well socialized with humans do not interact comfortably with a large group of people. Therefore, the more a puppy is socialized with humans, the more comfortably the puppy will interact with a large group of people.

(E) Individuals who take calcium supplements do not increase their risk of heart disease. Therefore, it stands to reason that individuals who do not take calcium supplements will increase their risk of heart disease.

GO ON TO THE NEXT PAGE

19. Some sports historians claim that professional tennis players develop unique playing styles that result from a combination of the peculiarities of each player's physical attributes and the influence of coaches during their early adaptation to the game. But when the increase in strength and endurance of modern players is discounted, it becomes readily apparent that the playing styles of the current crop of professional tennis players are no different from the styles of players from previous generations. Clearly, there is a universally efficient tennis style to which all professional tennis players conform.

Which of the following, if true, most weakens the argument above?

(A) The differences in physical attributes among tennis players are even more pronounced than the sports historians believe.

(B) Few current professional tennis players are familiar with the professional tennis players of 50 years ago.

(C) The increased strength of current tennis players contributes more to the development of individual playing styles than does increased endurance.

(D) All of the early coaches of today's professional tennis players were professional tennis players themselves earlier in their lives.

(E) Weight training and greater attention to diet are the primary factors in the increased strength and stamina of the current generation of professional tennis players.

20. Recently, the research and development departments at major pharmaceutical companies have been experimenting with new injections that provide the boost in iron that anemic children need to reverse their condition. These companies have expressed confidence that many children who are suffering from anemia will be cured by these injections.

In concluding that the biochemical remedy being developed will have its desired effect, the pharmaceutical companies assume that

(A) major pharmaceutical companies have the primary responsibility to cure childhood anemia.

(B) a low iron level in the body is the major factor influencing the incidence of anemia in children.

(C) a diet rich in iron cannot improve the conditions of children suffering from anemia to the point that biochemical supplements would become unnecessary.

(D) children afflicted with anemia will find out about and submit to injections that can reverse their conditions.

(E) the use of biochemical supplements is the safest way to cure anemia in children.

GO ON TO THE NEXT PAGE ⇒

2   **2**   **2**   **2**

21. When choosing pilots to participate in outer space missions, mission commanders subject applicants to challenging isolation tests. Commanders argue for the necessity of these tests by pointing out that performance on an isolation test may well indicate how safely a pilot could operate a craft during a long voyage home in the event that his or her crewmates were killed during a mission. But an individual's ability to withstand isolation may also arise from an antisocial personality disorder. Therefore, mission commanders should not use this test in selecting pilots.

The argument above is flawed because it fails to consider each of the following possibilities EXCEPT

(A) isolation tests may give applicants a more realistic idea of the dangers of an actual space mission, prompting some to re-evaluate their decision to apply.

(B) mission commanders may select more qualified pilots if the pilot tests are not subject to specific limitations.

(C) an applicant's ability to withstand isolation may indicate a capacity to cope with pressure.

(D) good performance in isolation testing may indicate a high level of stamina and endurance in an applicant.

(E) applicants who may not perform well under actual isolation conditions may nonetheless perform well in a simulated isolation test.

22. When Harry expressed frustration over the disarray of his baseball card collection, his older brother suggested that he organize the cards in a display album containing special pages to showcase his most valuable cards. After investigating albums available on the market, Harry concluded that his brother's suggestion would not help organize his collection because none of the albums with the special showcase pages were big enough to hold all of his cards.

Which one of the following assumptions is central to the reasoning behind Harry's dismissal of his brother's recommendation?

(A) Larger showcase display albums produced in the past were big enough to hold all of Harry's cards.

(B) Albums without showcase pages are never as effective for organizing baseball cards as are albums containing such pages.

(C) Any album large enough to hold all of Harry's cards would contain enough special showcase pages to display all of his most valuable cards.

(D) Harry's baseball card collection would not be well organized if displayed in several showcase albums.

(E) Harry's baseball card collection is in disarray because he has more cards in his collection than he did last year.

GO ON TO THE NEXT PAGE ⟩

2   2   2   2

23. A free press always informs the public of all aspects of a country's current military operations, except for cases in which the safety of troops or the success of a mission would be jeopardized by the public's knowing.

Which one of the following adheres most closely to the principle set forth above?

(A) A free press would publish editorials supporting a current military campaign but could repress dissenting opinions regarding the campaign.

(B) An unfree press would release information on the country's prisoners of war taken during a current military campaign, unless such information would hamper efforts to secure the prisoners' release.

(C) A free press would accurately report the number of casualties suffered on both sides of a battle but could withhold information regarding the possible targets of a future military strike.

(D) An unfree press would print inflammatory accounts of an international event to garner public support for an unpopular war.

(E) A free press would reveal any new information regarding the country's past involvement in secret military operations as soon as that information became available.

24. Lillian has expressed concern about maintaining cohesion in her drug addiction recovery group that she leads at her youth center. She has worked to develop cohesion by encouraging group members to share their experiences openly with the group. But some of the group members take advantage of this opportunity for openness by sharing long, violent stories primarily intended to shock the others. Aversion to these stories has caused some members to quit the group. These violent, lengthy stories also take time away from other members, preventing them from sharing their experiences. To ensure cohesion in the group, then, Lillian should delineate a specific time slot for each member to speak during each session.

Which one of the following best describes the logical flaw in the argument above?

(A) Two actions that merely occur simultaneously are presented as actions that are causally related.

(B) It fails to consider the possibility that the proposed solution might actually aggravate the problem.

(C) It overlooks the fact that the proposed resolution would address only one cause of the problem.

(D) A conclusion is based on evidence that is unrelated to the issue at hand.

(E) It ignores the likelihood that telling violent stories is therapeutic for some members.

GO ON TO THE NEXT PAGE

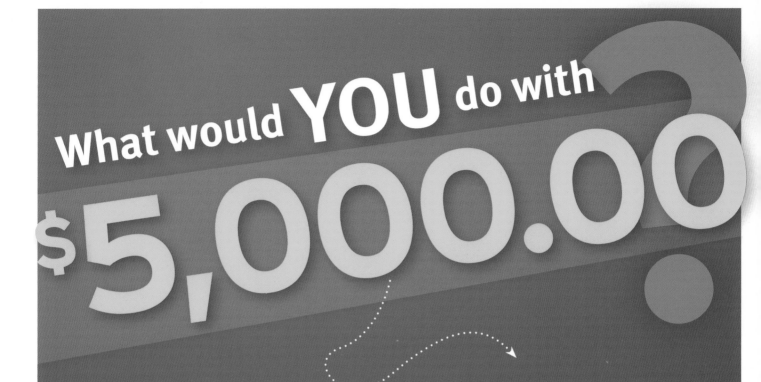

Kaplan $5,000 Brighter Future Sweepstakes 2010 Complete and Official Rules

1. NO PURCHASE IS NECESSARY TO ENTER OR WIN. A PURCHASE WILL NOT INCREASE YOUR CHANCES OF WINNING.

2. PROMOTION PERIOD. The "Kaplan $5,000 Brighter Future Sweepstakes" ("Sweepstakes") commences at 6:59 A.M. EST on April 1, 2010 and ends at 11:59 P.M. EST on March 31, 2011. Entry forms can be found online at kaptest.com/future. All online entries must be received by March 31, 2011 at 11:59 P.M. EST.

3. ELIGIBILITY. This Sweepstakes is open to legal residents of the 50 United States and the District of Columbia and Canada (excluding the Province of Quebec) who are sixteen (16) years of age or older as of April 1, 2010. Officers, directors, representatives and employees of Kaplan (from here on called "Sponsor"), its parent, affiliates or subsidiaries, or their respective advertising, promotion, publicity, production, and judging agencies and their immediate families and household members are not eligible to enter.

4. TO ENTER. To enter simply go to kaptest.com/future and fill-out the online entry form between April 1, 2010 and March 31, 2011.
As part of your entry, you will be asked to provide your first and last name, email address, permanent address and phone number, parent or legal guardian name if under eighteen (18), and the name of your undergraduate school.

LIMIT ONE ENTRY PER PERSON AND EMAIL ADDRESS. Multiple entries will be disqualified. Entries are void if they contain typographical, printing or other errors. Entries generated by a script, macro or other automated means are void. Entries that are mutilated, altered, incomplete, mechanically reproduced, tampered with, illegible, inaccurate, forged, irregular in any way, or otherwise not in compliance with these Official Rules are also void. All entries become the property of the Sponsor and will not be returned to the entrant. Sponsor and those working on its behalf will not be responsible for lost, late, misdirected or damaged mail or email or for Internet, network, computer hardware and software, phone or other technical errors, malfunctions and delays that may occur. Entries will be deemed to have been submitted by the authorized account holder of the email account from which the entry is made. The authorized account holder is the natural person to whom an email address is assigned by an Internet access provider, online service provider or other organization (e.g. business, educational institution, etc.) responsible for assigning email addresses for the domain associated with the submitted email address. By entering or accepting a prize in this Sweepstakes, entrants agree to be bound by the decisions of the judges, the Sponsor and these Official Rules and to comply with all applicable federal, state and local laws and regulations. Odds of winning depend on the number of eligible entries received.

5. WINNER SELECTION. One (1) winner will be selected for $5,000 USD from all eligible entries received in a random drawing to be held on or about May 11, 2011. The drawing will be conducted by an independent judge whose decisions shall be final and binding in all regards. Participants need not be present to win. Please note that if the entrant selected as the winner resides in Canada, he/she will have to correctly answer a timed, test-prep question in order to be confirmed as the winner and claim the prize.

6. WINNER NOTIFICATION AND VALIDATION. Winner of the drawing will be notified by mail within 10 days after the drawing. An Affidavit of Eligibility and Compliance with these Official Rules and a Liability and (unless prohibited) Publicity Release must be executed and returned by the potential winner within twenty-one (21) days after prize notification is sent. If the winner is under eighteen (18) years of age, the prize will be awarded to the winner's parent or legal guardian who will be required to execute an affidavit. Failure of the potential winner to complete, sign and return any requested documents within such period or the return of any prize notification or prize as undeliverable may result in disqualification and selection of an alternate winner in Sponsor's sole discretion. You are not a winner unless your submissions are validated.

In the event that a winner chooses not to accept his or her prize, does not respond to winner notification within the time period noted on the notification or does not return a completed Affidavit of Eligibility and Compliance with these Official Rules and a Liability and (unless prohibited) Publicity Release within twenty-one (21) days after prize notification is sent, the prize may be forfeited and an alternate winner selected in Sponsor's sole discretion.

7. PRIZES.

One (1) winner will be selected to win $5,000.00 USD.

Prize is not transferable. Any applicable taxes or fees are the winner's sole responsibility. All prizes must be redeemed within 21 days of notice of award.

8. GENERAL CONDITIONS. By entering the Sweepstakes or accepting the Sweepstakes prize, winner accepts all the conditions, restrictions, requirements and/or regulations required by the Sponsor in connection with the Sweepstakes. Unless otherwise prohibited by law, acceptance of a prize constitutes permission to use winner's name, picture, likeness, address (city and state) and biographical information for advertising and publicity purposes for this and/or similar promotions, without prior approval or compensation. Acceptance of a prize constitutes a waiver of any claim to royalties, rights or remuneration for said use. Winner agrees to release and hold harmless the Sponsor, its parent, affiliates and subsidiaries, and each of their respective directors, officers, employees, agents, and successors from any and all claims, damages, injury, death, loss or other liability that may arise from winner's participation in the Sweepstakes or the awarding, acceptance, possession, use or misuse of the prize. Sponsor reserves the right in its sole discretion to modify or cancel all or any portions of the Sweepstakes because of technical errors or malfunctions, viruses, hackers, or for other reasons beyond Sponsor's control that impair or corrupt the Sweepstakes in any manner. In such event, Sponsor shall award prizes at random from among the eligible entries received up to the time of the impairment or corruption. Sponsor also reserves the right in its sole discretion to disqualify any entrant who fails to comply with these Official Rules, who attempts to enter the Sweepstakes in any manner or through any means other than as described in these Official Rules, or who attempts to disrupt the Sweepstakes or the kaptest.com website or to circumvent any of these Official Rules.

9. WINNERS' LIST. Starting August 15, 2011, a winners' list may be obtained by sending a self-addressed, stamped envelope to: "$5,000 Kaplan Brighter Future Sweepstakes" Winners' List, Kaplan Test Prep and Admissions Marketing Department, 1440 Broadway, 8th Floor New York, NY 10018. All winners' list requests must be received by December 1, 2011.

10. USE OF ENTRANT AND WINNER INFORMATION. The information that you provide in connection with the Sweepstakes may be used for Sponsor's and select Corporate Partners' purposes to send you information about Sponsor's and its Corporate Partners' products and services. If you would like your name removed from Sponsor's mailing list or if you do not wish to receive information from Sponsor or its Corporate Partners, write to:

Direct Marketing Department
Attn: Kaplan Brighter Future Sweepstakes Opt Out
1440 Broadway
8th Floor
New York NY 10018

11. SPONSOR. The Sponsor of this Sweepstakes is: Kaplan Test Prep and Admissions and Kaplan Publishing, 1440 Broadway, 8th Floor New York, NY 10018.

12. THIS SWEEPSTAKES IS VOID WHERE PROHIBITED, TAXED OR OTHERWISE RESTRICTED BY LAW.

All trademarks are the property of their respective owner. PUB03812

2 **2** **2** **2**

25. The kuva weave fabric, produced by American Synthetics Inc., was once thought to be a miraculous invention due to its properties of strength and durability. However, industrial accidents over the past three years have proven that the material is extremely flammable. This discovery dealt a large blow to manufacturers who use the fabric in their products, as the fabric provided an excellent alternative to weaker textiles implicated in many product failures. Because the kuva weave fabric can no longer be used, manufacturers must eliminate all American Synthetics materials from their inventories.

The argument's conclusion logically follows if which one of the following statements is assumed?

(A) Early trial runs that testified to the safety of the kuva weave fabric have subsequently been shown to be incomplete.

(B) All materials produced by American Synthetics contain some form of the kuva weave fabric.

(C) The incidence of industrial fires in manufacturing plants that use the kuva weave fabric is relatively high compared to that in plants that do not use the fabric.

(D) Kuva weave fabrics are not as durable as originally believed.

(E) Manufacturers are likely to incur product liability lawsuits stemming from accidents caused by flammable products containing the kuva weave fabric.

IF YOU FINISH BEFORE TIME IS CALLED, YOU MAY CHECK YOUR WORK ON THIS SECTION ONLY. DO NOT WORK ON ANY OTHER SECTION IN THE TEST. STOP

3 3 3 3 3

Section III

Time—35 minutes 25 questions

Directions: This test is comprised of questions that ask you to analyze the logic of statements or short paragraphs. You are to choose as the answer to each question the one choice you consider best on the basis of your common-sense evaluation of the statement and its assumptions. Although a question may seem to have more than one acceptable answer, there is only one best answer, and it is the one that does not entail making any illogical, extraneous, or conflicting assumptions about the question. These questions do not presuppose any knowledge of formal logic on your part.

1. John's father: John has complained frequently that his psychoanalysis sessions are not helpful. But John has no knowledge of psychology, and he cannot accurately judge his analyst's techniques. His dissatisfaction in no way indicates that his analyst's methods are unsound and is, therefore, no reason for him to discontinue his counseling sessions.

   John's mother: But the purpose of his therapy is to help him adjust to our divorce. While it is true that John is not qualified to assess the analyst's methods, the important thing is whether or not he is making progress. If he believes that the sessions are a waste of time, he should stop seeing the analyst.

   Which one of the following is an assumption upon which John's mother's argument depends?

   (A) John's father is correct in concluding that John is unhappy with his counseling sessions.

   (B) Involvement in the therapeutic process does not hamper John's ability to perceive the value of his counseling sessions.

   (C) Psychoanalysts do not need to have extensive qualifications in order to be helpful to their clients.

   (D) If a psychoanalyst employs a sound method, then his or her clients will perceive the counseling sessions as helpful.

   (E) John is entitled to act on any belief concerning his own well-being, regardless of the origin or merits of that belief.

2. Harriet's husband: My wife, Harriet, has long desired to vacation in a region that is culturally rich. According to this travel brochure, income from the manufacture of industrial documentaries makes Sunshine Valley the second wealthiest region in the state. I have therefore decided to surprise Harriet with accommodations for a two-week trip to Sunshine Valley.

   Which one of the following best characterizes a flaw in Harriet's husband's method of reaching his decision?

   (A) He displays circular reasoning in his attempt to justify his decision.

   (B) He confounds similar but distinct terms that relate to a key factor in his decision.

   (C) He uses unreliable and potentially biased evidence as support for his decision.

   (D) He makes a major decision without consulting each party that the decision will affect.

   (E) He fails to demonstrate that his decision is economically feasible.

GO ON TO THE NEXT PAGE

3   **3**

3. Chocolate is derived from the beans of the tropical New World tree *Theobroma cacao*. When chocolate arrived in Europe around 1500, it was consumed only as a hot drink. In the mid-1800s, however, the Swiss invented the first method for producing it in a solid edible form. Today, millions more pounds of chocolate are produced for eating than for drinking.

Which one of the following can be inferred from the statements above?

(A) Today, *Theobroma cacao* is grown only in the tropical New World.

(B) When chocolate was introduced to Europe, it was most commonly used in a solid form.

(C) The number of pounds of chocolate made for eating today is greater than the number of pounds of chocolate that were made for drinking during the 1800s.

(D) Chocolate was not consumed in a solid form in the New World during the 1500s.

(E) If the Swiss had not invented a method for producing chocolate in a solid edible form, chocolate would not have become as popular as it is today.

4. Nuclear physicist: The *Fairmarch Times* should make an effort to include the protestors' views in their stories on the nuclear reactor controversy. The *Times* has covered the controversy for a week now, but so far it has presented only the industry side of the issue. No effort has been made to cover the protestors' side. Stories regarding that perspective are completely lacking.

Plant engineer: The protestors' views do not need to be included. The *Times* coverage is fine as is.

Which of the following principles best supports the nuclear physicist's position?

(A) Newspaper reporting must present the views of both sides of a controversy to be truly effective.

(B) A newspaper's reputation for impartially is built on its overall history, not a single story.

(C) Newspapers should present the view endorsed by the majority of their readers.

(D) Members of groups with a vested interest in an issue should not report on that issue.

(E) Industry groups should receive more media coverage than do protest organizations.

GO ON TO THE NEXT PAGE

3 3 3 3 **3**

5. Botanists once claimed that plants of the *faura* species required a balanced fertilizer comprised of the following elements to grow: nitrogen, boron, copper, and iron. This approach, however, inhibited *faura* propagation.

   The conclusion above is supported by each of the following EXCEPT

   (A) advocating that *faura* plants required a balanced composition of the four elements gave the impression that these elements would be sufficient for plant growth, but the plants cannot grow without an appropriate percentage of soluble potash as well.

   (B) the omission of zinc from the list of necessary elements conveys the false impression that zinc is less essential to *faura* plant growth than are the other four elements.

   (C) the emphasis on balance among the four fertilizer elements suggests that the elements should be present in the same amounts, but nitrogen and iron are more essential to *faura* plant growth and thus should be present in larger quantities.

   (D) the recommendation that the growth-promoting fertilizer should contain copper overlooks the fact that in order for the copper to function effectively, *faura* plants must also be fertilized with extremely small amounts of molybdenum.

   (E) the inclusion of the element boron in the list served to remind botanists to include this less well-known element in their fertilizer treatment for *faura* plants.

6. Three years ago, Ron and Crystal agreed that they would open a restaurant only when they both were prepared to put in the necessary long hours. At the beginning of this year, Ron assumed that Crystal was prepared to make this time commitment, but this erroneous belief was the product of wishful thinking: Crystal just took on a new year-long project at her current job that requires a great deal of travel and takes up most of her focus and energy.

   If the statements above are true, which of the following can be logically concluded?

   (A) Ron is more interested in eventually opening a restaurant than Crystal is.

   (B) Opening a restaurant requires a great deal of personal focus and energy.

   (C) Opening the restaurant would involve even longer hours than Crystal's current job.

   (D) Crystal was never truly interested in opening a restaurant with Ron.

   (E) Ron and Crystal will not open their restaurant this year.

GO ON TO THE NEXT PAGE

3 **3** **3** **3**

Questions 7–8

Center director: The number of volunteer applications for our elderly care center has doubled over the past five years. This clearly shows that community members are taking a greater interest in working with their aging parents.

Nurse: Unfortunately, my research indicates that just the opposite is true. If you look closely at our records, applications from patients' family members have decreased by 20 percent over the past five years. This would indicate that, contrary to your conclusion, community members' willingness and availability to work with their elderly parents has actually decreased.

7. If the statistics cited by both the center director and the nurse are correct, which one of the following must be true?

(A) The center has had a decline in its patient population over the past five years.

(B) The quality of care provided to patients at the facility has improved over the past five years.

(C) The center has received volunteer applications from individuals who are not related to patients at the center.

(D) The cost of maintaining adequate staff to care for the center's patients has risen enough to warrant the need for additional volunteers.

(E) Only a small percentage of all the people who apply to volunteer at the center actually assume volunteer positions.

8. Which one of the following, if true, would most seriously weaken the nurse's argument?

(A) Many community members living near the center have moved into newly constructed housing developments on the outskirts of town.

(B) Over the past five years, center funding for family-oriented activities has decreased significantly.

(C) Volunteering in elderly care facilities requires training for which most individuals do not have the time.

(D) Due to a recent change in policy, many family members who volunteer at the elderly care center do not fill out formal applications.

(E) The time commitment required by volunteers at elderly care centers is relatively modest compared to other volunteer opportunities in the region.

GO ON TO THE NEXT PAGE

9. Angie: If Bernard decides to allow his dog Pepe to sleep at the foot of his bed, Pepe will become spoiled, and his current disciplinary problems will worsen.

    Theresa: On the contrary, the dog's behavior would improve. Julian's dog used to chew his furniture at night just as Bernard's dog does now. When Julian followed a trainer's advice and allowed the dog to sleep in his bedroom, at the foot of his bed, his dog calmed down and stopped destroying the furniture within weeks. Similarly, if Bernard allowed his dog to sleep near his bed, the dog's destructive chewing would soon stop.

    In her argument, Theresa does which one of the following?

    (A) She provides a reinterpretation of evidence against a plan by pointing out how that evidence supports the plan.

    (B) She offers a general recommendation to resolve a specific problem.

    (C) She gives a rationale for why following a particular plan would cause difficulties for those who adhere to it.

    (D) She claims that the results of one course of action would be similar to the results of a different course of action.

    (E) She forecasts the results of following a plan in one instance by comparing that situation to a similar situation from the past.

10. A study sponsored by the Association of Educational Consultants has found that students learn and retain 20 percent of material they hear in class, 30 percent of material from written assignments, and 90 percent of material they teach to others. Based on these findings, the principal of Clarkstown Elementary School, interested in enhancing her students' learning and retention of typical grade-school material, has proposed the creation of a new curriculum in which the students conduct all of the teaching.

    Which one of the following best characterizes the flaw in the principal's proposal above?

    (A) It fails to take into account the fact that under the new curriculum, students would still be required to listen in class much of the time.

    (B) It mistakenly assumes that written assignments are as valuable a teaching aid as hearing material discussed in the classroom.

    (C) It fails to demonstrate how the new curriculum would directly lead to higher test scores.

    (D) It overlooks the possibility that the study's findings may be motivated in part by the self-interest of the sponsoring association.

    (E) It ignores the fact that most elementary school children are limited in the number of typical grade-school subjects they are qualified to teach.

GO ON TO THE NEXT PAGE

3   **3** **3**

11. Most students at Carmine University feel overwhelmed by the elective choices available to them in their course offering handbook. This could be because the elective courses are not properly categorized or because there is simply too much to read. A review of the lengths of typical elective course descriptions shows that each description is far less lengthy than the length that most students can absorb in any given reading. So it must be that the elective courses are not properly categorized.

   Which one of the following is an assumption upon which the argument above depends?

   (A) Improper categorization of elective course offerings makes it impossible to choose among those courses.

   (B) Some students are overwhelmed by the length of the course descriptions.

   (C) Some students find that the coursebook is not well organized.

   (D) The number of elective course offerings provided in the handbook is not the reason the students are overwhelmed.

   (E) Most students can absorb rather lengthy course descriptions.

12. Due to a rash of behavioral problems among a particular group of high school students, the principal has canceled all school extracurricular activities for the next month. The organizers of a pep rally scheduled to take place during this period have made the case that this event should be allowed because the increase in school spirit brought about by the pep rally will bond the participants together, which in turn will result in a decrease in aberrant behavior among the students in the long run.

   The organizers of the pep rally assume which one of the following in making their argument?

   (A) The principal did not intend to include the pep rally among the group of extracurricular activities canceled for the next month.

   (B) The students exhibiting behavioral problems will take part in the pep rally.

   (C) No other extracurricular activities besides the pep rally should be allowed to take place during the next month, unless it can be determined that such activities would bond the students together.

   (D) A pep rally is the most effective type of extracurricular activity to deal with the problem of aberrant school behavior.

   (E) The principal will allow other canceled events to take place once she sees the beneficial effect that the pep rally has on the students.

GO ON TO THE NEXT PAGE

3   **3**

13. Some individuals believe that attending cooking school in southern France teaches one all there is to know about French cooking. All branches of La Terrelle Cooking Academy are located in southern France. Yet a recent graduate of La Terrelle did not know how to make bechamel sauce, a sauce widely used in French gourmet cooking.

If the statements above are true, which one of the following must also be true?

(A) Attending cooking school in southern France does not always teach one all there is to know about French cooking.

(B) No graduate of La Terrelle Cooking Academy has learned all there is to know about French gourmet cooking.

(C) At least one branch of La Terrelle Cooking Academy is located outside of southern France.

(D) La Terrelle Cooking Academy does not provide an effective education in French gourmet cooking.

(E) Cooking schools located in southern France teach their students less about French gourmet cooking than do schools located in other parts of the country.

14. Tsumi bats are a rare breed of omnivorous bat found only in highly temperate climates. Most Tsumi bats living in captivity develop endocrine imbalances from their normal zoo diets, which consist mostly of fruits and berries. The healthiest way to feed the bats, therefore, is to provide them primarily with nuts, grubs, and vegetables and only minimal amounts of fruits and berries.

Which one of the statements below does NOT reflect an assumption upon which the argument depends?

(A) Tsumi bats living in captivity will consume diets that consist of nuts, grubs, and vegetables but no fruits or berries.

(B) Tsumi bats living in captivity will not be malnourished on diets that contain minimal fruits and berries.

(C) Those who care for Tsumi bats in captivity should avoid feeding them diets that produce endocrine imbalances.

(D) Tsumi bats living in captivity will be adequately nourished on a diet that consists primarily of nuts, grubs, and vegetables.

(E) For Tsumi bats living in captivity, no health problem stemming from diets consisting mostly of nuts, grubs, and vegetables would surpass in severity the health problems associated with endocrine imbalances.

GO ON TO THE NEXT PAGE

3   **3**

15. Before the advent of writing, each of the isolated clans of the Comaquogue tribe contained master storytellers whose function was to transmit orally the tradition of each clan from one generation to the next. When writing was developed within certain clans of the tribe, the master storytellers of these clans disappeared within a few generations. This stands to reason, considering that the availability of written records obviated the need for masterful oral communicators to keep the tradition of literate clans alive. What has puzzled anthropologists, however, is the total lack of masterful storytellers in modern illiterate Comaquogue clans.

Which one of the following, if true, best helps to explain the puzzling situation mentioned above?

(A) Modern illiterate Comaquogue clan members display personality characteristics that resemble those of their ancestors more closely than they resemble those of the characteristics of modern literate Comaquogue clan members.

(B) Modern illiterate Comaquogue clans participate in more ritual gatherings than most modern literate Comaquogue clans do, but they participate in fewer ritual gatherings than did their common ancestors.

(C) Modern illiterate Comaquogue clans are recently descended from long-time literate clans that failed to pass on the skills of reading and writing due to a devastating 75-year war.

(D) The celebrations of modern illiterate Comaquogue clans involve a great deal of singing and dancing, and children are taught clan songs and dances from a very young age.

(E) The traditions of modern illiterate Comaquogue clans are an amalgamation of the cumulative experiences of previous generations plus innovations to the heritage added by the current generation of clan members.

16. Playing in a rock band during college has caused Matthew's grades to suffer, which in turn has decreased his chances of being accepted to a prestigious graduate program. But being active in extracurricular activities, such as music, can in some cases compensate for bad grades and help a candidate's chances for admission to graduate school by demonstrating that one is a well-rounded individual with varied interests. However, the dean of Wentworth Business School refuses to allow Matthew's participation in the band to improve his acceptance chances.

Which one of the following principles best justifies the dean's position?

(A) The consequences of an action can only be evaluated with respect to the possible consequences of an opposing alternative action.

(B) Nothing that causes a condition can be used to compensate for the consequences of that condition.

(C) The overall value of an activity must not be overridden by a negative result of a single aspect of that activity.

(D) A decision that affects the future of an individual must not discount any factor relevant to that decision.

(E) A factor that eliminates a candidate from consideration in one instance should not be used to eliminate that candidate from consideration in a dissimilar situation.

GO ON TO THE NEXT PAGE

17. Computer scientists have discovered two particularly insidious computer viruses known as the alphatron and b-scan viruses. These viruses typically infiltrate a computer's systems files and prevent files from being stored properly, namely by storing them in incorrect locations. Fortunately, at present there is no evidence to prove that the alphatron and b-scan viruses erase computer files entirely, so computer users who detect one or both of the viruses can rest assured that their files will not be erased.

The argument above is flawed because it

(A) fails to consider the fact that causal relationships that cannot be proven may nonetheless influence people who assume that these relationships exist.

(B) fails to consider the possibility that a circumstance may exist even where it has not been demonstrated to exist.

(C) neglects to explain the technical mechanisms by which computer files may be erased by viruses.

(D) equivocates with respect to a key term.

(E) supports its conclusion with evidence that merely restates the conclusion.

18. If foods that require refrigeration are not kept at the proper temperature, they can become fertile environments for the growth of bacteria that invariably cause food poisoning in those who ingest them. Because the number of customers stricken with food poisoning at the Panhandler Restaurant rose significantly last month, the Panhandler must have served food that was not stored at the proper temperature.

Which one of the arguments below contains flawed reasoning similar to that in the argument above?

(A) Men over 65 with high blood pressure are at high risk for heart disease. Men over 65 from the Tonare tribe do not have high blood pressure, so they must not be at high risk for heart disease.

(B) Magelli is the only cabinetmaker who could have crafted a cabinet similar to this one. But the records show that Magelli died 15 years ago. This cabinet must therefore be a copy.

(C) PaintAll paint is sold at Decorator Outlet stores. Paint All paint is very popular among housepainters because of its brilliant pigment and its stain-resistant finish. Therefore, Decorator Outlets must sell more cans of PaintAll than any other kind of paint.

(D) Relief-O! is a new pain reliever that has been known to cause blurred vision in some people who take it. When Molly took a pain reliever last week to relieve a migraine headache, she experienced a bout of blurred vision. So the pain reliever Molly took last week must have been Relief-O!

(E) If tigermint is allowed to grow out of control in a garden, it can overrun other plants and kill them. Sally recently noticed that a number of plants in her garden looked better than ever. Clearly, her tigermint problem must be under control.

GO ON TO THE NEXT PAGE

3   **3**

19. The paintings of French painter Trianne Déjère sold best in the period following the production of *Le Triomphe*, now Déjère's most famous piece. In the 12-month period preceding the unveiling of this piece, Déjère sold 57 percent of the works she produced in this period, a far greater percentage than in previous years. In the 12-month period following a glowing review of *Le Triomphe* in a popular magazine, however, Déjère sold 85 percent of the paintings she produced. Interestingly, Déjère's revenue from painting sales was roughly the same in both periods, since she sold the same number of paintings in the 12 months before presenting *Le Triomphe* as she did in the 12 months following the favorable review.

Which one of the following statements can be properly concluded from the passage, if the information above is true?

(A) Due to the positive review, Déjère was able to charge substantially more for the works produced after *Le Triomphe* than the works produced before it.

(B) Déjère was more concerned with positive reviews than with increasing the prices of her paintings.

(C) The positive review of *Le Triomphe* brought Déjère's work to the attention of more art collectors than were previously aware of her work.

(D) Déjère painted fewer works in the 12-month period following the review of *Le Triomphe* than she had in the 12-month period preceding its unveiling.

(E) Déjère paid more attention to marketing her paintings after *Le Triomphe* received such a positive reception.

20. Most of the time, Doug has no stomach problems whatsoever when he eats dairy products. So it is unreasonable to claim that he has an allergy to dairy foods solely based on the fact that he has had stomachaches after eating dairy products on several occasions.

The argument above is most similar in reasoning to which one of the arguments below?

(A) A significant number of artists who take this fine arts program are later selected for fellowships to pursue their art. It is therefore unreasonable to believe that there is no connection between taking the program and receiving an art fellowship, even though many artists who attend the program never receive such fellowships.

(B) Sometimes, when Ella exercises in the evening, she has trouble sleeping. However, it would be erroneous to assume the exercise was to blame, because she often exercises in the evening and has no trouble sleeping.

(C) Many people who diet to lose weight put the weight back on over a fairly short period of time. Therefore, it is unreasonable to believe dieting is effective.

(D) Most theories must apply to a large number of cases before they are considered valid theories. It is therefore unreasonable to believe that a theory is valid when it has been applied to only a few cases, even if it has been applied successfully to those cases.

(E) Even though many businesses with decentralized operational structures earn a profit, it is unreasonable to believe the success of these businesses is solely attributable to their choice of operational structure. Only businesses with extensive capital resources can adopt a decentralized operational structure.

GO ON TO THE NEXT PAGE

21. Membership in the Theta Delta Psi fraternity is easily obtained by those who have previously had strong social connections with existing fraternity members before college. However, one must have attended high school with one or more of the members to forge such strong social connections. People who lack these social connections because they have not attended high school with one or more current fraternity members will, therefore, find it difficult to join the fraternity.

    This argument displays flawed reasoning because it neglects to consider the possibility that

    (A) many of those who went to high school with Theta Delta Psi fraternity members did not themselves become members of the fraternity.

    (B) it is more important in the long run to socialize with non–fraternity members than to develop strong connections with fraternity members.

    (C) it is more difficult to forge social connections with fraternity members than with non–fraternity members.

    (D) one may easily obtain membership in the fraternity through means other than having strong social connections with existing fraternity members.

    (E) some current members of the fraternity did not go to high school with other members.

22. The advantages of the new farm subsidy laws enacted last year do not warrant their continued enforcement. While these laws have enabled farmers to maintain their incomes despite overproduction and have at the same time stabilized the agricultural market, they will inevitably have negative long-term results stemming from the fact that they will encourage the production of surplus goods and lessen the need for competitive developments in agricultural technology.

    In the argument above, the statement about the negative results of the farm subsidy laws plays which one of the following roles?

    (A) It is used to disprove evidence cited in support of the laws.

    (B) It is used to imply that the laws may not have actually stabilized the agricultural market to the degree previously believed.

    (C) It is used to off set plausible reasons for supporting the laws.

    (D) It is used to prove that in the absence of the laws, the development of agricultural technology will remain a high priority.

    (E) It is used as evidence for the claim that market stabilization is less important to the agricultural industry than the development of competitive technology.

GO ON TO THE NEXT PAGE

3   **3**

23. Participants in Smallville's Annual Easter Egg Hunt search for special plastic Easter eggs containing valuable prizes. The top prize in the contest is an egg containing a three-carat diamond ring. The only way to locate the hidden eggs is by using clues provided to participants by the contest organizers. If every participant receives a complete list of clues for locating the eggs, then no participant will have any more information than any other participant about the whereabouts of the eggs. If no participant has any more information than any other participant, then no participant has a better chance of finding the diamond ring. However, the contest organizers did not provide a complete list of clues for locating the eggs to every participant. Therefore, some participant has a better chance of finding the diamond than all of the other participants.

Which one of the following points to a flaw in the argument's reasoning?

(A) Even if one participant received a more extensive clue list than all of the other participants, that participant might not necessarily find the diamond ring.

(B) The argument fails to consider the possibility that several participants received incomplete lists of clues.

(C) It ignores the fact that some participants may share a particular clue with other participants who did not receive that clue.

(D) It overlooks the possibility that all of the participants received identical clue lists.

(E) It fails to take into account that some participants who did not receive a complete list of clues will nonetheless be able to locate the egg containing the diamond ring.

24. Judges in the Fair Valley Children's Essay Contest disqualified an entry by student Samuel Carter on the grounds that Samuel's entry broke one of the contest rules. The rules specified that entrants should place their names only on the cover page of their essays, and not on any other page, to allow for unbiased judging. Samuel's name was included on each page of his essay. In contesting the judges' decision, Samuel's teacher argued that Samuel's essay should be allowed to qualify because Samuel had recently undergone the traumatic and difficult experience of his parents' divorce.

Samuel's teacher's argument presents a flawed response to the judges' decision because it

(A) presents a conclusion without providing supporting evidence.

(B) treats a factor that may cause a certain outcome as if that factor always causes that particular outcome.

(C) focuses only on a trivial aspect of the judges' argument.

(D) misrepresents evidence presented in the judges' argument.

(E) appeals to the judges' emotions instead of addressing their reason for disqualifying Samuel.

GO ON TO THE NEXT PAGE

3   **3**

25. For healthy individuals who wish to improve their overall fitness, cross-training in several sports is more beneficial than training with a single activity. Cross-training develops a wide range of muscle groups, while single-sport training tends to isolate a select few muscles. Single-sport activities, especially those that target slow-twitch muscles, tend to increase the tonic muscle fibers in the body. Cross-training works instead to increase the body's phasic muscle fibers, which burn more calories than tonic muscle fibers.

    Which one of the following, if true, best supports the argument above?

    (A) In healthy persons, overall fitness increases in proportion to the number of calories burned by the body.

    (B) Overall fitness is most effectively improved through athletic training.

    (C) Tonic muscle fibers are of greater value to overall fitness than are phasic muscle fibers.

    (D) Strenuous physical exertion on a single sport is not recommended for those recovering from a serious illness.

    (E) Some slow-twitch muscles contain many phasic muscle fibers.

4   4   4   4   4   4

The Frankenstein monster is the most
recognizable character in the horror genre, if not
in all of fiction. Beneath the endless Hollywood
adaptations and campy TV shows lies one of the
(5) great philosophical and prophetic works of the
19th century. While present generations associate
the name Frankenstein with the image of Boris
Karloff's movie portrayal of the monster, Mary
Shelley's story of the mad doctor Victor
(10) Frankenstein is best known to serious readers as a
cautionary tale of the danger of man's scientific
hubris.

I saw—with shut eyes, but acute mental
vision—I saw the pale student of unhal-
(15) lowed arts kneeling beside the thing he
had put together. I saw the hideous phan-
tasm of a man stretched out, and then, on
the working of some powerful engine,
show signs of life, and stir with an uneasy,
(20) half-vital motion. Frightful must it be; for
supremely frightful would be the effect of
any human endeavor to mock the stupen-
dous mechanism of the Creator of the
world.

(25) From this horrifying dream during the summer of
1816, Shelley conceived the story in which Victor
Frankenstein creates a man from body parts gathered from the dead. The clear clash of science and
nature ensues. The book is structured to refute
(30) science and technology's attack on nature, and the
most eloquent arguments come from the mouth
of the monster himself. For seven brilliant and
captivating chapters, he tells his story and pleads his
case for a companion. His point is clear: Man should
(35) not create that for which he is not ready to
take responsibility. The mad doctor ultimately
refuses to create a mate for the monster, and
Shelley portrays the horrifying consequences of
man's abdication of responsibility and of arro-
(40) gantly overstepping the bounds of nature.

How a 19th-century young woman crafted the
timeless tale that has resonated through every successive generation is still a great mystery. For many
years, the book was published anonymously, as

(45) society could not yet cope with the fact that such a
ghastly story was the work of a young woman. Yet
if *Frankenstein* were merely the story of a monster
run amok, we likely wouldn't know of it today. Its
enduring appeal can best be attributed to the rele-
(50) vance of the themes infused throughout the narrative: alienation of the outcast, the role of visual
appearance in society, science, versus nature, and
technology as man's salvation. These themes have
only grown in importance since the novel's publi-
(55) cation in 1818. The seriousness and complexity of
these issues, so magically and prophetically syn-
thesized in Shelley's tale of terror, account for the
inability to capture in cinematic form the deep
philosophical richness of the book. It can only be
(60) hoped that the visual adaptations will not entirely
eclipse in the public's mind the genius of the original masterpiece.

1. The passage suggests that the author would most
    likely agree with which one of the following
    statements?

    (A) No artistic work can be successfully adapted
    from one medium into another.

    (B) An artistic work that is likely to shock the
    sensibilities of its original audience should be
    presented anonymously.

    (C) An artistic work that does not gain critical
    acclaim during its period of origin cannot
    appeal to successive generations.

    (D) The resonance of thematic elements can
    contribute to the current relevance of an
    artistic work.

    (E) The complexity and seriousness of an artistic
    work is directly related to its prophetic
    capabilities.

4   4   4   4   4   4

1. According to the author, "The clear clash of science and nature" (lines 28–29)

   (A) is one of the major elements of *Frankenstein* that is mainly responsible for the current popularity of the cinematic adaptations of that work.

   (B) is one of the major elements of *Frankenstein* that is absent from the cinematic adaptations of that work.

   (C) is one of the major elements of *Frankenstein* that forced its author to publish that work anonymously.

   (D) is one of the major elements of *Frankenstein* that is less relevant today than it was at the time that work was first published.

   (E) is one of the major elements of *Frankenstein* that has contributed to the enduring appeal of that work.

3. The passage suggests that each of the following are relevant aspects of the current era EXCEPT

   (A) the belief in the power of technology to aid the human condition.

   (B) the appreciation of artistic seriousness and complexity.

   (C) the opposition between science and nature.

   (D) the physical appearance of societal members.

   (E) the isolation of individuals from society.

4. The author views the cinematic adaptations of Mary Shelley's *Frankenstein* with

   (A) unbounded appreciation for their artistic merit.

   (B) biting derision regarding the motivations of their producers.

   (C) concern for the effect they may have on the appreciation of their literary precedent.

   (D) guarded optimism as to the likelihood that they will spawn future efforts that will approach the philosophical richness of the original book.

   (E) unreserved condescension towards the public's demand for such unsophisticated reworkings of literary masterpieces.

5. The author's mention of "Hollywood adaptations" in the first paragraph serves which one of the following functions in the passage as a whole?

   (A) It provides a contrast that will resurface later as the basis of the author's central concern.

   (B) It introduces the background of a debate that the author will attempt to settle.

   (C) It reflects the main criticism of a work of art that the author will seek to deflect.

   (D) It offers an example of a form of art that the author will argue is the inevitable successor to literature.

   (E) It forms the basis of an artistic movement that the author will argue can never embody the seriousness and complexity of rich philosophical themes.

GO ON TO THE NEXT PAGE ▷

4 **4** **4** **4** **4** **4**

6. The passage is primarily concerned with

   (A) praising a work of art and voicing concern over its possible obsolescence.

   (B) describing the process by which works of art are degraded when adapted to different forms.

   (C) outlining the origin of a masterpiece of world literature.

   (D) arguing that the human race will face serious consequences for arrogantly overstepping the bounds of nature.

   (E) paying tribute to an art form that has been overshadowed by a more recent art form.

Max Weber's work is traditionally viewed as supporting a strictly objective, or value-neutral, approach to investigating social science issues. In many respects, Weber does uphold the notion of
(5) scientific objectivity throughout his writings. If we look at both his writings and his academic philosophies more carefully, however, it becomes clear that Weber's perspective on objectivity is more complicated than the traditional interpreta-
(10) tion would have us believe.

The term *objectivity* is used to denote that which lies outside the framework of subjective perception or bias. It is traditionally defined as that which "exists as an object or fact, independent
(15) of the mind." Indeed, Weber does appear to believe in the concept of strict objectivity concerning questions of reality and truth. Weber postulates that there exists a true reality that is inde- pendent of individuals' viewpoints. This position
(20) is illustrated through his use of the concept of "ideal types." Ideal types are theoretical construc- tions that can be used to help the social scientist analyze, investigate, and uncover reality. If ideal types can help the scientist uncover true reality,
(25) then it stands to reason that "true reality" must itself exist.

In discussing our ability to investigate objective reality, however, Weber moves away from the notion of strict objectivity. While he postulates
(30) that an objective reality exists, he seems to believe that our knowledge of this reality cannot be totally objective. According to Weber, individuals can only know truths insofar as we share communal presuppositions about particular realms of knowl-
(35) edge. Our methods of investigating truths are lim- ited to, and necessarily conditioned by, the value frameworks through which we approach issues. Thus, individuals who investigate issues can gener- ate only knowledge that is based upon assump-
(40) tions and perspectives shared by the community of scholars within which they work. Knowledge may not be purely subjective or influenced by individual bias, but it is only "objective" insofar as the scientific community upholds its presupposi-
(45) tions.

Weber goes even further afield from the traditional interpretation when discussing how individuals should use scientific knowledge to guide their actions. On this issue, Weber's stance
(50) approaches the purely subjective. He tells us clearly that each person should be free to choose how he or she acts upon the reality discovered by science. This position is put forth in his essay "Science as a Vocation," in which Weber argues
(55) that teachers must avoid personally imposing their own stances on their students and must rather help students to account for the ultimate meaning of their own conduct. In Weber's view, a professor must sit back and allow his students to reach their
(60) own conclusions. When it comes to action, Weber believes that individuals must make their own decisions and that not even a teacher can assert the truth for another person.

GO ON TO THE NEXT PAGE ⇒

7. Which one of the following best expresses the main idea of the passage?

   (A) Weber's theory on the topic of objectivity is more complicated than most other theories of objectivity.

   (B) Weber's views on objectivity are useful in supporting arguments against the notion of absolute truth.

   (C) Weber never clearly lays out his views on objectivity in his works.

   (D) Weber's views on the topic of objectivity are not as straightforward as is typically supposed.

   (E) Weber's views on objectivity are inconsistent and, therefore, cannot provide a reliable foundation for a belief in objective reality.

8. Based on the information in the passage, which one of the following statements would Weber most likely support?

   (A) Scientific knowledge about reality can never be completely free of subjective perceptions or biases.

   (B) The use of ideal types enables the scientist to perceive his or her own subjective biases concerning reality.

   (C) Teachers should refrain from imposing their personal views on students unless students are incapable of reaching their own conclusions.

   (D) The concept of objective reality is misleading because reality cannot exist apart from the value frameworks through which reality is perceived.

   (E) Ideal types are the only reliable method for investigating objective reality.

9. The primary purpose of the passage is to

   (A) resolve a debate over an author's theory.

   (B) summarize the complexities of an author's view.

   (C) reconcile two differing views of an author's works.

   (D) argue against an author's perspective.

   (E) present and test an author's hypothesis.

10. According to the passage, which one of the following is true about Weber's views on how individuals should use scientific knowledge to guide their actions?

   (A) Individuals may choose their own courses of action freely unless they are unable to account for the ultimate meaning of their own conduct.

   (B) Individuals should distrust scientific knowledge when making decisions that will determine their personal actions.

   (C) Individuals should be encouraged to determine their own courses of action based upon discovered scientific truth.

   (D) If a teacher determines that a particular course of action would be most beneficial for a given student, he or she should direct the student towards this course of action.

   (E) Teachers should follow their students' leads in determining the most appropriate course of action for themselves.

GO ON TO THE NEXT PAGE

4   4   4   4   4   4

11. Which one of the following best describes the organization of the passage?

    (A) An explanation is put forth and then rejected in favor of a second explanation.

    (B) An author's viewpoint is first criticized and then reclaimed for its redeeming values.

    (C) An argument is put forth and then negated by the presentation of conflicting evidence.

    (D) A hypothesis is advanced and then strengthened through empirical testing.

    (E) An interpretation of a view is presented and support for this interpretation is provided.

12. Which one of the following is mentioned in the passage as evidence for the assertion that knowledge of reality cannot be totally objective?

    (A) Scientific methods of investigation are always influenced by the subjective biases of the community of scholars within which the scientist operates.

    (B) Scientific methods of investigation are not legitimate unless they can be proven to be strictly objective.

    (C) Scientific investigations use ideal types, which at best help to approximate reality.

    (D) For truth to be objective, it must be independent of the mind of the investigating scientist.

    (E) The concept of objective reality is illusory.

13. The author presents the traditional interpretation of Weber's view of objectivity in the first paragraph primarily to

    (A) dismiss the relevance of all previous scholarship on Weber that does not accord with the author's line of reasoning.

    (B) argue that the concept of objective reality has been historically misunderstood by social scientists.

    (C) provide background for a contrasting interpretation of Weber's beliefs central to the argument that follows.

    (D) show how critics think that Weber's valueneutral approach to the notion of objectivity is more complicated than is traditionally believed.

    (E) illustrate the gist of a notion under attack that the author will subsequently attempt to vindicate

If one always ought to act so as to produce the best possible circumstances, then morality is extremely demanding, perhaps overly so. No one could plausibly claim that at every moment of
(5) their lives they have acted with maximum efficiency to improve the condition of the world. Because it would seem strange to punish those intending to do good by sentencing them to an impossible task, some ethical philosophers have concluded that
(10) morality has an "overdemandingness" problem.

From an analytic perspective, the potential extreme demands of morality are not a "problem." A theory of morality is no less valid simply because it asks great sacrifices. In fact, it is difficult
(15) to imagine what kind of constraints could be put on our ethical projects. Shouldn't we reflect on our base prejudices and not allow them to

GO ON TO THE NEXT PAGE

4   4   4   4   4   4

provide boundaries for our moral reasoning? Thus, it is tempting to simply dismiss the "overdemand-
(20) ingness" objection. However, in *Demands of Morality*, Liam Murphy takes this objection seri-ously.

Murphy does not tell us what set of "firm beliefs" we ought to have. Rather, he speaks to an
(25) audience of well-intentioned but unorganized moral agents and tries to give them principles that represent their considered moral judgments. Murphy starts with an initial sense of right and wrong but recognizes that it needs to be supple-
(30) mented by reason where our intuitions are con-fused or conflicting. Perhaps Murphy is looking for the best interpretation of our convictions, the same way certain legal scholars try to find the best interpretation of the U.S. Constitution.

(35) This approach has disadvantages. Primarily, Murphy's arguments, even if successful, do not pro-vide the kind of motivating force for which moral philosophy has traditionally searched. His work assumes and argues in terms of an inner sense of
(40) morality, and his project seeks to deepen that sense. Of course, it is quite possible that the moral view-points of humans will not converge and that some humans have no moral sense at all. Thus, it is very easy for the moral skeptic to point out a lack of jus-
(45) tification and ignore the entire work.

On the other hand, Murphy's choice of a starting point avoids many of the problems of moral phi-losophy. Justifying the content of moral principles and granting a motivating force to those principles
(50) is an extraordinary task. It would be unrealistic to expect all discussions of moral philosophy to derive such justifications. Projects that attempt such a der-ivation have value, but they are hard pressed to pro-duce logical consequences for everyday life. In the
(55) end, Murphy's strategy may have more practical effect than its more traditional counterparts, which do not seem any more likely to convince those that would reject Murphy's premises.

14. The passage is primarily concerned with

(A) highlighting the disadvantages of adopting a philosophical approach.

(B) illustrating a philosophical debate by comparing two current theories.

(C) reconciling the differences between two schools of philosophical thought.

(D) reviewing scholarly opinions of an ethical problem and proposing a new solution.

(E) evaluating the merits of a model of ethical inquiry.

15. The author suggests which one of the following regarding Murphy's philosophy?

(A) The application of Murphy's philosophy to the situations of two different groups would help to solve the problems of one group but not of the other.

(B) The application of Murphy's philosophy to the situations of two different groups could result in the derivation of two radically different moral principles.

(C) The application of Murphy's philosophy to the situations of two different groups would be contingent on the two groups sharing the same fundamental beliefs.

(D) The application of Murphy's philosophy to the situations of two different groups could reconcile any differences between the two groups.

(E) The application of Murphy's philosophy to the situations of two different groups would not provide definitive recommendations for either group.

GO ON TO THE NEXT PAGE

4 **4**   **4**   **4**   **4**   **4**

16. The passage implies that a moral principle derived from applying Murphy's philosophy to a particular group would be applicable to another group if

(A) the first group recommended the principle to the second group.

(B) the moral viewpoints of the two groups do not converge.

(C) the members of the second group have no firmly held beliefs.

(D) the second group shares the same fundamental beliefs as the first group.

(E) either group has no moral beliefs at all.

17. According to the passage, the existence of individuals who entirely lack a moral sense has which one of the following consequences?

(A) It confirms the notion that moral principles should be derived from the considered judgments of individuals.

(B) It suggests a potential disadvantage of Murphy's philosophical approach.

(C) It supports Murphy's belief that reason is necessary in cases in which intuitions are conflicting or confused.

(D) It proves that more traditional approaches to ethical theorizing will have no more influence over the behavior of individuals than will Murphy's philosophical approach.

(E) It is a necessary consequence of the "overdemandingness" problem.

18. The passage suggests that Murphy would agree that the application of reason is necessary for forming moral principles when

(A) the beliefs of one group supersede the beliefs of another.

(B) people's firmly held beliefs are conflicting or confused.

(C) the belief system of a group conflicts with an overriding ethical principle.

(D) individuals have no moral sense at all.

(E) the demands of morality seem too extreme.

19. A school board is debating whether or not to institute a dress code for the school's students. According to Murphy, which one of the following actions would constitute the best way to come to an ethical decision regarding the matter?

(A) Consulting the fundamental beliefs of the board members

(B) Analyzing the results of dress codes instituted at other schools

(C) Surveying the students as to whether or not they would prefer a dress code

(D) Determining whether or not a dress code has ever been instituted in the school's history

(E) Determining the best interpretation of the guarantees found in the U.S. Constitution

20. The primary purpose of the last paragraph of the passage is to

(A) describe the method of determining the best interpretation of an individual's firmly held beliefs.

(B) explain the origin of the "overdemandingness" objection.

(C) identify advantages associated with Murphy's approach to ethics.

(D) reconcile two opposing schools of philosophical thought.

(E) characterize Murphy's response to the "overdemandingness" objection.

GO ON TO THE NEXT PAGE

21. The passage suggests that the author would be most likely to agree with which one of the following statements?

   (A) Arguing from a set of firmly held beliefs is an important element of traditional moral philosophy.

   (B) Philosophical works that attempt to discover a motivating force behind moral principles have no value.

   (C) No one who lacks a moral sense can make a significant contribution to an ethical debate.

   (D) Those who are not well intentioned are unlikely to be influenced by traditional approaches to moral philosophy.

   (E) The "overdemandingness" objection does not represent a serious problem for traditional moral philosophy.

Passage A

Since the mid-1980s, it has been widely recognized by scientists that the "ozone layer" is in jeopardy. The ozone layer lies within the stratosphere— the layer of the earth's atmosphere begin-
(5) ning about 10 kilometers above the earth's surface. The ozone layer itself is about 25 kilometers overhead. That layer contains about 90 percent of the ozone in the earth's atmosphere, and that ozone isn't going to waste. The ozone layer absorbs more
(10) than 90 percent of the ultraviolet light from the sun; that ultraviolet light is potentially hazardous to life on earth.

The thinning of the ozone layer, which is caused at least in part by man-made pollut-
(15) ants, means that this ozone shield is diminished. Because of the unique atmospheric behavior in polar regions, those areas are especially vulnerable. Most scientists now attribute ozone depletion to chlorine and bromine compounds in the atmo-
(20) sphere, and a high percentage of those materials in the stratosphere comes from human activities.

In 2006 alone, the stratosphere lost more than 44 million tons of ozone. Although there are natural fluctuations based on temperature and the
(25) positioning of the thin spot in the ozone layer during different time periods, the destruction of the ozone layer has continued for the more than 20 years that scientists have monitored it. In 2007, the hole over the South Pole covered more than 10
(30) million square miles, roughly the size of the North American continent. Clearly, further research and action is required.

Passage B

The hole in the ozone layer shrank by 30 percent in 2007 and is projected to disappear completely within the next few decades. Early computer model projections suggested that the hole in the
(5) ozone layer over the South Pole might heal itself by 2050. While today's projections are somewhat more conservative, it seems that the damaged area over Antarctica may be entirely repaired by 2040 and that the larger, more serious South Pole prob-
(10) lem will resolve itself by some time in the 2060s. While there is some disagreement among scientists about the actual projected repair point, and recent adjustments have pushed the date back by a couple of decades, those changes are negligible
(15) when the age of the earth and its regular fluctuations are considered. The hole in the ozone layer over the South Pole reached its largest point in 2003, at about 11 million square miles. The computer models that attempt to pin down the exact date
(20) we can expect "success" and that test and retest and provide adjusted dates that are supposed to represent progress or a slowdown are speculative. The fact is that we're headed in the right direction; the hole is shrinking. Perhaps it is time to turn
(25) our attention and our extensive scientific resources toward more pressing issues.

GO ON TO THE NEXT PAGE ➤

4 **4** **4** **4** **4** **4**

22. About which of the following would the authors of Passage A and Passage B be most likely to disagree?

(A) The size of the hole in the ozone layer over the South Pole

(B) Whether or not the hole in the ozone layer is shrinking

(C) The approximate date on which we can expect the hole in the ozone layer to be "healed"

(D) Whether or not the hole in the ozone layer is a problem that requires the attention of scientists

(E) Whether or not the ozone layer is important for filtering out ultraviolet light

23. The figures offered by the two authors with regard to the size of the hole in the ozone layer over the South Pole

(A) directly conflict with one another.

(B) are not inconsistent, though they are used to support different conclusions.

(C) represent different interpretations of the same underlying data.

(D) indicate very different future outcomes.

(E) lack a scientific basis.

24. The relationship between the two passages can best be described as which of the following?

(A) Passage A describes a problem, and Passage B provides a different view that suggests that the problem is less serious.

(B) Passage A argues for a particular course of action, and Passage B explains why that course of action is likely to be ineffective.

(C) Passage A provides data regarding an environmental issue, and Passage B introduces different data that suggest that Passage A's figures are inaccurate.

(D) Passage B further builds on the issue introduced in Passage A by providing more detailed information about one specific aspect of the problem.

(E) Passage A provides scientific data relating to an issue, and Passage B counters with an emotional response.

25. The authors of the two passages would be most likely to agree that

(A) 44 million tons of ozone were lost in 2006.

(B) ozone loss can expose humans to dangerous levels of ultraviolet light.

(C) the ozone layer has suffered significant damage.

(D) scientists should act to protect the ozone layer.

(E) the ozone depletion problem is under control.

GO ON TO THE NEXT PAGE ▷

26. Which of the following is most analogous to the relationship between the two passages?

    (A) A father tells his son that his bedroom needs to be cleaned because it's dangerous to have the floor so cluttered, and the boy insists that a cluttered floor is not dangerous and no action is required.

    (B) One person in an office suggests that the process for submitting requests should be improved because there have been time delays and lost requests in the past, but another points out that those problems are already diminishing.

    (C) One doctor recommends treating a patient with medication, but another argues that surgery would be a more efficient and certain means of addressing the illness.

    (D) One veterinarian suggests exploratory surgery to find out whether a seriously injured animal can be saved, but another argues that it would be more humane to put the animal to sleep.

    (E) A tenant complains to her landlord about a problem with noisy neighbors, but the landlord tells her that the neighbors aren't unreasonably noisy and the problem is with her perception.

LSAT WRITING SAMPLE TOPIC

Snowridge Mountain is a small ski slope that fell into disuse when nearby Storey Peak was developed. Now the town of Snowridge, hoping to revive the area as a popular ski facility, has installed new lift s and access roads. The town is considering two proposals for the development of the 200-acre site at the base of the mountain. Write a well-reasoned argument in favor of one of these plans, keeping in mind the following two objectives:

1. Snowridge wishes to preserve its essentially rural character and small-town New England atmosphere, which it rightly feels are its most attractive features for tourists and native residents.

2. Snowridge has been hard hit by economic recession and declining farm prices. An infusion of new jobs, businesses, and tourists is essential to its survival.

Local real estate developers urge the adoption of a plan put forth by Condocorp. It plans to build a four-seasons condominium complex with 175 units selling at $100,000 to $175,000. The project would include an 18-hole golf course, indoor and outdoor swimming pools, a clubhouse with a restaurant, a sporting-goods shop, and a small convenience store. Condocorp has its own architects and construction crew but would supplement its crew with about 25 local workers. Once the project was completed, it would employ about 120 local workers, many in skilled jobs. A similar project in nearby Lake Mohasset generated serious problems for the town when sewage from the condominiums seeped into the water supply, creating high levels of pollution and a noxious odor during spring thaws. Condocorp later installed a sophisticated sewage system that alleviated the odor, although some problems remain. The company assures the town that new technology exists to prevent such problems at Snowridge.

New England Homes proposes to erect 60 single-family homes, each occupying a full-acre site and selling for about $150,000. Two acres of land would be preserved as wilderness for each acre developed. This plan includes a clubhouse with indoor and outdoor pools and a system of cross-country skiing and hiking trails. The project would employ about 100 local construction workers and would later employ a maintenance staff of 10. Previous experience with such projects indicates that restaurants and shops move into an area following the construction of a vacation village of single-family homes.

PRACTICE TEST TWO: ANSWER KEY

Section I Logic Games	Section II Logical Reasoning	Section III Logical Reasoning	Section IV Reading Comprehension
1. E	1. E	1. B	1. D
2. B	2. C	2. B	2. E
3. B	3. A	3. D	3. B
4. B	4. D	4. A	4. C
5. C	5. B	5. E	5. A
6. B	6. A	6. E	6. A
7. A	7. C	7. C	7. D
8. D	8. A	8. D	8. A
9. B	9. E	9. E	9. B
10. D	10. C	10. E	10. C
11. A	11. E	11. D	11. E
12. E	12. D	12. B	12. A
13. C	13. C	13. A	13. C
14. E	14. D	14. A	14. E
15. D	15. C	15. C	15. B
16. A	16. C	16. B	16. D
17. A	17. D	17. B	17. B
18. B	18. E	18. D	18. B
19. C	19. D	19. D	19. A
20. C	20. D	20. B	20. C
21. D	21. E	21. D	21. D
22. C	22. D	22. C	22. D
23. D	23. C	23. D	23. B
24. B	24. C	24. E	24. A
	25. B	25. A	25. C
			26. B

ANSWERS AND EXPLANATIONS

SECTION I: LOGIC GAMES

Game 1—Design Selections

The Action

A designer picks two out of five appliance designs and two out of three cabinet designs. So this a grouping game of selection, with the minor wrinkle that we'll have to keep track of both appliances and cabinets. The key issues are these:

- Which appliance designs can, must, and cannot be selected?
- Which cabinet designs can, must, and cannot be selected?
- Which designs can, must, and cannot be selected with which other designs?

The Initial Setup

A list of entities with two columns—one for those that are selected and one for those that aren't—will do just fine. You can distinguish appliance from cabinet designs by writing the former in ALL CAPS.

$$H J K L M \qquad t v w$$
$$\text{pick 2} \qquad \text{pick 2}$$
$$\text{IN} \qquad | \qquad \text{OUT}$$

The Rules

1) Be careful when you see "only if." When translated into a standard "if/then," the term that follows "only if " will follow the "then." So Rule 1 means that if H is selected, then both J and w must be selected. Taking the contrapositive, if either J or w is absent, we cannot have H.

2) "M cannot be selected unless J is selected," means that if M is selected, then J is selected. So if J isn't selected, then M isn't selected, either.

3) Rule 3 is a little easier: v implies H, and not-H implies not-v.

Key Deductions

There really isn't much you can deduce for sure. All the rules are hypothetical, so this isn't a great game to plumb the depths looking for deductions. You can combine Rules 1 and 3 to deduce that if v is selected, the selected designs must be v, H, J, and w. But this isn't such a big deal. Having done some investigation, hit the questions, keeping in mind that you're picking two of each design type.

The Final Visualization

$$H J K L M \qquad t v w$$
$$\text{pick 2} \qquad \text{pick 2}$$
$$\text{IN} \qquad | \qquad \text{OUT}$$

$H \rightarrow J$ and W
$no\ w$ or $no\ J \rightarrow no\ H$
$M \rightarrow J$
$no\ J \rightarrow no\ M$
$V \rightarrow H, J, w$
$no\ w$ or $no\ J$ or $no\ H \rightarrow no\ V$

The Big Picture

- The first game in a section isn't always the easiest, but as it happens, this was a good place to start. A straightforward grouping game can help you gain some quick points and boost your confidence.

- Never forget about the numbers governing a grouping game. This game seems wide open, until you remember that the initial paragraph specifies that the designer selects exactly two of each type.

- Know how to interpret and manipulate formal logic statements! "X cannot be selected unless Y is selected," simply means that X → Y. The contrapositive of Rule 1 offered another challenge. Remember that the negation of "A and B" is "not-A or not-B." In other words, if it isn't the case that they are both selected, then it must be the case that one or the other (or both) is not selected.

The Questions

1. E

First up is a straightforward hypothetical. Combining Rules 1 and 3, as you did in the Key Deductions, you see that if v is selected, then the complete group is v, H, J, and w. So choice (E) is correct. The others are impossible.

Remember: If you can handle formal logic statements, questions like this one are easy. But if you can't, Logic Games will be impossible. Make sure you have the basics under control before test day.

Always save your work. The correct answer to a hypothetical question is a scenario that could be true. So we know now that v, H, J, and w can be selected together. Having an acceptable scenario on hand often helps to eliminate wrong choices later on.

2. B

There's not much to do here except hit the choices one by one. But there's no need to handle this question second. Chances are, if you hit it last, you'll be able to eliminate most of the wrong choices by using your previous work. But if you attacked this question right away, you might have done something like this.

Choice (A) could be true, because we saw H and J together in the last question, and thus must be wrong. (B), however, is impossible. If we have H and M, then we can select no more appliance designs. But Rule 1 says that when we select H we need to select J. So (B) doesn't work and must be correct. For the record, (C), (D), and (E) are out, because if we select t and w as our cabinet designs, we can select any of these choices without violating any rules.

Remember: It's always worth seeing if your previous work can help you knock off a few choices.

You don't have to answer the questions in the order in which they appear on the page! Here, the question wasn't too brutal, anyway. But in another game, this strategy could be a real time-saver.

3. B

Without J, you can't have either H or M (contrapositives of Rules 1 and 2). Having eliminated three of the five appliance designs, you must select the remaining two. So K and L must be selected. Because we've rejected H, you must also reject v (contrapositive of Rule 3). Now you must select the only two cabinet designs left: t and w. That's the entire set. (B) must be true, while the other choices are impossible.

Remember: Always work out the contrapositive of if/then rules and then use those contrapositives to help you answer the questions quickly.

4. B

If L is selected, then you can select only one more appliance design. But if you select H, you must select J. And if you select M, you must select J. Either way, you'll select three appliance designs, so you can select neither H nor M. Having rejected H, you must also reject v, which in turn means you must select both t and w. So there are two possibilities: LKtw and LJtw. (B) has it right.

Remember: As you go through a game's questions, you should become familiar with the way the rules work. By now, you should be used to selecting t and w when you reject H, because that's what happened in the previous question.

5. C

For this one question, part of Rule 1 doesn't apply. Selecting H still requires you to select w, but now you can have H without J. Look at the choices.

(A) and (B) have the same problem. If you select M, you must select J, so these two choices force us to select three appliance designs. (C), however, is possible. Selecting v means you must select H and, therefore, w. Now that you can select H without selecting J, HKvw is an acceptable arrangement, so (C) is correct.

For the record, (D) is out, since selecting v means you must select H, selecting M means you must select J, and you have three appliance designs again. Likewise, selecting v means you must select H, which means you must select w, and now you have three cabinet designs, so (E) doesn't work, either.

Remember: Questions that change a rule should be handled last, if at all. You wouldn't want your work on this question to pollute your thinking on the other questions.

Game 2—Family Portrait

Rules and Deductions

This game is perhaps not as difficult (or as open-ended) as it may first appear if you realize the implications of the second rule, the one about the placement of Helen. There must be exactly two people between Helen and Feisal, which means either

$$H \_ \_ F \ or \ F \_ \_ H$$

and Helen is two places to the left of Gillian, or

$$H \_ G$$

When you combine these two, the first combination proves impossible:

$$H \_ G F \ No \ good!$$

—because you're told that Feisal cannot stand next to Gillian (Rule 1). The only combination that will work is

$$F \_ \_ H \_ G$$

—which is, therefore, a constant for every question! The only thing up in the air is where the remaining space goes, but it can only be at either end of what we've got so far. If you see this, you have only to note the conditions in the other rules:

$$no \ KG \ or \ GK \quad always \ IF \ or \ FI$$

—and you are ready to go.

The Questions

6.   B

Use the Kaplan strategy for Acceptability questions. Take each rule and test it against each choice. In this case, the requirement that Feisal and Gillian do not stand next to each other (Rule 1) eliminates (E). Exactly two people must stand between Helen and Feisal (Rule 2), so (A) and (C) must be wrong.

Khalia and Gillian do not stand next to each other (Rule 4), which kills (D), and you're left with (B), the correct answer.

7.   A

Being told that Laura is in position one solves the problem of the remaining space. The arrangement must be this:

$$\underline{L} \ \underline{F} \_ \_ \underline{H} \_ \underline{G}$$

Because Ian stands next to Feisal (Rule 3), we can fill in

$$\underline{L} \ \underline{F} \underline{I} \_ \underline{H} \_ \underline{G}$$

—and because Gillian and Khalia do not stand next to each other, the only space for Khalia is between Ian and Helen, leaving only one spot remaining for Jeremy:

$$\underline{L} \underline{F} \underline{I} \underline{K} \underline{H} \underline{J} \underline{G}$$

Jeremy is between Gillian and Helen, and the answer is (A).

8.   D

You have to be extra cautious when two questions in a game—especially two back-to-back—seem somewhat similar, even identical. Don't automatically assume that there's no further work that can be done. At first glance, it looks like the operational arrangement here is identical to that in question 2, and indeed the only way to put Laura next to Feisal is to add the remaining space on the far left. However, the final arrangement of people that you developed for the previous question is not the only one that works here. Ian could also fulfill Rule 3 by being in position one, giving us these two options:

$$\underline{L} \underline{F} \underline{I} \underline{K} \underline{H} \underline{J} \underline{G}$$

or

$$\underline{I} \underline{F} \underline{L} \underline{K} \underline{H} \underline{J} \underline{G}$$

Looking at these two options, what cannot be true? Jeremy is not between Helen and Ian in either scenario, so (D) is impossible. As for the others, Gillian must be in position seven, which kills (A), and the other three are possibly true.

9. B

Once you've added Jeremy to the far right,

$$\underline{F} \ \underline{\ } \ \underline{\ } \ \underline{H} \ \underline{\ } \ \underline{G} \ \underline{J}$$

—solving the problem is really a matter of three steps: Ian must be second, because of Rule 3; Khalia must be third, because of Rule 4; and Laura must be fifth, because that's the only space left. There is one person between Jeremy and Laura: Choice (B).

10. D

To put Ian and Jeremy next to each other, we of course need two adjacent spaces. Whichever end the remaining space is placed on, you won't get two adjacent spaces that way, so forget about that space for the moment. The only possible places for Ian and Jeremy are between Feisal and Helen, and because Ian stands next to Feisal, we get

$$\underline{F} \ \underline{I} \ \underline{J} \ \underline{H} \ \underline{\ } \ \underline{G}$$

Now you can deal with the seventh space. If it goes on the far right, you have to place Khalia next to Gillian, which is forbidden. Therefore the seventh space (and Khalia, for that matter) must go on the far left, leaving Laura to go between Helen and Gillian. There are four people between Laura and Khalia: choice (D).

11. A

Once again, the only possible locations for the adjacent Laura and Khalia are between Feisal and Helen, though this time we don't know which one goes to Feisal's right. But Laura and Khalia are in there. Now you've got to get Ian next to Feisal—on Feisal's left, in other words—leaving the space between Gillian and Helen for Jeremy. There is no one between Gillian and Jeremy: choice (A).

12. E

Use your previous work. You'll have to tackle this question choice by choice, but that process will go much faster if you don't repeat the work you did for previous questions. You're asked for the choice that cannot be true, so the possible scenarios we worked out in previous questions can help eliminate choices. The correct answer to the Acceptability question gives you

one of those possible scenarios. From question 6, we know the following scenario is possible:

$$\underline{F} \ \underline{I} \ \underline{K} \ \underline{H} \ \underline{J} \ \underline{G} \ \underline{L}$$

Does this help? Sure. You now know that Gillian can stand next to both Jeremy and Laura, which eliminates (B). You also know that Jeremy can stand next to Gillian and Helen, so (C) is possible.

Choice (A) asks if it's possible for Feisal to stand next to Ian and Laura. Back in question 7, you worked out this scenario, which shows that (A) is possible:

$$\underline{L} \ \underline{F} \ \underline{I} \ \underline{K} \ \underline{H} \ \underline{J} \ \underline{G}$$

(D) asks you whether Khalia can stand next to both Feisal and Laura. Khalia and Laura cannot be on Feisal's left, because that would force Gillian into a nonexistent eighth position:

$$\underline{L} \ \underline{K} \ \underline{F} \ \underline{\ } \ \underline{I} \ \underline{H} \ \underline{\ } \ \underline{G}? \ \textit{No good}$$

So if (D) is possible at all, then Khalia must be on Feisal's right. After placing Ian and Khalia, there's only one spot open for Jeremy, and you're left with this possible scenario:

$$\underline{I} \ \underline{F} \ \underline{K} \ \underline{L} \ \underline{H} \ \underline{J} \ \underline{G}$$

Because (A) through (D) are possible, (E) must be the right answer, and on test day, you would just select it. In case you're interested in why Laura cannot stand next to both Feisal and Jeremy, here it goes: You know from working out (D) that Laura and Jeremy cannot stand on Feisal's right, because this would force Gillian into an eighth position. So if (E) is possible at all, then Laura must be on Feisal's right. After placing Ian and Khalia, we're left with this scenario:

$$\underline{I} \ \underline{F} \ \underline{L} \ \underline{J} \ \underline{H} \ \underline{\ } \ \underline{G}$$

There's only one space left for Khalia, and unfortunately, that space is next to Gillian. because Khalia cannot stand next to Gillian, (E) is impossible.

Game 3—Sled Dogs

The Action

Five sled dogs are hitched together as the diagram indicates. You have to keep track of the positions of the sled dogs, so this game isn't too different from a sequence game; it's just that the entities are arranged in an odd formation instead of in a line. If we had to assign a game type here, we'd call this a spatial sequence game, but that's not important. What is important is that you identify the key issues:

- Which sled dogs can, must, and cannot occupy which positions?
- Which sled dogs can, must, and cannot be adjacent to which other sled dogs?

The Initial Setup

When the test maker gives you a picture, use it! The picture provided is a good framework for organizing your work. Add a list of entities, and you're set.

G H J K L

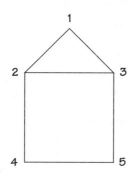

The Rules

1) This rule just defines "adjacency." This is pretty intuitive: Sled dogs that are connected to the same harness are adjacent.

2) Rule 2 brings in a new distinction: experienced and inexperienced. So now the game has become a bit more complicated. We can keep track of the experienced/inexperienced distinction by making a note under our list of entities. "2 XP, 3 non-XP," is one way to do this.

3) Here's one you can build in directly. Fill in an "XP" to remind you that the dog in position 1 is experienced.

4) and 5) These rules can also be built in directly by adding an "XP" to J and a "non-XP" to G.

6) Rule 6 is straightforward enough. The two experienced dogs cannot be adjacent. "No XP adjacent," is one way to represent this.

7) Rule 7 is similar to Rule 6: K and L aren't adjacent. "No KL adjacent," will do.

Key Deductions

Because the experienced dogs aren't adjacent and because an experienced dog is in position 1, positions 2 and 3 are occupied by inexperienced dogs. Therefore, J's assignment is limited. J is experienced, so J can't be in either 2 or 3 and J must be in 1, 4, or 5. Also, you know that since G is inexperienced, G can't be in position 1. That's plenty heading into the questions.

The Final Visualization

G(non-XP) H J(XP) K L
2 XP, 3 non-XP
No XP adjacent
No KL adjacent

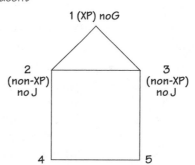

The Big Picture

- This wasn't an easy game, but it was easier than the previous game. This game was probably best handled third, after games 1 and 4.

- Games that require you to arrange characters in an odd formation aren't common on the LSAT, but they have appeared from time to time. Expect that your sequencing skills will help you with such games. You're still putting things in order, even though the order may not be a straight line.

- When the entities themselves are divided between different categories, make sure you recognize the distinction. You can bet that most of these questions will require you to recognize who must be experienced.

- To find deductions, you must translate the rules to find out what they mean in the context of the game. If the experienced dogs aren't adjacent, and we know that an experienced dog is in 1, what must be true? This is the kind of active thinking that leads to points.

The Questions

13. C

This question is a quick battle if you've done good work up front. You can't have an inexperienced dog in position 1, so (A) and (B) are wrong. Positions 2 and 3 must be occupied by inexperienced dogs, so (D), which omits the third position, and (E), which omits the second position, must be wrong. (C) is the only choice that remains, and yes, positions 2, 3, and 4 could all have inexperienced dogs.

Remember: Don't do more work than necessary! If you can eliminate four choices, pick the next one without further delay.

14. E

With J in 5, you have the experienced/inexperienced breakdown set. J is experienced, and position 1 has an experienced dog, and so positions 2, 3, and 4 must all have inexperienced dogs. The rest of the setup is pretty wide open, but (E) is inferable. Position 4 has an inexperienced dog, so (E) is correct. (A), (B), and (C) are all eliminated by this scenario:

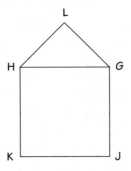

(D) is impossible. As you previously deduced position 3 is always occupied by an inexperienced dog.

Remember: As long as the deductions are coming to you, keep making them. But as soon as you're stuck, consult the choices. You may have deduced the correct answer without realizing it.

15. D

With L and H in 4 and 5, J is forced into position 1, because otherwise J would be adjacent to an experienced dog in 1. That leaves G and K to be placed, but K and L can't be adjacent, and so K must be in 3 and G must be in 2.

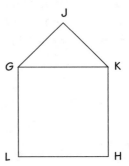

So all the choices must be true except (D): G and H aren't adjacent.

Remember: To make deductions, think about which rules and entities might be relevant. With slots 4 and 5 taken, you should think about where you can place J. With G and K yet to be placed, you should remember Rule 7, which states that K and L are not adjacent. Knowing where to look is often half the battle.

16. A

If K is in 5, what would guarantee that an experienced dog is in 4? From here, trying the choices is just as fast as anything else, and luckily, you don't have far to search. You must separate K and L, so if G were in 2, then L would have to go in 1. That means J must go in 4. So (A), if true, would guarantee that an experienced dog (i.e., Jinook) would be in 4.

(B), (C), (D), and (E)—If J were first, L were second, and either G or H were third, then the other of the

G/H pair must be fourth. Either way, K could be an experienced dog, and because we have only two experienced dogs (and one is first), all these choices fail to guarantee that the dog in position 4 is experienced.

Remember: Don't be afraid to postpone work on a tough question. Sometimes, a game that isn't that tough overall contains a killer question or two.

17. A

If J is next to K and L, where could J be? J can't be first, since that would place K and L in 2 and 3, next to each other. So J must be in either 4 or 5. If J is in 4, then K and L occupy the only positions adjacent to J: positions 2 and 5. That leaves G and H to place. G can't be in 1 (Rules 3 and 5), so G would go in 3, and H would go in 1. If J is in 5, we get much the same story: K and L split positions 3 and 4, G still can't go in 1 and so must go in 2, and H again goes in 1. So either way, Hira is adjacent to G, and choice (A) is correct.

(B) is impossible, because H is in 1 and J is in either 4 or 5.

(C) and (D) both could be true but need not be true—both K and L could be in either 4 or 5.

(E) also need not be true, because J and L could occupy positions 4 and 5.

Remember: Sometimes, you can't make any solid deductions, but you can break down a question into two distinct scenarios. That's okay. Work out those scenarios, and you'll know what must, could, and cannot be true.

Game 4—Animal Examinations

The Action

Seven animals must be examined, one at a time. Sounds like another basic sequence game. The familiar key issues are these:

- What is the order of the examinations?
- Which animals could, must, and cannot be examined before and after which other animals?

The Initial Setup

Seven slots representing the seven exams, plus a list of entities, will do just fine:

P Q R S T V W

__ __ __ __ __ __ __
1   2   3   4   5   6   7

The Rules

1) P is right before T. "PT" will do.
2) and 3) These rules are in if/then form, which means that we should determine their contrapositives, too. Because having Q fifth means that V is sixth, we also know that if V isn't sixth, Q cannot be fifth. Similarly, because having S second means that P is third, we also know that if P isn't third, then S isn't second.
3) This is easy enough to build in directly, with arrows pointing to both the fourth and sixth positions.
4) Rule 5 can also be built in directly. "No V" in the first and fifth positions will do.

Key Deductions

This one stays pretty wide open. There aren't major blocks of entities, the rules aren't too concrete, and lots of stuff is possible. A little time spent here wasn't wasted, but in general, simple sequencing games tend not to have big deductions that fill in large chunks of the picture.

The Final Visualization

P Q R S T V W

<u>No V</u> ___ ___ ___ <u>No V</u> ___ ___
1   2   3   4↘ 5↙ 6   7
                              W

PT
If Q 5th, then V 6th.
If V not 6th, then Q not 5th.
If S 2nd, then P 3rd.
If P not 3rd, then S not 2nd.

The Big Picture

- Never rush through the rules. Take your time to avoid sloppy mistakes that can make the entire game impossible.

- Whenever you see an if/then rule, determine its contrapositive. Make sure you know what conditions would bring a rule into play. Here, for example, Rule 2 comes into play whenever Q is fifth, but Rule 2 also comes into play whenever V cannot be sixth.

- Don't worry if you can't find a deduction on a game that's relatively simple. Simple games are less likely to contain big deductions. Check the most likely candidates but then move on.

The Questions

18. B

The question set begins with the usual Acceptability question, so use the familiar Kaplan strategy of using the rules to eliminate choices. Rule 1 is violated by no choice, but Rule 2 is violated by (E), which has Q fifth without V sixth. Rule 3 kills (C), which has S second without P third. Rule 4 axes (D), which has W fifth. Finally, Rule 5 eliminates (A), which has V fifth. Choice (B) remains and is correct.

Remember: Acceptability questions give you a shot at an easy point and give you the opportunity to practice applying the rules. That practice with the game's mechanics often helps on harder questions.

19. C

If S is second, then P is third (Rule 3), and thus T must be fourth (Rule 1). Because W isn't fourth, W must be sixth (Rule 4). Now who could be fifth? V is never fifth (Rule 5), and because V cannot be sixth, Q cannot be fifth either. So R is the only animal that can be fifth, and therefore (C) is correct.

Remember: When the stem provides concrete information in an "if clause," build the new information into a little picture and see where the new information takes

you. If you don't see where to go, use the choices to help you.

20. C

If Q is fifth, then V is sixth (Rule 2). Since W isn't sixth, W must be fourth (Rule 4). Only slots 1, 2, 3, and 7 are open, so the PT pair will have to go either first and second or second and third. Joining them in the first three slots is R (as the stem indicates), so the only entity that could be seventh is S. (C) must be true.

(A), (B), and (D) could be true, but R could also be first, placing P second and T third.

(E) is impossible. W is fourth here.

Remember: When you're definitely able to place a number of entities, ask yourself, "Who's left?"

21. D

If P is third, T is fourth (Rule 1), so W is sixth. Because V isn't sixth, Q isn't fifth, and you can eliminate (A), (C), and (E). The only difference between (B) and (D) is that (D) includes R. Could R be fifth? Sure. SVPTRWQ is one such acceptable arrangement. So R belongs on our list, and (D) is correct.

Remember: Don't do more work than necessary! Use the choices to help you answer "complete and accurate" questions more efficiently. Look to eliminate several choices at once and never check entities that appear in all the remaining choices.

22. C

If W is right after Q, where could they be? W cannot be sixth, since that would place Q fifth, which in turn would force V to be sixth. So W must be fourth, and Q must be third. Now where can we place the VS pair mandated by the stem? Placing them first and second would violate Rule 3, and V can never be fifth (Rule 5), so V and S must be sixth and seventh, respectively. Now the only place for the PT pair is first and second. So R, the only animal left, must be fifth, the only space left. (C) is correct.

Remember: When you're working with a block of entities, see where it could go. You may be surprised to see that it can go in only one place.

23. D

If P, T, and V all are examined after W, then W must be fourth and not sixth. V can never be fifth (Rule 5), and if we placed V sixth, you'd have to break up the PT pair. So V is seventh and P and T are fifth and sixth, respectively. Now we have to work out the possibilities for the first three slots. The only restriction that applies comes via Rule 3. S cannot be second because you know P cannot be third. If S is first, then the arrangement is either SQRWPTV or SRQWPTV. If S is third, the arrangement is either QRSWPTV or RQSWPTV. So four combinations are possible.

Remember: Straightforward sequencing games are usually quick and easy points, but not this time. The questions here were fairly complicated, so don't worry if you found them time consuming. Just remember, an easy game can be made harder by asking tough questions. But sometimes the test makers make a hard game easier by including easier questions.

24. B

If R is fourth, then W is sixth, but not much follows immediately from there. On to the choices:

(A) P can't be third because that would force T into the fourth position, and the stem places R fourth. So (A) is impossible.

(B), however, could be true. If Q is first, we could place P and T second and third, respectively. S could be fifth and V seventh, and presto! QPTRSWV is an acceptable arrangement. So (B) could be true and is, therefore, correct.

(C) If S is second, you have no place for our PT pair. (D) is nastier. If S is seventh, then who could be fifth? Not P or T, because they have to be together. Not Q, because V isn't sixth. Not V (Rule 5). So if S is seventh, then no one could be fifth, and (D) is impossible. Technically, you could have deduced that S must

be fifth before you consulted the choices, but that deduction was pretty subtle, so there's nothing wrong with discovering it here.

(E) is impossible, because P immediately precedes T and we already know that W is sixth.

Remember: If you don't see the next deduction, hit the choices. You may still be able to find the correct answer quickly.

Section II: Logical Reasoning

1. E

The problem: Channeling recycled wastewater into the harbor seems to have brought dangerous bacteria into this town's drinking water. The solution: Researchers recommend adding the enzyme tripticase to the water to eliminate those pestilent bacteria, which in turn will "solve the health problem." Because you're looking to weaken this argument, ask yourself if there could be a problem with this solution. It removes the bacteria, which will only solve the health problem if tripticase itself doesn't introduce any other problems. If, however, tripticase merely replaces one problem with another, as (E) has it, then the author's conclusion about its effectiveness as a solution is weakened.

Okay, so tripticase is supereffective because it solves the giardia problem as well as others. This certainly doesn't weaken the author's argument that tripticase is an effective solution (even though other illnesses are technically outside the scope), so (A) is wrong.

The frequency and severity of giardia isn't the issue here. The author addresses the effectiveness of a solution for a particular health problem. The relative size of that problem has no impact on the effectiveness of the solution, so eliminate (B).

Other illnesses are irrelevant to this consideration, as was mentioned above in (A), so eliminate (C).

The author discusses water-induced cases of giardia, so cases that arise from other causes aren't within the argument's scope. Therefore, (D) is incorrect.

Remember: When you're asked to weaken or strengthen an argument, remember to evaluate the impact that each answer choice has on that argument without questioning the information you're given. Assume that the stimulus is true and reconsider it in light of each answer choice. Does the new information make the conclusion more or less plausible? Don't question the information; just focus on its impact on the argument.

2. C

This is a Point-at-Issue question that basically asks, "What are they fighting about?" Look to see where they disagree. The marketing analyst only disputes the manufacturer's conclusion; each person presents completely different evidence. They can only disagree about something that they both discuss, and the only thing that meets that criterion in this dialogue is the conclusion. Therefore, they disagree about whether the company should switch to a less expensive brand of rubber, or (C).

The manufacturer certainly assumes that other brands cost less, but the analyst in no way disputes this or even directly mentions it. Both seem to agree that other brands would cost less. Eliminate (A).

(B) is not addressed by either person. The analyst mentions sales but not sales *quotas*, and the manufacturer doesn't even get close to discussing sales.

(D), like (B), brings up an issue that neither person directly addresses. Even if you thought the analyst's comments might have some relevance to customer preferences, the analyst never addresses them directly, and the manufacturer never gets near this subject.

(E) is addressed by the analyst but not by the manufacturer, whose argument deals only with cost.

Remember: Notice that all of the wrong answer choices mention issues that would be more relevant to the analyst's comments than the manufacturer's. Don't neglect the first argument; the right answer will have to be something discussed by both people.

3. A

Before hunting for an answer choice that will strengthen this argument, look for the assumptions in it. The salesperson argues that the system will provide safety because it will keep predators out, but this argument assumes that predators are the only real threats to the flock's safety. Perhaps the system provides its own dangers; the electronic gate that would apparently toast any wayward predator certainly sounds capable of hurting the flock surrounded by it. By affirming the argument's assumption that the system itself cannot harm the animals, choice (A) strengthens the argument.

So the system is being used for cattle. You don't know how effective it is, and in any case, this argument is about sheep, not cattle. You can eliminate (B).

(C) picks up on and intensifies the potential drawback discussed in the last sentence. That sentence is tangential to the argument, which would nevertheless certainly not be strengthened by such information about how often this system errs.

The argument concerns the efficacy of the contraption "when [the] flock is in danger of attack." The fact that some sheep predators are almost extinct does nothing to help the argument here; in fact, it makes the system seem, if anything, *less* necessary. Eliminate (D).

(E) is like (D) in that it would, if anything, weaken the argument. The system protects against predators, so if those predators don't provide a substantial threat, then it would be hard to sell this system as a splendid sheep protector. Again, the salesperson might protest that he simply touts the system *in the event* of attacks, which is fair enough—but that would only make (D) and (E) irrelevant and certainly not strengtheners.

Remember: Always try to identify the argument's assumption when dealing with Strengthen or Weaken questions. Making that assumption explicit is a surefire and common way to strengthen an argument.

4. D

Now you get to that tangential sentence in the stimulus. What role does the cliché play? Well, the salesperson mentions a potential drawback in the system and follows that with an important "but" that signals the shift in the second half of this sentence. While the system may not be perfect, the salesperson clearly suggests through the well-known adage that the problem is not that serious. "Better safe than sorry" therefore functions in the argument to downplay an imperfection in the system.

(A) takes the shift too far. The salesperson never suggests that the false alarms are actually a good part of the system but merely that they're not all that terrible.

Again, the false alarms aren't one of the salesperson's selling points as (B) suggests. (What kind of sales pitch would *that* be? "And best of all, the darn thing often misfires!") He presents the false alarms as a flaw but as a relatively unimportant one.

(C) does more to downplay the problem than the salesperson does. The salesperson only says that they happen, not that they happen rarely, and the statement in question can't play a role in the argument that *nothing* plays in the argument.

(E) entirely ignores the fact that "better safe than sorry" is said in relation to the false alarms flaw. It is uttered in reaction, not as *further* evidence for the need of such protection.

Remember: When you're dealing with a stimulus that has two questions, don't just rely on your memory when you get to the second question. A different question type means that you need to look for different things in the stimulus, so don't hesitate to do the necessary rereading before attacking the choices.

5. B

Next up is an Assumption question. The administrator concludes that Sandra would not be an effective teacher. Why not? She has two flaws: She's too lenient to fail students and too critical to reward any with high marks. But are failing students and rewarding high grades the only criteria for teacher effectiveness? Why can't she be effective even if she does neither of these things? The author doesn't say, and that omission is the basis of her assumption. In making her argument, the administrator assumes that to be effective, a teacher must be able to do one of these two things. This assumption is laid out for us in choice (B).

(A) is a distortion of the administrator's assumption. She doesn't assume that effective teachers have only two options: failing students or rewarding them with high marks. Instead, she assumes they must be capable of doing at least one thing or the other to be effective.

(C) gets the cause and effect of the argument mixed up by telling us what teachers must do to fail or reward students. You're interested in what teachers must do to be effective, so nothing regarding the reverse need be assumed here.

(D) and (E) fail to address the key issue at hand, which again concerns what it takes to be an effective teacher. Neither need be assumed here.

Remember: Straightforward Assumption questions lend themselves well to prephrasing. To determine the assumption, first isolate the conclusion and the evidence. Then ask, "What unstated yet necessary premise does the author rely on to draw her conclusion? What premise must she accept for the conclusion to follow logically from the evidence?" The assumption must bridge the gap between the conclusion and the evidence given.

6. A

Here you must choose an assumption upon which the argument in the stimulus depends. The conclusion is stated directly in the last sentence: In the coming years, Jenny will be less financially burdened by costs related to her job. The people most financially burdened by the costs associated with working are those making between $30,000 and $40,000 per year. Those who make less than $30,000 have lower job-related costs, so they generally are not as burdened—and folks who make more than $40,000 tend to make enough to compensate for their increased job costs, so they don't feel the burden as much either.

The author assumes that Jenny will move out of the $30,000–$40,000 income category in the coming years. Either she will start to make less than $30,000, or she will make more than $40,000 (for instance, if she receives a raise). If she stays in the same job, as the stimulus indicates, she's not likely to receive a pay cut, so the pay raise option is most feasible. Scanning the choices, you can see that choice (A) captures this last possibility nicely. If Jenny is promoted, her salary will probably go up, and the burden of her job-related costs will decrease.

(B) is tempting, because it provides one avenue through which Jenny's job-related costs could be reduced. Yet it doesn't address the issue of salary that is central to the evidence. The evidence tells us that job costs are less burdensome if an individual's salary surpasses $40,000. If Jenny's salary doesn't increase, she may still feel the burden of her job-related costs even if they're lessened.

(C) provides irrelevant information. You might try the Denial Test to eliminate this one: Even if $40,000 was an entry-level salary for Jenny's job, the argument could still work as is.

(D) may also be eliminated with the denial test. If Jenny's coworkers did find their job costs as burdensome as she finds hers, how would this affect the argument? Not at all—therefore, this choice cannot be a central assumption.

(E)—Irrelevant. You are not interested in what Jenny made at her previous job. You are merely interested in her current salary and how it and the financial burdens related to it are likely to change in the future.

Remember: Whenever possible, prephrase the answers to Assumption questions and scan quickly for your answer. If you can gain quick points through prephrasing here, you'll have more time to spend gaining points on more difficult questions later in the section.

7. C

This stimulus doesn't offer an argument with a conclusion but rather discusses two different qualities of physical beauty. Physical beauty can increase one's physical appeal, but the attention that physical beauty generates can also make someone arrogant and decrease that appeal. Because this is an Inference question and the stimulus is missing a conclusion, odds are pretty good that the right answer will be a conclusion supported by the stimulus as it stands. If you were to prephrase a conclusion, it would probably look something like "Therefore, physical beauty can both increase and decrease one's personal appeal."

(C) is entirely consistent with the information that the stimulus provides and could easily serve as the conclusion towards which this author is moving.

(A) directly contradicts the stimulus, which creates two links between one's beauty and one's physical appeal.

(B) distorts the stimulus, which doesn't say whether beauty's impact on personal appeal is more positive than negative or vice versa. The author merely mentions one positive effect and one negative; he doesn't rank them.

(D)—Again, the author doesn't say whether the positive trait and the negative trait are of equal or of varying weights. We can't infer a statement that the author doesn't directly support.

(E) might be a nice cliché, but it's certainly not consistent with the stimulus. The stimulus discusses beauty as something that exists and has two contradictory impacts on appeal; the author doesn't discuss what determines beauty.

Remember: When looking for a choice that is "best illustrated" by the statements in a stimulus, the right answer must above all be consistent with the stimulus and must also in some fundamental way reflect the essence of it. If a choice is inconsistent with the passage, kill it. If it's consistent but tangential, kill it. Something that is "best illustrated" by the stimulus must be better related to it than that.

8.   A

The educational consultant offers three reasons why school districts don't provide adequate educations: Teachers are inadequately trained tight budgets limit opportunities for afterschool academic programs, and parents aren't participating enough in the classroom. Those are the author's criteria for adequate education. The Prentice School District has experienced greater parental participation and is, therefore, "looking up" as a district. It is coming closer to meeting the third criterion and is, therefore, coming closer to providing an adequate education, according to the terms of the argument. You're looking to identify a valid inference, and it's not always easy to prephrase inferences in cases like this, so you're probably best off evaluating the choices one by one without spending much time trying to prephrase an answer of your own. In evaluating each choice, the key is to not read too much or too little into the Prentice School District's accomplishment.

Does (A) sound reasonable? Yup. This school district, because of its increased parental participation, displays at least one component of adequate education to a greater degree than it had. This inference is perfectly in line with the claims made about Prentice and about adequate education—and it doesn't overstep the bounds of the argument as do some of the other choices.

(B) is far more than you can infer. All you know is that Prentice is making some improvements in one of the three criteria that define an adequate education. With such limited information, you can't infer that the district's education is adequate.

Eliminate; (C), (D), and (E) you have no basis for comparing the Prentice School District to other districts, and all three remaining choices bite the dust on this account.

Remember: Often the key to answering Inference questions correctly is understanding the exact extent of the author's claims. Here, Prentice is improving in one particular category, but that allows us to infer nothing about its performance in terms of the other categories or about its educational system as a whole. Don't infer anything beyond what the argument specifically supports.

Beware of common wrong answer choices, such as (C) here, that offer to rank what the author never did.

9.   E

Again you're presented with two opposing views presented in a single argument. A survey showed that, as a group, action films were rated higher than romance films. Viewpoint number one comes from the survey organizers, who concluded from this that subject matter of popular movies must determine their appeal. Seems reasonable, but the author, making use of the contrast keyword *yet*, states that this conclusion is probably wrong and offers an alternative explanation. She notes that the producers of the action films were more experienced in successful film production. Notice that the author doesn't disagree that action films receive better ratings but rather supports a different explanation for that superiority; the effect is the same in both viewpoints, but the causes differ. You're looking for an inference based on this argument, so once you have a firm grasp of the content, it's time to move to the answer choices.

(A) confuses percentages and numbers. The survey is based on the percentage of films in each category to receive the highest rating, not on the actual number of films to receive the top rating. A lower percentage does not necessarily mean a lower number.

(B) is 180: The author does suggest a relationship between previous directorial successes and the popular appeal of the survey films.

The argument is about independent feature films. Based on that argument, we cannot infer anything about what a survey of big-budget mainstream films would show. So eliminate (C).

(D) distorts the information in the stimulus. Sure, of the filmmakers whose work is represented in this particular survey, some have a hit film to their credit, while some have never even made a movie before. Does that allow you to conclude who's "more likely" to produce a hit? For all you know, the folks with previous hits were new filmmakers themselves when they produced those hits.

(E) is all that's left. The author suggests that having a previous hit film to the director's credit is more important than subject matter in determining ratings, so it logically follows that subject matter may not be a significant factor in the popular ratings of films made by directors with an equal number of previous hits. By positing another factor besides subject matter that accounts for the survey results, the author's argument

allows for the possibility that subject matter *may* have no effect on the ratings.

Remember: Learn to recognize the kinds of wrong choices that appear again and again on the LSAT. Looking back over (A) through (E) here, you should notice some pretty common wrong answer types: confusing numbers and percentages (A), a 180 choice that suggests the opposite of what's in the passage (B), a choice that strays outside the scope (C), and a classic distortion (D).

10.   C

The second question based on this stimulus asks you to locate the one answer choice that doesn't strengthen the author's argument. You therefore want to eliminate the four choices that strengthen the connection between the popular appeal of a director's film and that director's having a past hit film, as well as those that strengthen the connection between lack of a hit film and lesser popular appeal.

If previous hits indicate talent, then the author's theory of the link between previous hit films and popular appeal of the survey films seems more plausible, and you're more likely to believe that the organizers are wrong, as the author maintains, about the effects of subject matter. So eliminate (A).

(B), (D), and (E) all strengthen the argument by tying past experience of success to present cinematic successes. (B) links previous experience to ratings directly. (D) takes it from another angle and explains that the films of first-timers do not often achieve the same popular appeal as that attained by previous hit makers. (E) links previous experience of success to the ability to obtain the best actors, offering another benefit that accrues to experienced directors and makes them more likely to produce hit films.

Why many first-time directors don't make action films has no impact on this argument. The fact remains that of the films in this particular survey, the action films were made by more experienced directors while the romances were made by novices, and the author uses this fact to counter a previous conclusion. (C) gives one possible explanation for this fact but has no effect on how this fact is used by the author, which, after all, constitutes the crux of her argument. This is the one choice that does not strengthen (or, for that matter, even affect) the author's argument.

Remember: Many question stems, like the one here, are not written in the clearest possible manner. Before proceeding to the answer choices, pause for a moment to consider what you're being asked and what type of answer choice you're looking for, even when you can't specifically prephrase an answer. Here we want a choice that doesn't support the author's causal link between previous directorial success and the popular appeal of that director's other films.

11. E

The question stem directs you to find a weakness in the manager's argument, and it lies in the survey. What if others who are skeptical about the candidate simply didn't respond to the survey? The fact that only 25 responded negatively does not necessarily mean that the other 975 are okay with the reports and have confidence in the candidate's ability to lead, although this is the interpretation the manager implies. (E) picks up on this problem in the manager's argument: If the skeptics were disinclined to respond to the survey, then the conclusion that the candidate need not worry may be unfounded, and the candidate's concern may be legit.

(A) is beyond the argument's temporal scope. The candidate and his manager only discuss the impact of the recent media coverage; the possible effects of future coverage don't play a relevant role in that discussion.

(B) identifies a possible use to which the candidate's opponent might put the media coverage, but that too is outside the scope. Maybe the opponent's survey won't show any residual concerns based on the survey, or maybe it will. By itself, (B) doesn't point out a weakness in the argument.

There's no indication that the survey was intended to hide its main focus; presumably, those surveyed knew that the survey was intended to measure the

fallout from the media coverage. So (C) need not be something that the campaign manager's argument fails to acknowledge.

(D) deals with television interviews, which show up in the candidate's argument but not in his campaign manager's. Therefore, (D) doesn't identify a problem with the manager's argument.

Remember: Be suspicious of surveys in Logical Reasoning stimuli. Whenever you see one, ask yourself if there are any problems with it. Particularly, ask yourself whether the supposed results accurately represent the views of the whole group surveyed. Here, the campaign manager fails to specify how the majority of the participants in the survey responded, if they responded at all.

12. D

You're asked to identify the role of the recommendation that shows up in the first sentence, and we can see that it constitutes the argument's conclusion based on the fact that the argument's evidence supports it. All of the information after sentence 1 answers the question "Why do you think Sarah's teacher should spend more time with her?" (If you were tempted to identify the last part of the last sentence as the conclusion, notice that it only pertains to that last sentence.) The proposal is the passage's conclusion, as choice (D) clearly states.

(A) is technically impossible, since the recommendation is actually stated in the argument and an assumption is never stated.

(B) would tempt those who saw the first sentence as setting the stage for the true conclusion in the last sentence. The fact that Sarah's teacher is not displaying good judgment is still subordinate to the overall proposal that she needs to spend more quality time with the student.

Remember that a *hypothesis* is not a synonym for a *conclusion* on the LSAT. A hypothesis is a working theory that has yet to be adequately proven, which is not how the author presents her recommendation. Further, (C) totally misrepresents the argument, because the evidence in the argument *does* support the principal's proposal, whether or not we erroneously accept that proposal as a hypothesis.

(E) gets the pieces of the argument mixed up, putting "evidence" where "conclusion" should accurately be and vice versa.

Remember: Identify conclusion and evidence only in the context of the argument as a whole. The first sentence appears to be the conclusion at first glance, but you can only be sure of that by seeing how that sentence plays into the rest of the argument. Withhold final judgment until all the information is in.

13.   C

Do you see the formal logic in this question? The author begins with the classic if/then formula: *If* there's too much pressure on the bottom shelf, *then* the bookcase will collapse. Because the stem directs you to find a weakness, you can anticipate that the logic will exhibit an error in the rest of the stimulus. A valid conclusion would be the contrapositive of this statement: If the bookshelf has not collapsed, then there is not too much pressure on the bottom shelf. This, however, is not what you get. Instead, the author concludes by flipping the original terms: If the bookcase has collapsed, then there must have been too much pressure on the bottom shelf. The correct choice is (C)—the author assumes that excessive pressure, because it's offered as one sure cause, is the *only possible* cause, even though there may be others.

(A)—The evidence and the conclusion are both about the same issues, even though the conclusion misinterprets the evidence. The problem isn't that the evidence is irrelevant but rather the way in which the conclusion distorts that evidence.

(B)—The author never mentions or implies the concept of a "partial collapse." It's impossible, according to the author, for just the bottom shelf to collapse. The author talks about an "entire" collapse and never deviates from this conception. There's no discontinuity in the meaning of *collapse*.

The author has no obligation to consider the existence of single-shelf bookcases. This argument is specifically about Sherry's bookcase, which has at least a bottom shelf, which implies it has at least one more. You can't tell whether the author has overlooked the possibility mentioned in (D), but even if she has, that has no bearing on the validity of her argument.

The conclusion is certainly too extreme, but it just deals with Sherry's bookcase, it would be hard to classify it as "broad." Also, the evidence doesn't contradict itself. As it stands, the evidence offers a perfectly valid formal logic statement; the problem comes in the conclusion drawn from this evidence. So eliminate (E).

Remember: This question offers a good example of the benefits of identifying the different parts of an argument. After isolating the evidence and the conclusion, look for the flaws. The evidence is fine, so (A) and (E) are out. That means the conclusion must be the problem, either in and of itself or because it rests on a weak assumption. Of the remaining answer choices, only (C) deals with the conclusion specifically. Even if you aren't sure what the weakness is, you can go far by identifying where it must be.

14.   D

To parallel a dialogue accurately, you'll want to understand the structure of each part individually. The first speaker in the right answer choice will explain that everyone within a certain group receives one of two items. The second part of the right answer will describe how, no matter which item is originally chosen, everyone in the group receives the same item. On its most basic general level, then, the right answer choice will start off with two options and will then narrow down to one of those options that's common to both choices. You can't quite predict how this is going to look, so let's evaluate the answer choices.

(A) starts off fine, but the second speaker concludes that "most" of the bouquets included silver roses, while the original argument concludes that "all" kids have loans. "Most" will never parallel "all."

(B) proceeds from discussing a group to discussing an individual. The original argument makes a conclusion about the group, not one of its members.

(C) follows the pattern you've seen by starting off okay but making its error in the second part. The psychiatrist discusses Ward A, but the nurse discusses an entirely different group residing in Ward B. The original argument deals with one and only one group.

(D) finally remains faithful throughout the second part of the argument. Margaret describes two options available to patients (corn or peas), and the cafeteria worker shows how the patients all share one of those options (peas) because anyone who chose one (corn) also chose the other (peas). Perfect.

(E) makes its error right away by describing the two choices as mutually exclusive. It can't parallel the original argument that combines the two options. You should have stopped reading this one at the phrase "but not both."

Remember: Be aware that many Parallel Reasoning questions can be cut down to size with strategic comparisons of the original to the choices. For example, (A)'s "most" and (E)'s "but not both" allowed us to chop through these choices rather quickly.

When time's running out, you may wish to focus on paralleling only one part of the original argument (for example, its conclusion). That may help you at least improve your odds if you have to guess.

15. C

Oddly, this stimulus presents you with nothing more than a list of different transportation vehicles and their definitions. With so much rather disconnected information, be prepared to refer back to the stimulus as you comb the answer choices for a proper inference. Choice (C) is the right answer, because any jeep meeting such criteria would also fulfill all of the criteria listed in the definition of a passenger vehicle. The author never says that a vehicle can't belong to more than one category.

(A) is incorrect. If the automobile in question were a passenger vehicle, then it *would* be fully enclosed with four wheels.

(B) knocks out three of the four vehicles described in the passage and, therefore, chooses the fourth, but that's only valid if there aren't any other vehicle options. Perhaps there are; nowhere does the author say that these are the only four vehicles in existence.

(D) makes an unsupported comparison among the vehicles. Even if the definitions of two of these vehicles are more similar, that doesn't suggest that the vehicles themselves are necessarily more *alike*. Too vague.

(E) may be true, but it may not. Because the stimulus doesn't discuss this possibility or provide any rules that would support it, we can't infer that the postal van and jeep categories overlap. It's possible that no postal vans are jeeps.

Remember: An inference is something that is well supported by the information and logically follows from it. Don't settle for choices that leave room for argument.

16. C

The evidence in this argument is the need for remedial programs in doctoral courses. The conclusion is that open admissions fails to accomplish what it is supposed to. Question 13 asks which reform would the author think most beneficial? In the passage, the author says, "Were our high schools more successful, we would have no need for open admissions," so presumably he or she would like to see an improvement in secondary education, and that's the reform in (C).

(D) is wrong because there's nothing in the passage to show that the author thinks a "higher teacher-student" ratio will necessarily result in improvement. (A), (B), and (E) are all harsh measures that would not constitute beneficial reforms. The author would probably like to see all of these things come about but after (C) had made open admissions unnecessary. (A), (B), and (E) recommend eliminations that would perhaps cover up the problem but not solve it. (C) would solve it.

17. D

We have a significant number of rats dying of liver disorder after exposure to sulfur dioxide, but most of the rats who died of liver disorder were not exposed to any environmental toxins. You should have realized immediately that the 65 percent and the 90 percent referred to two different groups and thus, that there is no discrepancy in the statistics. The 65 percent statistic refers to rats exposed to sulfur dioxide; the 90 percent statistic refers to all rats that died of liver disorder. (D) points this out. If only a small number of rats were exposed to sulfur dioxide, then it's not surprising that 90 percent of the rats that died of liver damage died of something other than sulfur dioxide exposure. After all, only a small number of them were exposed to sulfur dioxide in the first place.

In (A), the exclusivity of causes of liver damage is irrelevant to this study. Any of the rats could have had both causes but only one seriously enough to cause death. (B) explains nothing. If there is only one cause of liver disease in rats, then what killed the rats that were not exposed? As for (C), why did 65 percent of the exposed rats die, if environmental toxins are not very dangerous? (E) contradicts the evidence. If 65 percent of the rats exposed to low levels of sulfur dioxide died, then most rats will probably die from such exposure.

18. E

The stimulus begins with an absolute statement and takes you directly into formal logic territory. Thus, the first sentence can be restated: If children are guided by critical adults, then the children will not develop strong self-esteem. The question stem allows you to anticipate that the second sentence will offer an incorrect inference, as indeed it does. There the author concludes that if children are *not* guided by critical adults, then they *will* develop strong self-esteem. Expressing the stem algebraically, we can rewrite the first sentence as this: if A, then B. The second sentence alters the equation to this: if *not* A, then *not* B. That's an invalid

inference, so we'll look through the answer choices for another argument that makes the same mistake.

(A) doesn't give any formal logic statements, so it can't parallel the stimulus. The recommendation in (A) has no parallel in the original, either, so you may have axed (A) on that count as well.

(B) can be restated. If a solicitor has bad manners, then that solicitor won't sell any products (if A, then B). The second sentence concludes that if a solicitor has low sales (which, you'll note, is different from *no* sales), then that solicitor has bad manners (if C, then A). That's a flaw, but it's not the one we're looking for.

(C) contains a description of an event and a prediction based on that event. Moreover, the first sentence contains no formal logic. Not parallel.

(D) restated says that if a puppy is not well socialized, then it won't interact well with a group of people (if A, then B). The second sentence describes a proportional increase between socialization and comfortable interaction, which isn't a formal logic statement and, therefore, can't complete the parallel.

(E) is all that's left, so it had better work. In fact, on test day, you shouldn't even spend time checking it if you're totally confident that the others are lousy. But for the record: If one takes calcium supplements, then one does *not* increase one's risk of heart disease (if A, then B). In the next sentence, the author concludes that if one does *not* take calcium supplements, one *will* increase one's risk of heart disease (if NOT A, then NOT B). That's a perfect parallel of the flawed stimulus.

Remember: Always restate formal logic statements in an if/then format. That'll enable you to interpret them, form their contrapositives (by reversing and negating the terms), and, if necessary, compare them to one another accurately.

The logical opposite of a negative statement is a positive statement! Here, the opposite of "not increasing a risk" is "increasing a risk."

19. D

The author begins by describing the view of some sports historians who subscribe to a basic formula: physical attributes + a coach's influence = a player's "unique" tennis style. After dismissing the relevance of modern players' greater strength and endurance, however, the author argues that current styles are really no different from previous styles, implying that the historians' claim of the existence of "unique" tennis styles is bogus. And this implication is stated outright in the last sentence, where the author posits the existence of a universally successful tennis style shared by all professionals. In other words, the author uses the fact that tennis styles haven't changed over the years to argue that there's simply one best way to play tennis; in contrast to the historians' theory of uniqueness, the author proposes the theory of universality. But the author ignores the role of the tennis coach. If, as (D) has it, the early coaches of today's players were the professionals of yesteryear, then it becomes plausible that the style that the author considers "universal" may simply be the style (one possible one among many) that was handed down from one generation to the next. Perhaps if the current crop of tennis stars don't go on to teach the next generation, whole new styles will develop. If the current style is learned, then it may not be universally inherent to the game. If (D) is true, the author's claim of "universality" is weakened.

(A) emphasizes the truth of the first part of the sports historians' view regarding the individuality of physical attributes. Since the author doesn't explicitly disagree that players do vary in terms of some attributes, this choice doesn't weaken the argument. It just emphasizes a point on which the two views (historians and author) don't clearly disagree.

(B) if anything, strengthens the argument: If most current players don't know of the players of previous generations, yet their style is for the most part similar to that of those players, then we'd be more likely to believe that the author is on to something with the claim that a universally efficient style exists in the world of professional tennis. (B) is somewhat the converse of correct choice (D) in that it lowers the probability that current players have simply copied the successful styles of previous players.

(C) makes an irrelevant distinction between strength and endurance. Saying that one has a greater impact than the other has no effect on the argument, which never even begins to rank those two factors.

The factors that contribute to the greater strength and weight of today's players, (E), are beyond the scope of this argument.

Remember: When the author describes the view of some other people (in this case "some sports historians"), be ready to encounter a contrasting view. The author often mentions such groups to contrast their views to his or her own. At the first sign of conflict in a Logical Reasoning argument or Reading Comp passage, ask yourself where the views differ. The answer choices often test your ability to recognize the distinction.

One way to get through the more difficult questions is to pay extra attention to wrong answer choice elimination strategies. Even if choice (D) doesn't seem great to you, (A), (B), (C), and (E) all commit common errors. There's nothing wrong with eliminating four choices for good reasons and going with what remains.

20. D

The pharmaceutical companies conclude that anemic children will be cured with the new iron injection. The evidence presents itself in the first sentence: A new injection can apparently reverse children's anemia. Can you see any gaps between the conclusion and evidence? Notice that the evidence explains that something can be done, and the conclusion states that something will be done. Just because the cure is possible doesn't mean it will automatically be administered. The author assumes that children will receive the injection based on the fact that it exists. (D) expresses this more concretely: The author assumes that children are aware of and willing to receive this injection.

(A) focuses on the availability, not the production of this cure, so (A) is not necessary (or even relevant) to this argument.

(B) gives us irrelevant background information about causes. The author states that iron shots reverse children's anemia, regardless of the specific cause, so (B) may or may not be true without affecting the argument.

(C) basically states that a managed diet would not cure anemia. But the author doesn't state that the injection is the only cure for anemia, so the argument needn't assume that no other cure exists.

(E) is out of scope. The author only claims that the injection cures anemia "relatively simply." Safety never comes up as an issue—the injection could almost kill the kids and still not hurt the argument, which states only that the shot cures the condition, not that it does so safely.

Remember: Even though Logical Reasoning stimuli are shorter than Reading Comp passages, don't try to memorize the information in either situation.

Push yourself beyond recognizing the conclusion to considering how it operates in the context of the argument. Instead of stopping once you've recognized that the author concludes that a drug will provide a cure, really think about how that relates to the evidence. That'll make it easier to see the gap between them.

21. E

The author concludes that mission commanders should not choose pilots based on the candidates' performance on the isolation test. For evidence, the author says that a candidate who passes the test may have an antisocial personality disorder. Thus, the author argues against a current system of assessment by noting one particular instance in which the results might not indicate what they're meant to indicate. This is certainly not the strongest of arguments, offering as it does one apparently small disadvantage of the test and using it to condemn the test entirely, which is why we'll see four

of its flaws among the answer choices. Notice that the question stem informs us that the four wrong answers will offer information that the author fails to consider; they will describe errors of omission.

(A) describes one way in which the isolation tests might work to screen applicants accurately. It describes a possible benefit offered by the test. The argument is flawed for failing to consider and rebuff this possibility.

(B) operates in much the same way as (A). Here we're told that mission commanders may select pilots more accurately if the tests they administer aren't limited. Because the author argues that such tests should be limited (arguing that there should be one fewer test), her argument is flawed since it fails to consider and, again, rebuff this opposing argument.

(C) and (D) again indicate two possible advantages of the isolation test. The author doesn't mention or contest these advantages, which means that she makes her conclusion without addressing the relevant issues that they describe. That's certainly a flaw in the argument.

Rather than highlight a benefit of the test, (E) goes the other way by suggesting that the test itself may be flawed. The fact that a pilot may do well on the test and yet not do well under actual isolation conditions is, if anything, consistent with the author's conclusion that the test should be scrapped.

Remember: Be aware of the variations in the question stems throughout the exam. The stem here informs us that the four wrong answer choices will describe things relevant to the argument that the author doesn't consider, which is a particular type of flaw. If you are aware of that, you can approach the choices knowing what to expect.

22. D

The heart of the argument is the last sentence of the stimulus: Harry concludes that his brother's suggestion wouldn't help to organize his collection based on the evidence that no single special album could hold all his cards. Harry's argument depends on the assumption that the collection of cards cannot be organized if they're not all in one album. (D) expresses the same idea: Harry's dismissal of his brother's suggestion makes sense only if the collection cannot be organized in more than one album.

Harry needn't assume that the showcase albums from the olden days would have served his purposes. His argument isn't based on a comparison of what's available now compared to what used to be available, so (A) addresses a possibility that doesn't impact Harry's argument.

(B) isn't entirely relevant to this argument, since other album types don't figure in to this argument. Moreover, we're concerned only with Harry's predicament.

(C) contradicts the stimulus, which explicitly states that no showcase album on the market is large enough to contain all of Harry's cards.

(E) is irrelevant. The reason *why* Harry's collection is disorganized doesn't provide a link between the evidence and conclusion, because neither part of the argument concerns this issue.

Remember: Even when you aren't able to prephrase an assumption, you can still go far with a knowledge of the issues involved in the argument. Here, those issues are organization and showcase albums. Only (B) and (D) actually mention both issues, and only (D) stays focused solely on them.

23. C

You're asked for a situation that conforms to a principle, so your best bet is to understand the principle thoroughly and then test the choices against this understanding. The author offers an absolute truth with two restrictions. First the rule: A free press always reports all information about a country's military operations. There are two cases, and only two cases, in which this might not be true: first, if such information would jeopardize the safety of the troops and, second, if such information would jeopardize the success of a mission. With such clear rules, we'll be looking for the answer choice that follows them faithfully.

To make (A) work, you'd have to assume that such dissenting opinions would jeopardize the troops and/ or the success of the mission. This choice supports no such assumption, so based on the information that it alone provides, it is not consistent with the stimulus's principle.

(B) and (D) discuss unfree presses and, therefore, fall outside the scope of the argument. The rules pertain only to a free press, and we can't infer how an unfree press would behave in regard to these issues.

(C) succeeds where (A) fails because, while it doesn't directly state that the publication of future military targets would jeopardize the success of a mission, the link between the two is far clearer and more logical. According to the principle, a free press *could* withhold information that endangers the troops or mission, and it's reasonable to say that the info discussed in (C) could fall into that category.

The principle deals with *current* military operations and, therefore, doesn't shed any light on what's appropriate behavior in regard to previous engagements. Clandestine past military operations are outside the scope, so eliminate (E).

Remember: No correct answer choice will require you to make a significant, unfounded assumption in order to make it work. The right answer choice will be correct on its own merit, without requiring you to introduce extra information.

24. C

Lillian's goal is simple: to create cohesion in her drug addiction recovery group. To achieve this goal, she has encouraged members of the group to share their personal experiences openly. The problem: Some members have begun telling long and violent stories to shock the others, causing some members to quit and leaving inadequate time for others to share. The conclusion: Lillian should limit the time available for each member to speak. The stem alerts us that there's a flaw in this argument, and that flaw becomes apparent in the conclusion. The problem that the conclusion seeks to resolve stems from two causes: members telling both long and violent stories. The conclusion as it stands might prevent the stories from being long, but it doesn't prevent them from being violent. Therefore, the argument is flawed because its conclusion would only remedy one of two factors that create the problem it seeks to resolve, which is what (C) states.

Apparently, "two actions" refers to the telling of long scandalous stories and members dropping out. (A) is most immediately wrong because the author does not suggest that these incidents occur simultaneously. On the contrary, the author presents them sequentially: According to the argument, the stories "cause" other members to quit.

We have no evidence to indicate that time limits might aggravate the problem—they would clearly address one aspect of it. You can eliminate (B).

The evidence is all perfectly relevant to the conclusion. They are, after all, both focused on the same issues. Therefore, eliminate (D).

(E) is tempting but irrelevant—we're concerned only with whether time limits will solve a specific problem.

Remember: The correct answer to a Flaw question may be phrased in a variety of ways. Prephrase the flaw but be flexible about the way it's expressed.

25. B

This Assumption question picks up on a scope shift . The author's conclusion addresses all of the materials produced by American Synthetics Inc., but the evidence discusses only one particular material produced by the company: the kuva weave fabric. You're told that kuva weave, despite its impressive durability and strength, has an unfortunate tendency to burst into flames (a small drawback). Therefore, according to the author, manufacturers should eliminate *all* American Synthetics materials from their stocks. This would be a valid conclusion only if it were true that all of the materials produced by American Synthetics were equally likely to ignite. (B) states this assumption: If all of American Synthetics' materials contain kuva weave, then they're all flammable, and

manufacturers should indeed get rid of their stocks. (B) makes the evidence about kuva weave relevant to the conclusion regarding all American Synthetics products—it connects the evidence to the conclusion and, thus, qualifies as the assumption we seek.

Sure, they didn't catch that flammability problem, but you're not concerned with the accuracy of the trials or when the problem showed up. You're solely concerned with the flammability of the material and what that flammability means for the company's products as a whole. So eliminate (A).

Plants that don't use the fabric may suffer from just as high or even a higher incidence of fires due to other reasons. In other words, the author need assume nothing about the type of comparison stated in (C) to make an argument about what should be done as a result of kuva weave's flammability. You can negate (C) and the argument does not fall apart, which confirms that (C) is not a statement that's needed here.

Apparently they're not as durable as originally suspected if they're burning, but durability isn't the issue—flammability is. As you saw in (A), the early tests are irrelevant. Eliminate (D).

The manufacturers' liability is far off scope. While (E) may offer an additional reason for manufacturers to expunge their stocks, you're not looking to strengthen this argument but to identify its assumption, and this answer choice doesn't link kuva weave to American Synthetics' products as a whole.

Remember: An *assumption* has a very specific definition on the LSAT; it is an unstated yet necessary link between the evidence and the conclusion. After identifying the evidence and conclusion, look to eliminate all of the answer choices that don't relate to both elements. Even when you can't prephrase the assumption, you can evaluate the answer choices with very specific criteria in mind and increase your chances of finding the right answer correctly and quickly.

SECTION III: LOGICAL REASONING

1. B

For the mother to conclude from her evidence that the sessions should end, she needs to assume that John is capable of accurately analyzing the sessions' usefulness. If he's not, then his feelings on the matter may not be an accurate indicator of the value of the sessions, and it may not be a good idea to base any decisions on them. Basically, John's mother assumes that John is right in believing that the sessions aren't helping him, which is where answer choice (B) comes in. If she's assuming that John is right, then she must also assume that his judgment hasn't been impaired.

(A) is wrong because John's mother just discusses what should be done if John is unhappy with the sessions. Her conclusion does not depend on him being happy or unhappy.

(C) is far outside of the scope of the mother's argument. She never addresses the issue of the psychoanalyst's qualifications; she just discusses John's feelings and their indication of the sessions' value.

With (D), again, whether or not the analyst's methods are sound is not the issue for John's mother. For her, the central issue is John and how his feelings determine the helpfulness of the sessions. Therefore, the validity of her conclusion does not rest on whether John's perceptions accurately indicate the soundness of the analyst's methods but whether they indicate the value of the sessions in helping him to adjust to his parents' divorce.

By stating that John should "act on any belief," choice (E) exceeds the argument's scope. The argument does not deal with anything so broad as whether John should always act on his beliefs. Rather, it addresses whether his beliefs should be acted upon in this particular situation.

Remember: You can often eliminate a number of choices right off the bat that are simply too broad in scope to be necessary to the particular argument.

2. B

Harriet's husband concludes that he will plan a trip to Sunshine Valley for him and Harriet. His evidence: Harriet wants to vacation in a culturally rich area, and her husband has discovered that Sunshine Valley is financially rich. His error: He responds to her desire for cultural richness with a city steeped in financial richness. He therefore mistakes her definition of *richness.* (B) captures this. To *confound* can mean to fail to discern differences between things, which is precisely what Harriet's husband does when he equates cultural and financial wealth. Further, this richness certainly constitutes a key (even the key) factor in his decision.

(A) weakens the argument. An argument is circular when its evidence and conclusion are basically the same (e.g. "I should go to the store because I should go to the store"). That's not the case here, where the conclusion and evidence are clearly different.

All travel brochures are biased, (C), they want to convince the reader to visit that area. Relying on such evidence to decide where to go isn't the basis of a logical flaw. Moreover, nothing here indicates that the information in the brochure is unreliable. The problem here is how the husband *uses* the evidence to make his traveling decision.

He certainly does (D), but the fact that he doesn't consult Harriet doesn't constitute a flaw in the argument as it's presented. If anything, it's a subjective and personal, not a logical, flaw to make important decisions unilaterally.

(E), like (D), is certainly true, but why does he need to demonstrate the economic feasibility of his decision? We have no way of knowing whether they can afford the trip or not, but that's a separate issue. We're concerned only with the husband's decision as related to the evidence for it.

Remember: Flaw questions are distinct from Weaken questions in a few ways. A flaw is a logical error in the reasoning of the argument or an objective mistake committed by the argument. You'll often encounter wrong answer choices for Flaw questions that would weaken the argument. However, a flaw is an internal mistake in the argument, whereas anything that makes the conclusion less credible weakens the argument. You can sometimes weaken an argument by identifying its flaw, but remember that a choice that weakens an argument isn't a flaw unless it points out an internal, logical error in the argument as the stimulus presents it.

3. D

This stimulus just tells a story. Once you've grasped the basic contents of the stimulus, proceed to the answer choices.

The stimulus says that *Theobroma cacao* is a tropical New World tree, but that doesn't allow us to infer that this tree only grows in the tropical New World. The tree might very possibly exist in other countries. Therefore, eliminate (A).

(B) contradicts the stimulus, which tells you that chocolate was introduced to Europe as a liquid.

(C) makes an unsupported comparison. You do know that more pounds of chocolate today are produced for eating than drinking, but you have no idea how the amount of drinkable chocolate in the 1800s compares to the amount of solid edible chocolate produced today.

(D) is valid: If the Swiss invented the first way to produce solid edible chocolate in the 1800s, then solid edible chocolate wasn't consumed anywhere in the 1500s.

(E) is entirely unsupported by the stimulus. Just because the Swiss made chocolate into a solid, that doesn't necessarily mean that nobody else would have done so if the Swiss hadn't. Take the Swiss out of the picture, and chocolate might very well be just as popular today.

Remember: Every once in a while, you'll get a stimulus that isn't an argument (i.e., it doesn't have a conclusion and evidence, just a bunch of facts). The question that's attached to them will usually be Inference, because it's difficult to ask anything relating to how the evidence reaches the conclusion when there really is no conclusion to speak of.

Make sure you stay within the scope when looking for the choice that must be true.

4. A

The nuclear physicist argues that the *Times* should try harder to print the views of protesters in this particular controversy. She proceeds to state, three times and in three different ways, that such views are lacking. So the correct principle will support the idea that balanced coverage is for some reason important. (A) fits the bill because, if effective reporting needs to represent both sides of a controversy, the *Times's* coverage is not adequate.

(B) provides a reason why balance might not be critical in an individual story—the opposite of what we're looking for.

(C) doesn't say anything meaningful because we don't know who the newspaper's readers are.

(D) is irrelevant. We also have no reason to believe any reporter has such an interest.

(E) would support the situation the nuclear physicist is protesting.

Remember: Principle questions are closely related to assumptions—the principle is the same sort of "missing link."

5. E

The author of this rather skimpy argument only implies her conclusion that the botanists were wrong. Evidence? The botanists believed that the *faura* plants required a certain fertilizer composed of four specific elements, but adopting this approach actually hindered the growth of those plants. There's a lot of space available for information that would strengthen the author's conclusion, but since we can't predict anything concrete, let's go through them individually, crossing off anything that supports the conclusion.

(A), (B), and (D) all describe one negative effect of the botanists' belief. More specifically, each discusses the botanists' omission of one key ingredient that these plants need to grow. (A) explains in further detail that the botanists' advocacy of the fertilizer inhibited *faura* species plant growth because it led to the omission of the valuable potash. (B) doesn't directly state that the omission of zinc caused the problems experienced by the *faura* species plants, but it certainly implies it, calling zinc "essential" to the plants' growth and, therefore, suggesting that the lack of it harmed the plants. (D) directly states that the plants require a necessary ingredient that the botanists' fertilizer lacks. All three choices expand on the author's argument, more clearly defining *why* exactly the botanists' belief yielded such negative results. By adding to the evidence, all three choices strengthen the author's argument.

(C) doesn't identify a missing ingredient necessary for healthy plant growth but identifies a problem with the presentation of the list itself, as it fails to prioritize the most important elements. Despite this minor difference, (C) serves the same function as the aforementioned choices by explaining why the botanists' belief had negative results and, thus, strengthens the author's argument.

(E) is correct because it identifies one way in which the botanists' claim likely benefited the *faura* species plants. The author is concerned with the negative effects of the belief, so this piece of information certainly doesn't strengthen her case.

Remember: Don't expect the right answer choice for these "all except" questions to be 180 degrees different from the four others. The answer for this question doesn't need to weaken the argument; it only needs *not* to strengthen it. More often than not, the right answers for questions of this sort just have no effect on the argument one way or the other.

6. E

Ron and Crystal will open a restaurant when they can both put in the required hours. Accordingly, the argument offers this one condition that must be met before the two open the restaurant. The remainder of the stimulus focuses on the assertion that Crystal's year-long project won't give her enough time to focus

on the restaurant. Therefore, the condition required for the opening of the restaurant has not been met and clearly will not be met in the current year. It is therefore reasonable to conclude that the couple will not open the restaurant this year, answer choice (E). This could also be stated through formal logic: If the two open the restaurant, then that means they have enough time to dedicate to it. The contrapositive is that they don't have enough time (which the stimulus states), so, therefore, they won't open the restaurant (the implied conclusion).

Our information is all about the present—we can't infer anything about "eventually." So eliminate (A).

You can infer that Ron and Crystal would believe (B) to be true—hence their pact that they would wait to open the restaurant until they were ready to devote their time and energy to it. However, this general statement, while certainly sounding consistent with the stimulus, is not the conclusion the argument is leading to. What about Ron? What about Crystal? What about their proposed restaurant? These things are the crux of the matter; the statement in (B) is too broad to be what the author is ultimately after here.

(C) might or might not be true; the stimulus certainly doesn't support or lead to this statement either way.

(D) might touch on some bigger problems in the relationship, but it doesn't get any support from the stimulus.

Remember: The same formal logic skills you use to translate Logic Games rules will help to boil down many Inference questions.

7. C

This question asks you to determine what can be inferred from the statements in the passage. If the statistics cited by both of the speakers are true, which of the answer choices must also be true? A look at the statistics shows that over the past five years, the elderly care center has seen an increase in its applications from volunteers—the director says they've almost doubled.

The nurse points out, however, that applications from patients' family members have actually decreased by 20 percent. If overall applications have increased, but family members' applications have gone down, what can we infer? (C) provides a logical deduction—that the center is receiving applications from volunteers who are not patients' family members. Use the Kaplan Denial Test to check your accuracy here. If the clinic received no applications from persons who were not related to patients, then the statistics cited would not make sense.

(A) does not necessarily follow from the statistics in the passage. The statistics concern volunteer applications, not the size of the patient population. The data that you're given about the volunteer applications tells us nothing about the patient population one way or another.

(B) might be tempting, but it does not provide you with the inference we need. Based on the statistics given, you cannot know whether patient care has improved or not. You're told that the number of volunteer applications has increased, but you don't know whether the number of accepted volunteers has grown—and you certainly don't know whether the volunteers are providing better care to the patients.

With (D), again, you cannot be sure that this statement is true simply based on the passage. You merely know that more people are interested in volunteering. This doesn't necessarily mean that the extra volunteers are needed, and it tells you nothing about why they might be needed if they are.

(E) is again beyond the limits of what you can infer. You are told that the number of applications has increased and that the number of applications from family members has decreased. But that's all. This is not enough information to tell you anything about the selection process for volunteers—for all you know, every person who applies may actually become a volunteer.

Remember: If you're not sure after scanning the answers on a "must be true" Inference question, you can make eliminations based on known wrong answer patterns such as "outside the scope."

8. D

Next you're asked to find a statement that weakens the nurse's argument. Before you can choose a weakener, first isolate the nurse's conclusion and evidence. The nurse concludes that the director's interpretation is wrong and that community members are less willing and able to work with their parents than they were five years ago. She bases this conclusion on one piece of evidence: Applications from patients' family members have decreased over this time period. To weaken the argument, you might find another explanation for why volunteer applications from family members are down. (D) provides just such an alternative: If family members are no longer required to fill out formal applications, their applications will obviously not be on file, which could easily explain the 20 percent decrease. But they may continue to volunteer just the same.

(A) is irrelevant. This doesn't affect the nurse's argument one way or the other, because it refers to "community members" in general. You do not know if these community members are volunteer applicants or if they are related to the elderly at the center.

(B) touches on the issue of family activities, but it doesn't tell us anything about the center's volunteers.

(C) might be tempting, because it provides another reason, besides lack of interest, for why an individual might not volunteer. However, whatever the reason, "willingness and availability" are diminished.

(E) has no impact on the argument, which is concerned only with whether a decrease in applications means decreased willingness/ability to volunteer.

Remember: Make the most of "double" questions that rely on one stimulus. Read both question stems before approaching the stimulus and attack the one that seems most straightforward first.

9. E

You know from the question stem that you're concerned with Theresa's method of argument, so when reading the dialogue between them, look specifically at how Theresa responds to Angie. Angie argues that if Bernard allows Pepe to sleep at the foot of his bed, Pepe's disciplinary problems will worsen. Theresa disagrees and believes that the same course of action will have the opposite outcome. Her evidence is Julian's dog: When Julian allowed his dog to sleep at the foot of his bed, the dog's disciplinary problems lessened. (E) accurately characterizes this method of argument: She indeed makes a prediction about Bernard's dog based on a similar situation with Julian's dog.

If you identify the evidence in the two statements, (A) won't be tempting. Angie doesn't really provide any evidence, and Theresa's evidence about Julian is uniquely her own. There's no reinterpretation here.

Eliminate (B): Theresa's recommendation is quite specific—let the dog sleep on the bed, and he'll behave better.

Angie might almost do (C), but Theresa doesn't discuss the difficulties that might arise from a plan. She only discusses the benefits that would likely result given a certain course of action.

Within Theresa's argument, the course of action (letting the dog sleep on the bed) remains the same. Her whole point is that the same course of action would likely have the same result, so (D) is wrong because it states that Theresa offered two different courses of action.

Remember: It's easiest to evaluate the difference between two statements in a dialogue stimulus by sticking to the basics: Identify each person's conclusion and evidence, and you'll be able to see what the second person reacts to and how that person goes about it. The two views presented are always different, so be systematic to see where that difference lies.

10. E

Start by looking for the author's assumption. The study shows that students remember a good deal of the specific material that they teach, and the principal concludes that the students should teach everything. However, that conclusion assumes that the students are actually capable of teaching every subject. (E) expresses this flaw, noting that the assumption may not be true and that small-scale student teaching may not work on a large scale.

(A) isn't a flaw, because the principal doesn't suggest that teaching is the only way to learn and will be the students' only occupation.

(B) is not part of the principal's proposal, which makes no mention of written assignments or learning through hearing. Not even the study itself, which does mention these forms of learning, suggests that the two are equally valuable.

Well, the argument certainly doesn't discuss (C), but because the argument has nothing to do with test scores, this consideration wouldn't be relevant to the argument. Thus, its omission isn't a flaw.

(D) doesn't state that the survey is wrong but that it's motivations might not be pure. Even if the survey were intensely self-interested, the principal is not concerned with its motivations but with its results. Her argument might be flawed if we knew she relied on results that were grossly inaccurate or results that she herself misinterpreted, but that's not what (D) says.

Remember: Flaw questions are common, and so are a number of specific flaws. Some of the most common flaws are *unwarranted assumptions, ignored alternative possibilities*, and *scope shifts* and *causation*. Use your practice to become familiar with each of these types of flaws.

11. D

The author supports one explanation for why the students at Carmine University are overwhelmed by their elective course options. As the stimulus begins, he describes the problem and offers two possible explanations for it: improper categorization and too much reading. The author then concludes that, since each individual description isn't so long as to exceed the boundaries of what students can absorb (possibility #1), the problem must be with the categorization (possibility #2). Not so fast. Sure, each individual description isn't too long, but isn't it possible that all of the descriptions together are too long? (D) points out this missing step. If all the descriptions together are too much to absorb, then perhaps possibility #1 is the correct explanation after all.

(A) would certainly strengthen the argument, explaining as it does why students would be overwhelmed as a result of improper categorization, but it's not an assumption. The right answer choice somehow needs to address how the author selected his preferred explanation, and (A) does not.

(B) would weaken the argument because it offers an alternative explanation, but this is also not our task. An assumption doesn't undermine the argument's conclusion.

(C), like (A), supports the idea that the courses aren't properly categorized, but it isn't a necessary component of the argument.

Our argument deals with course descriptions, which are "far less lengthy" than what students can absorb. (E) discusses "rather lengthy" descriptions, which aren't necessarily the same thing and, therefore, aren't necessarily relevant to the argument.

Remember: While filling in an assumption is one surefire way of strengthening an argument, something that strengthens an argument is not necessarily an assumption. Don't be tempted by choices such as (A) and (C), which do support the author's conclusion but don't support it by connecting it to the evidence, which any valid assumption must do.

12. B

The organizers claim only that the participants in the rally will bond and will, therefore, be less inclined to display aberrant behavior. They do not claim that the entire student body will be less inclined to act up. If the pep rally really will help to remedy the student behavior problem as its organizers say it will, then the students with behavior problems must attend the rally.

(B) states this assumption quite directly: Only if the students creating the problem go to the pep rally can they receive the positive effects of that rally and be discouraged from their unpalatable behavior.

If (A) were true, then the whole argument would be unnecessary. The argument proceeds from the assumption that the pep rally *is* included among the extracurricular activities to be canceled or else the coordinators wouldn't need to argue against its cancellation.

(C) is outside of the argument's scope. The pep rally organizers make no claims about the value of *other* extracurricular activities. Thus, they don't need to assume anything about those activities for their conclusion to be valid.

(D) is too extreme. The organizers conclude that the pep rally will help, but (D) represents a much stronger version of that conclusion (i.e., that the pep rally will help *more than anything else*).

(E) again brings in the consideration of other events and adds to that error by focusing on what the principal will do in the future. Nothing regarding what effect the rally will have on the principal's consideration of allowing future events is necessary for the argument to stand.

Remember: Choices that deviate from the specific scope of the argument in question in any major way cannot function as necessary assumptions for that argument. Neither the pep rally organizer's conclusion or evidence for that conclusion deal with any other canceled activities, so choices like (C) and (E) can be eliminated quickly.

13. A

When you start off with a statement of what "some individuals" believe, be ready for the author to explicitly or implicitly disagree with their opinion. These individuals believe that the cooking schools in southern France teach all that there is to know about French cooking. Nevertheless, one recent graduate of a cooking school in southern France did not know how to make the ever-popular bechamel sauce. The keyword *yet* clearly suggests the author's belief that this piece of evidence undermines the first stated conclusion. The question stem directs you to look for an inference, and at this point in the argument, you can see that the author doesn't actually make her own conclusion. She provides evidence that would weaken the first conclusion, thereby implying her own conclusion that cooking schools in southern France do not necessarily teach a student all that there is to know about French cooking. Since the author doesn't directly state her conclusion and this is an Inference question, the right answer choice will likely state that implied conclusion, as (A) indeed does. Since the author provides an exception to the first conclusion, then it must not always be true.

(B) is too extreme. All you know is that *one* graduate didn't know everything, so La Terrelle doesn't necessarily teach all that there is to know about French cooking. Still, some graduates could have learned everything.

(C) contradicts the stimulus, which clearly states that all of La Terrelle's branches are in southern France.

Eliminate (D): Just because La Terrelle may not teach all that there is to know about French cooking to every student, it might still provide an effective education. *Incomplete* does not mean *ineffective*.

Schools outside the region lie beyond the scope of this argument. So eliminate (E).

Remember: If a question stem directs you to look for an inference and you read the stimulus and see that the author doesn't actually state his or her conclusion, prephrase the conclusion and seek it among the answer choices. Whenever you can prephrase an answer, you're much more likely to find the correct choice quickly and correctly, so always look out for possibilities to use that tool.

14. A

Four assumptions in the answer choices? Be prepared to see a pretty weak argument. The author concludes that, to achieve maximum healthiness, these bats should be fed certain nuts, grubs and veggies and a minimum amount of fruits and berries. The evidence comes in the second sentence: These bats, who are now fed mostly fruits and berries, develop endocrine imbalances. There's clearly a causality problem here.

The author provides no evidence that the fruits and berries cause this endocrine imbalance, but the author must assume that is the case in order to have a valid conclusion. It's not worth the effort to try to prephrase all the assumptions you might find, but if a few ideas jumped out at you, great. At the very least, proceed to the answer choices with a clear understanding of the evidence and conclusion.

(A) is too extreme. The conclusion states that the bats will be fed a minimal amount of fruits and berries, while this choice says that they will eat none. Must that be a necessary part of this argument? No: The author says straight away that eating some fruits and berries is okay, so it need not be assumed that the bats are denied these foods altogether.

(B) and (D) are valid assumptions. If the proposed diet will make the bats "healthiest," then the argument assumes that it will adequately nourish them (D) and that it won't malnourish them (B). Negate these choices via the Kaplan Denial Test, and the argument falls apart, confirming that these are necessary assumptions here.

(C) is also valid. The author suggests that the bat's endocrine imbalance is a problem and that a revised diet might fix that problem. Thus, the argument does assume that bats should not be fed endocrine imbalance-producing foods.

(E) focuses again on the author's claim that the recommended diet will make the bats healthiest. If that is true, then the author must assume that it won't create any health problems that are more detrimental to the bats' health than the endocrine imbalances that inspired the proposed diet in the first place.

Remember: Read the answer choices carefully! Reading the stimulus carefully and strategically will certainly get you on the right path, but you still need to be able to notice minor inaccuracies in the answer choices, like the difference between "no" fruits and berries and "minimal" fruits and berries.

15. C

The author clearly identifies the source of the confusion when he mentions what puzzles anthropologists. They're perplexed by two facts that seem inconsistent with each other. First, the advent of writing in certain Comaquogue clans seems to have caused the disappearance of the master storytellers within those tribes. Nevertheless, the second fact is that modern illiterate Comaquogue clans also lack master storytellers. The basic question is: Why do these modern illiterate clans lack storytellers when earlier clans lost their storytellers only after they learned how to read? Look at the answer choices and find one that specifically answers this question.

(A) does nothing to explain why the modern illiterate clans lack storytellers. Personality similarities don't have any clear relationship to literacy and storytellers.

Eliminate (B): A comparison of the frequency of clan gatherings also does not in any way explain why the current illiterate tribes lack storytellers.

(C) would explain the discrepancy. If it were true, then the storytellers did disappear when the clans became literate, but the clans subsequently lost that literacy. Thus, the modern tribes could both be illiterate and lack storytellers, as is the case in the stimulus, if they lost their storytellers during an earlier literate period.

(D) again touches on the issue of modern Comaquogue rituals without referring to literacy and storytelling, the central elements of the argument's paradox.

(E) is too broad. It might give you the room to start making assumptions, but it doesn't specifically address the issues of literacy and storytelling.

Remember: Don't read too much into a choice to try to make it work. A choice has to be right without any help from you.

In Paradox questions, rephrase the paradox as a question and go through the answer choices trying to answer it. The temptation in these questions is to lose track of the paradox; hence, we have answer choices like (A), (B), (D), and (E). If you stay focused on the seeming discrepancy, you can avoid this trap.

16. B

The question stem tells us to focus on the dean's position, but the author gives us a good deal of background information before we hear about the dean. Apparently, Matthew's membership in a rock band has lowered his grades, which has hurt his chances of getting into a good business school. Matthew might be able to rock on, however, because extracurricular activities like his could compensate for the lower grades. Finally, we get to the dean, who will not allow Matthew's musical hobby to better his chances of getting into Wentworth Business School. Focusing on this last piece of information, let's look at the answer choices to find one that generalizes the dean's position.

(A) sounds extremely official and says relatively nothing that relates to this situation. What action does (A) refer to? If it's Matthew's rock playing, then "consequences" probably would have to be his lower grades. If the action is the dean's refusal, the consequences for Matthew may be that he won't get in. Either way, there's no way to relate any of this to an evaluation of the action in light of "possible" consequences of an "opposing alternative action."

(B) is entirely consistent with the dean's position and would, if true, support its validity. We were told that participating in the band has hurt Matthew's chances for admission, so if something (like playing in a band) can't simultaneously hurt and help an applicant, then it makes sense that the dean sees no way for the rock band to increase Matthew's chances of getting into business school. (B) would, therefore, justify the dean's view that the band can have no positive effect. If you had trouble seeing this, match up the general terms in the choice with the specifics of the original: The "cause" is playing in the band; the "condition" is lower grades; the "consequence of that condition" is a lowered chance of admission. The dean simply refuses to allow Matthew's playing in the band to mitigate against the lower grades that resulted from his playing in the band.

(C) is inconsistent with the dean's position, since she is not stressing the positive value of Matthew's activities over their negative results. Rather, she sees no positive value in Matthew's musical activities.

(D) is irrelevant. Even if we argued that the dean's refusal is a decision that could affect Matthew's future, we have no idea how many factors go into admitting someone to business school and whether this particular dean has considered them all or missed a few.

(E), like (D), is irrelevant, because the candidate is never eliminated from consideration. The dean won't give him credit for playing in the band, but that doesn't mean that she's tossed out his application.

Remember: For Principle questions, the answer will contain the elements of the relevant portion of the stimulus rephrased and generalized but otherwise not significantly altered.

17. B

The two viruses clearly cause one problem: They mess up the file storage system, usually by putting the files in the wrong places. The author concludes that computer users who detect one or both of these viruses needn't worry about the destruction of their files, based on the evidence that there is no proof that either virus erases files entirely. Do you see the flaw? The author's evidence is basically that there is no evidence to suggest that files will be erased. Nevertheless, just because there's no proof that either virus destroys files, that doesn't mean that the viruses don't destroy files. (B) expresses this flaw; according to the argument, it is still entirely possible that the viruses destroy files, even though there is "at present" no evidence that they do.

(A) is outside the scope. The issue is whether the viruses pose a threat to files, not whether people believe that they do.

The author certainly doesn't discuss (C) but that doesn't constitute a flaw in the argument. A discussion about the mechanism of file erasure wouldn't be relevant to the conclusion, so its omission is not a flaw.

(D) suggests that a keyword has more than one definition in the argument, which is not the case.

(E) describes a circular argument, which exists when the evidence and the conclusion are the same. In this argument, the two are clearly different, and the extent of their difference is part of the real flaw.

Remember: The three most common types of flaws are unwarranted assumptions, unconsidered alternative possibilities, and scope shifts. This question gives us an example of the second type.

18. D

This Parallel Reasoning question lends itself well to algebraic characterization. The question stem itself gives us some critical information: We're told that the argument in the stimulus is flawed and that we're looking for an answer choice that is flawed in a similar manner. If foods aren't stored properly, they can give people food poisoning (if X, then possibly Y). Since people at the Panhandler got food poisoning, the restaurant must have served food that wasn't properly stored (Y, therefore X). This argument makes the mistake of concluding that a "reverse cause and effect" relationship is operating: Because the consequence occurred, the cause must have been in effect also. We know from formal logic that we simply can't get from "if X, then Y" to "if Y, then X." So all we need to do is find the choice that commits the same error. There's of course no way to prephrase the specifics of the right choice, only its structure, so the best bet is simply to work through the choices:

(A) tells us that if a man over 65 has high blood pressure, he is at risk for heart disease (if X, then Y). That has the first part of the argument right. But the second sentence tells us that Tonare males over 65 do not have blood pressure, so they are not at risk for heart disease—which translates into not X, therefore not Y. This conclusion simply negates the terms without switching them as in the original.

(B) and (C) can both be eliminated because neither of them presents a "reverse cause and effect" argument; in fact, neither contains anything that can be translated into a formal logic if/then statement. (B) contains a temporal flaw; for all we know, Magelli might have crafted the cabinet before he died. We would need information that the cabinet is less than 15 years old before the conclusion would be valid. (C)'s conclusion is certainly premature as well, but again, it does not contain the same formal logic structure as the original; there's nothing in there that can be translated into "if X, then Y."

(D) contains the kind of flaw we seek. This choice states that Relief-O! has been known to cause blurred vision in people who take it. We can translate that sentence as: "If people take Relief-O, they may experience blurred vision," (if X, then possibly Y). So far so good. The following sentences then tell us that Molly took a pain reliever and experienced blurred vision (Y), so she must have taken Relief-O! (therefore X). Perfect.

(E) deals with cause and effect but not in the same manner as in the stimulus. (E) lays out an initial cause: If tigermint grows out of control, it can kill other plants (if X, then Y). But its second sentence introduces a negative condition: Sally's plants did not get killed—in fact, they look better than ever. Therefore, the tigermint must not be out of control. This reduces to not Y, therefore not X—and not parallel.

19. D

When you see percents or ratios in a stimulus, you'll likely need to exercise your ability to distinguish between rates and numbers. This is an Inference question, as the stem makes clear, and you can prephrase an answer by considering what conclusion this evidence would support. If 57 percent equals the same number of paintings before the unveiling as 85 percent equals after the unveiling, then Déjère must have produced more paintings in the period before the unveiling—that's the only way that the numbers could work out. (D) states this from the other angle: Déjère must have painted fewer paintings after the unveiling.

The author tells us that revenue from both periods is equal because Déjère sells the same number of paintings in both. Therefore, if she had charged more in the second period, she would have made more money than she had in the first, which would contradict the stimulus. Because this is inconsistent with the passage, it certainly can't be inferred from it and you can eliminate (A).

(B) is outside of the scope because the author never mentions Déjère's motivations behind painting. Since there's no information about this, we can't reasonably conclude anything pertaining to it.

If anything, (C) might suggest that Déjère sells more paintings in the second period, which the stimulus explicitly contradicts. Further, the stimulus provides no information about how art collectors might have responded to the review, giving us no basis to make a conclusion about those collectors.

(E) would also act to explain why her sales are higher in the second period, but the author says that the sales were not any greater. Also, marketing is never discussed.

Remember: Percentages show up often in Logical Reasoning sections; make sure you're comfortable analyzing such data. Sometimes the difference between percentages and raw numbers forms the basis of a logical flaw. Other times, as is the case here, you'll simply need to understand what the percentages represent to draw an inference from the data.

20. B

Considering then the structure of the argument, the author states that something (the consumption of dairy products) doesn't usually create a certain result (stomachaches) and then concludes that something that might explain a causal relationship between the two (allergies) doesn't exist. In other words, if a causal relationship isn't usually present, then an explanation isn't present. Looking for another choice that demonstrates the same structure, we can hold onto (B): Exercise doesn't usually create a problem with sleeping for Ella, so we shouldn't believe it's the cause.

(A) is wrong because the conclusion argues *for* a correlation, while the stimulus argues against a correlation between two occurrences.

Eliminate: (C) The element of something occurring sometimes— but not all of the time—is missing here.

(D) presents an entirely different argument, arguing that a claim isn't valid because there isn't enough evidence to support it. The original argument says that a claim isn't valid because two factors usually aren't related. The notion of "validity," like "efficacy" in (C), is one step removed from the gist of the terms in the original argument.

(E) argues against a causal relationship, but it doesn't parallel the original evidence because it mentions what "many" businesses do, not what "most" do. More centrally, the conclusion veers away from the evidence: The evidence suggests that decentralized operations often yield a profit, while the conclusion suggests that the two aren't directly related. In the original, both the evidence and conclusion argue against a causal relationship.

Remember: It's often difficult to remember several pieces of information in your head without getting them mixed up, especially while you're evaluating five new pieces of information. Don't hesitate to make notes if they'll help keep you on track.

21.   D

The argument begins by offering one route through which a student can gain a coveted membership to the Theta Delta Psi fraternity. For those aspirants who attended high school with a current member of the house and developed a strong social connection with that member before college, entrance into the fraternity is easy. People who didn't attend high school with a current member can't easily attain membership through this route, but we are never told that this is the only easy way to get into the fraternity. The author concludes that the unconnected individuals will have difficulty joining the fraternity, but that's only valid if the route the author describes is the only possible easy route. But the author never says that. (D) thus gets at the major point the author fails to consider in issuing

her hasty conclusion: the possibility that there might be other easy ways to get into the frat.

You can eliminate. (A) First of all, those who attended high school with fraternity members are not necessarily the same people who have forged strong social connections with them. So the "many" referred to here may not even be relevant to the argument. Secondly, even assuming these guys *are* good high school buddies of the members, the author argues only about what conditions make for easy entry into the frat and need not consider the possibility that many high school classmates of the members would choose not to join.

(B) is irrelevant. Associations with non–fraternity members are not relevant to the argument and fall outside of its scope. Additionally, this choice discusses the long-term benefits of such connections; we only care about entrance into the fraternity, not about lifelong happiness.

The relative difficulty of building these connections has nothing to do with their necessity for membership. (C) also shares with (B) an interest in non–fraternity members, whom the author never mentions.

(E) is perfectly consistent with the author's argument, as it totally avoids the issue of the ease with which these "current members" got in. This choice falls outside of the author's scope, which is about the possibility of getting into the fraternity with ease, and we therefore can't fault the author for neglecting the possibility raised here.

Remember: Pay attention to author's topic and scope. Notice that answer choice (D) is the only one to address the difficulties of obtaining membership; most of the others fell outside of that scope.

22.   C

Again, the stimulus begins with the author's conclusion, which basically opposes the continued enforcement of the new farm subsidy laws. The author stipulates the advantages of the laws but nevertheless stresses their negative long-term results. The question stem directs you to determine the role of the second part of that second sentence, the part that discusses the negative effects of the laws. Before looking at the answer choices, it's possible to determine that this is evidence for the author's conclusion—it answers the question "Why do you oppose the continuation of the laws?" Correct choice (C) goes one step further: It shows more specifically how the statement functions as evidence. The author discusses the negative effects to counter the positive effects, which enables him to support his conclusion that the laws should be ditched.

Don't be thrown by the presence of the word *evidence* in (A). First, the author doesn't tell us that the positive effects of the laws have been used as evidence to support them. Second, the author doesn't use the negative effects to argue that the laws *haven't* enabled farmers to maintain their incomes or stabilized the market; he concedes those points but stresses that the negative effects outweigh those benefits.

(B) commits the same error as (A). It distorts the passage by suggesting that the author contradicts and discredits the benefits of the laws, but he acknowledges that they have stabilized the agricultural market. The author doesn't disagree with that statement but places it in the context of what he sees as the more serious negative effects.

(D) is way too strong: The author cannot "prove" that without the laws, agricultural technology will remain a high priority simply by stating that the laws discourage the need for competitive advancements. At most, the author suggests that in the absence of the laws, the opportunities for tech advances may improve, but that's far from "proving" anything.

(E) is half right and half wrong. It starts off on very strong footing by defining the statement as evidence, but it quickly takes a nosedive by making an irrelevant distinction between market stabilization and the development of competitive technology. The author does suggest that the negative effects of the laws outweigh the positive effects, and the author does mention these issues, but the author doesn't specifically rank one against the other. He shows that both of the negative effects outweigh both of the positive effects; he doesn't compare them piece by piece.

Remember: Be very careful when perusing the answer choices. Here, choices (A) and (E) use the word *evidence*, a sure temptation for those test takers who don't examine the answer choices carefully. (C) doesn't use the term *evidence* but basically defines what evidence is in the context of the passage. Even when you have a prephrase, remember to look at the answer choices carefully and not jump at the first one containing a term you had in mind.

23. D

Just because the organizers didn't give a complete list to everybody, it doesn't follow that they gave more complete lists to some people than others. You can use your formal logic skills on this one: We were originally told that if people are fully informed, then nobody has an advantage. It doesn't follow that if people are not fully informed, then somebody does have an advantage. That's a common formal logic error, and since the author commits it, the right answer choice will likely identify this as the flaw in the argument. (D) accomplishes this by stating what still could be true given the argument: Everyone could have received the same incomplete list. In concluding categorically that some lucky participant has a leg up on the others, the author doesn't allow for the possibility stated in (D).

Probably the easiest way to eliminate (A) is to recognize that the author discusses who has the best *chance* of finding the diamond ring. The author never suggests that having a better chance of finding the ring means actually finding the ring. If the author had made such a suggestion, it would be a flaw, but since the author never did, it isn't. (E) takes this issue from another angle by suggesting that people with incomplete lists might still find the ring. The author never suggests otherwise, since again the author solely discusses who has the best chance of finding the ring, not who will actually find it. So while (A) and (E) are indeed consistent with the stimulus, they don't point to a logical flaw in the argument.

(B) is tempting, but if many people have incomplete lists, it's still possible that no one has additional information that would give an advantage.

(C) just states one possible consequence of handing out different lists. The scenario in (C) is consistent with the facts in the stimulus, so it's okay on that count, but like (B), (C) still allows for the possibility that some person has a better chance than others, as the author maintains.

Remember: Reading critically means noticing small shifts in scope between the information in the passage and the focus of the choices. The author here is concerned with the participants' relative chances of finding the diamond. Choices like (A) and (E) that center around actually locating the ring are one step removed from this focus, so they aren't likely to point out a flaw in the logic.

24. E

The stem tells us that the teacher will make some error in her response to the judges' decision, so we can read knowing that we'll see at least two arguments and that the teacher's will be flawed. The judges decided to disqualify Samuel's essay from the contest only because he broke one rule: He put his name on every page of the essay when the rules required that he put it only on the cover page. Samuel's teacher disagrees with the judges' conclusion, but in her argument, she doesn't address the judges' reason for disqualifying him. She completely ignores the judges' evidence and introduces a new issue as her evidence: She believes that the personal problems in Samuel's life entitle him to have his essay considered in the contest. Her argument is flawed because she neglects to discuss the judges' reasoning and, thus, doesn't address the judges' argument. While the emotional appeal may work on *Oprah*, in the world of argumentation, it's a flaw to disagree with a conclusion without disputing the link between it and the evidence offered to justify it.

You can eliminate (A): The teacher does offer evidence when she explains that Samuel's essay deserves another chance because his parents got a divorce. Weak or irrelevant evidence is not the same as no evidence.

(B) is incorrect: The teacher doesn't make a causal argument. She thinks that personal considerations

should override the judges' decision, but she isn't concerned with whether one thing causes another.

(C) is out because the teacher doesn't address *any part* of the judges' argument, which is the real flaw. She merely disputes their action on grounds entirely divorced (so to speak) from their argument in support of that action.

(D) again suggests that the teacher actually addresses the judges' evidence justifying their decision. She doesn't.

Remember: To see where two arguments differ, compare their conclusions and their evidence. Here, the conclusions were different and the evidence was different in the two arguments, so right off the bat you could eliminate (A), (C), and (D). The more structured you are in the way in which you compare two arguments, the easier it'll be to see where one differs or goes awry.

25. A

The author begins by concluding that cross-training is more beneficial than single-sport training for those who wish to improve their overall fitness. The author presents two pieces of evidence to support this opinion: First, cross-training develops a wider range of muscle groups. Second, cross-training increases phasic muscle fibers, which burn more calories. Can you see any gaps (aka assumptions) between the conclusion and the evidence? The author assumes a link between developing a wide range of muscles/burning calories and overall fitness, so we can check to see if any answer choice strengthens the argument by asserting that assumption. We can stop at choice (A), since it establishes the connection between burning calories and overall fitness.

The fact that athletic training *in general* is the best way to improve overall fitness doesn't strengthen an argument that one kind of athletic training (cross-training) is better for fitness than another (single-sport training). So eliminate (B).

(C) is 180. This would actually weaken the argument. Tonic muscle fibers are exercised by single-sport training, so increasing their value would weaken the author's argument in support of cross-training.

(D) falls outside the scope: The author solely addresses which type of training works better to improve overall fitness in healthy individuals, so the danger of one type of training for those recovering from serious illness cannot have any bearing on the argument.

It might appear that (E) actually weakens the argument. Single-sport training targets slow-twitch muscle groups. If that exercise simultaneously exercises phasic muscle groups, then it provides one of the benefits of cross-training. Therefore, (E) would increase the value of single-sport training in achieving *overall fitness*, which would run counter to the conclusion. But the fact that slow-twitch muscles contain many phasic muscle fibers doesn't necessarily mean that single-sport training would increase these fibers; that's still up in the air. So the best thing to say about (E) is that it is too ambiguous to have any effect on the argument.

Remember: Whenever you see a central term that is unique to the conclusion, you're one step closer to prephrasing an author's assumption. Here, the conclusion contains a phrase—*overall fitness*—that shows up nowhere else in the argument. Because an assumption connects the evidence to the conclusion, it will make the evidence relevant to the dangling term in the conclusion. Specifically, developing a wide range of muscles and burning calories must lead to increased overall fitness if this argument is going to stand.

SECTION IV: READING COMPREHENSION

Passage 1—Frankenstein
Topic and Scope
Mary Shelley's novel *Frankenstein*; specifically, the great philosophical import of the book as compared to subsequent visual adaptations of it

Purpose and Main Idea
The author's purpose in writing this passage is to demonstrate the complexities of Mary Shelley's *Frankenstein* and to argue for an appreciation of the novel on its own terms, apart from film adaptations of it. The main idea is that cinematic versions of the story of Frankenstein are actually based on a complex and compelling novel, the richness of which cannot be fully captured on film but nonetheless should not be overlooked.

Paragraph Structure
The first paragraph immediately contrasts the aura that the Frankenstein monster has taken on in popular culture with the thematic purpose known to serious readers of the book; that is, to caution readers against the dangers of scientific hubris.

Paragraph 2 explains that the idea for the story came from a dream that Shelley had. The story is intended to refute the attacks of science on nature. It shows the negative consequences of not using our society's scientific capabilities responsibly.

In paragraph 3, we're told that the current appeal of the book is based on the many timeless themes that it contains, themes that have "only grown in importance" since its first publication. The full essence of the book cannot be captured by cinema, and the author hopes that film adaptations will not make people forget the book's richness.

1. D
This is a broad Inference question that asks us to choose the statement with which the author would most likely agree. Such an open-ended question is too difficult to prephrase, so the best approach is

to evaluate the choices. Choice (D) fits well with paragraph 3: The author tells us that the enduring appeal of Shelley's book is attributable to the relevance of themes that she raises. The author would thus likely agree that a work's relevance in general increases when its elements resonate with its current audience.

(A) is an exaggeration of the author's claim that visual adaptations have thus far not adequately captured the richness of Shelley's book. He believes this about film adaptations of *Frankenstein* but doesn't apply his claim to every artistic work.

(B) also misrepresents the author's argument. Shelley published her work anonymously because it was not acceptable at the time for women to write such "ghastly" stories. The author never suggests that every shocking work should be published anonymously.

Both (C) and (E) distort elements of the passage. As for (C), the author never addresses works that receive no critical acclaim when they are written. We're not sure, in fact, how Shelley's work was originally received; all we know is that it was too risqué at first to attach a woman's name to it. Further, the author never draws a relationship between the seriousness of a work and its ability to predict the future. Just because Shelley's work was both serious and prophetic doesn't allow us to infer the blanket statement in (E).

Remember: Wrong answer choices to Inference questions follow predictable patterns. Two of those patterns are represented in this question: extreme choices and distortions. Pay attention to the types of wrong answer choices that appear repeatedly and be prepared to avoid them on test day.

2.   E

This Detail question is signaled by the words "according to the author," which lets us know that the answer will come straight from the text. A line reference is given to make our work easier. This question doesn't seem tricky, but it turns out that the science-nature clash is mentioned in another place after the notion is introduced in the second paragraph—namely, in paragraph 3. Here the author tells us that the science

versus nature conflict increases the book's current relevance, an almost exact paraphrase of choice (E).

(A) is half right, half wrong. The science-nature clash is one of the factors responsible for the current appeal of the book itself, not its film versions.

(B) exaggerates the author's argument. The author merely suggests that movies are unable to portray the "science versus nature" theme in all its "seriousness and complexity." He never argues that the movie versions don't portray this central theme at all.

Here the issue of Shelley's anonymous publishing is again raised in (C) but, again, in an inappropriate context. We saw in choice (B) of the previous question that she published the book anonymously because society wasn't ready to accept women writing "ghastly" works. The science-nature clash itself doesn't seem to be the problem; the way in which that clash is *developed* (via the "ghastly" horror story device) is the reason she went underground for awhile.

(D) is 180: Paragraph 3 tells us that the science-nature clash is one of the themes of the work that has "grown in importance" since Shelley's day.

Remember: Keep an open mind concerning line reference questions and avoid focusing too narrowly. The correct answer will likely involve reading beyond the referenced line and may often involve connecting the reference to other relevant parts of the text.

3.   B

If we read the portion of paragraph 3 that discusses the currently relevant themes of the work, we see that all of the choices are listed except for choice (B). If this *Frankenstein* example is any indication, we'd have to say that the author's complaint suggests the opposite of (B), namely that appreciation for artistic seriousness and complexity is waning.

(A) is covered by the phrase "technology as man's salvation."

The theme in (C) comes up many times throughout the passage. Most relevant to this question is its appearance in the final paragraph as "science versus nature."

(D) is raised with "the role of visual appearance in society."

(E) is captured in the phrase "alienation of the outcast."

Remember: As always, watch the EXCEPT questions carefully. Be sure to choose the answer that is *not* implied or stated in the text. Sometimes the correct choice will simply be outside the scope. Other times, as is the case here, it may even go against the grain of the sentiments in the passage.

4.   C

This question addresses the author's attitude. To answer it, we should first determine whether the author's views on this issue are positive or negative. The wording of paragraph 1 gives us a clue: "endless Hollywood adaptations…campy TV shows…" Sounds like the author's not so hot on the visual adaptations, right? This is confirmed of course by the phrase in the final paragraph, "inability to capture in cinematic form the deep philosophical richness of the book." So this negativity kills (A) and (D) immediately. But just how negative are his views? Somewhat negative, although not drastic enough to say he displays "biting derision" (B) or "unreserved condescension" (E). We're therefore left with the more moderate (C).

Remember: Use the Kaplan strategy to make "attitude/ tone" questions easy to handle. Determine first whether the author's views are positive, negative, or neutral—then eliminate all of the choices that don't conform to the general category you choose. If you determine the views are somewhat negative, as is the case here, then look to cross off any choices that contain any positivity. Then weed out any exaggerations or choices that are too weak, and you should be left with the correct answer.

5.   A

This question tests whether you understand one part of the passage in the context of the overall argument. Why does the author mention Hollywood film adaptations early on in paragraph 1? As we see from paragraph 3,

he will argue eventually that film versions can't capture the depth of Shelley's original work. Citing film versions in paragraph 1 is, therefore, a means of setting up what will be the main idea, or as (A) describes it, the "basis of the author's central concern." The author certainly does return to this concept when developing the main idea in paragraph 3, so that part of the choice is accurate. But does the whole choice work? Is the example of film adaptations provided as a "contrast," as choice (A) would have it? Yes—the "endless" Hollywood adaptations, along with the other pop culture manifestations, are meant to stand in contrast to the philosophical and prophetic cautionary tale that spawned them. This contrast will build in paragraph 3 when it indeed "resurfaces" as the basis of the author's concern that the visual forms may one day eclipse the genius of the original work.

The author doesn't raise a debate, much less try to settle one. You can eliminate (A).

The author does support Shelley's work but doesn't deal with criticisms of it. No such criticisms appear in the passage. So eliminate (C).

(D) is 180. The author would not see film adaptations as an "inevitable successor" to literature. In fact, he believes that in this case, film cannot portray the literary work effectively.

(E) is both too general and exaggerated. The author doesn't describe Hollywood adaptations as part of a larger "artistic movement." Neither does he make the sweeping claim that film can *never* capture literary works well. He just doesn't believe that film versions of *Frankenstein* do justice to the original book.

Remember: Reading with a critical eye towards purpose and structure will always pay off in Reading Comp. When you encounter new characters or material, ask yourself, "Why are they here? What function do they serve?" When you come to a question like this one, prephrase an answer or at least eliminate a handful of wrong choices based on your initial understanding of the purpose of each element of the passage.

6. A

This question asks us for the author's purpose in writing the passage, so think about what you've been focusing on all along. We've seen how the author's purpose is to lay out the complexities of Shelley's work and to argue that it should be appreciated on its own terms and that the film versions should not overshadow the original story. The closest we get to this prephrase is found in choice (A), which is a bit more general than our prephrase but hits closest to the mark.

(B) and (E) are too broad. The problem with (B) is that the author does not discuss "works of art" in general but rather one work in particular. Similarly, with (E), the author does not pay tribute to the "art form" of literature in general; instead, he is praising one specific work of literature. Moreover, according to the author, this work has not yet *been* overshadowed but rather is in danger of being overshadowed by its visual adaptations.

(C) is too narrow. The author does discuss how Shelley's novel originated, but this is only a small part of what he does in the text.

Be careful with (D): This is the argument that Shelley makes in her novel, not the argument made by the author in the passage as a whole.

Remember: Choices like (D) reinforce why we must be careful to distinguish between the various views presented in a passage. Here we have an author of a passage presenting the views expressed by an author described in the passage. Make sure to keep the various views straight, and you won't be tempted by a choice like (D).

When answering Global questions, be on the lookout for choices that are overly broad or too narrow. The correct answer to a Global question will match the author's scope in the passage and will reflect the point of the passage as a whole—not just one part of it.

PASSAGE 2—WEBER AND OBJECTIVITY

Topic and Scope

Max Weber's views on objectivity; specifically, the degree to which Weber upholds a strict concept of objectivity in his work

Purpose and Main Idea

The author's purpose is to make an argument regarding how Weber views the concept of objectivity and employs it in his writing. The main idea is that Weber does not believe in strict objectivity across the board and that his views on objectivity are, therefore, more complex than they are traditionally portrayed.

Paragraph Structure

The first paragraph of this passage presents the "traditional" or conventional explanation of Weber's views: Scholars normally see him as upholding a strict concept of objectivity in his work. Whenever we're presented with a traditional view in the opening paragraph, it's a good bet that the author will counter or refute that view in what's to follow. This paragraph is no exception—sure enough, the author quickly counters the traditional interpretation by asserting that Weber's views are "more complicated" than the traditional view would have it.

Given this starting point, we might expect the following paragraphs to show us how and why Weber's views are complicated. This is exactly what happens. Paragraph 2 concedes that in certain respects, Weber does believe in the possibility of strict objectivity: We see it in his views on the nature of reality. When it comes to questions of truth, Weber does believe that a value-neutral reality exists.

In paragraph 3, however, the complexities of Weber's views are introduced. Here the author shows that Weber doesn't think our knowledge of reality can be totally objective. This is because knowledge is rooted in the assumptions and perspectives of those who investigate reality. Thus, some subjective bias enters in.

Paragraph 4 shows that Weber deviates most from strict objectivity on questions concerning ethics. When people use knowledge to decide how to behave, Weber thinks they should make their decisions subjectively, according to their personal biases. So as the passage progresses, so does Weber's deviation from the strict concept of objectivity "traditionally" ascribed to him.

7. D

This question asks the main idea of the passage, and in this case, the author presents an argument against a traditional view. Her opposing argument, or main idea, is laid out at the end of the first paragraph, where she tells us that Weber's views on objectivity are "more complicated than the traditional interpretation would have us believe." Choice (D) sums this up nicely.

(A) goes beyond the scope of the passage. Nowhere are other theories of objectivity discussed— the passage focuses only on Weber's views.

(B) contradicts what is stated in the passage. Paragraph 2 shows us that Weber upholds a strictly objective view concerning the nature of reality; he believes in the existence of an absolute truth. It is in our attempt to *investigate* objective reality that Weber believes subjectivity creeps in.

(C) and (E) are distortions of information in the passage. While the author argues that Weber's views on objectivity are complex, she never claims that these views are not clearly presented (C). Neither does she go so far as to claim that they are inconsistent (E).

Remember: If you focus on the author's purpose and main idea as you read, this type of question should be a snap. If you relate all of the content in the passage to the main idea as you read, you should be able to prephrase answers to questions like this one accurately.

8. A

It's difficult to prephrase an answer to such an open-ended Inference question as this, so we must proceed to the choices to see which view can be most readily ascribed to Weber. Luckily, we don't have to look far: (A) presents a good summary of Weber's views on scientific knowledge as presented in paragraph 3.

Here we learn that Weber believes that knowledge cannot be totally objective because it is influenced by the assumptions and perspectives of the particular scientific community involved in the investigation of reality.

(B) and (E) misrepresent Weber's use of "ideal types." Ideal types are presented in paragraph 2 as constructs that Weber believes can help scientists investigate reality, not their own biases regarding reality (B). And (E) goes way too far: Just because Weber believes that ideal types can be used to help the scientist investigate objective reality, that's far from saying that he believes this is "the *only* reliable method" possible.

In paragraph 4, we're told that Weber believes that teachers should refrain from imposing their views on students *period*—regardless of how capable those students are. So you can eliminate (C).

The fact that Weber believes that the *perception* of objective reality must be tinged by subjectivity doesn't mean that Weber finds the notion of objective reality itself "misleading". On the contrary, paragraph 2 tells us that Weber does believe in the existence of strict objective reality. So (D) is incorrect.

Remember: Inference questions are usually not easy to prephrase, so the best approach to these questions is to quickly evaluate each answer choice. A good Road Map can help you determine whether a given choice fits with the ideas in the passage.

9. B

This question would have been a good one to prephrase, particularly if you looked for the author's purpose and main idea as you read the passage. Since this passage focuses only on Weber, the correct answer will indicate that one author's views are discussed. (B) throws in the key word *complexities*, describing the author's purpose succinctly.

It can be said that the author enters into a debate by countering the traditional view of Weber's scholarship, but that's not the same as "resolving" a debate. If (A) were the intended right answer, two independent views would have to be presented, with the author choosing one over the other. Similarly, she does not "reconcile" opposing perspectives (C). She merely develops her own position regarding Weber's views.

The author does not argue against Weber's perspective but rather describes it for the reader. So eliminate (D).

The author presents Weber's views but does not *test* them as (E) suggests. Furthermore, Weber's views represent his position on objectivity, but they do not take the form of a formal hypothesis.

Remember: Reading for topic, scope, and purpose has many benefits. Not only does it allow you to gain a better grasp of the passage overall, it can also lead to quick points if you're handed a straightforward Global question like this one.

10.   C

The phrase "according to the passage" here clues us in that this is a Detail question; we can thus expect the answer to draw on a specific detail from the passage. Which paragraph discusses how individuals should use knowledge to guide their actions? Exactly—paragraph 4.

A good road map would have quickly led you to this part of the passage, and the phrase "free to choose how he or she acts upon the reality discovered by science" is the one that best captures the gist of Weber's position regarding the uses of scientific knowledge. Choice (C) stands out as the best paraphrase of this.

(A) distorts the author's meaning in the passage. Paragraph 4 tells us that teachers should help students account for the meaning of their own conduct. It does not tell us that students should be restricted from making decisions if they cannot account for the meaning of their conduct.

Eliminate (B): According to paragraph 4, Weber believes that individuals should use scientific knowledge in making decisions about action, not that they should distrust it.

(D) is 180: We are told that Weber believed that teachers should not guide their students' actions but should allow students to make their own decisions.

(E) also goes against the grain of the passage. "Weber believes that individuals must make their own

decisions…" suggests that teachers should *not* follow the lead of their students but should also act on knowledge independently when determining their own course of action.

Remember: Explicit Text questions can often be answered by referring back to the part of the passage that contains the detail in question. If you must quickly reread the relevant parts of the paragraph to make your selection, do so.

11.   E

Next up we're asked for the passage structure, and hopefully your work on the passage so far will help you prephrase an answer or at least quickly eliminate choices that stray beyond your Road Map. We know from our answer to question 9 that only one author's views (Weber's) are presented here, and our Road Map tells us that different aspects of these views are described in each paragraph. This fits with the gist of choice (E): The "interpretation" expands on the traditional position regarding Weber's view of objectivity, and the author certainly does support this interpretation throughout the passage with specific references to Weber's views and teachings.

The author spends her time in this passage developing Weber's views. She does not reject his views as (A) indicates, nor does she first criticize these views as (B) states.

(C) is 180. As we saw with choice (A), the author does not negate Weber's views. Instead, she supports them.

(D) tries the same trick we saw in (E) in question 9. We know that no hypothesis is presented here and that no testing is accomplished, so we can reject this choice.

Remember: The choices in "passage structure" questions are often phrased in general terms. The wrong answer choices will contain terms such as "reject" and "criticize" that violate the spirit of the passage and others such as "hypothesis" and "empirical testing" that sound nice and official but don't apply to the passage at all. Put the choices through their paces before settling on the one you prefer.

12. A

Our road map can again come in handy here by helping us locate the assertion that "knowledge of reality cannot be totally objective." A quick review shows us that this point is raised in paragraph 3, where the author discusses scientific knowledge. This Detail question asks for evidence specifically mentioned in the passage that supports the assertion in the stem, and again we return to the same idea that we've discussed previously: The interpretation of objective reality is biased by underlying assumptions. (A) speaks to this with its reference to "subjective biases."

(B) reflects the opposite of what is stated in the passage. The author claims that Weber believes that methods of investigation can never be strictly objective by their very nature.

(C) and (D) present ideas raised in the passage, but neither of these statements reflects evidence for the assertion in question. Ideal types are discussed in the passage but only in paragraph 2. We're looking for evidence given in paragraph 3. The definition of "objective truth" is also raised in paragraph 2 but not as evidence for the point that knowledge can't be objective.

(E) once again plays off the distinction between objective reality and the *knowledge* of objective reality. Weber does believe in the concept of strict objectivity, so to say that objective reality is "illusory" goes against the grain of the passage, and it can't be evidence for something else in the passage.

Remember: When asked about specific details, make sure to locate the part of the text from which the relevant details will be drawn. Then stick strictly to the author's argument. If you're asked for evidence, choose only the choice that provides support for the point or conclusion in question. Avoid choices taken from other parts of the text.

13. C

Why would the author have given us the "traditional" interpretation of Weber's view? To let us know which view she was reacting against—to provide an introduction into her opposing interpretation of his views. Choice (C) describes this reason well.

(A) is an exaggeration. Although the author rejects the traditional view, it would be going too far to say that she "dismiss[es] the relevance of all previous scholarship" on Weber.

(B) again distorts the author's purpose. She does not argue that objectivity has been historically misunderstood in general but rather that Weber's views on objectivity have been misunderstood.

(D) and (E) state the opposite of the author's reason for presenting the traditional view. She does not use it to develop critics' views of Weber but rather her own interpretation. Neither does she attempt to vindicate the traditional view; on the contrary, she refutes it.

Remember: Questions that end with the words "in order to" require you to look for how something functions to support the author's overall argument or purpose in the passage. When you're asked why an author includes something, think about the entire passage. What role is played by the part in question?

How does it contribute to the passage? Some parts of the text may provide support or evidence; others may lay out the author's conclusions; still others may serve as introductions or as background information. Focus on how the part in question fits within the whole.

PASSAGE 3—MURPHY'S LAW

Topic and Scope:

Morality; specifically, the pros and cons of Liam Murphy's views on morality

Purpose and Main Idea

The purpose of the passage is to assess the value of Murphy's view. The main idea is that Murphy's argument may lack motivating force for those who don't have an inner sense of morality, but it also avoids having to justify the content of particular moral principles and is more practical than traditional views.

Paragraph Structure

Paragraph 1 introduces us to the "overdemandingness" problem in moral philosophy. If we define morality as requiring us to always act to produce the best circumstances, then morality may seem to ask too much of people. Paragraph 2 tells us that some people reject the idea that morality is overdemanding. The philosopher Liam Murphy, however, takes the "overdemandingness" problem seriously.

In paragraph 3, Murphy's philosophy is described. Murphy doesn't give people a set of firm beliefs or particular moral principles. Instead, he argues that each person should make moral decisions based first upon his or her own inner sense of right and wrong. If a person's inner sense of right and wrong is confused, the person can then use his or her reason to make the final decision.

Paragraph 4 lists the disadvantages of Murphy's view. The main disadvantage is that people who have no moral foundation aren't likely to get one through his approach. Paragraph 5 then gives the advantages of Murphy's perspective. Murphy's view starts with the individual's own inner sense of morality, so it doesn't have to go through the difficult task of justifying specific moral principles. This view ends up being more practical than traditional approaches.

14.   E

Here's a case where the first question of the set is a good question to answer first. This overall purpose question is a good one to prephrase based on your road map. The author's purpose, which we determined earlier, is "to assess the value of Murphy's view." This answer is summed up well in choice (E), because the author is evaluating the merits of Murphy's model of ethical inquiry.

(A) is too narrow. The author does discuss the disadvantages of Murphy's view but only in one paragraph. The answer to a primary purpose question must apply to the entire passage, not just one part.

(B) and (C) are incorrect because they suggest that two views are addressed in the passage. Choice (B) suggests

that two theories are discussed, whereas choice (C) suggests that two schools of thought are reviewed. In fact, only one view— Murphy's—is developed in the passage.

The author does not pose a solution to an ethical problem. So eliminate (D).

Remember: Prephrasing is a good strategy for answering questions rapidly and correctly. If you can prephrase an answer, do so before looking at the answer choices. A quick scan of the choices will tell you whether your prephrase is on target.

15.   B

Here we're asked to draw an inference, as is denoted by the word *suggests*. This Inference question is too broad to prephrase, so it's best to evaluate each answer choice, eliminating obviously incorrect choices. Each answer choice describes what might happen if Murphy's philosophy is applied to the situations of two different groups. Which outcome is more likely, based on the passage? We're told in paragraph 3 that Murphy's view starts with individuals' innate sense of right and wrong. We're also told in paragraph 4 that people's moral viewpoints might not converge. Thus, answer choice (B) is the most likely outcome: It's possible that the two groups could start with entirely different innate senses of right and wrong and, therefore, come out with principles that radically differ. It's also possible that the groups could come out with principles that were relatively similar. This doesn't negate answer (B), however. Depending on how similar the groups' starting views are, their principles could either be alike or very different.

If two groups were using the approach, it's possible that one group might come up with a resolution while the other did not—but there's no reason to believe that this necessarily would be the case, so eliminate (A).

(C) misrepresents the author's argument. Murphy's view could be applied to two groups regardless of what views those groups held. Its outcome in each case, however, would depend on the group's particular beliefs. It is true that the outcomes would be similar only if the groups held similar views. But the philosophy itself could be applied to any group, regardless of whether they shared the same beliefs.

(D) is beyond the scope of the author's argument. The author never discusses using Murphy's view to reconcile differences between groups. He merely describes how the view can be used to help individuals determine moral behavior.

(E) is a bit tricky. As with choice (A) above, we must pay attention to the statement's wording. It's possible that Murphy's philosophy could be applied to two groups and that neither group would use the philosophy effectively to determine a course of action. This would be the case if both groups had no moral sense to begin with. This type of outcome is only possible, however—it's not certain.

Remember: When choosing an answer about potential outcomes, be careful to scrutinize the verbs in each answer choice. In LSAT Reading Comp, there is a significant difference between stating that something *would* happen and stating that something *could* happen. Pay attention to the difference as you choose your answer.

16. D

This Inference question deals with the same issue as the previous question: What happens when you apply Murphy's philosophy to two groups? We know from question 15 that Murphy's philosophy can be applied to different groups but that it would produce the same outcome for both only if both groups started with the same moral foundation. Another way of putting this is to say that two groups could apply Murphy's philosophy to their problems, but they would only come up with the same moral principles of action if they both started with the same beliefs. Therefore, a principle derived by one group would only apply to another group if the second group shared the same beliefs as the first, as stated in (D).

(A) is beyond the scope of the passage. Nowhere does the author discuss individuals sharing

recommendations regarding Murphy's principles. The author tells us instead that principles are developed by starting with individuals' own sense of right and wrong (as opposed to recommendations from others).

(B), (C), and (E) are all 180. Each of these choices gives an answer that conflicts with the author's argument. If the moral viewpoints of the two groups did not converge, as (B) states, then the principle derived by one group might not apply to the other group at all. With (C), if the members of the second group had no firmly held beliefs, a principle developed using Murphy's view would be difficult to apply to them. Finally, if (E) were true, it would be difficult even to come up with the first group's principle, much less apply it to another group.

Remember: LSAT Reading Comp questions aren't always unique. Often one question will test the same concept as a another question in the set. When this occurs, use your previous work to help you answer the second question. This will save you time and increase your score.

17. B

Here we are given a question that starts out with the words "according to the passage." That lets us know that we're being asked for specific detail from the passage—a good bet for a question to answer early on in the set. Where does the passage mention individuals who have no moral sense? In paragraph 4, where it tells us that individuals without moral beliefs would have no justification for using Murphy's system. This point describes one disadvantage of Murphy's approach, as we're told with answer (B).

(A) is 180. The existence of individuals without moral beliefs provides one reason for refuting Murphy's views. These individuals might not follow Murphy's views at all.

(C) misrepresents the author's argument. The author does tell us that reason is necessary when people's beliefs conflict. But he tells us this in paragraph 3, as he's describing Murphy's approach. The issue of individuals without moral beliefs is not raised until the following paragraph, in the discussion of the philosophy's disadvantages.

(D) misrepresents the author's argument. The author does mention that traditional approaches might not be any more influential for some people than Murphy's approach would be. But he states this in paragraph 5 when discussing the advantages of Murphy's view. He doesn't raise the issue of people without moral beliefs to prove this point.

(E) is beyond the scope of the argument. The author never discusses the consequences of the "overdemandingness" problem. He merely describes this problem for us.

Remember: Watch out for choices that slap together two separate parts of the passage, comparing them in a way that the author doesn't.

Don't let the test dictate the order in which you'll do the questions. Scan the question set before you begin answering and knock the easier questions out of the way first.

18. B

This question asks us for an inference regarding Murphy's views (as distinct from the author's views). We can look back to the text to help us with the answer. Where is the issue of "reason" discussed? In paragraph 3, we're told that a person can use reason to determine moral principles if his or her fundamental beliefs are conflicting or confused. This would be a good prephrase to approach the answer choices with. As it turns out, choice (B) reflects the prephrase exactly.

The issue of some beliefs superseding others is not discussed in the passage. Neither (A) nor (C) is the issue of a belief system conflicting with an ethical principle.

(D) is 180. An individual who had no moral sense would not be able to apply Murphy's philosophy because he would lack an innate sense of right and wrong, which is Murphy's starting point.

(E) explains the meaning of the overdemandingness problem, discussed in paragraphs 1 and 2. Murphy's philosophy responds to this problem in general—but the problem itself doesn't explain when reason should be used.

Remember: Prephrasing doesn't work with most Inference questions, but it can help with some. If an Inference question is phrased specifically and you can posit a reasonable prephrase, it's worth a scan of the answer choices to see if your prephrase shows up. If not, you can always rule out choices by elimination.

19. A

This unusual question requires us to take information from the passage and apply it to a situation not presented in the passage. We know from paragraph 3 that the use of Murphy's philosophy requires two steps: First, the person or group starts with innate beliefs about right or wrong, then uses reason if necessary to derive moral principles. The first step for the school board, then, is reflected in (A): Members would have to determine their fundamental beliefs regarding the dress code issue.

(B) and (D) are irrelevant to the application of Murphy's philosophy. The author never states that analysis of other situations or historical precedents is necessary for determining moral principles with Murphy's view.

Because the school board members are deciding the policy, according to Murphy, they would need to start with their own beliefs—not those of the students. So eliminate (C).

(E) misrepresents the author's argument. In paragraph 3, the author is merely comparing Murphy to legal scholars who interpret the Constitution. He doesn't imply that people using Murphy's view must also consult the Constitution.

Remember: Application questions require you to apply ideas from the passage to alternative scenarios not raised in the passage. Make sure that the answer choice fits within the scope of the author's argument and can reasonably be deduced from the text.

20. C

A good road map can help us answer this efficiently. What does the author discuss in paragraph 5? We might prephrase here that he presents the pros of Murphy's view. A quick scan of the answer choices reveals the credited answer: (C) matches our prephrase almost exactly.

(A) is not discussed in the passage. Murphy doesn't give us any means of determining the best interpretation of beliefs—at least not in what we're told here.

The "overdemandingness" issue is discussed in paragraph 1. So eliminate (B).

The author does not address two schools of thought. This point is raised in the explanations for question 14, answers (B) and (C). So (D) is out.

(E) is addressed in paragraph 3, where Murphy's views are summarized.

Remember: This question again demonstrates why it's vital to choose your own order for answering the questions. Also Logic questions are good candidates for prephrasing, thanks to the power of the Road Map.

21. D

Which one of the answer choices would Murphy be likely to agree with? There's no way to form a prephrase here, so on to the choices:

(A) is 180. People who argue from firmly held beliefs would be following Murphy's approach, not a traditional approach.

(B) is 180. Paragraph 5 tells us that these sorts of works have value—they just aren't as practical as Murphy's approach.

(C) exaggerates the author's argument. In paragraph 4, we're only told that people who lack moral sense won't be able to apply the particular approach developed by Murphy. However, they might still have contributions

to make to ethical debates. We can't be sure from the passage that they would not contribute anything.

(D) is the winner. In the last paragraph of the passage, the author tells us that people who reject Murphy's premises aren't likely to accept traditional views either. What kind of people would reject Murphy's views? Moral skeptics, or those who have no moral sense at all, according to paragraph 3. So (D) provides the best answer choice here.

We cannot determine whether the author himself believes that "overdemandingness" is a serious problem for traditional philosophy. We're only told that some scholars think it's not a serious problem and that Murphy does take it seriously. The author's tone in the passage implies that he sides with Murphy—but we don't have enough information to be sure. So this statement is either definitely incorrect or too poorly supported to evaluate. Either way, (E) gets ruled out.

Remember: Know your strengths and weaknesses when answering Reading Comp questions. This will help you determine which questions to answer last in the set. If Inference questions are a weak point, you might have left this question until last or even skipped it altogether. Don't be afraid to skip questions that look as though they'll take a long time.

Questions 22–26

The general topic of the passages is the same: the ozone layer. Their scope is close as well; both authors talk about the problem of the hole in the ozone layer. In Passage A, however, the author is primarily concerned with driving home the seriousness of the problem, while Passage B focuses on the strides that have already been made.

Passage A: The author's main idea is that we have a serious problem in the depletion of the ozone layer. His purpose is simply to inform us of the problem and describe it.

Passage B: The main idea in Passage B is that the ozone layer is repairing itself, so we shouldn't worry so much about it. The author's purpose is to persuade us that the ozone layer problem is well in hand and it's time to move on to other matters.

Having assessed topic, scope, purpose, and main idea just as we do in regular passages (except that we have two purposes/main ideas), we move on to the one step that differs in reading comparative passages: Before moving on to the questions, we need to get a handle on the relationship between the passages.

The best starting point is to examine each passage's purpose/main idea. Passage A spells out the problem of depletion of the ozone layer. Passage B, on the other hand, focuses on the improvement that's already taken place and the likelihood of a full recovery. In other words, Passage B asserts that we needn't worry much about the problem set forth in Passage A; it's already on the mend.

Since comparative passages are so short, we won't need Road Maps. Once we have T/S/P/MI and the relationship between the passages in hand, we can jump into the questions. Remember to look first to see whether any questions refer to only one passage and then follow your usual order of operations with regard to question types.

22. D

Although our authors reach very different conclusions, they don't actually disagree on many of the specifics. They provide different figures for the size of the hole in the ozone layer over the South Pole, but the numbers are from different time periods, so there's no inconsistency there—eliminate answer choice (A). Answer choice (B) might be tempting as well, since it's the key point author B introduces to show that the problem isn't as serious as some scientists hold it out to be. But in fact, Passage A doesn't mention that issue at all, and nothing in the passage is inconsistent with the idea that there's been some shrinkage. Likewise, the author of Passage A doesn't make any mention of when we can expect the hole to "heal," so (C) is out. (D) is correct; the author of Passage A states directly that further research and action is required, whereas author B tells us that we're headed in the right direction

and should turn our attention elsewhere. (E) is raised by author A only; it's important to note that the author of Passage B never downplays the importance of the ozone layer itself, only says that it's repairing itself so we needn't concern ourselves about it.

23. B

Use your work from previous questions. In eliminating answer choice (A) in question 22, we determined that the data on the size of the hole came from different time periods. Thus, we can rule out answer choice (A) here, as well—they don't conflict. Correct answer choice (B) strikes the right balance; the data itself doesn't conflict, but the way the authors use the figures leads to very different conclusions. (C) might be tempting—the authors certainly make different interpretations in the broader sense. However, this question asks us specifically about the figures cited. In (D), again, the data itself doesn't indicate an outcome; even if it did, nothing in Passage A indicates that the author disputes the suggestion that the ozone layer is slowly repairing itself. The fact that he thinks the issue deserves further attention could be the result of wanting to see quicker results or to ensure that the trend isn't reversed by human activity. (E) may or may not be true, but we have no reason to believe that the numbers supplied are questionable.

24. A

Like all "relationship between the passages" questions, this one was done as soon as you'd analyzed the passages. Correct answer choice (A) is a match for the relationship we determined up front. (B) goes wrong in the second half—there's no suggestion in Passage B that efforts would be ineffective, simply that they're not necessary. (C) is incorrect because the author of Passage B doesn't suggest that A's figures are inaccurate, only that they don't mean we need to act. (D) is wrong because Passage B doesn't build on Passage A—it presents a conflicting view. And (E) can be eliminated because Passage B is founded in scientific data just as is Passage A—the conclusion is different, but the approach is not.

25. C

This is a bit tricky because the authors of the two passages don't actually *disagree* about many of the details. However, they don't often address the same points, so we can't infer that they'd agree about those that one or the other hasn't mentioned. Answer choices (A) and (B) both fall into that category—the author of Passage A talks about them, and we have no reason to believe that the author of Passage B would disagree, but he hasn't said anything to indicate agreement and we can't guess. Eliminate. Correct answer choice (C), on the other hand, is directly stated by both authors. Although the author of Passage A thinks we should act and the author of Passage B thinks the problem will resolve itself, both clearly agree that there is a problem, and both provide fairly dramatic statistics regarding the extent of the damage. (D) is the point of conflict between the two authors and the one thing we can be sure that they *don't* agree on. (E) is simply another way of stating that issue; one author thinks we need to act, and the other thinks we're on the right track and can move on.

26. B

Again, we have a handle on the general relationship: Passage A introduces a problem and calls for action, while Passage B says the problem is already resolving itself. Answer choice (A) isn't a match because the boy doesn't say there's a solution in the works—he says there's not a problem at all. (B) is correct; here, the second person acknowledges the problem but says it's getting better. (C) is incorrect because the two physicians are recommending different courses of action, whereas in our passages, one is recommending action and the other inaction. (D) similarly reflects two different courses of action, not action versus inaction. In (E), the second party claims that there is no problem, which our author B does not do—he simply says we don't need to do anything more about it.

PRACTICE TEST 3

LSAT PRACTICE TEST 3 ANSWER SHEET

Remove (or photocopy) the answer sheet and use it to complete the Practice Test.

How to Take the Practice Tests

Before taking each test, find a quiet place where you can work uninterrupted for about two and a half hours. Make sure you have a comfortable desk and several No. 2 pencils.

Each Practice Test includes four scored multiple-choice sections. Keep in mind that on the actual LSAT, there will be an additional multiple-choice section—the experimental section—that will not contribute to your score, plus an unscored Writing Sample.

Once you start a Practice Test, don't stop (except for a 5- to 10-minute break after the second section) until you've gone through all four sections. Remember, you can review any questions within a section, but you may not go back or forward a section.

Good luck!

Start with number 1 for each section. If a section has fewer questions than answer spaces, leave the extra spaces blank.

Section I

1. Ⓐ Ⓑ Ⓒ Ⓓ Ⓔ	9. Ⓐ Ⓑ Ⓒ Ⓓ Ⓔ	17. Ⓐ Ⓑ Ⓒ Ⓓ Ⓔ	25. Ⓐ Ⓑ Ⓒ Ⓓ Ⓔ
2. Ⓐ Ⓑ Ⓒ Ⓓ Ⓔ	10. Ⓐ Ⓑ Ⓒ Ⓓ Ⓔ	18. Ⓐ Ⓑ Ⓒ Ⓓ Ⓔ	26. Ⓐ Ⓑ Ⓒ Ⓓ Ⓔ
3. Ⓐ Ⓑ Ⓒ Ⓓ Ⓔ	11. Ⓐ Ⓑ Ⓒ Ⓓ Ⓔ	19. Ⓐ Ⓑ Ⓒ Ⓓ Ⓔ	27. Ⓐ Ⓑ Ⓒ Ⓓ Ⓔ # right in
4. Ⓐ Ⓑ Ⓒ Ⓓ Ⓔ	12. Ⓐ Ⓑ Ⓒ Ⓓ Ⓔ	20. Ⓐ Ⓑ Ⓒ Ⓓ Ⓔ	28. Ⓐ Ⓑ Ⓒ Ⓓ Ⓔ Section I
5. Ⓐ Ⓑ Ⓒ Ⓓ Ⓔ	13. Ⓐ Ⓑ Ⓒ Ⓓ Ⓔ	21. Ⓐ Ⓑ Ⓒ Ⓓ Ⓔ	29. Ⓐ Ⓑ Ⓒ Ⓓ Ⓔ
6. Ⓐ Ⓑ Ⓒ Ⓓ Ⓔ	14. Ⓐ Ⓑ Ⓒ Ⓓ Ⓔ	22. Ⓐ Ⓑ Ⓒ Ⓓ Ⓔ	30. Ⓐ Ⓑ Ⓒ Ⓓ Ⓔ
7. Ⓐ Ⓑ Ⓒ Ⓓ Ⓔ	15. Ⓐ Ⓑ Ⓒ Ⓓ Ⓔ	23. Ⓐ Ⓑ Ⓒ Ⓓ Ⓔ	# wrong in
8. Ⓐ Ⓑ Ⓒ Ⓓ Ⓔ	16. Ⓐ Ⓑ Ⓒ Ⓓ Ⓔ	24. Ⓐ Ⓑ Ⓒ Ⓓ Ⓔ	Section I

Section II

1. Ⓐ Ⓑ Ⓒ Ⓓ Ⓔ	9. Ⓐ Ⓑ Ⓒ Ⓓ Ⓔ	17. Ⓐ Ⓑ Ⓒ Ⓓ Ⓔ	25. Ⓐ Ⓑ Ⓒ Ⓓ Ⓔ
2. Ⓐ Ⓑ Ⓒ Ⓓ Ⓔ	10. Ⓐ Ⓑ Ⓒ Ⓓ Ⓔ	18. Ⓐ Ⓑ Ⓒ Ⓓ Ⓔ	26. Ⓐ Ⓑ Ⓒ Ⓓ Ⓔ
3. Ⓐ Ⓑ Ⓒ Ⓓ Ⓔ	11. Ⓐ Ⓑ Ⓒ Ⓓ Ⓔ	19. Ⓐ Ⓑ Ⓒ Ⓓ Ⓔ	27. Ⓐ Ⓑ Ⓒ Ⓓ Ⓔ # right in
4. Ⓐ Ⓑ Ⓒ Ⓓ Ⓔ	12. Ⓐ Ⓑ Ⓒ Ⓓ Ⓔ	20. Ⓐ Ⓑ Ⓒ Ⓓ Ⓔ	28. Ⓐ Ⓑ Ⓒ Ⓓ Ⓔ Section II
5. Ⓐ Ⓑ Ⓒ Ⓓ Ⓔ	13. Ⓐ Ⓑ Ⓒ Ⓓ Ⓔ	21. Ⓐ Ⓑ Ⓒ Ⓓ Ⓔ	29. Ⓐ Ⓑ Ⓒ Ⓓ Ⓔ
6. Ⓐ Ⓑ Ⓒ Ⓓ Ⓔ	14. Ⓐ Ⓑ Ⓒ Ⓓ Ⓔ	22. Ⓐ Ⓑ Ⓒ Ⓓ Ⓔ	30. Ⓐ Ⓑ Ⓒ Ⓓ Ⓔ
7. Ⓐ Ⓑ Ⓒ Ⓓ Ⓔ	15. Ⓐ Ⓑ Ⓒ Ⓓ Ⓔ	23. Ⓐ Ⓑ Ⓒ Ⓓ Ⓔ	# wrong in
8. Ⓐ Ⓑ Ⓒ Ⓓ Ⓔ	16. Ⓐ Ⓑ Ⓒ Ⓓ Ⓔ	24. Ⓐ Ⓑ Ⓒ Ⓓ Ⓔ	Section II

Section III

1. Ⓐ Ⓑ Ⓒ Ⓓ Ⓔ
2. Ⓐ Ⓑ Ⓒ Ⓓ Ⓔ
3. Ⓐ Ⓑ Ⓒ Ⓓ Ⓔ
4. Ⓐ Ⓑ Ⓒ Ⓓ Ⓔ
5. Ⓐ Ⓑ Ⓒ Ⓓ Ⓔ
6. Ⓐ Ⓑ Ⓒ Ⓓ Ⓔ
7. Ⓐ Ⓑ Ⓒ Ⓓ Ⓔ
8. Ⓐ Ⓑ Ⓒ Ⓓ Ⓔ

9. Ⓐ Ⓑ Ⓒ Ⓓ Ⓔ
10. Ⓐ Ⓑ Ⓒ Ⓓ Ⓔ
11. Ⓐ Ⓑ Ⓒ Ⓓ Ⓔ
12. Ⓐ Ⓑ Ⓒ Ⓓ Ⓔ
13. Ⓐ Ⓑ Ⓒ Ⓓ Ⓔ
14. Ⓐ Ⓑ Ⓒ Ⓓ Ⓔ
15. Ⓐ Ⓑ Ⓒ Ⓓ Ⓔ
16. Ⓐ Ⓑ Ⓒ Ⓓ Ⓔ

17. Ⓐ Ⓑ Ⓒ Ⓓ Ⓔ
18. Ⓐ Ⓑ Ⓒ Ⓓ Ⓔ
19. Ⓐ Ⓑ Ⓒ Ⓓ Ⓔ
20. Ⓐ Ⓑ Ⓒ Ⓓ Ⓔ
21. Ⓐ Ⓑ Ⓒ Ⓓ Ⓔ
22. Ⓐ Ⓑ Ⓒ Ⓓ Ⓔ
23. Ⓐ Ⓑ Ⓒ Ⓓ Ⓔ
24. Ⓐ Ⓑ Ⓒ Ⓓ Ⓔ

25. Ⓐ Ⓑ Ⓒ Ⓓ Ⓔ
26. Ⓐ Ⓑ Ⓒ Ⓓ Ⓔ
27. Ⓐ Ⓑ Ⓒ Ⓓ Ⓔ
28. Ⓐ Ⓑ Ⓒ Ⓓ Ⓔ
29. Ⓐ Ⓑ Ⓒ Ⓓ Ⓔ
30. Ⓐ Ⓑ Ⓒ Ⓓ Ⓔ

right in
Section III

wrong in
Section III

Section IV

1. Ⓐ Ⓑ Ⓒ Ⓓ Ⓔ
2. Ⓐ Ⓑ Ⓒ Ⓓ Ⓔ
3. Ⓐ Ⓑ Ⓒ Ⓓ Ⓔ
4. Ⓐ Ⓑ Ⓒ Ⓓ Ⓔ
5. Ⓐ Ⓑ Ⓒ Ⓓ Ⓔ
6. Ⓐ Ⓑ Ⓒ Ⓓ Ⓔ
7. Ⓐ Ⓑ Ⓒ Ⓓ Ⓔ
8. Ⓐ Ⓑ Ⓒ Ⓓ Ⓔ

9. Ⓐ Ⓑ Ⓒ Ⓓ Ⓔ
10. Ⓐ Ⓑ Ⓒ Ⓓ Ⓔ
11. Ⓐ Ⓑ Ⓒ Ⓓ Ⓔ
12. Ⓐ Ⓑ Ⓒ Ⓓ Ⓔ
13. Ⓐ Ⓑ Ⓒ Ⓓ Ⓔ
14. Ⓐ Ⓑ Ⓒ Ⓓ Ⓔ
15. Ⓐ Ⓑ Ⓒ Ⓓ Ⓔ
16. Ⓐ Ⓑ Ⓒ Ⓓ Ⓔ

17. Ⓐ Ⓑ Ⓒ Ⓓ Ⓔ
18. Ⓐ Ⓑ Ⓒ Ⓓ Ⓔ
19. Ⓐ Ⓑ Ⓒ Ⓓ Ⓔ
20. Ⓐ Ⓑ Ⓒ Ⓓ Ⓔ
21. Ⓐ Ⓑ Ⓒ Ⓓ Ⓔ
22. Ⓐ Ⓑ Ⓒ Ⓓ Ⓔ
23. Ⓐ Ⓑ Ⓒ Ⓓ Ⓔ
24. Ⓐ Ⓑ Ⓒ Ⓓ Ⓔ

25. Ⓐ Ⓑ Ⓒ Ⓓ Ⓔ
26. Ⓐ Ⓑ Ⓒ Ⓓ Ⓔ
27. Ⓐ Ⓑ Ⓒ Ⓓ Ⓔ
28. Ⓐ Ⓑ Ⓒ Ⓓ Ⓔ
29. Ⓐ Ⓑ Ⓒ Ⓓ Ⓔ
30. Ⓐ Ⓑ Ⓒ Ⓓ Ⓔ

right in
Section IV

wrong in
Section IV

1 $\boxed{1}$ **1**

Section I
Time—35 minutes 26 questions

Directions: Each selection in this test is followed by several questions. After reading the selection, choose the best response to each question and mark it on your answer sheet. Your replies are to be based on what is stated or implied in the selection.

Every day the mailboxes of America are filled with millions upon millions of solicitations provided by the direct-marketing industry. Most often they are straightforward advertisements for goods
(5) and services, but they also include such things as fund-raising solicitations, sweepstakes entries, and free trial offers. America's response to this deluge has been strangely mixed. On the negative side, poorly executed direct marketing produces unwanted,
(10) annoying, and wasteful solicitations, also known as "junk mail." The deluge of these solicitations constitutes an imposition on each household, putting a condition on that household's use of the mail system. Even worse, aggressive direct marketing
(15) techniques represent a serious threat to informational privacy. Rapid increases in technology have allowed direct marketers to have access to the personal characteristics of virtually everyone. Further, sophisticated computer-matching programs can
(20) produce intrusive personal profiles from information that, standing alone, does not threaten individual privacy. Direct mailers disseminate this personal information originally revealed with an expectation of privacy. This information is dis-
(25) closed without the subject's consent, and the target is typically never notified of the transfer.

The 1991 Harris-Equifax Consumer Privacy Survey addressed popular attitudes towards direct-mailing practices and their impact on informa-
(30) tional privacy. When asked how they viewed direct mail offers in general, 46 percent said they were a "nuisance," 9 percent considered them to be "invasions of privacy," and only 6 percent said they were "useful." But if Americans have such a nega-
(35) tive opinion of the direct marketing industry, they have a strange way of showing it. Direct marketing is an effective technique that has grown in influence. Direct mail advertising expenditures rose from $7.6 billion in 1980 to $23.4 billion in 1990.

(40) The laws of the market dictate that companies would not have made these efforts without prospects of success. Moreover, in the Equifax survey mentioned above, almost half of the citizens who considered direct mail offers to be "invasions
(45) of privacy" had themselves bought something in response to a direct mail ad in the past year. Why, then, did not more of them express more positive opinions of direct marketing offers?

Analysis of this seeming contradiction reveals
(50) the central problem of regulation in this industry: Everyone hates receiving "junk mail," and everyone ought to be concerned about informational privacy. Still, direct marketing offers real advantages over other means of shopping, and the
(55) industry as a whole probably offers something for everyone. Even those who believe that the direct mailing industry has a generally negative societal impact probably would prefer to remain on some mailing lists. We like shopping by mail, and we
(60) don't want to throw out the good with the bad.

GO ON TO THE NEXT PAGE ⟩

1. Which one of the following best expresses the main idea of the passage?

   (A) Increases in technology have been the main catalyst for the direct marketing explosion during the 1980s.

   (B) Concerns over privacy issues as expressed in popular opinion polls have influenced the way direct marketers have targeted their audience.

   (C) The discrepancy between the public's stated views of unsolicited "junk mail" and individuals' actual reaction to direct-marketing materials has fueled the recent boom in the direct-marketing industry.

   (D) The mixed response of Americans toward direct marketing stems from aggressive marketing techniques that threaten individual privacy.

   (E) The success of the direct marketing industry in the face of apparent public opposition to its practices can be explained in the light of consumer tendencies.

2. Which one of the following, if true, would best strengthen the author's explanation of the "seeming contradiction" expressed in line 49?

   (A) Awareness of commercial infringements on the rights of citizens has never been higher.

   (B) The number of people on more than one mailing list has increased in direct proportion to the increase in direct-marketing expenditures.

   (C) Consumers do not perceive a connection between their individual purchasing behavior and infringements on their personal rights.

   (D) Some people believe that the benefits associated with the recent success of the direct-marketing industry will filter down to consumers over time.

   (E) Some opinion polls on other topics indicate a similar discrepancy between what people say about an issue and how they act in relation to that issue.

3. Which one of the following critiques most approximates the logic underlying the author's concern regarding the effects of the computer-matching programs mentioned in lines 18–22?

   (A) An ecologist who states that because each of three species individually would not damage an ecosystem, it is safe to introduce all three into the ecosystem overlooks the possibility that the dominance of one species may lead to the extinction of one or both of the other two species.

   (B) An ecologist who states that because each of three species individually would not damage an ecosystem, it is safe to introduce all three into the ecosystem overlooks the possibility that the three species taken together may very well pose a serious threat to the ecosystem.

   (C) An ecologist who states that because each of three species individually would not damage an ecosystem, it is safe to introduce all three into the ecosystem overlooks the possibility that the addition of the three species to the ecosystem may preclude the addition of any further species.

   (D) An ecologist who states that because each of three species individually would not damage an ecosystem, it is safe to introduce all three into the ecosystem overlooks the possibility that the ecosystem may not be the optimal environment for the species in question.

   (E) An ecologist who states that because each of three species individually would not damage an ecosystem, it is safe to introduce all three into the ecosystem overlooks the possibility that any one of the three species may have posed a risk to the previous ecosystem in which it lived.

GO ON TO THE NEXT PAGE

4. Which one of the following can be inferred from the passage about direct mail advertising expenditures in the years between 1980 and 1990?

(A) The rise in expenditures during this period is suggestive of the expectations of companies engaged in direct marketing at the time.

(B) The profit derived from sales linked to these expenditures in 1990 was more than double the profit derived from such sales in 1980.

(C) The lowest yearly expenditure on direct mail advertising during this period occurred in 1980.

(D) Direct marketing companies expect the pattern of expenditures during this period to continue in the decades to come.

(E) The rise in expenditures during this period closely parallel the laws of the market.

5. According to the passage, the author believes that the American public's reaction to the direct mail phenomenon

(A) is in accordance with the true dangers posed by the enterprise.

(B) demonstrates an unusual willingness of people to consistently act against their deeply held convictions.

(C) stems primarily from its fear of the loss of privacy that results from direct mail practices.

(D) is unusual at first glance but more understandable once the motivations of the public are considered.

(E) signals that the direct mail industry will need to alter its practices to respect informational privacy.

6. The opinions expressed in the Harris-Equifax Consumer Privacy Survey in lines 27–34 serve as

(A) a justification for the increase in direct mail advertising expenditures in the 1980s.

(B) the basis for the solution to a seemingly paradoxical situation.

(C) the primary evidence for the author's conclusion about computer-matching programs.

(D) a contrast to additional evidence derived from another part of the survey.

(E) an indication that the boom in direct marketing is not likely to continue.

7. The author would most likely agree with which one of the following statements?

(A) Despite its drawbacks, direct marketing has had an overall positive effect on American society.

(B) The attitudes revealed in opinion polls can provide useful insights.

(C) Regarding the effects of commercial enterprises, presenting a nuisance is a more serious offense to society than is invasion of privacy.

(D) Everyone who would prefer to remain on at least one mailing list thinks that direct marketing negatively affects society in some way.

(E) The growth in direct marketing would be even more significant in the future if the percentage of people who find direct mail offers to be a nuisance were to decrease.

GO ON TO THE NEXT PAGE

For at least 300 years prior to the beginning of the 20th century, people had noticed that the bulge along the eastern edge of South America fits remarkably well into the bight of Africa. Indeed,

(5) Francis Bacon suggested in 1620 that the fit could not be accidental. Several 19th-century scientists offered explanations for the fit, but when Alfred Wegener first published the continental-drift hypothesis in 1912, his novel explanation for why

(10) the continents seem to fit together like pieces of a jigsaw puzzle drew explosive criticism from many geologists. Wegener used gravity measurements and observations of the earth's surfaces to deduce that the continents are composed of lighter rock than

(15) the basalt that lies beneath the ocean floors. The continents, he suggested, float on the denser layer of basalt like icebergs on water. Wegener's early critics excoriated him for not proposing a mechanism for propelling the continental "icebergs"

(20) through solid basalt, although now there is some theoretical basis for thinking that convection might drive the process.

    Wegener did not live long enough to find the clear and convincing evidence his hypothesis

(25) required, but since his death in 1930, geologists have learned much that supports his revolutionary idea. For example, belts of complementary rock formations found along the African and South American shorelines of the Atlantic Ocean

(30) make a strong argument for continental drift. In one experiment, geochronologists determined the age of a distinctive layer of crystalline basement rock in Ghana, Africa, and then predicted where the same rock layer would be found at the edge of

(35) South America if the two continents had indeed once been contiguous. By sampling and dating rocks in northeastern Brazil, the scientists demonstrated that the layer does occur in its predicted location. Another belt of two-billion-year-

(40) old rock that abruptly ends at the edge of the West African continental mass and begins again at the expected location along the coast of South America adds additional proof that the two continents once formed part of a larger land mass.

(45)   The fossil record contains additional evidence that Africa and South America were once connected. Large bodies of water act as barriers to the migration of many types of animals, yet the fossils of identical animal species are found on

(50) both sides of the southern Atlantic Ocean. For example, the remains of Mesosaurus, a small reptile of the Permian that lived in shallow, brackish swamps, are found in only two locations—in the Early Permian Dwyka Formation in South Africa

(55) and in the Irarare Formation in Brazil. The rock formations are the same age, are similar in composition, and lie directly across the ocean from each other, thus enhancing the plausibility of Wegener's theory of continental drift.

8. Which one of the following best expresses the main point of the passage?

(A) Several 19th-century scientists have offered explanations for the apparent fit of the coastlines of South America and Africa but none as intriguing as the hypothesis proposed by Wegener.

(B) Fossil evidence and the dating of certain rocks in South America and Africa has recently undermined the continental drift hypothesis.

(C) Scientists have uncovered a growing body of evidence for continental drift since the death of the theory's original proponent.

(D) The study of fossils and rock formations is an important aspect of geochronology.

(E) Scientists cannot conclusively prove the validity of Wegener's continental-drift hypothesis until the mechanism that causes it is understood.

GO ON TO THE NEXT PAGE

9. The author's conclusion about the two-billion-year-old rock formations in West Africa and South America implies which one of the following?

    (A) The rock formations would not be in their current locations if the continents had never been connected.

    (B) Similar rock formations must be present in at least one other continent.

    (C) The rock formations were formed by the same geological process that separated the continents.

    (D) The rock formations must contain fossils common to both Africa and South America.

    (E) Although much older, the rock formations resemble the crystalline basement rock found in Ghana.

10. According to the passage, Wegener's continental-drift hypothesis was originally

    (A) a modification of an earlier 19th-century hypothesis about the structure of continents.

    (B) rejected by most geologists because it was inconsistent with Francis Bacon's suggestion regarding the apparent fit between Africa and South America.

    (C) an attempt to explain why South America and Africa share common rock formations.

    (D) formulated with the use of scientific observations but lacking in supporting evidence.

    (E) used to explain why certain fossils are found on both sides of the South Atlantic.

11. Which one of the following, if true, would most weaken Wegener's theory of continental drift?

    (A) Far more Mesosaurus reptile fossils were uncovered in the Early Permian Dwyka Formation in South Africa than in the Irarare Formation in Brazil.

    (B) A new mechanism has been discovered that could displace convection as the motive force behind continental drift.

    (C) Francis Bacon based his observation on the nonaccidental nature of the structural fit between continents purely on speculation and not on scientific fact.

    (D) Many rock formations around the world are the same age but not of similar composition.

    (E) In many cases, continents that do not appear to have interlocking coastlines nonetheless share common rock formations and fossils of identical animal species.

12. It can be inferred that the author of the passage would most likely agree with which one of the following statements about fossil evidence?

    (A) Fossil evidence is less conclusive than rock formation evidence in substantiating Wegener's theory of continental drift .

    (B) Fossil evidence can contribute to the plausibility of a geological model.

    (C) No fossil evidence links the animal species of South America to those of Australia.

    (D) Fossil evidence proves that identical animal species once lived in widely separated locations.

    (E) Fossil evidence suggests that convection is the underlying mechanism responsible for continental drift .

GO ON TO THE NEXT PAGE

13. The primary purpose of the passage is to

   (A) describe some of the evidence for the continental-drift hypothesis.

   (B) detail how belts of complementary rock formations can be used to support geochronological hypotheses.

   (C) argue that the continental-drift hypothesis has been conclusively proven.

   (D) assess certain types of evidence relied upon by modern geochronologists.

   (E) describe Wegener's evidence for continental drift.

   Sensing that government defined by the Articles of Confederation did not meet the needs of the newly born United States, the Congress of the Articles of Confederation authorized commission-
(5)   ers to "devise such further provisions as shall appear to them necessary to render the Constitution of the federal government adequate to the exigencies of the Union." These provisions were to be reported to Congress and confirmed by
(10)   every state and were to consist of alterations to the Articles of Confederation. Having given these instructions, Congress was quite surprised by the terms of the Constitution as submitted, and even claimed that the commissioners did not have the
(15)   legal authority to submit such a revolutionary constitution.
   In the *Federalist Papers*, James Madison defended the commissioners by returning to the terms of their mandate. Given the goals expressed by
(20)   Congress, and the principle that conflicts ought to be resolved in favor of more important goals, Madison argued that the degree to which the Constitution departs from the Articles could not make the Constitution illegal. Where the goal of
(25)   amending the Articles conflicted with the goal of creating good government, the Articles must yield, because the goal of good government is an overriding consideration. This same argument, however, did not apply to the commissioners' decision to

(30)   allow the Constitution to be ratified by only three-quarters of the states. Unanimous approval was a fundamental aspect of national government under the Articles. Requiring nonratifying states to be bound by the new Constitution was thus a power-
(35)   ful diminishment of their sovereignty, because the Constitution changed the national government from a weak union of independent states to a strong union in which the interests of the many states could outweigh the protests of the few.
(40)   Although history has validated the wisdom of the change, the question of whether the change was legal is another matter.
   In authorizing the commissioners, the independent states requested a proposal for the
(45)   alteration of the national government but never intended to waive their veto power. So even if Madison was correct, and the commissioners could have proposed anything they deemed likely to fulfill the goal of good government, it does not follow
(50)   that their proclamations should have impinged upon the legal rights of the states. This does not, however, imply that the Constitution ratified by the states has no moral authority. No government ought to have the power to entrench itself against amend-
(55)   ment, and so the fact that the government under the Articles of Confederation did not consent to the alteration of the ratification process does not establish the moral illegitimacy of the Constitution. The case for rebelling against the
(60)   government under the Articles was further strengthened by the fact that the government itself admitted its unfitness for the exigencies of the Union.

GO ON TO THE NEXT PAGE ▷

1   **1**   **1**

14. It can be inferred that Congress's surprise over the radical nature of the Constitution submitted by the commissioners could be attributed in part to the fact that its members did not foresee

    (A) the inevitability that the Constitution it requested would be adopted without the unanimous ratification of the states.

    (B) the possibility that the Constitution it requested would contain provisions that jeopardized the government's moral authority.

    (C) a conflict between the modification of the Articles of Confederation and the creation of a Constitution adequate to the needs of the nation.

    (D) the possibility that the Constitution it requested would differ from the Articles of Confederation.

    (E) the likelihood that one such as Madison would invoke a principle as part of an argument attempting to justify the legality of the Constitution submitted.

15. Which one of the following views can be attributed to Madison?

    (A) In the case of conflicting interests, priority should be given to the course of action that best promotes peace in the nation.

    (B) Applications of conflict resolution principles can be used to determine the legality of an action.

    (C) Unanimous approval is the most important objective in drafting a new Constitution.

    (D) The Constitution drafted by the commissioners corresponded precisely to the expectations of the Congress of the Articles of Confederation.

    (E) In drafting the new Constitution, the commissioners had a moral obligation to forge a strong nation out of the weak union of independent states.

16. If a government decrees that it is illegal to make any changes to the structure or practices of the state, the author would most likely view a group within the state that attempts to violate the decree

    (A) with skepticism regarding its motivations.

    (B) with admiration, since any law passed by such a government has no moral authority.

    (C) with concern regarding the government's reaction to the group's act of dissent.

    (D) with disdain for its violation of the orders of the state.

    (E) with approval regarding its moral right to disobey the decree.

17. Which one of the following, if true, would most seriously weaken the argument put forth in defense of the legality of the Constitution submitted by the commissioners?

    (A) Nonunanimous ratification of such a new Constitution is incompatible with the goal of creating a good government.

    (B) Extensive debate among statesmen is necessary in order to create a fair and legal Constitution.

    (C) It is nearly impossible to create an effective Constitution out of the pieces of a previous Constitution.

    (D) No legal Constitution can include provisions to safeguard the power of the ruling elite that commissioned the document.

    (E) In regard to heated political issues, arguments presented orally are generally more persuasive than arguments presented in written form.

GO ON TO THE NEXT PAGE ⟩

18. According to the passage, which one of the following provided justification for the revolutionary nature of the new Constitution?

   (A) The current government's admission of its inadequacy in national affairs

   (B) The right of any given state to refuse to ratify the new Constitution

   (C) The moral right of a new government to entrench itself against amendment

   (D) The recommendation that the new Constitution be created from alterations of the current Articles of Confederation

   (E) The analysis presented by Madison that showed that the new Constitution did not differ from the Articles of Confederation to the extent asserted by Congress

19. Which one of the following relationships between legal and moral authority is implied by the author?

   (A) The morality of a constitution is the primary determinant of its legality.

   (B) A principle lacking moral authority can still be legally binding.

   (C) The morality of an action can never be determined irrespective of the legality of that action.

   (D) A document of questionable legal authority can still carry moral weight.

   (E) The moral justification for an action can be used by a court to override the illegality of that action.

20. The primary purpose of the passage is to

   (A) reconcile two opposing viewpoints.

   (B) illustrate the argumentative power of a principle.

   (C) argue for the reconsideration of an established doctrine.

   (D) support the establishment of one form of government over another.

   (E) assess the authority of a political event on two grounds.

Passage A

   In the 1980s, a new breed of author sprang up in the United States. America's disaffected youth rose up to be heard, and writers in their 20s—some just barely—asserted themselves as
(5) the voice of their generation. Brett Easton Ellis, Jay McInerny, Michael Chabon, and others flatly narrated tales of the new "lost generation," their characters scarcely reacting to slices of life once considered shocking.
(10)   Many critics, striving to establish themselves as cutting-edge, likened these works to classics such as J. D. Salinger's masterpiece, *Catcher in the Rye*, and Ernest Hemingway's debut, *The Sun Also Rises*. In truth, though, this new generation of
(15) novels contained none of the nuances that made their supposed ancestors great, any more than the overindulged artistes from exclusive colleges possessed the genius and insights of their predecessors.
(20)   Instead, these modern writers seized on the drugs, disconnect, and lack of direction of their peers and glamorized it, without regard to one important distinction: The true lost generation of writers and thinkers gave us insight into a
(25) world disillusioned by war and the changes it had wrought on the world they knew. The youth of

GO ON TO THE NEXT PAGE ⟶

1

1

1

the '80s found its disillusionment and rebellion in theory, borrowing it from generations or foreign cultures that faced real problems, and turned it
(30) into little more than an excuse for increasingly outrageous behavior and a practiced ennui that made it sophisticated to take it in stride.

Passage B

In the early 1980s, author Brett Easton Ellis took the literary world by storm, not simply through the insights of his work but because the novel that captivated open-minded critics and a
(5) generation of readers came into being on a dormitory room floor. Ellis, then 20 years old and a full-time student at one of the most expensive liberal arts colleges in the country, wrote the book with a portable typewriter on his lap.
(10) For the first time, a generation of youth overwhelmed by rapid technological development, blossoming economic opportunity, and the introduction of drug use as a regular staple of upper-middle-class life found a voice of its own—a voice that used simple, stark relation of events to convey
(15) the radical disconnection of that sector of society from the goals and values previous generations had taken for granted.

Through the vivid but judgment-neutral picture he painted, Ellis—and other writers of
(20) his time and ilk—clearly conveyed the missing pieces of a life otherwise portrayed as enviable, even golden. Unfortunately, some critics managed to miss the point, accusing Ellis of trading on or even glorifying the empty, promiscuous, and drug-
(25) intensive lifestyle of his characters.

21. Which of the following would the authors of both passages be most likely to agree on?

  (A) Brett Easton Ellis made an important contribution to the literary landscape of the 1980s.

  (B) Brett Easton Ellis brought a new voice and perspective to the literary world in the 1980s.

  (C) Writing that glorifies negative aspects of society like drug use should not find favor with critics.

  (D) Critics who favorably reviewed Ellis's work did so based largely on inaccurate perceptions.

  (E) The generation represented by Ellis's work and the work of other authors like him added little if any value to the literary world.

22. The author of Passage A intends primarily to

  (A) describe the impact of the work of Brett Easton Ellis on literary traditions in the 1980s.

  (B) argue that Ellis and the other writers in his tradition who rose to popularity in the 1980s never received the critical acclaim they deserved.

  (C) dispute the literary value of Brett Easton Ellis's first book.

  (D) point out that Ellis's work was not truly unique within his generation and that other authors in the same tradition deserve more attention.

  (E) argue that the critical acclaim received by Ellis and his compatriots was unwarranted.

GO ON TO THE NEXT PAGE ▷

1　　　　　　　　1　　　　　　　　1

23. The relationship between the two passages is best described by which of the following?

    (A) Passage A rejects an assessment that Passage B advances.

    (B) Passage B refutes claims raised in Passage A and draws a differing conclusion.

    (C) Passages A and B rely upon the same evidence to reach conflicting conclusions.

    (D) Passage A relies on critical analysis to draw a conclusion about an issue that Passage B addresses directly.

    (E) Both authors reach the same conclusion, but rely on different evidence to support their views.

24. The authors of the two passages disagree about which of the following?

    (A) Some critics were erroneous in their assessment of the works of Brett Easton Ellis and his peers.

    (B) Of the generation of young writers addressing similar issues, Brett Easton Ellis was the most significant.

    (C) Writers should not glorify negative aspects of society in literature.

    (D) The writings of Brett Easton Ellis provided important insights into the issues faced by his generation.

    (E) The contributions of Ernest Hemingway and other writers of the original "lost generation" were greatly exaggerated by critics.

25. The author of Passage A would be most likely to agree with which of the following?

    (A) The literary work of J. D. Salinger was superior to that of Brett Easton Ellis.

    (B) Michael Chabon's writing made a valuable contribution to the literary world.

    (C) There were no important literary voices among the writers who appeared on the literary scene in the 1980s.

    (D) *The Sun Also Rises* was neither as insightful nor as significant as some critics have suggested.

    (E) The novels of Brett Easton Ellis, Jay McInerny, and others of their genre would be better compared to the more modern novels of Salinger than to those of Ernest Hemingway.

26. Which of the following most closely mirrors the relationship between Passage A and Passage B?

    (A) A music critic writes a scathing assessment of an entire new genre of music, then another writer builds on that with a specific critique of one musician within the genre.

    (B) A reviewer raves about a new movie, only to have another reviewer directly respond to his review by harshly criticizing the film.

    (C) Two judges in a speech competition give the same student very different scores and provide comments that directly conflict with each other.

    (D) One music critic explains why he is unimpressed by a particular genre of music, and another writes a positive review about a particular musician in that genre.

    (E) One reviewer finds little value in a book, and another responds to his review by suggesting that the first reviewer overlooked critical aspects of the novel.

IF YOU FINISH BEFORE TIME IS CALLED, YOU MAY CHECK YOUR WORK ON THIS SECTION ONLY. DO NOT WORK ON ANY OTHER SECTION IN THE TEST.　STOP

2 2 2

Section II
Time—35 minutes 25 questions

Directions: This test is comprised of questions that ask you to analyze the logic of statements or short paragraphs. You are to choose as the answer to each question the one choice you consider best on the basis of your commonsense evaluation of the statement and its assumptions. Although a question may seem to have more than one acceptable answer, there is only one best answer, and it is the one that does not entail making any illogical, extraneous, or conflicting assumptions about the question. These questions do not presuppose any knowledge of formal logic on your part.

1. Cross-species studies of animal groups indicate that offspring who are separated from their mothers during the first months of life frequently develop aggression disorders. During group feedings, for example, separated offspring exert excessive force in the struggle over food, continuing to strike at other offspring long after the others have submitted. The best explanation for this observed behavior is the hypothesis that aggression disorders are caused by lack of proper parent-led socialization during the first stage of an offspring's development.

Which one of the following, if true, provides the most support for the hypothesis above?

(A) Some wildebeests who are not separated from their mothers during infancy display excessive aggression in conflicts that establish their place in the dominance hierarchy.

(B) Human babies adopted in the first three months of life often display aggressive behavior disorders during early childhood.

(C) Chimps raised in captivity in environments simulating traditional parent-led socialization display far less aggression in mating-related conflicts than do chimps raised without such social interaction.

(D) Many polar bears display more aggression in conflicts over food and social dominance than they do in mating-related conflicts.

(E) Elephants who are separated from their mothers during the first months of life do not display excessive aggression in food or social dominance struggles.

2. Sarrin monks practice the Pran meditation technique only when extremely damaging weather conditions confront the farming villages surrounding Sarrin monasteries. Pran meditation is a more highly disciplined form of the ritual meditation that the monks practice daily and involves unique practices such as isolation and fasting.

Which one of the statements below does NOT follow logically from the passage above?

(A) Some meditation practices are less disciplined than Pran meditation.

(B) Pran meditation among Sarrin monks does not take place according to a precisely regulated schedule.

(C) The ritual meditation that a typical Sarrin monk practices daily does not take place in an atmosphere of isolation.

(D) Monks practice some types of meditation in response to threats faced by the local population.

(E) The ritual meditation that Sarrin monks practice daily is largely undisciplined.

GO ON TO THE NEXT PAGE

3. Movie pirating, the illegal videotaping of a new theater release and subsequent selling of the tape on the black market, is a major concern to the film studios that produce today's mainstream movies. When pirating sales are high, individual studios whose movies are being taped and sold illegally lose a large amount of revenue from black market viewers who would otherwise pay the full theater price. A low level of pirating sales during a specific period, however, is a fairly reliable indicator of an economic downturn in the movie industry as a whole during that period.

Which one of the following, if true, most helps to reconcile the discrepancy noted above?

(A) The film studios that produce today's mainstream movies occasionally serve as distribution outlets for smaller budget independent films that are also susceptible to pirating.

(B) Movie piraters exclusively target blockbuster hits, the existence of which is inextricably tied to the financial success of the movie industry during any given period.

(C) Most movie piraters use small, handheld video cameras that are specially designed to record images in the darkened environment of a movie theater.

(D) The five largest film studios take in a disproportionate amount of movie revenue compared to hundreds of smaller and independent film studios, regardless of whether pirating activity during a specific period is high or low.

(E) A movie pirater who is highly active in selling movies on the black market can sometimes make a full living doing so, while a less active pirater will usually have to supplement the income generated from pirated movies.

4. Six months ago, a blight destroyed the cattle population in the town of Cebra, eradicating the town's beef supply. Since that time, the only meat available for consumption in Cebra has been poultry, lamb, and other nonbeef meats.

If the above statements are true, which one of the following must also be true on the basis of them?

(A) Villagers in the town of Cebra consume only beef raised by Cebra farmers.

(B) Cebra villagers prefer lamb and poultry to beef.

(C) The town of Cebra has not imported beef for consumption during the last six months.

(D) Most of the residents of Cebra are meat eaters.

(E) Before the blight occurred, Cebra villagers ate more beef than any other type of meat.

GO ON TO THE NEXT PAGE ⟹

5. The food critic who writes for the magazine *Dining Today* was misguided in his review of Fabri's Restaurant. He criticized the cold strawberry soup because it contained cilantro and sun-dried tomatoes. But Fabri's roasted chicken dish contains cilantro and sun-dried tomatoes, and the same critic awarded that dish the highest rating possible. Clearly, such blatant inconsistency proves that the critic is unqualified.

The argument above is based upon which one of the following assumptions?

(A) Fabri's roasted chicken dish is disliked by some of Fabri's customers.

(B) The evaluation of Fabri's cold strawberry soup should not suffer on account of its inclusion of a few ingredients that the critic happens to dislike.

(C) As enhancing ingredients, cilantro and sun-dried tomatoes are less appropriate for appetizers than for main dishes.

(D) Cilantro and sun-dried tomatoes enhance roasted chicken and cold strawberry soup dishes in a comparable manner.

(E) Cilantro and sun-dried tomatoes are best used in chicken dishes that are not roasted.

6. Peter Dovak has stated that his soon-to-be released new novel, *From Bad to Worse*, will exhibit the same literary form as his previous six novels. Each of these previous books was a "philosophy novel," also known as a "novel of ideas," in which characters and events represent various expressions of the author's deeply held philosophical convictions. Therefore, while the plot will surely be different from those of his previous books, any astute literary critic will know in advance what underlying issues will dominate Dovak's forthcoming book.

The argument above assumes which one of the following?

(A) Dovak is consistent in the philosophical convictions that he expresses through the characters and events of his books.

(B) The plot of *From Bad to Worse* will have nothing in common with the plots of any of Dovak's previous six books.

(C) Nothing written by Dovak prior to the publication of his previous six books took the form of the philosophy novel.

(D) One of the functions of literary critics is to predict what will be in an author's forthcoming book.

(E) The plot of *From Bad to Worse* is less important than the underlying philosophical convictions expressed through its characters and events.

GO ON TO THE NEXT PAGE ⟹

7. Despite the threat of legal prosecution, many agencies gather personal data from phony telephone solicitations, often luring details from the respondent through the promise of nonexistent prizes. Such solicitors sell this data to individuals and agencies that are willing to pay for information on people's personal lives, buying habits, and political views. Politicians, however, have relied less on phony solicitors thanks to recent advances in public opinion polling, which generally supplies them with reliable information regarding voter attitudes on major issues. It is therefore likely that the phony solicitation industry will dwindle significantly in the years to come.

Which one of the following, if true, most seriously undermines the conclusion above?

(A) Public opinion polling is not only effective at discerning the political attitudes of individuals but also at revealing their buying habits and details of their personal lives.

(B) Most people are unwilling to share personal information on their preferences and attitudes with strangers over the telephone.

(C) Large retailers are by far the largest consumers of pirated personal information and do not benefit from the information gathered in public opinion polls.

(D) Those politicians who rely on legal public opinion polls for information on voter attitudes are nonetheless hesitant to encourage the prosecution of the illegal datagathering agencies.

(E) Due to the recent success of public opinion polling, the phony solicitors have begun to co-opt the public opinion agencies' techniques for getting people to disclose information on their personal lives.

Questions 8–9

Albert: The CEO's proposal to conduct free career seminars for high school students does not make business sense. Teenagers do not use our products, since they do not have the disposable income to purchase luxury items.

Bill: I disagree. Any activities that improve the company's image can enhance our profit margins in the long run. The positive publicity received from the seminars will boost the company's image in the public's eye. Image enhancement, it has been proven, increases sales significantly.

8. A point at issue between Albert and Bill concerns whether

(A) the business has suffered from recent problems with its image.

(B) the CEO's plan to offer career seminars makes financial sense for the company.

(C) the publicity received from the seminars is likely to be highly positive.

(D) the advice given in the free career seminars would enable high school students to buy the company's products.

(E) teenagers would be more likely to buy the company's products if the company maintained a stronger public image.

GO ON TO THE NEXT PAGE

2   **2**   **2**   **2**

9. Bill responds to Albert by

(A) broadening the scope for the determination of whether offering the career seminars will be financially beneficial for the company.

(B) comparing the values of short-term versus long-term business gains.

(C) providing examples that demonstrate that image is more important to a company's financial health than its profit margins.

(D) showing that Albert's argument relies on the erroneous presupposition that increased product sales are not the only route to financial growth.

(E) presenting evidence that clarifies the issue of whether teenagers have enough disposable income to purchase the company's products.

10. Veterinary technician: I disagree with Dr. Markey's analysis concerning the medical problems of Wisecrack, the Smiths's horse. Dr. Markey recommends that Wisecrack undergo hoof surgery because his hoof problems are causing him great pain. But the Smiths cannot afford to pay for this procedure, much less the cost of Wisecrack's hospital stay.

The argument above is logically suspect because it

(A) supports its conclusion on the basis of evidence that fails to take into account the emotional or financial costs of not treating Wisecrack's condition.

(B) fails to draw a conclusion that is in the best interest of the owners of the horse.

(C) resorts to attacking the personality of an individual involved in order to direct attention away from the relevant issue.

(D) uses evidence regarding the feasibility of acting on a recommendation as grounds for questioning the validity of the analysis supporting that recommendation.

(E) supports its main point with evidence that is derived from sources that cannot be independently verified.

11. Pharmaceutical scientist: Any bone marrow taken from lab rats after their primary growth phase is degenerative and will not function properly in transplants. All marrow in this shipment was extracted from laboratory rats provided by Chronin Labs. Chronin Labs has a policy of supplying only rats that are four months of age or older. Therefore, the marrow in this shipment is degenerative and should not be used.

Which one of the following, if true, most helps to justify the conclusion that leads to the pharmaceutical scientist's recommendation?

(A) The degenerative quality of a particular bone marrow supply is not a valid reason for definitively ruling out its use in transplants.

(B) All rat bone marrow that displays degenerative properties comes from rats that are more than four months old.

(C) Some bone marrow extracted from laboratory rats during the rats' primary growth phase is degenerative.

(D) Laboratory rats go through their primary growth phase between birth and four months of age.

(E) In rare instances, Chronin Labs agrees to supply rats under four months of age to certain experiment sites containing appropriate environmental conditions.

GO ON TO THE NEXT PAGE

12. Many Maids, a well-known commercial cleaning franchise, has always relied heavily on income from its major clients and would have been forced to close down this year if any of its major clients had closed their accounts. However, Many Maids has not only been able to continue its operation throughout the year, but it has also announced the grand opening of its second office.

The above statements, if true, support which one of the following conclusions?

(A) During this year, Many Maids's clients have placed a larger than usual number of special cleaning orders.

(B) Over the past few months, Many Maids developed many new small client accounts, which made the company less dependent on its major clients for income.

(C) None of Many Maids' major clients closed an account with the company this year.

(D) Corporate use of cleaning services like Many Maids has recently increased.

(E) Major clients were the source of more than half of Many Maids's income for the current year.

13. The Fines Museum has a totem pole that was too tall to be stored in the museum's temperature-controlled storage vault. Fortunately, the totem pole can now be stored in the temperature-controlled vault, thanks to the efforts of restoration artists who have discovered a way to separate the pole into two parts for storage purposes while allowing it to be reassembled later without any noticeable change in the appearance of the artifact.

The argument above depends on which one of the following assumptions?

(A) Neither of the separated parts of the totem pole is too tall to fit into the vault.

(B) The totem pole can be separated into two equal-sized parts.

(C) The procedure for separating the parts of the totem pole will not cost more than it would cost to replace the totem pole if it deteriorated.

(D) Placing the two parts of the totem pole into the vault would not require removing other key artifacts from the vault.

(E) The optimal temperature required to preserve the totem pole can be attained in the temperature-controlled vault.

2   **2**   **2**   **2**

14. Psychologists who wish to have one of their book reviews nominated for the prestigious *Boatwright Psychology Review* award should not submit book review articles that review more than three books at a time. This is because editors for the *Boatwright Psychology Review* will not publish a book review article if it is too lengthy and cumbersome to read. In their submission guidelines, the editors explicitly state that review articles that cover more than three books at a time are considered too lengthy and cumbersome to read.

Which one of the following statements represents an assumption upon which the argument above depends?

(A) The book review article that covers the most books must be the lengthiest and most cumbersome article to read.

(B) If a book review article is published in the *Boatwright Psychology Review*, that article will receive the prestigious *Boatwright Psychology Review* award.

(C) All articles published in the *Boatwright Psychology Review* must be limited to a certain length specified by the editors.

(D) The *Boatwright Psychology Review* editors generally prefer book review articles that cover one book rather than two books.

(E) To be nominated for the *Boatwright Psychology Review* award, a psychologist's book review article must be published in the *Boatwright Psychology Review*.

15. The best-tasting premium ice cream requires milk from organically raised cows. When milk supplies are obtained from nonorganic sources, ice cream manufacturers are unable to ensure that their products are free of pesticide residues, and taste tests have shown that only those products that are free of pesticide residues meet the highest-quality standards for taste.

The claim that ice cream products can meet the highest-quality taste standards only if they are free of pesticide residues plays which of the following roles in the argument?

(A) It serves as support for the argument's conclusion.

(B) It represents a logical consequence of the argument.

(C) It is an assumption upon which the argument depends.

(D) It is a statement that must be proven false in order to weaken an opposing viewpoint.

(E) It functions as the argument's conclusion.

GO ON TO THE NEXT PAGE ⟶

Questions 16–17

The proliferation of colloquialisms is degrading the English language. A phrase such as "She was like, 'No way!', you know?"—a meaningless collection of English words just a few decades ago—is commonly understood by most today to mean "She was doubtful." No language can admit imprecise word usage on a large scale without a corresponding decrease in quality.

16. The argument relies on which one of the following assumptions?

(A) Colloquialisms always evolve out of a meaningless collection of words.

(B) The colloquialisms appearing in the English language introduce imprecision into the language on what would be considered a large scale.

(C) The Russian, French, and German languages cannot admit imprecise word usage on a large scale without an inevitable decrease in the quality of those languages.

(D) The English language would not be degraded if there did not exist an alternative informal way to express the sentiment "She was doubtful."

(E) The widespread use of colloquialisms represents the most serious form of language degradation.

17. Which one of the following, if true, most weakens the argument above?

(A) Linguists have shown that the use of imprecise language on a small scale does not generally impair understanding.

(B) Many colloquialisms that appeared in earlier forms of the English language disappeared over time as the people who used those particular phrasings were assimilated into larger groups with different language patterns.

(C) Dissemination of a new word or phrase by the mass media is an important factor in whether or not the new word or phrase will become a colloquialism.

(D) Colloquialisms are more likely to be coined by the youth in a culture than by any other segment of the population.

(E) Languages of the highest quality often evolve over time out of a collection of colloquial usages woven into the formal dialect of a given people.

GO ON TO THE NEXT PAGE ⇨

2　　　2　　　2　　　**2**

18. To teach in the writing program at Brenton University, graduate student instructors must complete the writing program themselves. The course directors justify this policy by invoking the principle that those who teach must thoroughly understand the subject matter, and they point out that the best means of learning the course material is to take the course as a student. Without taking the course, potential instructors might underemphasize certain key concepts in their preparation.

The principle relied upon in the argument above is most applicable to which one of the following situations?

(A) Dog trainers should be required to obtain kennel licenses before they open their practices, since most dog trainers end up boarding their clients' dogs for a period of time during the dogs' schooling.

(B) Youth probation officers should be required to take a psychological development class as part of their on-the-job training, because it is difficult to document which officers previously completed such a class before they applied for their jobs.

(C) Paramedic trainers should be required to ride as patients in ambulances before they become certified trainers, since only by experiencing the plight of the patient firsthand can the paramedic trainer truly convey the patients' needs to paramedic students.

(D) Vocal coaches should train their students extensively before allowing their students to compete in singing competitions because untrained singers often waste a good deal of judges' time in these competitions.

(E) Zookeepers should be required to have in-depth training in the botanical sciences, because serious illnesses can occur if animals are placed in environments containing plants that are poisonous to the animals' species.

19. Without a fund-raising specialist, foundations have trouble meeting their fund-raising targets. Research shows that fund-raising specialists help foundations raise the majority of their yearly funds. Financial planners serve a key organizing and advisory role, but financial planners raise only a small percentage of foundation funds, if they raise any funds at all. Therefore, _____.

The argument above can be best completed by which one of the following?

(A) a foundation interested in raising funds should entrust its fund-raising activities to fund-raising specialists rather than financial planners

(B) no foundation that does not employ fund-raising specialists can raise the same amount of funds as a foundation that employs financial planners

(C) fund-raising specialists lacking financial planning knowledge will provide less help to foundations than will financial planners with no fund-raising knowledge

(D) foundations that employ fund-raising specialists meet their annual fund-raising targets

(E) foundations should not routinely engage the services of financial planners

GO ON TO THE NEXT PAGE ⟩

20. It would be futile to ask any of the runners to move that boulder on the path. None of the runners individually could move the bolder, so it will not be possible for the runners to move the boulder as a group.

Which one of the following arguments contains reasoning that is flawed in a manner most similar to that in the argument above?

(A) Charlotte should not be appointed for the new position. She has not succeeded in her previous position, so there is no reason to think that she would perform well in the new position.

(B) Our board of trustees is incorrect in suggesting that a committee should be appointed to oversee treasury matters. We would not trust any individual member with the responsibility of overseeing these matters, so we should have no more trust in a committee, which after all is merely a conglomerate of individuals.

(C) This code will remain unbroken. Detective Tally cannot break the code, so none of the other detectives will be able to break it either.

(D) Wearing fashionable clothing will not ensure that a person is considered stylish. Many styles go quickly in and out of fashion, so clothing that is considered stylish by one group may not be seen as stylish by all.

(E) It is useless to argue with Arthur. No one but Margaret can win an argument with him, so it will not be possible to win no matter how hard we try.

21. Leroy could not possibly have given the flu to his coworker on Monday. In fact, Leroy's records lead to only one conclusion: that Leroy did not have the flu himself on Monday. It is true that Leroy spent the day on Sunday visiting a friend who had the flu, but there is no evidence to show that Leroy had the flu on Monday. His records show only that Leroy had the flu on Tuesday, the day he went to see his doctor.

The reasoning in the argument is flawed because the argument does which one of the following?

(A) It concludes that there is a lack of evidence for Leroy having the flu based on evidence suggesting that Leroy did not have the flu.

(B) It fails to consider that Leroy's coworker might have caught the flu from exposure to someone other than Leroy.

(C) It overlooks the possibility that Leroy's flu diagnosis on Tuesday serves as an indicator that Leroy had the flu on Monday.

(D) It assumes that an individual's association with an ill person is relevant to the question of whether he or she contracted an illness from that person.

(E) It raises the question of Leroy's professional ethics without providing evidence to document the relevance of his ethics to the issue at hand.

GO ON TO THE NEXT PAGE

22. Until 1990, the results of the Reading Level Assessment Test given in junior high schools of school districts X and Y indicated that the reading ability of students in the two districts was nearly identical. Since 1990, however, the average score on the test has been markedly higher in district Y than in district X. The superintendent of district Y theorizes that the difference is due to the reinstatement of the minimum reading level requirement in all junior high schools in his district, which mandates that students reading below grade level attend afterschool reading workshops one day a week.

If the statements above are true, which one of the following must also be true?

(A) The average score on the Reading Level Assessment Test in district Y has increased dramatically since the reinstatement of the minimum reading level requirement.

(B) There was a minimum reading level requirement in the junior high schools of district X at some point before 1990.

(C) There was no minimum reading level requirement in the junior high schools of district Y at some point before 1990.

(D) There was no minimum reading level requirement in the junior high schools of district X at some point after 1990.

(E) Since 1990, the Reading Level Assessment Test score of every student in district Y has been higher than the Reading Level Assessment Test score of every student in district X.

23. An economic or political crisis in a poor country can lead to a lack of faith in the country's leaders, which is often followed by violent behavior, dissent, and even revolt among specific segments of the population. In many cases, propaganda is immediately issued from media outlets that quells such reactions by downplaying the extent of the recent crisis, thereby helping to restore belief in the efficacy of the government. However, the habitual violence exhibited by certain groups of disaffected youths in such countries generally has nothing to do with a lack of faith in their leaders but rather is the consequence of endemic boredom and lack of any vision of a positive future for themselves.

Which one of the following statements follows most logically from the statements in the passage above?

(A) It is easier to quell periodic revolts in poor countries than it is to solve the habitual problem of youth violence.

(B) In all poor countries, propaganda alone cannot entirely diffuse dissent stemming from an economic or political crisis.

(C) Economic and political crises do not lead to any instances of youth violence in poor countries.

(D) The effect that propaganda has in putting down revolts in poor countries is primarily related to its ability to alter people's fundamental beliefs.

(E) To the extent that propaganda may help to decrease youth violence in a poor country, it is probably not the result of restoring the youths' faith in their country's leadership.

GO ON TO THE NEXT PAGE

2 **2** **2** **2**

24. Derek won this year's school science fair and is a star on both the school's football and basketball teams. Outside of school, he runs his own successful business and is an accomplished musician. Obviously Derek is good at everything he does and, thus, will undoubtedly make an excellent student government president if elected.

    The argument above is flawed because it overlooks the possibility that

    (A) Derek participates in only those activities at which he knows he will excel.

    (B) presiding over the student government requires different skills than those necessary to become an accomplished musician.

    (C) school, athletics, music, and business are the only activities in which Derek is engaged.

    (D) there may be other students as qualified as Derek to preside over the student government.

    (E) Derek's business requires many of the same skills that would make an effective student leader.

25. Pediatric nurses in Downs Valley have typically been willing to accept overtime emergency home-care cases on short notice, despite the fact that this work is stressful, difficult, and not well compensated relative to the demands related to home-based pediatric care. Many accepted these voluntary assignments because of the professional and personal satisfaction that comes from personally helping a child and the child's family through a true time of need, especially after a relationship with the patient has been forged. Over the past six months, however, the cynicism pervading the Downs Valley medical establishment has clearly taken root among the pediatric nurses. They are now less willing to sacrifice for the well-being of their patients, as

evidenced by the steep decline during this period in nursing assignments to home-care cases, despite an overall increase in available pediatric nurses.

Which one of the following, if true, best strengthens the argument above?

(A) Over the past six months, the total number of medical cases in Downs Valley requiring a nurse's care in a hospital setting has greatly increased.

(B) Despite certain advances in the treatment of childhood diseases, there has been no decrease in the last six months in the number of illnesses in Downs Valley requiring the service of an at-home pediatric nurse.

(C) Over the past six months, an increase in the paperwork required by insurance companies has obligated pediatric nurses to spend more time producing reports and less time with patients and their families.

(D) The financial compensation for home-care nursing assignments in Downs Valley is far greater than that in communities of neighboring states due to differences in state funding of pediatric home-care treatment.

(E) The cynicism pervading the Downs Valley medical establishment stems from disgruntled doctors who are furious over recent substantial increases in the cost of malpractice insurance.

3 **3** **3** **3**

Section III
Time—35 minutes 24 questions

Directions: Each group of questions is based on a set of conditions. You may wish to draw a rough sketch to help you answer some of the questions. Choose the best answer for each question and fill in the corresponding space on your answer sheet.

Questions 1–6

A stadium has two walls available for advertisements, one circling its upper deck and one circling its lower deck. Each of six companies places exactly one ad on one of the two walls. Three of the companies—F, G, and H—sell beverages, and the other three companies—M, N, and P—sell clothing. No other companies will advertise at the stadium. The ads will be placed according to the following conditions:

> Each wall must contain at least one beverage ad and at least one clothing ad.
>
> M will advertise on the lower wall only if the upper wall contains exactly four ads.
>
> Neither F nor N will advertise on a wall containing exactly two ads.

1. If the upper wall contains exactly four ads, which one of the following companies must advertise on the upper wall?

   (A) G
   (B) H
   (C) M
   (D) N
   (E) P

2. If G is one of exactly two companies that advertise on the upper wall, all of the following companies must advertise on the lower wall EXCEPT

   (A) F.
   (B) H.
   (C) M.
   (D) N.
   (E) P.

3. Which one of the following could be a complete and accurate list of companies advertising on the upper wall?

   (A) F, G, M
   (B) G, H, N, P
   (C) G, N
   (D) H, N, P
   (E) M, P

4. If N and P advertise on the upper wall, which one of the following must be true?

   (A) F advertises on the upper wall.
   (B) G advertises on the upper wall.
   (C) H advertises on the lower wall.
   (D) H advertises on the same wall as M.
   (E) P advertises on a wall containing exactly three advertisements.

5. F cannot be the only beverage company to advertise on the lower wall UNLESS

   (A) G advertises on the same wall as N.
   (B) H advertises on the lower wall.
   (C) M advertises on the lower wall.
   (D) M advertises on the same wall as P.
   (E) N advertises on the lower wall.

6. If one wall contains exactly two beverage ads and exactly two clothing ads, then which one of the following must be true?

   (A) F and H cannot advertise on the same wall.
   (B) G and H advertise on the same wall.
   (C) G and N advertise on the same wall.
   (D) M and N cannot advertise on the same wall.
   (E) M and P cannot advertise on the same wall.

GO ON TO THE NEXT PAGE ▷

3 **3** **3**

Questions 7–12

Three divers—Xavier, Yulissa, and Zeke—perform exactly six dives, numbered one through six from first to last, as part of a theme park exhibition. Exactly one diver performs each dive. The following additional restrictions apply:

> Xavier performs exactly three dives but none consecutively.

> Yulissa performs exactly two dives, at least one of which must be the first dive or the second dive.

> Zeke does not perform a dive immediately before or immediately after Yulissa performs a dive.

7. Which one of the following could be an acceptable ordering, from first to sixth, of divers performing in the exhibition?

    (A) Xavier, Yulissa, Xavier, Zeke, Yulissa, Xavier

    (B) Yulissa, Xavier, Xavier, Zeke, Xavier, Yulissa

    (C) Yulissa, Xavier, Yulissa, Xavier, Zeke, Xavier

    (D) Yulissa, Xavier, Zeke, Xavier, Xavier, Yulissa

    (E) Zeke, Xavier, Yulissa, Xavier, Yulissa, Xavier

8. If Zeke performs the fifth dive, which one of the following must be true?

    (A) Xavier performs the first dive.

    (B) Xavier performs the second dive.

    (C) Xavier performs the third dive.

    (D) Yulissa performs the first dive.

    (E) Yulissa performs the third dive.

9. Which one of the following CANNOT be true?

    (A) Xavier performs the first dive.

    (B) Yulissa performs the fourth dive.

    (C) Yulissa performs the sixth dive.

    (D) Zeke performs the first dive.

    (E) Zeke performs the sixth dive.

10. If Xavier performs the third dive, which one of the following must be false?

    (A) Xavier performs the first dive.

    (B) Xavier performs the sixth dive.

    (C) Yulissa performs the second dive.

    (D) Yulissa performs the fourth dive.

    (E) Zeke performs the fourth dive.

11. If Yulissa performs two consecutive dives, then each of the following must be true EXCEPT

    (A) Xavier performs the first dive.

    (B) Xavier performs the sixth dive.

    (C) Yulissa performs the second dive.

    (D) Yulissa performs the third dive.

    (E) Zeke performs the fourth dive.

12. If the restriction that Xavier's performances must not be consecutive is changed to the requirement that Xavier's performances must be consecutive, but all other conditions remain the same, then the number of possible orderings of divers performing the six dives is

    (A) 1.

    (B) 2.

    (C) 3.

    (D) 4.

    (E) 5.

GO ON TO THE NEXT PAGE

3 3 3 3

Questions 13–18

Seven instructors—J, K, L, M, N, P, and Q—teach adult education courses at a community college. Each instructor teaches during exactly one semester: the fall semester, the spring semester, or the winter semester. The following conditions apply:

> K teaches during the winter semester.
> L and M teach during the same semester.
> Q teaches during either the fall semester or the spring semester.
> Exactly twice as many instructors teach during the winter semester as teach during the fall semester.
> N and Q teach during different semesters.
> J and P teach during different semesters.

13. Which one of the following could be an accurate matching of instructors to semesters?

  (A) M: the fall semester; P: the spring semester; Q: the fall semester

  (B) J: the winter semester; L: the winter semester; P: the winter semester

  (C) L: the fall semester; N: the spring semester; P: the winter semester

  (D) J: the fall semester; M: the winter semester; N: the spring semester

  (E) K: the spring semester; L: the winter semester; P: the winter semester

14. Which one of the following CANNOT be true?

  (A) L teaches during the fall semester.

  (B) M teaches during the spring semester.

  (C) M teaches during the winter semester.

  (D) N teaches during the spring semester.

  (E) P teaches during the fall semester.

15. If exactly one instructor teaches during the spring semester, which one of the following must be true?

  (A) J teaches during the winter semester.

  (B) L teaches during the fall semester.

  (C) M teaches during the winter semester.

  (D) P teaches during the spring semester.

  (E) Q teaches during the fall semester.

16. Each of the following is a list of instructors who can all teach during the same semester EXCEPT

  (A) J, K, M.

  (B) J, L, M.

  (C) K, L, P.

  (D) K, P, Q.

  (E) L, M, P.

17. Which one of the following could be a complete and accurate list of instructors who do NOT teach during the winter semester?

  (A) J, L, Q

  (B) J, Q

  (C) L, M, Q

  (D) N, P, Q

  (E) N, Q

18. If more instructors teach during the spring semester than teach during the fall semester, then which one of the following instructors must teach during the spring semester?

  (A) J

  (B) M

  (C) N

  (D) P

  (E) Q

GO ON TO THE NEXT PAGE

3 **3** **3** **3**

Questions 19–24

Medland has exactly seven doctors—Alice, Barbara, Camille, Dianne, Ed, Fred, and Gretchen—each of whom practices one of the following specialties— Neurology, Psychiatry, Radiology, Surgery, or Urology—in one of five adjacent offices, numbered 1–5 from left to right. Each office has a different specialty and at least one doctor.

> Offices 4 and 5 have the same number of doctors.
> The number of radiologists equals the number of surgeons.
> There are fewer psychiatrists than neurologists.
> Barbara and Gretchen work in the same office.
> Only Fred works in office 2.

19. Which one of the following must be true?

    (A) There are more neurologists than urologists.

    (B) There are as many psychiatrists as urologists.

    (C) There are fewer psychiatrists than surgeons.

    (D) There are more neurologists than radiologists.

    (E) There are as many radiologists as urologists.

20. If Fred practices urology, then which one of the following must be false?

    (A) Surgery is practiced in office 3.

    (B) Radiology is practiced in office 1.

    (C) Neurology is practiced in office 4.

    (D) Psychiatry is practiced in office 5.

    (E) Urology is practiced in office 2.

21. If Barbara practices urology in office 1, then which one of the following must be true?

    (A) Alice's office is next to urology.

    (B) Fred's office is next to neurology.

    (C) Camille's office is next to psychiatry.

    (D) Dianne's office is next to radiology.

    (E) Ed's office is next to surgery.

22. Which one of the following could be true?

    (A) Barbara and Camille practice urology.

    (B) Gretchen practices radiology.

    (C) Alice and Ed practice neurology.

    (D) Barbara practices surgery.

    (E) Camille and Gretchen practice psychiatry.

23. If the neurology office is next to Barbara's, then all of the following could be true EXCEPT

    (A) Fred's office is next to Dianne's.

    (B) Camille practices psychiatry.

    (C) Alice shares an office with Camille.

    (D) Fred's office is next to Gretchen's.

    (E) Ed's office is next to Barbara's.

24. If Gretchen and Ed practice in the same office, then which one of the following would make it possible to determine precisely the office in which they practice?

    (A) Urology is practiced in office 4.

    (B) Surgery is practiced in office 2.

    (C) Psychiatry is practiced in office 5.

    (D) Urology is practiced in office 3.

    (E) Radiology is practiced in office 2.

4 **4** **4** **4** **4** 4

Section IV
Time—35 minutes 25 questions

Directions: This test is comprised of questions that ask you to analyze the logic of statements or short paragraphs. You are to choose as the answer to each question the one choice you consider best on the basis of your commonsense evaluation of the statement and its assumptions. Although a question may seem to have more than one acceptable answer, there is only one best answer, and it is the one that does not entail making any illogical, extraneous, or conflicting assumptions about the question. These questions do not presuppose any knowledge of formal logic on your part.

1. Attention Deficit Disorder (ADD) is a condition characterized by an inability to focus on any topic for a prolonged period of time and is especially common among children 5–10 years old. A recent study has shown that 85 percent of seven-year-old children with ADD watch, on average, more than five hours of television a day. It is therefore very likely that Ed, age 7, has ADD, because he watches roughly six hours of television a day.

   The argument above is flawed because it

   (A) cites as a direct causal mechanism a factor that may only be a partial cause of the condition in question.

   (B) fails to indicate the chances of having ADD among seven-year-old children who watch more than five hours of television a day.

   (C) limits the description of the symptoms of ADD to an inability to focus for a prolonged period of time.

   (D) fails to consider the possibility that Ed may be among the 15 percent of children who do not watch more than five hours of television a day.

   (E) does not allow for other causes of ADD besides television watching.

2. Industry analyst: Individuals typically buy Internet access accounts from American providers for about $19.95 a month, which includes email but no other services. Recently, however, foreign Internet providers have begun offering website design and management in addition to Internet access and email for the same fee of $19.95. Representatives of these foreign Internet providers have boldly predicted that their services will put the American providers out of the Internet access business in the next few years. But they have yet to demonstrate that their companies will provide quality, reliable customer service that is as good as or better than that currently offered by American Internet providers.

   In the argument above, the industry analyst

   (A) demonstrates that any concern on the part of certain companies regarding the threat of foreign competition is entirely unfounded.

   (B) suggests that the proponents of a view are basing their conclusion on erroneous information.

   (C) reconciles a prediction with analogous facts from a previous situation.

   (D) casts doubt on a contention by introducing an additional consideration.

   (E) proposes a way for one group of companies to ward off competition from another group of companies.

GO ON TO THE NEXT PAGE

Questions 3–4

The incidence of suicide in the country of Travonia has increased dramatically in recent years, as evidenced by the fact that since the introduction of several nonprescription brands of sleeping pills, the number of deaths from overdoses alone has nearly doubled. However, certain types of suicides have not increased in number during this period. It is true that elderly suicides have seen a greater than 70 percent increase, but teen suicides now account for only 30 percent of all suicides in the country. This is a significant decrease from 1985, when teen cases represented 65 percent of all countrywide suicides.

3. The argument above is most vulnerable to criticism on the grounds that it does which one of the following?

    (A) It discounts the possibility of suicides occurring in groups other than the elderly and teenagers.

    (B) It takes for granted that the introduction of nonprescription sleeping pills has had the same effect on two different demographic groups.

    (C) It assumes that a decrease in the percentage of teen suicides necessarily signifies a decrease in the number of teen suicides.

    (D) It overlooks the possibility that the total number of deaths in Travonia has increased since 1985.

    (E) It relies on evidence that contradicts its conclusion.

4. The assertion that suicides are increasing in Travonia is most justified if which one of the following is assumed?

    (A) The elderly suffered the greatest number of overdoses from the nonprescription sleeping pills.

    (B) Overdosing on sleeping pills was not the most pervasive method of suicide in Travonia 10 years ago.

    (C) The number of deaths from natural causes in Travonia has decreased in recent years.

    (D) The majority of deaths resulting from overdosing on nonprescription sleeping pills were not accidental.

    (E) Travonia's suicide rate is higher than the worldwide average suicide rate.

5. Log for log, with its improved convection features, the Wotan wood-fired stove produces more heat than does the more traditional Vulcan stove. A Wotan stove, however, produces less heat than a Vulcan does.

    Which one of the following, if true, best explains how the statements above can both be true?

    (A) The Wotan's convection features are not energy-efficient.

    (B) Various types of wood produce varying degrees of heat.

    (C) The Vulcan holds more logs than the Wotan does.

    (D) The Vulcan has been in working use longer than the Wotan has.

    (E) Convection features are not the most important heat-producing characteristics.

GO ON TO THE NEXT PAGE

6. City planner: The businesses along Maple Street are struggling, while the shops along the much broader Walnut and Crescent Streets have been prospering recently. Therefore, I propose to widen much of Maple Street, which will benefit the stores along the widened portion of the road by increasing vehicle traffic and bringing more shoppers to the stores.

Which one of the following, if true, best supports the city planner's recommendation?

(A) Widening Maple Street will make the sidewalks narrower, making it less appealing to pedestrian shoppers.

(B) The increased traffic on Maple Street will consist almost entirely of drivers using the widened street to get to distant destinations more quickly.

(C) Maple Street is farther from the densely populated city center than is Walnut Street or Crescent Street.

(D) Walnut Street was once a thoroughfare and is now a pedestrian mall.

(E) Widening Maple Street will create room for many more parking spaces near the shops on the street.

7. In theory, establishing the democratic principle of respecting the basic rights of individuals is unambiguous, but in actual practice, it may involve some rather interesting scenarios. For example, recently in country Q, major reforms of the legal system were enacted to prevent the violation of the basic rights of its minorities. However, these reforms were only possible because country Q is led by a nonelected dictator who may act directly contrary to the popular will without fear of being voted out of office.

The argument relies on which one of the following assumptions?

(A) In a democracy, when a political figure acts directly contrary to the popular will, that figure will be voted out of office.

(B) Nonelected dictators who act directly contrary to the popular will have no reason to fear being removed from office.

(C) The principles of democratic government and of respect for basic individual rights are inconsistent.

(D) The popular will in country Q does not support the protection of the basic rights of minorities in the country.

(E) The rights of minorities in dictator-led countries such as country Q are more restricted than they are in democratic countries.

GO ON TO THE NEXT PAGE

4　4　4　4　4　4

8. The city is required by federal environmental regulations to build a new water treatment plant. If this plant is built inside the city limits, it will disrupt the lives of many more citizens than if it is built on vacant land near the city. However, despite the availability of the vacant land, the plant should be built inside city limits because of the increased economic benefits its construction would provide to the city in the form of jobs.

Which one of the following, if true, most weakens the argument above?

(A) The available land outside of the city is privately owned, whereas there is an adequate site within the city that is city owned.

(B) Regardless of the site location, most of the jobs created by the plant's construction will go to residents of the city.

(C) A municipal plant like the water treatment plant will pay no taxes to city government regardless of its location.

(D) Most citizens of the city will tolerate brief disruptions in their daily lives if such disruptions will secure better water quality in the future.

(E) The amount of taxes paid by workers depends both on where they work and where they live.

9. School chancellor: Just one school in this school district has failed to meet newly enacted minimum achievement standards for the three years the standards have been in existence. An investigation has shown that at this school, counterproductive work habits have become entrenched among most of the teachers and administrators so that simply firing a few "bad apples" will not solve the problem. Therefore, the best solution is to close the school and send the students to neighboring schools in order to improve overall educational performance in the district as a whole.

Each of the following, if true, weakens the argument above EXCEPT

(A) nearby schools in the district do not have the resources to accommodate the children from the closed school.

(B) the school had failed to meet the recently imposed minimum standards for over 10 years but has recently shown significant improvement.

(C) in other districts, a thorough retraining program has been successful in improving the work habits of most subpar teachers and administrators.

(D) earlier in her career, the principal at the school had proven herself to be a competent administrator outside the district.

(E) the children from the school are academically so far behind the children from the other schools in the district that teachers in neighboring schools will be forced to slow down and teach at the level of the new students, thus disadvantaging the current students.

GO ON TO THE NEXT PAGE ▷

4 **4** **4** **4** **4** **4**

10. If ad pages in Fission magazine have increased in December, then either ad rates have decreased or circulation has increased for the month, but not both. If circulation has increased in December, then the editors will receive year-end bonuses. If ad pages have not increased in December, then the editors will not receive year-end bonuses.

If all of the above statements are true, which one of the following can be concluded from the fact that the editors of *Fission* will not receive year-end bonuses?

(A) Ad rates have not increased in December.

(B) Ad pages have increased in December.

(C) Ad pages have not increased in December.

(D) Circulation has increased in December.

(E) Circulation has not increased in December.

11. Historian #1: The metis were a distinct people within Canadian society, the offspring of Native Americans and Europeans. Rejected by both groups, they sought to forge an identity for themselves and made claims for land and political autonomy much as did the Native Americans. Tragically, these requests were not granted, with the result that the metis have gradually lost a distinct identity to the great detriment of Canada's cultural diversity.

Historian #2: I disagree that this denial of the metis' demands was tragic. The metis were an artificial creation who lacked long-standing cultural traditions of their own. They were not so much a separate cultural group as a name given to all those who were neither fully European nor fully Native American—a wide range forming a necessary continuum connecting the two cultural poles.

A point of disagreement between the two historians is whether

(A) the denial of a people's request for identity can be considered tragic.

(B) the metis were a distinct cultural entity within Canadian society.

(C) the metis were offspring of Native Americans and Europeans.

(D) the denial of a people's request for identity can diminish a country's cultural diversity.

(E) the metis' claims for land and autonomy resembled the claims of the Native Americans.

GO ON TO THE NEXT PAGE

12. Before it closed last year, Betty's Beauty Parlor had been in the same location for 25 years. Two years ago, Felix's Hair Salon opened one block away, offering similar services, and Betty's business began to decline. The opening of Felix's Hair Salon directly caused the demise of Betty's Beauty Parlor. This provides yet another example of the effects of competition in a free marketplace.

Which one of the following can be inferred from the statements in the passage above?

(A) Competition is ultimately destructive in a free marketplace.

(B) Betty's Beauty Parlor did not face competitive pressures other than from Felix's Hair Salon.

(C) Felix's Hair Salon served some of the same customers who would have gone to Betty's Beauty Parlor.

(D) Betty's Beauty Parlor would be open today if Felix's Hair Salon had not opened nearby.

(E) Two businesses that offer the same services cannot both survive for long in close proximity.

13. General: The commander of the Air Force has recommended that we deploy the G28 aircraft in the reconnaissance mission because the G28 can fly lower to the ground without being detected and could, therefore, retrieve the necessary information more efficiently than the currently stationed D12. But the D12 is already in the area and poised for takeoff and would have just enough time to accomplish the mission if deployed immediately, while the G28 would require four days just to arrive in the area and get outfitted for the mission. Because the mission's deadline is immovable, I am forced to overrule the commander's recommendation and order the deployment of the D12.

Which one of the following is assumed in the general's argument?

(A) The quality of information retrieved from the mission would be higher if the D12 were deployed than if the G28 were deployed.

(B) By the time the G28 arrived in the area and was outfitted for the mission, the D12 would have already completed the mission if deployed immediately.

(C) The ability of an aircraft to fly low to the ground is not a significant consideration when choosing aircraft for a reconnaissance mission.

(D) It would take longer for any aircraft not currently in the area besides the G28 to arrive in the area and get outfitted for the mission.

(E) Any time saved during the mission due to the operation of the more efficient G28 would not offset the additional time required to deploy the G28.

GO ON TO THE NEXT PAGE ▷

4 **4** **4** **4** **4** **4**

14. In his *History of Oracles*, de Fontanelle maintained that it was not the obvious and true facts, for which we lack a cause or explanation, that had convinced him of our ignorance, but rather the obvious falsities we take for facts, and for which we have elaborate causes and explanations. He felt the greatest indication of our foolishness was not that we lack principles and methods to arrive at what is true, but that we possess others that coexist so peacefully with what is false.

Which one of the following can most reasonably be inferred as an opinion de Fontanelle would hold?

(A) Facts are more important than explanations or causes.

(B) We are ignorant of the true nature of the oracles of ancient Greece and Rome.

(C) The truth can be arrived at if, and only if, we have principles and methods.

(D) The quantity of our knowledge is far more important than the quality of our knowledge.

(E) It is better to be ignorant of a fact and aware of this ignorance than to be in error about a fact and unaware of this error.

15. The influence of McTell's work on Waters's formulation of psychosocial theory has long been recognized in the academic community. McTell was Waters's mentor and main confidant during the 1950s, the time just before Waters published his revolutionary findings. There is ample evidence of communication during this time between the two regarding the core issues that would eventually coalesce in Waters's theory. However, a recently discovered letter dated 1947—years before Waters met McTell—indicates that Waters had already formulated the basic conceptions of his psychosocial theory. While McTell may certainly have helped Waters develop his theories, it is not possible that McTell influenced the formulation of Waters's scholarship in the manner originally believed.

The author of the argument above assumes that Waters

(A) did not know of and read McTell's work before he met him.

(B) did not model his theory on the work of some scholar other than McTell.

(C) did not have a mentor and confidant during the 1940s.

(D) did not allow McTell to influence any aspect of his psychosocial theory.

(E) did not benefit in any way from his association with McTell in the 1950s.

GO ON TO THE NEXT PAGE

16. Fewer geniuses have emerged from the present era than emerged in previous eras. In the 17th century, there were only about one one-hundredth as many people as today, yet in Europe alone, geniuses like Galileo, Descartes, Newton, and Shakespeare flourished. In the 20th century, Einstein is the only accepted genius of that stature.

Which one of the following, if true, provides the most support to the argument above?

(A) Geniuses are widely recognized during their lives or soon after their deaths.

(B) There are many different kinds of geniuses, some of which are not easily comparable.

(C) The very idea of genius has been questioned and seriously criticized.

(D) The 20th century has seen the spread of education to a much greater proportion of the population, reducing the extremes in educational attainment present in previous centuries.

(E) Scientific knowledge has been expanding at an ever-increasing rate for hundreds of years.

17. Sylvia: The public has a false perception that Banner clothes dryers are dangerous machines that frequently catch on fire. In fact, the number of Banner dryers that have caught on fire is quite small. Moreover, that number is minuscule compared to the number of major manufacturers' dryers that have caught on fire.

Alice: It is possible, however, that the percentage of Banner dryers that catch on fire is larger than the percentage of dryers from major manufacturers that do so. After all, the total number of dryers manufactured by the Banner company is relatively small compared to the extremely large numbers of dryers that major dryer companies have produced.

In responding to Sylvia's argument, Alice does which one of the following?

(A) She accepts Sylvia's conclusion but shows that different evidence may be used to reach that conclusion.

(B) She disproves Sylvia's conclusion by bringing up evidence that contradicts the evidence used by Sylvia to support her conclusion.

(C) She proves the irrelevance of Sylvia's evidence by pointing out that Sylvia is comparing two groups of items that cannot be compared.

(D) She refutes the evidence that Sylvia uses to support her conclusion.

(E) She demonstrates that Sylvia's conclusion is suspect because it is based on a faulty comparison involving total numbers instead of percentages.

GO ON TO THE NEXT PAGE ▷

4   4   4   4   4   4

18. A building that does not have adequate ventilation and natural light cannot be well designed. A building with many windows will have adequate natural light, so the presence of many windows in a building ensures that it is well designed.

The argument above is flawed in that it fails to establish that

(A) adequate ventilation is only possible with many windows.

(B) natural light ensures the presence of many windows.

(C) the presence of many windows suffices to provide adequate ventilation.

(D) some buildings without many windows are well designed.

(E) some buildings that have adequate ventilation and natural light may not be well designed.

19. It is not illegal to use hairspray, air conditioners, or vacuum-pressurized aerosol food containers, but it is well known that the use of such products damages the ozone layer, which may in turn have serious negative ecological consequences for future generations. It is therefore incumbent upon us to stop using these products so as to preserve the environment as best we can, even though we believe these products may enrich our lives and there are no legal sanctions against them.

Which one of the following principles is most consistent with the line of reasoning presented above?

(A) The legality of one's self-interested actions should be determined in light of the moral quality of that action.

(B) The morality of one's self-interested actions should be judged in light of the legal ramifications of performing those actions.

(C) The legality of one's self-interested actions should be determined based on the consequences such actions had on previous generations.

(D) The morality of one's self-interested actions should be judged in light of the consequences those actions may have for others.

(E) The severity of punishment for an illegal action should be determined based on the moral quality of that action.

GO ON TO THE NEXT PAGE ▷

20. Public service announcements attempt to persuade teenagers to follow useful advice but cause them to resent being preached to. Teenagers will follow advice only if they do not resent being preached to. Therefore, public service announcements are ineffective and should be discontinued.

Which one of the following exhibits reasoning most similar to the reasoning displayed in the argument above?

(A) Mandatory seat belt laws are directed at those who do not like to feel constricted when they drive. Freedom from unnecessary restrictions is one of the fundamental principles of this country. Thus, mandatory seat belt laws damage one of the fundamental principles of this country and should be repealed.

(B) Zoning restrictions prevent the development of neighborhoods that include both industrial and residential buildings. Including both industrial and residential buildings in the same neighborhood is dangerous and very harmful to residential property values. Therefore, including both of these types of buildings in the same neighborhood should be prevented.

(C) The estate tax applies to those who possess large estates when they die but encourages them to reduce their savings. Savings are needed to stimulate growth in the economy. Thus, the estate tax causes more economic harm than good and should be repealed.

(D) Conservation laws are intended to protect endangered wildlife, which induces their expansion into land presently occupied by people. People will not support conservation laws when their land is occupied by the animals under protection. Thus, the conservation laws are self-undermining and should be abandoned.

(E) The use of 12-hour shifts at a company is intended to maximize production by employees but encourages them to work inefficiently. Employers will increase production only if they are not working inefficiently. Therefore, the use of 12-hour shifts fails to further the company's objective and should be abolished.

Questions 21–22

In addressing the regionwide recession, the comptroller of County X has asserted that the depressed economy of County X is indicative of the inevitable consequences of the recession for all counties in the region. But that must be false, considering that the economy of neighboring County Y is as robust as ever, despite the overall current financial difficulties of the region.

21. Which one of the following, if true, most helps to explain the fact that the economy of County X is suffering while the economy of County Y is not?

(A) The level of economic recession in the region is less severe than that of its neighboring regions.

(B) In overall revenue generated, the economy of County X surpasses that of County Y, even during recessionary periods.

(C) Unlike County Y, County X's economy relies almost entirely on tourism, which has been crippled by the region's recession.

(D) County Y relies on imports for most of its nonessential consumer items, most of which come from County X.

(E) When the recession struck, a few retail businesses relocated from County X to County Y.

GO ON TO THE NEXT PAGE ▷

4   4   4   4

22. The previous argument does which one of the following?

(A) It counters a claim by providing evidence that directly conflicts with that claim.

(B) It contests the relevance of one piece of evidence on the grounds that it is categorically dissimilar from an opposing piece of evidence.

(C) It counters a claim by asserting the impossibility under the current circumstances of that which is claimed.

(D) It supports its conclusion by appealing to an authority.

(E) It provides evidence in the form of a generalization that counters the claim being opposed.

23. While it is expected that some vaccinated children develop immunities, researchers have long been perplexed by the development of measles immunity in children who were not given the measles vaccination. However, they now believe that they understand this phenomenon. The children in question were all raised from birth on a baby formula produced by the manufacturer Dihydro. The Dihydro formula contains a synthetic chemical known as dihydron-X, which has been shown in lab tests to destroy cells infected with measles rapidly. Researchers have concluded that those children who ingest the Dihydro formula maintain dihydron-X in their bloodstreams indefinitely. When measles-infected cells proliferate in the child's body, the dihydron-X responds to the invasion by quickly killing off all infected cells, thus arresting the progress of the disease so rapidly the child is perceived to have a measles immunity.

Which one of the following most accurately characterizes the role played in the passage by the statement that some children who receive vaccinations develop an immunity?

(A) It is a point that, taken together with the fact that some children who do not receive the measles vaccine develop an immunity to measles, generates the problem that motivated the research described in the passage.

(B) It is a generalization assumed by the researchers to prove that the explanation of their puzzling case must involve a reference to the chemical composition of measles-resistant cells.

(C) It is a generalization that, if true, makes impossible the notion that some children who do not receive a measles vaccine develop an immunity to measles.

(D) It is a hypothesis that the researchers take to be proven conclusively by the findings put forth in the passage.

(E) It is a conclusion that is overturned by the researchers' discovery that some children who do not receive vaccines nonetheless develop a measles immunity.

GO ON TO THE NEXT PAGE

4   4   4   4   4   4

24. The chief of personnel declared yesterday that no human resource employees were fired due to the embezzlement scandal. However, the records show that some human resource employees were fired in March, and they also show that some employees who were fired in March were fired due to the embezzlement scandal. It thus stands to reason that the chief of personnel made a false declaration.

(A) Which one of the following arguments contains reasoning that is flawed in a manner most similar to the reasoning in the argument above?

(B) Candy must have extremely good manners. She is a member of the hospitality team at the summer lodge, and all hospitality team members at the lodge have extremely good manners.

(C) Some of the summer theater actors who starred in *Icarus* also starred in *Mrs. Jones,* and some of the actors who starred in *Mrs. Jones* were schooled at the Zeller Drama School. Therefore, some of the summer theater actors who starred in *Icarus* were schooled at the Zeller Drama School.

(D) Many of the Parkers's neighbors have young children. People with young children tend to stay home on weekend nights. So at least some of the Parkers's neighbors probably stay home on weekend nights.

(E) Some artificial Christmas trees have white branches. Other types of artificial Christmas trees have blue branches. Therefore, some artificial Christmas trees have both white and blue branches.

(F) This is Bradley's third year on the delivery crew for Arlene's Grocery. Arlene's Grocery is famous for its efficient delivery service, so Bradley must be a fast worker.

25. Principal: Excellence Learning Services offers reading and math programs for elementary school children. In its promotional literature distributed last year, the company argued that the deficiencies in the current educational system put children at risk of failing statewide math and reading tests. The literature further claimed that the company's programs will remedy these problems. Our school responded to this message by enrolling our children in Excellence Learning Services's programs. However, this year, the percentage of our students that passed the statewide math and reading tests is the same as it was 20 years ago. Therefore, the claims in Excellence Learning Services's promotional literature were misleading.

The principal's reasoning is most vulnerable to criticism on which one of the following grounds?

(A) It merely criticizes the math and reading programs without offering an alternative method of addressing the problems of the current educational system.

(B) It assumes that the parents of the enrolled children were not capable of critically evaluating Excellence Learning Services's promotional literature.

(C) It uses emotionally charged terms as a substitute for relevant evidence.

(D) It does not demonstrate that the programs did not provide benefits in areas other than math and reading skills.

(E) It fails to consider the possibility that the programs were effective in improving math and reading scores.

IF YOU FINISH BEFORE TIME IS CALLED, YOU MAY CHECK YOUR WORK ON THIS SECTION ONLY. DO NOT WORK ON ANY OTHER SECTION IN THE TEST.  STOP

LSAT WRITING SAMPLE TOPIC

Roberto Martinez, owner of a small used bookstore, has recently purchased an adjacent store and is deciding how best to use it to expand his business. Write an argument in support of one plan over the other based on the following criteria:

- Martinez wants to attract a significant number of new customers.
- Martinez wants to retain the loyal clientele who look to him for out-of-print books and first editions.

One plan is for Martinez to begin carrying bestsellers and popular fiction. Because of his downtown location, publishers of these works are likely to put his store on their book tours; although the large bookstore chains have taken hold in the suburbs, none has yet located in the downtown area. Under this plan, however, Martinez would have enough room to keep only the best books from his current inventory. To capitalize on this collection, he is considering an occasional evening series called "Rediscoveries," featuring discussions of authors whose out-of-print books he carries, particularly several authors who are currently enjoying a resurgence of critical attention.

An alternative plan is for Martinez to use the new space to open a small coffeehouse with a limited menu. He would furnish the area as a sitting room with couches and chairs and a few regular dining tables. Although there are several restaurants nearby, they primarily offer full meals in more formal settings. Retaining much of his inventory of used books, he would add novels, poetry, and nonfiction published by small presses to feature lesser-known writers whose work is difficult to find in this community. These small presses include a number of local authors who are eager to read and discuss their work in the coffeehouse.

PRACTICE TEST THREE: ANSWER KEY

Section I Reading Comprehension	Section II Logical Reasoning	Section III Logic Games	Section IV Logical Reasoning
1. E	1. C	1. D	1. B
2. C	2. E	2. C	2. D
3. B	3. B	3. A	3. C
4. A	4. C	4. A	4. D
5. D	5. D	5. E	5. C
6. D	6. A	6. E	6. E
7. B	7. C	7. C	7. D
8. C	8. B	8. E	8. B
9. A	9. A	9. D	9. D
10. D	10. D	10. B	10. E
11. E	11. D	11. E	11. B
12. B	12. C	12. A	12. C
13. A	13. A	13. D	13. E
14. C	14. E	14. A	14. E
15. B	15. A	15. C	15. A
16. E	16. B	16. D	16. A
17. A	17. E	17. D	17. E
18. A	18. C	18. B	18. C
19. D	19. A	19. D	19. D
20. E	20. B	20. C	20. E
21. B	21. C	21. B	21. C
22. E	22. C	22. C	22. A
23. A	23. E	23. D	23. A
24. D	24. A	24. D	24. B
25. A	25. B		25. E
26. D			

ANSWERS AND EXPLANATIONS

SECTION I: READING COMPREHENSION

Passage 1—Direct Marketing

Topic and Scope

Direct mail marketing; specifically, the discrepancy between Americans' attitudes towards direct mail and their behavior in response to it

Purpose and Main Idea

The author's purpose is to explain why direct mail marketing has been so successful despite Americans' seemingly negative attitudes towards direct mail techniques. The main idea is that even though Americans dislike receiving "junk mail," they value the advantages of shopping by mail and continue to respond positively to direct mail marketing, increasing the industry's success.

Paragraph Structure

Paragraph 1 introduces us to the notion that Americans' response to direct mail marketing has been "strangely mixed." We get the "negative side" of the American response in the first paragraph when the author explains why Americans view direct mail marketing as annoying and invasive.

Paragraph 2 then helps us to see why the American response can be considered "mixed." It starts out by providing evidence from an opinion survey that supports the author's claim that Americans view direct mail negatively. It then shows that despite their attitudes, Americans' behaviors in response to direct mail have been positive: Direct mail has become a highly successful marketing industry. Evidence from the same opinion survey cited earlier is given to show that Americans buy items through direct mail even though they dislike its techniques.

This "seeming contradiction" is explained in paragraph 3, where the author tells us that Americans shop by direct mail even though they dislike it because it is convenient and offers distinct advantages over other types of shopping. In essence, Americans like shopping by mail—so they put up with the drawbacks of direct mail techniques.

1.   E

First off is a standard Global question looking for the main idea of the passage. If you've properly developed your road map and put some thought into the author's purpose and main idea up front, this question should be a good one to prephrase. The author argues that direct mail has been successful, despite negative attitudes about it, because people like the advantages of shopping by mail. This point is nicely summarized in choice (E).

(A) distorts the technology issue presented in the passage. Increases in technology are seen as responsible for the fact that direct mail marketers now have access to individuals' private information, but technology is not cited as a reason for the success of direct marketing.

You are never told that concerns over privacy issues have affected the targeting of direct mail audiences, (B). In fact, the opposite may be true—direct marketers seem to ignore individuals' concerns over privacy.

(C) misrepresents the author's argument. The boom in direct mail marketing appears to be the result of individuals' actual reaction to the technique, not a result of the discrepancy between attitude and reaction.

(D) is too narrow. Part of America's "mixed response" does stem from the perceived threat to privacy caused by aggressive marketing techniques—but what about the other reasons for this mixed response, especially the positive reasons?

Remember: When choosing the answers to Global questions, be careful to avoid choices that are either too narrow or too broad. Choices that are too narrow focus only on part of the passage, while overly broad choices go beyond the passage's scope.

2.   C

This Strengthen question requires that we first understand how the author explains the "seeming contradiction" in paragraph 3. He argues that

Americans respond to direct marketing because of its conveniences, even though Americans don't like the annoyance or the invasion of privacy. This evidence assumes that Americans are willing to maintain certain shopping habits despite the drawbacks associated with them. Choice (C) bolsters this assumption and, therefore strengthens the argument.

(A) and (B) focus on one portion of the author's argument but do not help strengthen it as a whole. In (A), the fact that awareness of infringement is high would strengthen only one part of the author's claim—that people don't like direct mail. It doesn't bolster the full argument that direct mail marketing is successful despite these infringements because of the fact that Americans like to shop by mail. Similarly, with (B), the increased number of people on multiple mailing lists does not necessarily strengthen the argument that people use direct mail despite its drawbacks because they like its conveniences. These individuals may be on multiple lists simply because their names were sold to direct mail companies.

(D) contradicts the author's explanation of why direct mail marketing is successful. It states that direct marketing may eventually benefit consumers—its success will filter down to consumers over time. But the author tells us that people respond to direct mail marketing because they like its advantages—in other words, they benefit from it now, as they are using it. That's why they put up with its annoyance and invasion of privacy. If (D) is true, perhaps there's more to the story than the author perceives.

The only thing that (E) may strengthen (and it's tenuous at best) is the notion that the "seeming contradiction" that the author describes exists.

Remember: The answer to any Strengthen/Weaken question will always be linked to the author's argument concerning the issue in the question. To find a strengthener, first determine the components of the author's argument in that portion of the passage. Once you've isolated the evidence and conclusion, you'll be in a better position to look for the author's assumptions. As in Logical Reasoning, strengtheners and weakeners in Reading Comp often work by bolstering or damaging the assumptions in an author's argument.

3. B

This question asks you to identify the criticism that most closely approximates the logic of the author's concern over the use of computer-matching programs. Well, why is the author concerned about these? The line reference brings us right to the crux of the matter: "Further, sophisticated computer-matching programs can produce intrusive personal profiles from information that, standing alone, does not threaten individual privacy." Extracting the general logical structure of this, you have a situation in which harmless individual elements, when combined, become harmful in some way. That's the situation you need to find among the choices, and (B) best approximates this situation: The species alone aren't dangerous to the ecosystem, but put them together and look out!

It's helpful to restate exactly what you're looking for to eliminate the wrong choices: The logic of the original example in the passage states that things (bits of information) that individually don't have a certain effect (i.e., threaten privacy) *do* have that effect when put together.

(A) has a species that individually don't harm the ecosystem (so far so good) but when put together may harm each other. Not the same thing.

(C) again starts out okay with individual species that by themselves don't harm the ecosystem, so you have to look at the end of the choice to see where it goes awry. In this case, the ecologist is chastised for asserting the safety of throwing the three species together into the ecosystem on the grounds that they may not allow other species to join later. This result would not necessarily cause damage to the ecosystem.

With (D), this time, the ecologist's assertion is bashed on the grounds that the species in question may be happier somewhere else. Again, the "overlooked possibility" is not one that necessarily causes harm: The ecosystem might not be an optimal environment for the species, but that doesn't necessarily mean that the ecosystem itself will be damaged.

Their previous ecosystems? What does (E) have to do with putting them together here in the ecosystem in question? This is far from the logic underlying the example in the passage.

Remember: Some questions ask you to apply something you've learned in the passage to another issue in a different context. If the question seems difficult and you're having trouble making the connection, it might be a good one to save until the end of the passage—or to skip altogether.

Questions with long answer choices may not be as difficult as they seem. Notice that every choice in this question starts with the same 29 words. Once you picked up on that, you should have had an easier time—in truth, you really only needed to read the last part of each choice to see how it differed from the others.

4.   A

The mention of expenditures from 1980–1990 brings you squarely to paragraph 2, where the author informs you that expenditures increased significantly during that stretch and that "companies would not have made these efforts without prospects of success." Inference questions are not great candidates for prephrasing, so you probably moved on to the choices at this point. Hopefully, you saw that (A) is a reasonable inference based on this information. It stands to reason that companies spent more money on advertising because they expected to benefit from it (in accordance with the "laws of the market"). Therefore, the rise in direct marketing expenditures can be reasonably said to reflect their expectations regarding success.

The passage implies that companies benefited from direct marketing—meaning, they made greater profits—but you have no idea how much they benefited. Thus, a specific claim like (B)'s assertion that they made "more than double" the profit at the end than at the beginning of the period is not warranted. Similarly, you are told that expenditures increased from 1980 to 1990, but you don't know how much they increased in any given year. In fact, you can't be sure that expenditures increased every single year—you're

only told that the 1990 figure was greater than the 1980 figure, so we don't have enough information to infer choice (C). The same is true of choice (D). We're only told that expenditures increased 1980–1990. We cannot infer anything about what companies might expect expenditures to be in the future.

(E) distorts information in the passage. The author tells us that "the laws of the market dictate" that companies would not have invested in direct marketing unless they expected it to be successful. But to say that the rise in expenditures "parallels" the laws of the market is a distortion of this concept. The rise in expenditures may be explained with reference to the laws of the economic market, but that's about it. (E)'s manner of combining these two elements of the passage is unwarranted.

Remember: Inference questions often refer to only a small part of the passage. Zero in on the relevant section using the specific words of the stem as your guide.

5.   D

The words "according to the passage" clue you in that this is a Detail question. The answer to a Detail question like this will most likely not restate the passage's information directly but will often be recognizable, nonetheless, as a close paraphrase. Because a number of parts of this passage deal with Americans' reaction to direct mail, perhaps the best method is to move right to the choices, seeing if any jump out. (D) is, in fact, a very close paraphrase of the author's main idea that emerges along the way and is summarized rather explicitly in the final paragraph.

(A) goes beyond the scope of the passage. The author does not discuss the "true dangers" of the enterprise (whatever these may be).

(B) exaggerates material from the passage. The author states in paragraph 3 that Americans are willing to put up with the drawbacks of direct mail because they like its conveniences. You might interpret this as meaning that people are willing to overlook some problems to receive certain benefits. To say that people "consistently act against their deeply held convictions," however, is going too far. Besides, the dislike of direct mail probably doesn't qualify as a deeply held conviction in most people's books.

(C) only gives you part of the author's view and is a distortion to boot. The author distinctly tells you that the public's reaction is mixed—it's not just negative, as this answer choice portrays it. In addition, the negative attitude of the American public revolves around both the privacy issue and the "annoyance" factor. It's a distortion to say that privacy is the primary issue.

(E) is 180: The author tells you that the industry has been very successful despite the public's negative attitudes. There is no indication that the industry will need to alter its practices.

Remember: The answers to Explicit Text questions will be drawn directly from material given in the passage. Rule out any answer choices that stray too far from the details in the passage and look for those that convey what the author has already stated.

6. D

This Logic question asks you to determine what function is served by the opinions expressed in the survey mentioned in the beginning of paragraph 2. These opinions are provided as evidence for the public's negative view of direct mail. But later in paragraph 2, these opinions seem to contradict further findings of the same survey, which show that people who don't like direct mail buy from direct mail ads anyway! This function is captured in choice (D)—these opinions are brought up to form a contrast to the behavior of consumers described later in the paragraph, which in turn forms the basis of the author's main concern.

(A) goes beyond the scope of the passage. The negative attitudes revealed in this part of the survey would make it rather unlikely that the opinions were used by the author to justify increased direct mail spending.

The author does not provide a "solution" to a paradoxical situation, (B), but rather an explanation for a seemingly contradictory phenomenon. If anything, the opinions cited contribute to a contradictory phenomenon, not to its explanation.

The information about computer-matching programs is presented in paragraph 1 and is unrelated to the author's discussion of the survey. The author develops his conclusion about the problem of the matching program without resorting to any opinion data. You can eliminate (C).

(E) is possible, the opinions expressed in the survey could reasonably be used to argue that the direct-marketing industry will fall on hard times; after all, the opinions expressed are quite negative. But that would be a different passage altogether—here, the author goes on to say that the industry seems to be booming in spite of these opinions.

Remember: A good Road Map can help you answer Logic questions more quickly by providing an outline of the entire argument and the author's main idea. Once you know the full argument and how each paragraph fits within it, you're in a better position to determine how any given part of the passage serves the whole.

7. B

This Inference question requires you to determine which statement could most likely be attributed to the author, based on the information presented in the passage. Again, your grasp of the author's purpose in writing the passage comes into play. This passage looks at the difference between Americans' attitudes about direct mail and their behaviors in response to it. Evidence for the public's attitudes is provided through opinion surveys, which suggests that the author believes that those surveys provide useful information, choice (B). If the author didn't agree with (B), he wouldn't rely on the opinion poll data in his analysis. The passage as is can exist only if the author believes that polls can provide insight.

(A) exaggerates the author's conclusion. We are told that Americans respond to direct mail because they perceive its benefits, but it would be going too far to conclude from this that the author believes that direct mail has "an overall positive effect on American society."

(C) presents an unwarranted comparison that in no way can be attributed to the author. Nuisance and privacy invasion are two categories of responses from the poll of paragraph 2, with the former outranking the latter in the public's mind, but we can't infer from this that the author believes that presenting a nuisance is a greater offense than invading privacy when it comes to direct marketing, certainly not in the context of "commercial enterprises" as a whole.

(D) switches the terms of the second-to-last sentence of the passage. It also fails to take into account the qualified nature of the author's assertion indicated by the word "probably."

With (E), again, you are not given enough information to draw this inference. The author does not discuss the future growth of direct marketing, so it's too much of a stretch to infer how the author thinks the industry might increase or decrease. In addition, the passage states that the direct-marketing industry has grown despite people's negative attitudes about it. Growth in the industry does not, therefore, seem directly proportional to negative attitudes, which is another reason why it is unwarranted to ascribe the belief in (E) to the author.

Remember: Watch out for answer choices to Inference questions that exaggerate the author's points or go beyond the scope of the passage. If a choice contains information about a subject that the author doesn't discuss, be wary of it. The correct answer to an Inference question will stick closely to the topic and scope of the passage.

Passage 2—Continental Drift

Topic and Scope

Continental-drift theory; specifically, support for Wegener's continental-drift theory

Purpose and Main Idea

The author's purpose is to demonstrate support for the theory of continental drift, first posed by Alfred Wegener. The main idea is that since Wegener's death, geologists have learned much that supports Wegener's revolutionary continental-drift hypothesis.

Paragraph Structure

Paragraph 1 introduces continental-drift theory. This theory was first posed by Alfred Wegener in 1912 as a way of explaining why the edges of South America and Africa seemed to "fit" with one another. There follows some technical description of the theory, but for our purposes, it's best to simply note at this point that Wegener's theory was at first rejected by scientists on the grounds that no causal mechanism had yet been discovered to explain how continents could "float" like icebergs on top of the denser basalt lying beneath them.

Things look up for Wegener in paragraph 2—or at least for his theory, since he didn't live to see its acceptance. The second clause of the paragraph's first sentence essentially outlines the direction of the remainder of the passage: The author states that "since his death in 1930, geologists have learned much that supports [Wegener's] revolutionary idea." Well, what have they learned? That alone is the subject of paragraphs 2 and 3. The support described in paragraph 2 concerns rock formations on the edges of South America and Africa. Scientists used continental-drift theory to trace rock formations on the African continent and predict the location of similar rock formations in South America. Empirical findings upheld the theory's predictions.

Paragraph 3, not surprisingly, provides further evidence for continental drift, this time in the form of fossils. Both Africa and South America contain fossils of identical animal species, despite the fact that these continents are separated by an ocean that today would prevent animals from migrating from one continent to the other. The final sentence returns to rock formation evidence that further enhances the plausibility of Wegener's theory.

8.   C

This Global question is a great one to get you off to a quick start. It lends itself well to prephrasing if you picked up on the huge importance of the first sentence of paragraph 2, as discussed above. The main idea of the passage appears in that sentence, namely that geologists have discovered support for Wegener's theory since his death. You know this is the main idea because everything in paragraph 1 serves as background for this notion and everything in the rest of the passage serves to demonstrate it. Choice (C) captures this main point perfectly.

Nowhere is it stated that Wegener's hypothesis is "more intriguing" than other theories, (A), but even if this were implied, it still wouldn't constitute the passage's main point. What about all the support for Wegener's theory that makes up the bulk of the passage?

(B) is 180: The evidence discussed concerning fossils and rock dating clearly supports the continental-drift hypothesis.

(D) is too broad. The author is concerned specifically with continental-drift theory, not simply "geochronology."

(E) may have been the main idea of Wegener's early critics, but even then, it's possibly shot down by the end of the first paragraph by the mention of "convection," a factor that may bypass their objection. In any case, the author doesn't discuss "conclusive proof" of Wegener's theory but rather evidence that makes that theory more likely to be valid.

Remember: Always strive to determine the purpose, main idea, and structure of each passage. If you do, you'll have an excellent shot at prephrasing an answer to Global questions that address these three issues.

9. A

This Inference question asks you about an issue that is developed in paragraph 2. The two-billion-year-old rock formations are mentioned as evidence to lend support to the continental-drift theory. The author tells you that this example lends proof to the idea that Africa and South America were once connected. If this is correct, the author must believe the statement in choice (A): The rocks would not be located where they are if the continents had not been connected.

Nothing is suggested by the passage regarding rock formations on other continents, (B); for all you know, the rock formations on Africa and South America that are mentioned in the passage are unlike any formations anywhere else in the world.

(C) takes a rather large leap: You're never told how the rock formations were formed—what would make us believe that they were formed by the same force that drove them apart? You're merely told that scientists can use rock formations to predict accurately the location of similar rock formations.

(D) makes a false connection. Fossil evidence doesn't come into the picture until paragraph 3, where the author maintains that in some places, fossils of identical species are found on both sides of the Atlantic. The example given concerns formations in South Africa and Brazil. But the rock formations that are the focus of this question need not have any fossils in common, or even if they do, nothing says these formations need to contain fossils that are common to both continents.

There is simply no evidence given to indicate that the two-billion-year-old rock formations resemble the basement rock in Ghana. Therefore, eliminate (E).

Remember: In Inference questions, beware of choices that attempt to link elements of the passage that have no logical connection. Sometimes, as in (D) here, facts from two different paragraphs are erroneously linked. Other times, facts from the same paragraph are tied together in a bogus way, such as (E)'s attempt to relate the two-billion-year-old rock formations to the basement rock of Ghana.

10. D

The word *originally* in the stem of this Detail question is a good indication of where this answer is likely to be found: Your Road Map should point you right to paragraph 1, where Wegener's theory and the original reception to it are introduced. Paragraph 1 tells you that the theory was developed through gravity measurements and observations and was originally rejected for lack of a propelling mechanism. You're then told in the first sentence of paragraph 2 that Wegener never found clear and convincing evidence for his theory while he was alive. It is certainly fair to say, based on these pieces of evidence, that Wegener's work was developed through observation but was not fully supported with evidence, choice (D).

(A) is a 180: Wegener's theory didn't modify an early hypothesis. It was a "novel" approach to the problem it addressed.

(B) is a 180 again. The theory wasn't originally rejected because it was inconsistent with Bacon's but rather because it provided insufficient evidence for its physical plausibility. Contrary to (B), Wegener's theory seems to have supported Bacon's suggestion that the "fit" between the continents was not merely a coincidence.

(C) and (E) distort the author's meaning in the passage. Wegener's theory attempted to explain why the edges of the two continents seemed to "fit together." Analysis of shared rock formations was one means of supporting Wegener's hypothesis; so was the evidence given regarding fossils on both sides of the South Atlantic. Wegener's theory wasn't used to explain these things—it was rather supported by them.

Remember: Beware of wrong answer choices that reverse the relationship between evidence and conclusion. In this case, rock formations and fossils are discussed as support for the continental-drift hypothesis, not the other way around.

11. E

To answer this Weaken question, first understand Wegener's theory and the support provided for it. The author describes two pieces of evidence that uphold Wegener's claims about continental drift: (1) Studying rock formations in Africa successfully helps predict the location of rock formations in South America and (2) fossils found on both continents suggest that the continents were once contiguous. These details are given as evidence that the continents were once locked together, but (E) weakens this argument significantly. If common rock formations and fossils exist on continents *without* interlocking coastlines, there is much less reason to believe that the existence of common rock formations and fossils points to a previous history of interlocked coastlines.

Regardless of whether or not more fossils were uncovered in South Africa, (A), the fact remains that identical fossils were found on continents now

separated by an ocean, so this statement does not weaken the argument at all.

If a new explanation for the cause of continental drift were discovered, (B), this could only strengthen Wegener's theory, not weaken it.

(C) and (D) are irrelevant to Wegener's argument. Even if Bacon's argument was based on speculation, this does not affect Wegener's views. Further, the relationship between age and composition of rock formations in general does nothing to cast doubt on evidence regarding the age, composition, and structure of rock formations in Africa and South America or what these factors portend for the validity of Wegener's theory.

Remember: A weakener need disprove not an argument, only make it less likely to be accurate.

12. B

This Inference question relates to fossil evidence, an issue discussed only in paragraph 3. You're told that fossil evidence supports Wegener's theory of continental drift. In general, therefore, the author would be likely to believe (B)—that fossil evidence can contribute to the plausibility of a geological model. If the author didn't believe this, it would be hard to understand why he introduces the fossil evidence at all.

(A) offers a classic unwarranted comparison. The author presents rock formation evidence and fossil evidence, but he never compares their relative merits. You have no way of knowing which kind of evidence the author thinks is stronger.

Australia is not mentioned or alluded to in the passage, nor does the author suggest that the fossil similarity described is unique to South America and Africa, so you have no way of knowing what the author would think about possible fossil links between South America and other continents. You can eliminate (C).

(D) is 180: According to paragraph 3, fossil evidence suggests that certain species now greatly separated once lived in the same location. It is only now that those locations are separated because, according to the theory, the continents drifted apart. If you need another reason to reject (D), consider that the word *proves* is way too strong here—fossil evidence is used merely to support a hypothesis.

Fossil evidence appears in the last paragraph, convection in the first. Nothing in between even remotely suggests any link between them, so (E) should have been a quick kill.

Remember: Be on the lookout for inferences that move from the specific to the general while staying within the argument's scope. If an author uses a particular piece of evidence (fossils in Africa and South America) to uphold a claim (continental-drift theory), he or she is likely to believe that this category of evidence (fossils in general) is valid for supporting this sort of claim (geochronological hypotheses).

13. A

This straightforward Global question is found at the end of the question set, but good section management would recommend that you answer the question earlier rather than later. This might have been a great question to tackle second, after the first question on the author's main idea; after all, the answers to these two must be related. You saw early on how the author's purpose is to demonstrate support for continental-drift theory. Here you find this paraphrased in answer choice (A), which gives a more general depiction of the author's purpose.

(B) is too narrow. The author does discuss rock formations but only in one part of the passage. (B) is part of the author's support for the main idea, but it does not represent the author's full intention.

(C) is too extreme. This harks back to choice (D) of the previous question, where we discussed how the concept of "proof" is too strong for this passage. Here, the author doesn't set out to convince us that continental drift is beyond question, merely that it has strong support.

The author doesn't assess evidence in this passage, (D); rather, he presents evidence to support a theory.

(E) is tricky because it tests your eye for detail. The author does describe evidence for continental drift, but it's not Wegener's evidence. He tells us in paragraph 2 that

this evidence wasn't discovered until after Wegener's death.

Remember: Read critically! Take out the creator of the theory in choice (E), and we're pretty much back to correct choice (A). If you blew past Wegener in (E), you'd surely have the darndest time choosing between the two.

Passage 3—Illegal Constitution
Topic and Scope
The Constitution; specifically, the legality and moral legitimacy of the Constitution

Purpose and Main Idea
The author's purpose is to evaluate whether the Constitution is legal and morally legitimate. The main idea is that while the Constitution may not be legal (because its adoption by three-quarters ratification violated the sovereignty of nonratifying states), it nonetheless carries moral weight.

Paragraph Structure
The first paragraph tells us that although Congress authorized a group of commissioners to create the U.S. Constitution by revising the Articles of Confederation, Congress was surprised by the revolutionary nature of the Constitution that the commissioners submitted.

Paragraph 2 starts by explaining James Madison's argument that the commissioners were justified in submitting a revolutionary Constitution because the document served the goal of creating good government, a goal that was more important than adhering strictly to the Articles. Despite Madison's argument, the author questions the legality of the Constitution, because it was ratified by only three-quarters of the states.

In the final paragraph, the author expands her argument from paragraph 2 by showing that the "three-quarters ratification" provision violated the rights of nonratifying states. At the same time, however, she claims that the Constitution's questionable legality does not cast doubt on its moral legitimacy and gives two reasons why this is so.

14. C

This Inference question asks for a reason why Congress may have been surprised by how much the Constitution differed from the Articles of Confederation. What possibility might the Congress have overlooked? This topic is discussed in the very beginning of the passage, where we see that Congress authorized the commissioners to revise the Articles to create an "adequate" federal government. They asked for some alterations and got back something they deemed to be an illegal revolutionary document. To carry out Congress's wish, the commissioners felt they had to depart radically from the Articles, not just modify them. You can infer from its reaction that Congress did not foresee that mere modification of the Articles would not suffice to carry out its charge, choice (C).

(A) distorts information from the text. While the Constitution was adopted without unanimous ratification, this fact is not described by the author as an "inevitability" or as something that was bound to occur. Any lack of foresight on this issue cannot be blamed for Congress's surprise.

Moral authority, (B), appears later in the passage and has no recognizable connection to Congress's surprise over the revolutionary Constitution. Congress certainly felt that the document submitted lacked legal authority, but the issue of moral authority is not raised at this point.

(D) is 180: Congress was presumably aware that the Constitution would differ from the Articles, because it specifically commissioned a revision of the Articles. What the Congress did not anticipate was the extent of this difference.

The reaction of an individual such as Madison is irrelevant to Congress's surprise. The question concerns why Congress was surprised about the content of the Constitution, not how or why someone would later justify this content. So eliminate (E).

Remember: Because Inference questions are often not suited for prephrasing, the best tactic on such questions is to evaluate each answer choice and eliminate wisely. If you're having trouble spotting an attractive choice, ruling out two or three answer choices will still greatly improve your odds.

15. B

Next up is a question that asks you to draw an inference based upon Madison's views. In other words, given the discussion of Madison's perspective, which statement could he be expected to uphold? Since Madison's views are primarily discussed in paragraph 2, look at that paragraph to determine an answer. Madison based his argument about the legality of the Constitution on the principle that conflicts ought to be resolved in favor of more important goals, so choice (B) represents a statement he would be likely to agree with.

Madison used the principle that conflicts should be resolved in favor of more important goals, but the author never stated or implied that Madison viewed "peace in the nation" to be an overriding national goal that should be used to resolve conflicts of interest. So eliminate (A).

(C) misrepresents the author's meaning in the passage. The author never specifies that unanimous approval is the most important objective in drafting a new constitution, nor does he imply that Madison believed this. The issue of unanimous approval comes up later in a different context.

(D) is 180: The reason Madison raised his voice to justify the new Constitution in the first place was because it did not meet Congress's expectations.

(E), like (C), appeals to an issue that comes up later in the passage: moral obligation. The author states that the result of the Constitution was to forge a strong union of the states, but he does not indicate that Madison believed that the commissioners were morally obligated to create a Constitution that did so.

Remember: Some Inference questions can be answered by reference to one specific part of a passage. When this is the case, take advantage of it—keep your review limited to just the relevant portion and dismiss choices like (C) and (E) here that attempt to bring in irrelevant elements of the passage.

16. E

With this third Inference question, you are asked for a deduction based on the author's views. Where are the author's views about the legality of making changes to government? In paragraph 3, the author states flat out that "no government ought to have the power to entrench itself against amendment." So the author would be likely to support a group that rebelled against a state's decision to protect itself from changes. Choice (E) expresses this view.

(A) and (D) are 180 choices that violate the spirit of the author's view on this matter. These choices can be eliminated at first glance, because we're looking for a positive or supportive attitude.

(B) is too extreme. First of all, it can be argued that "admiration" is too strongly positive; the author's views are more moderate than that, and "approval" matches her tone a little better. Secondly, the author would certainly believe that opposition to the law in question would carry moral weight, but would she believe that "any law passed by such a government has no moral authority"? You can't tell—that's a different issue. You can speculate, but this is too extreme to be fully inferable here.

The most you can infer here is how the author would react to the legitimacy of such an act of dissent. How she would feel about the reaction to the reaction against such a law, (C), is one step beyond the scope. While you can infer that she would support such dissent on moral grounds, there's no way to tell if she would be concerned about government reprisals or not.

Remember: Questions about author's attitudes lend themselves well to quick scanning of the main characterization in each answer choice. Once you've determined whether the author's attitude is likely to be positive or negative, scan the choices looking for appropriate terminology. Here, you could have skipped over any negative terms and focused on only the choices with positive characterization.

17. A

To choose the best weakener, first understand which argument the question is referring to. You are asked to determine which statement would best weaken the argument put forth in defense of the legality of the Constitution. Where is this argument made, and by whom? A quick reference to your Road Map should reveal that Madison argued in defense of the Constitution's legality, and this argument is presented at the beginning of paragraph 2. Here Madison claims that the Constitution is justified despite its radical nature because it upholds the over arching goal of creating a good government. Choice (A) serves as a good weakener: If one of the Constitution's provisions (nonunanimous ratification) prevented it from creating a good government, then Madison's argument would be far less convincing.

(B), (D), and (E) are irrelevant to Madison's argument. The issue of "extensive debate" (B) is not addressed in his justification. Neither are the issues of safeguarding the power of the ruling elite (D) or the relative merits of oral versus written arguments (E). Because an argument can only be weakened on its own terms, these answer choices do not accomplish the task at hand.

(C) if anything, supports the necessity for the radical nature of the Constitution handed in by the commissioners. However, it does not relate to Madison's reason for why he believed the Constitution to be legal. He viewed it as justified because it upheld the overriding goal of good government. If anything, (C) might strengthen Madison's cause (defending the Constitution), but since it does not address Madison's reasoning, it has no effect on his particular argument.

Remember: LSAT Reading Comp arguments can only be weakened on their own terms. To choose a weakener, therefore, you must first understand the argument at stake. When a specific argument is referenced in a question stem, read back in the passage to make sure you understand the evidence and conclusion of that particular argument and make sure the choice you select is directly relevant to them.

18. A

"According to the passage" lets you know that you're being asked for something that is found directly in the text. Find something that provided justification for the revolutionary nature of the new Constitution. Justification is given in two places: Madison justifies the Constitution's legality, and the author justifies the Constitution's moral authority. Choice (A) relates to the final sentence of the passage, in which the author justifies rebelling against the government under the Articles on the grounds that government itself admitted it wasn't up to the task of dealing with the "exigencies"—that is, pressing needs—of the nation.

(B) is incorrrect the author uses this reason to argue against Madison's justification of the Constitution's legality.

(C) is 180: In paragraph 3, the author states that no government has the right to entrench itself against amendment.

(D) also presents the opposite of what you're looking for: If the commission followed Congress's recommendation, it would not have submitted such a radical document. Far from justifying the revolutionary Constitution, (D) describes a factor that would presumably guard against the creation of such a document.

(E) is false. Madison did no such thing: His analysis attempted to justify the differences between the Articles and the Constitution. Nowhere does the author state that Madison questioned the extent of these differences.

Remember: In Detail questions, be on the lookout for choices that describe the opposite of what is stated in the passage.

19. D

Nowhere does the author directly relate legality to morality, but since you know about the author's attitude toward each independently, you must be able to infer a connection—otherwise, this question wouldn't exist. Briefly review what you learned about each: The author believes that the legality of the Constitution is questionable but that its moral authority is not. It's a simple matter of putting these facts together. Inferably, the author believes that moral authority can exist without clear legality, choice (D).

The remaining choices may seems difficult insofar as they include all of the same terms as the correct choice, but each choice somehow fouls up the relationship between morality and legality.

(A) is 180: In stating that a document with questionable legal validity can nonetheless carry moral weight, the author evidently sees moral authority and legality as two separate issues.

First of all, the author is concerned with the morality and legality of a written document, not a principle. But even if you overlook that fact, (B) reverses the situation in the passage, where there's something that could be illegal yet moral. Would the author think that something lacking morality can be legal? It's doubtful, since morality seems to carry lots of weight with this author. But still, there's no real way to tell.

(C), like (B), switches the scope from documents to "action." Still, had you overlooked that, you should have recognized that (C) runs counter to the author's beliefs: Despite its possible illegality, in the author's mind the new Constitution can still have moral authority.

(E) goes beyond the scope of the passage. The author's argument does not address court decisions but rather the country's governing documents.

Remember: In Inference questions, beware of choices that shift the scope from the focus of the passage.

20. E

The last question of this set is a straightforward Global question, showing that it pays to scan the question set before answering the questions! Your Road Map should have helped you to determine the author's purpose in writing the passage: to evaluate the legality and moral legitimacy of the Constitution. Answer choice (E) expresses this purpose in a more general manner to "assess the authority of a political event [i.e., the Constitution] on two grounds [i.e., legal and moral]."

What two viewpoints are reconciled? The author argues against Madison's view, but that's about as close as we come in this passage to opposing viewpoints. So (A) is incorrect.

The author does make an argument, (B), but she isn't interested in illustrating the "argumentative power" of anything (except perhaps the evidence she provides).

(C) misrepresents the author's purpose. She doesn't argue for a reconsideration of the Constitution (after all, she states that "history has validated the wisdom of the change") but apparently for an initial consideration of it. And besides, the Constitution can be considered a governing document, not a "doctrine" per se.

The author's argument does not support the establishment of the Constitution over the Articles as much as it reviews some legal and moral considerations of the Constitution itself. You can eliminate (D).

Remember: Global questions are usually among the easier questions to answer in any Reading Comprehension question set. Don't let their positions in a question set lead you to answer them last! You can maximize your points on test day by scanning a passage's questions and answering the easiest ones first, no matter where they're located in the set. This strategy will allow you to accumulate points quickly at the outset of the passage, raising your confidence and giving you extra time to spend on the harder questions.

Questions 21–26

Of course, both passages loosely have the same topic: the new literary tradition that included writers like Brett Easton Ellis. The scope of the passages is very different, though. In Passage A, the author is primarily concerned with what he considers to be the misplaced critical acclaim granted to Ellis and his peers, while Passage B focuses in on the merits of Ellis's work.

Passage A: The author's main idea is that Brett Easton Ellis and other writers from the same time frame and literary genre were overrated by some critics and didn't make a meaningful literary contribution. His purpose is simply to argue that point.

Passage B: The main idea in Passage B is that Ellis did provide new insight through his literary view of his generation. The author's purpose is to describe how Ellis's writing gave a voice to a sector of his generation.

Having assessed topic, scope, purpose, and main idea just as we do in regular passages (except that we have two purposes/main ideas), we move on to the one step that differs in reading comparative passages: Before moving on to the questions, we need to get a handle on the relationship between the passages.

The best starting point is to examine each passage's purpose/main idea. Passage A takes a negative view of Ellis and his cohorts and suggests that the critics have misstated the literary value of their works. Passage B, on the other hand, sets forth the positives of Ellis's work.

Because comparative passages are so short, we won't need road maps. Once we have T/S/P/MI and the relationship between the passages in hand, we can jump into the questions. Remember to look first to see whether any questions refer to only one passage, then follow your usual order of operations with regard to question types.

21. B

The authors of these two passages don't agree on much. Certainly not on answer choice (A)—the author of Passage A definitely doesn't believe that Ellis made an "important contribution." Correct answer choice (B) looks very similar at a glance. The critical difference, of course, is that there's no value judgment here. Both authors agree that Ellis's voice was new; they simply have differing perspectives on whether or not that was a good thing.

(C) is outside the scope, though it might have been tempting because the author of Passage B specifically talks about critics thinking that Ellis glorified drugs and promiscuity. (D) is dead on with Passage A, but the author of Passage B doesn't even mention critics who favorably reviewed the books—and we have no reason to believe that he would disagree with such critics. (E) is the flip side of answer choice (A) and wrong for the same reason—it accurately represents the view of one author but directly contradicts the other.

22. E

This is a straightforward Global question just like one you'd see in a single Reading Comprehension passage. We've already done the groundwork on this one and know that the author of Passage A wants us to know that the critics who hailed Ellis and his contemporaries were wrong and the voice they brought to the literary world didn't really add anything of value. That's correct answer choice (E).

(A) is too neutral—the author of Passage A is definitely taking a position. (B) is the opposite of author A's position; he thinks the critics gave them too much credit. (C) is close but too narrow. The author of Passage A takes issue with a whole genre and group of writers of whom Ellis is one, not just one book by one writer. (D) is a distortion—Passage A does not advocate more attention to any other writers.

23. A

The relationship between the passages is fertile ground for comparative reading passages, and the work is already done before you've ever reached the question stage. When we broke down the passages, we already said that the author of Passage A rejected the value of the work of Ellis and his compatriots, while the author of Passage B advanced the idea that Ellis had added an important literary voice for his generation. That's correct answer choice (A), though it might have been a little trickier to recognize with the focus on Passage B as the primary source of the view in question.

(B) is incorrect because the author of Passage B doesn't directly refute the evidence advanced by the author of Passage A. (C) might look good at a glance, since the authors definitely reach different conclusions, but where is the common evidence? (D) suggests that the author of Passage A is getting his information secondhand, from critics, but the fact is that he disagrees with the critics he mentions. (E) is clearly incorrect, since the two authors reach conflicting conclusions.

24. D

There are many possibilities—these two authors disagree about almost everything. So we'll have to check the answer choices one at a time. (A) looks like a winner at first glance, but in fact, each author finds fault with some of the critical response to these writers. (B) is an issue neither author takes a position on. (C) draws on familiar language, but it isn't actually a position either writer takes—or one that can be inferred from what they've said. (D) is correct; the author of Passage A doesn't think that Ellis added much (if anything) of value, but the author of Passage B considers him an important literary force. (E) is a distortion; the only reference to Hemingway is in the author of Passage A's assessment that the comparison between Ellis's generation of writers and Hemingway's is misplaced.

25. A

Few comparative passage questions relate to only one passage, but attack them right away when you see them—the individual passages are so short that locating the correct answer is a quick and efficient process. And in fact, answer choice (A) is right on target. The only thing the author of Passage A said about Salinger was that the critics who thought Ellis and the others approached the quality of a Salinger were way off base.

(B) contradicts the author's position. (C) is too extreme; the author's assessment related to only a particular group of writers, not all writers of the time period. (D) is a distortion, and (E) is an irrelevant comparison—it pulls familiar names from the passage, but the author didn't make a distinction between Hemingway and Salinger.

26. D

You've already determined the relationship between the passages; now match those pieces up with the answer choices to find the one that fits. The author of Passage A negatively assessed a group of writers, and the author of Passage B described the favorable attributes of one of those writers. Answer choice (A) is a serious trap for the careless reader—it's almost exactly right except that the second writer in answer choice

(A) makes a negative assessment rather than a positive one. (B) reverses the positions of the authors. (C) may be tempting because of the very different perspectives of the two judges, but they are each reviewing a single student, whereas the author of Passage A is addressing a wider group. Correct answer choice (D) accounts for that, with the first reviewer addressing a genre negatively and the second positively reviewing a single artist within that genre. Finally, (E) introduces two elements not present in our original passages: The author of Passage B does not write in response to Passage A, nor does he indicate that the author of Passage A overlooked anything.

SECTION II: LOGICAL REASONING

1. C

The author explains that animals who get separated from their mothers early in life don't play and live well with the other animals. Specifically, they acquire aggression disorders, possibly leading to food fights and other unattractive behavior. The author's conclusion: These animals acquire aggressive disorders because they lack early, proper, parent-led socialization training. To strengthen this argument, you want to reinforce the causal relationship between the lack of parent-led socialization training and aggressive disorders. (C) gets at this issue, and the fact that it approaches the issue from the other angle, saying that simulated parent-led socialization leads to less aggression, doesn't make it any less right. This choice strengthens the link between the two terms of the conclusion and, therefore, strengthens the argument by making it more likely that the causal mechanism cited by the author is valid.

(A), if anything, weakens the hypothesis by linking aggressive disorders with animals not separated from their mothers. If separation and the resulting lack of parent-led socialization are the cause of aggression disorders, how would the hypothesis explain the excessive aggression of these nonseparated wildebeests?

To make (B) work, you'd have to assume that a child who is put up for adoption inherently lacks access to parent-led socialization. If that were the case, then this

would help support the hypothesis. But the assumption is unsupported; for all we know, adopted human babies receive plenty of parent-led socialization. (B), thus, has no direct bearing on the argument.

You don't know whether these polar bears did or did not have early parent-led socialization, so their aggressiveness does not strengthen (or weaken or do anything to) this argument. The argument discusses aggressive behavior in terms of socialization, so any information about aggression outside of that context doesn't affect the argument. Therefore, eliminate (D).

(E) is the exact opposite of what you're looking for. The proposers of the hypothesis would feel better about their idea if these elephants were rude, ornery, stampeding, aggressive beasts.

Remember: Always be prepared to see and eliminate an answer choice that would weaken an argument in a Strengthen question and one that would strengthen an argument in a Weaken question. They're often present to tempt less-focused test takers.

2. E

Because you'll need to find the one choice that isn't an inference, be prepared to keep track of the boundaries around the argument. That way you'll be better prepared to spot what isn't there. The author begins by noting that the Sarrin monks use Pran meditation only in cases of severe weather. The author then explains the differences between Pran meditation and ritual meditation. Understanding the differences will likely be key to getting this question right. Pran meditation is different than ritual meditation because it's more highly disciplined and uniquely involves isolation and fasting. Thus, there are three ways in which Pran meditation is different than ritual meditation. Go to the choices.

The author states that Pran meditation is more disciplined than ritual meditation, so (A) must be true. Remember that "some" in the LSAT means "one or more." You have one example of less disciplined meditation, and that means that some practices are less disciplined. This is a valid inference, so it's not the answer.

The monks only practice Pran meditation when there's severe weather, and because weather isn't precisely scheduled, then Pran meditation must not be precisely scheduled either. Sure, that's an inference. You can eliminate (B).

If Pran meditation involves the unique practice of isolation, then no other meditation, including ritual meditation, involves isolation. So (C) can be eliminated.

With (D), again, "some" means "one or more," so since the monks practice Pran meditation in response to local weather threats, some types of meditation do in fact exist as a response to local threats.

(E) is correct because, even though the author implies that ritual meditation is less disciplined than Pran, that doesn't mean that it's *un*disciplined. (E) goes beyond what the passage supports, so it's not a valid inference and is the correct answer here.

Remember: Get comfortable with the specifics of LSAT vocabulary well before test day so that you don't have to take time to think about what words like *some* or *unique* mean when you're taking the exam.

3.   B

Following the lead of the question stem, your first task is to understand the discrepancy. The author says that a high volume of pirating sales causes studios to lose a great deal of money. However (a keyword that signals the discrepancy in the stimulus), a low volume of pirating sales generally indicates a period of economic weakness in the movie industry. Why does a low level of pirating sales, which would seem to benefit the industry, actually signal a period of economic weakness in the industry? This is the question that we need to answer, so let's proceed to the answer choices.

(A) doesn't address the issues involved in the discrepancy, focusing as it does on whether these studios distribute smaller films.

(B) is correct because it creates a direct connection between pirating and the financial success of the entire industry. If pirating is related exclusively to big hits,

then a low level of pirating signals a lack of blockbuster hits, in which case it's more understandable how a low level of pirating would correspond to periods of economic downturns in the industry.

(C) is off base, focusing as it does on the methods of pirated tape production and not on the connection between pirating and the economic health of the movie industry.

(D) is similarly off base, since it offers a comparative analysis between the largest and not-so-large studios, which isn't a comparison relevant to the original discrepancy.

(E) gives us information about the profitability of selling pirated movies, which may be interesting but doesn't explain why low pirating sales would signal an economic low point in the entire movie industry.

Remember: When dealing with complex discrepancy questions like this one, make sure to identify the primary issues involved and then search for a choice that addresses those issues. Here, note how only (B) actually keeps focused on the issues at hand.

4.   C

The author concludes that no beef has been available in Cebra for the past six months. The evidence is the first sentence: A blight wiped out the town's beef supply six months ago. With such a skimpy argument, anticipate that the correct inference will require you to have read it carefully. Since Inference questions are often tough to prephrase, there's not much else to do but to go to the answer choices.

If you interpret (A) to mean that Cebra folks consume nothing but Cebra beef (i.e., no fruits, veggies, etc.), then (A) is easy to dismiss—there's been no Cebra beef for six months, and these people must eat something. The more plausible reading of (A) is that the only type of beef Cebra residents consume is that raised by Cebra farmers. Still, this is going too far: Although for the past six months, no non-Cebra beef has been brought into town (which is, incidentally, correct choice (C)), for all you know, plenty of outside beef was consumed in Cebra prior to the blight.

(B) makes an unsupported distinction between the categories of meat and discusses the issue of preferences. According to the author, lamb and poultry are available for consumption while beef is not. What's available is clear; what's preferred is not.

(C) must indeed be true if the conclusion and evidence are true. If the elimination of the town's beef supply means that no beef is available, then the town must have had no external beef provider during the last six months.

(D) goes too far. Technically, you don't even have enough information to infer that one resident is a meat eater, although they do have meat available for consumption, it's likely that someone's eating it—otherwise, why would they have various kinds of meat available? However, you certainly can't infer that most people eat the stuff.

(E) pushes outside the stimulus's time frame. It provides no information about consumption patterns before the blight or even after. The argument concerns meat availability, not its consumption, so the comparison stated in (E) has no support in the passage.

Remember: What's the difference between an inference and an assumption? Both are unstated and must be true if the statements in the argument are true. However, an assumption is central to the argument, connecting its evidence to its conclusion, while an inference can come from any part of the argument.

5. D

The author concludes that the food critic's review is flawed based on the following evidence: The critic criticized the soup for containing cilantro and sun-dried tomatoes but praised a chicken dish with those same ingredients. The author calls this an inconsistency that shows the critic to be unqualified. Thus, the critic's review is misguided because the critic is inconsistent. For the author's conclusion to be valid, one must assume that the two pieces of the comparison in the evidence are fully relevant to one another. Only if the two dishes are comparable can the critic's difference of opinion about the two be construed as an inconsistency. Therefore, the author must assume

that cilantro and sun-dried tomatoes have the same culinary impact on strawberry soup and roasted chicken, which is what (D) says.

(A) is irrelevant because the author is concerned with the critic's inconsistent reviews, not with some customers' preferences.

(B) contradicts the argument. The critic clearly does like cilantro and sun-dried tomatoes in the chicken dish, so it's not the ingredients that he dislikes.

(C) would weaken the argument, showing how these particular ingredients are more appropriate to some dishes than others. If (C) were true, you'd be more likely to see the critic's supposed "inconsistency" as warranted and the author's criticism of the critic as off base. Nothing that would weaken an argument need be assumed by that argument.

(E) is entirely irrelevant to the argument, since the author never discusses nonroasted chicken. Information about that dish has no relationship to the author's conclusion.

Remember: Whenever an author uses one fact to prove the truth of another, make sure that the two objects of comparison really are fully comparable. If that comparability isn't demonstrated, then the author must assume it.

6. A

The author concludes that any astute literary critic will be able to anticipate correctly which underlying issues are addressed in Dovak's new book. The evidence comes earlier in the stimulus: Dovak's new novel will have the same form as his six previous works, all of which were philosophy novels in which the plot and characters demonstrated the author's own philosophical convictions. Thus, it seems clear that Dovak's new book will also demonstrate his philosophical convictions, but it will only deal with the same underlying issues if the author assumes that Dovak's philosophical convictions have remained constant. The author's evidence provides information about Dovak's motivations for writing, but they only support the conclusion's prediction about the content of Dovak's new book if those motivations (i.e., his philosophical convictions) have remained constant. (A) clearly states this assumption.

The author says that the plot will "surely be different," but (B) makes that assertion even stronger by claiming that the plots have absolutely not one thing in common. (B) is wrong both because an assumption doesn't make the author's assertions more extreme and because the plot of the text, unlike its underlying issues, is not the central concern in this argument.

(C) journeys outside of our scope as soon as it mentions the novels that Dovak wrote before the seven in which we're interested.

The stimulus states that competent critics can make such predictions but doesn't suggest that their jobs involve making such predictions on a regular basis. Also, the critics are less central to the conclusion than the underlying content of Dovak's new book, and that's what the correct assumption must address. So eliminate (D).

(E) ranks two elements in the stimulus—plot and underlying convictions—that aren't ranked by the author and that needn't be ranked for the author's conclusion to stand.

Remember: Be suspicious of comparisons and rankings that appear in the answer choices. The first thing you must ask yourself about such comparisons is "Is this relevant?" The "irrelevant comparison" is a common wrong answer choice in Assumption and Strengthen/Weaken questions.

7. C

We get a lot of information before the author finally gets to the point, which is that the phony solicitation industry will likely "dwindle significantly" in the years to come. To support this opinion, the author explains that politicians are using phony solicitors less often and that's basically the extent of the evidence. For the loss of some politicians' business to affect the phony solicitation industry so dramatically, the author must assume that politicians represent a significant portion of that industry's clientele. Since this is a Weaken the

Argument question, you can scan the answer choices to see if one might deny this central assumption. (C) fits the bill—it basically says that politicians are not the industry's major clients and suggests that the really major clients, the large retailers, are not following the politicians out the door. This weakens the argument because it downplays the importance of the politicians in this industry's survival; that is, it undercuts the author's central assumption.

You already know that some politicians find public opinion polling useful enough to make them stop using the solicitors. Anything that further suggests the efficacy of public opinion polling, as (A) does, could only strengthen the argument by suggesting that more than just politicians may begin to take advantage of it, to the detriment of the phony solicitors.

(B), if true, wouldn't hurt or help the argument. The stimulus says that some people do share such information; whether or not most people share personal information isn't important in terms of this argument.

Prosecution itself is not an issue central to the argument's conclusion or evidence, so (D) is largely irrelevant.

(E) deals with the solicitors' techniques, when all you really care about in terms of the argument is whether the solicitors are going to go out of business due to the withdrawal of some politicians' business.

Remember: When evaluating the answer choices for Strengthen/Weaken questions, it's crucial that you be able to distinguish between choices that provide useless background information and those that really have some impact on the argument. The easiest way to make this distinction is to evaluate each answer choice in terms of the author's conclusion and evidence. If a choice doesn't directly affect the way in which the evidence leads to the conclusion, then it cannot strengthen or weaken the argument.

8. B

This dialogue stimulus begins with Albert arguing that the CEO's proposal doesn't make business sense. His evidence: Teenagers can't afford luxury products. Bill disputes Albert's conclusion with the evidence that image enhancement boosts sales in the long run. The point at issue between them will be something that both men address and on which both men offer differing opinions. They use different evidence, so that's not the point of contention. They only explicitly disagree about whether the CEO's proposal will create sales. (B) captures that perfectly. Bill would vote yea on (B), believing as he does that the CEO's proposal will financially benefit the company (albeit down the road). That opinion is certainly one with which Albert, who's focusing only on immediate sales, disagrees.

(A) and (D) present views that neither person supports. Looking at (A), since neither man addresses any recent image problems, they certainly aren't disagreeing about that. Albert never discusses image at all, and Bill merely states a correlation between image enhancement and sales, which is not nearly strong enough to say that he feels the company's image is suffering. Sure, positive publicity can help image, but that doesn't mean that the company's image is bad as is. (D) directly contradicts Albert's evidence that teenagers would not be able to purchase the products, and it's an issue that Bill does not address.

(C) presents a view with which only one person, specifically Bill, would agree. This is a fundamental assumption in Bill's argument, but Albert never addresses the issue of publicity.

(E) distorts Bill's statement. He discusses the long-term financial benefits of a good public image but doesn't suggest that teenagers could buy the products. Furthermore, Albert never addresses the issue of publicity.

Remember: Dialogue stimuli are very similar to single stimuli that present different views: The second person in a dialogue never says, "Yeah, you're 100 percent right! I have nothing to add." In both cases, you need to recognize what distinguishes the two views, as well as the scope of each view presented.

The answer to a Point-at-Issue question has to revolve around an issue that's addressed by both people. If one of the parties has nothing to say regarding the subject of a particular choice, that choice must be wrong.

9. A

Next up is a Method of Argument question based on this same conversation between Albert and Bill, so you'll need to characterize the way in which Bill responds to Albert's argument. Bill disagrees with Albert's conclusion and offers supporting evidence for his claim. More specifically, Bill introduces the new issue of publicity and uses it to dispute Albert's conclusion. By adding a consideration of the long-term benefits of image enhancement, Bill certainly does "broaden the scope" of the argument to argue for the financial benefits of the CEO's proposal, as stated in (A).

(B) is tempting insofar as it mentions long-term gains. However, this answer choice is far too broad. Bill does not offer a general assessment of the values of short- versus long-term gains but merely discusses one instance in which long-term considerations might benefit the company.

With (C), first of all, Bill doesn't offer examples, or even one singular example. Second, he doesn't rank the issues of image and profit margins as competing factors in financial health; he suggests that a good image leads to higher sales, which leads to enhanced profit margins (returning to his first sentence).

(D) is 180: Bill does not argue that product sales do not lead to financial growth but quite the opposite. Bill argues that a positive image leads to sales, which leads to financial growth. He introduces a new variable but maintains the direct relationship between sales and financial growth.

(E) is incorrect, Bill does not address Albert's concern with teenagers' disposable income. Bill immediately embarks on a different approach (the image enhancement theory of financial well-being), and he neither argues against or supports Albert's contention that teenagers can't afford the company's products.

Remember: Method of Argument answer choices sometimes seems difficult, since they often depend on general terms like *presupposition*, *scope*, and *evidence*. It's particularly easy to get lost in them if you aren't clear about what you're seeking. Tie the general terms back into the argument. In (A), for instance, consider what the scope really is and then ask yourself if Bill has broadened it. Relate the general terms of the answer choices to the specific elements of the stimulus in order to assess them and throw out any choice that deviates from the stimulus in even one respect.

10. D

The veterinary technician does not discuss the medical merits or weaknesses of Dr. Markey's recommendation but solely discusses Wisecrack's owner's financial situation. Because the Smiths cannot afford the procedure, the technician disagrees with the doctor's analysis concerning the horse's medical problem. The technician's flaw is her shift in the discussion—did you spot the scope shift? Just because the Smiths can't afford the surgery is no reason to disagree with the doctor's analysis; the fact that they can't pay for the surgery doesn't allow one to conclude that, therefore, the doctor was wrong in his diagnosis and subsequent recommendation. In other words, just because the Smiths can't act on Markey's recommendation doesn't mean that the analysis that prompted the recommendation is suspect. What's suspect here, as the stem puts it, is this form of logic—and (D) captures the technician's flaw perfectly.

Indeed, the technician is not quite the animal advocate that you might want your veterinary technician to be, but (A) doesn't characterize how her argument is flawed in this particular context. Her evidence is concerned only with the costs of treatment; she has no real obligation to take the costs of not treating Wisecrack into consideration.

Who's to say what's in the "best interest" of the owners? As uncaring as it may sound, perhaps not spending money they can't afford is a higher priority for them than is treating the suffering horse. "Best interest" is too ambiguous here for (B) to be the flaw in this argument. And once again, one is obligated only to draw a logical conclusion—not one that's in the best interest of some party or another.

Just in case (C) comes up in your own life, a disagreement is not necessarily a personal attack!

The technician disagrees with the doctor's analysis, but she doesn't attack him personally.

The technician's evidence concerns the inability of the Smiths to pay for the procedure. Certainly this can be independently verified, therefore (E) is incorrect.

Remember: Often among the wrong answer choices for an LR question, you'll see an answer choice that confuses what *can* be done for what *should* be done. For instance, if an argument argues for a certain course of action, it doesn't strengthen the argument to say that the course of action is actually achievable. By the same logic, it doesn't weaken an argument to assert that a course of action cannot be achieved. An argument that discusses what should happen is not weakened by a consideration of what can happen—they are entirely different arguments.

11. D

First things first: The recommendation is that the marrow in the shipment should not be used. What is the conclusion justifying this recommendation? It's the conclusion that the marrow shipped is degenerative. The author presents two key pieces of evidence to support this. (1) The shipment comes from rats supplied by Cronin Labs, which has a policy to supply rats that are four months old or older. Somewhat separated from this is (2): Degenerative marrow comes from rats who are beyond their primary growth phase. If the rats provided by Cronin Labs do in fact provide degenerative marrow, then the author must assume a connection between the two pieces of evidence. Specifically, she must assume that rats four months old or older are past their primary growth phase. Since you're looking to strengthen this argument, see if any choice states this assumption. (D) is perfect because it informs us that four-month-old rats are indeed past their primary growth phase.

(A) contradicts part of the evidence, so it certainly doesn't strengthen the argument.

(B) doesn't help to justify the author's conclusion, which concerns a particular shipment of marrow derived from rats four months old or older. (B) just gives information on rats more than four months old. Assuming (B) were true, the shipment still could have come from rats exactly four months old, and you aren't given any information about whether their marrow is degenerative. Therefore, this doesn't support the argument because it only discusses part of the group of rats involved in it.

(C) wouldn't justify why this particular batch of marrow is degenerative because it doesn't link its information to the rats in the stimulus. Were those rats in their primary growth phase? Were they the ones with degenerative marrow? You don't know, so this information needn't underlie the argument.

Even if you assume that the argument constitutes one of these rare instances, (E) would seem to weaken the argument, suggesting that the marrow may not have been degenerative because it might have come from younger rats in their primary growth phases.

Remember: When you have two pieces of disconnected evidence, often an assumption is necessary to tie them together, enabling them to lead to the conclusion as the author intended. Remain on the lookout for gaps in the argument and don't neglect to prephrase assumptions in Strengthen/Weaken questions when possible. Questions like this one reward you for that effort.

12. C

You can view this Inference question from a formal logic angle: If a client had pulled out, the company would have closed. The company didn't close, so you can continue with the contrapositive to infer that no major client closed an account. You could pause at this point to scan the answer choices, and indeed you would see that (C) takes you exactly where you want to go. After all, the author says that a certain action would inevitably result in the company's closure. Since the company expanded, the death blow wasn't dealt—it must be the case that no major client pulled out.

There's no information in the stimulus that would support (A). It could be true, but it might not be, so we really can't infer it.

(B) and (D) basically suggest ways in which Many Maids's business might have increased in the past year. But nothing in the stimulus suggests that business must have increased in these particular ways. In fact, (B) mildly runs counter to the argument, which states that Many Maids absolutely depends on the major clients to stay in business. Sure, it's possible that this dependence has been lessened by the acquisition of small accounts, but the fact remains that if one biggie pulls out, it's bye-bye cleaning company. So you can quibble over whether (B) is possible, possible but not probable, or what have you—but you can definitely say that it is not inferable.

Consider (E), again, this might be true, and it seems reasonable that major clients provide this company with much of its revenue, but you have no information that would enable you to make such a precise statement as (E) offers.

Remember: When you see formal logic in the stimulus of an Inference question, you'll often see the statement's contrapositive among the answer choices as your correct answer. Consider that your reward for recognizing the formal logic and knowing how contrapositives work.

13. A

The author here begins by explaining a certain problem that the Fines Museum had: Its totem pole was too tall to fit into the storage vault. The author then concludes that the problem has been solved and the totem pole can now be stored in that vault. The author's evidence is the ensuing explanation: The pole can now be separated into two pieces and then later reassembled without damage. If you don't see the assumption, scan the answer choices while keeping the central issues of the conclusion and evidence in mind, which are size and storage. To work on a prephrase, consider the relationship between the pieces of the argument. The author argues that dividing the totem pole into two pieces will enable its storage in the vault, thereby overcoming the initial problem concerning the height of the pole. Size offered the only barrier to putting the pole in the vault, so if the pole can presently fit into the vault, it must have overcome the size problem. Accordingly, the author assumes that each piece of the separated pole can fit into the storage vault, as (A) states.

(B) is more precise than you need it to be. For the divided totem pole to fit into the storage vault, it just needs to be short enough to fit. That may not require that it be divided into equal pieces.

(C) focuses on the issue of expense, which the author never addresses as a relevant factor. The argument's only real issues are size and storage, so the correct assumption needs to maintain that focus.

Again, (D) strays from the central issues of size and storage. The author really only cares about this particular totem pole. How its storage would affect the other pieces doesn't matter, so nothing about this need be assumed.

Whereas the vault is temperature controlled, the actual temperature of the vault isn't a crucial issue in the author's argument. You can't even presume that temperature is a motivation for putting the pole in the vault—it seems likely, sure, but you're not told one way or the other. Therefore you must eliminate (E).

Remember: Prephrasing doesn't necessarily mean that you should have a full sentence in your head that you seek to more or less match with an answer choice. It means that you recognize the key issues that the right answer choice will likely address and understand the ways in which the choice should address them. If you identify the conclusion and evidence in this argument and recognize that the divided totem pole has to be short enough to fit into the vault, only (A) and (B) will have any appeal, and only (A) will survive a closer analysis.

14. E

The author concludes that psychologists who want their work to be nominated for the *Boatwright Psychology Review* award should only submit articles

containing reviews on three or fewer books. The evidence: *Boatwright Psychology Review* will not publish any book review article that reviews more than three books. Look back over the conclusion and evidence, and you'll realize that they aren't really talking about the same thing. The conclusion is about what one should do to get work nominated for the award, and the evidence is about what one should do to get work published. That's a classic scope shift. The only way to make these two subjects relate to one another is to assume that one must have a review article published in *Boatwright* in order to be eligible for the award. Otherwise the evidence about publication requirements would have no relevance to the conclusion about nomination requirements. (E) expresses this central assumption faithfully, tying the evidence concerning publishing to the conclusion concerning nominations.

Whereas the stimulus suggests that articles covering more books are longer, it nowhere suggests that this proportional relationship carries out to the extremes. What makes for the longest articles isn't central to the evidence and conclusion and, hence, need not be assumed for this argument to work, so eliminate (A).

(B) overstates the link between the two subjects. The argument in the stimulus assumes that publication is necessary for a book to be nominated, whereas (B) says that publication guarantees that a book will win the award.

(C) is too broad. The argument concerns book review articles, which do come with certain length restrictions. But (C) deals with all articles, and you don't know nor do you really care anything about articles besides book reviews that *Boatwright* may contain.

(D) makes an irrelevant distinction that doesn't directly pertain to the central issue: what must be done with an article before it can be nominated for the prestigious award. One book and two books are both on the acceptable side of the length restriction—no distinction between them need be assumed here.

Remember: A scope shift occurs when the nature of the evidence differs in some fundamental way from the nature of the conclusion but the author treats them as if they were the same. The gap that results from this is often bridged by an assumption. In other cases, you'll be asked to recognize the discrepancy as a flaw in the logic.

15. A

The question asks you to determine the role played by a specific piece of information in the argument, so it stands to reason that we should begin by identifying the basic pieces of the argument. The author concludes that milk from organically raised cows is a necessary ingredient for the best-tasting ice cream. The evidence focuses on one factor: pesticides. Pesticide residues can make their way into the milk of non-organically raised cows and lower the quality of taste for ice cream made from that milk. Since you are asked to consider how the statement about taste and pesticides fits into the argument, you can see before you reach the answer choices that the statement is part of the author's evidence: It supports the author's conclusion that the best-tasting ice cream must come from organically raised cows—choice (A).

(B) is outside the scope. A logical consequence is something that follows from the author's conclusion or takes the author's conclusion one step further. The statement you're told to look at doesn't extend beyond the author's conclusion but rather serves to support that very conclusion as it is.

The claim about taste and pesticides is stated in the argument, so by definition it cannot be an assumption, which, remember, is an unstated yet necessary component of the argument. Therefore, eliminate (C).

(D) is a confusing answer choice, and the logic is a bit circuitous, but if you pick it apart, you'll see why it's wrong. To the extent that the statement in question supports the author's argument, proving it false would, if anything, strengthen a viewpoint that opposes the one set forth by our author. To weaken an opposing viewpoint, you'd want to shore up, not falsify, the statement in the stem.

The statement we're looking at explains the results of a taste test and, thus, present facts that contribute to

the author's larger point, which is the conclusion in the first sentence. So eliminate (E).

Remember: To help identify the evidence and the conclusion in an argument, distinguish the facts from the opinions. Since an LSAT conclusion has evidence that supports it, that conclusion cannot be self-evident; it cannot be presented as an uncontested fact, or else it wouldn't need support. Surveys, statistics, and other facts usually support the opinion (aka the conclusion) and, thus, take the form of evidence.

16. B

The author begins with his conclusion that the increase in colloquialisms degrades the English language. For evidence, he then gives an example of a colloquialism and states that imprecise word usage present on a large scale decreases the quality of the language—hence, the tie-in with the conclusion in the first sentence. The assumption resides in the gaps between these pieces of information; you were never told that these colloquialisms were rampant or imprecise. Indeed, the author states that imprecise words admitted on a large scale decrease a language's quality without showing that colloquialisms really fall into either category. For the author's conclusion to be valid based on this evidence, he must assume that the evidence is relevant to the conclusion and that colloquialisms are both imprecise and prevalent in English. The right answer choice, (B), picks up on both: Colloquialisms are both imprecise and appear on a large scale. Without this, the evidence doesn't lead all the way to the conclusion.

(A) focuses on the source of colloquialisms, which the author addresses but which plays a central role in neither the evidence nor the conclusion. This could or could not be true without impacting the conclusion.

(C) basically restates the evidence. If "no language" can permit such laxity, then these three languages would logically follow along, but since the stimulus already tells us this much, (C) is not a necessary assumption here.

(D), if anything, presents us with a flawed inference, which would only be accurate if the author assumed that the stated colloquialism were the only colloquialism in English and that only colloquialisms degrade the English language. He assumes neither, so if this were an Inference question, (D) would be wrong on these counts. As far as being assumed—that is, being something that's required by the argument—(D) is even further off base.

(E) is too extreme. The author identifies one cause (proliferating colloquialisms), which leads to one effect (like degraded English). To make this argument, he does not need to assume that this cause is more or less serious than any other. Even if colloquialisms were a minor part of this problem, the author's conclusion could still be valid.

Remember: When in doubt on an Assumption question, use the Kaplan Denial Test. If you denied, for example, (A) or (E), the conclusion might still be true. However, if (B) were false, then the conclusion would no longer be supported by the given evidence, and the argument would fall apart. Thus, (B) is necessary if the conclusion is to be true, which is why it's the assumption we seek.

17. E

Now you're asked to weaken the same argument. The right answer probably won't involve denying the argument's assumption, because the first question for this stimulus already focused on that element. Therefore, go through the choices one by one, looking for a choice that will decrease the viability of the conclusion.

(A) discusses imprecise language "on a small scale," while the stimulus focuses on such language "on a large scale." Therefore, (A) is outside of the argument's scope.

(B) is irrelevant. Because the author's argument relates colloquialisms to the quality of a language, information about their historical longevity does not impact the argument one way or the other. The real issue is the damage they do to the language while they're around.

(C) explains the media's role in determining the fate of a potential colloquialism, and since the argument itself does not concern the media or the mechanisms by

which a colloquialism becomes a colloquialism, (C) has no effect on this argument.

Like (C), (D) brings up the issue of the source of colloquialisms. The argument focuses on the effect of colloquialisms; their source plays no role in that focus.

(E) breaks apart the author's causal argument. The author asserts that colloquialisms lower the quality of a language, while (E) explains that they actually often contribute to the "highest-quality" languages in the long run. (E) thus addresses a possibility that the author doesn't consider and that would weaken the author's argument.

Remember: The two most common ways of weakening an argument are by breaking down the argument's assumption and by locating alternative possibilities relevant to the argument. If you have a sense of what types of answers you might be looking for (even just knowing the common categories that they fall into), they'll be easier to find.

18. C

The author kindly identifies the relevant principle in the second sentence of the stimulus. Basically, the principle is that a teacher should learn his or her subject matter as a student because that will enable the teacher to understand the subject matter well enough to then teach it. In other words, one should be on the receiving end of instruction before proceeding to train others in that same skill. The other parts of the stimulus provide additional information, but since the question instructs you to apply this specific principle to another situation, the principle is what you should focus on as you evaluate the answer choices.

(A) is off track because it emphasizes that dog trainers need to be licensed, not trained. Education and instruction are the key elements of the stimulus's principle, and this answer choice focuses on neither.

(B) starts off well but then falls apart, because the officers aren't going to use their psychological training to teach others about the same subject; they simply need to make sure they take the class. According to the stimulus, a group needs to learn a skill to then proceed to teach it to others.

(C) is entirely consistent with the original principle because it explains that one must be taught how to treat a patient from the patient's perspective before teaching others the same skill. One must receive another's instruction before instructing others. This is, therefore, the situation that relates best to the principle in the passage.

(D) discusses the importance of training but is wrong. These students aren't using their training to teach others the same skill but rather to prepare themselves to perform in competitions.

(E) again tells you why training is necessary to perform a job well but misses the element central to the stimulus where the trained individual then proceeds to train others.

Remember: When applying a principle to a new situation, bear in mind that the new situation must contain every important part of the original situation. Incomplete applications, like those in answer choices (D) and (E), are never correct, so develop a clear sense of the precise elements that need to be applied before looking through the answer choices.

19.   A

The argument begins by explaining that fund-raising specialists help foundations to raise much of their money, unlike financial planners who raise much less money but serve an important function as organizers. Before the blank is the ever-important keyword *therefore*. That means that the right answer choice will provide a conclusion based on the information thus far provided. Remember that this is still an Inference question, so the right answer will need to be perfectly consistent with and supported by the information already provided in the stimulus. (A) is perfectly consistent with the argument and represents a logical conclusion for it. If fund-raising specialists raise more funds, then it is certainly logical that a foundation seeking to raise funds should entrust such activities to those specialists.

(B) is too extreme. The stimulus discusses general trends but never states or supports the notion that companies lacking fund-raising specialists can't still raise lots of money. It's not difficult to imagine how a huge company lacking fund-raisers may still raise as much if not more money than a tiny company with fund-raisers.

(C) ranks fund-raising specialists based on what knowledge they do or don't possess. The author never breaks the specialists into these groups or provides information about the specialists in terms of their knowledge of financial planning, so the stimulus as it stands provides no direct support for this conclusion.

(D) again takes you far beyond what you can reasonably infer from the stimulus. Fund-raising specialists generally raise more money than financial planners, but whether or not that enables foundations who use specialists to meet their goals is more than we have the information to determine.

(E) isn't consistent with the passage, which states that financial planners serve a "key" role as organizers and advisors. Maybe they shouldn't be in charge of fund-raising, but the stimulus does explain that financial planners serve important and useful functions for foundations. It doesn't follow that they therefore shouldn't be hired.

Remember: Fill-in-the-blank questions are always Inference questions, so they always follow the rules of Inference questions. This means that the right answer will make statements entirely consistent with the argument without unsupported innovation and that it won't stray beyond the scope of the argument.

20.   B

To parallel the flaw, figure out what exactly that flaw is. The author argues that, since every individual in a group is unable to accomplish a certain task, the individuals working together must also be unable to accomplish that task. In general terms, an individual's deficiency must also imply a communal deficiency. Let's look for that in the choices.

(A) discusses only one individual without tying that individual to a group.

Because something is true of individuals, it is therefore true of a group comprising those individuals. (B) is flawed, parallel, and the correct choice here.

(C) says that if one person can't do something, then none of the others can either, but it doesn't mention whether they could do it working together. That's what you're after.

(D), like (A), has the wrong method of argument. (D) is a causal argument, arguing that one thing won't create a certain effect. The original argument doesn't argue against causation but makes a conclusion about a group based on the individual qualities of its members.

(E) mentions one person who can do something and others who cannot. In the stimulus, all individuals are equally incapable by themselves and as part of the group.

Remember: The key to Parallel Reasoning questions is characterizing the stimulus in such a way that you recognize the key elements that the right answer must contain, while recognizing which elements are changeable. For instance, the order of the evidence and conclusion can change, but the relationship between them cannot. The subject matter can (and almost always will) change, but the method of argument cannot. Focus on what must remain the same and quickly axe any choice that deviates in any fundamental way.

21.   C

The author concludes that Leroy did not have the flu on Monday. His evidence is that Leroy had the flu on Tuesday and visited a friend with the flu on Sunday and that "there is no evidence to show that Leroy had the flu on Monday." Just because there's no evidence to show that Leroy had the flu on Monday doesn't mean that he definitely did not have it—you know it's certainly possible to be sick the day before seeing a doctor and receiving official proof of the illness. Lack of evidence to prove an event doesn't mean that the event itself didn't exist. (C) expresses this argument's error by pointing out that it is indeed possible that the

diagnosis on Tuesday suggests that Leroy had the flu on Monday.

(A) gets the conclusion and evidence mixed up. Actually, the argument concludes that Leroy didn't have the flu based on the fact that there is no evidence to prove that he did have the flu.

The author nowhere discusses how Leroy's coworker got the flu, (B), and there's no flaw in something that isn't part of the argument.

(D) isn't consistent with the argument, which suggests that Leroy's association with an ill person isn't entirely relevant to his own health status.

(E) is just strange. Leroy's professional ethics aren't discussed at all in the argument and certainly aren't central to the argument, as (E) suggests.

Remember: In every section of the LSAT, it is absolutely crucial that you maintain a structured approach. By breaking arguments like this one into conclusion and evidence, you can more easily ascertain whether the flaw comes up in one, the other, or both and then proceed to define what that flaw is. If you don't take the time to understand the argument, you have less odds of getting the question right.

22.   C

The author says that two school districts were running neck and neck until about 1990 as far as their junior high school students' reading scores were concerned. After 1990, district Y consistently took the lead, with its students demonstrating much higher average scores on the reading test. The superintendent of district Y attributes this to her district's reinstatement of a minimum reading requirement in the junior high schools.

(A) is more than you know because it deals with a non-relative increase in the average scores themselves. All you know is that district Y's average score is higher than district X's, but you were given no information to suggest that the actual average score in district Y has been increasing.

(B) deals with minimum reading requirements in district X before 1990, which isn't a subject that the stimulus even addresses.

(C) is inferable. The superintendent attributes her district's successes to the reinstated reading requirement, and these successes began in 1990. This means that the program must have been reinstated sometime around when the change in relative average scores occurred. Otherwise, it couldn't account for the district's post-1990 achievements. This leads to (C): If the requirement was reinstated around 1990 when district Y began to outpace district X, then it must be true that the requirement was not in effect at some point in district Y before 1990.

(D) is wrong for the same reason as (B): You know nothing about district X's history with the reading requirement, so you can't infer either answer choice.

(E) confuses averages with individual students. The stimulus states that the average score has increased in district Y relative to district X, but that certainly doesn't mean that each and every student in district Y is beating each and every student in district X.

Remember: Choices like (B) and (D) exist for those students who don't read answer choices carefully enough and miss the fact that both choices discuss district X. Don't put your critical reading skills aside once you get to the answer choices; read them at least as carefully as the stimulus.

23.　E

This argument begins with a chain of causality: A crisis (step 1) can lead to a decrease in people's faith in their country's leaders (step 2), which can in turn lead to violence in unspecified segments of the population (step 3). Propaganda limits the perception of the crisis, thereby keeping the first domino from falling and favorably impacting at least the second step in the chain. This is the author's first explanation for violence, and the propaganda solution refers only to it. The author then gives an entirely different explanation for violence, this time more specifically explaining youth violence. Youth violence is caused by boredom and

lack of vision regarding a promising future. You have two paths explaining violence, and the answer to this Inference question will certainly test your ability to distinguish between them. Evaluate the answer choices, keeping the distinctions in mind.

While the author offers one potential antidote to the first type of violence without making any such reference in regards to the second, that doesn't mean that there is no solution for the second type. Just because something isn't mentioned, that doesn't mean it doesn't exist, so you have no way of inferring which type of violence is easier to quell, so eliminate (A).

In (B), for all you know, propaganda alone may be enough to diffuse dissent entirely in some poor countries, possibly those without disaffected youth or even those with disaffected youth who are not driven to dissent by such crises.

(C) is too extreme and distorts the argument. The author writes that economic and political crises lead to violence among "specific segments of the population," which may include youth; the author certainly doesn't rule out that possibility. Further, because boredom and lack of vision lead to habitual youth violence, that doesn't mean that only boredom and lack of vision lead to youth violence. The two explanations aren't mutually exclusive.

(D) also goes too far out on a limb. The author mentions two effects of the propaganda—it downplays the extent of the crisis and restores faith in the government. However, you don't know that an alteration in people's "fundamental beliefs" is inherent in either of these cases. You simply know that the propaganda has an effect on their immediate actions at the time of the crisis.

(E) is correct. Because the author does not directly link habitual youth violence to economic or political crises or to the decrease in faith which such crises create, propaganda probably doesn't decrease that violence by restoring faith in the country's leaders. The author says that habitual youth violence is not caused by a loss of such faith, so restoring the faith probably wouldn't help matters any. If propaganda helps to quell habitual youth violence, then it probably does it in some other way.

Remember: Beware of extreme answer choices in Inference questions. Notice all of the overly eager claims in answer choices (A) through (D): (A) mentions which revolt is "easier" to quell, (B) discusses the powers of "propaganda alone," (C) affirms that crises don't lead to "any" instance of youth violence, and (D) discusses the "primary" effect of propaganda. All of these choices go farther than our author, who doesn't make such assertive claims. The right choice won't intensify the argument but, like choice (E), will discuss the possibilities that the argument leaves open.

24. A

The question stem directs you to locate a particular type of flaw in the stimulus; specifically, find what the stimulus is wrong to neglect. The author states that Derek is good at everything he does and then predicts that Derek will be a good student president. We can immediately be suspicious of the word *everything*, since the author's evidence shows that Derek is good at science, two sports, capitalistic ventures, and music. Is this a representative sample? Because Derek is good at these four things, does that mean that he'll be good at anything one asks him to do? You don't really know if being a good president necessarily follows from the fact that he's good at the activities mentioned. Perhaps he's particularly interested in and suited for those things, and that's why he does them in the first place. This argument's flaw of omission is its failure to mention whether or not the four successes described accurately indicate that Derek will be good at anything he does. (A) captures the flaw: The author fails to consider that the causal mechanism may be the other way around; that is, Derek may only do those things he knows he's good at. If that's the case, the prediction of his presidential prowess may be a miscalculation.

The author doesn't necessarily overlook the possibility presented in (B). In painting Derek as a "Renaissance man" and making the bold prediction, the author evidently believes that any skill is within his grasp. His flaw lies there, not in overlooking the fact that the president's job will call on skills other than his musicianship.

(C) comes close, because it would be a viable answer choice if those four skills weren't Derek's only skills. The author assumes that they are, so this answer choice states an assumption rather than identifying a flaw.

(D) is irrelevant because the conclusion only asserts that Derek would be a good president, not that nobody else would do the job as well. The argument is only about Derek, so the author's failure to mention other people isn't a flaw.

(E) would actually serve to strengthen the argument, since we need to know that Derek's success in business is a relevant prediction of his success as president.

Remember: When you have a question stem that's an incomplete sentence, like the one in the question above, make sure that you read each answer choice as an extension of that sentence, meaning you may want to reread the stem with each answer choice.

25. B

The first two sentences of this argument provide background information explaining why pediatric nurses were willing to take the difficult home-care assignments. The heart of the argument is the last two sentences. The author concludes that the nurses have clearly become cynical and supports that conclusion by citing an increase in the number of nurses but a decrease in the number of home-care nursing assignments. The author argues that nurses have consciously rejected these home-care cases and assumes that no other factor besides cynicism might be responsible for this situation. Because you are asked to strengthen this argument, look to support the author's argument that the decline in home-care nursing assignments is the result of growing cynicism among the nurses and not the result of other factors. (B) strengthens the argument precisely because it eliminates a possible alternative explanation. If there were simply fewer cases requiring at-home pediatric nurses, you'd be able to argue that cynicism is not really the reason for the decrease in such assignments. The author assumes that this very plausible alternative (less demand) is not the case. (B), by explicitly shoring up this assumption, strengthens the argument: If the demand for home-care pediatric nurses has remained constant, the author's explanation for the decline in accepted cases seems more reasonable.

On the face of it, cases in a hospital setting may seem to fall outside the scope. The author is concerned with home-care cases, so your correct answer choice will most likely maintain that specific focus. On another reading, however, (A) may be seen to weaken the argument. If demand for hospital nurses in this area is way up, that could explain the steep decline in home-care assignments—it may simply be a matter of prioritizing finite resources. If that were the case, then the author's cynicism theory would take one on the chin.

(C) would provide a different reason for the nurses to take fewer home assignments. Like (A), if anything, it would weaken the argument by providing an alternative explanation for the decline in accepted nursing home-care assignments.

This comparison of compensation rates across communities, (D), doesn't strengthen this argument because it doesn't add anything new. The author states that the assignments pay poorly; the relative degree to which they pay poorly doesn't change the stated fact that money is not a strong incentive to take such cases. Because the information has no real impact, it doesn't strengthen the argument.

The reason why the cynicism exists, (E), is irrelevant to this argument. You only care whether it's the cause of the decrease in nursing assignments to home-care cases.

Remember: In a Strengthen the Argument question in which an author constructs a causal relationship offering one way to explain a certain situation, you'll want to strengthen that link. The right answer choice will often do that directly. However, it may strengthen the argument indirectly by ruling out another possible cause, as (B) does here.

SECTION III: LOGIC GAMES

Game 1—Stadium Ads The Action

Six companies each advertise in one of two places— either the upper wall or the lower wall. So this is a grouping game of distribution, but you'll also have to keep track of beverage and clothing companies. The key issues are these:

- Which beverage companies can, must, and cannot be advertised on each wall?
- Which clothing companies can, must, and cannot be advertised on each wall?
- Which companies can, must, and cannot be advertised with which other companies?

The Initial Setup

A list of entities with two rows—one for the upper wall and one for the lower wall—will do just fine. Distinguish beverage companies from clothing companies by writing the former in ALL CAPS:

```
    F G H m n p
  upper |
  lower |
```

The Rules

1) Now see how the beverage/clothing distinction will play itself out. Each wall will have at least one of FGH and at least one of mnp. Build this in directly by placing a "1+ in each" below the clothing ads and the beverage ads.

2) This one requires some translation. Remember, when an "only if" statement is translated into a standard if/then, the statement that follows the "only if" will follow the "then." So Rule 2 means that if M is on the lower wall, then the upper wall must have four ads, which in turn means that the lower wall must have two ads. "M (lower) → 4/2 upper/lower," is one way to capture this. Taking the contrapositive, you can deduce that if you don't have a 4/2 upper/lower distribution, then M cannot be on the lower wall, which in turn means that M must be on the upper wall.

3) This also requires some translation. Neither F nor N can be on a wall with exactly two ads. What does this mean in the context of this game? Let's turn to the Key Deductions.

Key Deductions

When you get a grouping game, always pay attention to the numbers governing the game. Here, each deck gets at least one ad from each of two groups. In that case, the minimum number of ads on each wall is two, and the maximum number of ads on each wall is four. We can also expand on Rule 3. Because the minimum number of ads on a wall is two, and because neither F nor N will advertise on a wall containing exactly two ads, any wall with either F or N will have at least three ads.

The Final Visualization

F G H   m n p

1+ in each   1+ in each

       upper |
       lower |

M (lower) → 4/2 upper/lower

no 4/2 upper/lower → M (upper)

F or N on a wall → 3+ on that wall

The Big Picture

- This wasn't a bad place to start your Logic Games section. As it happens, the next game is probably easier, but a straightforward grouping game is a good place to build some points and confidence.

- When you see a grouping game, examine the numbers, looking for minimums and maximums. When you do, you'll probably discover that the game isn't as wide open as it seemed initially.

- Treat "only if" statements with care! "X only if Y," means "If X, then Y."

- Keep driving the abstract to the concrete, especially when forming contrapositives. Here, if M isn't on the lower wall, M must be on the upper wall, since those are the only two possibilities.

The Questions

1. D

First up is a straightforward hypothetical. If the upper wall has four ads, then the lower wall contains exactly two. In that case, neither F nor N can be on the lower wall (Rule 3), so they must both be on the upper wall. F isn't among the choices, but N is choice (D). The other choices are possible only. (E) is tempting but does not answer the question. Remember that M is on the lower wall only if there are four on the upper wall, but just because there are four on the upper wall doesn't mean that M has to be on the lower wall.

Remember: When you get a hypothetical, build in the new information and see where it takes you. Don't look at the choices without looking for some deductions.

2. C

If G is one of only two companies that advertise on the upper wall, then Rule 2 comes into play. You don't have four companies on the upper wall, so M can't be on the lower wall, and therefore M is on the upper wall. That's (C).

Remember: You could have found this answer by deducing that the other companies must advertise on the lower wall; it just would have taken a little longer. That's okay, though. You can always find the correct answer by eliminating the other choices.

3. A

Here's a partial Acceptability question. You get only part of the setup, which means that some of the choices will likely be wrong because of their implications for the other deck. Eliminate (C) and (E) fairly easily, because they contain pretty straightforward violations of Rules 3 and 1, respectively. Getting rid of (B) and (D) is a little harder. Rule 2 gets rid of (D), because (D) places M on the lower wall but places only three companies on the upper wall. Rule 3 gets rid of (B), which places only F and M on the lower wall, and you know that any wall with F must contain at least three ads. So (A) is correct.

Remember: When you get an Acceptability question that only gives you part of the arrangement, expect that you'll have to make deductions concerning the entities that aren't mentioned.

4. A

With N and P on the upper wall, M will have to go to the lower wall since M is the only clothing company left. That brings Rule 2 into play. Because M is on the lower wall, the upper wall will have four ads. Now Rule 3 comes into play. Because the lower wall has two ads, F must be on the upper wall. You can place every ad definitively except G and H. One of these two goes on each wall, but you can't tell which. So (A) must be true and is correct.

(B) and (C) and (D) are possible only because you don't know where G and H are.

(E) is impossible. P is on the upper wall, which has four ads.

Remember: To find deductions, look for the most relevant rule. Placing N and P on the upper wall should direct you to Rule 1. Once M is placed on the lower wall, Rule 2 comes into play, and so on. Sometimes success in Logic Games is just a matter of knowing where to look.

5. E

In a different way, this question is asking what must be true if F is the only beverage company on the lower wall. In that case, G and H must be on the upper wall, and according to Rule 1, they must be joined by at least one clothing company. Now Rule 3 comes in. Because F is on the lower wall, the lower wall needs at least three ads. So the ads are split 3/3, which in turn means that M is on the upper wall (contrapositive of Rule 2). So N and P, the only ads left, must go on the lower wall. Here's what you've just deduced:

upper	G H M
lower	F n p

All the choices must be false except (E). N must be on the lower wall.

Remember: "X cannot be true unless Y," means "If X, then Y."

6. E

This question is a little tougher since you don't know which wall has two of each ad type. So start by seeing what happens when the upper wall has two of each type. You know that F and N will have to be on the upper wall, because they can't be on a wall with only two ads. Beyond that, there isn't much to deduce. Each wall will have one of G and H, and each wall will have one of M and P.

upper	F n	G/H	m/p
lower		G/H	m/p

From here, you can eliminate all the wrong choices. This scenario demonstrates that F and H could be together, (A); G and H could be apart, (B); G and N could be apart, (C); and M and N could be together, (D). So (E) must be true.

At this point, you don't have to explore what happens when the lower wall has two of each ad type, but if you did, here's what you might have found: F and N still have to be on the wall with four ads, and they still have to be joined by exactly one of G and H. However, you can make one extra deduction: Because the upper wall doesn't have four ads, M cannot be on the lower wall (contrapositive of Rule 2). So M is on the upper wall, which means P must be on the lower wall. Here's what you've deduced:

upper		G/H	m/p	
lower	F n	G/H	p	

In either scenario, M and P are on separate walls, so again, (E) must be true.

Remember: If a question breaks down into two distinct scenarios, work them both out. Then you'll know what must, could, and cannot be true.

Game 2—Six Dives
The Action

Six dives are performed, one after the other in a row, so we're dealing with another sequencing game. This one is a little different in that some divers will dive more than once, but otherwise this is business as usual. The key issues are:

- Which dives can, must, or cannot be performed by which people?
- Which dives can, must, or cannot be performed by the same person as which other dives?

The Initial Setup

Nothing fancy is required here. A list of the entities (X, Y, Z) and six slots will do just fine.

X Y Z

$$\frac{\quad}{1} \quad \frac{\quad}{2} \quad \frac{\quad}{3} \quad \frac{\quad}{4} \quad \frac{\quad}{5} \quad \frac{\quad}{6}$$

1) So X performs three dives, and none in a row. At this point, you should be asking: How many different ways are there for this to happen? There aren't too many, and that leads to the Key Deduction below.

2) Y gets two dives, and you know you'll need to place at least one Y in one of the first two slots.

3) The meaning of this is clear enough: You can't have YZ.

Key Deductions

X gets three dives but none consecutively. With only six slots, there aren't many ways to fit this in. So explore them. If X is first, then Y must be second (Rule 2). Now, if another X is third, where can the last X be? It can't be fourth or sixth, since that would leave YZ together. So the last X would have to be fifth. Y and Z will split the fourth and sixth slots, in either order. Call this Option I.

Option I

$$\frac{X}{1} \quad \frac{Y}{2} \quad \frac{X}{3} \quad \frac{Y/Z}{4} \quad \frac{X}{5} \quad \frac{Y/Z}{6}$$

If X dives first and fourth, then X's third dive must be sixth. Now you have to split up YZ. The two Y's go second and third, and Z goes fifth. Call this Option II.

Option II

$$\frac{X}{1} \quad \frac{Y}{2} \quad \frac{Y}{3} \quad \frac{X}{4} \quad \frac{Z}{5} \quad \frac{X}{6}$$

Finally, if X dives second, then X's other dives must be fourth and sixth. Y then dives first (Rule 2), and Y and Z split the third and fifth slots. Call this Option III.

Option III

$$\frac{Y}{1} \quad \frac{X}{2} \quad \frac{Y/Z}{3} \quad \frac{X}{4} \quad \frac{Y/Z}{5} \quad \frac{X}{6}$$

That's it! There's no other way to spread out the three Xs. So the entire game breaks down into three options. It takes a little time to find them, but once you do, the questions will drop like flies.

The Final Visualization

Option I

$$\frac{X}{1} \quad \frac{Y}{2} \quad \frac{X}{3} \quad \frac{Y/Z}{4} \quad \frac{X}{5} \quad \frac{Y/Z}{6}$$

Option II

$$\frac{X}{1} \quad \frac{Y}{2} \quad \frac{Y}{3} \quad \frac{X}{4} \quad \frac{Z}{5} \quad \frac{X}{6}$$

Option III

$$\frac{Y}{1} \quad \frac{X}{2} \quad \frac{Y/Z}{3} \quad \frac{X}{4} \quad \frac{Y/Z}{5} \quad \frac{X}{6}$$

The Big Picture

- Knowing when to stop looking for deductions is an acquired skill. Early on, expect to stop looking too early in some instances and too late in others. That's okay—it's part of the learning process. In time, though, develop a sense for the "likely suspects" but move on when they aren't there.

- One of those "likely suspects" is Limited Options. If a game breaks down into only two or three scenarios, work out those scenarios. You'll fly through the questions.

The Questions

7. C

First up is a standard Acceptability question. Again, the Kaplan method of using the rules to eliminate choices yields a quick point. Rule 1 kills (B) and (D). Rule 2 kills (E). Rule 3 kills (A). (C) remains and is correct.

Remember: When you get an Acceptability question, use the rules to eliminate four choices, then pick the one that remains without checking it.

8. E

If Z is fifth, then you're either in Option II or Option III. In Option III, X dives neither first nor third, so (A) and (C) are wrong. In Option II, X doesn't dive second and Y doesn't dive first, so (B) and (D) are wrong. So (E) must be true. You don't have to check it, but Y is always third in Option II, and Y must be third in Option III whenever Z is fifth, because Y and Z split the third and fifth positions.

Remember: When you have set out a game's options, use the stem to tell you which scenarios are in effect.

9. D

This one is a quick battle once you have the options. In Option I, X is first, Y can be fourth, Y can be sixth, and Z can be sixth. So (A), (B), (C), and (E) are all wrong. So (D) must be correct, and yes, Z can never be first.

Remember: When you've worked out all the possibilities up front, you always know what could, must, and cannot be true.

10. B

If X is third, then you're in Option I. (A) and (C) must be true. (D) and (E) could be true, but (B) must be false and is, therefore, correct. X can't be sixth because that wouldn't allow us to break up Y and Z.

Remember: If things are going well, don't second-guess yourself. Move swiftly and save time for harder games.

11. E

If Y performs two dives consecutively, then you're in Option II:

Option II

$$\underline{\overset{X}{1}} \qquad \underline{\overset{Y}{2}} \qquad \underline{\overset{Y}{3}} \qquad \underline{\overset{X}{4}} \qquad \underline{\overset{Z}{5}} \qquad \underline{\overset{X}{6}}$$

Remember: Always read the question stem carefully! It can be easy to miss a word like EXCEPT, even when it's in ALL CAPS.

12. A

Now the test makers have switched things around. Now X's dives must be consecutive. So how many ways can they be placed? X's dives cannot be first through third because we need a Y in the first two. If X's dives are second through fourth, then you can place Y first, but now you have YZ in fifth and sixth in violation of Rule 3. So can X's dives be third through fifth? Sure. Y's dives will be first and second, and Z will be sixth. That's one combination so far. Now can X's dives be fourth through sixth? No, because we wouldn't be able to split up Y and Z. So (A), one combination, is correct.

Remember: If a question involves a rule change, don't panic. You may have to rethink part of your understanding of the initial setup, but your experience working with the other rules will see you through.

Game 3—Seven Instructors, Three Semesters

The Action

Seven instructors—J, K, L, M, N, P, and Q—each teach during exactly one of three semesters. In other words, you have to distribute the seven instructors among the three semesters. So this is another grouping game of distribution, and the key issues will be these:

- Which instructors can, must, or cannot teach during which semesters?

- Which instructors can, must, or cannot teach during the same semester as which other instructors?

- How many instructors teach during each semester?

The Initial Setup

A list of the entities and three columns (one for each of the semesters) will allow you to keep track of the action here

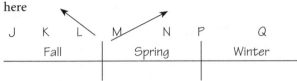

The Rules

1) Here's a concrete rule: You can place K in the winter column permanently.

2) Rule 2 is a familiar enough grouping rule. L and M are always together. "Always LM," captures this.

3) Rule 3 can be built in directly, with arrows pointing to the fall and spring semesters.

4) The winter semester gets twice as many as the fall semester. Okay, what does that mean in the context of this game? With seven instructors, there really aren't that many ways to split them up so that exactly twice as many wind up in the Winter semester. So how many combinations are there? If one instructor taught in the fall, then you'd need two in the winter, and the remaining four would teach during the spring semester. Or you could have two in the fall, four in the winter, and one in the spring. That's it. It's either 1/4/2 or 2/1/4. You can't have three or more in the fall, because that would force you to have six or more in the winter, and that's no good because there are only seven instructors.

5) and 6) are familiar enough grouping rules. You cannot have an NQ, and you cannot have a JP.

Key Deductions

The Big Deduction here was the 1/4/2 or 2/1/4 breakdown of the instructors. This essentially comes straight out of Rule 4, but if you noticed it at this point, that's okay, too. From here, you could have explored different scenarios, seeing if they set off any chains of inferences, but there wasn't anything else that qualifies as a major deduction. On to the questions!

The Final Visualization

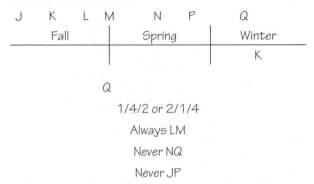

The Big Picture

- This wasn't an easy game, but it is less complicated than Game 4. This game was probably best handled third, after Games 1 and 2.

- Get to know the usual suspects that appear in Logic Games. Grouping games are very common, so you should get a feel for their mechanics. This will help should you encounter a similar game on test day.

- Always investigate the numbers behind grouping games always turn abstract rules into concrete rules. Here, the game was pretty tough if you didn't make the numbers deduction early. But don't get down if you didn't make it. Instead, focus on the clues that will lead to similar deductions on test day.

- When a rule is abstract, think of concrete scenarios that would violate it and see if there are a limited number of scenarios that don't violate it. Rule 4 is tough to deal with without paraphrasing, but once you see how it applies in context, you have the key to the game.

The Questions

13. D

This is a harder Acceptability question than most since we're only given part of the lineup. So you may have been forced to work out scenarios for each choice. Only (B) and (E) contain a straightforward violation of a rule. (According to Rule 6, we can't have J and P together, and according to Rule 1, K teaches during the winter). The rest of the choices require some work:

(A) doesn't work: With Q and M in the fall, you need L there as well (Rule 2). That's three in the fall, which is no good, because it would force you to place six in the winter.

If L is in the fall, then so is M. Because the fall can hold no more, Q must go in the spring (Rule 3). That leaves K, J, P, and N for the winter. But we can't have J and P together, so (C) doesn't work. So (D) is correct by the process of elimination.

For the record: Placing J, M, and N as the stem dictates means you must also place L in the winter. Because the winter now has three instructors, it will need a fourth to satisfy the 2/1/4 distribution. We also need to split up J and P. So you can place Q in the fall and P in the winter, and (D) is an acceptable arrangement.

Fall	Spring	Winter
J	N	K
Q		M
		L
		P

Remember: Acceptability questions are usually quick points, but they can be harder when you only see part of the arrangement. Often, the wrong choices in these questions don't contain obvious violations of the rules. Rather, they violate the rules by virtue of their implications for the other entities.

14. A

This one was quick if you worked out the scenario in (C) from the previous question. In that choice, you saw what happens when you put L in the fall: You need to put M there as well, and you're forced to place J and P together in the winter. So you can never put L (or M, for that matter) in the fall, and choice (A) is correct.

If you didn't see this, you still could have attacked this question strategically by postponing working on it until after you've built some acceptable scenarios from the other questions. (B) must be true in question 18, (E) could be true in question 18, and both (C) and (D) are true in the correct answer to question 13.

Remember: Postpone working on questions when your work in the other questions will eliminate some choices.

Don't forget about the correct answer to the Acceptability question. It often eliminates a few wrong choices elsewhere.

15. C

If only one instructor teaches in the spring, then we have a 2/1/4 setup. You've seen we can't place L and M in the fall, since that would force J and P together in the winter. So L and M teach in the winter, and (C) is correct.

(A), (D), and (E) are all possible only.

(B) is impossible. L teaches in the winter.

Remember: Sometimes a game's questions are similar to each other. So once you build some experience, you should be able to make inferences more quickly as the game goes on.

16. D

Here's another question that allows you to benefit from previous work. In the last question, we had K, L, and M together in the winter. They could be joined by either J or P without any violations. Once you know that we can have KLMJ or KLMP together, you can eliminate all four wrong choices because they all contain a subset of one of those groups. You also might have spotted correct choice (D) directly: K must be in the winter, and Q can never be in the winter. So (D) is correct.

Remember: Use your previous work whenever possible. It saves time.

17. D

Who doesn't teach in the winter semester? Since the winter semester has either two or four instructors, either three or five instructors don't teach during the winter semester. So (B) and (E) are wrong. Eliminating the other wrong choices was a little harder:

(A) splits up L and M, in violation of Rule 2.

(C) places J and P in the winter and thus violates Rule 6. So (D) is correct.

For the record, we could place Q and P in the fall, N in the spring, and K, L, M, and J in the winter. (D) is therefore correct.

Remember: Numbers deductions are key in grouping games. Always look for minimums and maximums and then use that information to cut down on your work later on.

18. B

If more instructors teach during the spring semester, then you're dealing with the 1/4/2 setup. So where could L and M go? They can never go in the fall, and they can't go in the winter, because there are only two winter instructors and K is always there. So they must go in the spring. So (B) is correct. The wrong choices are possible only.

Remember: The challenge with this game was timing. Lots of people could find the right answers given unlimited time, but the real challenge is to find the right answers as quickly as possible. Take a second look at your work on these questions and ask yourself how you could have used good test-taking strategies to save time. Then practice these strategies until you apply them automatically.

Game 4—Doctors in Offices
The Action

Who's here? Doctors

How many? Seven

What are their names? a, b, c, d, e, f, and g

What do you want to know about them? The specialty (N, P, R, S, or U) and the office (1, 2, 3, 4, and 5) in which they practice

Rules and Deductions

All rules are not created equal. Which, if any, of the rules answers something you want to know directly? Right, Fred is in office 2. Moreover, he's alone. Here's how that might look:

Of course, you also want to know his specialty. It can't be N, because more doctors practice N than P and each specialty, P included, has at least one doctor. If Fred practiced N, he'd be the only one. So he must practice one of the others.

Now that you've realized that at least two doctors practice N, you might be tempted to think that b and g, who work in the same office, practice N. Don't jump to any conclusions until you've considered all the possibilities.

Although b and g *might* practice N, they don't have to. With seven doctors and five offices, there might well be *more* than one office/specialty with more than one doctor. In fact, there would have to be two such office/specialties unless there were three doctors practicing N.

You're well on your way once you realize that the distribution of doctors among the office/specialties must be 3-1-1-1-1 or 2-2-1-1-1.

And because R = S, they must both have only one doctor, as does P, which has fewer doctors than N. Checking out the possibilities, only U can join N in having more than one doctor.

So perhaps b and g practice U, in which case two other doctors practice N. And maybe N and U are practiced in offices 4 and 5 (which have the same number of doctors):

And maybe they're not:

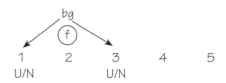

But may be b and g and someone else all practice N, in which case they can't be in office 4 or 5 or 2.

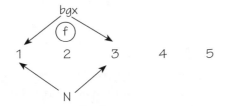

But you shouldn't be worrying about what you don't know. Instead, you should be delighted at how much you've been able to figure out.

The Questions

19. D

What must be true is something you've been able to figure out so far. The deduction that specialty N has multiple doctors, whereas specialties P, R, and S don't, steers you to (D).

Note that there is at least one possible scenario in which each of the other answers might not happen. But always remember that the best way to avoid wrong answers is having a sense of what you're looking for before diving into the answer choices.

20. C

Whenever a question gives you additional information, take it as far as you can. In this case, knowing that Fred practices U leads to the conclusion that three doctors (including b and g) must practice N. And, as you've already noted, they must do so in office 1 or 3.

You have no clue as to which of the two possible offices N is in; neither do you have any other hint as to where the other specialties may be located.

Since the question asks what must be false, you should be looking for a claim that N isn't where we know it is.

That's (C). Once again, each of the wrong answers can be shown to be wrong because each could happen (in fact, (E) must happen).

21. B

You know that b and g are always together. Therefore, being told that b practices U in 1 tells you quite a bit. With two doctors practicing U, there must be two

practicing N, and they must be in office 3. After all, lonesome Fred is in 2 and the same number must be in both 4 and 5.

Once again, taking the information to its logical extreme allows you to look for and find the right answer, however disguised, quickly and confidently. You knew that Fred was sandwiched between U and N, and that's exactly what it says in (B).

22. C

What could be true is anything consistent with (i.e., not in conflict with) the possibilities you outlined before you started answering questions. Because you'll have to try out answer choices, you might want to skip this one on your first pass through the questions in favor of questions with additional concrete information.

It's actually pretty easy to "try out" these answers. Can b and c practice U? Nope; b and g go together and—since no more than two doctors can practice U— b, c, and g would be too many. Can g practice R? Not without b at her side, and you know that there's only one R. Can a and e practice N? Well, that would force b and g into U, but there's certainly no rule against that. So the answer must be (C).

For the record, b can't practice S, (D), for the same reason that g couldn't practice R in the preceding paragraph. And c can't join g in P, (E), because there's only one P.

23. D

This seemingly innocuous "if" clause is *loaded* with information. It tells you that b (and g) do not practice N but are next door to the two doctors who do. So b and g practice U, and two others practice N in offices 4 and 5, not necessarily respectively. Taking the information as far as you can is relatively easy.

The hard part is understanding this question. What does it mean to say, "All of the following could be true EXCEPT"? Except what? Except something that must be false.

So what must be false? N and U (which includes g and b) must be in 4 and 5, so putting them anywhere else must be false. And, sure enough, that is answer (D), which puts g next to f.

24. D

If g and e practice together, they must be joined by b, according to Rule 4; they must practice N, as N is the only specialty that can possibly have three doctors; and they must do so either in office 1 or office 3, the only offices open to three doctors. You have it narrowed down to two offices, and the question requires that we go one step further: You need to find the piece of information that will allow us to determine precisely the office in which these three neurologists practice. Skimming the choices, the only one that mentions either relevant office (1 or 3) is (D). If, as (D) says, you must assign urology to office 3, then clearly the only office available for g, e, and b is office 1. None of the other choices does anything to clear up the ambiguity.

SECTION IV: LOGICAL REASONING

1. B

The author's conclusion pops up at the end, where she states that Ed is likely to have ADD because he watches television a lot and is 7. The key piece of evidence is a recent study that the author cites, which states that 85 percent of seven-year-olds with ADD watch more than five hours of television per day. The study only discusses the television-watching habits of seven-year-olds who have ADD. The author's conclusion is flawed because it makes a conclusion about a seven-year-old television watcher based on a study about seven-year-old television watchers with ADD. In other words, there's a scope shift between the evidence and the conclusion. The author errs in accepting the survey as relevant to Ed. To make conclusions about Ed and whether he might have ADD, the author must come up with evidence that pertains to Ed because the original evidence does not. She needs a statistic that states the likelihood that a seven-year-old who watches more than five hours of TV a day would have ADD. The evidence provided sounds like that, but isn't, and (B) captures the gist of the author's mistake.

(A) is confusing, but the argument above isn't really about degrees of causation. The author doesn't suggest that age and television watching cause a child to contract ADD but that those factors generally appear with the disorder. (A) distorts the author's conclusion by suggesting that it says that Ed's television watching has caused him to contract ADD, but the author never suggests this.

(C) is true, but that's not a problem. Perhaps some doctors might disagree with the author's definition, but its validity is not the issue at the heart of this argument. Rather, the argument's concerned with Ed's chances of having ADD based on a particular study.

(D) is easiest to remove for the fact that it contradicts the stimulus, where you learn that Ed does watch more than five hours of television per day. You may have also noticed that the 15 percent figure is bogus—it's derived from the 85 percent figure in the stimulus, but that figure refers to the percentage of children with ADD who watch more than five hours of TV a day. You can therefore infer that 15 percent of children with ADD do not watch more than five hours of TV a day, but you can't turn this into 15 percent of children in general who don't watch more than five hours, as (D) attempts to do.

(E) again distorts the argument, which never suggests that television watching causes ADD. Since no causality is mentioned, you can only assume that the data represents a correlation.

Remember: Scope shifts are often hard to spot, but the rewards are great when you find them. They often involve subtle distinctions between the evidence and the conclusion, so look carefully at the terms of each, especially in Logical Flaw questions, to determine whether the author shifts gears en route.

2. D

Even though the stem is skimpy, it does indicate that this is a Method of Argument question, so track the argument carefully. Basically, American and foreign Internet providers charge the same monthly fee, but foreign providers offer more services. Representatives for these foreign providers predict that their services will put the American providers out of business. The industry analyst clearly disagrees with this assertion in the sentence that begins with the contrast keyword *but*. In that sentence, the analyst mentions two services offered by American providers that foreign providers may not be able to match. The analyst therefore disagrees with the representatives' conclusion and does so by introducing new factors into the equation. (D) perfectly captures this: The analyst's additional consideration (quality and customer service) does weaken the initial contention (that foreign providers will drive American providers out of the Internet industry).

(A) is too extreme. The analyst does suggest that foreign takeover may not be imminent, but he never suggests that American companies needn't have any fear of foreign competition.

The analyst does not dispute (B), the representatives' evidence that foreign providers offer two perks that most American providers do not. The analyst offers additional elements to consider but does not disagree with those that have been mentioned previously.

(C) starts off badly with the verb *reconciles* and doesn't get any better. The analyst disagrees with the representatives' prediction, neither offering his own nor harmonizing his view with that of the representatives. Also, the analyst doesn't refer to a "previous situation," so this choice is zero for three.

Again, with (E), the analyst doesn't really make any proposals, so we can be suspicious right off the bat. The analyst doesn't offer a plan by which American companies might ward off foreign competitors; he merely mentions an additional consideration that might make the representatives rethink their "bold" prediction.

Remember: Always be attuned to the presence of different views. This is more or less a dialogue stimulus without the dialogue formatting, since it begins with the explanation of one view and offers a second

opinion in response to the first. Therefore, the analyst's method of argument is tied to the way in which he responds to the representatives' argument.

3. C

The author states that Travonia's suicide rate has increased, citing an increase in the number of overdoses following the recent release of certain brands of sleeping pills. Getting to the heart of the argument, the author then asserts that certain types of suicides have not increased in number, conceding that the percentage of elderly suicides has increased but noting that the percentage of teen suicides has decreased. The flaw is the author's blurred distinction between numbers and percentages. Just because the percentage represented by teen suicides has decreased, that doesn't mean that fewer teens are committing suicide. A decreased *percentage* needn't signify a decreased *number* of suicides, and the author's flaw comes in failing to recognize this, as (C) expresses.

The argument doesn't explicitly discuss other groups (we don't really know where the sleeping pill poppers fall), but it certainly doesn't discount the possibility that other groups might exist. So eliminate (A).

(B) is incorrect because the author doesn't link the sleeping pill takers to either demographic group, as mentioned in the explanation for (A).

(D) goes too far. The total number of deaths in general is outside the scope of the argument, which deals exclusively with deaths from suicides and overdoses. The author need not consider the overall death figures in Travonia to make this argument.

(E) is too vague. The evidence about percentages doesn't contradict the author's conclusion; it just doesn't necessarily support it.

Remember: Whenever you see numbers and percentages discussed in a stimulus, see if the author is maintaining the distinction between them. You'll be rewarded for your effort in questions like this.

4.   D

Re-evaluating the argument, you can see that the author presents one piece of evidence to support this assertion: Deaths resulting from sleeping pill overdoses have almost doubled since new nonprescription sleeping pills have been released. To use these overdoses to support the assertion that suicides have increased dramatically, the author must assume that the overdoses were indeed deliberate and, hence, qualify as suicides.

(A) brings up the same problem that we saw in the previous question's answer choices: The author makes no links between the people overdosing on the sleeping pills and the teens and elderly folk discussed later in the stimulus. The author needn't assume such a connection to assert that suicides have increased dramatically.

(B) is irrelevant. Knowing what was the most pervasive suicide method 10 years ago doesn't have any bearing on the claim in the first sentence of the passage.

(C) is far outside the scope. Deaths from natural causes have no necessary relation to this argument about suicide.

(E)'s comparison of Travonia's suicide rate to the world's is not relevant to the assertion in question. The author only asserts that suicides in Travonia have increased; there is no mention of their relative increase or of the suicide rate in other countries.

Remember: Assumptions play a key role not just in Assumption questions but in many other question types as well. You may have picked up on the central assumption that's tested in this question as soon as the author cited the evidence about the doubling of overdose deaths. Thinking ahead, you may have asked yourself right then and there, "But are these overdoses necessarily suicides?" Such proactive thinking is what allows you to prephrase answers and select choices with greater confidence.

5.   C

Log for log, the Wotan stove produces more heat than the Vulcan stove, but the Vulcan produces more heat overall. The only possible explanation is that the Vulcan contains more logs (i.e., is a bigger stove). Thus, choice (C) is the correct answer.

(A) appears to contradict the first sentence, which tells us that the Wotan's convection features are improved. In any case, if (A) were true, it wouldn't explain how the Wotan produces more heat than the Vulcan "log for log." The same phrase allows you to disregard choice (B), implying as it does that the same logs are used or can be used when comparing the two stoves. (D) implies that the Vulcan is older and perhaps in worse condition than the Wotan, but offers no explanation of why one stove produces more heat than the other while producing less per log. As for choice (E), the passage doesn't specify what the convection features contribute to the heat-producing capabilities of either stove. Therefore, questioning the importance of convection features cannot help explain why a Wotan stove would produce less heat than a Vulcan does.

6.   E

The planner wants to broaden Maple Street, an action that he thinks will help the shops on that street. He supports this recommendation by noting that the shops on Maple Street aren't doing well but the shops on two wider streets are doing quite well. This argument demonstrates a classic causal flaw. The author assumes that because the shops on Walnut and Crescent Streets are doing well and the streets are wide, the width of the streets in some way *causes* the success of the shops. You're looking to strengthen this argument, and a good candidate would be an answer that supported this assumption and showed how wide streets really do help the businesses that reside on them. (E) works because it shows how wide streets will make it easier for people to shop, strengthening the connection between the two key elements of the argument.

(A) weakens the argument by explaining how wider streets deter shoppers. Wrong way.

(B) also heads in the other direction, explaining that the planner's recommendation will not bring more shoppers to the stores, only more congestion from drivers looking to get somewhere else.

(C) actually weakens the argument by providing an alternative explanation for the fact that fewer shoppers visit Maple Street.

Oh good, street history. If anything, (D) might suggest why Walnut does so well, but it doesn't suggest that Maple would achieve the same success. Indeed, it doesn't draw any connection between or even discuss wide streets and shopping.

Remember: If you notice a logical flaw in the argument, it's tempting to weaken the argument by noting that flaw, which perhaps explains why many of the wrong choices here would, if anything, weaken the argument. Even if an argument is deeply flawed, if your task is to strengthen it, then you don't get to criticize it. Resist the temptation and look instead for something that will bolster one of the argument's major assumptions.

7. D

The author concludes (though not explicitly) that the democratic principle of respecting basic individual rights can be ambiguous. As evidence, he discusses country Q, where minorities' basic rights were protected through the laws enacted by a nonelected dictator. According to the author, the dictator was able to enact such laws only because he didn't have to fear being ousted from office and could, thus, act contrary to public will. If country Q really does provide an accurate example of a situation where the principle of respecting individual rights is ambiguous (which it must for the author's argument to hold), then there needs to be some sort of confusion around the issue of individual rights in that country. The author says that the dictator "may" act against the public will to protect certain individuals' rights. The situation in country Q is only ambiguous if the dictator actually does act against the public will to bring about this particular democratic principle—otherwise; he wouldn't need to be a dictator to enact his reforms. (D) states this assumption: The author's conclusion is only valid if it is assumed that the public would not have supported such reforms. Try the Denial Test: If popular will did support the protection

of minorities' rights, then this example would not serve as an illustration of how establishing democratic principles leads to some "interesting scenarios." Everything would be harmonious—there would be no ambiguity and, therefore, no argument for that matter.

(A) is outside of the argument's scope because it focuses on situations in democracies. Since the author never discusses democracies, you have no way to relate this information back to the stimulus. In any case, (A) certainly isn't necessary for the validity of the author's conclusion.

If nonelected dictators can be ejected from office, then the dictator of country Q might have been taking a chance if he was acting against the popular will. But even so, it's still possible that the dictator's immunity to being voted out was the key factor. So (B) fails the Denial Test.

The author never discusses democratic government, (C). He only discusses one democratic principle, and even in that case, he doesn't suggest that it's incompatible with individual rights but that situations involving individual rights can sometimes become ambiguous.

(E) makes an irrelevant comparison regarding minority rights in dictator- and nondictator-led countries. (E) doesn't seem consistent with the argument as regards country Q, and its comparison clearly does not link the author's evidence to his conclusion.

Remember: This stimulus offers a clear example of a quite common argument structure, where the author will make a claim in his conclusion and support it with an example in his evidence. The validity of such arguments rests on whether the example illustrates the claim(s) made in the conclusion. When answering Assumption questions for such arguments, look to fill any gaps between the example and the conclusion. The right answer will be the one that allows the example to illustrate the author's primary point.

8. B

The author's conclusion comes toward the end, when she says that the plant should be built inside the city limits. Despite her acknowledgment that a plant built inside the city limits will disrupt more lives, she advocates this option because it will create jobs for the city residents and, therefore, offer economic benefits to the city. She's deciding between two options, and she concludes that one option is better than the other because it promises a certain benefit to the inhabitants of the city. For that conclusion to be valid, she must assume that the other option does not promise such a benefit. Thus, she must assume that only the inside-city-limits option would create jobs for the city's residents. (B) weakens the argument by denying this assumption, stating that either alternative will create jobs for the residents of the city.

(A) doesn't do a whole lot unless you assume more than the answer choice tells you (a sin for any LSAT test taker). Perhaps private owned land is more expensive, in which case this choice would strengthen the argument, or perhaps it isn't. As it stands, there's no clear link between (A) and the central issues of the argument.

(C) shows how the location of the plant doesn't matter in terms of taxation. It's wrong because taxation isn't one of the criteria determining which option the author prefers. Choice (B) also notes a similarity between the options, but it's right because the similarity there pertains to job creation, which is central to the argument and which determines the option the author prefers.

(D) would, if anything, strengthen the argument by suggesting that the possible defect of the author's choice, disruption, isn't so bad.

(E) brings up taxes again, though this time the choice is about the workers' taxes and not the plant's. Still, the issue of taxation isn't even mentioned by the stimulus, and neither (C) nor (E) makes it relevant to the issues discussed in the argument.

Remember: When more than one choice addresses an issue that you don't remember encountering in the stimulus, it's tempting to reread the stimulus to see if you missed something. Resist that. If you've read carefully, you'll know what's important in the stimulus, and you can stay on track even when the answer choices might tempt you to question your understanding of the passage.

9. D

Four choices are going to weaken the argument? The argument's probably going to be pretty bad. The chancellor concludes that the lackluster school should be closed and the students redistributed so as to improve the performance of the whole district. His evidence is that firing a few people at that school won't help and that the school isn't meeting minimum achievement standards. There are lots of questionable assumptions tied into this argument, but it's not a good use of time to try to prephrase all four. Instead, evaluate the choices keeping the terms of the argument in mind and keeping in mind that the choice we seek will most likely be irrelevant to the argument.

(A) would indeed weaken the argument, since it suggests that redistributing the students will not strengthen the overall educational performance of the entire district.

(B) would also weaken the argument by suggesting that the school may not need to close since it's actually improving.

(C) weakens the author's evidence where he indicates that the school employees' poor work habits are untreatable. (C) suggests otherwise.

(D) is entirely irrelevant to the argument, since the school principal's previous successes don't have a clear relationship to the current problems at the school or the chancellor's "solution." Even if she's a "competent administrator" now (which we can't even be sure of), the fact remains that most of her teachers and administrators stink, so nothing's really changed. (D) is correct because it has no impact on the argument.

(E), like (A), weakens the argument by indicating that the students' redistribution won't improve the educational performance of the entire district. In fact, both choices strongly suggest that if the plan is carried out, the neighboring schools will suffer.

Remember: In these sorts of questions, don't expect to find a choice that would strengthen the argument. It's possible, sure, but usually the right answer to a "weaken EXCEPT" or "strengthen EXCEPT" question will be the choice that just has no impact on the argument one way or the other.

10. E

That's a pretty user-friendly question stem because it tells you which part of the argument the inference will address. And with so many formal logic statements to choose from, it's a good thing you know where to start. The question stem gives us the first half of an if/then statement; the correct answer will likely be the second half. So if the editors don't receive year-end bonuses, then what do you know? Scoping out the part of the stimulus that deals with bonuses, you come to sentences 2 and 3. See if sentence 2 helps: If circulation has increased, then editors get their bonuses. Form the contrapositive of an if/then statement by reversing and negating the terms—the contrapositive of sentence 2 will read, "if editors DO NOT get bonuses, then circulation has NOT increased." You're given the first part, the, "If" clause in the stem; the second part, the "then" clause that must follow, is found in correct choice (E).

(A) deals with ad rates, about which you can make no inferences based on what we're told about bonuses.

(B) and (C) offer the two options regarding ad pages, but neither is right because, according to what you know, ad pages might have increased or not. There's no accurate inference that you can draw on this subject based on the information we're given.

(D) is 180: As you saw above, forming the contrapositive allowed us to deduce that circulation has not increased. Be careful when constructing contrapositives to flip the statement and negate each part.

Remember: In detailed formal logic questions like this one, use the information in the question stem whenever possible to provide you with a starting point. Find the relevant statement in the stimulus and work

backwards from there, employing the contrapositive whenever you can.

11. B

The two historians here offer two different views on the metis, a Canadian group derived from Native American and European heritage. The first historian thinks that the rejection of the metis' request for some autonomy was tragic since it led to their loss of a distinct identity and weakened Canada's cultural diversity. The second historian clearly expresses where she disagrees: She doesn't think that the rejection of the metis' request was tragic because the metis never constituted a culturally distinct group. They therefore disagree about whether the rejection of the metis' request was tragic and about whether the metis comprised a culturally distinct group. (B) picks up on that second difference: The first historian clearly believes that the metis were a distinct cultural group, while the second historian clearly believes they weren't.

(A) is off track because it focuses on the denial of a "people's" request and not on the metis in particular. Both historians only express views on that one particular group without making generalizations from it. The fact that historian #2 believes that the denial of the metis' requests was not tragic doesn't mean that she necessarily believes that such a denial can never be considered tragic.

(C) is stated by the first historian and uncontested by the second. In fact, the second historian's argument suggests that she also believes the metis were a mixture of both cultures.

The first historian certainly believes that the denial of a people's request for identity can be detrimental to a country's cultural diversity—he says this is the case with the metis and Canada. The second historian, however, doesn't venture an opinion on this issue of the effect of denying identity; she merely argues that the denial in this specific case was the right thing to do. So eliminate (D).

(E) is again something suggested by the first historian but that's not discussed, much less disputed, by the second historian.

Remember: The correct answer to a Point-at-Issue question must relate to an issue taken up by both participants of the dialogue. It's common for wrong choices to focus on an issue that's addressed by only one speaker, so make sure when you evaluate a choice to check to see that both care about the issue it contains.

12.   C

The author says that Betty's bad fortune was directly caused by Felix's salon and then proceeds to hold forth on the subject of competition in a free-market economy. Taking all of this to be true (accepting, for example, that Felix's store really did drive Betty's out of business), proceed to the answer choices to find a logical inference based on this information.

(A) might seem consistent with the author's attitude, but even then, it's a little too strong to be a view you can attribute to the author. Of course, that's not what you're looking for anyway—you simply want a statement that must be true based on the facts of the passage.

(B) might or might not be true. Because the author gives us no information about other salons, you can't make inferences on that topic.

(C) is valid. If Felix's store caused the decline in Betty's clientele and ultimately drove Betty out of business, then he must have taken some customers from Betty.

(D) is too extreme. The author says that Felix's store caused the closure of Betty's store, but that doesn't necessarily mean that Betty's store would still be open were it not for Felix's. Perhaps someone or something else would have had the same effect; the author identifies one cause but doesn't suggest that it's the only possible cause.

(E) makes a generalization that would be more appropriate to a Principle question. You're given information only about two specific stores; you don't know if their free-market experience is representative of all businesses everywhere.

Remember: One of the reasons why it's so important to start off with the question stem is that different question types have different sets of rules. If you were supposed to find a flaw in this question, you wouldn't want to assume that the conclusion were true, but because it's an Inference question, you do. The difference is entirely a result of the different question types, so it's a good idea to become very familiar with them and with what's expected of you in each.

13.   E

In this argument, the general determines which of two types of aircraft would better the needs of the Air Force for an upcoming mission. While the commander of the Air Force prefers the G28 because it could perform the necessary task more efficiently, the general orders that the D12 be used instead. He provides one piece of evidence to support this decision: Only the D12 can perform the task in time to meet the mission's deadline. We've seen this type of argument before. When an author argues for one option over another, the author must assume that the benefit provided by the preferred option can only be found in that option. In other words, the author must assume that the G28 would not fulfill the mission in the allotted period of time. The general says that it would take four days for the G28 to be ready for the mission, but he doesn't say that the G28 couldn't meet the deadline. Perhaps the plane's greater efficiency would enable it still to complete the mission in the allotted period of time. (E) expresses this assumption, because for the general's conclusion to be valid, he must assume that the G28 could not perform the mission by the immovable deadline. Thus, he assumes that the G28's efficiency would not save the time that it would take for the G28 to begin the mission.

(A) is unrelated to the argument. The stimulus doesn't state that one aircraft retrieves higher-quality information than the other.

(B) goes too far. The author never states how long the mission would take, so there's no basis for stating that the D12 would be done before the G28 arrived. All the author needs to assume is that only the D12 could meet the mission's deadline, not that it would do so in the next four days.

(C) contradicts the stimulus, in which such an ability is a significant consideration to the commander. The general never contests the importance of the consideration; he just overrides it by making the deadline a more significant consideration.

(D) focuses on aircraft other than the G28. Aren't two enough to deal with? The author seems to think so, because he only discusses two types of aircraft between which he has to choose. Any others aren't relevant.

Remember: This assumption might be difficult to prephrase, since the author comes quite close to saying that the G28 couldn't meet the mission's deadline. Don't worry if you can't prephrase; just stay focused on the author's evidence and conclusion, and you'll find only one choice that links the two.

14. E

De Fontanelle's conclusion is that we, inferably human beings, are ignorant and foolish. The evidence from which he drew this conclusion is not, as might be expected, our lack of knowledge but rather our possession of incorrect knowledge—our possession of causes and explanations for falsities. This he attribute to our having certain methods and principles that fail to contradict falsities and error. Thus, if the possession of falsities is his ground for judging us foolish, rather than our not possessing certain truths, de Fontanelle must assume choice (E), that humble ignorance is better than unknowing error. Because he assumes (E) in his argument, it is an opinion he is likely to hold.

Choices (A) and (C) are too strong for a good inference. Nowhere does he stress the importance of either facts or explanations over the other, as (A) would have it. Nor does he anywhere hinge uncovering the truth solely on the possession of principles and methods, regardless of their quality. He actually contradicts this claim in the last sentence. (B) draws a conclusion about his view on oracles, but nowhere does the passage mention this view, and for all we know, he may have believed the exact opposite of (B). Choice (D) also fails because de Fontanelle stresses the quality of knowledge, where it is true knowledge, over

a greater quantity of knowledge, where that quantity is composed of falsities.

15. A

The author concludes that Waters was not influenced by McTell in his formulation of the key elements of his psychosocial theory (although McTell may have aided in the theory's subsequent development). As evidence, she notes that Waters had already determined the basic components of his theory by 1947, years before Waters ever met McTell. The author gives you lots of other information about the two theorists and their relationship in the 1950s, but that's just extra information; the author's argument basically consists of the final two sentences. For the author's conclusion to be valid, she must assume that McTell could only influence Waters in person. Note that the author says that the two theorists had never "met" before the 1950s; she doesn't say that they had never communicated or that Waters knew nothing of McTell's ideas. Therefore, if she's correct in arguing that McTell didn't influence the formulation of Waters theory at all, she must assume that Waters was not influenced by McTell in any way before they met. (A) gives a more concrete expression of this assumption: The author assumes that Waters hadn't read anything by McTell prior to their meeting and, thus, that Waters wasn't influenced by McTell in 1947. The Denial Test confirms this: What if Waters did know of and read McTell's work before he officially met him? Could the author then be so sure that the formulation in 1947 of Waters's theory was not influenced by the ideas of McTell? No, she couldn't, so (A) is necessary for this argument to work.

(B) is outside the scope. The author only discusses whether Waters got his ideas from one particular scholar, McTell. Waters could have completely plagiarized from someone else, and the conclusion might still be valid.

(C) is outside the scope. The author's claim isn't that Waters's ideas were completely original, in which case (B) and (C) would be relevant, but that he didn't get them from McTell. Other scholars, confidantes, and mentors just aren't relevant.

(D) goes against the grain—the author strongly suggests that McTell did influence Waters's ideas in the 1950s and helped him develop his theory. The only part the author feels McTell did not influence was the initial formulation.

(E) would be sad for McTell, but it's wrong because it deals with the 1950s. Technically, whether or not Waters benefited from his association with McTell in the 1950s has no impact on whether Waters's 1947 ideas were influenced by McTell. However, like (D), (E) seems to contradict the passage, which suggests that Waters did in fact benefit from his association with McTell in the 1950s.

Remember: Read actively! Often, when we hear that something has "long been recognized . . . ," it will be followed up by opposition of some sort to the long-held theory. This is common in both Logical Reasoning and Reading Comp passages. Be on the lookout for this shift in sentiment. Here, the classic contrast keyword *however* in the second-to-last sentence signals the onset of the author's major point, which, not surprisingly, is a reworking of the academic community's long-held belief.

16. **A**

Too bad you don't get to weaken this one. The author states that there are fewer geniuses nowadays than there were, oddly, in the 17th century. The argument is pretty flimsy, based primarily on the assumption that it's legitimate to compare the two periods. To strengthen this argument, you'll want a choice to demonstrate that this comparison is more likely to be valid. This is where (A) comes in, stating a more specific element of this assumption. If people are indeed able to recognize geniuses while they're alive or soon after they die, then it's more valid to compare modern genius production to 17th-century genius production. After all, to make a valid comparison about the number of geniuses by period, the author must assume that you can count them accurately. If it took, say, a hundred years or more to recognize genius stature, then the comparison wouldn't allow the author to form the categorical conclusion in the first

sentence; you'd just have to wait and see. Maybe in the year 2100 CE, notables such as James Joyce and Howard Stern will grace the genius list, too.

(B) doesn't help the argument since the author concerns himself only with the geniuses of one certain (though undefined) stature. If anything, (B) might weaken the argument by suggesting the author's comparison is not valid. Maybe there's only one 20th-century genius (Einstein) who's in the same category as the 17th-century geniuses listed, but if there are other types of geniuses besides scientists and writers to consider, the author's conclusion may be a bit hasty.

(C) also does nothing to help the author's case, because the author relies on a stable definition of the term *genius* in his argument. Throwing that definition into question would only weaken his argument.

(D) would only be relevant if it could be shown that extremes in educational attainment were somehow related to the development of geniuses. You have no support to make such a leap, so (D) can't assist our author here.

At first glance, (E) would seem inconsistent with the author's argument: If scientific knowledge is increasing at an ever-greater pace, then why do we have so few geniuses? Still, this is all too vague. We can't be sure of the relationship between the expansion of scientific knowledge in general and the production of geniuses; maybe geniuses create themselves through the process of being forced to discover stuff on their own without simply looking it up on the Internet, for example. Besides, (E) is also too specific, focusing as it does only on science; Shakespeare was no scientist. All in all, no help here.

Remember: Arguments that rely on a central comparison are so common that it's useful to recognize them as a type. When they show up for Weaken questions, you can usually weaken the argument by undermining the comparison, and for Strengthen questions, you can look for a choice that somehow validates the comparison. Be on the lookout for specific information that could serve those purposes.

17. E

According to Sylvia, the public's belief that Banner clothes dryers are particularly fire-prone is false since the number of such dryers that actually erupt into flames is small. She also compares this number to that of major manufacturers' dryers that catch on fire, stating that the number of Banner dryers fires (a rhyme which must plague their marketing department) is smaller. Alice does not offer an alternative argument but merely notes a flaw in Sylvia's evidence. Like a good LSAT student, Alice recognizes that Sylvia compares the number of Banner dryers and the number of major manufacturers' dryers that catch on fire rather than their rates of occurrence. Looking through the answer choices, you find (E): Alice does indeed note a flaw in Sylvia's argument, and that flaw does involve a distorted use of numbers where percents would be more appropriate.

Alice neither accepts nor rejects Sylvia's conclusion; rather, she identifies a problem in Sylvia's evidence. She certainly doesn't offer another path toward proving that the public is wrong to distrust Banner clothes dryers. So eliminate (A).

(B) is partially right because Alice does present new evidence, but that evidence doesn't contradict Sylvia's, nor does it show how Sylvia's conclusion is wrong. Alice only criticizes the appropriateness of Sylvia's evidence in getting to where she's trying to go. She suggests that Sylvia's conclusion may be hasty, but she certainly doesn't "disprove" it.

(C) can be axed because Alice herself compares the same two groups of items (she simply compares them in a different and what she believes to be a more appropriate way).

(D) is too extreme. Alice doesn't refute Sylvia's evidence but merely demonstrates a flaw in using it to get to her conclusion. She never says or suggests that Sylvia's evidence (that Banner has fewer dryer fires than the major manufacturers) is incorrect.

Remember: Notice how frequently Method of Argument answer choices mention the *conclusion* and *evidence* of the initial argument. The prominence of those terms just underscores how important it is to identify the conclusion and evidence in the initial argument and to determine precisely what the respondent says in terms of them.

18. C

The first step in this stimulus is to recognize these assertions as formal logic statements and to translate them into if/then statements. The author first states that IF a building lacks sufficient ventilation and natural light, THEN it is not well designed (if A and B, then C). You can also form that statement's contrapositive: IF a building is well designed, THEN it has sufficient ventilation and natural light. Next: IF a building has many windows, THEN it has natural light (if D, then B). Finally, the author's conclusion is this: IF a building has many windows, THEN it is well designed (if D, then C). Do you see the problem? The author first identifies two qualities necessary for a building to be considered well designed. The author then proceeds to discuss only one of those elements, completely neglecting to mention whether the building has sufficient ventilation. Instead of maintaining that a well-designed building needs good ventilation and natural light, the author concludes that natural light itself (coming from many windows) can determine whether a building is well designed. The author fails to consider whether the building is also well ventilated, which is what (C) states. (You may have noticed that there's another major flaw here: Even if it were ascertained that a building had good ventilation and natural light, that would still not "ensure" that it is well designed; those factors are necessary, but not necessarily sufficient, for well-designed buildings. The stem asks for a flaw in the argument, most likely because there are two big ones here.)

(A) is too extreme. The author needn't show that ventilation is only possible through windows but that windows provide adequate ventilation.

(B) is not established by the argument, but that's not a flaw. The author shows that windows provide natural light, which is sufficient for the author's conclusion in terms of the natural light issue. The author has no obligation here to switch the first clause of sentence 2 around.

(D) could be true, but it isn't really relevant to this argument, which concerns a building that does have many windows. Remember, windows are not part of the original rule but come in later as one possible factor that ensures the presence of one of the elements (natural light) of the main rule. That's why the author need establish nothing about buildings without windows.

(E) points out a possibility that conflicts with the stimulus; failing to consider the impossible isn't a logical problem.

Remember: You will definitely see some Logical Reasoning questions involving formal logic on your exam, so try to get comfortable with spotting formal logic statements, translating them, finding their contrapositives, and differentiating between necessity and sufficiency.

19. D

The author concludes that we should stop using certain products that harm the ozone layer despite the fact that their use is both legal and enjoyable. Rather, we should focus on our obligation to act in the best interests of future generations. Rephrase to make this sound more like a principle. The author argues against a course of action by stressing our obligation to consider the consequences of those actions for future generations. Thus, we shouldn't do something now because it'll hurt people later on. According to (D), the morality, or rightness, of an action depends on its future consequences, which is entirely in line with the logic underlying the author's argument.

(A) and (C) have no bearing on the argument. The author doesn't suggest what should determine the legality of one's actions. According to the stimulus, it's legal to use the mentioned products, so what determines legality isn't the issue.

(B) goes against the grain of the argument. It's legal to use the products, but the author argues that they still shouldn't be used, therefore arguing that the legality of an action does not necessarily determine its morality.

(E) discusses appropriate punishment, which the author never addresses. Also, the author never discusses any "illegal action." Out on two counts.

Remember: Try to generalize the stimulus before you get to the answer choice when dealing with Principle questions. The answer choices often sound so abstract, and sometimes even so similar to each other, that you can get lost in them without some sort of guide. Prephrase an answer by abstracting from the stimulus and putting the specifics of the situation into more general terms.

20. E

A Parallel Reasoning question with some formal logic thrown in—proceed carefully. The stimulus starts off by telling us that public service announcements try to advise teens but really just annoy them. Then comes the formal logic "only if" statement, which, when properly translated, means that IF teenagers follow advice, THEN they do not resent the delivery of that advice. (If you have any trouble translating "only if" statements into standard if/then statements, stop and work through this translation again until you see it.) The author then concludes that the announcements should be discontinued. Since this is a Parallel Reasoning question, we should get a better sense of the general structure of the passage. The author shows that a certain program has a goal and an unintended negative side effect. The author then explains that the goal can't be met if the side effect exists (which we know it does) and concludes, therefore, that the program doesn't work and should be scrapped. It's a pretty solid argument, and we can proceed to look for the same elements in the answer choices.

(A) identifies the goal of a certain program but never identifies an unintended negative side effect. You can stop there without having to delve too deeply into the touching patriotism in the remainder of the choice.

(B) never discusses the goal of zoning restrictions and so never survives past consideration of the very first element of the stimulus.

(C) again never explains the goal of the estate tax. Don't be fooled by the fact that it does include what could be called a side effect and a negative consequence of it—if every element is not present, then you have to move on.

(D) identifies the goal of a certain program and explains a negative side effect. But the second sentence shifts away from the success of the conservation laws to their ability to get support. The original argument stays focused only on the program's potential for success.

(E) is correct because it outlines the goal of a program, discusses an unintended negative side effect, shows that the program can't succeed in the presence of that side effect, and concludes that the program should be eliminated. All the necessary elements are present.

Remember: Make a mental (or written) checklist for yourself when dealing with Parallel Reasoning. The absence of one key element invalidates any choice.

21. C

This argument discusses the effects of a regionwide recession on two counties (X and Y). The comptroller of County X has stated that County X's depressed economy represents what will happen to all counties in the financially struggling region (the "inevitable" consequences). However, County Y is not currently suffering any financial difficulties, so the author concludes that County X's comptroller must be wrong. Your task is not to determine whether or not this conclusion is correct but explain the apparent contradiction presented in the stimulus. More specifically, you want an answer choice that will show how County X could be adversely affected by the recession while County Y is not. Keeping that in mind, look through the choices.

(A) doesn't explain the situation within the region, which is all the stimulus addresses. Comparing this region to any other doesn't shed light on the different situations occurring in Counties X and Y.

(B) compares the overall revenue generated by the two counties, which has no relationship to the issue at hand. Maybe X is 10 times bigger than Y, accounting for the greater revenue. That wouldn't alter the fact that X is suffering compared to its usual economic state and that Y is robust.

(C) explains one important way in which County X is different than County Y, which certainly does help to

explain the counties' different financial situations. If the region's recession decreased tourism, and County X depends on tourism for revenue more than County Y, then it makes sense for County X to be more affected by the recession than County Y.

(D) doesn't make its information relevant to the recession and its different impact on the two counties. Both (C) and (D) discuss one factor contributing to one county's revenue, but (D) is wrong because, unlike (C), it doesn't show how the issue relates to the recession's impact.

(E) doesn't do quite enough to explain the initial situation. Would the relocation of "a few retail businesses" hurt County X and stabilize County Y? We don't know; we can't even be sure that the businesses that relocated were successful. In (C), we were told that County X relied "almost entirely" on tourism that was "crippled" by the recession; the terms in that choice are far stronger. In contrast, (E)'s discussion of the relocation of a few businesses doesn't help to explain the larger differences in the financial situations of the two counties.

Remember: It's pretty common to see an argument in which an author discusses a difference existing between two apparently similar people or groups. The trap is to assume that because two groups are similar in one way, they're similar in all ways. That's seldom the case, and, as we see in this question, it's often important that you allow that dissimilarities might account for the differences between the groups.

22. A

For your second question relating to this stimulus, you're asked about the author's method of argument. Looking at the structure of the stimulus, we can see that the author begins by expressing the views of County X's comptroller, who makes a generalization about all of the counties in the state. The author then notes an exception to the comptroller's generalization and uses it to show that the comptroller must be wrong. Therefore, to make his argument, the author provides evidence that disproves a generalization. (A) best expresses this: The author counters the comptroller's claim with evidence about County Y that directly contradicts the comptroller's assertion that a depressed economy is the inevitable consequence for all counties in the region.

The author doesn't dismiss any part of the comptroller's statement as irrelevant; he just says that the statement is wrong. Further, the comptroller doesn't provide any real evidence for his claim, so there's no evidence for the author to contest. You can eliminate (B).

(C) starts off well but goes awry in the second half. The author clearly believes that the comptroller is wrong, but (C) misrepresents the way in which the author expresses his opinion. The author doesn't dispute the comptroller's statement by saying that it's impossible in this situation for all of the region's counties to be economically depressed. Rather, he provides opposing evidence (the booming economy of County Y), which proves that this is simply not the case.

Who would be the authority appealed to in this scenario? No one in the stimulus would fit this description, so (D)'s out.

(E) gets the argument all muddled up. The author doesn't make the generalization; the comptroller does. The author gives a specific example, and while it does counter the claim he opposes, a specific example is not a generalization.

Remember: In Method of Argument questions, test the general terms of the choices against the specifics of the stimulus. Here, ask yourself: "Is there an impossibility asserted? Is there an authority here?" Every aspect of the right choice must pan out.

23. A

The author begins by explaining a paradox: Kids who weren't vaccinated seemed to be immune to measles. The idea that vaccinated children sometimes form immunities is accepted without question. How does this function in the argument? Well, it helps to set up the strange situation that the rest of the stimulus will strive to explain or, in other words, the problem that requires a solution provided in the argument. (A) captures this by noting that the first sentence creates

the confusion, which the researchers then worked to explain.

(B) would tie the statement into the evidence regarding dihydron-X, but this assumption doesn't come from the part of the passage in question.

(C) contradicts the passage, which explains how the kids were able to achieve such an immunity. Therefore, such immunity is not impossible.

(D) might be tempting. Researchers do seem to take this to be proven but not by the findings in the passage.

Just because the kids became immune through their formulas, that doesn't overturn the assumption that vaccinations also create immunity. The researchers' conclusion does not contradict or undermine this particular assumption. Therefore eliminate (E).

Remember: Questions that ask you to determine the role of a statement can be great time-savers— you're doing that anyway when you break down the argument.

24. B

Next up is a "parallel the flaw" type of Parallel Reasoning question, so first find the flaw. This one is particularly amenable to an algebraic treatment. The author tells us that the chief of personnel claimed that no human resource employee was fired in the embezzlement scandal, but he ends up asserting that this claim must be false. So the author actually concludes that some human resource employees were fired in the embezzlement scandal. Find the evidence for this and begin your algebraic representation there (it's easier in a case like this to build the argument in order from evidence to conclusion). "Some human resource employees were fired in March," can be represented as "Some X are Y." And "Some employees fired in March were fired in the embezzlement scandal," breaks down to "Some Y are Z." The conclusion mentioned above would then be "Some X are Z,"—which you know is not necessarily true, because the group of human resource folks canned in March and the group of embezzlers who were tossed can be totally distinct groups. Searching the choices, you find that (B)'s logic is botched in the same way as the original: Some stars of *Icarus* starred in *Mrs. Jones* (some X are Y). Some *Mrs. Jones* folks went to Zeller (some Y are Z).

Therefore, some *Icarus* actors went to Zeller (some X are Z). Same structure, and the same flaw: The stars of *Icarus* who were also in *Mrs. Jones* may not have been the same *Mrs. Jones* folks who attended Zeller.

(A) is out immediately because it doesn't commit any flaw. All members have good manners, and Candy is a member, so she must have good manners. That's fine, at least in terms of logic. No flaw, no good.

(C), like (A), commits no logical error. If the neighbors have young kids, and many people with kids stay home on weekend nights, then it's certainly reasonable to conclude that some of the neighbors probably stay home on weekend nights. The qualified nature of this argument—that is, the use of the word *probably*—makes this a very reasonable conclusion and differentiates it from the original argument, in which the author claims that the chief was wrong and that some human resource employee definitively was fired.

(D) is flawed, but not parallel. Some X are Y. Some X are Z. Therefore, some X are both Y and Z.

(E) contains no "some" terms to play with, so it's impossible for this choice to mimic the original. Kill it for that reason alone.

Remember: Algebraic representation is valuable in Parallel Reasoning questions made up of (or that can be translated into) formal logic terms. When you see words like *some*, *all*, *no*, *none*, *if*, and *then*, think of breaking down the terms in the original and in the choices into letters to find the one that matches.

25. E

The principal concludes that the Excellence Learning Services's promotional materials were "misleading" and supports this conclusion by discussing his own school's experience with the service. Even though the school used the Excellence program to improve its students' reading and math scores, the students' performances on the tests were the same as they were 20 years ago.

The principal uses this information to demonstrate that the Excellence program does not improve test scores, but there's an unwarranted assumption involved in his argument—did you spot it? Just because the students' scores equal those of the students 20 years ago, that doesn't necessarily mean that the Excellence program was wholly ineffective. Perhaps the students' scores would have been lower than those of the students 20 years earlier without the program. Perhaps equaling the scores of 20 years ago is a marked improvement over the score levels of recent years. The principal assumes that the Excellence program did not improve the students' scores, but that assumption is unwarranted because it's unsupported by the argument's evidence. (E) picks up on this flaw, noting that the principal does not demonstrate that the Excellence program did not improve student test scores.

Because the author's conclusion solely concerns the accuracy of the Excellence program's advertisements, and solely intends to criticize the program, it needn't offer alternative solutions for support. You can eliminate (A).

(B) is wholly irrelevant because the author never directly or indirectly discusses parents and their capacities. Parents are outside the scope here. (C) criticizes the author's language, but it's hard to identify any language that might be called "emotionally charged" in the argument. "Misleading" certainly doesn't qualify, and that's the author's strongest term, so (C) identifies a flaw that the argument doesn't commit.

(D) is not relevant, because the author's argument only concerns the program's claims to help students improve their math and reading scores. Other possible benefits aren't discussed or pertinent to the program's ability specifically to raise these test scores.

Remember: Many answer choices for Logical Flaw questions discuss issues that the author never addresses. Those choices only constitute correct flaws if the issues they introduce are directly relevant to the argument. Alternative solutions in choice (A), parents' capabilities in (B), and benefits in other areas in (D) do not fit this requirement.

Part Four

GETTING INTO LAW SCHOOL

CHAPTER 8: LAW SCHOOL ADMISSIONS

- Where to Apply
- When to Apply
- How to Apply

WHERE TO APPLY

The question of where you should apply has two parts. What schools should you consider, regardless of your chances, and which of these schools can you actually get into? Let's begin with the first question.

WHAT SCHOOLS SHOULD YOU CONSIDER?

According to one study, 58 percent of all law students end up living and working within a one-hour drive of where they went to law school. That's nearly 6 out of every 10 students!

There are many reasons for this surprising statistic. Obviously, a lot of people attend the local law school in the town where they have always lived and want to continue living. Also, since employers tend to interview and hire from nearby law schools, many recent grads stay put. Whatever the explanation, a majority of all law students end up spending more than just the required three years in the city or region where they attend law school.

Despite the importance of law school selection, however, it's frightening how lightly many applicants treat the whole process, even students who spend a great deal of time studying for the LSAT or working on their applications. Horror stories abound—of distant relatives convincing someone to attend State University Law School just because they themselves did 40 years ago or of a student who decides not to apply to a school because his girlfriend's cousin heard that the social life was not so hot.

This point cannot be stressed enough. *Choosing a law school is a major decision in your life and should be treated as such.* There are several factors to consider when choosing where to apply, including reputation, location, and cost.

Reputation

How much does a law school's reputation matter? The short answer is that it matters very much in your first few years out of law school, when you're looking for your first job or two. Most employers evaluating you at this time will have little else to go on and so will tend to place a lot of weight on school reputation. After a few years, when you've established a reputation and a record of your own, the importance of your alma mater's rep will diminish.

The long answer to the question of academic reputation, however, is a little more complex. Each applicant must look at his or her situation and ask several questions:

- **Am I looking to work for a law firm or to do public service work?**
  Law firms tend to put more emphasis on the reputation of the school.

- **Do I want to stay in the area or have more mobility nationwide?**
  Some schools enjoy strong local reputations as well as strong alumni bases, whereas other schools have a nationwide appeal.

- **How competitive do I want my law school experience to be?**
  Although there are exceptions, as a general rule, the schools with better reputations tend to be very competitive.

- **Do I want to consider teaching as an option?**
  Virtually all law school professors come from a handful of top-notch law schools. The same also applies for the most prestigious judicial clerkships.

- **To what extent am I willing to go into debt?**
  The schools with the biggest reputations also tend to have the biggest price tags.

Studies rank the top 50 schools or the top 15 schools or categorize all schools into four or five levels. (Most of these books can be found in the reference section of your local bookstore.) Many law firms rely heavily on such rankings in making their hiring decisions.

But there are other methods to determine a school's reputation. Speak to friends who are lawyers or law students. Lawyers have a habit of noting who their most formidable opponents are and where they went to law school. Look through law school catalogs and see what schools the professors attended. Finally, ask the placement offices how many firms interview on campus each year and compare the numbers. Their answers can give you a strong indication of what the law firm community thinks of a school.

Location

Location is of prime importance because of the distinct possibility that you'll end up spending a significant part of your life near your law school—three years at the very least. Even under the best of conditions, law school will be a difficult period in your life. You owe it to yourself to find a place where you'll be comfortable. Pick cities or areas you already know you like or would like to live. Pay particular attention to climate. Think about rural areas versus urban centers.

Visit as many law schools as possible, your top two or three choices at the very least. You may be surprised at what you find. Spend some time researching location by visiting *when school is in session*, which is when you'll get the most accurate picture. You should also do the following:

- Buy a local newspaper and scan the real estate ads for prices near campus; check out campus housing to determine whether it's livable.
- Check out transportation options at the law school.
- Take the school's tour so you can hear about the area's good points.
- Look at bulletin boards for evidence of activities.

Finally, don't be afraid to wander into the student lounge and just ask several law students what they think. Most are more than willing to provide an honest appraisal, but be sure to get more than one opinion.

Costs

Among the cost issues to consider are these:

- **State Schools**
  State schools tend to have lower tuition for in-state residents.

- **Urban versus Rural Living Costs**
  Schools in large urban areas will almost invariably have higher living costs than those in rural areas (although the larger cities also tend to have more part-time jobs for second- and third-year students, which can offset the extra cost).

- **Special Loan Programs**
  Many schools now offer special loan repayment or loan forgiveness programs for students who take low-paying public service jobs.

- **Special Scholarship Programs**
  Many law schools offer special scholarship programs that range from small grants to full three-year rides.

The law school application will tell you what the annual tuition was for the previous year. Many applications will even give you an estimate of living expenses. If you want to dig deeper, call the financial aid office and ask them to send you the breakdown of living expenses of the average law student. Also, ask them to send information about any loan forgiveness programs and about scholarships offered by the law school.

Job Placement

With the legal job market shrinking, the proficiency of a law school's placement office is now a major factor to be considered. If interviews with law students can be believed, the competency of placement officers varies widely. Some see their job as simply setting up on-campus interviews and making sure they run smoothly. Others call and write letters on behalf of students and are constantly selling the school to employers. Some schools direct almost all of their efforts into placing students into private law firms. Other schools provide information on an entire range of opportunities. At some schools, students are lucky if the placement office even provides them with a list of alumni in cities in which they'd like to live. At other schools, the office calls alumni to hunt for leads.

Ask the placement office for the percentage of graduates in the most recent class who had jobs upon graduation. Don't be fooled by statistics that show 98 percent of all graduates employed. Almost all law students are eventually employed, even if they drive taxis. The key is to determine how many are placed in law jobs *before* they leave law school.

Second, stop by the placement office on your visit and look around. Ask to see the placement library and check whether it's well organized and up-to-date. Note whether it carries materials on public interest or teaching jobs and how large this section is. Also, ask whether a newsletter is published to keep alumni informed of any recent job openings.

Again, talk with law students. Most have very strong opinions about the performance of their placement office. Most students recognize and appreciate when the placement office is making an extra effort.

Course Selection

One of the nicest things about law schools today is their growing number of course selections and the new areas of law that are opening up. International trade, employment discrimination, sports and entertainment, and environmental law are areas in which schools are providing more offerings. Many law students nowadays are becoming specialists, because of both personal preference and better marketability. If you're one of the many students who enter law school without a clue about what kind of law they want to practice, look for schools that offer a lot of different areas of study.

Schools list the courses most recently taught in their recruiting brochure, which they will gladly send you. One note of caution: Just because a class has been taught in the past and is listed in the brochure doesn't mean that it's taught every year or will be taught in the future. If you're interested in a particular class, call the registrar's department and find out how often the class has been taught in the past and whether it will be offered again in the future. Ask to speak with the professor who has taught the course in the past.

Social Life

Although it's an important part of the law school experience, social life should rank near the bottom of the list of factors to consider when choosing a law school. Why? Because your social life at any law school is what you make of it. Almost all law schools have monthly parties or weekly Thursday night get-togethers at local bars. And if you choose to expand that schedule, you can always find a willing accomplice. Furthermore, most schools now have a comparably full range of social organizations.

Examine the area surrounding the law school. During your first year, locale probably won't matter much. But as you get into your second and third years, you'll likely find that you do have some free time, particularly on weekends. Think about whether you want a quiet rural area where canoeing or skiing are readily available or whether you'd prefer a larger city with a vibrant restaurant and nightlife scene.

Additional Considerations

There are a few other factors that you may want to toss into the equation when deciding which law school is right for you.

Class Size: This factor is not as important as it is when choosing a college because, despite what you may read in a catalogue, virtually all first-year classes will be large. Nevertheless, there are some differences between a school such as Georgetown, with more than 2,000 students, and a school such as Stanford, with fewer than 800. In the second and third years, the larger schools tend to have more course offerings, whereas the smaller schools focus on smaller class size and more contact between professors and students. Smaller schools also tend to encourage a greater sense of camaraderie and less competition. Larger schools, on the other hand, produce more alumni and thus more contacts when it comes time for your job search.

Attrition Rates: Law schools generally try to keep their attrition rate below 10 percent. There are exceptions, however, and if the school you're interested in has an attrition rate above 10 percent, you should ask an admissions officer why. There may be a reasonable explanation, but you should probably approach the school with some caution.

Joint-Degree Programs: These are designed to help students pursue two degrees jointly in less time than it would take to earn them separately. Some common examples are the Master of Public Policy (MPP) or the Master of Business Administration (MBA) combined with the law degree. These programs generally take four to five years to complete. Most schools are becoming more daring in this field—indeed, some are now encouraging students to create their own joint-degree program in any area that they choose, as long as it meets both departments' approval. It's not uncommon now to see joint degrees in law and foreign languages, music, or sociology. Check with the schools to see what joint-degree programs are routinely offered but don't be limited by what you hear. If you have a specialized program in mind, call the registrar's office and see how flexible the school is.

Clinical Programs: Every law school in the country now offers one or more clinical programs. A clinic is a unique, hands-on opportunity that allows law students to see how the legal system works by handling actual civil cases for people who can't afford an attorney (and getting credit for it at the same time). Not only are these clinics a tremendous learning tool, but they are also the highlight of many law students' three years of study.

Usually the workload is heavy on landlord/tenant disputes or other debt-collection cases. However, many schools are branching out and offering specialized clinics in such areas as child abuse, domestic violence, and immigration. One word of caution: Clinics tend to be popular with students. In many cases, it's very difficult to get a spot in the class, and admission usually depends on the luck of the draw. As a general rule, the schools in large cities have bigger and more clinics because they tend to have more clients.

Internships: Like clinical programs, internships are becoming more popular and varied. Internship programs vary widely from school to school and may include anything from working for an international trade organization in Europe for an entire year to getting three hours of credit for part-time work at the local prosecutor's office. Internships are often overlooked by students who are afraid to veer from the traditional path. Yet they can be a welcome break from regular law studies and may also help in the later job search.

Computer Facilities and Law Library: Legal research is a big part of your three years in law school. Nothing will frustrate you more than to have a brief due the next day only to find that your library lacks essential volumes on the subject or that the few computers are either occupied or not working. If you make a visit to the law schools, check out their facilities. Again, don't be afraid to ask students for their opinions.

WHERE CAN YOU GET IN?

Let's turn to the second major question in the selection process: "Where do you have a chance of being accepted?"

Anyone who tells you that he can predict where you'll be accepted is fooling himself and, worse, fooling you. Stories of students accepted by a Harvard, Stanford, or Michigan only to be turned down by schools with far less glamorous reputations are common. Yet what is often overlooked is how well the process does work, considering the volume of applications and the amount of discretion exercised by admissions officers.

One reason the admissions process runs smoothly is that all law schools use the combined LSAT score and GPA as the most important determinant in making the decision. This provides a degree of consistency to the admissions process and gives the applicants some direction in deciding where to apply.

Those Legendary Law School Grids

Each year, LSAC publishes the *Official Guide to ABA-Approved Law Schools* (at bookstores or freely searchable available at **officialguide.lsac.org**). This guide includes a wealth of information on all the accredited law schools in the United States. The schools themselves provide most of the information for the book, including the LSAT scores and GPAs of the most recently admitted class. These are generally presented in grid form and are the single most valuable tool in determining your chances of being accepted at any particular law school.

Assembling a List of Schools

Most students apply to too few schools. According to LSAC, the average applicant applies to only about five schools. Admittedly, the cost of applications is rising, and sending out 10 or more applications can result in an outlay of $500 or more. But keep in mind that if the cost of application presents a real hardship, most schools will waive the application fee—provided you give them a good, credible reason.

Using the grid numbers as a guide for determining your chances of acceptance, you should create a list of schools to apply to, dividing the list into three categories: preferred schools, competitive schools, and safe schools.

Preferred Schools: These are schools you'd love to attend, but your numbers indicate a less than 40 percent chance of admission. Apply to two or three schools in this group. Long shots rarely pay off, but daydreaming about them is always nice.

Competitive Schools: Competitive (or "good fit") schools are those where your grid numbers are in the ballpark and where, depending on the rest of your application, you have a decent chance of getting admitted. These are schools where your numbers give you a 40–80 percent chance of admission. These are the schools on which you should focus most of your attention. Applying to four to seven schools in this group is reasonable and increases your odds of getting into at least one school where you are competitive.

"Safe" Schools: These schools are not high on your preference list, but your odds of admission are excellent there. Look at the grids and determine two or three schools where your chances of getting in appear to be 80 percent or better. One suggestion for this list would be to pick schools in locations that you particularly like.

WHEN TO APPLY

Schools send out application forms in August and September, begin accepting applications in October, and start sending out acceptance letters by November. (As proof that they have a heart, most law schools will not begin sending out rejection letters until after the holiday season.) Application deadlines may be in February or March, but because the schools have begun filling their classes in the fall, it is not unusual for more than 75 percent of the anticipated acceptance letters to have been sent by the spring deadline date. This is what's known as rolling admissions, which creates the scenario of unaware applicants who proudly deliver their applications on the deadline date only to find that they have put themselves at a distinct disadvantage.

THE ADVANTAGES OF EARLY APPLICATION

Does applying early really provide you with an advantage? Yes! Here are the major reasons why.

Rising Index Numbers

The first reason has to do with index numbers. Your index number is based on the combination of your LSAT score and your GPA. At the beginning of the application process, most schools set an automatic admittance index number. Applicants whose index numbers surpass that figure are admitted quickly with only a cursory look at their application to confirm that they are not serial killers. At the beginning of the process, law schools are always afraid that they'll have too few applicants accepting their offers, which would mean less tuition money and almost certainly some complaints from the school's administrative office. Thus, they usually begin the application process by setting the automatic admittance index number on the low side. Then they gradually increase it as the admission season wears on and they discover that their fears are unfounded.

Fewer Available Places

Because schools have a tendency to be a little more lenient early in the process, they begin reaching their admission goals fairly quickly. By February, the school may well have sent out more than 75 percent or more of all the acceptance letters it plans to send. Yet at this point, all of the earlier applicants haven't been rejected. Instead many people are left hanging, just in case better applicants don't start coming through the system. This means that if you apply in March, you're now shooting for fewer possible positions, yet you're still competing against a fairly substantial pool of applicants.

The "Jading" Effect

If they are candid, admissions officers will admit that by the time they get to the two thousandth essay on "Why I want to go to law school," they're burned out and more than a little jaded. Essays or applications that might have seemed noteworthy in the beginning now strike the reader as routine.

WHEN TO START

For the most part, a pre-Halloween application is overdoing it. When schools are just gearing up, you run the risk of documents being misplaced. Pre-Thanksgiving is the preferable choice and ensures that you'll be among the early entries. Shortly before Christmas is not as desirable but should still hold you in good stead. After Christmas and the holidays, however, you're on the downside and may well find yourself among the last 30 percent of all applications received. And if you go with a post–Valentine's Day application—well, you'd better have strong numbers.

Remember that this discussion applies to the date on which your application is *complete*, not just the date on which the school receives your application forms. Applications are not considered complete until the LSAT score, LSAC's Credential Assembly Service reports, transcripts, and all recommendations have been received. Even though other people are sending these pieces, it's your responsibility to see that they arrive at the law school promptly. This does *not* mean calling the law school three times a week to see if they've arrived. It means prodding your recommenders or your college to send in the necessary documentation. Explain to them the importance of early applications.

If you want to have a complete application at the law schools by, say, late November, you can't start planning just a few weeks in advance. Your campaign for admission should begin five or six months before that deadline (i.e., 18 months before your first day as a law student). We've included below a schedule that you can use to organize your campaign. As you'll see, you should plan to devote plenty of time to your applications the summer before they're due.

AN IDEAL LAW SCHOOL APPLICATION SCHEDULE

Your campaign for law school admission should start up to 18 months before you step into your first law classroom. Here's a schedule of what you should be doing when.

SPRING

- ❏ Get the *Official Guide to U.S. Law Schools*.
- ❏ Register for the June LSAT. (You can retake it in October if you blow it.)
- ❏ Prepare for the LSAT.
- ❏ Go to LSAC.org to register for the CAS (so you can apply to schools online).

SUMMER

- ❏ Take the June LSAT.
- ❏ Start drafting your personal statement.
- ❏ Think about whom you'll be asking for recommendations.
- ❏ Make a list of schools you'll be applying to, using the grids from the *Official Guide* as an aid.
- ❏ Send away for applications or download them online if you're going to mail them in. Start visiting as many schools as you can.
- ❏ Register for the October LSAT if you're not satisfied with your June score.

EARLY FALL

- ❏ Familiarize yourself with the applications as they roll in.
- ❏ Make a checklist and schedule for each application and photocopy all forms.
- ❏ Send transcript request forms to all undergraduate and graduate schools you've attended.
- ❏ Line up your recommendation writers. Give them the specific info they need to write an outstanding recommendation of you.

- ❏ Apply for financial aid.
- ❏ Revise your personal statement. Tailor it to specific essay topics, if any, on individual applications.
- ❏ Fill out your applications online.

MID-FALL

- ❏ Finalize your personal statements.
- ❏ Transfer application information from the photocopies to the actual application forms.
- ❏ Make sure your recommendation writers are on board.
- ❏ Take the October LSAT (if necessary).
- ❏ Send in your applications if you're mailing them in.

LATE FALL

- ❏ Remind your recommendation writers to send in recommendations ASAP.
- ❏ Get Master Law School Report from CAS, summarizing transcripts, etc.

WINTER AND THE FOLLOWING SPRING

- ❏ Receive monthly updates from CAS, telling you which schools your records have been sent to.
- ❏ Cross your fingers while you wait for the acceptances to roll in.
- ❏ Decide which offer to accept.
- ❏ Send in acceptance.

HOW TO APPLY

All ABA-approved law schools now make their applications available online via the CAS online registration service. Moreover, some schools require and many schools prefer that applicants apply online.

This free service will help you apply to multiple law schools with ease. You enter basic background information into the Common Information Form, and the program will transmit your answers to each law school application you select. Typing the information into one application versus having to retype the information multiple times will help you avoid making careless mistakes. All of your information is saved in a secure, central database, enabling you to work on your applications on any computer you choose. Information can be saved and revisited and revised on an ongoing basis.

Further, the service will alert you to supplementary information that needs to accompany a particular application. You can electronically attach your personal statement(s), résumé, addendum(s), and other written materials. You can pay for most application fees via LSAC as well. And you control the timing of the submission of each application and need not send them all at once.

To apply using the CAS online registration, begin by going to **lsac.org**. Step-by-step instructions can be found online. However, the process generally requires:

(1) downloading the necessary plug ins;

(2) entering personal information into the Common Information Form;

(3) selecting the applications for the schools you wish to apply to and preparing and attaching any supplementary materials requested; and

(4) mailing in any documentation (e.g., certification letter) or payments that cannot be transmitted electronically.

Furthermore, the CAS online registration service enables you to track the date your electronic and paper application was transmitted from LSAC to your selected schools and confirms when the law school report has been requested and processed as well.

If you choose instead to apply manually, make photocopies of all forms to be filled out, unless you use the application software option. (If you're applying using law school application software, the cumbersome photocopying step can be eliminated.) Admittedly, this is time consuming, but the photocopies are what you'll work on. Changes and corrections will have to be made no matter how careful you are. These changes should not be made on the original form, which will go to the school. Neatness is a big factor for both admissions and financial aid applications. The feeling is that if the application is sloppily prepared, the student is not very serious about attending that law school. Make photocopies for every form and write on the copies until you are sure you are ready to transfer items to the original application.

The most important thing to keep in mind about your law school application is that it is, above all else, a sales pitch. The application is your single best opportunity to sell yourself. Remember, every person who applies will have strengths and weaknesses. It's how you *present* those strengths and weaknesses that counts. *You* are in control of what that admissions committee sees on your application and how they see it.

So what's the best way to sell yourself? We all know that some people are natural-born sellers in person, but the application process is written, not spoken. The key here is not natural talent but rather organization—carefully planning a coherent presentation from beginning to end and paying attention to every detail in between. But be careful not to focus so much on the overall theme that you neglect the details. That can be disastrous.

THE APPLICATION FORM

For the most part, filling out the Common Information Form (application form) requires simply putting down factual information. But even in something so apparently mindless, you can still make sure you present yourself as a thorough, organized person who can follow directions. The key to filling out the C.I. form can be summed up in a single sentence: Don't make the admission officers do more work than they have to. Make sure that they have all of the information they need at their fingertips. If they have to hunt up your statistics, if your application is full of unexplained blanks, if they can't read what you've written—all of these things will just serve to annoy the very people you want to impress. Look for opportunities to provide additional information. If they ask you to describe in priority order your honors or extracurriculars, this is another opportunity to compel them to see your readiness for law school. Avoid simply listing this information dryly or saying, "See Résumé."

Addendums

An important part of the application form will not be in the package sent from the law school. It is your addendums. Addendums (or *addenda*, if you want to be fancy) are the additional page or pages that you staple onto the forms when the space they give you to answer a question is too small.

This is where an addendum comes in. If you are sending hard copies, simply write, "Continued on addendum," on the application form after you've used up its space and then clearly mark what you are listing at the top of the addendum. Staple this addendum at the back, and you've solved a tricky problem. Law schools appreciate addendums because they're much neater than attempts to cram things into a limited space—*and* they show careful organization. But don't overdo it. One or two addendums should be sufficient for any application.

Addendums can be used to preserve neatness when the application blanks are of insufficient length. But they can also be helpful if an answer requires further explanation. For example, if you won the Grant R. Humphrey Science award, it's not enough just to list it. You need to explain what it is, what it's given for, and possibly how many others were competing for it or how prestigious it is.

Honesty

One final topic about the application form that needs to be discussed is honesty. If you think you can get by with a lie or two on your application—well, you may be right. Law schools as a rule don't have the resources to verify all aspects of every application. But before you go overboard and decide to put down that you were once the Prince of Wales, you should realize that you're taking a big chance.

First of all, many schools are beginning to devote more time to checking up on applicants' claims. Secondly, there's always the chance that, if you lie, some other part of your application will contradict the lie and get you booted.

Finally, even if you fool the law school, get in, and graduate with honors, you'll find that any state in which you apply to take the bar exam will do a much more extensive background check than that done by the law school. This check very well might include looking for contradictions in your law school application. Lying on a law school application, in fact, is considered grounds for refusing admittance to a state bar.

THE PERSONAL STATEMENT

There are about as many theories on what constitutes a winning personal statement as there are theories on the Kennedy assassination—and, unfortunately, many of them have about the same validity. To begin with, how can you tell 85,000 annual applicants with 85,000 different personalities and backgrounds that there is one correct way to write a personal statement? Furthermore, if even a small percentage of those applicants read and come to believe that a certain way is the correct way, it automatically becomes incorrect, because law schools despise getting personal statements that are familiar—that are, in other words, *im*personal.

For that reason, this section on personal statements has been broken down into two parts. First, we'll look at the procedure of putting together a personal statement. Then we'll look at a list of the DOs and DON'Ts that admission officers most frequently mention.

Putting Together an Outstanding Personal Statement

Next to your LSAT score and GPA, the personal statement is probably the most important part of your application. If your numbers are excellent or very poor, the essay may get only a cursory glance. But if your numbers place you on the borderline at a school, then it may very well make the difference between acceptance and rejection.

What Kind of Essay to Write: The personal statement is exactly what its name implies—a statement by you that is meant to show something about your personality and character. But that doesn't mean you are to create a lengthy essay detailing every aspect of your life since birth. Nor is the personal statement intended to be a psychological profile describing all of your character attributes and flaws. Several admissions officers have said that the best essays are often only remotely related to the applicant. The point is that you need not write an in-depth personality profile baring your innermost soul. Admissions officers are adept at learning what they want to know about you from your essay, even if it doesn't contain the words *me, myself,* and *I* in every sentence.

One exception, however, should be noted. Although most schools still provide wide latitude in their directions about what the personal statement should be about, some schools are becoming more specific. The problem with specific requirements like these is that you may well have to write a separate essay for that school alone. Be sure to check the instructions carefully and follow them closely. If a law school asks for a specific type of essay and you provide it with a more general one, the admissions committee will likely feel that you're not very interested in attending that particular school.

But take heart. Most schools provide few restrictions on what you can write about, so unless you're very unlucky, you should be able to limit the number of essays you must write to two or three.

How Long an Essay to Write: How long should the personal statement be? Some schools place a word limit on the essay; others specify one or two typed pages. Always follow the specific directions, but you should be in good shape with virtually all schools if your essay is one and a half to two pages in length.

Writing the Essay: The personal statement shouldn't be done overnight. A strong personal statement may take shape over the course of months and require several drafts. One practice that many have found particularly effective is to write a draft and then let it sit for four to six weeks. If you leave it alone for a significant period of time, you may find that your first instincts were good ones. On the other hand, you may shudder at how you could ever have considered submitting such a piece of garbage. Either way, time lends a valuable perspective.

Try to start the essay sometime during the summer before you apply. Allow at least three months to write it, and don't be afraid to take it through numerous drafts or overhaul it completely if you're not satisfied. Get several perspectives. Ask close friends or relatives to scrutinize it to see if it really captures what you want to convey. Be sure to ask them about their initial reaction, as well as their feelings after studying it more carefully. Once you've achieved a draft that you feel comfortable with, try to have it read by some people who barely know you or who don't know you at all. If certain criticisms are consistently made, then they're probably legitimate. But don't be carried away by every suggestion every reader makes. Stick to your basic instincts because, after all, this is your personal statement, no one else's.

Proofreading is of critical importance. Again, don't be afraid to enlist the aid of others. If possible, let an English teacher review the essay solely for spelling and grammar mistakes.

Essay Content: As stated earlier, there's no one correct way to write an essay, but admissions officers do provide some helpful tips about what they like and don't like to see in a personal statement. Let's begin with a list of the things that officers most often mentioned they disliked seeing.

Personal Statement DON'Ts

Don't turn your personal statement into a résumé. This is the personal statement that begins at birth and simply recites every major (and sometimes minor) event of the person's life. Most of this information is repetitive since it's included on other parts of the application. But worse than that, it's just a boring format.

Avoid the "why I want to go to law school" essay. Although this can be a *part* of any law school essay, too many people make it the entire focus of their statement. The problem is that there are not many new variations on this theme, and the admissions officers have likely heard them all before, probably many times.

Avoid talking about your negatives. The personal statement is not the place to call attention to your flaws. Don't forget that you're selling yourself and the personal statement is your most prominent sales tool.

Don't be too personal. Stories of abuse or trauma are often very moving and can be particularly effective if tied into a person's reason for wanting to practice law. Several admissions officers, however, have noted a trend towards describing such problems in graphic detail in personal statements. This kind of confessional essay can easily cross the line and become too personal.

Don't discuss legal concepts. Along those same lines, don't try to impress the reader with how much you already know about the law. The school assumes that it can teach you what you need to know, regardless of the level at which you start. By discussing a legal concept, you also run the risk of showing a certain amount of ignorance about the subject while at the same time appearing arrogant enough to have tried to discuss it.

Don't put down lawyers or the legal profession. Although it may seem that spewing cynicism about the legal profession is a clever device, trust us when we tell you that it isn't. Once you become a member of the legal profession, you can make as many lawyer jokes as you want. Until then, watch your step.

Don't try to cover too many subjects. Focus on one or two areas you really want to talk about. One of the worst mistakes applicants make is writing essays that ramble from one subject to another and back again. Fight the desire to talk about every highlight of your life.

Now that you've got a sense of what not to do in your personal statement, let's turn to a list of suggestions for things that you *should* do.

Personal Statement DOs

Tell stories. Readers respond much better to a concrete story or illustrative anecdote than to an abstract list of your attributes. Instead of just writing how determined you are, for instance, tell a story that demonstrates it. Stories stick in people's memories. The same holds true when you're trying to make sure the admissions officers remember you.

Be funny—if you can pull it off. Humor, particularly self-deprecating humor, is a very effective device. Admissions officers appreciate occasional flashes of irony. However, be careful in your use of humor. Don't overdo it—a couple of funny lines or a funny story can be great, but include too many jokes and you start to sound flippant. Finally, think about using *self-deprecating* humor. Law schools often complain about the lack of humility among students and appreciate those who show some.

Be unique. The term *unique* has been overused. Even some applications now ask you to describe what is unique about you. Applicants rack their brains trying to figure out how they're different from the other 5,000 people applying to that law school. Or worse, some interpret *unique* to mean disadvantaged and rack their brains trying to think how they have suffered more than others. But what the admissions officers want to know is what qualities or experiences in your life would make you a particularly valuable member of a law school class.

Start strong. In private moments, admissions officers will often admit that they don't read every essay carefully. They may just glance at an essay to get a general impression. That's why it's important to grab them from the beginning. Tell the ending of a story first and make them want to read on, to see how it all started, for example.

The above points are as much general advice as one can responsibly give about the personal statement in a book such as this. We hope that they'll provide you with some ideas or keep you from making some costly mistakes. In the end, however, it *is* a personal statement, and it must come from you.

RECOMMENDATIONS

During the last 10 years, as law school applications have increased dramatically and the odds against being accepted at any particular school have increased, applicants have taken various approaches to stand out from the crowd. Too often overlooked in this mad pursuit, however, is one of the very best ways for an applicant to stand out—that is, by getting terrific, vividly written recommendations.

Because so many recommendations tend to be blasé, an outstanding recommendation that goes beyond the standard language can really make an applicant stand out. Not only does such a recommendation serve the purpose of pointing out an applicant's strengths, it also shows that the recommender thought enough of the person to put time and effort into carefully writing it.

What Makes a Recommendation Outstanding?

Outstanding recommendations can vary in format, but they all tend to have in common several qualities.

An outstanding recommendation must be personal. By far the most common mistake made by applicants is believing that the prestige or position of the recommender is more important than what that person writes. Admissions officers tend to treat recommendations from senators, governors, and chief executive officers of major corporations with a great deal of skepticism, because very few applicants have a truly personal relationship with such people. To make matters worse, these officials tend to respond with very standard recommendations that rarely offer any real insight into the applicant's character; in a worst-case scenario, they may even be computer generated.

Find people who truly know you and are able to make an honest assessment of your capabilities. This means that it may be better to have the teaching assistant with whom you had daily contact write the recommendation rather than the prestigious professor you spoke to once during the year.

An outstanding recommendation compares you to others. When an admissions officer reads a recommendation, he or she often has to put into perspective the meaning of overused phrases—such as *hardworking* and *quick mind*—as they relate to the applicant. A much better format, and one that admissions officers appreciate, is the comparison recommendation, one that compares the applicant to other people that the recommendation writer previously knew in the same position or (in a best-case scenario) to people he or she has known who are alumni of that particular law school.

An outstanding recommendation tells stories. A concrete and specific recommendation stands out. Rather than merely listing attributes, a good recommendation engages the reader by telling an insightful story about the applicant. Recently, a professor of political science chose not to submit the standard phrase about what a quick study a student was. Instead, he related a story about the student in class. It seems the professor introduced a new and difficult concept in class that the student discussed intelligently and actually took further than the professor was prepared to do. That kind of story sticks in a reader's mind.

An outstanding recommendation focuses on scholastic abilities. Although recommendations often cover a lot of ground, from the applicant's attitudes about school to his or her personality traits, admissions officers focus on comments about a person's scholastic ability. Obviously, this means that a strong recommendation from a professor carries a great deal of weight. However, a lot of people are in a position to observe a person's intellectual aptitude. Employers, friends, clergy, and workers at volunteer agencies are all usually able to discuss an applicant's scholastic abilities—and should.

How to Ensure You Receive Outstanding Recommendations

Now that you know what makes for an outstanding recommendation, all you have to do is ensure that each of your recommenders produces one. While you can't actually write the recommendations yourself, you *can* have a great deal of influence over how accurate and persuasive they are.

Choose the right people to recommend you. What are the qualities of a good recommender? Obviously, you should choose someone who likes you and who thinks you're good at what you do. This doesn't mean that you have to be intimate pals, but sworn enemies don't often write good recommendations. It helps if the person is a good writer so that he or she can clearly express an opinion about you.

Most, if not all, of your recommendations for academic programs should come from professors or other academic faculty. If you've been out of school for a few years and haven't kept in touch with your professors, call or write the admissions offices of the schools to which you're applying. Don't assume that it's okay to send fewer letters than required or to substitute other kinds of information for recommendation letters. Most likely, schools will allow you to submit recommendations from employers or from other nonacademic people with knowledge about your background, skills, and goals.

Balance your list of recommendation writers. Three professors from your undergrad major department probably will have similar things to say about you, so why not include someone from another field who can speak to your thinking and writing skills?

Be considerate of your recommendation writers. As soon as you decide to go to law school, you should start sizing up potential recommenders and letting them know that you may ask them for a letter. This will give each plenty of time to get to know you better and to think about what to say in the letter. Once they've agreed, let them know about deadlines with plenty of lead time to avoid potential scheduling conflicts. The more time they have, the better the job they'll do recommending you.

Make sure your recommendation writers know what they need to know. Once someone has agreed to consider writing a letter for you, you should arrange an appointment to discuss your background and goals for your future. If you live thousands of miles away from your recommender, arrange a telephone appointment.

Bring to the appointment copies of appropriate documentation such as your transcript, papers you've written, your résumé or curriculum vitae, your personal statement, and a sheet of bullet points that you plan to feature in your application and essay. Supply the appropriate form or forms, as well as stamped, addressed envelopes and a copy of your home address and phone number.

Keep the appointment relatively brief—you're already taking up enough of their time. Give your recommenders a good idea of why you want to go to law school. Play up your good points, of course, but be reasonably humble. If you have a very specific "marketing" image that you're trying to project, let your recommenders in on it—they may want to focus on some of the same points you're trying to stress. But don't tell your recommenders what to write—don't even give them the impression that you're doing so! Recommenders tend to resent any attempts at manipulation and may, as a consequence, refuse to write your letter. What recommenders *do* appreciate, however, is some direction as to what you'd like to see.

Keep your recommendation writers on schedule. Finally, make sure your recommenders know how important it is to complete the letters as early as possible. If they procrastinate, gently remind them that their deadline is approaching and be sure to remind them of the importance of early applications.

A Final Check

After you've completed everything and are getting ready to place it in a manila envelope and mail it, make sure you go through one more time and check each document. Law schools frequently receive documents that were intended to go to another law school. With all of this paperwork, it's easy to see how that can happen, and the law schools expect a certain amount of it. However, it can be embarrassing if you've written in your personal statement that ABC Law School is the one and only place for you—and then you accidentally send it to XYZ Law School instead.

APPLICATION CHECKLIST

The three major parts of your law school application:

1. Application form
2. Personal statement
3. Recommendations

APPLICATION FORM

- ❏ Working photocopies of applications made.
- ❏ Information/addresses/other data gathered.
- ❏ Addendums (if any) written.
- ❏ Information transferred to actual application.
- ❏ Application proofread.
- ❏ Final check done.

PERSONAL STATEMENT

- ❏ Theme finalized.
- ❏ Readers selected and notified.
- ❏ First draft written.
- ❏ Self-evaluation made.
- ❏ Second draft written.
- ❏ Comments from readers received.
- ❏ Final draft written.
- ❏ Final statement proofread.

RECOMMENDATIONS

- ❏ Recommendation writers chosen.
- ❏ Recommendation writers on board.
- ❏ Informational meeting with recommendation writers conducted.
- ❏ Reminders to all recommendation writers sent.
- ❏ Notice of complete application received.

CHAPTER 9: SPECIAL NOTE FOR INTERNATIONAL STUDENTS

In recent years, U.S. law schools have experienced an increase in inquiries from non-U.S. citizens, some of whom are already practicing lawyers in their own countries. This surge of interest in the U.S. legal system has been attributed to the spread of the global economy. When businesspeople from outside the United States do business with Americans, they often find themselves doing business under the American legal system. Gaining insight into how the American legal system works is of great interest around the world.

This new international interest in the U.S. legal system is having an effect on law schools. Many schools have developed special programs to accommodate the needs of this special population of lawyers and students from around the globe. If you are an international student or lawyer interested in learning more about the American legal system, or if you are considering attending law school in the United States, Kaplan can help you explore your options.

Getting into a U.S. law school can be especially challenging for students from other countries. If you are not from the United States but are considering attending law school in the United States, here is what you'll need to get started.

- If English is not your first language, you'll probably need to take the TOEFL® (Test of English as a Foreign Language) or provide some other evidence that you are proficient in English. Most law schools require a minimum computer TOEFL score of 250 (600 on the paper-based TOEFL) or better.

- Depending on the program to which you are applying, you may also need to take the LSAT® (Law School Admissions Test). All law schools in the United States require the LSAT for their JD programs. LLM programs usually do not require the LSAT. Kaplan will help you determine if you need to take the LSAT. If you must take the LSAT, Kaplan can help you prepare for it.

- Because admission to law school is quite competitive, you may want to select three or four programs and complete applications for each school.

- You should begin the process of applying to law schools or special legal studies programs at least 18 months before the fall of the year you plan to start your studies. Most programs will have only September start dates.

In addition, you will need to obtain an I-20 Certificate of Eligibility from the school you plan to attend if you intend to apply for an F-1 Student Visa to study in the United States.

KAPLAN ENGLISH PROGRAMS*

If you need more help with the complex process of law school admissions, assistance preparing for the LSAT or TOEFL, or help building your English language skills in general, you may be interested in Kaplan's programs for international students.

Kaplan English Programs were designed to help students and professionals from outside the United States meet their educational and career goals. At locations throughout the United States, international students take advantage of Kaplan's programs to help them improve their academic and conversational English skills; raise their scores on the TOEFL, LSAT, and other standardized exams; and gain admission to the schools of their choice. Our staff and instructors give international students the individualized attention they need to succeed. Here is a brief description of some of Kaplan's programs for international students.

GENERAL ENGLISH SELF-STUDY

For students needing a flexible schedule, this course helps improve general fluency skills. Kaplan's General English Self-Study course employs the communicative approach and focuses on vocabulary building, reading, and writing. You will receive books, audio, and video materials as well as three hours of instructor contact per week.

TOEFL AND ACADEMIC ENGLISH

Kaplan has updated its world-famous TOEFL course to prepare students for the new TOEFL iBT. Designed for high-intermediate to advanced-level English speakers, our new course focuses on the academic English skills you will need to succeed on the new test. The course includes TOEFL-focused reading, writing, listening, and speaking instruction and hundreds of practice items similar to those on the exam. Kaplan's expert instructors help you prepare for the four sections of the TOEFL iBT, including the new Speaking Section. Our new simulated online TOEFL tests help you monitor your progress and provide you with feedback on areas where you require improvement. We will teach you how to get a higher score!

*Kaplan is authorized under federal law to enroll nonimmigrant alien students. Kaplan is accredited by ACCET (Accrediting Council for Continuing Education and Training) and is a member of FIYTO and ALTO.

LSAT TEST-PREPARATION COURSE

The LSAT is a crucial admission criterion for law schools in the United States. A high score can help you stand out from other applicants. This course includes the skills you need to succeed on each section of the LSAT, as well as access to Kaplan's exclusive practice materials.

OTHER KAPLAN PROGRAMS

Since 1938, more than 3 million students have come to Kaplan to advance their studies, prepare for entry to American universities, and further their careers. In addition to the above programs, Kaplan offers courses to prepare for the SAT®, GMAT®, GRE®, MCAT®, DAT®, USMLE®, NCLEX®, and other standardized exams at locations throughout the United States.

APPLYING TO KAPLAN ENGLISH PROGRAMS

To get more information or to apply for admission to any of Kaplan's programs for international students and professionals, contact us at

Kaplan English Programs
700 South Flower Street, Suite 2900
Los Angeles, CA 90017
Phone (if calling from within the United States): 800-818-9128
Phone (if calling from outside the United States): (213) 452-5800
Fax: (213) 892-1364
Email: world@kaplan.com
Web: *kaplanenglish.com*

FREE Services for International Students

Kaplan now offers international students many services online—*free of charge*! Students may assess their TOEFL skills and gain valuable feedback on their English language proficiency in just a few hours with Kaplan's TOEFL Skills Assessment. Log onto www.kaplanenglish.com today.